Common Lisp Recipes

A Problem-Solution Approach

Edmund Weitz

Apress®

Common Lisp Recipes: A Problem-Solution Approach

Edmund Weitz
Hamburg, Germany

ISBN-13 (pbk): 978-1-4842-1177-9 ISBN-13 (electronic): 978-1-4842-1176-2
DOI: 10.1007/978-1-4842-1176-2

Library of Congress Control Number: 2015960959

Distributed to the book trade worldwide by Springer Science+Business Media New York, 233 Spring Street, 6th Floor, New York, NY 10013. Phone 1-800-SPRINGER, fax (201) 348-4505, e-mail orders-ny@springer-sbm.com, or visit www.springeronline.com. Apress Media, LLC is a California LLC and the sole member (owner) is Springer Science + Business Media Finance Inc (SSBM Finance Inc). SSBM Finance Inc is a Delaware corporation.

For information on translations, please e-mail rights@apress.com, or visit www.apress.com.

Apress and friends of ED books may be purchased in bulk for academic, corporate, or promotional use. eBook versions and licenses are also available for most titles. For more information, reference our Special Bulk Sales-eBook Licensing web page at www.apress.com/bulk-sales.

Any source code or other supplementary materials referenced by the author in this text is available to readers at www.apress.com/9781484211779. For detailed information about how to locate your book's source code, go to www.apress.com/source-code/. Readers can also access source code at SpringerLink in the Supplementary Material section for each chapter.

Printed on acid-free paper

For Heike and Mouna

Table of Contents

About the Author

Edmund Weitz is well known in the Common Lisp community for his open source libraries and for being one of the organizers of the European Common Lisp Meeting. He has a PhD in mathematics and has been a freelance Common Lisp consultant for clients in the United States, Europe, and Asia since 2002. He now works as a professor for math and computer science at the University of Applied Sciences in Hamburg, Germany.

About the Technical Reviewer

Hans Hübner has been a professional programmer for three decades. After becoming proficient in the then-ubiquitous BASIC, he was an enthusiastic follower of the object-orientation wave, mostly programming in C++. Perl led him into the dynamic programming language field, where he eventually picked up Common Lisp and applied it in a multitude of industrial projects for clients in various industries. He is now leading a small company developing Lisp-based applications in the health-care space.

Preface

I don't know about you, but for me, discovering COMMON LISP and learning to program in it was kind of a revelation. I came to it around 1999 when I was earning my money with "mainstream" languages and tried out various others just out of interest. I was immediately hooked and I've never looked back. Although it is probably fair to say that COMMON LISP is nowadays a *niche* language, I managed to make a living out of programming in it for more than a decade and met lots of others who did the same. I still think that COMMON LISP is the most enjoyable language to work with in spite of its inevitable shortcomings. If you have bought this book, or if you are considering buying it, you probably have the same feeling.

However, more than 15 years ago, the situation compared to today was quite bleak. There weren't even half as many COMMON LISP implementations as now; there were only very few ready-to-use and useful open source libraries, and there was no infrastructure. Plus, while for something like, say, PERL, there were quite a few high-quality and recent books available, for COMMON LISP all books were, although at least partly quite good, simply outdated and didn't reflect the current situation anymore. One of the many things that changed for the better in this century is that one really good new Lisp book finally appeared (more on it shortly) and I believe that it was a very important contribution to Lisp's resurgence. And I also believe that—although some claim that nobody reads book anymore—more good books are needed.

I was thus glad that Apress asked me to author a Lisp book and I accepted immediately. I started the *Common Lisp Cookbook* project many years ago (which, unfortunately, petered out due to various reasons) and at that time may have had hopes to turn it into a "real" book. But looking back to it today, I'm actually happy this didn't happen, as I feel that with several more years of experience and given the current state of the COMMON LISP "world," I'm in a much better position to write a useful book.

Who This Book Is For

In order to get the most out of this book, you should be somewhat familiar with COMMON LISP. This means you should have at least one COMMON LISP compiler on your hard drive which you should have already used to write a few simple programs. You should know how to define functions with DEFUN and how to call them;

you should know how to declare local variables with LET and how to use them; you should have used some basic arithmetic and list functions like + or LIST; you should not be surprised by strings or characters; you should be familiar with forms like IF for branches or DOTIMES for iteration. And so on. It would also be good if you knew your way around in the HyperSpec (see page XXIV), so that you can look up things that you don't know.

Apress, the publisher of this book, has also published Peter Seibel's *Practical Common Lisp* (2005), which in my opinion is the best from-scratch introduction to COMMON LISP that has been written so far. If you haven't read it yet, please give it a try—it's really worth it! The book you have in your hands right now assumes you have understood at least the basic concepts of most of what Peter explains in his book, and I'll sometimes refer you to specific sections of it instead of repeating things.[1]

Who This Book Is (Probably) Not For

Due to its very nature as a collection of "recipes," this book can't be considered a textbook. If you're totally new to COMMON LISP, you shouldn't read this book as an *introduction*. Rather, I'd recommend starting with Peter's book, which I already mentioned in the previous paragraph. Once you've mastered it, please return to this book for the next steps.

Also, if you're a seasoned professional and have used COMMON LISP for years, this book is likely not for you.[2] I'd be pleased if you'd find something in this book you didn't know yet. (And chances are you will, as COMMON LISP is such a huge language. I myself learned or relearned a lot when writing the book.) But you'd probably have been able to figure this out yourself if necessary.

How to Read This Book

In a way, like all authors, I'd wish that you'd read the whole book from cover to cover. But that's pretty unlikely, given how it is organized. You'll probably look at individual recipes or chapters whenever the need arises. Still, some topics are too complex to cram into a few pages. That's why I tried to provide lots of cross-references to related recipes or places where more information can be found. I also endeavored to create a comprehensive index, which will hopefully help you to find things which are "hidden" in not so obvious places.

But even with all these pointers, it might be a good idea to at least skim the table of contents for a rough idea about what's covered in the book. And maybe you'll read

[1] In my opinion, it is definitely worth buying the book, but Peter has been nice enough to make its contents available online for free. So, if you just need a refresher here and there, bookmark a link to `http://www.gigamonkeys.com/book/`.

[2] And I'm wondering if you even made it this far in the preface.

some of the chapters just out of interest, and not only because there's a deadline that you have to meet...

What's In and What Not

If you look at the table of contents, you'll notice that the book covers a lot of different areas, from core features of the language, to third party additions, to tasks like debugging. And it is, to my knowledge, the first COMMON LISP book which discusses topics such as environment access, logical pathnames, foreign function interfaces, multithreading, graphical user interfaces, persistence, delivery of executables, and optimization.

But although the book is quite big, it still can't do full justice to *all* of COMMON LISP and to all interesting open source libraries written in the last decades. I tried to find a healthy mixture and let myself be guided by features I've used myself.[3] My apologies in advance if I missed exactly those parts you were looking for.

Having said that, there are two areas where the book is scarce on purpose.[4] One is the absolute basics. I mentioned *Practical Common Lisp* and I've been trying not to repeat what Peter already explained thoroughly. There will be some inevitable overlaps, but in general, if there's something you're missing, you should first check if there isn't already a chapter in Peter's book devoted to that topic.

(Still, there *will* be basics explained and discussed here, which you'll already know very well, and you might be wondering why I "wasted" time and space for them. Well, this is a book of recipes that also aims to serve as some kind of reference. And each reader is different. If a recipe is called *Understanding Foo*, and you already understand Foo, just skip it...)

The other area this book doesn't spend a lot of time on is macros. They make cameo appearances here and there, but they don't get their own chapter. The reason is that there are at least two books solely devoted to this topic. One is the "classic" *On Lisp* by Paul Graham (Prentice Hall, 1993)[5] and the other is *Let over Lambda* by Doug Hoyte (Lulu.com, 2008).[6] Once you've read and understand these two books, and Peter's book, there won't be anything left I could teach you about macros.

Finally, from giving university lectures in mathematics for several years I've learned that it's not always a good idea from a pedagogical perspective to provide all the

[3]I tend to think that for every COMMON LISP pro, there are some parts of the language they've never used and probably don't even know (or care) about.

[4]Well, *at least* two. For example, I also rarely mention structures (the ones defined by `DEFSTRUCT`) anyhwere in the book because I view them as an historical artefact superseded by CLOS. And there are certainly other things I only treat negligently.

[5]Available as a free download from `http://www.paulgraham.com/onlisptext.html`.

[6]Be careful with these books, though, if you're new to COMMON LISP. In my opinion, some people have the tendency to be overly impressed by macros and to (mis)use them just because they seem to be "cool."

"dirty" details at once. More often, it is beneficial to "lie" a bit or to at least "hide" the full truth. I've certainly *not* written anything in this book that's actually wrong (at least not on purpose), but I might have left out some rare special cases in order to be more concise or in order to not spoil the overall narrative. If you're in doubt, you can always consult the standard (more on this next).

The HyperSpec

COMMON LISP is a language defined by a standard. That means there's an official document which describes in painstaking detail how the individual parts of the language are expected to work and interact. Not only is this standard very detailed and comprehensive, it is also (for a technical document) surprisingly easy to read. The bad news is that the "real" standard is only available as an ugly PDF through ANSI's online store for a rather steep price. (At least that was the situation when I wrote this preface and it has been like that for years.)

The good news is that there's a wonderful online version of the standard which is actually much more useful than the PDF because of its extensive cross-referencing and additional material. From a legal point of view, this so-called *HyperSpec* is not "the standard," but for all practical purposes it is. This is why, whenever I'm talking about "the standard" in this book, I'm referring to this online version (which also goes by the acronym *CLHS*).

You should have the standard on your hard drive already, but if you don't, you can find it at `http://www.lispworks.com/documentation/common-lisp.html`.[7] And see also page 488.

Which Implementation

Unlike many other popular programming languages (but like C++, for example) there are lots of different implementations of COMMON LISP. As long as we're talking about standard COMMON LISP, it shouldn't matter which implementation you're using. But this book also talks extensively about non-standard additions. On the one hand, it would have been a pretty bad idea to base the whole book on one particular implementation.[8] On the other hand, I needed to actually run and test my code somehow. I eventually decided to use a mixture of different compilers and different platforms.[9] That's why, for example, you might see different prompts in different

[7] It can be found at the LISPWORKS web site because its creation (by Kent Pitman) was funded by LISPWORKS's predecessor company, HARLEQUIN.

[8] There are simply too many which are quite good (see Recipe 17-15). And although one may be the most popular now, this might change over time. Also, popularity on one particular operating system doesn't necessarily translate to popularity on other platforms.

[9] For what it's worth I mostly used LISPWORKS on Windows, OS X, and Linux, SBCL on Windows and Linux, ALLEGROCL on Windows and Linux, and occasionally CLOZURECL on Linux or OS X.

recipes. Whenever possible I tried to pinpoint where your results may differ if you're not using the same Lisp I happened to use for that recipe.

Source Code

This book doesn't contain large pieces of code but consists mostly of small demonstration snippets. Still, if you want to save some typing, everything that can be found in the framed boxes is available for download; from the Apress web site (at `www.apress.com`) as well as from `http://weitz.de/cl-recipes/`.

The Index

I personally like books with extensive indexes and thus tried to provide for my own book an index as comprehensive as possible. This means, for example, that you won't only find one entry for a specific COMMON LISP function (the one for the recipe where it is explained), but usually several such entries, including references to pages in other recipes where it is "just" *used* so that you can see it "in action." Likewise, you might, say, find an index entry for *Gaussian integers*. This is not because this books explains what Gaussian integers are, but because maybe you remember one specific example and later want to look it up.

So, the general policy when compiling the index was to provide as many ways of finding stuff as possible. I hope you'll find it useful. (And maybe you'll even browse the index to find stuff you might have otherwise overlooked.)

For technical reasons, if an index entry refers to page n, you will in some cases have to search for a code excerpt on page $n+1$ instead.

Typographical Conventions

Many of the recipes in this book will show examples where we interact with Lisp images. They'll look like so:

```
CL-USER 1 > (* 6 7)
42
```

Here the "`CL-USER 1 >`" part is the *prompt* of the REPL, so `(* 6 7)` is what you're supposed to enter and 42 is what your Lisp is expected to return. Depending on the implementation we're using for a specific example, the prompt can also be something different, such as simply "`*`" and nothing else.

I also used other Lisps, like CLISP, ECL, or ABCL for specific recipes.

Also, my technical reviewer used OS X as his main testing platform, so that platform should be covered even if I myself used it only sparingly.

The output of the REPL has sometimes been edited a bit in order to increase readability or to save space.

Although Common Lisp behaves as if it were case insensitive (see Recipe 1-8), we'll follow the usual convention to use uppercase letters (as in "`LIST`") in running text.

The names of programming languages and libraries are set in small caps (as in "Quicklisp"). Wherever possible I tried to follow typical usage regarding the distribution of lowercase and uppercase letters in those names but I'm sure I got it wrong in some cases.

Acknowledgements

I would like to thank my technical reviewer, Hans Hübner, (who, by the way, is also one of the best and knowledgeable hackers I personally know) for his great work. He found some really embarassing mistakes...

Arthur Lemmens (another great Lisp hacker and a good friend) gave the whole book another very thorough review. And both Hans and Arthur not only found errors but also provided many useful suggestions to improve the text.

Any remaining errors in this book (and whatever else you might not like about it) are, of course, my responsibility.

Zach Beane has done a lot of things for the Common Lisp community already,[10] but I think his most important contribution to date has been the invention of Quicklisp (see Recipe 18-2), which made finding and installing Lisp libraries so much easier than it was before. Without Quicklisp, writing a book like this, which talks about so many open source libraries from diverse sources, would have been almost impossible. Zach was also nice enough to review the recipes which pertain to his own code.

Thanks to all the implementors and to all authors of open source libraries for their contributions to the Common Lisp ecosystem. Thanks to the members of the PRO mailing list[11] and specifically to Thomas Burdick for helping me with some tricky issues with respect to the standard. Thanks to Wes Henderson for his help with the MOCL recipe.

Since I started to work with Common Lisp "in earnest," I've met a lot of Lisp hackers through conferences or joint projects. I've learned tons of stuff from them because these guys (and girls) are all very intelligent and knowledgeable. But apart from that they are also just nice persons of whom I'm glad I made the acquaintance. In addition to Arthur, Hans, and Zach, I'd like to mention Jans Aasman, Marc

[10]For example, he maintains the blog aggregrator *Planet Lisp* at `http://planet.lisp.org/` and publishes useful and interesting tips on his blog *Common Lisp Tips* at `http://lisptips.com/`. He's also a prolific creator of open source software. See more at `http://xach.com/lisp/`.

[11]See `https://mailman.common-lisp.net/listinfo/pro`.

Battyani, Dave Fox, Luke Gorrie, Jeremy Jones, Nick Levine, David McClain, Scott McKay, Christophe Rhodes, Martin Simmons, Dimitri Simos, Robert Strandh, Ernst van Waning, Didier Verna, Gail Zacharias, and the late Dan Weinreb. (And I'm sure I forgot some. My apologies!)

The whole book was written and typeset using Donald Knuth's TEX. All graphics, execpt for a few screenshots in Chapter 20, were generated using Till Tantau's TikZ and PGF packages.

Many thanks to the people at Apress who made this all happen, especially to Mark Powers.

And finally, my love to Heike and Mouna (without whom the book would probably have been finished earlier but life would certainly be less fun).

1. Symbols and Packages

Symbols are one of the most important building blocks of COMMON LISP. Many other programming languages either don't have symbols, or if they have them, they are just one of many data types. But in Lisp, symbols play a central role because they are used to name things like variables and functions, are indispensable in macros, but are also objects in their own right. Thus, they deserve some attention.

Although symbols are superficially easy to "get," they are complicated compound objects under the hood, so if you want to use them in advanced ways, a deeper understanding of them and their interaction with packages is necessary. That's what main parts of this chapter are about.[1]

There's one thing you definitely should *not* use symbols for: don't use them when strings (see Chapter 3) would be more appropriate. While symbols can "behave" like strings (see for example Recipe 1-9), that's not what they are for. You will occasionally find older code where symbols are used for *everything*; but that is most likely because it was written for a Lisp dialect that didn't have strings or because it was written by someone who didn't know better.

Also, code that creates new symbols automatically and constructs their names by gluing things together smells fishy in my opinion.[2] You should at least think twice before doing that.

Note that for didactical reasons the recipes in this chapter generally use the functional interface to the package system. In practice, you will almost always use `DEFPACKAGE` in your code, as for example on pages 27 and 29.

1-1. Understanding the Role of Packages and the Symbol Nomenclature

Problem

Symbols can be *accessible, inherited, internal, present,* and so on. They have a *home package* but can live in several different packages at the same time or in none at all. This

[1] And if you read the first recipes one by one, you might sense some repetition. Which is on purpose, as we'll be talking about the same processes but from different perspectives.

[2] Yes, this includes `DEFSTRUCT`!

can all be pretty confusing at first, but it is vital to develop a good understanding of how packages and symbols interact in order to get the finer points.

Solution

We'll work through the various notions and interdependencies using an example. Let's create three new packages using these forms and then dissect what we get:

```
(defpackage :p1
  (:intern :alpha)
  (:export :bravo :charlie))

(defpackage :p2
  (:intern :alpha :delta)
  (:use :p1)
  (:export :bravo :echo))

(defpackage :p3
  (:intern :alpha)
  (:use :p2 :cl)
  (:export :charlie)
  (:import-from :p2 :delta))
```

How It Works

We now have a situation that can be depicted graphically, like so:

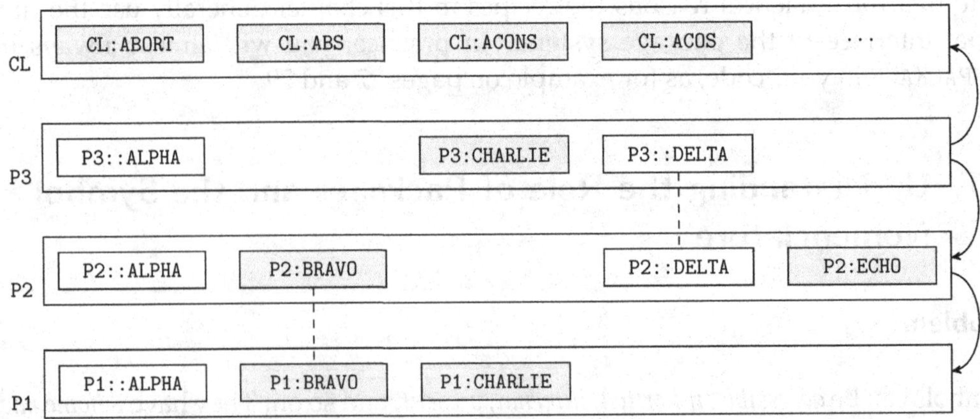

Each of the four large boxes above is a package; the smaller rectangles denote symbols. We see the three packages, P1 through P3, which we explicitly created, and the

CL (or COMMON-LISP) package, which is already there when we start our Lisp image and of whose many symbols we only show a sample of four.

A *package* is a container of symbols (that's why they are drawn as boxes "holding" the symbol rectangles); and it is probably fair to say that the main job of packages is to help us *find* symbols and to organize them into groups. This can also be put differently: packages can help us name and find symbols, but symbols can have an existence on their own; that is, *without* packages. (As we'll see in Recipes 1-2 and 1-3.)

Symbols are usually created automatically (by the Lisp reader; see Chapter 8) when you type them;[3] and they are then put into a package (which is the *current* package, the one in `*PACKAGE*`, unless you explicitly create a symbol in a different package). This process is called *interning* (see also Recipe 1-3) because it creates a new *internal* symbol of the package.

Of course, most of the time symbols are *not* created because, when it reads them, the Lisp system firsts checks if they are already there; that is, whether they are *accessible* using the name and (implicit or explicit) package prefix you provided. So, in the following situation (assuming you just started your Lisp image)

```
CL-USER > 'foo
FOO
CL-USER > 'foo
FOO
```

when your Lisp reads `foo` it is as if it had read `cl-user::foo` because (as the prompt shows) the `CL-USER` package is the *current* package. Because no symbol with the name `"FOO"` is accessible via the package `CL-USER`, a new symbol (with *that* name and in *that* package) is created (viz. *interned* into the package).

When your Lisp now reads `foo` *again*, a symbol described by this sequence of characters *is* available (the one that was just created) and is returned.

In our example code from page 2 we didn't create any symbols this way but we created them implicitly or explicitly through the `DEFPACKAGE` forms. Let's see what we got this way:

- Symbols are either *present* in a package or not. In our picture, the symbols present in a package are those that are contained within the surrounding box.
- Symbols become present in a package either if a new symbol is *interned* (see above) or if an existing symbol is *imported*.

[3]It is not totally accurate to say that you "typed the symbol" because this conflates the symbol itself with its representation. (See Recipe 1-3 for why this distinction is important.) But we'll use this slightly sloppy manner of speaking for now.

Also, as should be made clear by the allusion to the Lisp reader, the process of *typing* isn't really relevant. The things mentioned here happen at *read time*.

The `DEFPACKAGE` form for `P3`, for example, explicitly interned a symbol named `ALPHA` and explicitly imported the symbol named `DELTA` from the `P2` package.

- When a symbol is imported into a package, the effect is that the *same* symbol is now present in (at least) two different packages. In the picture, we used dashed lines to show identity; that is, symbols connected with dashed lines are actually the same symbol and symbols *not* connected are really different symbols.
- Once a symbol is present in a package, it can only be removed using the function `UNINTERN` (see Recipe 1-3).
- If a symbol is present in a package, it can be *exported*[4] from that package. This means that it can now be accessed using only one colon between the package's and the symbol's name. Exported symbols are shown with a gray background in our picture.

  For example, the package `P1` exports the symbol `CHARLIE`, but not the symbol `ALPHA`. We didn't explicitly intern `CHARLIE`, but because we instructed the system to export it, it had to be present and was thus created (and interned) automatically.
- Exported symbols are called *external* and the other ones are called *internal*.
- A package can also have *inherited* symbols. This happens if a package *uses* another package. All external symbols of the used package become inherited symbols of the package using this package. Inherited symbols are not shown directly in our picture but rather by means of the arrows on the right that show which packages use which other packages.

  For example, package `P3` uses package `P2` and thus `P2:ECHO` is an inherited symbol of `P3`. Likewise, `P3` also uses `CL` and thus all of the 978 exported symbols of `CL` (see footnote on page 19) become inherited symbols of `P3`. You can thus refer to `P2:ECHO` as `P3::ECHO` and to `CL:ABS` as `P3::ABS`.
- Inheritance is *not* transitive. The fact that `P3` uses `P2` and `P2` in turn uses `P1` does *not* mean that the symbol `P1:CHARLIE` is an inherited symbol of `P3`.[5]

  `P3` has its own symbol named `CHARLIE`, which was implicitly created because it was exported, but this symbol is *different* from `P1:CHARLIE`.
- A symbol is *accessible* in a package (in other words, it can be found through that package) if it is either present or inherited in that package.

  As accessibility means that a symbol can be found in a package by name, it

---

[4] I personally think that some of these notions aren't such a great fit. While *importing* a symbol means that the symbol moves *into* a new package, it doesn't mean that it *leaves* its home package. Likewise, a symbol which is *exported* is not leaving at all, it is just *exposed*, kind of.

[5] `P1:BRAVO` is, though, because it was explicitly "re-exported."

implies that no two *different* accessible symbols can have the same name. This would be called a *name conflict*.[6] To provoke such a conflict, try something like this:

```
(import 'p2::alpha :p3)
```

Some parts of our example might deserve closer inspection:

- What about the dashed line between P2:BRAVO and P1:BRAVO? And why is P1:BRAVO present in P2 in the first place?

  P2 uses P1 and as P1:BRAVO is external to P1 it should be an inherited symbol of P2. But in the DEFPACKAGE form, we say that we want to export the symbol with the name BRAVO, and as only present symbols can be external symbols, the symbol was automatically "upgraded" from inherited to present by importing it.

- Why are the symbols called ALPHA all different?

  Why should they not be? Each DEFPACKAGE form explicitly creates a symbol called ALPHA, but none of these symbols is exported nor are any of them imported.

This is the gist of it; although some of the following recipes will show that it can be even more complicated. One last thing worth mentioning is that symbols were drawn as rectangles to allude to the fact that they are compound objects with a life of their own. Most importantly, each symbol has a *home package*[7] which is typically the package it was first interned in. For example, although P2:BRAVO (née P1:BRAVO) is present in both P1 and P2, its home package still is P1.

1-2. Making Unique Symbols

Problem

You want to create symbols that can't be reached by their name; for example, to avoid inadvertent name capture in macros.

Solution

A situation where you most typically want to avoid such name clashes is when writing macros. Let's suppose you want to create a macro to swap two variables (but see Recipe 10-7!) and you do it like so:

[6] See Recipe 1-4.

[7] Well, usually. But see Recipes 1-2 and 1-3.

```
(defmacro swap (var-1 var-2)
  `(let ((temp ,var-1))
     (setf ,var-1 ,var-2
           ,var-2 temp)
     (values)))
```

The problem with this definition is this:

```
CL-USER > (defparameter *a* 42)
*A*
CL-USER > (defparameter *b* 23)
*B*
CL-USER > (swap *a* *b*)
CL-USER > (list *a* *b*)
(23 42)
CL-USER > (defparameter temp 100)
TEMP
CL-USER > (swap temp *a*)
CL-USER > (list temp *a*)
(100 23)
```

Swapping `*A*` and `*B*` worked fine, but swapping `TEMP` and `*A*` didn't because the second use of `SWAP` was expanded into this form:

```
(let ((temp temp))
  (setf temp *a*
        *a* temp)
  (values))
```

This should make clear what went wrong.[8]

Obviously, the reason this could happen is that one of the arguments to `SWAP` used the same symbol that was used for the temporary variable in the macro. You can now try all sorts of "clever" things to make such a conflict pretty unlikely; for example, by using long and strange symbol names, as in

```
(defmacro swap (var-1 var-2)
  `(let ((my-own-temp-var-name-please-do-not-use ,var-1))
     (setf ,var-1 ,var-2
           ,var-2 my-own-temp-var-name-please-do-not-use)
     (values)))
```

[8]The technical term used by the standard is that the newly created binding of `TEMP` *shadowed* the binding we actually wanted to modify. This is not to be confused with *shadowing symbols* (see Recipe 1-4).

or by using your own package just for this purpose; but none of them is totally safe because you'll always have to ask the users of your macros to follow certain rules that they'll likely forget or accidentally break.

The classical way to solve this problem is to write the macro like so:

```
(defmacro swap (var-1 var-2)
  (let ((temp-var (gensym)))                              ;; <- added
    `(let ((,temp-var ,var-1))                            ;; <- changed
       (setf ,var-1 ,var-2
             ,var-2 ,temp-var)                            ;; <- changed
       (values))))
```

If we now look at the macro expansion, we see this:[9]

```
CL-USER > (macroexpand '(swap *a* *b*))
(LET ((#:G42 *A*))
  (SETF *A* *B*
        *B* #:G42)
  (VALUES))
T
```

And now there's not even a theoretical chance for a name conflict anymore. We'll explain why next.

How It Works

To fully explain this we need to step back a bit first. Let's assume that you are in a fresh Lisp image with the package `CL-USER` being your current package. You want to define a function using the well-known macro `DEFUN`, and thus you need to refer to the macro's *name*, which is a symbol. There are several ways to do this:

(i) You can type `CL::DEFUN`. This works (no matter what the current package is) because the *home package* of the symbol is the `COMMON-LISP` package and `CL` is a standardized *nickname* of this package.

(ii) You can save one colon and type `CL:DEFUN`. This works because the symbol is by default *exported* from its home package.

(iii) You would usually just type `DEFUN`. This works because the package you're in (the standardized `COMMON-LISP-USER` package nicknamed `CL-USER`) *uses* the `CL` package, which means that the symbol we're interested in is now also an *inherited* symbol of `CL-USER`.

[9]Output edited for readability. And you will almost certainly see a number that is different from 42.

There are even more ways.[10] But what they all have in common is that in order to *access* the symbol, we need its name, and then we somehow need to go through a package, either by naming the home package explicitly or by making a detour via another package as in (iii).

But this also works the other way around: if a symbol is not accessible through any packages, it is not accessible at all; that is, there's *no* way to refer to it (although you might know its name) unless you already have a reference to it.

There are various ways to create[11] new symbols without a home package that fulfill the above criterion of not being accessible:[12]

(i) Use the function GENSYM which gives you a symbol with a generated name (in a way that you can influence).[13]

(ii) Use the function MAKE-SYMBOL which creates a symbol with a name that you specify.

(iii) Use the function COPY-SYMBOL which allows you to create a symbol with the same name that an existing symbol has, and to optionally also copy the existing symbol's "behavior," that is, its property list (see Recipe 6-9) and that it might name a value and a function.

(iv) Use the *reader syntax*[14] `#:` which is just a shortcut. Something like `#:FOO` is essentially equivalent to `#.(MAKE-SYMBOL "FOO")`.

You'd usually use GENSYM with a prefix so that you can later make sense of the macro's expansion; a variable name like `#:HEIGHT123` is certainly more meaningful than `#:G123`.

What all of these methods have in common is that they create a *fresh* symbol on each invocation, which means that if you invoke them twice to create two symbols with the *same* name, the symbols will nevertheless be different:[15]

```
CL-USER > (make-symbol "FOO")
#:FOO
CL-USER > (make-symbol "FOO")
#:FOO
CL-USER > (eql * **)
```

[10]You could, for example, use FIND-SYMBOL or INTERN directly.

[11]You can also make *existing* symbols inaccessible. See Recipe 1-3.

[12]There's also a function called GENTEMP, but you should not use it.

[13]See the preceding example. Try several invocations of GENSYM in a row and try something like `(GENSYM "FOO")`. You can also play around with the global special variable `*GENSYM-COUNTER*`.
By the way, "gensym" is like "car" or "cons" one of those words that became nouns in the Lisp world. It is a synonym for "uninterned symbol."

[14]See Chapter 8 for more about the Lisp reader.

[15]See Recipe 16-11 for the meaning of * and **.

```
NIL
```

This implies that, although it is *temp*ting (pun intended), you could *not* write your macro like so:

```
(defmacro swap (var-1 var-2)
  `(let ((#:temp ,var-1))
     (setf ,var-1 ,var-2
           ,var-2 #:temp)
     (values)))
```

Try it...

This will work, though:

```
(defmacro swap (var-1 var-2)
  (let ((temp '#:temp))
    `(let ((,temp ,var-1))
       (setf ,var-1 ,var-2
             ,var-2 ,temp)
       (values))))
```

Avoiding name capture in macros might not be the only reason you'll ever need inaccessible symbols, but it is certainly the most common one. That's why many Lisps offer a "semi-standard" macro called `WITH-UNIQUE-NAMES`,[16] which you can use to create several such names in one go. If you don't have it, you'll find it as part of the ALEXANDRIA library (see Recipe 18-4).

1-3. Making Symbols Inaccessible

Problem

You have a "normal" symbol with a name and a home package and you want to get rid of it.

Solution

This seems easy enough: just use `UNINTERN`. But this action can have some interesting consequences...

[16]Sometimes also called `WITH-GENSYMS`.

```
CL-USER> (defun test () 42)
TEST
CL-USER> (defparameter *s* 'test)  ;; or (DEFPARAMETER *S* *) instead
*S*
CL-USER> (test)
42
CL-USER> (unintern 'test)
T
CL-USER> (test)
;; at this point you'll get an error message
;; about an undefined function...
CL-USER> (funcall *s*)             ;; or (#.*s*) instead
42
CL-USER> *s*
#:TEST
```

How It Works

As part of our `DEFUN` form above, the Lisp reader came across the character sequence `TEST`, which was meant to *name* the function we defined. Upon reading this character sequence, there are two things that can happen:

(A) There is already a symbol with the name `"TEST"` accessible in the `CL-USER` package. In this case, this symbol is the one denoted by the character sequence and it is used to name the function.[17]

(B) If, on the other hand, there is no symbol of this name accessible in the `CL-USER` package, then one will be created, with `CL-USER` being its *home package*.[18]

    This process is known as *interning* the symbol[19] and when we evaluate `(TEST)` afterward, the reader will, as in (A) above, return the same symbol that was just interned.

So, when we then *uninterned* the symbol by calling `UNINTERN`, we denuded the symbol of its home package (effectively setting it to `NIL`), which in turn meant that it was no longer accessible in the `CL-USER` package. When we then tried to evaluate `(TEST)` again, the process described in (B) happened *again*, except that the Lisp system was required by the standard to produce a *new* symbol that is *different* from the old one. And this brand-new symbol has an empty function cell and it can't be used to find the function anymore.

[17]Technically, the symbol's *function cell*, accessible via `SYMBOL-FUNCTION`, is now pointing to the new function.

[18]This can be queried using the function `SYMBOL-PACKAGE`.

[19]You could have achieved the same effect by calling `(INTERN "TEST")`.

What we did with `*S*` shows that the symbol itself is still there and can still be used to refer to the function. It just *looks* different. Specifically, what we could once refer to by the character sequence `TEST` can no longer be reached this way. Instead, if we now type `TEST`, we're referring to *another* symbol instead.

It is tempting to mentally identify a symbol with its representation (i.e., how the system displays it and what we have to type to access it), but what we've just done shows that this is wrong! The character sequence `TEST` denoted different symbols at different times. (This is in contrast to, say, the character sequence `42.0`, which always denotes the *same*[20] number.)

Symbols are objects in their own right (compound objects even, with various properties) and their "surface syntax" is essentially just a convenience feature to create and find them.[21] The process of uninterning symbols should be viewed as a maintenance measure which can potentially be dangerous.

In fact, you could even do silly things like this:

```
CL-USER > (eval-when (:execute) 42)
42
CL-USER > (unintern :execute :keyword)
T
CL-USER > (eval-when (:execute) 42)
NIL
```

Which shows that there is no such thing as *the* keyword symbol `:EXECUTE`!

How Can We Fix This?

How can we "get back" our function from above so that we can again call it using `(TEST)`? One way to do it would be like so:

```
(setf (symbol-function 'test) (symbol-function *s*))
```

The character sequence `TEST` would still refer to the new symbol, but the new symbol's function cell would now point to the same function that the old symbol's function cell pointed to.

A more "radical" alternative would be this:

```
(unintern 'test)
(import *s*)
```

[20]See Recipe 10-1.

[21]Well, I'm exaggerating here of course. You could as well say that their surface syntax is the *raison d'être* for symbols.

This would first make the new symbol inaccessible and then reinstantiate the old symbol as the one accessible by the character sequence TEST in the CL-USER package.

1-4. Avoiding Name Conflicts

Problem

You want to *use* a package to avoid typing package prefixes, but when you try it, you get an error message about "name conflicts."

Solution

The solution to this problem is called *shadowing*.

As usual, we'll walk through an example. Let's assume you are working on a biological problem. You have created a package called BIO and one of the classes you have defined is called TREE:

```
CL-USER> (defpackage :bio
           (:use :cl))
#<PACKAGE "BIO">
CL-USER> (in-package :bio)
#<PACKAGE "BIO">
BIO> (defclass tree () ())
#<STANDARD-CLASS TREE>
```

You now want to use a graph theory library for some of your computations. This library has defined a package called GRAPH. Among the symbols it exports, there's also one called TREE, because this is not only a biological term, but also one used in mathematics:

```
BIO> (defpackage :graph
       (:use :cl)
       (:export :vertex :edge :tree))
#<PACKAGE "GRAPH">
```

If you want to employ this library, you have to type things like GRAPH:VERTEX or GRAPH:EDGE. As this gets tedious pretty quickly, you decide to *use* the package, but you get an error message:

```
BIO> (use-package :graph)
USE-PACKAGE #<PACKAGE "GRAPH"> causes name-conflicts in
#<PACKAGE "BIO"> between the following symbols:
```

```
GRAPH:TREE, BIO::TREE
;; and so on...
```

At this point, you might want to have a look at the *restarts* (see Recipe 12-6) your system offers you, and then select the ABORT restart to do nothing for now.

What you'll most likely want in this case is:

```
BIO> (shadow 'tree)
T
BIO> (use-package :graph)
T
```

How It Works

As discussed in Recipe 1-1, each combination of package and symbol name has to be unique; that is, there can't be two *different* symbols of the *same* name accessible through the same package.

When we evaluated the USE-PACKAGE form above, we created the following conflict:

- There was already a symbol named TREE *present* (and thus *accessible*) in the BIO package.
- By *using* the GRAPH package we would have *inherited* its *exported* symbol named TREE and thus also made it accessible from the BIO package.
- But that's the name conflict. We'd have two *different* symbols of the same name accessible in the same package.

You can only have one of them and the solution essentially boils down to which of the two you want to keep (as an accessible symbol in your package) and what your decision would mean for the *other* symbol you "neglect:"

(A) If you opt for BIO::TREE as we did above, then BIO::TREE is added to the list of *shadowing* symbols of the BIO package. Whenever a package is *used* (as is GRAPH above), only those external symbols with names different from all shadowing symbols will be inherited.

So, after adding BIO::TREE to the list of shadowing symbols, GRAPH:TREE will simply not be inherited. But, of course, you can still access it using the package prefix; that is, as "GRAPH:TREE."

(B) If, for whatever reason, you want to opt for GRAPH:TREE instead, then you must make GRAPH:TREE one of BIO's shadowing symbols. But only present symbols can be shadowing symbols, so you first need to import GRAPH:TREE, which in turn only works if BIO::TREE is uninterned first. The function SHADOWING-IMPORT does all of this for you in one go, but the consequences are grave:

```
CL-USER> (defpackage :bio
           (:use :cl))
#<PACKAGE "BIO">
CL-USER> (in-package :bio)
#<PACKAGE "BIO">
BIO> (defclass tree () ())
#<STANDARD-CLASS TREE>
BIO> (find-class 'tree nil)
#<STANDARD-CLASS TREE>
BIO> (defpackage :graph
       (:use :cl)
       (:export :vertex :edge :tree))
#<PACKAGE "GRAPH">
BIO> (shadowing-import 'graph:tree)
T
BIO> (use-package :graph)
T
BIO> (find-class 'tree nil)
NIL
```

Because the original BIO::TREE is gone, you can no longer access the class you've defined! (More about this in Recipe 1-3.)

The situation is slightly different if you want to use two libraries that export conflicting symbols:

```
CL-USER> (defpackage :graph
           (:export :node :vertex :tree))
#<PACKAGE "GRAPH">
CL-USER> (defpackage :bio
           (:export :cat :dog :tree))
#<PACKAGE "BIO">
```

If you now try (USE-PACKAGE '(:GRAPH :BIO)), you get an error message, because there are two symbols called TREE competing to become an inherited symbol.

Shadowing is still the solution, but as we already know, only present symbols can be shadowing symbols; one of the two TREE symbols needs to be imported. Either

```
(shadowing-import 'graph:tree)
```

or

```
(shadowing-import 'bio:tree)
```

will solve the problem, but you have to make a decision.

When Name Conflicts Do Not Occur

Here's a situation where name conflicts don't happen, although you might expect so initially:

```
CL-USER> (defpackage :foo
           (:export :quux))
#<PACKAGE "FOO">
CL-USER> (defpackage :bar
           (:use :foo)
           (:export :quux))
#<PACKAGE "BAR">
CL-USER> (eql 'foo:quux 'bar:quux)
T
CL-USER> (use-package '(:foo :bar))
T
```

Both FOO and BAR export a symbol named QUUX, but it's the *same* symbol in both cases, so there's no conflict.

1-5. Using Symbols As Stand-Ins for Arbitrary Forms

Problem

You want to abbreviate an often-used form with a simple symbol.

Solution

Use *symbol macros*.

As an example, let's assume that your program uses a specific directory where images are stored. You could do something like

```
(defvar *pics-dir* #p"/data/pictures/")
```

and whenever you needed to access a specific picture you'd use a form like this:

```
(merge-pathnames "nanook.jpg" *pics-dir*)
```

However, a requirement of your program is that the image directory might change over time so that whenever you need it, you must query for the *current* image directory by using a form like this

```
(resource-information :type :directory :data :images)
```

to receive a value like `#p"/data/pictures/"` or whatever is current at the time of the call.

With a symbol macro you can do this

```
(define-symbol-macro %pics-dir%
  (resource-information :type :directory :data :images))
```

and then treat `%PICS-DIR%` like `*PICS-DIR*` in the `MERGE-PATHNAMES` form above, although now it would expand into the correct call to `RESOURCE-INFORMATION`.

How It Works

To a first approximation, a symbol macro is like a macro without parameters. You could have achieved a very similar effect using[22]

```
(defmacro pics-dir ()
  '(resource-information :type :directory :data :images))
```

but then you'd have to use it like this:

```
(merge-pathnames "nanook.jpg" (pics-dir))
```

That is, you'd have to wrap parentheses around it.

But the more important difference is that symbol macros are designed to *behave* like variables which in particular means two things:

- They can be *shadowed* by `LET` bindings. In a form like

  ```
  (let ((%pics-dir% #p"/tmp/"))
    (merge-pathnames "nanook.jpg" %pics-dir%))
  ```

  the result will always be `#"/tmp/nanook.jpg"`, no matter what the current image directory is.

[22]But note the quote sign.

- You can use them with special operators like SETQ or macros like MULTIPLE-VALUE-SETQ and they will "do the right thing."

  For example, if RESOURCE-INFORMATION were a *place* (see Recipe 10-8), then a form like

```
(setq %pics-dir% #p"/tmp/")
```

  would be expanded into this:

```
(setf (resource-information :type :directory :data :images)
      #p"/tmp/")
```

There's also a "local" variant called SYMBOL-MACROLET, which is to DEFINE-SYMBOL-MACRO what MACROLET is to DEFMACRO.

One burden that symbol macros don't take off your shoulders is the decision on whether their usage is actually a good idea in terms of style. If someone is reading your code and sees something like %PICS-DIR%, they might think that what they see is a variable and might be very surprised to learn that this "variable" metamorphoses into a (possibly expensive) function call each time it is used.

1-6. Searching for Symbols by Name

Problem

You want to know whether a symbol with a specific name exists.

Solution

You can use FIND-SYMBOL to search in one package and FIND-ALL-SYMBOLS to search in all packages:

```
CL-USER> (find-symbol "FOO")
NIL
NIL
CL-USER> 'foo
FOO
CL-USER> (find-symbol "FOO")
FOO
:INTERNAL
CL-USER> 'bar
BAR
```

```
CL-USER> (export *)
T
CL-USER> (defpackage :quux (:use :cl))
#<PACKAGE "QUUX">
CL-USER> (in-package :quux)
#<PACKAGE "QUUX">
QUUX> (find-symbol "FOO")
NIL
NIL
QUUX> (find-symbol "BAR")
NIL
NIL
QUUX> (use-package :cl-user)
T
QUUX> (find-symbol "FOO")
NIL
NIL
QUUX> (find-symbol "BAR")
BAR
:INHERITED
QUUX> (find-all-symbols "FOO")
;; output is implementation-dependent
(COMMON-LISP-USER::FOO :FOO SB-C::FOO SB-IMPL::FOO
                        SB-KERNEL::FOO)
```

How It Works

FIND-SYMBOL searches for symbols by *name* and its first argument has to be a string.[23] (And note that this search is case sensitive; see Recipe 1-8.) Its second argument is the package to search in; if there's no second argument, the current package is searched.

As you can see, the function not only returns the symbol (if found) but also a second return value describing the symbol's status.[24]

FIND-ALL-SYMBOLS searches *all* packages[25] for symbols of a specific name and returns a list of them.

---

[23] And thus isn't a *string designator* (see Recipe 1-9).

[24] For which see Recipe 1-1.

And because of one edge case the second return value is not only additional information but really needed: try (FIND-SYMBOL "NIL") and (FIND-SYMBOL "nil").

[25] Technically, it searches all *registered* packages. In theory, you could call DELETE-PACKAGE on a package, but keep a reference to it so that it would still be "there." It wouldn't be *registered* anymore, though.

As an alternative, you could use DO-ALL-SYMBOLS to loop through *all* symbols of *all* packages and collect only those you're interested in. For example, the following two forms create equal sets (see Recipe 6-10) of symbols, but the second one will likely do less work:

```
(union (find-all-symbols "VECTOR-ADD")
       (find-all-symbols "VECTOR-MULT"))

(let (result)
  (do-all-symbols (s)
  (when (member s '("VECTOR-ADD" "VECTOR-MULT")
                :test 'string=)
    (pushnew s result)))
    result)
```

(See also Recipe 16-8.)

1-7. Iterating Through All Symbols of a Package

Problem

You want to perform some action on all symbols of a package.

Solution

You can do this with LOOP:[26]

```
(loop for s being each external-symbol of :cl count s)
```

But there are other ways to do it. Keep reading.

How It Works

We've shown above how to go through all *external* symbols of a package with LOOP; that is, through those which can be accessed if there's one colon between the pack-

[26] The standard stipulates that the CL package must have exactly 978 external symbols which are all listed in its section 1.9. If you evaluate the form above in a conforming implementation, the result will be 977. Fun question: Why is it not 978?

Answer: One of the 978 symbols is NIL which this loop won't count.

age name and the symbol name, as in CL:DEFUN. You can instead replace EXTERNAL-SYMBOL with one of the following:[27]

- SYMBOL: This loops through all symbols *accessible* in the package; that is, those that can be reached if there are two colons between the package name and the symbol name.
- PRESENT-SYMBOL: This loops through all symbols that are *present* in the package; that is, those that would still be accessible if PACKAGE-USE-LIST applied to the package would return NIL.

As we've already seen, behind OF you can place the *name* of a package, but of course you can also use a package object itself. And you can also omit the OF part completely in which case it is understood that the *current package* is meant. Here's an example:

```
CL-USER > (defpackage :quux (:use :cl))
#<The QUUX package, 0/16 internal, 0/16 external>
CL-USER > (in-package :quux)
#<The QUUX package, 0/16 internal, 0/16 external>
QUUX > (loop for s being each present-symbol collect s)
(COLLECT PRESENT-SYMBOL S OF BEING EACH FOR)
QUUX > (loop for s being each symbol of (find-package "QUUX")
             count t)
985
```

What To Do If You Don't Like LOOP

There are two other ways to iterate through the symbols of a package. One is with "DO-" macros like so:

```
CL-USER > (do-symbols (s ':cl)
            (when (eql (char (symbol-name s) 0) #\Y)
              (return s)))
Y-OR-N-P
```

There's also DO-EXTERNAL-SYMBOLS but there's no equivalent to LOOP's ability to go through all present symbols. (See also Recipe 1-6 for DO-ALL-SYMBOLS.)

The second alternative is to use WITH-PACKAGE-ITERATOR, which roughly works like the macro WITH-HASH-TABLE-ITERATOR (see Recipe 6-4). It has yet another way to specify the symbols that you want (for example, only those that are *inherited*) and it can iterate more than one package at once. But in this case, I refer you to the HyperSpec for details.

[27]See Recipe 1-1 for a more detailed explanation of the terms *external*, *accessible* and *present*.

Note that for all of these iteration constructs, it is possible that you'll come across the same symbol more than once. Again, see the HyperSpec for more information.

1-8. Understanding Common Lisp's Case (In)Sensitivity

Problem

If you type `:foo` into the REPL, it will reply with `:FOO`, so COMMON LISP is obviously case insensitive, isn't it?

Solution

Of course, it isn't. And you knew that. What you're seeing is the combination of three different effects:

- How the Lisp reader interprets what you're typing.
- How symbols are stored internally.
- How the Lisp printer displays objects.

Both the reader's and the printer's behavior can be changed (about which more in Chapters 8 and 9), but their default is to behave *as if* COMMON LISP were case insensitive. Let's look at the details next.

How It Works

It's a common misconception (usually among people who have never used the language) that COMMON LISP is case insensitive. Of course, nobody doubts that strings (see Chapter 3) can contain lowercase as well as uppercase characters and that the language can distinguish between them. However, you typically only ever see *symbols* shown in uppercase, whereas Lisp hackers typically always type in lowercase. So, it is not too far-fetched to assume that symbols can only consist of uppercase characters and that the Lisp system helpfully converts lowercase characters (which are easier to type) into uppercase characters.

While the latter is true (although only as a default setting), the former is simply wrong. Let's start with symbols.

A symbol has two important constituents: its name and its package. Both are internally strings and *every* string you can create can act as a name. Likewise, two symbols (or packages) can't be identical unless they have the same name;[28] and "sameness" for names means STRING=.[29] In other words, it is possible to have three symbols with names "foo", "FOO", and "Foo" and they're all mutually distinct.

This already settles the question of whether COMMON LISP is case insensitive (it really, really isn't!), but it doesn't explain its "case insensitive behavior." So, what exactly happens if you type, say, :foo into your REPL and why does it end up as :FOO?

What we're concerned with here is what happens once the Lisp reader (see Chapter 8) has figured out it has just read a symbol (as opposed to, say, a number or an opening parenthesis). It will have read the symbol's name and that would mean in our example that it has read "foo". The next step would be to hand this name over to the *evaluator* telling it to treat it as a symbol with this name. However, *before* it'll do this, it consults its readtable (see Recipe 8-7) and as a result, it might *manipulate* the name!

Let's do some experiments. (If you want to type along, make sure to replicate exactly what is done here; otherwise, you might end up in a confusing state that you'll have trouble getting out of again.)

```
* (readtable-case *readtable*)
:UPCASE
* (symbol-name :foo)
"FOO"
* (symbol-name :FOO)
"FOO"
* (symbol-name :Foo)
"FOO"
* (symbol-name :F\oo)
"FoO"
* (setf (readtable-case *readtable*) :preserve)
:PRESERVE
* (SYMBOL-NAME :foo)
"foo"
* (SYMBOL-NAME :FOO)
"FOO"
* (SYMBOL-NAME :Foo)
"Foo"
* (SYMBOL-NAME :F\oo)
"Foo"
* (SETF (READTABLE-CASE *READTABLE*) :DOWNCASE)
:|DOWNCASE|
```

[28]Note that this does *not* mean that symbols with the same name are always identical. There's a crucial difference between a *necessary* and a *sufficient* condition.

[29]See Recipe 3-4.

```
* (|SYMBOL-NAME| :foo)
"foo"
* (|SYMBOL-NAME| :FOO)
"foo"
* (|SYMBOL-NAME| :Foo)
"foo"
* (|SYMBOL-NAME| :\Foo)
"Foo"
* (|SETF| (|READTABLE-CASE| |*READTABLE*|) :|INVERT|)
:invert
* (symbol-name :foo)
"FOO"
* (symbol-name :FOO)
"foo"
* (symbol-name :Foo)
"Foo"
* (symbol-name :f\oo)
"FoO"
* (setf (readtable-case *readtable*) :upcase)
:UPCASE
```

Let's take this in step by step. We're using the function READTABLE-CASE, which can be used as a reader as well as a writer, and we're manipulating the current readtable through the variable *READTABLE*, so each change immediately affects how the next input is read. There are four allowed values—:UPCASE, :DOWNCASE, :PRESERVE, and :INVERT—of which the first is the default. :UPCASE means that every alphabetic character within a symbol's name is upcased no matter how you typed it.[30] That's the main reason your Lisp seems to be case insensitive.

In the next part of our example we change the readtable case to :PRESERVE, which as the name implies, just means that case is always preserved. This seems simple except that it wouldn't have worked if your next line had been this one:

```
* (symbol-name :foo)
```

The reason is that all the symbol names in the COMMON-LISP package are in uppercase (because of the default readtable case, obviously), whereas typing symbol-name while :PRESERVE is active means asking for the function named "symbol-name", which doesn't exist. That's why you have to write the following instead:

```
* (SYMBOL-NAME :foo)
```

We're then trying out how the reader behaves if the readtable case is :DOWNCASE, and

[30] *Unless*, that is, you *escaped* it (as was the case for the second character in :F\oo) in which case no conversion happens.

this is not really surprising; it's like `:UPCASE`, only in the other direction. The only interesting question is how to get out of this because neither

```
* (setf (readtable-case *readtable*) :invert)
```

nor

```
* (SETF (READTABLE-CASE *READTABLE*) :INVERT)
```

would have worked. In both cases, the downcase conversion would have resulted in the wrong symbols. The only cure is to escape all characters because the readtable case doesn't affect escaped characters:[31]

```
* (|SETF| (|READTABLE-CASE| |*READTABLE*|) :|INVERT|)
```

Finally, we're looking at the `:INVERT` case, which is arguably the strangest of the four; it will *invert* the case (from lowercase to uppercase or vice versa), but *only* if all (unescaped) characters have the same case. In other words, sequences of characters with mixed case won't be changed at all. You can't help but wonder who might have a use for this one.

But this is not all. Our little experiment used the `SYMBOL-NAME` function on purpose because just returning the symbol itself could have been more confusing. We'll do that now, and maybe you should first try to make sense of this yourself:

```
* (readtable-case *readtable*)
:UPCASE
* (symbol-name :foo)
"FOO"
* :foo
:FOO
* (symbol-name :|foo|)
"foo"
* :|foo|
:|foo|
* *print-case*
:UPCASE
* (setf *print-case* :downcase)
:downcase
* :foo
:foo
* :|foo|
:|foo|
* (setf *print-case* :capitalize)
```

[31]You could also type `\S\E\T\F` instead of `|SETF|` but that doesn't seem very desirable.

```
:Capitalize
* :foo
:Foo
* :|foo|
:|foo|
* (setf *print-case* :upcase)
:UPCASE
* (setf (readtable-case *readtable*) :downcase)
:|DOWNCASE|
* (|LIST| :foo :|FOO|)
(:FOO :|FOO|)
* (|SETF| |*PRINT-CASE*| :|DOWNCASE|)
:|DOWNCASE|
* (|LIST| :foo :|FOO|)
(:foo :|FOO|)
* (|SETF| |*PRINT-CASE*| :|CAPITALIZE|)
:|CAPITALIZE|
* (|LIST| :foo :|FOO|)
(:Foo :|FOO|)
```

The description of this behavior in the HyperSpec, while technically correct, is not exactly enlightening. The underlying mechanism is quite simple, though: the Lisp printer "knows" about the current readtable case and will always[32] print a symbol in such a way that using this printed representation as input with the same readtable would result in the same symbol.

This allows for some leeway, though, as with readtable cases like `:DOWNCASE`, there are several ways of entering the same symbol. That's what `*PRINT-CASE*` is for: it controls how these symbols are printed. This can then lead to the strange behavior that while in readtable case `:DOWNCASE`, and with the default value for `*PRINT-CASE*`, you type `:FOO` and the printer responds with `:FOO`, although the symbol's name really consists of lowercase letters.

Finally, literal strings are never affected by the settings discussed in this recipe. This means that if you use `INTERN` or `MAKE-SYMBOL` (see Recipe 1-2), the string argument will always be used exactly as provided.

Style Hint: Don't Use CamelCase!

You knew it before but even if you didn't you know it now: With the default settings (which is what everybody will use 99.9% of the time) it makes no difference for COMMON LISP whether you use `RocketVelocity` or `rocketvelocity` (or even

[32]Well, unless you also fiddle with `*PRINT-ESCAPE*`. But let's talk about that on a rainy day...

rOCkEtveLOciTy) as a variable name; it'll all end up as ROCKETVELOCITY where you can't see anymore that this was meant to consist of two words. If a language is always case sensitive (as are JAVA and other C-syntax languages), then it makes sense to use the so-called "CamelCase" convention to name objects, but for Lisp it is nonsense, so don't do it. (It won't hurt either, but the other kids won't want to play with you.)

An alternative (also common in many programming language cultures) is to use the underline character to separate words as in rocket_velocity. That's not as bad as the CamelCase variant, but arguably it's also not as good as the Lisp-y way to use hyphens as in rocket-velocity. The underline is used in languages that *can't* use hyphens in identifiers. Lisp can. And hyphens are simply more natural and also a bit easier to type on most keyboards.

But the most compelling reason to not use CamelCase should be that your Lisp IDE will be better suited to deal with hyphens in symbol names: in a good IDE (see Recipe 16-2), you should be able to type m-v-b and have it automatically completed to MULTIPLE-VALUE-BIND. Try that with MULTIPLEVALUEBIND...

So: when in Rome, do as the Romans do.

1-9. Using Symbols As String Substitutes

Problem

You want to understand the differences between the strings "foo" or "FOO" and the symbols FOO, :FOO, and #:FOO, and when they can be used interchangeably.

Solution

Some COMMON LISP functions don't care whether their argument is a string or a symbol. Let's try some experiments.

If you enter this form

```
(length
 (remove-duplicates
  (mapcar #'find-package '(CL :CL #:CL "CL"))))
```

your Lisp returns the number 1. We call the function FIND-PACKAGE with four different arguments (three symbols that are really distinct and one string), and after removing duplicates, it turns out the result is always the same. In all cases, the package with the name "COMMON-LISP" is found.

And some functions even have STRING- in their name, but will happily accept symbols, too:

```
(string-capitalize :foo)
```

(This should return the *string* "Foo".)

So, what's happening here?

How It Works

What these functions have in common with several other Lisp functions is that they are intended to work with strings, but will also happily accept what the standard calls a *string designator*—something that can stand in for a string. Of course, a string itself can be a string designator, but as we saw above, so can a symbol. The crucial point here is that the symbol's *name* will be used as the string.[33] Of course, case still matters, as always (see Recipe 1-8), so neither of the following two forms would have found the COMMON-LISP package:

```
(find-package "cl")
(find-package '|cl|)
```

By the way, characters can also act as *string designators*, but that's rather boring, as a character simply stands in for the string of length one, which only consists of this character.

And here's something that won't work: if a function works on strings and relies on their being arrays (like the function CHAR) or if it is designed to *destructively* modify a string (like NSTRING-CAPITALIZE), then it will only accept *real* strings as arguments, no surrogates.

So, What Should You Use?

If you're looking at the package definitions (a place where string designators can be employed) in several open source libraries, you will find at least three styles in use:

```
(defpackage :my-package-1
  (:use :cl)
  (:export :important-function))

;; ... or ...
```

[33] Which implies that the symbol's *package* is completely ignored. That's why :CL and CL had the same effect in our example.

```
(defpackage #:my-package-2
  (:use #:cl)
  (:export #:important-function))

;; ... or ...

(defpackage "MY-PACKAGE-3"
  (:use "CL")
  (:export "IMPORTANT-FUNCTION"))
```

The first variant uses keyword symbols. This is short and succint, and arguably aesthetically the most pleasant form, but some think that it will "litter" your Lisp *image* (see Recipe 16-1) with unnecessary symbols.[34] For example, after reading the first `DEFPACKAGE` form, symbols like `:MY-PACKAGE-1` and `:IMPORTANT-FUNCTION` will have been interned into the keyword package, although you'll probably never need them again.

The second variant doesn't have this problem, because the symbols are explicitly *not* interned (see Recipe 1-3). It is, however, a bit ugly and it entails typing one extra character per name.

The third variant also uses more characters, but it doesn't create any symbols at all and is probably not as ugly as the second one. It also explicitly shows that all names are meant to be uppercase. This might be construed as a good thing by some, but it will cease to work if you're using the so-called *modern mode* of ALLEGROCL. That's why it's not a good idea to use this style if you're interested in wide dissemination of your code.

I'd say that which of these styles you use is largely a matter of taste and not worth bickering about. But now you'll at least know what your options are.

1-10. "Overloading" of Standard Common Lisp Operators

Problem

C++ has "operator overloading" in the sense that you can, say, give the addition symbol + its own specific meaning, if it is used with instances of classes that you've defined.[35] You want that in COMMON LISP as well.

[34] You could also say that if you did this in an open source library, you'd be littering *other people's* Lisp images.

[35] See `https://en.wikipedia.org/wiki/Operator_overloading`.

Solution

The short answer is that (a) in Lisp there can only be *function overloading*, as something like + is just a function like SIN or CONS, and (b) you can't do it, as + is not a generic function and you are not allowed to redefine it.

But, as almost always, there is a way to do it if you really want...

How It Works

Let's suppose you want to have a class VECTOR and you'd like to be able to add your vectors using the same notation as for numbers.

You could do something like this:[36]

```
CL-USER > (defpackage :vec
            (:use :cl)
            (:shadow :vector :+))
#<The VEC package, 2/16 internal, 0/16 external>
CL-USER > (in-package :vec)
#<The VEC package, 2/16 internal, 0/16 external>
VEC > (defclass vector ()
        ((x :initarg :x :reader x)
         (y :initarg :y :reader y)))
#<STANDARD-CLASS VECTOR 200A309B>
VEC > (defgeneric + (arg &rest other-args)
        (:method ((arg number) &rest other-args)
         (apply 'cl:+ arg other-args)))
#<STANDARD-GENERIC-FUNCTION + 200928CA>
VEC > (defmethod + ((arg vector) &rest other-args)
        (make-instance 'vector
                       :x (apply 'cl:+ (x arg)
                                       (mapcar 'x other-args))
                       :y (apply 'cl:+ (y arg)
                                       (mapcar 'y other-args))))
#<STANDARD-METHOD + NIL (VECTOR) 201097F3>
```

Now, as long as you are in the VEC package, this will work as always:

```
(+ 3 4 5)
```

But something like this will now also work:

[36]See also Recipe 13-3.

```
(+ (make-instance 'vector :x 3 :y 4)
   (make-instance 'vector :x 5 :y 6)
   (make-instance 'vector :x 7 :y 8))
```

The relevant part, as far as the subject of this chapter is concerned, is that we work in our own package VEC. We *use* the CL package so that all the usual symbols are accessible, but we make sure that two standard symbols, + and VECTOR, are *not* inherited. (This is called *shadowing*; see Recipe 1-4.)

This enables us to define a class called VECTOR and a generic function called +.[37] Both of these names are symbols in our own package, and whereas they have the same *name* as the corresponding CL symbols, they are different objects.

If we want to use the *"real"* +, we must access it as CL:+; that is, with its package prefix, as we do it in the method definitions.

This technique of selectively shadowing CL symbols and replacing them with our own implementations gives us something akin to "operator overloading." The only downside is that the indirection of going through the generic function VEC::+ will make something like (+ 3 4) a little bit slower than it used to be (and it will make it harder for the compiler to optimize our code). But that's the usual antagonism of convenience and efficiency.

[37] Although you aren't allowed to define a class called CL:VECTOR or a generic function called CL:+.

2. Conses, Lists, and Trees

While you also have hash tables (see Chapter 6) and arrays (see Chapter 5), conses and lists remain the most important building block for data structures in COMMON LISP, if only because that's how the internal representation of your code is realized and you'll thus need them if you want to write macros and domain-specific languages. Also, because COMMON LISP has such a plethora of built-in convenience functions to manipulate conses and lists, and because conses are at the same time very simple yet extremely versatile, there are lots of situations where you should just use them (whereas if you're coming from another programming language, your first instinct might tell you to use, say, arrays). Some of the recipes in this chapter will thus show how widely-used data structures can be implemented on the basis of cons cells.

Peter Seibel explained the basics of conses and lists in chapters 12 and 13[1] of *Practical Common Lisp* (Apress, 2005).[2] I will thus try to concentrate on things that he omitted or only mentioned in passing. But I'll also revisit some things that I think are important enough to repeat.

Conses are also what's underneath *alists*, *plists*, and *sets*, of which you'll find more in Chapter 6. And lists are *sequences* and you'll thus meet them again in Chapter 7.

2-1. Understanding Conses

Problem

You want to know how lists (and trees) are built internally.

Solution

Although, as you'll know, *Lisp* is short for "**LISt** Processing," the most basic structure in Lisp is *not* the list but the *cons* which is constructed with the eponymous function

[1]Online at `http://www.gigamonkeys.com/book/they-called-it-lisp-for-a-reason-list-processing.html` and `http://www.gigamonkeys.com/book/beyond-lists-other-uses-for-cons-cells.html`.

[2]Another good source for how lists work is the book *Common Lisp* by David S. Touretzky (Dover Publications, 2013), which is available online at `https://www.cs.cmu.edu/~dst/LispBook/`.

CONS:[3]

```
CL-USER> (cons 42 #\X)
(42 . #\X)
CL-USER> (car *)
42
CL-USER> (cdr **)
#\X
```

A cons always has two parts and their order is significant; that is, it works exactly like an *ordered pair*[4] in mathematics (as opposed to a *doubleton*, a set of two elements). As we saw above,[5] these two parts can be accessed using the functions CAR and CDR.[6] COMMON LISP also has FIRST and REST, which do exactly the same thing as CAR and CDR. It is rather a matter of style which you prefer. I tend to use CAR and CDR for conses and the other two if I'm working with lists, but I'm not religious about it.

Conses have a printed representation where the two parts are enclosed in parentheses and separated by a dot surrounded by spaces. You can also use this dot notation for input:[7]

```
CL-USER> (cons 'foo 'bar)
(FOO . BAR)
CL-USER> '(foo . bar)
(FOO . BAR)
```

Any Lisp object whatsoever can be the car or cdr of a cons:

```
CL-USER> (cons (make-array 1 :initial-element 23)
               "23")
(#(23) . "23")
```

And thus also conses can be put into conses:

```
CL-USER> (cons (cons 1 2) :foo)
((1 . 2) . :FOO)
```

A *list* is nothing more than a chain of conses; the cdr of the first cons is a cons the cdr of which is again a cons and so on, until finally one cdr is NIL which ends the list:

[3]That's an abbreviation for *constructing*; in the Lisp world, it is used as a noun like above but also as a verb (see Recipe 17-6).

[4]See https://en.wikipedia.org/wiki/Ordered_pair.

[5]See Recipe 16-11 for the meaning of * and **.

[6]And like with *cons*, these two are also used as nouns: "The car of (4 . 2) is 4."

[7]And in case you're wondering: there's no way to confuse the dot in the middle with a symbol the name of which is only a dot. A stand-alone dot is only allowed as a separator in conses, and if you want to use it as a symbol name, it has to be escaped (see Recipe 8-8 and section 2.3.3 of the standard).

```
CL-USER> (cons 'a (cons 'b (cons 'c (cons 'd nil))))
(A B C D)
```

This also shows that there's a special notation for lists, or rather for conses where the cdr is a cons or `NIL`:[8]

- If the cdr is a cons, then the dot in front of it and the parentheses around it are suppressed:

```
CL-USER> (cons 1 (cons 3 4))
(1 3 . 4)                          ;; instead of (1 . (3 . 4))
```

- If the cdr is `NIL`, then it and the dot in front of it are suppressed:

```
CL-USER> (cons 42 nil)
(42)                               ;; instead of (42 . NIL)
```

How It Works

While you can get pretty far with the mental image that lists are, well, "just lists," it is in the long run much more instructive to look beneath the surface and view lists in terms of conses. This will not only enable you to construct other data structures like trees from lists, it'll also help you understand the performance characteristics of lists.

A cons is nothing more or less than an abstract data structure (which you can image as a kind of C `struct` if you like) that can hold two objects. So, the first cons from above could be represented graphically like so:

42	#\X

Here, the cons itself would consist of the two boxes and each box is a container that can contain anything, like, for example, the integer 42 or the character `#\X`.

But a more fitting representation would look like this:

[8] Interestingly, and although you can customize almost everything else in COMMON LISP, there's no portable way to convince the Lisp printer to use the dot notation for lists. But there's a nice little library called DRAW-CONS-TREE that can be used to draw ASCII pictures of conses similar to the pictures in this chapter.

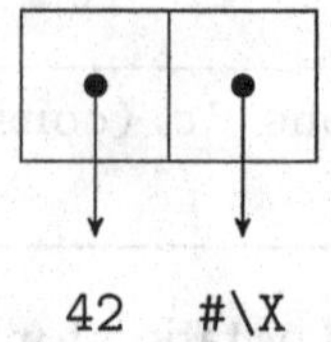

This shows the car and the cdr as being *references*[9] (represented as arrows) to objects. (Some authors prefer to make a distinction between "simple" or "immediate" objects being drawn within the box, whereas others are drawn outside with arrows pointing to them. I find this distinction rather arbitrary and potentially misleading, although it might be close to how most implementations store conses internally.)

The `((1 . 2) . :FOO)` cons-within-a-cons would then look like this:[10]

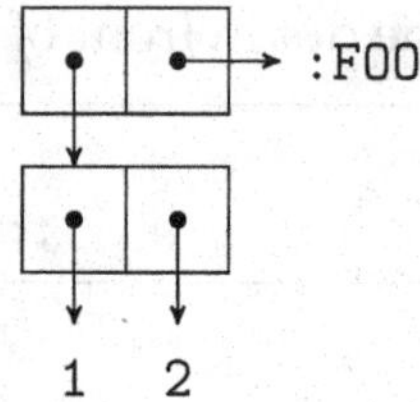

And it is now also obvious how a list as `(A B C D)` looks like:

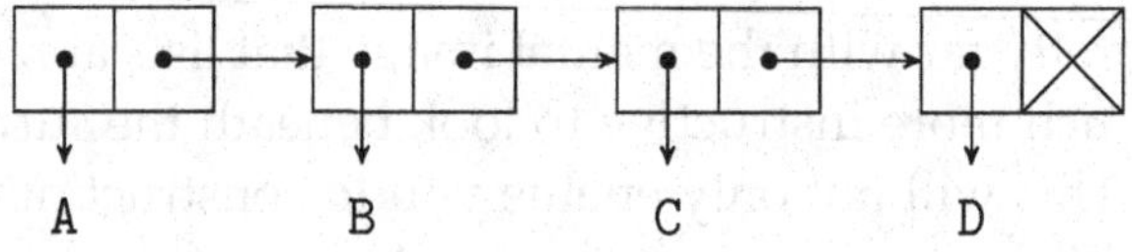

Here `NIL` is symbolized by crossing out the cdr box.[11]

List Access

And that's all there is to it. A list is really nothing more than a bunch of conses with absolutely no additional information attached to it. This makes conses and lists data structures that are lightweight, easy to handle, and versatile. But it also comes with a couple of drawbacks:

- If you hold a reference to a list, then all you really have is a reference to the beginning of the list; that is, to its first cons cell.
- If you now want to know the length of the list or access its, say, 42nd element, then the only way to achieve that is to traverse it "cons by cons," counting the conses that you pass, until you are at the end or where you wanted to end up.

[9]You can also imagine them as *pointers* except that there's no pointer indirection; the car of this cons *is* the number `42` and not a pointer to it.

[10]I will generally lay out conses so that they somehow "look nice," which is to say that it, of course, doesn't matter whether an arrow points down, or to the right, or somewhere else.

[11]And it is not too far-fetched in this context to think of `NIL` as the `NULL` pointer in C.

- You can't even be sure whether the reference you have is really a reference to a *proper list* (see below) unless you've traversed it completely.
- If a variable "points" somewhere into the middle of a list, there's *no* way to go back and find the beginning of the list from there. (You could just as well be at the beginning of a list that just happens to be the *tail* of some other list someone else has a reference to.)

In computer science parlance, Lisp lists are *singly-linked lists* and their main disadvantage is that random access to list elements is $\mathcal{O}(n)$; whereas for arrays and hash tables it is $\mathcal{O}(1)$.[12] But if you're aware of these shortcomings and don't use lists for data for which arrays or hash tables would be a better fit, then conses are a great tool that can not only be used for lists, alist, plists, sets, and trees, but for almost any ad hoc data structure that you can think of.

Testing Whether Something Is a Cons or a List

To check whether something is a cons, use the function CONSP. There's also the corresponding type CONS and you can also create *compound type specifiers* (see Recipe 13-1) based on this type. The following form would for example check whether A is a cons whose car is a number and whose cdr is a string:[13]

```
(check-type a (cons number string))
```

The complement of the type CONS is the type ATOM; that is, it is *as if* ATOM had been defined by this form:

```
(deftype atom ()
  '(not cons))
```

This implies that every object in COMMON LISP is either an atom or a cons but never both. There's also a test function of the same name; so it is *not* called "ATOMP," as you might expect.

(The term "atom" is a bit misleading because it derives from the Greek word for *indivisible* and in Lisp applies to things like arrays or hash tables which are clearly "divisible" in the sense of being compound objects. This is a remnant from the times when the only compound objects in Lisp where conses.)

Although it is obvious what a cons is, it is not so clear what a *list* should be. There are at least two different meanings:

[12]This is the *Landau notation* typically used in computation complexity theory (see https://en.wikipedia.org/wiki/Big_O_notation).

[13]See Recipe 12-1 for CHECK-TYPE.

- A list is an object of type `LIST` and can be tested with the function `LISTP`. This type and the type `NULL`[14] behave *as if* they had been defined like so:

```
(deftype null ()
  '(member nil))

(deftype list ()
  '(or cons null))
```

So, by this definition, all of the following six objects are lists.

```
CL-USER> nil
NIL                                              ;; proper list
CL-USER> (cons 1 2)
(1 . 2)
CL-USER> (cons (cons 1 2) 3)
((1 . 2) . 3)
CL-USER> (cons (cons (cons 1 2) 3) 4)
(((1 . 2) . 3) . 4)
CL-USER> (cons 1 (cons 2 (cons 3 4)))
(1 2 3 . 4)
CL-USER> (cons 1 (cons 2 (cons 3 nil)))
(1 2 3)                                          ;; proper list
```

And *circular lists* (see Recipe 7-6) are, of course, also of type `LIST`.

- A *proper list* is a list like above with the added requirement that it is either `NIL` or, if you follow the chain of cdrs from the first cons, ends in a cons with the cdr `NIL`. This excludes circular lists (because they don't end) and *dotted lists* like the second to fifth examples above because they end in something that's not of type `NULL`.

If people are talking about "lists," they usually mean *proper* lists. But to check whether something is a proper list can be pretty expensive, because you'd have to walk through all conses and also check for circularity. The `LISTP` check, on the other hand, is very simple and never looks beyond the first cons. The ALEXANDRIA library (see Recipe 18-4) offers types and tests for proper and circular lists.

For information on how to *compare* conses, lists, and trees, see Recipe 10-1.

[14]There's also a corresponding function `NULL` (*not* "`NULLP`"). `NULL` does exactly the same as `NOT`. Which of the two you use should depend on which intention you want to convey to the reader of your code.

2-2. Creating Lists

Problem

You want to create lists without constructing them from individual conses.

Solution

Well, of course nobody uses CONS to construct lists as we did in Recipe 2-1. There are actually a lot of different ways to create lists. To begin with, here are the most common ones:

```
CL-USER> (list 1 2 3)
(1 2 3)
CL-USER> (list 1)
(1)
CL-USER> (list)
NIL
CL-USER> (list 1 2 (list 3 4))
(1 2 (3 4))
CL-USER> (list* 1 2 (list 3 4))
(1 2 3 4)
CL-USER> (make-list 4 :initial-element 42)
(42 42 42 42)
CL-USER> (make-list 4)
(NIL NIL NIL NIL)
```

But there's more...

How It Works

It should be pretty obvious what LIST and MAKE-LIST do. The only difference between LIST and LIST* is that the last argument of the latter function doesn't become the last element of the newly-created list but rather its tail. The structural difference looks like so:

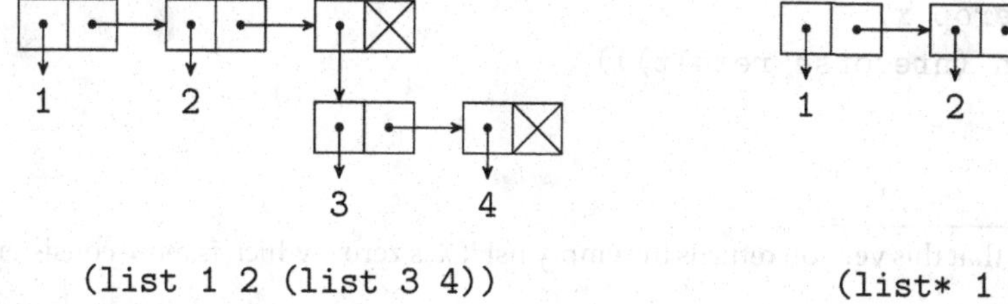

Converting Vectors to Lists

You can also easily convert any vector (see Recipe 5-2) to a list by means of the function COERCE:

```
CL-USER> (coerce #(3 2 1 0) 'list)
(3 2 1 0)
```

Or you could have done it like so:

```
CL-USER> (map 'list 'identity #(3 2 1 0))
(3 2 1 0)
```

And as strings are vectors, this will also work:

```
CL-USER> (coerce "Frunobulax" 'list)
(#\F #\r #\u #\n #\o #\b #\u #\l #\a #\x)
```

There's no built-in way to convert an integer to a list of its bits, unfortunately. For your amusement, here's one way to do it which is horribly inefficient but "elegant" in a certain way as it's a one-liner (but for the page width):

```
(defun integer-to-bit-list (x)
  (check-type x (integer 0 *))
  (reverse
   (mapcar 'parse-integer
           (mapcar 'string (coerce (format nil "~b" x) 'list)))))
```

We first use FORMAT to get the binary representation of X as a string (see Recipe 4-4), and then we convert the string to a list of characters. Next, we convert these characters to strings again so that we can eventually apply PARSE-INTEGER (see Recipe 4-9). As the very last step, we reverse the result so that the least significant bits come first (or in other words, so that the last element of the list is a one unless X is zero).

A more reasonable version is this one:[15]

```
(defun integer-to-bit-list (x)
  (check-type x (integer 0 *))
  (let (result)
    (loop (when (zerop x)
            (return (nreverse result)))
```

[15]With the slight difference that this version returns the empty list if X is zero—which is more consistent anyway.
For the use of NREVERSE see the footnote on page 43.

```
        (push (logand x 1) result)
        (setf x (ash x -1)))))
```

The ALEXANDRIA library (see Recipe 18-4) has functions to "listify" hash tables (or only their keys or values).[16]

(See also Recipe 2-4 for yet another way to create lists.)

2-3. Transposing a Matrix

Problem

You want to *transpose*[17] a matrix.

Solution

If your matrix is stored as a list of lists, then it's as simple as this:

```
(apply 'mapcar 'list matrix)
```

How It Works

Let's use this transposition as an example:

$$\begin{pmatrix} 11 & 12 & 13 & 14 \\ 21 & 22 & 23 & 24 \\ 31 & 32 & 33 & 34 \end{pmatrix} \rightsquigarrow \begin{pmatrix} 11 & 21 & 31 \\ 12 & 22 & 32 \\ 13 & 23 & 33 \\ 14 & 24 & 34 \end{pmatrix}$$

In Lisp, it'd look like this:[18]

```
CL-USER> (defparameter *m*
           '((11 12 13 14)
             (21 22 23 24)
             (31 32 33 34)))
*M*
CL-USER> (let ((*print-right-margin* 20))
```

[16]Although what you'll get isn't a list in a narrower sense but rather an *alist*, a *plist*, or a *set*. (See Chapter 6.)

[17]See `https://en.wikipedia.org/wiki/Transpose`.

[18]We used the *pretty printer* to make the result look good (see Recipe 9-9).

```
          (pprint (apply 'mapcar 'list *m*)))
((11 21 31)
 (12 22 32)
 (13 23 33)
 (14 24 34))
; No value
```

The "trick" here is that APPLY "deconstructs" the matrix and works as if we had done this:

```
(mapcar 'list '(11 12 13 14) '(21 22 23 24) '(31 32 33 34))
```

And now it should be pretty obvious what's happening: MAPCAR (see Recipe 7-12) traverses all three lists in parallel and LIST combines the corresponding elements.

If, however, you're using arrays to store your matrices, you will have to implement transposition with loops like everybody else...

2-4. Using List Interpolation

Problem

You want to create lists based on a "template" that is to be filled.

Solution

Use the *backquote* syntax.

In its simplest form, the backquote character has exactly the same effect as a single quote (which is itself, as you'll know, just an abbreviation for the special operator QUOTE):

```
CL-USER> `(a b c)
(A B C)
CL-USER> '(a b c)
(A B C)
CL-USER> (quote (a b c))
(A B C)
```

But inside the form following the backquote the comma acquires a special meaning: it "unquotes" the form following it.

```
CL-USER> (let ((b 42))
           `(a ,b c))
(A 42 C)
```

And if the comma is immediately followed by an at-sign (@), the form following this pair of characters will also be evaluated, but afterward it is "spliced" into the containing structure:[19]

```
CL-USER> (let ((b (list 23 42)))
           `(a ,@b c))
(A 23 42 C)
```

How It Works

Many people who learn COMMON LISP have their first contact with the backquote syntax in the context of macros and some think that it is only useful there. But the backquote character is simply a standard *macro character* (see Recipe 8-8) and thus this syntax can be used everywhere.

And although the name of this recipe contains the word *list*, the backquote syntax can be used with arbitrarily complex structures built out of conses. You can, for example, regenerate the example tree from Recipe 2-8 like so:

```
CL-USER> (let ((x 'f)
               (y (list 'g nil nil)))
           `(a (b (d nil nil) (e nil nil)) (c (,x nil nil) (,@y))))
(A (B (D NIL NIL) (E NIL NIL)) (C (F NIL NIL) (G NIL NIL)))
```

Or you can mix this with the dot syntax (see Recipe 2-1):

```
CL-USER> (let ((list '(3 4)))
           `(1 2 . ,list))
(1 2 3 4)
```

And it can be used with vectors (see Recipe 5-2) as well:

```
CL-USER> (let ((list '(3 4)))
           `#(1 2 ,@list 5))
#(1 2 3 4 5)
```

[19]Which implies that the form must evaluate to a list.

Beware, though, that the backquote syntax will typically *not* produce a completely *fresh* object each time it is invoked. Rather, objects generated this way will very likely share structure (see Recipe 2-7):

```
CL-USER> (flet ((foo (x)
                  `(,x b c)))
           (let ((a (foo 23))
                 (b (foo 42)))
             (list a b (eq a b) (eq (cdr a) (cdr b)))))
((23 B C) (42 B C) NIL T)
```

This shows that the two lists A and B are (of course) different objects but that the cdr of A is *identical* (see Recipe 10-1) to that of B.

How the backquote syntax is implemented internally usually remains hidden from a COMMON LISP programmer, but there are several portable implementations available; for example, the FARE-QUASIQUOTE library (see Recipe 2-11 for a usage example).

2-5. Adding Objects to the End of a List

Problem

You want to add something to the end of a list and you're wondering why COMMON LISP doesn't have a specific operator for this.[20]

Solution

The short answer is: Don't do that!

There are ways to add something to the end of a list; for example, like so:[21]

```
CL-USER> (defparameter *list* (list 'a 'b 'c))
*LIST*
CL-USER> (setf *list* (append *list* (list 'd)))
(A B C D)
```

But there's a reason why this feels clumsy and why COMMON LISP's PUSH (see Recipe 2-9) doesn't have an equivalent for the "other end" of a list.

[20]Like, for example, JAVASCRIPT's **push** in addition to **unshift**.

[21]Note that ***LIST*** will now have the value you wanted it to have, but the *original* list wasn't changed. See more below.

How It Works

From Recipe 2-1 it should be clear why adding something to the start of a list and adding something to the end are two completely different operations; to add something to the start, you just create a new cons cell where the car is the new object and the cdr is the list you add to. To add something to the end of a list, you must walk through the whole list until you reach its end and then replace the last cdr (which will be `NIL`) with a new cons. So, if in your application, you constantly need to add objects to a list's end, then you should reconsider and maybe use a data structure that is a better fit.

Having said that, there are situations where using a list might still be a valid choice. One technique often used in the Lisp world in such a case is to "turn things upside down." If extending the list happens more often than accessing it, you might consider adding from the start and then reversing it when needed.

For a simple example let's build an ordered list of perfect squares (leaving aside for now that this would be much easier with `LOOP`). The wrong way of doing it would be like above:

```
CL-USER> (let (list)
           (dotimes (i 10)
             (setf list (append list (list (* i i)))))
           list)
(0 1 4 9 16 25 36 49 64 81)
```

And the typical "Lisp-y" way would be like so:[22]

```
CL-USER> (let (list)
           (dotimes (i 10)
             (push (* i i) list))
           (nreverse list))
(0 1 4 9 16 25 36 49 64 81)
```

This is not only a matter of efficiency (which is not so important in this case) as mainly one of style. Pretty much every experienced Lisper will prefer the second version and consider it more elegant.

(See Recipe 4-9 for a function that uses this technique.)

[22] By the way, this is one of the few situations where the use of a *destructive* operation (see page 534) like `NREVERSE` instead of `REVERSE` would not be dangerous at all; you have created the list yourself, the original list (the one in the wrong order) will be thrown away anyway, and nobody else holds a reference to it or some tail of it. Still, for a list as short as this one, it is probably premature optimization (see the introduction to Chapter 17).

The Tail Wagging the List

Another technique that might be helpful at times is to keep a reference to the *tail* of the list. In order to understand how this is done, let's revisit the list (A B C D) from Recipe 2-1:

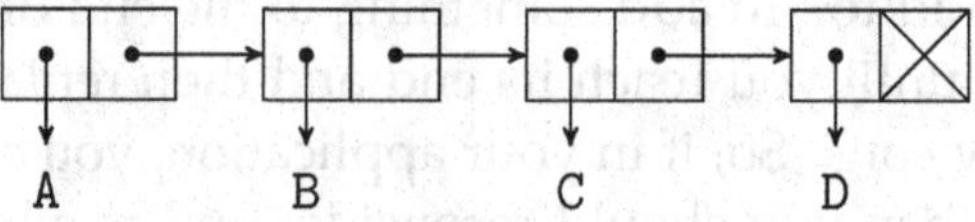

To add something to the end, we need to modify the last cons; that is, we need a reference to it:[23]

```
CL-USER> (defparameter *list* (list 'a 'b 'c 'd))
*LIST*
CL-USER> (defparameter *tail* (cdddr *list*))       ;; or (LAST *LIST*)
*TAIL*
CL-USER> *tail*
(D)
```

What we now have is this:

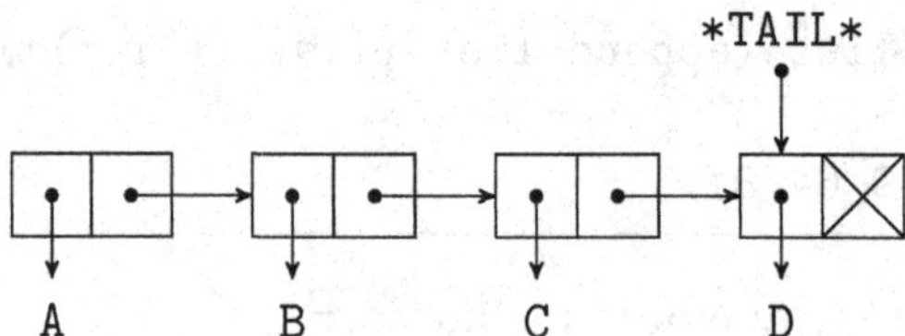

And we can add something to the end, like so:

```
;; continued from above
CL-USER> (setf (cdr *tail*) (cons 'e 'nil)
               *tail* (cdr *tail*))
(E)
CL-USER> *list*
(A B C D E)
```

This can be translated to our perfect square example:

```
CL-USER> (let (list tail)
           (dotimes (i 10)
             (let ((new-tail (cons (* i i) nil)))
               (cond ((null list) (setf list new-tail))
                     (t (setf (cdr tail) new-tail)))
```

[23]LAST gives you the last cons (or the last *n* conses if used with an optional argument) of a list. Of course, it still has to traverse the list in order to achieve that.

```
                (setf tail new-tail)))
            list)
(0 1 4 9 16 25 36 49 64 81)
```

The important point here is that TAIL "keeps moving;" that is, we don't have to find the end of the list on each iteration as in our first example. In this particularly simple case, that's certainly overkill, but it showcases the general idea, which, for example, can be used to implement a *queue*, as in Recipe 2-10.

You should be aware, though, that this is a *destructive* (see page 534) technique that is error-prone and potentially dangerous. Such code can be very efficient, but its complexity should better be hidden. That's why, as I already alluded to, for our example, LOOP would certainly be the most elegant choice:

```
CL-USER> (loop for i below 10 collect (* i i))
(0 1 4 9 16 25 36 49 64 81)
```

It might be instructive to look at the macro expansion of this form in various Lisps to see how they do it. Chances are that they'll also use some tail-chasing technique under the hood.

2-6. "Splicing" into a List

Problem

JAVASCRIPT has this nice splice method[24] that you can use to replace a subsequence of an array with some other sequence not necessarily of the same length. You want that for COMMON LISP's lists as well.

Solution

COMMON LISP doesn't have a standard function to do that, but of course it can be done somehow.

First of all, both NTH (access the *n*th element of a list) and SUBSEQ (access an arbitrary subsequence of a list, or actually of any sequence) are "setf-able" (see Recipe 10-8) which means that you can already replace parts of a list. However, this will only work as expected if the replacement sequence has exactly the same length as the part of the list we want to modify:

[24]See https://developer.mozilla.org/en/docs/Web/JavaScript/Reference/Global_Objects/Array/splice.

```
CL-USER> (defparameter *list* (list 1 2 3 42 5))
*LIST*
CL-USER> (nth 3 *list*)
42
CL-USER> (setf (nth 3 *list*) 4)
4
CL-USER> *list*
(1 2 3 4 5)
CL-USER> (subseq *list* 2 4)
(3 4)
CL-USER> (setf (subseq *list* 2 4) (list :three :four))
(:THREE :FOUR)
CL-USER> *list*
(1 2 :THREE :FOUR 5)
```

To really reproduce JAVASCRIPT's `splice`, we need to invest a bit more work...

How It Works

Suppose we have the list `(A B C D E)` stored in the variable `*LIST*` and we want to substitute the subsequence comprised of the symbols `B` and `C` by the list `(X Y Z)`.

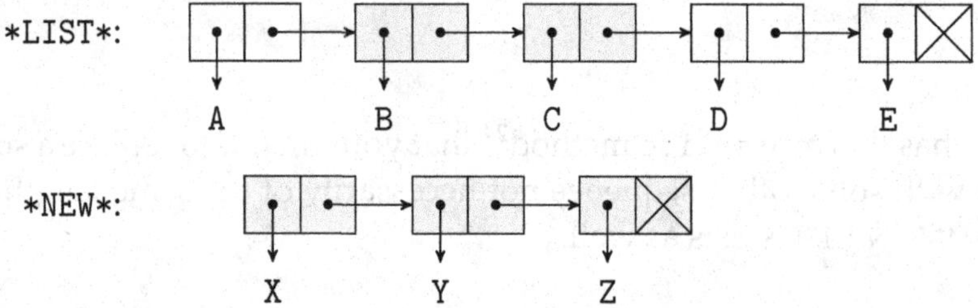

We want to be able to do this like so:

```
(defparameter *new* (list 'x 'y 'z))
(setf *list* (splice *list* :start 1 :end 3 :new *new*))
```

And it is OK for us if `*LIST*` is destructively modified by this operation.

It is tempting to create a "detour" by "bending some pointers" like so:

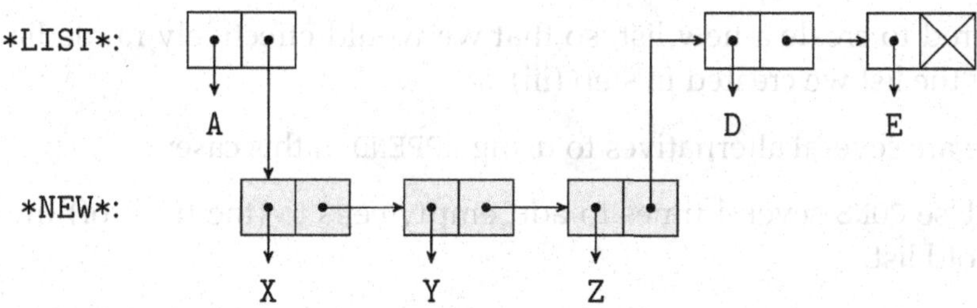

But this is wrong.[25] If we do that, then afterward `*NEW*` will be the list `(X Y Z D E)`, which is *not* what we want.

We rather need to do it like so:

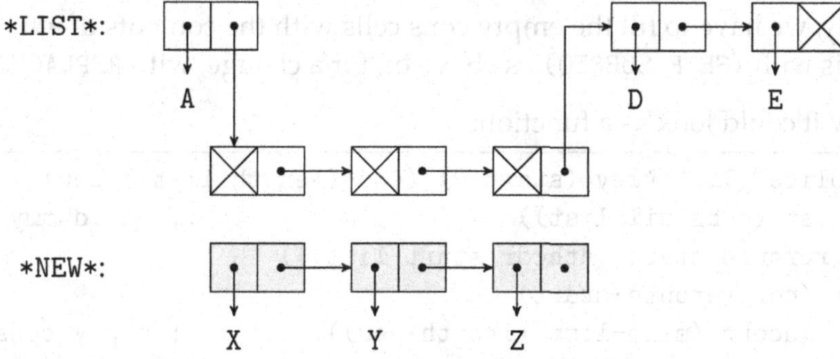

This means that we need to insert new empty cons cells (as many as `*NEW*` has) into `*LIST*` and then afterward fill their cars by copying from `*NEW*`. So, let's summarize the whole process:

(i) We first need to find the cons where we start our "rerouting." (In our picture that's the one where we changed the arrow pointing to the right into a long arrow pointing down.) If the first element to remove from the list is at position `START`, we find this cons with `(NTHCDR (1- START) LIST)`.[26]

(ii) The previous step is wrong, though, if `START` is zero. We could fix this by distinguishing two different cases as in the code on page 44, but here we will instead perform the following "trick:" we will temporarily add a dummy cons cell to the front of our list, which we'll later remove.

(iii) Now we need a bunch of empty cons cells, which we create with `MAKE-LIST` (see Recipe 2-2).

(iv) And to the end of this new list, we want to attach the rest of the old list; in our example, that's the `(D E)` part. We could do this by simply using `APPEND` to concatenate the two lists, but that would be a bit wasteful because `APPEND` is

[25] Unless you don't care whether the `:NEW` argument is destructively modified.

[26] `NTHCDR` does what its name says: it finds the *n*th cdr of a list. Like any other list function it has to traverse the list to do so.

required to create a new list, so that we would effectively immediately throw away the list we created in step (iii).

There are several alternatives to using APPEND in this case:

- Use CONS several times to add empty cells to (the front of) the tail of the old list.
- Modify the last cdr of the new list to point to the tail of the old list (as we did in the picture).
- Use APPEND's *destructive*[27] sibling NCONC, which does exactly that: it destroys the structure of its first argument by bending its last cdr.

(v) Finally, we have to fill the empty cons cells with the contents of *NEW*. We can do this with (SETF SUBSEQ) as above or, for a change, with REPLACE.

This is how it could look as a function:

```
(defun splice (list &key (start 0) (end (length list)) new)
  (setf list (cons nil list))                        ;; add dummy cell
  (let ((reroute-start (nthcdr start list)))
    (setf (cdr reroute-start)
          (nconc (make-list (length new))            ;; empty cons cells
                 (nthcdr (- end start)               ;; tail of old list
                         (cdr reroute-start)))
          list (cdr list)))                          ;; remove dummy cell
  (replace list new :start1 start)                   ;; fill empty cells
  list)
```

And this is how it works:

```
CL-USER> (defparameter *list* (list 'a 'b 'c 'd 'e))
*LIST*
CL-USER> (defparameter *new* (list 'x 'y 'z))
*NEW*
CL-USER> (setf *list* (splice *list* :start 1 :end 3 :new *new*))
(A X Y Z D E)
CL-USER> *new*
(X Y Z)
CL-USER> (splice *list* :start 1 :end 4)
(A D E)
CL-USER> (splice *list* :start 2 :new (list 1 2 3))
(A D 1 2 3)
CL-USER> (splice *list* :start 3 :end 3 :new (list 42))
(A D 1 42 2 3)
```

[27]See page 534.

```
CL-USER> *list*
(A D 1 42 2 3)
```

Our function SPLICE has one flaw, though, that we can't fix, at least as long as we're talking about *functions*: it returns the new list and at the same time modifies the old list (which is what we want), but if someone has a reference to the old list, this reference won't "pick up" the new list if the :START keyword parameter happens to be 0:[28]

```
CL-USER> (defparameter *list* (list 'a 'b 'c 'd 'e))
*LIST*
CL-USER> (splice *list* :end 3 :new (list 1 2 3))
(1 2 3 D E)
CL-USER> *list*
(A B C D E)
```

In a way, this is similar to how destructive functions like SORT behave (see Recipe 7-3).

Perhaps you should, as an exercise, write a *setf expander* (see Recipe 10-8) which ameliorates this.

2-7. Detecting Shared Structure in Lists

Problem

You want to know if two lists share structure.

Solution

The function TAILP tests if its first argument is the *tail* of its second argument (which must be a list):

```
CL-USER> (defparameter *a* (list :a :b :c :d :e))
*A*
CL-USER> (defparameter *b* (list :b :c :d :e))
*B*
CL-USER> (list *a* *b*)
((:A :B :C :D :E) (:B :C :D :E))
CL-USER> (tailp *b* *a*)
NIL
CL-USER> (tailp (cdr *b*) *a*)
```

[28]See step (ii) above.

```
NIL
CL-USER> (let ((tail (list :c :d :e)))
           (setf *a* (append (list :a :b) tail)
                 *b* (cons :b tail)))
(:B :C :D :E)
CL-USER> (list *a* *b*)
((:A :B :C :D :E) (:B :C :D :E))
CL-USER> (eql *a* *b*)
NIL
CL-USER> (tailp *b* *a*)
NIL
CL-USER> (tailp (cdr *b*) *a*)
T
```

How It Works

After we redefined `*A*` and `*B*` above, in the "cons notation" from Recipe 2-1, we have this situation:

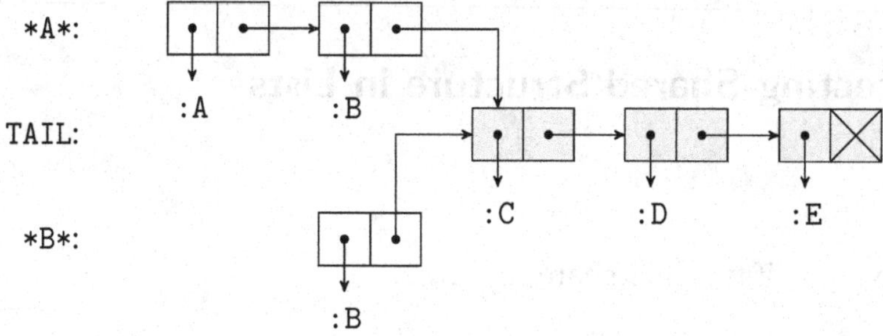

"Shared structure" means that two lists have at least one cons cell in common. It is obvious that once they have one cons cell in common, they share the whole tail following this cons cell. In our picture above, that's the gray part.[29] We can't figure out if two lists share structure just by looking at their printed representation, we have to compare individual cons cells for identity (see Recipe 10-1) in order to achieve that.

`TAILP` will do this for you; it'll check whether its first argument is some tail of its second argument. You could write `TAILP` yourself without much effort although you'd have to make sure to get the edge cases right:

```
CL-USER> (tailp nil '(1 2 3))    ;; NIL is a tail of every proper list
T
```

[29]Note that this happened *although* we used `APPEND`. While `APPEND`—in contrast to `NCONC`—is required to construct a new list structure, it will reuse its *last* argument.

```
CL-USER> (tailp 42 '(1 2 . 42)) ;; TAILP accepts dotted lists
T
```

Here's one of many ways to do it:

```
(defun my-tailp (object list)
  (check-type list list)
  (loop for tail = list then (cdr tail)
        until (prog1 (atom tail)
                (when (eql object tail) (return t)))))
```

(Note how the terminating condition is `(ATOM TAIL)`, but due to the `PROG1` form, we perform the `EQL` test even in the last case.)

Isolating the Non-Shared Part

If `TAILP` returns a true value, then `LDIFF` will give us the part of the list that is *not* shared:[30]

```
;; continued from above
CL-USER> (tailp (cdr *b*) *a*)
T
CL-USER> (ldiff *a* (cdr *b*))
(:A :B)
```

`LDIFF` can come in handy when combined with a function like `MEMBER`, which always returns a tail (!) of its argument:

```
CL-USER> (defparameter *a* '(42 "3" 5.3 :x #\u :a 23/12))
*A*
CL-USER> (ldiff *a* (member-if 'symbolp *a*))
(42 "3" 5.3)
```

2-8. Working with Trees

Problem

You need trees[31] for one of your algorithms.

[30]Note that the order of the arguments has to be reversed!

[31]This is about the abstract data structure called *tree*. If you were thinking of plants, you bought the wrong book.

Solution

You can represent any tree with conses. Each node is represented as a list, where the first element is the node's value and the other elements are the node's children.

How It Works

If you don't already have trees in your language, you have to create them somehow. This is typically done with objects or structs. In C, for example, you could use this for binary trees:

```
struct node tree {
  int value;
  struct node *left;
  struct node *right;
}
```

And, of course, you can do the same in COMMON LISP, with CLOS objects (see Chapter 13) or with structures.

But in a way, COMMON LISP already has trees. Let's look at a simple structure built out of conses:

```
(cons (cons 'A 'B) (cons 'C 'D))
```

This is how it looks using our "cons notation" from Recipe 2-1:

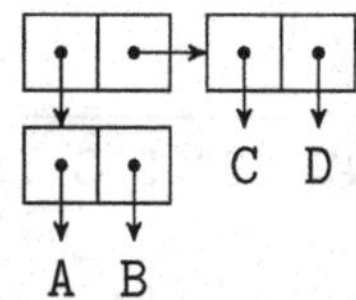

With a bit of "artistic freedom," we can draw the same thing like below on the left.

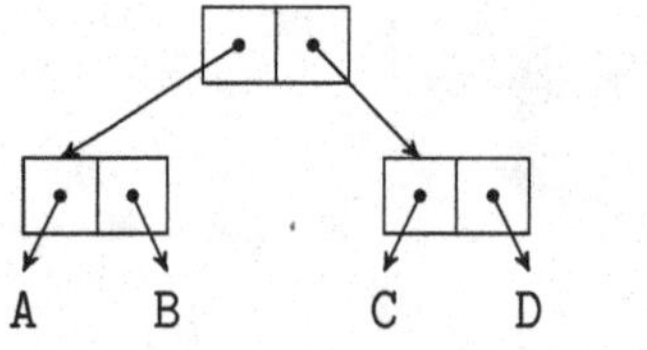

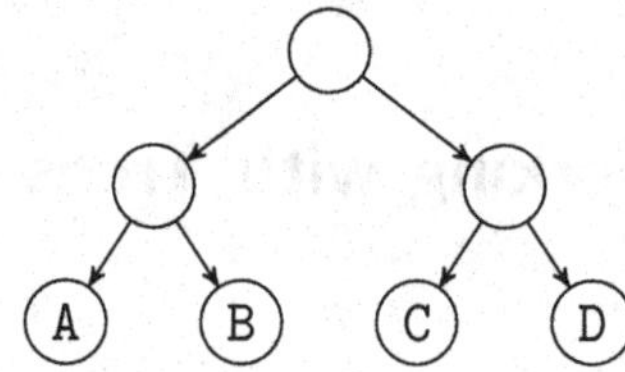

And if we compare this with what's shown on the right, we realize that we *almost* already have what's usually called a *binary tree*.

Except that binary trees look more like what's shown below left; that is, *all* nodes have values and not only the leaves. And for that, it looks like we'd need something like our C `struct` from above, which would lead to a structure like below right.

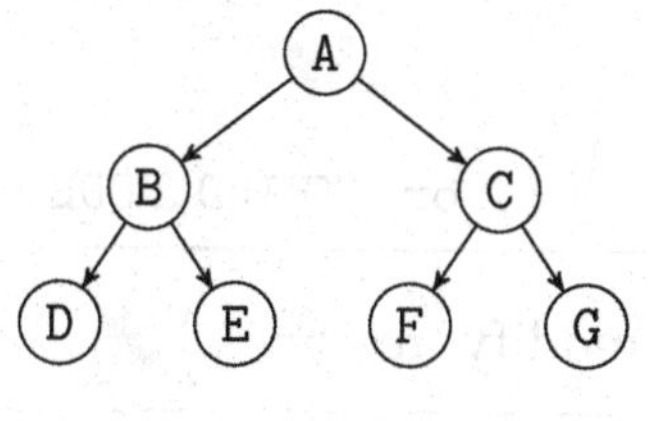

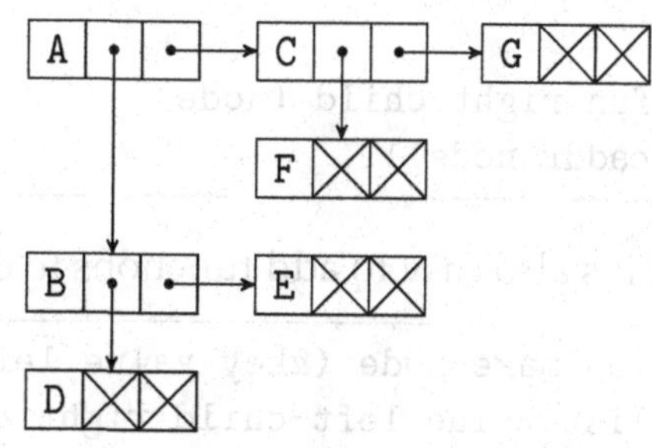

But that's not really necessary; we can do it with conses. The "trick" is to represent like , or for aesthetic reasons, more like ; that is, we represent the three components of the "C `struct`" as three elements of a Lisp list. At first sight, the picture is more convoluted, but once you understand its structure, it's no more complicated than before:

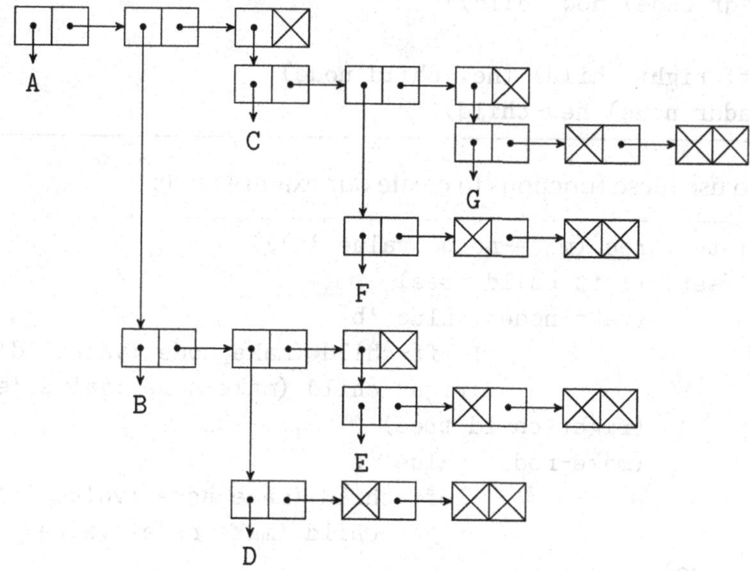

In Lisp: `(A (B (D NIL NIL) (E NIL NIL)) (C (F NIL NIL) (G NIL NIL)))`.

So let me repeat what I said in the beginning:

- Each node is a list.
- The first element of the list is the node's value.
- The following elements of the list are the child nodes.

You can now even mirror our C `struct` from above with these reader functions:

```
(defun node-value (node)
  (car node))                                    ;; or (FIRST NODE)

(defun left-child (node)
  (cadr node))                                   ;; or (SECOND NODE)
```

```
(defun right-child (node)
  (caddr node))                                      ;; or (THIRD NODE)
```

And it's also easy to add functions to create, grow, and modify trees:[32]

```
(defun make-node (&key value left-child right-child)
  (list value left-child right-child))

(defun (setf node-value) (new-value node)
  (setf (car node) new-value))

(defun (setf left-child) (new-child node)
  (setf (cadr node) new-child))

(defun (setf right-child) (new-child node)
  (setf (caddr node) new-child))
```

Here's how to use these functions to create our example tree:

```
CL-USER> (let ((tree (make-node :value 'a)))
           (setf (left-child tree)
                 (make-node :value 'b
                            :left-child (make-node :value 'd)
                            :right-child (make-node :value 'e))
                 (right-child tree)
                 (make-node :value 'c
                            :left-child (make-node :value 'f)
                            :right-child (make-node :value 'g)))
           tree)
(A (B (D NIL NIL) (E NIL NIL)) (C (F NIL NIL) (G NIL NIL)))
```

Using the three simple rules mentioned earlier, it should now also be obvious how to translate arbitrary trees (not only binary ones) into structures built out of cons cells with very little effort.[33]

More Complicated Trees

You usually not only want to *represent* trees as was done here, but also to do something with them, like looking up, inserting, or deleting nodes according to some

[32] For the setf functions, see Recipe 10-8.

[33] Which is not to say that you shouldn't represent tree nodes as CLOS objects if you think it'll fit your problem domain better. But this is a chapter about conses and what you can do with them.

application-specific pattern. There are many tree variants; for example, *AVL trees* or *red-black trees*, which offer specific advantages and disadvantages, and it is beyond the scope of this book to discuss them all. (That would rather be a topic for a computer science textbook.)

But I should at least mention that for most of the common tree data structures, there are already good COMMON LISP implementations available. You might want to start looking for them with something like this:[34]

```
(ql:system-apropos "tree")
```

Common Lisp's Standard Tree Functions

The standard includes two functions with "TREE" in their name: `TREE-EQUAL` (see Recipe 10-1) and `COPY-TREE` (see chapter 13 of *Practical Common Lisp*). And there are also functions like `SUBST`, `SUBST-IF`, and so on. These function are not meant to operate on some specific tree implementation like ours from above. "Tree" here just means that they descend recursively into the cdr *and* the car of every cons cell they visit, whereas the typical list functions only descend into the cdrs.

2-9. Working with Stacks

Problem

You need to implement a *stack* (or *LIFO*).

Solution

Just use a list and the standard macros `PUSH` and `POP`:

```
CL-USER> (defparameter *stack* nil)
*STACK*
CL-USER> (push :plate *stack*)
(:PLATE)
CL-USER> (push :another-plate *stack*)
(:ANOTHER-PLATE :PLATE)
CL-USER> (pop *stack*)
:ANOTHER-PLATE
```

[34]See Recipe 18-2.

```
CL-USER> *stack*
(:PLATE)
```

How It Works

Like trees (see Recipe 2-8), it is very easy to implement stacks with conses. You could even argue that stacks are already a built-in data structure in COMMON LISP; they are just called "lists" there. The two basic operations you need even have the same name they usually have in computer science: PUSH to add an item to the stack and POP to remove an item. (Note that these two are macros that work with *generalized references*; see Recipe 10-8.)

The "peek" operation that stack implementations sometimes have would be just CAR or FIRST. And obviously you don't have to worry about the size of your stack when you "create" it (unless it grows so big that it uses up all of your memory).

2-10. Implementing a Queue

Problem

You need to implement a *queue*[35] (or *FIFO*).

Solution

Here's some example code to give you an idea. For production purposes this should of course be ameliorated with error checks.

```
(defclass queue ()
  ((list :initform nil)
   (tail :initform nil)))

(defmethod print-object ((queue queue) stream)
  (print-unreadable-object (queue stream :type t)
    (with-slots (list tail) queue
      (cond ((cddddr list)
             ;; at least five elements, so print ellipsis
             (format stream "(~{~S ~}... ~S)"
                     (subseq list 0 3) (first tail)))
             ;; otherwise print whole list
            (t (format stream "~:S" list))))))
```

[35]See https://en.wikipedia.org/wiki/Queue_%28abstract_data_type%29.

```
(defmethod dequeue ((queue queue))
  (with-slots (list) queue
    (pop list)))

(defmethod enqueue (new-item (queue queue))
  (with-slots (list tail) queue
    (let ((new-tail (list new-item)))
      (cond ((null list) (setf list new-tail))
            (t (setf (cdr tail) new-tail)))
      (setf tail new-tail)))
  queue)
```

And here's a usage example:

```
CL-USER> (defparameter *q* (make-instance 'queue))
*Q*
CL-USER> *q*
#<QUEUE ()>
CL-USER> (enqueue 42 *q*)
#<QUEUE (42)>
CL-USER> (enqueue :foo *q*)
#<QUEUE (42 :FOO)>
CL-USER> (dotimes (i 5 *q*)
           (enqueue i *q*))
#<QUEUE (42 :FOO 0 ... 4)>
CL-USER> (dequeue *q*)
42
CL-USER> *q*
#<QUEUE (:FOO 0 1 ... 4)>
CL-USER> (dequeue *q*)
:FOO
CL-USER> *q*
#<QUEUE (0 1 2 ... 4)>
```

How It Works

The main point here is that we deploy the technique discussed on page 44; the queue itself is just a Lisp list, but we keep a pointer to its *tail*. Therefore, the *dequeue* operation is just POP (see Recipe 2-9), whereas for *enqueue* we have to make the same distinction of cases as on page 44.

For other parts of the code, see also Recipes 9-3 and 9-8.

2-11. Destructuring and Pattern Matching

Problem

You want to extract information out of a complicated structure built out of conses.

Solution

If you have read *Practical Common Lisp*, you already know the DESTRUCTURING-BIND macro; but if you haven't used it often, then maybe you're not aware of the many possibilities that it offers.

For one, you can destructure arbitrary *trees* (see Recipe 2-8) built out of conses, not only lists:

```
CL-USER> (destructuring-bind (a (b &rest c) (d (e . f)))
             '("A" (:b 2 3) (#\D (1.0 . 3.0)))
           (list a b c d e f))
("A" :B (2 3) #\D 1.0 3.0)
```

You can also use it to destructure *plists* (and even provide defaults):

```
CL-USER> (destructuring-bind (&key a (b :not-found) c
                                   &allow-other-keys)
             '(:c 23 :d "D" :a #\A :foo :whatever)
           (list a b c))
(#\A :NOT-FOUND 23)
```

(Note that order doesn't matter, as you might expect.)

How It Works

DESTRUCTURING-BIND accepts as its first argument anything that could be a valid lambda list for DEFMACRO.[36] These lambda lists can be nested, and thus have a much richer syntax than the so-called *ordinary* lambda lists used for things like DEFUN.

However, DESTRUCTURING-BIND has the shortcoming that it doesn't lend itself well to testing *if* an object has a certain structure (it will signal an error if it can't match) and it also can't match against constant parts of a structure. These tasks fall into the domain called *pattern matching* and languages like HASKELL or ML are particularly good at that.

[36]Minus the &ENVIRONMENT parameter, but including a &WHOLE parameter.

But as everybody can extend COMMON LISP, it is not surprising that several libraries that integrate pattern matching into the language are available.[37] We'll show a quick session with one of them, OPTIMA by Tomohiro Matsuyama (available via QUICKLISP; see Recipe 18-2). This is not so much about giving you an introduction to OPTIMA (you will have to read its documentation), but rather to demonstrate how easy it is to add new control structures and new syntax[38] to COMMON LISP.

```
CL-USER> (ql:quickload '(:optima
                         :fare-quasiquote-optima
                         :fare-quasiquote-readtable))
;; output elided for brevity
CL-USER> (named-readtables:in-readtable :fare-quasiquote)
;; output elided for brevity
CL-USER> (optima:match (list 42 23)
           (`(,x ,_ ,_) (list :three x))
           (`(,x ,_) (list :two x)))
(:TWO 42)
CL-USER> (optima:match (list 42 23)
           (`(41 ,x) x)
           (`(,x 23) x))
42
CL-USER> (optima:match '(1 (2 (3 4 5 6) 7 8) 9)
           (`(1 (2 (3 ,x) 7 8) 9) (list :one x))
           (`(1 (2 (3 ,x . ,_) 7 8) 9) (list :two x)))
(:TWO 4)
```

OPTIMA can do a lot more than I showed here. In particular, it can not only match against cons structures but also against other Lisp objects including your own CLOS instances.

The ALEXANDRIA library (see Recipe 18-4) also offers a `DESTRUCTURING-CASE` macro, with limited pattern matching capabilities.

[37] `http://www.cliki.net/pattern%20matching` provides a (probably incomplete) list of them.

[38] Note the special *quasiquote* notation (see Recipe 2-4) used here.

3. Strings and Characters

Whereas "computing" was mostly about numbers in its earlier days, strings and characters are ubiquitous now—just think about XML and Internet protocols like HTTP. In COMMON LISP, characters, as well as strings, are first-class data types.

The ANSI COMMON LISP standard was finalized before there was a usable Unicode standard; it gives much leeway to implementors about how they want to represent and support strings and characters. But now that Unicode seems to be widely adopted, most Lisps have full Unicode support. It is a testament to the foresight of the ANSI committee that this was possible without breaking adherence to the standard. COMMON LISP never felt tempted to identify characters with numbers or deal with "convenient" units like 8-bit bytes, and was thus able to support "legacy" systems as well as upcoming standards. However, some aspects of Unicode are, nevertheless, impossible to align with the Lisp standard (see Recipes 3-4 and 3-6). This is where newer languages like JAVA clearly have an advantage.

One important fact that you should keep in mind when you read the recipes in this chapter is that in Lisp, strings are actually vectors and, therefore, also "sequences." In other words, all the recipes from Chapter 7 (and those from Chapter 5 about vectors) apply to strings as well. (There will be some inevitable overlaps, though, where we explain some thing and then explain it again in a different setting in a different chapter.)

3-1. Getting the ASCII Code of a Character

Problem

You want to know the ASCII code (or the Unicode code point) of a character.

Solution

Try CHAR-CODE which is the right thing in almost all Lisp implementations. (But make sure to double-check.)

```
CL-USER 1 > (char-code #\a)
97
```

```
CL-USER 2 > (char-code #\A)
65
CL-USER 3 > (char-code #\ü)
252
CL-USER 4 > (char-code #\א)
1488
```

These are the results that I got with LISPWORKS. The first two characters are from the standard 7-bit ASCII repertoire; the third one is a small German *umlaut* U[1] and the fourth character is the Hebrew letter *alef* (also known as *aleph*).

Of course, you need to be able to type these non-ASCII characters and your IDE needs to be able to display them. An alternative in LISPWORKS for the fourth example would have been (char-code #\U+05D0), but in this case, we'd be using a non-standard *character name*.[2]

How It Works

The COMMON LISP standard defines a function CHAR-CODE, which is an injective[3] mapping from the set of characters into the set of integers (the *character codes* of the corresponding characters). However, there's not much else that's said about this mapping in the standard, except for the fact that the ordering on the set of characters induced by < and their character codes has to be consistent with CHAR<.[4]

So, in a completely portable program, there's *no* way to solve this recipe's problem. Luckily, for all current implementations on Unix/Linux, Mac OS, and Windows that I know of, the following holds:

- If a character is a member of the 7-bit ASCII characters set (Unicode code points 0 to 127), then CHAR-CODE maps it to its ASCII code (which incidentally is also its Unicode code point).
- If a Lisp implementation supports the full Unicode character set, then the CHAR-CODE function maps each character to its Unicode code point.

So, if you forget about compatibility with all COMMON LISP implementations of the past and the future, then CHAR-CODE is pretty much what you want.

[1]Which is also sometimes called "Latin u with diaeresis."

[2]For more about character names, see Recipe 3-2.

[3]Meaning that different characters have different character codes.

[4]Modulo *character attributes*, actually. But that's already too much detail...

The Other Way Around

The inverse function to `CHAR-CODE` is `CODE-CHAR`; that is, it maps character codes to characters:

```
CL-USER 5 > (code-char 97)
#\a
CL-USER 6 > (code-char 65)
#\A
CL-USER 7 > (code-char 252)
#\ü
CL-USER 8 > (code-char 1488)
#\א
```

(There's also another function called `CHAR-INT`, which is completely useless unless you want to play with implementation-specific features of your Lisp.)

The Limit

The standard defines the constant `CHAR-CODE-LIMIT` as the upper exclusive bound on the values of `CHAR-CODE`. In other words, every character code in this particular implementation is strictly smaller than `CHAR-CODE-LIMIT`. This does not mean, however, that every positive integer below `CHAR-CODE-LIMIT` is actually a character code.[5]

3-2. Naming Characters

Problem

You want to refer to a character by name; perhaps because you can't type it with your keyboard or because your IDE can't display it.

Solution

Use `CHAR-NAME` to get the name of a character. This name can then be used with the standard character syntax or alternatively with `NAME-CHAR`.

Here's a small example session with SBCL:

[5]So the `CHAR-CODE` function is injective, but not surjective.

```
* (char-name #\A)
"LATIN_CAPITAL_LETTER_A"
* (char-name #\a)
"LATIN_SMALL_LETTER_A"
* (name-char "Latin_Small_Letter_A")
#\a
* #\latin_small_letter_a
#\a
* (char-name (code-char 1488))
"HEBREW_LETTER_ALEF"
* #\HEBREW_LETTER_ALEF
#\HEBREW_LETTER_ALEF
* #\U+05D0
#\HEBREW_LETTER_ALEF
* (name-char "U+05D0")
#\HEBREW_LETTER_ALEF
* (name-char "A")
NIL
```

(See also Recipe 3-5.)

How It Works

In COMMON LISP, characters can have *names*. The foremost reason for the existence of character names is that characters are first-class objects in the language (as opposed to, say, JAVASCRIPT) and you thus need a way to refer to them even if they can't be displayed like whitespace (the standard calls these *non-graphic* characters) or if they can't be entered or displayed in your IDE. For example, the first letter of the Latin alphabet can be easily entered as `#\a` in the standard character syntax; but for a space character, you need to type `#\Space`.

That's why the standard defines `"Space"` and `"Newline"` as required names for the corresponding characters and also recommends other names, like `"Backspace"` and `"Tab"`. *Graphic* characters, on the other hand, don't need to have a name, and if they have one, it is not covered by the standard. Should they have a name, then it must be usable with the `#\` syntax, though.

As I already explained in the introduction to this chapter, the standard was finalized too early for Unicode, so there's no requirement that a COMMON LISP implementation must use and understand the official Unicode character names. But many will, as we saw in the SBCL example above. Many also understand the typical numerical (hexadecimal) Unicode syntax in the form of `U+2135`, which is then understood to be (another) character name for the character `(code-char #x2135)`.

If your Lisp doesn't support all Unicode names or if you want a portable way to refer to non-ASCII characters, have a look at the CL-UNICODE library (installable with QUICKLISP; see Recipe 18-2), which among other things can install its own character syntax[6] so that your Lisp will "understand" something like `#\Alef`, although it otherwise might not.[7]

Finally, I'll explicitly mention three things you might already have noticed in the example:

- By definition, a character name must be at least two characters long; for example, `"A"` is *not* a character name, although `#\A` works. That's the reason why `(NAME-CHAR "A")` above failed.
- When character names are looked up (whether by `NAME-CHAR` or via the character syntax), case is irrelevant.
- Characters can have more than one name.

3-3. Using Different Character Encodings

Problem

You need to control the way textual data you read from or write to a file or network connection is decoded or encoded, respectively.

Solution

That's what COMMON LISP's *external formats* are for. Here's an example of their usage in LISPWORKS:

```
CL-USER 1 > (with-open-file (out "/tmp/foo.txt"
                                 :direction :output
                                 :if-exists :supersede
                                 :element-type '(unsigned-byte 8))
              (write-byte 195 out)
              (write-byte 156 out))
156
CL-USER 2 > (with-open-file (out "/tmp/foo.txt"
                                 :direction :output
                                 :if-exists :append
                                 :element-type 'character
```

[6]For how to change the syntax of COMMON LISP, see Chapter 8.

[7]CL-UNICODE won't magically extend your Lisp's supply of characters. It'll just provide it with Unicode information about the characters it already has.

```
                                :external-format :latin-1)
          (write-string "berjazz" out))
"berjazz"
```

First, we create a new file and use a binary (see Recipe 14-10) stream to write two octets to it. We then open a character stream to the same file and *append* some text to it, instructing LISPWORKS to use the *Latin-1* encoding, which is also known as ISO 8859-1. This means that we're writing one octet per character, namely its ASCII code. The file will now have these contents (shown as octets in hexadecimal):

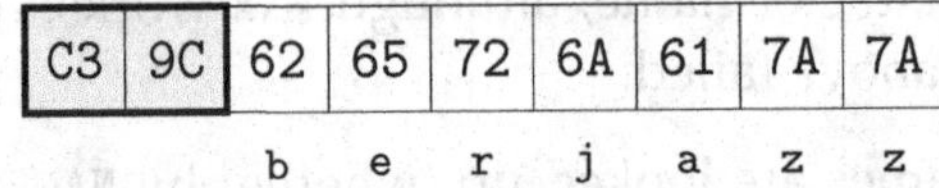

Nothing remarkable so far—and this would have worked just as well without even mentioning the external format.

But now we're reading from the file that we just created, and this time we're using UTF-8[8] as the external format:

```
CL-USER 3 > (with-open-file (in "/tmp/foo.txt"
                                :element-type 'character
                                :external-format :utf-8)
          (read-line in))
"Überjazz"
T
```

Because UTF-8 works differently, the first two octets (the gray ones in the picture) are not considered to be individual characters but are combined to form an *umlaut* character.

How It Works

Whatever a stream is used for, at the lowest level, the data sent back and forth consists of individual bits, and in the case of textual data, your computer is only *pretending* that characters are involved. And in order to do that, it needs a means of translating between bits and characters in a reproducible way. That's what *character encodings* are for, which in the COMMON LISP world are traditionally called *external formats*. You won't be surprised by now to hear that implementations can decide which external formats they support and how they call them, but these days, it is probably safe to assume that each self-respecting implementation will at least support UTF-8, UTF-16, UTF-32, and (some of) the ISO 8859 encodings (which are all

[8]See `http://en.wikipedia.org/wiki/UTF-8`.

"supersets" of ASCII); and some will, of course, support many more.[9]

Unfortunately, they will not generally agree on how these external formats are to be specified. (For example, to get UTF-8, do you use the keyword `:UTF-8`, or the keyword `:UTF8`, or the string `"UTF-8"`, or what?) This is something you'll have to look up.

Also, this is not the end of the story. There are two other things that at least sometimes have to be considered. One is which line endings are used (see Recipe 14-9) and the other is the endianness of the data (see Recipe 14-11) once characters can be larger than one octet. Both of these aspects are usually added to the external format so that, for example, in LISPWORKS a fully-specified external format could look like

```
'(:utf-16le :eol-style :crlf)
```

for UTF-16, little-endian, with DOS-like line endings.

The FLEXI-STREAMS library (installable with QUICKLISP; see Recipe 18-2) might be helpful if you're working with more than one Lisp. It provides external formats that are independent of a specific implementation and a reasonable set of encodings, which will work no matter whether the underlying Lisp has them or not. The price you'll have to pay for this is a possible decrease in performance as a Gray stream (see Recipe 14-14) is layered over a "raw" binary stream to perform the encoding.

3-4. Comparing Strings or Characters

Problem

You want to compare characters or strings, either in the sense of testing whether they are equal or for the purpose of ordering them.

Solution

COMMON LISP has a whole slew of functions for such tasks, of which we'll demonstrate some in the following example:

```
CL-USER 1 > (char= #\a #\a)
T
CL-USER 2 > (char= #\a #\b)
NIL
CL-USER 3 > (char= #\a #\A)
```

[9] That an implementation supports a specific character encoding doesn't necessarily imply that it supports all characters this encoding can encode (see Recipe 3-1).

```
NIL
CL-USER 4 > (char-equal #\a #\A)
T
CL-USER 5 > (char< #\a #\b)
T
CL-USER 6 > (char< #\A #\b)
T
CL-USER 7 > (char< #\a #\B)
NIL
CL-USER 8 > (char-lessp #\A #\b)
T
CL-USER 9 > (char-lessp #\a #\B)
T
CL-USER 10 > (eql "foo" "foo")
NIL
CL-USER 11 > (string= "foo" "foo")
T
CL-USER 12 > (equal "foo" "foo")
T
CL-USER 13 > (string= "foo" "Foo")
NIL
CL-USER 14 > (equal "foo" "Foo")
NIL
CL-USER 15 > (string-equal "foo" "Foo")
T
CL-USER 16 > (equalp "foo" "Foo")
T
CL-USER 17 > (string< "adam" "eve")
0
CL-USER 18 > (string< "aardvark" "aardwolf")
4
CL-USER 19 > (string< "werewolf" "aardwolf")
NIL
CL-USER 20 > (string< "aardvark" "Aardwolf")
NIL
CL-USER 21 > (string-lessp "aardvark" "Aardwolf")
4
```

How It Works

CHAR= does what you expect; it returns a true value if the two (Lisp) characters you're comparing denote the same ("real world") character. Incidentally, you could also use

EQL for this test,[10] but if you know you're comparing characters, CHAR= will make your code easier to understand. #\a and #\A are *not* the same character for CHAR=. If you want them to be equal (i.e., if you want to ignore case), use CHAR-EQUAL instead.

The string versions of these function are STRING= (case sensitive) and STRING-EQUAL (case insensitive). Note that you can't rely on EQL here.[11] Depending on whether case is relevant or not, you have to use EQUAL or EQUALP.

Functions like CHAR< compare characters by their character codes (see Recipe 3-1), so for the 26 characters of the English alphabet, this corresponds with the order you had to memorize in school. For everything else, the situation is more complicated (more on this later).

Each of the character comparison functions comes in two versions: one that is case sensitive (and has a mathematical symbol like = or < in its name) and one that is case insensitive (with a name consisting solely of letters and hyphens). The whole bestiary looks like this:

Case Sensitive	Case Insensitive
CHAR=	CHAR-EQUAL
CHAR/=	CHAR-NOT-EQUAL
CHAR<	CHAR-LESSP
CHAR<=	CHAR-NOT-GREATERP
CHAR>	CHAR-GREATERP
CHAR>=	CHAR-NOT-LESSP

For strings, the situation is very similar: they are compared character by character as if by the functions just discussed (which results in what is usually called *lexicographic order*). The only difference is that all functions except STRING= and STRING-EQUAL will return, instead of T, the index of the first character where the two words differ.[12] (See the examples with the wolves and with Adam and Eve.) Other than that, the string functions use the same names as the character functions, only with CHAR replaced with STRING:

Case Sensitive	Case Insensitive
STRING=	STRING-EQUAL
STRING/=	STRING-NOT-EQUAL
STRING<	STRING-LESSP
STRING<=	STRING-NOT-GREATERP
STRING>	STRING-GREATERP
STRING>=	STRING-NOT-LESSP

[10]Note that while EQ might accidentally work for you, it is nothing you should rely on. See Recipe 10-1 for more on this.

[11]The technical reason is that strings are *compound* objects (vectors) internally and two strings will likely be two different vectors although they might denote the same sequence of characters. See Recipe 10-1 for more on this.

[12]Which is, of course, fine because every value that is not NIL is a *true* value in COMMON LISP.

Internationalization

Sorting characters or strings by character code (whether that's the Unicode code point or not) is not a good idea if, say, you want to display a list of names to a user because it will fail as soon as non-English characters come into play. Moreover, different countries might have different ideas about how the *same* characters should be ordered.[13] To make matters even worse, sometimes it might not even be sufficient to use lexicographical ordering for words even if you get the order for the individual characters right.[14]

These issues are usually subsumed under the term *collation*, and as you might have guessed, the standard doesn't mention them. You will have to check if your Lisp implementation provides means to help you with collation if you need it. (One example is ALLEGROCL with `EXCL:STRING-SORT-KEY` and `EXCL:PARSE-UCET`.)

Another complicated area is case (see also Recipe 3-6). As an example, take the so-called "long s" (`U+017F`), which you might encounter in older books.[15] According to Unicode, this is a lowercase letter and its uppercase variant is the usual *S* that we all know (and which appears all over this book). Now, the lowercase variant of *this* letter is *s* and *not* the *long s*. That's something that can't be mapped to COMMON LISP's concept of case because the standard clearly states[16] that there must be a one-to-one correspondence between uppercase and lowercase letters.

So, the standard essentially mandates this behavior:

```
* (both-case-p (code-char #x17F))
NIL
* (char-equal #\S (code-char #x17F))
NIL
```

This means that the *long s* doesn't have case (although it has according to Unicode) and that a capital *S* and the *long s* are different, even if case doesn't matter. (But according to Unicode's *case folding* rules they shouldn't be.)

Again, your Lisp might have ways to deal with this and you'll have to browse its documentation. LISPWORKS, for example, has functions like `LW:UNICODE-STRING-EQUAL` or `LW:UNICODE-CHAR-EQUAL` (and several others) that take Unicode's rules into account.

13For example, in Swedish, *z* comes before *ö*, whereas in German, it's the other way around. And even in German, dictionaries and phone books disagree about whether *of* or *öf* comes first.

14See `http://www.unicode.org/reports/tr10/` for some interesting examples.

15See `https://en.wikipedia.org/wiki/Long_s`.

16In 13.1.4.3, in case you want to look it up.

3-5. Escaping Characters in String Literals and Variable Interpolation

Problem

Many programming languages offer a way to insert arbitrary characters into string literals by an "escape" mechanism. In JAVA you can write `"\u00DCberjazz"` to get the string `"Überjazz"`, for example. In addition to that, languages like PERL, RUBY, or PYTHON offer *variable interpolation*, which means that you can write (in PERL) `"${foo}berjazz"` which is converted to `"Überjazz"` if the variable `$foo` has as its value the string `"Ü"`.

You want something like this in COMMON LISP, too.

Solution

The short answer is that this is not in the standard.

One could, however, argue that all of the above can be done pretty easily with `FORMAT`:[17]

```
CL-USER 1 > (format nil "~Cberjazz" #\U+00DC)
"Überjazz"
CL-USER 2 > (let ((foo "Ü"))
              (format nil "~Aberjazz" foo))
"Überjazz"
```

How It Works

The standard dictates that the only escape character allowed in literal strings is the backslash and that it only escapes the next character so that it can essentially only be used to escape itself or the string delimiter (i.e., the double quote character).

So, although you can do this with `FORMAT` as shown above, you might be a bit disappointed because you don't get the *syntax* you have in other languages. If that's an issue for you, consider using the CL-INTERPOL library (installable with QUICKLISP; see Recipe 18-2), which offers an alternative string syntax[18] that makes COMMON LISP's strings similar in expressiveness to PERL's.

[17]See Recipe 3-2 for the (implementation-dependent) meaning of `#\U+00DC`.
[18]More about how you can change the syntax of COMMON LISP in Chapter 8.

Is It Still a Literal?

Even if you're OK with using FORMAT as a surrogate for more flexible escaping in strings, you might ask yourself whether something like

```
(format nil "~Cberjazz" #\U+00DC)
```

(where no variables are involved) would still "behave" like a literal string. Well, in theory, a sufficiently clever compiler might be able to see that this is a constant expression and replace it with a literal string; but it must not do that, because the programmer might expect a new (or *fresh*, in Lisp parlance) string each time the form is evaluated. If you really want a constant string that behaves like a literal, use the syntax described in Recipe 8-3:

```
#.(format nil "~Cberjazz" #\U+00DC)
```

(For variable interpolation in S-expressions instead of strings, see Recipe 2-4.)

3-6. Controlling Case

Problem

You want to change the case of a character—be it a stand-alone character or one within a string.

Solution

There are many functions in the standard to control the case of characters. Here are most of them in action (in ALLEGROCL):

```
CL-USER(1): (char-upcase #\a)
#\A
CL-USER(2): (char-downcase #\A)
#\a
CL-USER(3): (char-downcase #\a)
#\a
CL-USER(4): (char-downcase #\Space)
#\Space
CL-USER(5): (char-downcase #\greek_capital_letter_alpha)
#\greek_small_letter_alpha
CL-USER(6): (upper-case-p #\A)
T
```

```
CL-USER(7): (lower-case-p #\a)
T
CL-USER(8): (upper-case-p #\Space)
NIL
CL-USER(9): (lower-case-p #\Space)
NIL
CL-USER(10): (both-case-p #\Space)
NIL
CL-USER(11): (both-case-p #\hebrew_letter_alef)
NIL
CL-USER(12): (string-upcase "miles davis")
"MILES DAVIS"
CL-USER(13): (string-downcase "MILES")
"miles"
CL-USER(14): (string-capitalize "miles DAVIS")
"Miles Davis"
CL-USER(15): (string-upcase "miles davis" :start 0 :end 6)
"MILES davis"
```

How It Works

CHAR-UPCASE is used to change a lowercase character to its uppercase counterpart (and vice-versa for CHAR-DOWNCASE). The examples above show the following:

- Downcasing (upcasing) a character that already is in lowercase (uppercase) does nothing.
- Changing the case also works with non-ASCII characters.[19]
- You can check the case of a character with LOWER-CASE-P and UPPER-CASE-P.
- There are characters that don't have "case" (which can be checked with the function BOTH-CASE-P), like the space character, but also graphical characters like Hebrew *aleph*.
- Applying CHAR-UPCASE or CHAR-DOWNCASE to these characters is the identity operation.

There are "bulk" versions of CHAR-UPCASE and CHAR-DOWNCASE that work on entire strings, STRING-UPCASE and STRING-DOWNCASE, and as usual, they accept :START and :END keyword parameters so that you can selectively modify only parts of the string.

[19]Well, of course the standard technically doesn't require this but you can be *very* sure that every self-respecting Lisp implementation will do this.

Finally, there's STRING-CAPITALIZE, which upcases the first letter of each "word"[20] in the string (see also Recipe 1-9).

By using CHAR or AREF[21] you can directly hit single characters within a string and change their case if you want:

```
CL-USER(16): (let ((string (copy-seq "Grover Washington, jr.")))
               (setf (char string 19)
                     (char-upcase (char string 19)))
               string)
"Grover Washington, Jr."
```

STRING-UPCASE, STRING-DOWNCASE, and STRING-CAPITALIZE have destructive counterparts, NSTRING-UPCASE, NSTRING-DOWNCASE, and NSTRING-CAPITALIZE, which enable you to modify the string "in place" instead of creating a new one. The usual warnings (see page 534) for destructive operations apply.

Also, the mighty FORMAT function has a directive for case conversion:

```
CL-USER(17): (format nil "Downcase: ~(~A~)" "FOO")
"Downcase: foo"
CL-USER(18): (format nil "Capitalize: ~:(~A~)" "FOO BAR BAZ")
"Capitalize: Foo Bar Baz"
CL-USER(19): (format nil "Capitalize first word, ~
downcase rest: ~@(~A~)"
                     "FOO BAR BAZ")
"Capitalize first word, downcase rest: Foo bar baz"
CL-USER(20): (format nil "Upcase: ~:@(~A~)" "Foo BAR baz")
"Upcase: FOO BAR BAZ"
```

What About Unicode?

Let's just say that Unicode can make things complicated. (Or rather this is just a consequence of natural languages being complicated beasts.) For example, if you're from Western Europe or the United States and you feed the letter #\i (U+0069) into CHAR-UPCASE, you'll likely expect #\I (U+0049) as the result. (And I'd bet that every current COMMON LISP implementation will give you exactly that.) However, if you are from Turkey, you have two distinct forms of "*LATIN SMALL LETTER I,*" namely one with a dot above and one without (U+0131). If your Lisp had adhered to the rules of the Turkish language, then the outcome of CHAR-UPCASE #\i should have been a dotted uppercase letter (U+0130).

[20]The HyperSpec defines exactly what a "word" means in this context, but it's pretty intuitive and very likely does what you mean.

[21]See Chapter 5.

So, you probably wish that functions like CHAR-UPCASE behaved according to the current *locale*.[22] But this is not going to happen because it would contradict the standard. You'll rather have to check if your implementation provides additional internationalization functions. (See also Recipe 3-4.)

3-7. Accessing or Modifying a Substring

Problem

You want to access (and maybe also modify) a substring of a string.

Solution

Use SUBSEQ (which you can also use together with SETF) or use REPLACE:

```
CL-USER 1 > (subseq "Cookbook" 4)
"book"
CL-USER 2 > (subseq "Cookbook" 4 7)
"boo"
CL-USER 3 > (let ((string1 (copy-seq "Harpo Marx"))
                  (string2 (copy-seq "Groucho, Harpo, and Chico")))
              (setf (subseq string1 0 5) "Zeppo")
              (print string1)
              (setf (subseq string1 0 5) "Groucho")
              (print string1)
              (setf string1
                    (replace string1 string2
                             :start1 0 :end1 5
                             :start2 9 :end2 14))
              (print string1)
              (setf (subseq string1 0) "Groucho")
              string1)
"Zeppo Marx"
"Grouc Marx"
"Harpo Marx"
"Grouchoarx"
```

[22]See https://en.wikipedia.org/wiki/Locale.

How It Works

As SUBSEQ can return subsequences of arbitrary *sequences*, it can, of course, also work with strings in particular. Its second argument is the index into the sequence denoting where to start the subsequence. Its (optional) third argument denotes where to stop. If there is no third argument, the subsequence extends to the end of the original sequence.

SUBSEQ can also be used together with SETF to manipulate a part of the original sequence. REPLACE is similar but allows you to specify that you only want to use a part of its second argument. So,

```
(replace string1 string2 :start s1 :end1 e1
                         :start2 s2 :end2 e2)
```

is essentially the same as

```
(setf (subseq string1 s1 e1) (subseq string2 s2 e2))
```

but the important difference is that in the second case Lisp first has to *create*[23] a new object, namely the subsequence of STRING2, while REPLACE just copies existing objects into STRING1 without the need to allocate memory.

Note that the third argument to SUBSEQ is an index into the string and *not* the length of the substring, as in some other languages, so (SUBSEQ STRING X X) always yields a sequence (string) of length zero no matter what the value of X is.[24]

The result of SUBSEQ is guaranteed to be a *fresh* sequence that doesn't share structure with the original sequence, even if you ask the function to return the whole sequence:

```
CL-USER 4 > (let* ((string1 "walk")
                   (string2 (subseq string1 0)))
              (setf (char string2 0) #\t)
              (values string1 string2))
"walk"
"talk"
```

By the way, SUBSEQ and REPLACE are actually functions that work on arbitrary sequences, not only on strings. See Chapter 7 for more about sequences.

[23]See also Recipe 7-5.

[24]It has to be a *bounding index*, of course, which is to say that it must not be greater than the length of the string.

3-8. Finding a Character or a Substring Within a String

Problem

You want to know if (and where) a sequence of one or more characters occurs in a given string.

Solution

Use FIND, POSITION, or SEARCH:

```
CL-USER 1 > (find #\o "We're Only In It For The Money")
#\o
CL-USER 2 > (find #\o "We're Only In It For The Money"
                  :test 'char-equal)
;; uppercase!
#\O
CL-USER 3 > (position #\o "We're Only In It For The Money")
18
CL-USER 4 > (position #\O "We're Only In It For The Money")
6
CL-USER 5 > (search "on" "We're Only In It For The Money")
26
CL-USER 6 > (search "on" "We're Only In It For The Money"
                    :test 'char-equal)
6
```

How It Works

Again, as in Recipe 3-7, we're actually talking about general *sequence* functionality here, so I'll refer you to Recipe 7-2 for the details.

(Note that depending on your needs you might also want to consider regular expressions for this task. See more in Recipe 18-6.)

3-9. Trimming Strings

Problem

You want to trim certain characters off of the start and/or end of a string.

Solution

Use STRING-TRIM or its friends STRING-LEFT-TRIM and STRING-RIGHT-TRIM.

```
CL-USER> (string-trim '(#\Space #\Linefeed) "
  This is a sentence.  ")
"This is a sentence."
CL-USER> (string-left-trim "([" "([foo])")
"foo])"
CL-USER> (string-right-trim ")]" *)
"foo"
```

How It Works

In the first example we've removed all space and linefeed characters from the beginning and the end of the sentence. (Note that the string started with a linefeed and two spaces.) In the second example, we have removed the opening parentheses and brackets from the beginning of the string. In the third example, we took the result of the second example (see Recipe 16-11 for the meaning of *) and removed closing parentheses and brackets from its end.

The first argument is a *sequence* (i.e., a list or a vector) containing the characters to trim. Note that a string is also a vector, so the second example means that we want to trim #\(or #\[. The second argument is the string itself.

Your Lisp implementation is free to return the original string if there's nothing to trim, so you cannot count on the result being a *fresh* string:

```
CL-USER> (let* ((string1 (copy-seq "abc"))
                (string2 (string-trim "x" string1)))
           (setf (char string2 0) #\A)
           (list string1 string2))
;; SBCL result:
("Abc" "Abc")
```

The preceding example is implementation-dependent. The results could as well have been ("abc" "Abc") instead.

For trimming and more complex operations on strings, you might also want to look into regular expressions (see Recipe 18-6).

3-10. Processing a String One Character at a Time

Problem

You want to process each character of a string in turn.

Solution

Use LOOP or MAP or use another (possibly homegrown) iteration construct and index into the string:[25]

```
;; assumes something like ASCII - see footnote
;; see https://en.wikipedia.org/wiki/Digital_root
* (defun digital-root (string)
    (assert (every (lambda (char)
                     (char<= #\0 char #\9)) string)
            (string)
            "~S doesn't denote a non-negative decimal integer."
            string)
    (loop for char across string
          sum (- (char-code char) (char-code #\0)) into result
          finally (return
                   (if (> result 9)
                     (digital-root (princ-to-string result))
                     result))))
DIGITAL-ROOT
* (digital-root "12")
3
* (digital-root "1234")
1
;; assumes something like ASCII - see footnote
;; see https://en.wikipedia.org/wiki/ROT13
* (defun rot13-char (char)
    (cond ((char<= #\a char #\z)
           (code-char (+ (mod (+ (- (char-code char) (char-code #\a))
                                 13)
                              26)
                         (char-code #\a))))
```

[25]These functions make certain assumptions about the ordering of the characters which aren't necessarily portable between all *theoretical* COMMON LISP implementations. For example it would be perfectly legal if `(char<= #\a #\B #\c)` returned *true* or if `(code-char (1+ (char-code #\A)))` weren't `#\B`. However, for all current COMMON LISP implementations it is safe to assume that our examples will work as intended (see Recipe 3-1).

```
          ((char<= #\A char #\Z)
           (code-char (+ (mod (+ (- (char-code char) (char-code #\A))
                                  13)
                               26)
                            (char-code #\A))))))
ROT13-CHAR
* (map 'string #'rot13-char "foobar")
"sbbone"
* (map 'string #'rot13-char *)
"foobar"
```

How It Works

The first example—a contrived way to compute the digital root of an integer (written in decimal notation) represented as a string—uses the ACROSS keyword of LOOP to bind CHAR to each character of STRING in turn. ACROSS works with arbitrary *sequences* (see Chapter 7) and thus with strings in particular. Note that we have to convert the result back to a string with PRINC-TO-STRING (see Recipe 9-2) if we call DIGITAL-ROOT recursively.

The *assertion* (see Recipe 12-2) at the beginning of DIGITAL-ROOT shows a different string iteration technique: it uses one of the standard sequence functions.

Another way to iterate through a string (any sequence, that is) is to use MAP (see Recipe 7-12), as demonstrated with the second example. The first argument to MAP is the return type, which should also denote a sequence (or NIL if you're only interested in side effects). The second argument is a function that will be applied to each element (each character in this case) in turn.

Again, strings are sequences, so we can access individual characters with AREF. We can also uses AREF's "cousin" CHAR, which returns the same value but might be more efficient because it only works with strings. SCHAR might be even more efficient because it only works with *simple* strings—strings without fill-pointers and that aren't explicitly requested to be adjustable.[26] Obviously, you can iterate an integer from 0 to the length of a string and use it together with one of these accessors to get at the individual characters.

```
* (let ((string "frob"))
    (values (aref string 0)
            (char string 1)
            (schar string 2)
            (subseq string 3 4)))
#\f
```

[26]These terms are explained in Chapter 5.

```
#\r
#\o
"b"
* (let ((string "baz"))
    (loop for i below (length string)
          collect (char string i)))
(#\b #\a #\z)
```

Note that SUBSEQ above returns a string of length 1, not a character.

You can also convert a string into a list of characters; for example if you want to manipulate the result with functions that only work on lists. COERCE is probably a more efficient way to do this than our LOOP example above:

```
* (coerce "Recipes" 'list)
(#\R #\e #\c #\i #\p #\e #\s)
```

LOOP ACROSS and MAP both bind each character to a variable and thus prevent you from modifying the characters within the string. You have to use AREF, CHAR, or SCHAR together with SETF to do that. The following function will *destructively* modify a string:

```
* (defun n-rot13-string (string)
    (loop for i below (length string)
          do (setf (char string i)
                   (rot13-char (char string i)))))
N-ROT13-STRING
* (defparameter *string* (copy-seq "foobar"))
*STRING*
* (n-rot13-string *string*)
NIL
* *string*
"sbbone"
```

3-11. Joining Strings

Problem

You want to join strings—as with the `join` operator that many languages (like PERL or JAVASCRIPT) have.

Solution

You have to implement this yourself, but it's easy.

Here's one possibility:

```
* (defun join (separator list)
    (with-output-to-string (out)
      (loop for (element . more) on list
            do (princ element out)
            when more
              do (princ separator out))))
JOIN
* (join #\Space '("This" "is" "it"))
"This is it"
* (join #\- '(2003 12 31))
"2003-12-31"
* (join ", " '("C" "C++" "C#"))
"C, C++, C#"
* (join "" '("Hallo" "ween"))
"Halloween"
* (join #\- '())
""
* (join #\- '("One item only"))
"One item only"
```

If you don't like the so-called *extended* form of LOOP, here's a simpler variant of the same idea:

```
(defun join (separator list)
  (with-output-to-string (out)
    (loop (princ (pop list) out)
          (unless list (return))
          (princ separator out))))
```

How It Works

In some situations, a function like PERL's join (which "chains" together a list of strings using a supplied separator) comes in handy. Although there's no such function defined in the COMMON LISP standard, it's really easy to roll your own and there are lots of ways to do it. Above you'll see one which uses LOOP[27] to iterate through the (cdrs of the) list and destructure it on the fly. If there's more to come

[27] See Recipe 7-8, for example.

(i.e. if `MORE` is not `NIL`) it'll `PRINC` the separator, otherwise it'll only `PRINC` the (last) element. Note the use of `WITH-OUTPUT-TO-STRING`, which is explained in more detail in Recipe 14-7.

If your separator is constant you can use some `FORMAT` black magic[28] to achieve what you want:

```
* (format nil "~{~A~^, ~}" (list "C" "C++" "C#"))
"C, C++, C#"
```

(Note how the `", "` part is hard-coded into the format string.)

There are several other ways to skin this cat. You might want to try your luck with, say, `MAPCAR` or `REDUCE`. It should also be clear from the preceding code that you're not limited to strings here. The same technique can be used for lists, for example:

```
* (defun list-join (separator list)
    (loop for (element . more) on list
          collect element
          when more
            collect separator))
LIST-JOIN
* (list-join '+ (loop for i below 5 collect i))
(0 + 1 + 2 + 3 + 4)
```

3-12. Reading CSV Data

Problem

You want to read a comma-separated values ("CSV") file generated by other programs.

Solution

For simple CSV data, you can get by with a slight modification of the readtable. However, some widespread applications (notably Microsoft Excel) may interpret "comma-separated" in a completely different way, and you'll have to parse the data with other means.

Here's the approach that is probably the most straightforward. We'll first create a file `/tmp/test.csv` with these contents:

[28]See `http://www.gigamonkeys.com/book/a-few-format-recipes.html`.

```
"a string",3,3.2
"another string","string with \"quotes\"",12
"string, with comma","",3.5E3
```

Now, in our Lisp:

```
* (defparameter *csv-readtable* (copy-readtable))
*CSV-READTABLE*
* (set-syntax-from-char #\, #\Space *csv-readtable*)
T
* (defun read-csv-line (string)
    (let ((*readtable* *csv-readtable*))
      (with-input-from-string (stream string)
        (loop for object = (read stream nil nil)
              while object
              collect object))))
READ-CSV-LINE
```

We create a new readtable `*CVS-READTABLE*` by copying the standard readtable and then setting the syntax of the comma to be that of the space character (so that, like whitespace, it separates Lisp objects from each other).[29] Now we can (in our function `READ-CSV-LINE`) simply use the built-in `READ` function to read numbers and strings from a line with comma-separated values.

That's all there is to it. We can now parse our file, like so:

```
* (with-open-file (stream "/tmp/test.csv")
    (loop for line = (read-line stream nil nil)
          while line
          collect (read-csv-line line)))
(("a string" 3 3.2)
 ("another string" "string with \"quotes\"" 12)
 ("string, with comma" "" 3500.0))
```

How It Works

If CSV data is formatted according to the rules of RFC 4180,[30] and strings are enclosed in double quote, then except for the comma separating the individual entries, this is identical to the way COMMON LISP prints and reads its data; so we can use

[29]See Chapter 8 for the mechanics of modifying the syntax of COMMON LISP.

[30]See `https://tools.ietf.org/html/rfc4180`.

our Lisp's `READ` function to read this data if we instruct it to treat a comma like whitespace.

Unfortunately, this is not sufficient for real-life usage. Not all applications agree on how to format CSV data, so you'll very likely need a tool that's a bit more flexible. In May 2015, there were at least five libraries listed on QUICKDOCS (see Recipe 18-2), which claimed to be able to parse CSV data, so you should very likely find something that suits your needs.[31]

Finally, another way would be to use regular expressions (see Recipe 18-6). You'll figure it out yourself...

[31]Or have a look at `http://xach.com/rpw3/articles/2qydnU8FD8--BOCiXTWc-w@speakeasy.net.html`.

4. Numbers and Math

Out of the box, COMMON LISP is exceptionally well suited to numerical mathematical calculations.[1] Integers are not limited to a specific size (see Recipe 4-1). It comes with rational numbers so you can do arithmetic with unlimited precision (see Recipe 4-5). And it has complex numbers (see Recipe 4-8).

All of these numerical types are part of the standard and thus not only available in every COMMON LISP implementation but also fully integrated into the language. This chapter will look at them in detail—how they are used, how they can be printed and parsed, and what to look out for. It'll also discuss arbitrary precision floats (see Recipe 4-7), which aren't part of the standard but can be added with the help of a library.

4-1. Using Arbitrarily Large Integers

Problem

You are afraid of integer overflow.

Solution

Don't be!

Here's a session showing off a few computations with large integers:

```
;; see <http://en.wikipedia.org/wiki/Fermat_number>
* (defun fermat (n) (1+ (expt 2 (expt 2 n))))
FERMAT
* (fermat 7)
340282366920938463463374607431768211457
* (fermat 8)
;; wrapped around so that it fits on the book page
115792089237316195423570985008687907853269984665640564039457584007 9
```

[1]And to symbolic computations as well. Some of the earliest computer algebra systems (CAS) were based on Lisp dialects. And today MAXIMA, arguably one of the best open source CAS, is written in COMMON LISP.

```
13129639937
* (gcd * **)
1
```

(The function GCD computes the greatest common divisor of two or more integers.)

How It Works

Integer overflow is an ailment that plagues many popular programming languages these days.[2] What it means is that they usually have a datatype called `int` or similar, which stands for *integer* but doesn't really mean integer numbers in the mathematical sense but rather a finite subset of them. The set of all numbers of type `int` is restricted to mean those integers that can be represented with a fixed amount of bits. The consequence is that if, for example, this bit length is 32 and you want to multiply 1000000 with 2000000, the result, 2000000000000, isn't an `int` anymore. What's worse, you have to be prepared to be presented with the "result" 2840207360 instead without any warning.[3] What your computer is really doing here is what mathematicians call *modular arithmetic* (see also Recipe 4-3) where numbers "wrap around" like the time on a clock.[4]

In COMMON LISP, the situation is completely different. There's a type called `INTEGER` and as long as you're just adding, subtracting, or multiplying[5] integers, you won't ever have to worry about integer overflow; the result will be correct and again be of type `INTEGER`. This also applies to powers; if you compute `(EXPT A B)` (i.e., a^b in mathematical notation), and if `A` and `B` are integers, then the result returned will be exact and an integer as well.[6]

Other operators that work fine with integers no matter how big they are include `ABS`, `MAX`, `MIN`, `PLUSP`, `MINUSP`, `ZEROP`, `1+`, `1-`, `INCF`, `DECF`, `GCD`, `LCM`, `EVENP`, `ODDP`, `SIGNUM`, `MOD`, `REM`, and various functions operating on bits (see also Recipe 4-5).

There are, of course, still some limitations. Integers can't be *arbitrarily* big because

---

[2] And it has caused far too many problems in the last decades—from security bugs to the explosion of an Ariane 5 space rocket in 1996.

[3] This is assuming that you're working with *unsigned* integers. (To be fair, some languages like ADA *will* warn you, but that doesn't necessarily mean that they also have something like COMMON LISP's bignums.)

[4] And, of course, this doesn't change if you substitute `long` for `int`.

[5] For division of integers, see Recipe 4-5.

[6] And presumably your compiler will internally use exponentiation by squaring or a similar technique to make this reasonably fast, even if `A` and `B` are pretty large. Unfortunately, this is not true in general for the `LOG` function. You might hope that the result of evaluating `(LOG (EXPT 2 100) 2)` would be the integer `100`, but implementations are allowed to return the floating-point number `100.0` instead, and most do—with the notable exception of CLISP (see also Recipe 4-7), which follows the policy that whenever the compiler is able to compute an exact rational result, it will be returned even if the standard would allow a floating-point approximation.

they have to fit into your computer's memory somehow. But it's hard to conceive of situations where you might reach this limit (except maybe in experimental number theory).

A limitation that might seem more serious to some is that COMMON LISP's correctness in integer arithmetic comes at the price of a potential decrease in speed (compared to modular arithmetic, which is the way it is because it exactly matches how arithmetic is implemented in today's processors). This is actually more of a topic for Chapter 17, which deals with optimization, but the next recipe investigates some implementation details of integer arithmetic (and finally explains what the word "bignums" in *this* recipe's title means).

4-2. Understanding Fixnums

Problem

You've learned that COMMON LISP has integers that can be as large as you need, but you want to know whether it also has "small" integers like in C or JAVA that fit into the machine's registers.

Solution

It has. And these numbers are called *fixnums*. If you run the following code, the output should be (T NIL T NIL T T) no matter which Lisp you use:[7]

```
(loop for n in (list most-positive-fixnum (1+ most-positive-fixnum))
      append (loop for type in '(fixnum bignum integer)
                   collect (typep n type)))
```

This shows that there's a constant MOST-POSITIVE-FIXNUM, which is an integer (see Recipe 4-1) but is also of a type called FIXNUM, whereas its successor is not and has the type BIGNUM instead.

Fixnums are (except for implementation-specific goodies; see Recipe 4-3) the closest you'll get to int or long in C, but their behavior is a bit different. Read on...

[7]See Recipe 13-1 for TYPEP.

How It Works

The set of all integers in COMMON LISP is divided into two disjoint[8] sets: *fixnums* and *bignums*. The fixnums are the integers with small[9] absolute values; the other integers are the bignums. Your Lisp system will automatically switch between fixnums and bignums as needed; so if, for example, you add two fixnums and the sum is too big to be a fixnum, then it'll be a bignum. No matter what, it'll always be an integer and the result will be correct. COMMON LISP never uses modular arithmetic in way that could cause incorrect results.[10]

If you're only concerned about correct results, you can stop reading here and pretend you've never heard of fixnums and bignums. Only if you're forced to think about space or speed optimizations are fixnums something you should know about. So, what's the deal?

The standard doesn't enforce any specific kind of implementation but it is probably fair to say that on modern hardware, all Lisp compilers use so-called *tag bits* to distinguish between different types of data. A few bits (usually the least significant ones) are set aside so that when looking at a machine word, the compiler knows if this word is meant to represent an integer (and that's what will be called a *fixnum*) or something else like, for example, a pointer. This is a pretty clever technique, as it allows the compiler to use the CPU's normal arithmetic instructions on these tagged integers as long as it makes sure to mask out the tag bits.[11]

For the sake of an example, let's assume we're dealing with a Lisp implementation with 16-bit words and one tag bit (marked with a gray background below) where a zero tag denotes a fixnum and a one means any other Lisp object.[12] Let's have a look at three words in this machine's memory:

A:	0	0	0	0	0	0	0	0	0	0	0	0	0	0	1	0
B:	0	0	0	0	0	0	1	1	0	1	0	0	1	0	0	0
C:	0	0	0	0	0	0	1	1	0	1	0	0	1	0	0	1

The word at address A is a fixnum because its tag bit is 0. That means it stands for the value `#b000000000000001` or simply 1 as a decimal number. (Note that it's *not* the number 2, which would be the case if the tag bit were a part of the number.) The

[8]This means that the two sets are mutually exclusive; an integer is either a fixnum or a bignum, but never both.

[9]In case you're wondering what exactly "small" means in this context—it depends. Please read on...

[10]Well, unless you're forcing the compiler to do it (see for example Recipes 17-3 and 4-3.)

[11]There's another bit of cleverness involved here. As most datums are aligned on 4-byte boundaries, you don't really need the two least significant bits of a pointer, and thus it doesn't hurt to use them for other purposes.

[12]Using a zero tag for fixnums is common but not the only strategy used. ECL, for example, tags fixnums with `01`.

second word is also a fixnum and means `#b0000001101001 00` or 420. If we want to add these two numbers, we can ask the CPU to simply add the two 16-bit words, including the tag bits, and the result will be the correct sum as a fixnum, including the tag bit!

Finally, the word at address C would presumably be a pointer to some other (non-fixnum) Lisp object. Its value would be `#b0000001101001000` or the decimal 840. (And not 420! Typically, the tag bits for pointers will be replaced by zeros and not cut off, as with fixnums.)

The consequence of all this, of course, is that now fewer bits are available for the integers. On our 16-bit machine, only 15 bits are available for integers; that is, instead of the integers from -2^{15} to $2^{15}-1$ only the integers from -2^{14} to $2^{14}-1$ can be represented in two's complement.

Bignums on the other hand consist of several parts. You just use as many machine words as needed to represent the corresponding integer. That means that there's no limit (except for the size of your RAM) for how big they can be, but it also implies that bignum computations can't be performed with a single machine instruction. Thus, arithmetic with fixnums is usually significantly faster than bignum arithmetic.

Therefore, you sometimes need to know where the fixnums end and the bignums start. As each implementation can decide for itself how many tag bits it wants to use,[13] there are two constants guaranteed to be available—`MOST-POSITIVE-FIXNUM` and `MOST-NEGATIVE-FIXNUM`—and they mean exactly what you think they mean: if an integer is larger than the first value or smaller than the second, it'll be a bignum, otherwise it is a fixnum.

That is usually all you need to know, but if you're curious how many tag bits your Lisp uses, that's easy to find out, too:

```
(1+ (max (integer-length most-positive-fixnum)
         (integer-length most-negative-fixnum)))
```

This form gives you the number of bits available for fixnums in binary two's complement. (That's exactly what the function `INTEGER-LENGTH` is for: figuring out how many bits are needed to represent a number. We then add 1 for the sign bit.) If your result is, say, 30 and you're on a 32-bit machine, you now know that your compiler uses two tag bits.

Incidentally, the standard is pretty careful here in that it in theory allows the most positive and most negative values to have different magnitudes, and so we're careful too. In practice, I'd be very surprised to see an implementation where `MOST-NEGATIVE-FIXNUM` were not the value of `(- (1+ MOST-POSITIVE-FIXNUM))`.[14]

---

[13]And, as I said, it doesn't even have to use tag bits if someone comes up with a better technique.

[14]The standard even goes as far as not forcing implementations to represent integers as binary numbers in two's complement; there are merely a couple of places where functions have to behave *as if* this

4-3. Performing Modular Arithmetic

Problem

You want modular arithmetic the way it is implemented in your computer's CPU.

Solution

Once you know about the MOD function, it seems pretty obvious that if you want to, say, multiply 58 with 74051161 and simulate a 32-bit processor, you'd do something like this

```
(mod (* 58 74051161) (expt 2 32))
```

and the result will be 42 as expected.

You could now start writing your own little "modular arithmetic library" like so:

```
(defconstant +mod+ (expt 2 32))
(defun plus (x y) (mod (+ x y) +mod+))
(defun times (x y) (mod (* x y) +mod+))
;; etc.
```

But this probably won't work as you expected for negative numbers and you might also be concerned about efficiency. Read on...

How It Works

Although in general one should be quite happy that COMMON LISP provides arbitrarily large integers out of the box (see Recipe 4-1), sometimes you want or need modular arithmetic. This might, for example, be the case if you're doing experimental number theory or if you're working on cryptographic algorithms.

As you might expect, COMMON LISP has a function to compute the *modulus* of a number, similar to what is called % in languages with C syntax. But what maybe you didn't expect is that there are actually two such functions. One of them is called REM (for *remainder*) and it works like % in C or JAVA; the other one is called MOD (for *modulus*) and it works like % in PYTHON. So, what's the difference?

MOD and REM yield the same results as long as their arguments are positive, but they differ for negative arguments. Let's assume we're only dealing with integer arguments and the second argument is always positive. (Both functions can deal with

were the case.

arbitrary Lisp reals, but you'll rarely need that.) The simple rule then is that the result of MOD is always non-negative, irrespective of the sign of its first argument; whereas the result of REM always has the same sign as its first argument (unless the result is zero). Here's an example:

```
(defconstant +mod+ (expt 2 32))
(defun plus-mod (x y) (mod (+ x y) +mod+))
(defun plus-rem (x y) (rem (* x y) +mod+))
```

If you call these functions with the arguments -58 and 74051161, then PLUS-REM yields -42 while PLUS-MOD gives you 74051103.

Both results are mathematically correct, but MOD behaves as people working in number theory would prefer, whereas REM is "closer to the metal," so to say. If you wanted to simulate binary two's complement arithmetic, you'd go with REM.

(Note, by the way, that MOD and REM are just "shortcuts" for FLOOR and TRUNCATE; see Recipe 4-5.)

Efficiency Considerations

Now, although modular arithmetic can lead to wrong results if you expect it to work like arithmetic on "real" (no pun intended) integers, it is what virtually every computer available today does internally, and therefore many important algorithms, especially in cryptography, have adopted it and use it to their advantage. If you want to write them in COMMON LISP with its emphasis on correctness, you'll have to invest some work to make such code as efficient as in C or C++. I'll briefly cover two implementation-dependent features that can help you here:

Consider again PLUS-MOD from above. If the compiler doesn't know what kind of numbers X and Y are in an expression like (+ X Y), it has to compile the call to + into the most generic function call that works for all types. And even if, say, it knew that X and Y were fixnums (see Recipe 4-2), the result of adding them could be a bignum.[15] However, the call to MOD following the addition implies that the *correct* result of the addition is irrelevant and only its least significant 32 bits are asked for. So, if we rewrote PLUS-MOD like below, then a sufficiently smart compiler could deduce that the function's body can be reduced to one 32-bit machine instruction:[16]

```
(defun plus-mod (x y)
  (declare (type (unsigned-byte 32) x y))
  (mod (+ x y) (expt 2 32)))
```

[15]Not to mention that fixnums wouldn't help much for algorithms optimized for 32-bit word sizes.
[16]See Recipe 17-3 for DECLARE.

The good news is that such a smart compiler does indeed exist. SBCL will compile code like this into extremely efficient machine code on par with C (see for example their `sb-md5` implementation of the MD5 message digest algorithm).[17]

Another approach is the INT32 API provided by the LISPWORKS compiler. It introduces a new Lisp type called `SYS:INT32`, representing integers with at most 32 bits and functions like `SYS:INT32+` to do modular arithmetic on them. With the right optimization settings, the compiler will convert a form like `(SYS:INT32+ X Y)` to a single machine-language instruction if it knows that `X` and `Y` are `SYS:INT32` objects (which in optimized code will, of course, be replaced by "raw" 32-bit integers). LISPWORKS recently also added an INT64 API with similar capabilities for 64-bit modular arithmetic. For details, see the LISPWORKS reference manual.[18]

4-4. Switching Bases

Problem

You want to input or output binary, octal, or hexadecimal numbers. (Or actually numbers in any base from 2 up to 36.)

Solution

For input, use the sharpsign (`#`) notation;[19] for output, use `FORMAT`. Try this:

```
(list (list #b101010 #o52 #x2A)
      (loop for fmt in '("~B" "~O" "~X")
            collect (format nil fmt 42)))
```

But you can also directly manipulate the Lisp reader and/or the Lisp printer (you'll read more on this next).

How It Works

To enter a number in binary form, precede it with `#b` and use only the digits 0 and 1. (An optional sign at the beginning, as in `#b-10` is allowed, though.) For octal numbers, it's the same with `o` instead of `b` and with digits from 0 up to 7. For hexadecimal

[17] For a detailed account see the article *Efficient Hardware Arithmetic in Common Lisp* by Alexey Dejneka and Christophe Rhodes which can be found at `http://jcsu.jesus.cam.ac.uk/~csr21/papers/modular/modular.pdf`.

[18] Example code that uses this INT32 API can be found in the LISPWORKS-specific parts of `http://method-combination.net/lisp/ironclad/` or at `http://weitz.de/cl-dongle/`.

[19] See more about it in Chapter 8.

numbers, use x. In this case, as usual, the characters A to F are used (to denote 10 to 15) in addition to the decimal digits. Case isn't relevant, whether directly behind the sharpsign or in non-decimal digits, so #x2A, or #X2a, or #x2a all mean the same thing.

These are the bases most often used in computer science, but if you need something else, that's also possible. For this, you'd use an r and precede it with the base itself. So, to enter 42 in base 7 you'd use #7r60 and instead of #x2A you could have written #16r2A. The largest base you can use is 36. Why is it 36? Because for bases larger than 10 you need additional digits (as in hexadecimal numbers) and there are only 26 characters available in the Latin alphabet.

You can't enter floating-point numbers in bases other than 10,[20] but you can do all of the above with rationals (see Recipe 4-5) as well; so, for example, #xA/C will yield the fraction $\frac{5}{6}$.

To output numbers in other bases, you don't have to learn other letters; it's b, o, and x again (plus d for decimals); see the FORMAT example above. Plus, r is also available as, for example, in (FORMAT NIL "~7R" 42) to create a base 7 representation of 42. All this works with rationals, too.

And while we're at it, you can output integers in even more ways with the ~R format directive; as English cardinals or ordinals, or as Roman numerals. Try this:

```
(loop for fmt in '("~R" "~:R" "~@R")
      collect (format nil fmt 42))
```

A more radical way to deal with different bases is to modify the way your Lisp reads and prints numbers. (Although you probably will do this only in special circumstances.) Use the global special variables *READ-BASE* and *PRINT-BASE*. As a safety measure, you can set *PRINT-RADIX* to a true value so that the Lisp printer reminds you for each number in which base it is in.[21] The following example session should give you an idea:

```
;; the default values
* *read-base*
10
* *print-base*
10
;; switch to binary input
* (setf *read-base* 2)
```

[20]But by setting *READ-BASE* (we'll get to this shortly) to a high enough value, you can, for example, make 42d0 an integer, although with standard syntax, this is understood to be a floating-point number.

[21]Try it out with various settings for *PRINT-BASE*. Note how numbers get a prefix so that you can read them back in again this way. The only exception is base ten, where there's no prefix for integers and they are instead printed with a dot as a suffix.

```
2
* 101010
42
;; you can still override this with #
* #x2A
42
;; this does NOT switch back to decimal because "10" is read
;; as a binary number...
* (setf *read-base* 10)
2
;; this works
* (setf *read-base* 1010)
10
;; now switch to hexadecimal output
* (setf *print-base* 16)
;; this is the sixteen we just entered, but already in hex
10
* 42
2A
* (setf *print-radix* t)
T
* 42
#x2A
```

4-5. Performing Exact Arithmetic with Rational Numbers

Problem

You want to do exact arithmetic with rationals (as opposed to working with floating-point numbers which usually are approximations).

Solution

COMMON LISP has a type called RATIONAL, which represents rational numbers (in the mathematical sense) without any loss of precision; that is, they are stored and displayed as fractions where the numerator and the denominator are arbitrarily large integers (see Recipe 4-1). Here are a few examples:

```
* (/ 3 4)
3/4
* (floor 3 4)
```

```
0
3
* 6/8
3/4
* (* 3/4 8/3)
2
* (+ 1/3 3/7)
16/21
* (/ (expt 2 30) (1+ (expt 3 30)))
536870912/102945566047325
```

How It Works

The example shows that the result of dividing two integers is a fraction if it's not an integer. This is different from most mainstream programming languages where `(/ 3 4)` would have yielded zero as a result.[22] Also note how the fraction `6/8` is automatically canceled down to `3/4`; that is, fractions are always represented in a canonical form: as an integer, or otherwise with a positive denominator that is as small as possible.

In case that wasn't obvious, let me mention that the form `(/ 3 4)` is a *function call* to the function `/` while the form `6/8` is the *literal representation* of a fraction. Negative fractions can be entered[23] as in `-3/4` but *not* in the form `3/-4`, although that might make sense mathematically.

The example `(* 3/4 8/3)` that returns `2` is nothing special except that it again shows cancelation, which in this case makes the result an integer. But this is still a rational; in mathematics, all integers are rationals[24] and in the COMMON LISP type hierarchy (see Recipe 13-3) as well. If you want to be able to distinguish between integers and *other* fractions, use the Lisp type `RATIO`.

The individual parts of a Lisp rational can be accessed with the aptly named functions `NUMERATOR` and `DENOMINATOR` (which use the canonical form mentioned above); so, for example, the form

```
(denominator (/ 2 -10))
```

evaluates to `5` and *not* to `10` or `-5`.

(See also Recipes 9-9 and 20-4 for code, which uses rational numbers explicitly.)

[22] Read on if you want to know how to "simulate" this behavior with COMMON LISP.

[23] And you can enter rationals using a different basis; see Recipe 4-4.

[24] Integers are simply fractions where the denominator is 1.

Various Ways of Converting Numbers to Integers

The behavior of C-like languages where you get 0 if you divide 3 by 4 is sometimes actually what you want. You can think of this as first computing the correct result and then cutting off the part behind the decimal point, so you might be tempted to use FLOOR:

```
* (/ 3 4)
3/4
* (floor (/ 3 4))
0
3/4
* (floor 3 4)
0
3
* (floor -3 4)
-1
1
```

This actually works and you can see that FLOOR will accept two arguments so that you don't have to perform the division in a separate step (more on this shortly). However, that last result is -1, whereas C and JAVA would have given you zero instead. This is because FLOOR truncates toward negative infinity; that is, if the result is not an integer, it will return an integer, which is always *smaller* than the correct result. What you need to simulate C in this case is TRUNCATE, which truncates toward zero. But there are actually four[25] functions that do roughly the same thing:

```
* (dolist (fn '(floor ceiling truncate round))
    (dolist (args '((3 4) (-3 4)))
      (format t "~A -> ~A   " (list* fn args) (apply fn args)))
    (terpri))
(FLOOR 3 4) -> 0   (FLOOR -3 4) -> -1
(CEILING 3 4) -> 1   (CEILING -3 4) -> 0
(TRUNCATE 3 4) -> 0   (TRUNCATE -3 4) -> 0
(ROUND 3 4) -> 1   (ROUND -3 4) -> -1
NIL
```

As promised, TRUNCATE does what C does when performing division, while FLOOR and CEILING (you'll find functions with similar names in many programming languages) always have a "bias" to one direction.[26] ROUND is the function you'd use for

[25]To be completely honest with you, there are *eight* such functions. Each of the four mentioned here has a variant with an extra F in front. The variant performs the same calculations as its counterpart, but returns the resulting integer as a Lisp float.

[26]This corresponds to the $\lfloor x \rfloor$ and $\lceil x \rceil$ notation you'll find in math and computer science textbooks, which can essentially be traced back to Carl Friedrich Gauß.

actual *rounding* because it tries to minimize the distance between the argument and the resulting integer. ROUND will even go as far as alternating between rounding up and rounding down numbers that are exactly halfway between two integers in order to prevent what is called *sign bias*:[27]

```
* (loop for i in '(1/2 3/2 5/2 7/2)
        collect (round i))
(0 2 2 4)
```

As you'll have noticed in the case of FLOOR at the beginning of this recipe, all of these functions return two values. This is because they all implicitly perform a division (if you call them with one argument the divisor is understood to be 1). The second value returned is then the remainder (see also MOD and REM in Recipe 4-3).

How Not to Use FLOOR and Friends

You will have noticed that (FLOOR 3 4), for example, gives the same result as (FLOOR (/ 3 4)), at least if you're only interested in the first return value. There's a slight difference, though. In the second variant, your Lisp must create a rational number to store the result of the division; whereas in the first, there's no need for that. This might make a difference in a tight loop.

Converting Floating-Point Numbers to Rationals and Vice Versa

In a language that has a type like RATIONAL, you'll rightly expect a function to convert floats to rationals. In fact, COMMON LISP has *two* functions for this task: RATIONAL and RATIONALIZE. They both have the property that if you use one of them to convert a float to a rational number and then convert this rational number back to a float of the same type (see below), you'll get exactly the float you started with. That the two functions might still generate different rationals from the same float is due to the nature of floating-point numbers and their internal representation as binaries.

Let's look at two simple examples. The number $\frac{1}{2}$ can be expressed exactly in binary, namely as 0.1, which would mean $0 \cdot 2^0 + 1 \cdot 2^{-1}$. This is why RATIONAL and RATIONALIZE don't disagree in this case:

```
* (rational 0.5)
1/2
* (rationalize 0.5)
1/2
```

[27]If you always rounded up in such cases, then if you were rounding a large amount of numbers, more numbers would be rounded up than down.

But like $\frac{1}{3}$ can't be represented as a *terminating* decimal fraction (because it'd be `0.3333333333...` without ever ending) there are also lots of numbers that can't be represented as binary fractions with a finite number of digits, even if they can be in decimal notation: $\frac{1}{5}$, which is `0.2` in decimal, is

$$\texttt{0.001100110011...} = 2^{-3} + 2^{-4} + 2^{-7} + 2^{-8} + 2^{-11} + 2^{-12} + \ldots$$

as a binary number. As your computer doesn't have infinite memory, it will cut this sequence of digits off at some point and thus *round* the number somehow. In other words, the floating-point representation of $\frac{1}{5}$ will be that of a number that is *almost* $\frac{1}{5}$ but not quite.

Still, if you enter `0.2` or (see Recipe 4-6) `0.2d0` into your REPL, you will almost certainly see `0.2` as a reply and not some other number that is very close to $\frac{1}{5}$.[28] This is because your Lisp *knows* that the number it's dealing with might not be exact, and thus doesn't take the least significant bits for granted but rather prints a rounded result that, in most cases, is more to our liking, because humans are used to decimal representation. And this is exactly the difference between `RATIONAL` and `RATIONALIZE`. The first function "believes" that the floating-point number it sees is exact and returns a corresponding rational. The second function takes its input with a grain of salt and rounds it first:[29]

```
* (rational 0.2)
13421773/67108864
* (rationalize 0.2)
1/5
;; see next paragraph
* (list (float *) (float **))
(0.2 0.2)
```

Because both functions operate within the accuracy of the underlying floating-point representation, converting back to a float will yield the same result.

As we've just seen, there's, of course, also a function to convert rationals to floats; it is aptly called `FLOAT` and, in principle, does exactly what you expect. But watch out:

```
* (float 1/7)
0.14285715
* (float 1/7 1d0)
0.14285714285714285d0
;; see below
* (float 0.1f0 1d0)
0.10000000149011612d0
```

[28]But see the end of this recipe.

[29]See Recipe 16-11 for the meaning of `*` and `**`.

FLOAT will *always* give you a single float (see Recipe 4-6) unless you provide a so-called *prototype* as its second argument. The numerical value of the prototype is completely irrelevant, only its type is used. (Granted, this is a bit unwieldy, but there's not really an elegant way to do it. You might want to look up COERCE, though.)

The last example shows that you can, of course, also convert, say, single floats to double floats, but it also demonstrates the inexact internal representation explained a few paragraphs ago.

Mixing Rationals and Floats

If one of the standard functions (including, of course, the arithmetic ones like + or *) is given floating-point arguments of different types, then the one with higher precision "wins," meaning that if, for example, you do this

```
(* 2f0 2d0)
```

then the result will be 4.0D0 and not 4.0F0.[30] This is probably what you would have expected as it is the same in other languages.

However, what if some arguments are rational and some are floating point? One could argue that rational numbers are (infinitely) more precise and should thus "win." But this is not what happens. To make life easier for implementors, something like

```
(* 2 2d0)
```

will evaluate to 4.0D0 and *not* to 4. So, you should keep in mind that when you're working with rationals because of their precision, one floating-point number will suffice to "taint" the result.[31] Funnily, the one exception to this rule are comparison functions, where in mixed situations the floats are first converted by means of RATIONAL (see above). This can lead to seemingly strange results, like

```
(< 6/7 (float 6/7))
```

being true in Lisps with IEEE floats (see Recipe 4-6).

[30]Unless SINGLE-FLOAT and DOUBLE-FLOAT are identical in your Lisp, which is pretty unlikely.

[31]As will applications of non-rational functions, like SQRT or SIN (see also Recipe 4-8).

4-6. Controlling the Default Float Format

Problem

You want to make sure that float literals are always interpreted as double floats. (And you should!)

Solution

Change the value of the variable `*READ-DEFAULT-FLOAT-FORMAT*`. The following is from a fresh SBCL session and should look more or less the same in any current COMMON LISP:

```
* *read-default-float-format*
SINGLE-FLOAT
* (- 1.00000001 1)
0.0
* 1.00000001
1.0
* (- 1.00000001d0 1)
9.99999993922529d-9
* (setf *read-default-float-format* 'double-float)
DOUBLE-FLOAT
* (- 1.00000001 1)
9.99999993922529e-9
```

How It Works

The COMMON LISP standard provides for four types of floating-point numbers; there's actually nothing preventing a COMMON LISP implementation from having even more than four different floating-point types. However, in most implementations[32] there are only two floating-point types that are actually *different* from each other; you can probably count on the types `SINGLE-FLOAT` and `DOUBLE-FLOAT` corresponding to 32-bit and 64-bit IEEE[33] floating-point numbers, respectively.

Double floats use twice as much space but should otherwise almost always be preferred over single floats as they offer higher precision and smaller rounding errors. And on modern hardware, computing with double floats is not even slower than

---

[32]But see Recipe 4-7.

[33]This refers to the IEEE 754 standard. You can actually check the *features* (see Recipe 10-10) of your Lisp implementation and look for the keyword `:IEEE-FLOATING-POINT`. If it's there, your compiler claims to conform to this standard.

computing with single floats; it might even be faster. That's why in languages like C++ and JAVA, float literals are understood to be doubles unless they're explicitly qualified as singles.

Unfortunately, when the COMMON LISP standard was written, the situation wasn't quite as clear-cut as it is today, and so they decided to make `SINGLE-FLOAT` the default for float literals. That's why in the preceding example, the first computation returns zero instead of 10^{-8}: the precision of an IEEE 754 single float doesn't suffice to hold the value `1.00000001` and it is thus converted to `1.0` *before* the function `-` is called.[34]

One way to fix this is to always make sure to use an explicit *exponent marker* like `D` in your code; that is, to write `42D0` instead of `42E0` or `42.0`. But this gets tedious pretty quickly and you might forget it in critical places. Luckily, you can actually *change* the way float literals are interpreted. There's a global special variable called `*READ-DEFAULT-FLOAT-FORMAT*` that by default has (and must have) as its value the symbol `SINGLE-FLOAT`. But that can be changed, as in the preceding example. It is probably a good idea to do this in your *init file* (see Recipe 22-5) so you can always be sure you're not inadvertently using insufficient precision.

Note that the value of this variable also affects how floating-point numbers are printed. A floating-point number will always be printed with an explicit exponent marker—one of the characters `F`, `S`, `D`, or `L` for `SHORT-FLOAT`, `SINGLE-FLOAT`, `DOUBLE-FLOAT`, and `LONG-FLOAT`, respectively—if its type doesn't agree with the current default format. For example:

```
* *read-default-float-format*
SINGLE-FLOAT
* 1.0f0
1.0                    ;; <--
* 1.0d0
1.0d0
* (setf *read-default-float-format* 'double-float)
DOUBLE-FLOAT
* 1.0f0
1.0f0
* 1.0d0
1.0                    ;; <--
```

(Implementations have some leeway in what exactly they output here, but in the two

[34]In case you're wondering why the result at the end is `9.99999993922529e-9` instead of `1.0e-8`—that's a typical artifact of representing floating-point numbers using (only finitely many) binary digits, and not specific to COMMON LISP. You'll find a bit about this on page 100, but essentially this is beyond the scope of this book. There are numerous good resources available, though. One of the classic texts is *What every computer scientist should know about floating-point arithmetic* by David Goldberg (Computer Surveys, 1991).

marked places they should all agree; see section 22.1.3.1.3 of the standard.)

4-7. Employing Arbitrary Precision Floats

Problem

You need higher floating-point precision than double (or long) floats have to offer.

Solution

Use an implementation that has that built-in (like CLISP) or use the COMPUTABLE-REALS library.

As a toy example, let's look at the following test function:

```
(defun foo (orig &optional (n 10))
  (let ((x orig))
    (loop repeat n do (setf x (sqrt x)))
    (loop repeat n do (setf x (* x x)))
    (list x (* (/ (abs (- x orig)) orig) 100))))
```

FOO will take a number as input and will then iteratively compute its square root *n* times, and afterward square the result *n* times. If this were your math homework, you should immediately see that the result must be the same as the input and a good computer algebra system should be able to figure that out as well. A program computing with floating-point numbers, however, will inevitably introduce rounding errors that will accumulate. That's why FOO returns not only the result but also the relative error as a percentage of the input.

If you call (FOO 2F0)—that is, if you're using single floats—the error will be roughly 0.002%; whereas with (FOO 2F0 20) (with 20 iterations), you'll have reached a shocking seven percent already. It looks a bit better with double floats, where (FOO 2D0) will report a mere 10^{-12} percent; but if you then try (FOO 2D0 50), you'll have an error of almost 18%.[35]

Here's how this can be made to look better in CLISP:

```
> (setf (ext:long-float-digits) 256)
256
> (foo 2L0 50)
;; numbers wrapped so that they fit into the book
```

[35]This is assuming that your implementation uses the usual IEEE floats for single and double floats; see Recipe 4-6.

```
(2.000000000000000000000000000000000000000000000000000000000002448
  529853516406L0
 1.224264926758202845716226042678028278168919039455233077172546776621
  080703188262L-60)
```

That's a relative error of only 10^{-60} percent!

With the COMPUTABLE-REALS library, we'll have to modify FOO a bit:

```
(defun foo-r (orig &optional (n 10))
  (let ((x orig))
    (loop repeat n do (setf x (cr:sqrt-r x)))
    (loop repeat n do (setf x (cr:*r x x)))
    x))
```

There are just two relevant changes: we replace SQRT and * with their arbitrary-precision counterparts. And note that we don't compute the relative error anymore. You'll see below that this wouldn't make sense.

If you now call (FOO-R 2) (note that we use the *rational* 2 as input because the library wouldn't accept inexact floats), the result will look like this:

```
+2.00000000000000000000...
```

Read on to see what the dots at the end mean.

How It Works

The COMMON LISP implementation CLISP has a LONG-FLOAT type the precision of which can be changed at run time;[36] just set (EXT:LONG-FLOAT-DIGITS) to a multiple of 16 as in the example above. You'll still have floats with a finite number of bits, but in theory you can make rounding errors as small as you want.[37]

The library COMPUTABLE-REALS (loadable via Quicklisp; see Recipe 18-2), uses a different approach.[38] In this library, you can set the precision *a posteriori*; that is, *after* the computation is finished. This works essentially like a human or a computer algebra

[36] In a typical COMMON LISP, LONG-FLOAT will just be a synonym for DOUBLE-FLOAT and thus for 64-bit IEEE floats. If you're lucky, then maybe in the future you'll get 128-bit floats instead.

[37] An interesting side note is that while this is a cool feature, it is not completely "legal." For example, according to the standard, PI is a long float constant. However, if you change the long float precision in CLISP, then the value of PI changes as well, so it *isn't* constant...

[38] The library was originally written by the mathematician Michael Stoll. The library's name actually has a deeper meaning, because to a theoretical computer scientist, most real numbers aren't computable (and "most" has a precise meaning in this context); whereas those that are could be defined as exactly those which a library like this can approximate to any desired precision; keeping in mind that computers usually only deal with (a finite subset of the) rational numbers.

system would do it: computations are performed only if they don't "taint" the result with approximations, so that the "result" will actually be more of a formula (a "delayed" computation or a *continuation* if you will) than a number. Only if requested will COMPUTABLE-REALS then compute a numerical approximation.

The library is pretty easy to use; you just replace the normal math functions and constants of COMMON LISP with ones where the name ends with `R` or `-R` as above. "Numbers" will be output with `...` at the end, unless you use the `CR:PRINT-R` function to ask for a specific precision (specified in decimal digits):[39]

```
> (cr:sqrt-r 2)
+1.414213562373095048880...
> (cr:print-r * 30)
+1.414213562373095048801688724210...
> (cr:print-r ** 40)
+1.4142135623730950488016887242096980785696...
> (cr:print-r *** 50)
+1.41421356237309504880168872420969807856967187537695...
;; and so on...
```

4-8. Working with Complex Numbers

Problem

You need complex numbers.

Solution

No problem, COMMON LISP has them. And they are well-integrated into the whole system. If you've never dealt with complex numbers in COMMON LISP before, try this:

```
(sqrt -1)
```

This means that you want to compute the square root of -1. In a typical mainstream programming language, you'll get an error message at this point. COMMON LISP will instead return something like `#C(0.0 1.0)`, which is the representation of a complex number with real part 0 and imaginary part 1.

[39]See Recipe 16-11 for the meaning of *, *, and ***.

You can enter complex numbers using this syntax and they will in almost all respects behave like any other Lisp number; that is, you can use them with all the mathematical functions you're used to.

(See also Recipe 20-3 for an example that actually uses complex numbers.)

How It Works

There are certainly lots of hackers and computer scientists who'll never need complex numbers in their whole life. However, there are situations where these numbers are extremely helpful, and although it's not that hard to simulate them with pairs of real numbers, it's much more convenient to have them available as first-class numbers.

A complex number in mathematics is a number usually written as $a + bi$, where a and b are real numbers—the so-called *real part* a and the *imaginary part* b—and i is the *imaginary unit* with the property $i^2 = -1$.

All numbers which are *not* complex—that is, rationals (see Recipe 4-5) and floating-point numbers—are called *reals* in COMMON LISP.[40] You can use any combination of two Lisp reals to create complex numbers. Here are some examples:

```
* #C(8 -9)
#C(8 -9)
* #c(2/4 1/2)
#C(1/2 1/2)
* #c(2/4 .5)
#C(0.5 0.5)
* #c(2d0 2f0)
#C(2.0d0 2.0d0)
* (complex 1/2 3)
#C(1/2 3)
* (complex 1 0)
1
```

The first examples show the literal syntax for complex numbers and how integers, rationals, and floats can be used to construct them. The last two examples show how complex numbers can be constructed programmatically from reals using the function COMPLEX.

We can now start working with these numbers:

```
> (* #c(2.0 3.0) #c(-1.0 2.0))
#C(-8.0 1.0)
```

[40]And there's actually a corresponding type REAL.

```
> (sin #c(2.0d0 3.0))
#C(9.15449914691143D0 -4.168906959966566D0)
> (abs #c(3 -4))
;; CLISP and ClozureCL will return the integer 5, which is neat:
5.0
> (+ #c(61/2 3) #c(23/2 -3))
42
```

We can, of course, use arithmetic like addition and multiplication with complex numbers, but also all transcendental functions (with `SIN` as our example here) will accept complex arguments. We also note that complex numbers follow the same rules as floating-point numbers; specifically, if one part of a complex number has a higher precision than the other one, then the higher one "wins" (see the `SIN` example where the result consists of double floats).

But perhaps the most interesting example is the last one because the result is a Lisp rational (actually an integer in this particular case). The rule is that as long as both parts of a complex number are rational and the imaginary part is zero, the number must be treated as *identical* (as in `EQL`; see Recipe 10-1) to its real part; that's why we see the result 42 above.[41] As long as you're performing only rational computations with complex numbers comprised of rational parts, the result must again be a "rational" complex number. (This means that you can use COMMON LISP to play with *Gaussian integers*.[42])

Alas, this breaks once you start using functions like `SQRT`, `EXPT`, or `ATAN`, where the standard understandably allows approximations even if the arguments are exact. For example, the expression `(EXPT (SQRT -4) 2)` should, in theory, evaluate to the integer `-4` but in most Lisps (again with the notable exception of CLISP), the result will be `#C(-4.0 0.0)`. (You might want to have a look at Recipe 4-12 once you're finished with this one.)

This is not a math book, so I expect that if you're using complex numbers, you'll know a bit about them. That's why I'll only mention in passing that, of course, you have functions like `REALPART` and `IMAGPART` to access the parts of a complex number, `PHASE`[43] and `ABS` to convert to polar coordinates, and `CONJUGATE`. Likewise, you will know that many irrational and transcendental functions are "multivalued" in the complex plane and thus a branch cut has to be selected if they are implemented in a computer. Suffice it to say, this is not at the discretion of implementors, but all of this is clearly specified in the HyperSpec, where you can look it up if necessary.

---

[41]The CLISP COMMON LISP implementation goes even one step further and converts *all* complex numbers where the imaginary part satisfies `ZEROP` to their real parts.

While I personally like this feature, I understand it could be argued that this isn't compliant with the standard which specifically says (in 12.1.5.3 in case you want to look it up) that the objects `#C(5.0 0.0)` and `5.0` must *not* be `EQL`. (But see also 12.1.3.3.)

[42]See also page 363.

[43]See also Recipe 4-11.

Let's end this chapter with what most mathematician's think is the most beautiful formula in history:[44]

```
(1+ (exp (* pi #c(0 -1))))
```

Euler has taught us that the result should be (the integer) zero. Check your Lisp to see what it says!

4-9. Parsing Numbers

Problem

You want to convert the textual representation of a number into an actual (Lisp) number.

Solution

If you only have to deal with integers, this is very easy because the function PARSE-INTEGER is part of the standard. For example, evaluating the form

```
(parse-integer " 42")
```

will return the integer 42. (Note that whitespace is ignored.)

If you want to parse arbitrary rationals, floats, or complex numbers, the situation is a bit more involved; see below.

How It Works

Let's first have a closer look at PARSE-INTEGER. Its first argument is a string from which the integer will be read. In addition to that, it has four keyword parameters that can be used to control the parsing process. Something like

```
(parse-integer "42 quux")
```

will signal an error because of the characters behind the number. But you can tell PARSE-INTEGER to ignore this like so:

```
(parse-integer "42 quux" :junk-allowed t)
```

[44] I have to admit it looks nicer without S-expressions: $e^{i\pi} + 1 = 0$.

Note that with `:JUNK-ALLOWED T`, the function will also happily return without an error if there's no number in the string at all. In this case the return value will be `NIL`.

You can use `:START` and `:END` to ensure that only a specific part of the input string will be parsed. As the function also returns as a second value, the position within the string where it stopped parsing, you can combine these features to easily parse a string consisting of several numbers:

```
(defun parse-integers (string)
  (let ((start 0)
        (end (length string))
        (result '()))
    (loop
     (when (>= start end)
       (return (nreverse result)))
     (multiple-value-bind (number pos)
         (parse-integer string :start start :junk-allowed t)
       (cond (number
              (push number result)
              (setf start pos))
             (t (setf start end)))))))
```

The code above isn't meant to be "production quality," but it should give you an idea. It will, for example, convert a string like `" -3 42 18 junk"` into `(-3 42 18)` (and stop once it encounters "junk").

The fourth keyword parameter enables you to not only parse decimal integers but also binary, octal, or hexadecimal numbers or numbers in any base from 2 to 36, inclusive. If you try the following form, the return value will be `(7 73 111 273)`.

```
(loop for radix in '(2 8 10 16)
      collect (parse-integer "111" :radix radix))
```

Unfortunately, there is no standard function to parse non-integer numbers.[45] You can utilize the Lisp reader to do this and use the function `READ-FROM-STRING`,[46] though, but I wouldn't recommend this unless you're absolutely sure that the string you're reading from really contains only numbers in correct Lisp syntax and nothing else. Using the Lisp reader on untrusted textual data is very dangerous; for example, if you evaluate the following form in LispWorks, then your Lisp image will be gone...

```
(read-from-string "#.(lw:quit)")
```

[45] But check your implementation. LispWorks, for example, offers the function `HCL:PARSE-FLOAT`.
[46] See Recipe 8-1.

A better way to do this is to use code someone else has already written. There are two libraries loadable with QUICKLISP (see Recipe 18-2) that seem to fit the bill.

The PARSE-NUMBER library can parse any number that is in valid Lisp syntax. For example, the following form will return what you expect:

```
(loop for input in '("-42" "2/84" "#c(3 4)" "2.34" "2d3")
      collect (parse-number:parse-number input))
```

As with PARSE-INTEGER, there are several keyword arguments available to control parsing behavior.

The PARSE-FLOAT library will only parse floating-point numbers, but it allows more fine-tuning.

There's one caveat, though: parsing a floating-point number in such a way that its printed representation agrees with the string you started from is not trivial and sometimes even impossible. See footnote 34 in this chapter.

```
CL-USER> 1.1234567890123456D0
;; in many Lisps (note last digit):
1.1234567890123457d0
```

4-10. Testing Whether Two Numbers Are Equal

Problem

You want to check whether two numbers are equal (which seems easy enough).

Solution

The general rule should be to use the function = which was made specifically for this task. But watch out:

```
CL-USER 1 > (= 42 42.0)
T
CL-USER 2 > (eql 42 42.0)
NIL
CL-USER 3 > (= 0.33333333 1/3)
NIL
;; assuming 32-bit IEEE floats:
CL-USER 4 > (= 0.33333333 11184811/33554432)
T
```

```
CL-USER 5 > (eql 0.33333333 11184811/33554432)
NIL
CL-USER 6 > (= #c(3 0) 3)
T
CL-USER 7 > (eql #c(3 0) 3)
T
CL-USER 8 > (= #c(3.0 0) 3)
T
CL-USER 9 > (eql #c(3.0 0) 3)
NIL
CL-USER 10 > (= (1+ most-positive-fixnum)
                (1+ most-positive-fixnum))
T
CL-USER 11 > (eql (1+ most-positive-fixnum)
                  (1+ most-positive-fixnum))
T
```

How It Works

= is the preferred predicate to test for the equality of two numbers. As you can see above, it'll give you a positive answer if its two arguments represent the same *mathematical value* irrespective of their internal *representation* (that is, their Lisp type). Note, for example, that `#c(3.0 0)` and `3` are correctly considered to represent the same number.

Essentially, the only situation where you might be surprised is when you compare rationals to floating-point numbers. The rule here is that the floating-point number is first converted to a rational using the function `RATIONAL` (see Recipe 4-5) and only then will the numbers be compared. That results in the somewhat unintuitive replies involving `1/3` and `0.33333333` above. (The same conversion rules apply to <, <=, and so on.)

If you want to avoid this, you can use `EQL` (see Recipe 10-1) instead of =. `EQL` will only return a true result if both of its arguments not only represent the same *number* but are also of the same *type*. (In case you're wondering whether this isn't contradicted by `(EQL #C(3 0) 3)` being true, have a look at Recipe 4-8. The short answer is that the complex number `#C(3 0)` that you typed is converted to the integer 3 before `EQL` even had a chance to look at it.)

Don't Ever Use `EQ` with Numbers!

The following is technically implementation-dependent, although I'd expect the same result in all current Lisps:

```
CL-USER 1 > (eq (1+ most-positive-fixnum) (1+ most-positive-fixnum))
NIL
CL-USER 2 > (eq 3d0 3d0)
NIL
```

This example is meant to discourage you from using EQ to compare numbers. There'll always be numbers that represent the same value *and* have the same type but will *not* be identical according to EQ.[47] And there's nothing in the standard that specifies for which kinds of numbers this will be the case, and for which not. Therefore, it is a bad idea to do this (see also Recipe 10-1).

4-11. Computing Angles Correctly

Problem

You want to compute angles using the arc tangent function and you always get angles between −90 and 90 degrees.

Solution

Use the two-argument version of ATAN:[48]

```
(dolist (x '(1 -1))
  (dolist (y '(1 -1))
    (print (list x y
                 (round (* (/ 180 pi) (atan (/ y x))))
                 (round (* (/ 180 pi) (atan y x)))))))
```

This will print the following:

```
(1 1 45 45)
(1 -1 -45 -45)
(-1 1 -45 135)
(-1 -1 45 -135)
```

Note how in the third column, the angle is always 45 or −45 degrees, while in the fourth we have four different values corresponding to the compass points NE, SE, SW, and SE.

---

[47]Technically, this is because the compiler doesn't have an *immediate* representation for them.

[48]We multiply by $\frac{180}{\pi}$ to convert from radians to degrees.

How It Works

The arc tangent function is typically used to compute angles if Cartesian coordinates (or vectors) are given. As the tangent is defined to mean the ratio of the opposite side and the adjacent side of an angle, once you know this ratio, the inverse function of the tangent (called *arc tangent* because its results can be interpreted as an arc) gives you the corresponding angle.

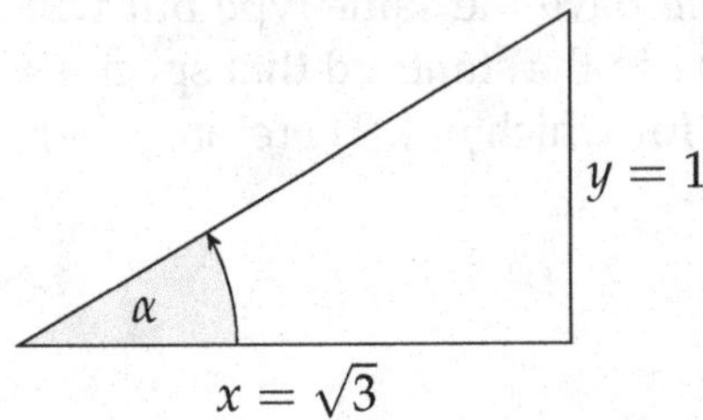

In the image above, the angle α is $\frac{\pi}{6}$ or 30 degrees,[49] the adjacent side x is $\sqrt{3}$, and the opposite side y is 1. This means that we have $\tan(\frac{\pi}{6}) = \frac{y}{x} = \frac{1}{\sqrt{3}}$. So, if we know x and y, and we want to know the angle, we compute $\arctan(\frac{y}{x})$.

However, you might remember from school that because the tangent function is a periodic function (and thus not injective), it can't be inverted; you can only invert the restriction of it to a primitive period. The common convention is to restrict the tangent to the interval from $-\frac{\pi}{2}$ to $\frac{\pi}{2}$ so that as a consequence, the arc tangent will only have values in this interval.[50] On the other hand, the tangent function, like all trigonometric functions, is defined for arbitrary real (or complex) arguments; specifically, it is also defined for angles larger than 90 degrees. Consider this:

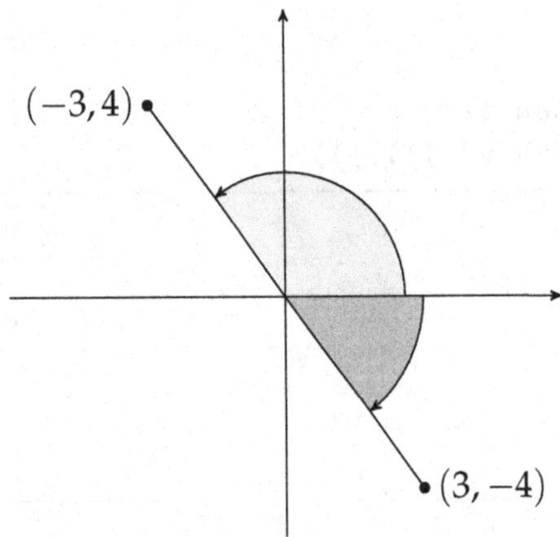

[49]Mathematicians and computers prefer radians over degrees because it's easier and more elegant once you get used to it. Conversion is a simple cross-multiplication, where π corresponds to 180 degrees.

[50]In case you're mathematically inclined, it would be more correct to talk about *branches* because the trigonometric functions in COMMON LISP also work with complex numbers (see Recipe 4-8). The HyperSpec has more detailed information about this.

What you wanted here was the light-gray angle from the x axis[51] to the line between the origin and the point with coordinates $(-3,4)$, which should have been approximately 127 degrees, or 2.214 in radians. However, for the reasons explained above, evaluating the form `(ATAN (/ 4 -3))` will return something like `-0.927...`, which is about -53 degrees, and is the dark-gray angle corresponding to the point at $(3,-4)$.

You could figure out the correct result by checking the signs of the x and y coordinates and distinguishing several cases. But the good news is that you can just call `(ATAN Y X)` instead of `(ATAN (/ Y X))` and it will do the right thing. The result will be an angle the tangent of which is `(/ Y X)`, but it will be "corrected" by 180 degrees if `X` and `Y` are the coordinates of a point on the left side of the y axis.

4-12. Calculating Exact Square Roots

Problem

You'd prefer the square root of a perfect square to be an integer.

Solution

COMMON LISP actually has a neat little function called `ISQRT`.

How It Works

If you evaluate `(SQRT 25.0)`, you won't be surprised to get `5.0` as a result, and if you enter `(SQRT 26)`, you won't be surprised to see `5.0990195` as an answer.[52]

But what about `(SQRT 25)`? The standard leaves it at the discretion of implementors if they want to return `5.0` or `5` here. Most[53] opt for `5.0` (and you will find the same behavior in other programming languages), as things like square roots are usually implemented with approximating algorithms and computed with floating-point numbers.

However, you can *force* every COMMON LISP to come up with an integer result with the function `ISQRT`, which by definition must return "the greatest integer less than or equal to the exact positive square root."

[51]Of course, this is how angles are typically measured in mathematics and also how COMMON LISP does it—starting from the x axis and going counterclockwise from there. This has to be taken into account if you use trigonometric functions for computer graphics because screen coordinates usually have the "wrong" orientation.

[52]Unless maybe you haven't read Recipe 4-6 yet.

[53]Most, but not all. The venerable CLISP gives us `5` indeed.

5. Arrays and Vectors

In theory, everything that can be done with arrays can also be done with lists. But just because lists are the ubiquitous data type in Lisp and Lisp is an abbreviation for "**LIS**t Processing," you shouldn't be tempted to use lists *exclusively*. Lists are extremely flexible and lend themselves incredibly well for prototyping (see Chapter 2), but for many algorithms arrays are the better choice because of their constant-time access characteristics.

Arrays in COMMON LISP have many facets and can be used like arrays in C or JAVA (which are essentially structured, fixed-size memory blocks), but also like arrays in PERL or RUBY (where in a way they behave like lists with array access characteristics). That's what this section is about.

For the printed representation of arrays, see Recipe 9-1, and specifically the variable `*PRINT-ARRAY*`. (See also Recipes 6-7 and 8-4.)

5-1. Working with Multiple Dimensions

Problem

You want to create an array with two or more dimensions (like a matrix) and access its elements.

Solution

Use `MAKE-ARRAY` with a list as its first argument. To create, say, a 365 × 24 matrix for a table with 365 rows (one for each day of the year) and 24 columns (one for each hour) and store it in the special variable `*HOURS*`, you'd use this form:[1]

```
(defparameter *hours* (make-array '(365 24)))
```

Then, to set the value for the third hour of the 42th day to `"foo"`, do something like this:

[1]But see also Recipe 5-4.

```
(setf (aref *hours* 41 2) "foo")
```

(Note that array indices in COMMON LISP start at zero like in most programming languages.)

How It Works

The first thing to note here is that what you might be tempted to call the *dimension* of the array (i.e., the number 2 in our example above) is in COMMON LISP called the array's *rank*; while the *dimensions* (note the plural) in this case are the two numbers 365 and 24. In other words, the rank is the number of dimensions.

The first argument to `MAKE-ARRAY` is a list of positive integers,[2] where the length of the list is the just-mentioned rank of the resulting array. So, a vector has rank 1, and a matrix in the classical mathematical sense has rank 2, but you can also use higher ranks. (You might, for example, wish to use an array of rank 3 to represent the vertices of a three-dimensional grid.) The standard says that each COMMON LISP must support arrays of rank at least 7, but your implementation will almost certainly allow much higher values that'll be good enough for all practical purposes. The constant variable `ARRAY-RANK-LIMIT` holds the actual limit for the Lisp you're currently using.[3]

Each number in the list (i.e., each individual *dimension*) can be as high as the value to be found in the constant variable `ARRAY-DIMENSION-LIMIT`. The standard only says that this value must not be smaller than 1024, but again you'll see that in practice you'll probably only be limited by the amount of available memory.[4] (There's also `ARRAY-TOTAL-SIZE-LIMIT` for—you guessed it—the *total* number of elements an array can have; see Recipe 5-3. Again, you'll rarely have to worry about this limit, although the standard is pretty conservative.)

If you want to read or write individual array elements, you use `AREF`. An `AREF` form denotes a *place* (see Recipe 10-8), and thus can be used to read array elements and also to change their values with `SETF`, as shown above.

`AREF` wants (in addition to the first argument, which is the array itself) exactly as many arguments (which are called *indices*) as the rank of the array. This will get a tad unwieldy once you're using ranks higher than three or so. However, as `AREF` is a function, you can use `APPLY`. So, if you've really found a use for an array of rank 100

[2]If so far you only used calls like `(MAKE-ARRAY 42)` and are wondering how 42 is a list: this is a shortcut expressly allowed by the standard. If the first argument is a number, then it is interpreted as a one-element list; that is, you're creating a *vector* (see Recipe 5-2 for more).

[3]I just checked, and in SBCL on a 64-Bit Linux machine the value is 65529, for example.

[4]Checking on SBCL again, I get 4611686018427387901!

that is stored in the variable TENSOR and you have a 100-element list IND of indices, you can use

```
(apply #'aref tensor ind)
```

to access the element denoted by the indices in IND. And this even works with SETF (see Recipe 10-8). Neat, isn't it?

5-2. Understanding Vectors and Simple Arrays

Problem

You want to know what the terms *vector* and *simple array* mean.

Solution

A vector is an array with rank 1. A simple array is a no-frills array that doesn't have any of the special features detailed in other parts of this chapter. (Or in other words: a simple array is very similar to a plain old C or C++ array.)

How It Works

When reading the HyperSpec, you sometimes come across the notions *vector* and *simple array*. Both are used to denote specific kinds of arrays although they mean very different things.

A *vector* is just an array with rank 1 (see Recipe 5-1). The important thing to note is that as far as COMMON LISP is concerned, a vector is a so-called *sequence*, which is also true for our beloved lists. There are about four dozen functions (like LENGTH, MAP, FIND, or SORT) that work on sequences; that is, they work as well on vectors as they do on lists. (See chapter 17 of the HyperSpec for an exhaustive list of all sequence functions and see also Chapter 7 of this book.)

A *simple array* is an array that is neither displaced (see Recipe 5-8) nor adjustable[5] (see Recipe 5-7), nor does it have a fill pointer (see Recipe 5-6). You can't do anything with simple arrays that you can't do with arrays in general; they are just there so that your implementation can use them for optimization purposes. (See Chapter 17 for more.)

[5]To be as exact as possible, to be simple an array must not be expressly adjustable but *might* be actually adjustable. As said in Recipe 5-7, nowadays this won't make any difference in practice.

Another species from the COMMON LISP array zoo is the *simple vector*. That's a vector that is at the same time a simple array and also *not* specialized (see Recipe 5-9). Again, this type exists solely for the purpose of optimization. There's even a special accessor for simple vectors called SVREF which semantically does exactly the same thing as AREF but can presumably aid the compiler in generating more efficient code. You probably shouldn't bother with this unless you really, really need it.

5-3. Obtaining the Size of an Array

Problem

You want to know how big a specific array is.

Solution

Well, it depends on what you're actually asking for. If you want to know how many elements an array has, use ARRAY-TOTAL-SIZE. But there's also ARRAY-RANK, ARRAY-DIMENSIONS, and ARRAY-DIMENSION. Try it:[6]

```
(let ((a (make-array '(4 5 6))))
  (list (array-total-size a)
        (array-rank a)
        (array-dimensions a)
        (array-dimension a 1)))
```

But that's not the whole story...

How It Works

The function ARRAY-DIMENSIONS will return a list of the dimensions[7] of an array; that is, the list you gave as an argument to MAKE-ARRAY if you yourself created the array. ARRAY-DIMENSION is just a convenience function you use to query for an individual dimension. If it weren't there, you could create it yourself like so:

```
(defun my-array-dimension (array i)
  (nth i (array-dimensions array)))
```

Likewise, ARRAY-RANK will give you the array's rank, so you could write this one yourself, too:

---

[6] $4 \cdot 5 \cdot 6 = 120$, so this should return a list with the four elements 120, 3, (4 5 6), and 5

[7] For terms such as *dimensions* and *rank* see Recipe 5-1.

```
(defun my-array-rank (array)
  (length (array-dimensions array)))
```

Finally, ARRAY-TOTAL-SIZE tells you how many elements the array can hold, and again, this is something you could implement by yourself if needed:[8]

```
(defun my-array-total-size (array)
  (reduce #'* (array-dimensions array) :initial-value 1))
```

There's one catch, by the way. If your array has a fill pointer (see Recipe 5-6), all of the functions above will ignore the fill pointer; that is, the answer returned by these functions will be as if the array didn't have a fill pointer. The good news is that only arrays of rank one (i.e., *vectors*, see Recipe 5-2) can have fill pointers, and for such arrays you can use LENGTH instead of ARRAY-TOTAL-SIZE. And LENGTH *does* observe fill pointers. Try this:

```
(let ((a (make-array 10 :fill-pointer 3)))
  (list (array-total-size a)
        (length a)))
```

5-4. Providing Initial Contents

Problem

You want to create an array and at the same time fill it with initial contents.

Solution

If you want the same initial value for all elements of the array, use the :INITIAL-ELEMENT keyword argument to MAKE-ARRAY:

```
(make-array '(8 8) :initial-element #\x)
```

If you want to specify different values for each element, use (nested) sequences with :INITIAL-CONTENTS like so:

[8]You might ask yourself why I provided an initial value here. Well, it is legal to create an array with (MAKE-ARRAY '()), which will have rank zero and a total size of one. You would access the one and only element of such an array A with (AREF A). This makes sense mathematically and actually shows that consistency was important when COMMON LISP was invented.

(And if you're now asking yourself why you should ever want to use such an array, think of macros that generate code.)

```
(make-array '(2 3) :initial-contents '((2 3 5) (7 11 13)))
```

I guess it's obvious that these two alternatives are mutually exclusive.

How It Works

It should be noted that our first example in Recipe 5-1 was a bit sloppy. If you want to write programs that are guaranteed to work with all conforming implementations, you should never try to read an element of an array that hasn't been initialized before.[9] You can do this (and sometimes you have to) by setting all the values individually, but the easier way, of course, is to fill the array already when it is created as shown above.

If you use :INITIAL-CONTENTS, you must provide a structure that exactly matches the dimensions of your array. So if your array has two rows and three columns, you must provide a list of two lists with three elements and each of the two lists. It's probably easier to see a few examples:

```
(make-array '(2 3) :initial-contents '((1 2 3) (4 5 6)))
(make-array '(3 2) :initial-contents '((1 2) (3 4) (5 6)))
(make-array '(2 3 2) :initial-contents '(((1 2) (3 4) (5 6))
                                         ((7 8) (9 10) (11 12))))
```

Also, you can use vectors instead of lists and you can mix and match lists and vectors at your discretion. So, all of these combinations (and more) are fine too and will result in the same array contents:

```
(make-array '(2 3) :initial-contents '#(#(1 2 3) #(4 5 6)))
(make-array '(2 3) :initial-contents '#((1 2 3) (4 5 6)))
(make-array '(2 3) :initial-contents '#(#(1 2 3) (4 5 6)))
(make-array '(2 3) :initial-contents '((1 2 3) #(4 5 6)))
```

A Warning About Identical Objects

One important thing you should not forget is that when you use :INITIAL-ELEMENT to fill an array, you can't expect to get *copies* of the initial element. In fact, almost always the *same* object will reside in the array in various places. This is usually not

[9]Technically, you'd be asking for the dreaded *undefined consequences* which essentially means that all bets are off. In practice, there's a good chance your Lisp will assign meaningful default values to uninitialized array elements, but that doesn't mean you should rely on it. Also, different Lisps will definitely use different default values.

an issue with numbers and characters, but it can lead to unexpected behavior with composite objects. Here's an example:

```
(let ((a (make-array '(4 4) :initial-element (list 1 2 3))))
  (setf (second (aref a 0 1)) 42)
  (aref a 2 2))
```

In case you expected this form to return `(1 2 3)`, you're in for a surprise, as the result will actually be `(1 42 3)`. The reason is that the array `A` has 16 elements, but they are all the *same* list. (In other words, `(AREF 0 1)` and `(AREF 2 2)` are not only `EQUAL`, they are actually `EQ`; see Recipe 10-1.) So, if you're modifying `(AREF 0 1)`, you are at the same time modifying `(AREF 2 2)` and all the other places in the array as well. If you wanted to create such an array with 16 *different* lists, one way to do it would be like this:[10]

```
(let ((a (make-array '(4 4))))
  ;; initialize array
  (dotimes (i 16)
    (setf (row-major-aref a i) (list 1 2 3)))
  ;; now the same test as above
  (setf (second (aref a 0 1)) 42)
  (aref a 2 2))
```

5-5. Treating Arrays As Vectors

Problem

You want to access the elements of a multidimensional array as if the whole array were one contiguous sequence of elements. (This might, for example, come in handy if you want to apply a function to all elements of such an array in turn.)

Solution

Use `ROW-MAJOR-AREF` instead of `AREF`:

```
(let ((a (make-array '(20 10))))
  (dotimes (i 20)
    (dotimes (j 10)
      (setf (aref a i j) (* i j))))
```

[10]See Recipe 5-5 for `ROW-MAJOR-AREF`.

```
(list (aref a 6 7)
      (row-major-aref a 67)))
```

The return value here will be (42 42) because both the AREF as well as the ROW-MAJOR-AREF form access the same element of A.

How It Works

The language standard actually prescribes how multidimensional arrays are to be stored. As is the case in C, C++, or PYTHON,[11] they must be stored in linear storage in so-called *row-major order*, which means that a (two-dimensional) matrix is stored as (all elements of) the first row, followed by the second row, followed by the third row, and so on. And more generally, the contents of a multidimensional array are stored in such a way that the indices are ordered lexicographically with indices to the right varying faster than those on their left.

If you created an array as

```
(make-array '(3 2 4) :initial-contents '((( 2  3  5  7)
                                           (11 13 17 19))
                                          ((23 29 31 37)
                                           (41 43 47 53))
                                          ((59 61 67 71)
                                           (73 79 83 89))))
```

then it would be stored in memory in 24 consecutive cells like so:

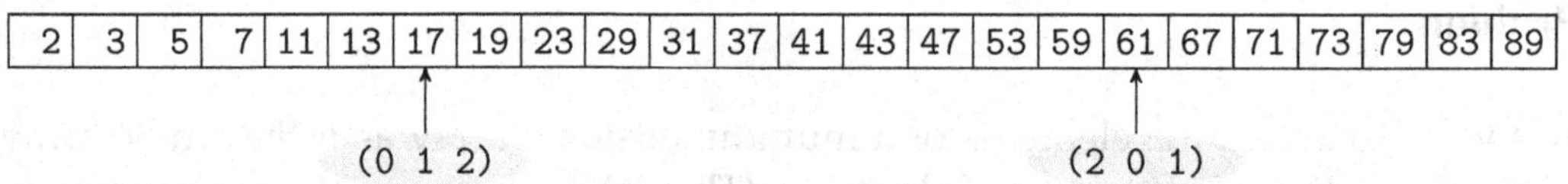

(As examples, I denoted where the elements with indices (0 1 2) and (2 0 1) would be.)

If instead you had created an array with

```
(make-array '(4 6) :initial-contents '(( 2  3  5  7 11 13)
                                       (17 19 23 29 31 37)
                                       (41 43 47 53 59 61)
                                       (67 71 73 79 83 89)))
```

then in memory it would look exactly the same:

[11]And, incidentally, as is *not* the case in FORTRAN. And what about JAVA? Well, JAVA doesn't have multidimensional arrays...

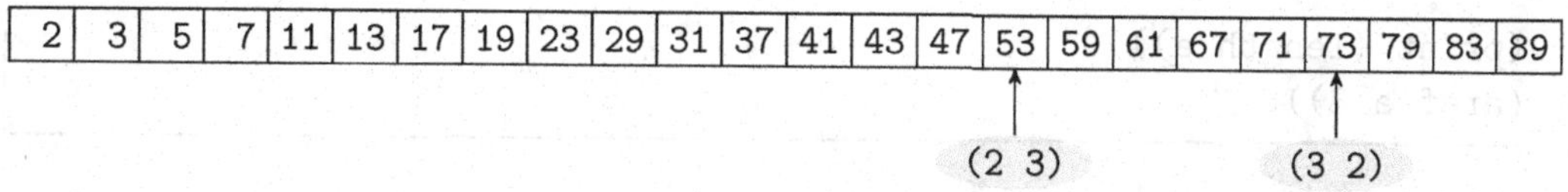

This entails that in a multidimensional array, each element has a specific position, as seen from where the array begins; this position is what you use as the second argument for ROW-MAJOR-AREF. In the example at the beginning of the recipe, the position of the element with indices (6 7) is 67 because each row has ten elements and there are six rows (with indices 0 to 5) before row 6 begins.

Luckily, you don't have to do such computations yourself because the function ARRAY-ROW-MAJOR-INDEX will do it for you:[12]

```
(let ((a (make-array '(5 10 20))))
  (dotimes (i 5)
    (dotimes (j 10)
      (dotimes (k 20)
        (setf (aref a i j k) (* i j k)))))
  (list (aref a 2 3 7)
        (row-major-aref a (array-row-major-index a 2 3 7))))
```

This should again yield (42 42).

But the typical usage of ROW-MAJOR-AREF is more like in the piece of code at the end of Recipe 5-4.

5-6. Making the Length of Vectors Flexible

Problem

You need a *vector* (see Recipe 5-2) the size of which isn't known in advance.

Solution

Use a *fill pointer*:

```
(let ((a (make-array 10 :fill-pointer 3)))
  (print (length a))
  (vector-push 42 a)
```

[12] ARRAY-ROW-MAJOR-INDEX is one of those functions you could write yourself if it weren't already there. It's a nice exercise to write a concise version of this function that works for arrays of arbitrary rank.

```
  (print (length a))
  (aref a 3))
```

This will first print 3, then 4, and then return 42.

How It Works

Vectors can have *fill pointers,* which are non-negative integers. If such vectors are used with sequence functions such as LENGTH or SEARCH, they behave as if only the elements with indices smaller than the fill pointer (the so-called *active* elements) were present:

```
(let ((a (make-array 30
                     :initial-contents
                       (loop for i below 30 collect i)
                     :fill-pointer 20)))
  (print (aref a 23))
  (find 23 a))
```

This will print 23 and then return NIL, which shows that AREF does *not* observe fill pointers, but the sequence function FIND does. Specifically, FIND doesn't find the number 23 in A because it lies beyond the fill pointer (i.e., is not active).

As a rule of thumb, operators that act on arrays as if they were "just arrays," usually *ignore* fill pointers (see also page 121). Fill pointers are intended to cooperate with the VECTOR- functions discussed in this recipe and with functions that treat arrays as sequences (see Chapter 7).

Your mental picture of the example array above should look like this (with inactive elements grayed out and the fill pointer shown):

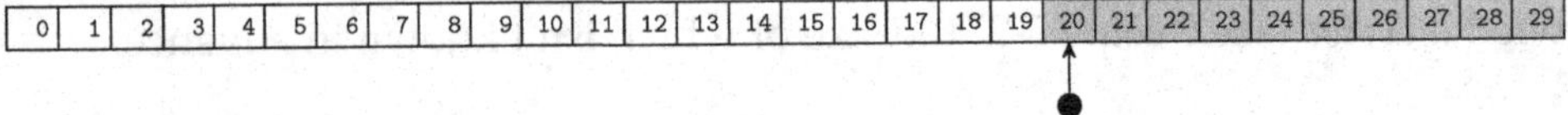

You can access the current value of the fill pointer with the function FILL-POINTER and you can also use (SETF FILL-POINTER) to modify it. But you will typically use the functions VECTOR-PUSH and VECTOR-POP instead. VECTOR-PUSH adds an element directly after the last active element, and then increases the fill pointer; whereas VECTOR-POP returns the last active element, and then decreases the fill pointer:

```
(let ((a (make-array 10 :fill-pointer 0)))
  (print (length a))
  (dotimes (i 3)
    (vector-push (* i i) a))
  (list (length a)
```

```
    (vector-pop a)
    (length a)))
```

This example will first print 0 (indicating that a vector with fill pointer 0 is treated like an empty sequence) and will then return (3 4 2): After pushing the three numbers 0, 1, and 4, the vector had length 3 and then we popped the 4 off the vector, which shortened it to length 2.

As you might have expected, using VECTOR-POP if the fill pointer is already zero will signal an error. Likewise, there's a limit to how large the fill pointer can become and that's simply the size you specified when you created the array. However, it doesn't have to be like this; see Recipe 5-7 where you'll see VECTOR-PUSH-EXTEND in action.

5-7. Adjusting Arrays

Problem

You already have an array, but you need to change its size and/or dimensions after its creation.

Solution

Use the function ADJUST-ARRAY. Here's an example where we create an array and afterward enlarge it and change its dimensions:

```
(defun adjust-test (adjustable)
  (let* ((a (make-array '(4 6)
                        :initial-element 42
                        :adjustable adjustable))
         (b (adjust-array a '(5 5) :initial-element 23)))
    (list (array-dimensions b)
          (eq a b)
          (array-dimensions a)
          (aref b 1 1)
          (aref b 4 4))))
```

If you evaluate (ADJUST-TEST T), the return value is ((5 5) T (5 5) 42 23), which shows that some parts of A—which was a 4×6 matrix—have been metamorphosed into the 5×5 matrix B (and B is now just another name for A).

If you call ADJUST-TEST with the argument NIL, you will *probably*[13] see the return

[13]In current implementations, this is what I would expect. However, keep reading for more details.

value `((5 5) NIL (4 6) 42 23)`, meaning that you now have two arrays, one of which is `B` with the new dimensions and inheriting some of `A`'s contents, while `A` itself is unchanged.

How It Works

You usually create arrays with a fixed size—either you know in advance exactly how much data you have to store or you make the array "big enough" by estimating the maximum size needed.[14]

However, COMMON LISP can do more than that; it can *adjust* an array for you by means of the function `ADJUST-ARRAY`. This function accepts as arguments an existing array and *new* dimensions, where it doesn't matter whether the new dimensions amount to the same total size or to less or more.[15] The function will return an array with the new dimensions and those elements of the original array copied over, which are accessible with the same indices in the old as well as the new array.

Here's a graphical representation of what happens in the initial example:

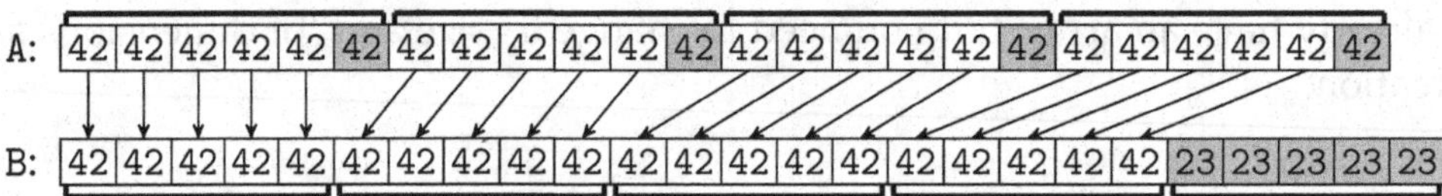

The arrows show which elements are copied. The grayed out elements in `A` have indices with no counterpart in `B`, and are thus not copied. The grayed out elements in `B` have indices with no counterpart in `A`, and were thus initialized with the value 23.

A simplified and inefficient version of `ADJUST-ARRAY` could be implemented like this:

```
(defun my-adjust-array (old-array new-dimensions
                        &key initial-element)
  (let ((new-array (make-array new-dimensions
                               :initial-element initial-element))
        (copy-dimensions (mapcar #'min new-dimensions
                                 (array-dimensions old-array))))
    (labels ((copy-elements (indices dimensions)
               (if dimensions
                 (dotimes (i (first dimensions))
                   (copy-elements (cons i indices)
                                  (rest dimensions)))
                 (setf (apply #'aref new-array (reverse indices))
                       (apply #'aref old-array (reverse indices))))))
```

[14]If you only need a one-dimensional array, you can even use fill pointers (see Recipe 5-6) and thus add some leeway to your vector in case it needs to grow at some point.

[15]The only restriction is that you can't change the *rank* (see Recipe 5-1).

```
        (copy-elements nil copy-dimensions)
        new-array)))
```

And at this point you're probably wondering why this function deserves its own recipe and why it isn't called COPY-ARRAY.

The interesting part is that if you create an array (using MAKE-ARRAY) with a true argument for the keyword parameter :ADJUSTABLE,[16] then the array returned from ADJUST-ARRAY will be *identical* (in the sense of not begin distinguishable by EQ; see Recipe 10-1) to the original array; that is, all variables which pointed to the old array will now point to the adjusted array. Which is really cool if you need it. It is definitely not something you could hack yourself without digging into the guts of your Lisp.

Now, once we know about adjusting arrays, we can return to the function VECTOR-PUSH that we met in Recipe 5-6. If you use VECTOR-PUSH and you run out of fill pointer (so to say), an error will be signaled. If, however, you are using the function VECTOR-PUSH-EXTEND instead, then the vector will be enlarged (by means of ADJUST-ARRAY) instead. You can even (using an optional third argument) tell your Lisp by how much the vector is to be enlarged.[17]

Finally, as I said above, MY-ADJUST-ARRAY is an oversimplification. The real ADJUST-ARRAY of COMMON LISP can also deal with fill pointers (see Recipe 5-6), displacement (see Recipe 5-8), element types (see Recipe 5-9), and initial contents (see Recipe 5-4). But that's beyond the scope of this recipe and you'll need to look up the details in the HyperSpec.

See Recipe 5-10 for an unusual application of ADJUST-ARRAY.

5-8. Using an Array As a "Window" into Another Array

Problem

You want an array that doesn't occupy space of its own but rather acts as a "window" into another array (or a part of it).

[16]The wording in the standard is actually a bit more involved, as it distinguishes between *expressly adjustable* and *actually adjustable* permitting implementations to allow "in-place" adjustments of arrays even if they were not explicitly created as being adjustable. As a rule of thumb, with the COMMON LISP compilers currently available, you can act on the assumption that expressly adjustable and actually adjustable mean the same thing. If you're really paranoid, use the function ADJUSTABLE-ARRAY-P to check.

[17]It is probably worth noting that adjustable arrays and fill pointers are independent of each other; you can have fill pointers in arrays that aren't adjustable and you can have arrays that are adjustable but don't have a fill pointer. However, VECTOR-PUSH-EXTEND will only work with vectors that have a fill pointer *and* (in case they need to be enlarged) are adjustable.

Solution

Use a *displaced* array:

```
(let* ((a (make-array '(5 5)))
       (b (make-array '(3 6)
                      :displaced-to a
                      :displaced-index-offset 4)))
  (dotimes (i 5)
    (dotimes (j 5)
      (setf (aref a i j) (+ (* 10 (1+ i)) (1+ j)))))
  (print (list (aref a 3 1) (aref b 2 0)))
  (setf (aref b 2 0) 23)
  (aref a 3 1))
```

This little example should print (42 42) and then return 23. So, what happened? While A is a normal array (a 5×5 matrix in this case), B doesn't have an existence of its own but acts as an "intermediary" to A. B looks and feels like a 3×6 matrix, but if you access one of its elements, you're actually accessing the corresponding elements of A.

How It Works

When you displace an array (i.e., if you create it with MAKE-ARRAY,[18] as in the preceding example) to another array, there isn't actually any memory allocated for the displaced array. Instead, it shares memory with the array it is displaced to. The original array and the displaced array don't have to have the same dimensions; they don't even have to have the same rank.[19] As far as displacement is concerned, arrays are always simply viewed as linear blobs of memory in row-major order (see Recipe 5-5).

A graphical representation of the initial example would look like this:

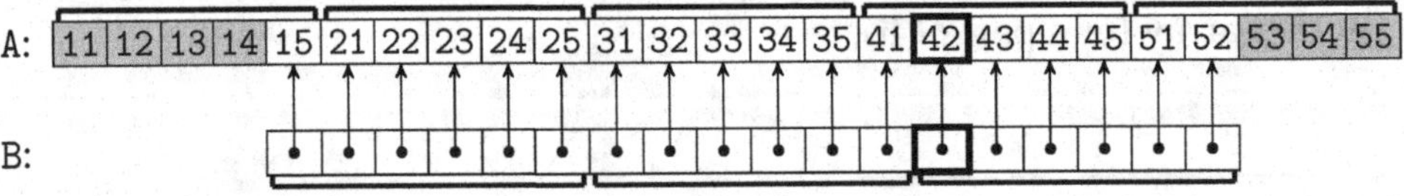

The elements of B are just "virtual" elements[20] that you can imagine as references to the "real" elements in A. (The grayed out elements in A are also there, but not

[18] You can also create displaced arrays with ADJUST-ARRAY, but that's beyond the scope of this recipe.

[19] The only restriction (which is quite obvious) is that the array you displace to must be large enough so that all of the displaced array "fits in."

[20] What the picture can't show is that the elements of B actually don't occupy any space, so they're really only virtual.

accessible via B. The ones to the left are not accessible because of the offset; the ones to the right aren't accessible because B is shorter than A.) The element 42 can, for example, be accessed from A with indices (3 1) or from B with indices (2 0).

Technically, every access to B of the form

```
(aref b i1 i2 ... in)
```

is translated into one to A of the form

```
(row-major-aref a (+ (arrow-row-major-index b i1 i2 ... in) δ))
```

where δ is the offset that was specified when the array was displaced.

For an application of displaced arrays, see Recipe 7-5.

5-9. Restricting the Element Type of an Array

Problem

You want to restrict an array to store only elements of a specific type.

Solution

That's what the :ELEMENT-TYPE keyword argument to MAKE-ARRAY is for. If, say, you wanted to create a 100 × 100 matrix of double floats, you'd do it like this:

```
(make-array '(100 100) :element-type 'double-float)
```

Such an array is called *specialized*.

How It Works

But why would you want to do this? COMMON LISP arrays are very flexible and you can use them to store whatever you want—numbers, strings, other arrays, functions, you name it. Why would you voluntarily give up this freedom?

Well, there are at least three reasons—safety, space, and speed. Let's tackle them one at a time:

- The point about safety is that once you have declared an array to be of a specific element type, your Lisp should[21] warn you once you try to stuff something into it that *isn't* of that type. As a Common Lisp hacker, you're probably used to using a language that isn't statically typed, and thus you likely don't care as much about these warnings as a safety net as a Java or C++ programmer might, but if you want it, you can have it.

- The second reason for specializing an array (especially a large one) can be saving space. Although not mandated by the standard, all Common Lisp implementations nowadays use a mechanism by which some values (the so-called *immediate* objects) can be represented by one word (let's say 64 bit) while all others must be "boxed" which means such a value is not stored directly but rather as a pointer to the actual object.[22] A small array of boxed floats could look like so:

  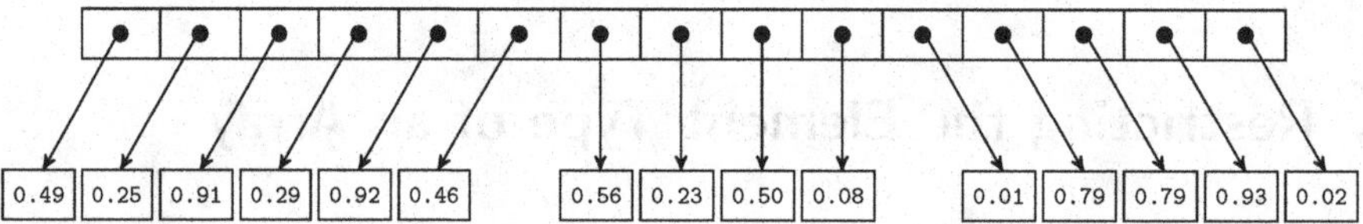

  The cells in the upper row are the actual array elements which are pointers, and each of them points to another cell, which holds the actual float.[23]

  So, if you have a normal array of 100,000 double floats, you'll need 100,000 words for pointers and another 100,000 words for the numbers themselves. If instead your array is specialized to hold only double floats, your Lisp compiler can arrange the array to use only 100,000 words.

  As a specialized array, the example from above could look like this:

0.49	0.25	0.91	0.29	0.92	0.46	0.56	0.23	0.50	0.08	0.01	0.79	0.79	0.93	0.02

- The third reason, speed, is tightly related to the second one. Once the compiler, for example, knows that a form like `(AREF ARR 42)` will definitely return a double float because `ARR` is specialized, it might be able to replace generic code surrounding this form by something more specific and thus more efficient (see Recipe 17-14, for example).

Be aware, though, that just because an array is specialized your code won't automatically use less space or become faster. You'll probably have to use the right declarations (see Recipe 17-3) to persuade your compiler to take action.

---

[21] I'm writing "should" here because technically your Lisp could, by default, have a very low safety level, or it could decide not to warn you even at the highest safety level. But that's pretty unlikely. A Lisp implementation that acted this way would probably not gain a lot of mindshare. (But it is certainly true that you can't rely on warnings if you have lowered the safety level on purpose.)

[22] The actual implementation might be different and more clever than what I'm describing here, but this should suffice to provide the right mental picture (see also page 525).

[23] The cells with the floats have deliberately not been neatly arranged because it is neither necessary nor always possible that they are all allocated in one large linear block.

Upgrading Element Types

And there's one more aspect of specialized arrays that might surprise you. Your Lisp might refuse to do what you want! The typical reason for such a refusal to obey orders will be that it doesn't make sense as far as the memory layout of the array is concerned. Let's look at an example:[24]

```
(let ((a (make-array 10 :element-type '(unsigned-byte 3))))
  (array-element-type a))
```

If you enter this form, your Lisp will very likely *not* return (UNSIGNED-BYTE 3), but probably (UNSIGNED-BYTE 4). The reason is that with all microprocessors currently in use, it would be extremely inefficient to read the contents of the machine's RAM one bit at a time. Instead, it is typically read in larger chunks, the smallest of which usually is an octet, which consists of eight bits. Now, if your Lisp were to store the array at the address #x2A00, and if it would really use 3 bits per array element, then—because 3 doesn't divide any power of two—the 22nd array element would end up partly in the eighth and partly in the ninth octet. So, even if the processor were able to fetch 64 bits at a time, to execute (AREF A 21) it would need to retrieve 64 bits from #x2A00 and then another 64 bits from #x2A08, and it would then have to glue the last bit from the first fetch together with the first two bits from the second fetch to finally end up with what you wanted.

Here's a graphical representation of our example with the first 64 bits grayed out. (Each dot represents one bit and you see that they're in groups of three.)

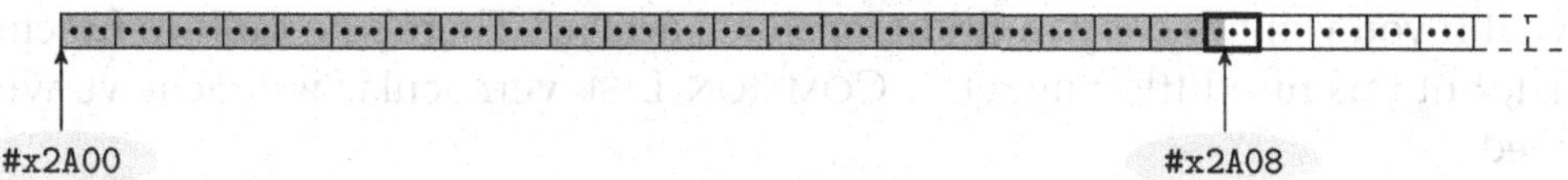

This doesn't sound like a good plan and so it should be understandable that instead it decides to allocate a bit (no pun intended!) more space for the array and use 4 bits per element (so that two of them neatly fit into one octet).

This process of using a more general type than requested is called *upgrading* in COMMON LISP. In the preceding example, the type (UNSIGNED-BYTE 3) was upgraded to the type (UNSIGNED-BYTE 4). While certain kinds of upgrading are identical on all Lisps,[25] the standard gives a lot of leeway to the compiler writers. The only types for which there are rules about upgrading (namely, that they must *not* be upgraded) are characters (for strings, see Chapter 3) and bits (for bit vectors). In all other cases you might be in for a suprise. Of two up-to-date Lisps currently on my hard drive, one upgrades (UNSIGNED-BYTE 23) to (UNSIGNED-BYTE 32), the other one to (UNSIGNED-BYTE 31)...

[24]This obviously also shows how you can query an array for its element type.

[25]I would, e.g., expect all current Lisps to not upgrade the type DOUBLE-FLOAT.

The good news is that you can programmatically ask in advance what your implementation will do in terms of upgrading. That's what the function UPGRADED-ARRAY-ELEMENT-TYPE is for.

5-10. Copying an Array

Problem

You need a copy of a whole array.

Solution

If your array is a vector (see Recipe 5-2), there's a standard function to do that:

```
(let* ((a (make-array 3 :initial-contents '(1 2 3)))
       (b (copy-seq a)))
  (setf (aref b 1) 42)
  (list a b (eq a b)))
```

This will return (#(1 2 3) #(1 42 3) NIL), which shows that B is an array that is a *different* object from A (thus the NIL at the end) but to which the contents of A were initially copied.

But what if you want to copy multidimensional arrays? There's no built-in function for that, but this nice little nugget of COMMON LISP vernacular will achieve what you need:

```
(defun copy-array (array)
  (let ((dimensions (array-dimensions array)))
    (adjust-array
     (make-array dimensions
                 :element-type (array-element-type array)
                 :displaced-to array)
     dimensions)))
```

Keep reading to see why and how this works.

How It Works

As is pretty obvious from its name, COPY-SEQ is a function to copy sequences; that is, (proper) lists or vectors. That already answers this recipe's question for one-dimensional arrays. COPY-SEQ is also required to honor the original vector's element type (see Recipe 5-9), so that too is taken care of. However, the value returned by `COPY-SEQ`—if applied to vectors—will always be *simple* (in the sense of Recipe 5-2), so if you want to copy special features of your array, like fill pointers or adjustability, you'll have to roll your own copy function.

(Incidentally, `(COPY-SEQ A)` is in no way different from `(SUBSEQ A 0)`. The compiler won't care, but you should probably use `COPY-SEQ` for copies to convey your intent to human readers of your code.)

Now, how does our little `COPY-ARRAY` achieve the same thing for multidimensional arrays? It should be obvious (maybe after reading Recipe 5-8) that the "intermediate" array created with `MAKE-ARRAY` doesn't occupy any new space but is rather only a "window" into the original array. Given this point of departure, the complicated rules for `ADJUST-ARRAY` (see Recipe 5-7) force it to make a copy, which is exactly what we want. Neat, isn't it?

As an alternative, you could use the function `COPY-ARRAY` of the ALEXANDRIA library (see Recipe 18-4), which offers more flexibility via various keyword arguments.

A Warning About Object Identity

This is not specific to COMMON LISP, but be aware that if you copy an array, then the elements of the copy are *identical* (see Recipe 10-1) to the corresponding elements in the original array. That's not a problem with numbers or characters, but it might be with compound objects. If say, the first element of your vector `A` is a list and `B` is the result of `(COPY-SEQ A)`, then if you change the second element of the list, this will modify the first element of `A` *and* the first element of `B`—because they are the same:

```
(let* ((a (make-array 3
                      :initial-contents (list (list 1 2) 3 4)))
       (b (copy-seq a)))
  (setf (nth 1 (aref a 0)) 42)
  (list a b))
```

(See also Recipes 2-7 and 8-2.)

6. Hash Tables, Maps, and Sets

As stated in the introduction to Chapter 5, lists aren't the only data structure in COMMON LISP. In addition to arrays, the standard also offers *hash tables* which are data structures that map *keys* to *values* by means of a *hash function*. Ideally, the cost of hash table lookups, as well as insertions or deletions of new entries, is independent of the number of elements stored in the table (although, see Recipe 6-5), which makes them a powerful alternative to other ways of organizing data.

Practical Common Lisp provides a brief introduction to hash tables on pages 138 to 140, but if you've never used hash tables before, reading through Recipes 6-1 to 6-6 (in that order) might serve as an introduction as well.[1]

Hash tables are an example of a more general data structure that is called an *associative array* in computer science. COMMON LISP has another means to represent associative arrays, called an *alist*, which we'll also discuss in this chapter (together with *plists*, which are kind of a variant of alists).

Furthermore, as you saw in Chapter 2, the versatile *cons* pair can be employed for other things than lists. Toward the end of the chapter, we'll have look at how it can be used for *sets*.

6-1. Understanding the Basics of Hash Tables

Problem

You want to create and use a basic, no-frills hash table.

Solution

To create the hash table, use `MAKE-HASH-TABLE`. To look up, set, and change values, use the accessor `GETHASH`:

```
* (defparameter *h* (make-hash-table))
*H*
* (gethash 'batman *h*)
```

[1] Although it can't replace a decent textbook about data structures, of course.

```
NIL
NIL
* (setf (gethash 'batman *h*) 'gotham-city)
GOTHAM-CITY
* (gethash 'batman *h*)
GOTHAM-CITY
T
* (setf (gethash 'superman *h*) 'duckburg)
DUCKBURG
* (gethash 'superman *h*)
DUCKBURG
* (setf (gethash 'superman *h*) 'metropolis)
METROPOLIS
* (gethash 'superman *h*)
METROPOLIS
T
* (gethash 'spider-man *h*)
NIL
NIL
```

We created a hash table and stored it in the special variable `*H*`. We then added the first key/value pair that associated the symbol `BATMAN` with the symbol `GOTHAM-CITY` and immediately asked the hash table to give us the value associated with the key `BATMAN`, which it duly did. (We did the same right after the creation of the hash table, and in this case, the answer was `NIL`.)

We then added another key/value pair (with the key being the symbol `SUPERMAN`) and demonstrated how we can change the value associated with this key by simply calling `(SETF GETHASH)` again.

How It Works

After the preceding example, the hash table conceptually looks like this:

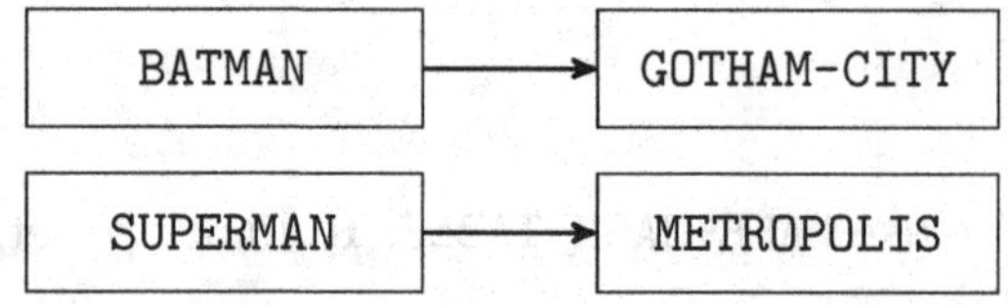

And that's essentially all there is to it. The things on the left side are called *keys*; the things on the right side are called *values*. The "job" of the hash table is to tell you if it knows about a key and if so, which value it points to. (In a way, the hash table *consists of* these *associations* and nothing more, so the mental picture you should have is that in the diagram above, the arrows comprise the hash table.)

Keys and values always come in pairs. Keys are mapped to values, but not vice versa; that is, there's no efficient operation to find out, say, which key points to the value GOTHAM-CITY.[2]

Associations are unique: a key can only be associated with one value, not with two or more.[3] But different keys can be associated with the same value. We could, for example, add a new hash table entry with

```
(setf (gethash 'lois-lane *h*) 'metropolis)
```

giving us this structure:

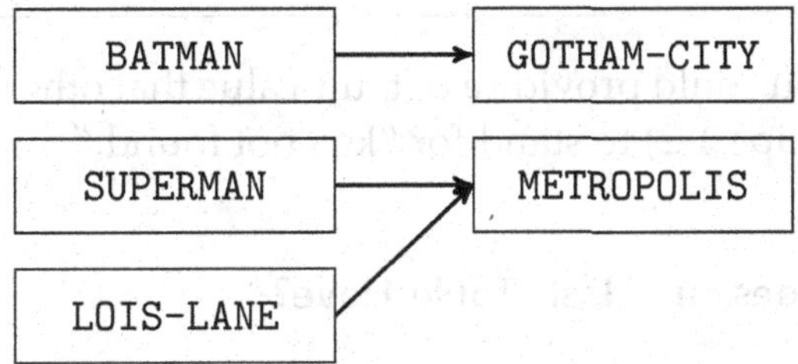

We would then still be able to look up the value associated with the key SUPERMAN.[4]

Every Lisp object can be used as a key or as a value for a hash table, not only symbols as in our example. However, if you've never worked with hash tables, you might want to look at Recipe 6-5 first.

Why Does GETHASH Return Two Values?

Because every Lisp object can be used as a value, NIL is also a legitimate value. This means that generally you can't interpret the return value of GETHASH as a *generalized boolean* in the Lisp sense. If (GETHASH 'HULK *H*) is NIL, this could mean that there's no value associated with the key HULK, or it could mean that the value NIL is associated with that key.

Of course, if you, as the programmer, know that NIL will never be a value in your hash table, you can simply check if GETHASH returns NIL to catch nonexistent associations. If, however, NIL is a possible value, you can always look at the second return value of GETHASH which provides exactly this information:

---

[2]And if you need to do that often, then a hash table is probably not the right data structure for your task.

[3]You can, of course, associate a key with, say, a *list* of several objects. But technically it'd still be only *one* value—the list.

[4]So, if you're mathematically inclined, a hash table is just a way to represent a *function*, which is not necessarily *injective*. The set of keys is the *domain* of this function, while the set of values is its *range*.

```
* (defparameter *h* (make-hash-table))
*H*
* (gethash 'batman *h*)
NIL
NIL                                              ;; second value is NIL
* (setf (gethash 'batman *h*) nil)
NIL
* (gethash 'batman *h*)
NIL
T                                                ;; second value is now T
```

See also Recipe 6-2: you could provide a default value that otherwise can never occur (e.g., a *gensym*; see Recipe 1-2) to stand for "key not found."

How Many Entries Does the Hash Table Have?

If you want to know how many entries (keys) you have, just use the function `HASH-TABLE-COUNT`. (Which, by the way, should not be confused with `HASH-TABLE-SIZE`. For the latter, see Recipe 6-6.)

6-2. Providing Default Values For Hash Table Lookups

Problem

As we've seen in Recipe 6-1, `GETHASH` returns `NIL` if it is used with a key not found in the hash table. Sometimes this is not what you want.

Solution

Let's suppose you want to associate the inhabitants of Duckburg with their species. This could be done like so:

```
* (defparameter *h* (make-hash-table))
*H*
* (setf (gethash 'gladstone-gander *h*) 'goose)
GOOSE
* (setf (gethash 'gyro-gearloose *h*) 'chicken)
CHICKEN
* (defun duckburg-species (name)
```

```
    (gethash name *h*))
DUCKBURG-SPECIES
```

You could now use the function DUCKBURG-SPECIES to find out the species of a character by name:

```
* > (duckburg-species 'gyro-gearloose)
CHICKEN
T
```

However, you're thinking that the majority of Duckburg's citizens are ducks, so it would make sense to *not* add Donald Duck, Scrooge McDuck, and hundreds of other ducks to your hash table, but to provide a default to your function. This is very easily done. Replace the function definition from above with this one:

```
(defun duckburg-species (name)
  (gethash name *h* 'duck))
```

And the result will be like this:[5]

```
* (duckburg-species 'gyro-gearloose)
CHICKEN
T
* (duckburg-species 'donald-duck)
DUCK
NIL
```

How It Works

There's not much to explain here: GETHASH accepts an optional third argument: the value to be returned if the key (the first argument) is not found in the hash table (the second argument). The default (if you don't provide a third argument) is NIL, which explains the behavior in Recipe 6-1.

Of course, you could have written DUCKBURG-SPECIES like so:

```
(defun duckburg-species (name)
  (or (gethash name *h*) 'duck))
```

But this approach will *not* work if NIL is a legitimate value in your hash table. Also, the three-argument version of GETHASH provides more information due to the second return value (see page 139).

[5]The second return value shows that DONALD-DUCK is not a key of the hash table *H* (see Recipe 6-1).

Another typical idiom where default values are used is for a hash table that counts something. You want counters to be initialized with the value 0 and this can be done automatically if you increment the counter for the key KEY like this:

```
(incf (gethash key hash-table 0))
```

If there already is a value associated with the key KEY, it will be incremented. If there is no such value yet, it will be set to the result of incrementing the default value (0). This works because the macro expansion[6] of the form above will essentially do something like the following (although the actual expansion will certainly look quite different in your Lisp):

```
(let ((temp (gethash key hash-table 0)))
  (setf (gethash key hash-table) (+ temp 1)))
```

6-3. Removing Hash Table Entries

Problem

You want to completely get rid of a key/value pair in your hash table.

Solution

Let's start with this hash table:

```
* (defparameter *h* (make-hash-table))
*H*
* (setf (gethash 'batman *h*) 'gotham-city)
GOTHAM-CITY
* (setf (gethash 'superman *h*) 'metropolis)
METROPOLIS
```

If you wanted to get rid of Superman, you could be tempted to do this:

```
* (setf (gethash 'superman *h*) nil)
NIL
```

You will now get NIL as a result if you evaluate (GETHASH 'SUPERMAN *H*), but the second return value (see page 139) will be T, and HASH-TABLE-COUNT (see Recipe 6-1) will still return 2; both indicate that the hash table still consists of two key/value pairs.

[6]For macros like INCF, see also page 291.

The right solution is to use REMHASH:

```
* (remhash 'superman *h*)
T
* (gethash 'superman *h*)
NIL
NIL
* (hash-table-count *h*)
1
```

How It Works

The key to understanding this is actually Recipe 6-1. If you have the mental picture of viewing a hash table as a collection of *associations* (shown as arrows in the pictures), then you'll understand that (SETF GETHASH) will only ever add associations or manipulate existing associations, so you need a different function to *remove* associations. That's what REMHASH does; it removes the association starting at the key, which is the only argument to this function.

Note that REMHASH returns a boolean indicating success. It won't complain if you're trying to remove a nonexistent key, but it will return NIL in this case.

Also, there's CLRHASH, which in one fell swoop removes *all* entries from the hash table, leaving it intact but empty. (And see also Recipe 6-6 to understand why after CLRHASH, a hash table isn't necessarily the same as directly after its creation.)

6-4. Iterating Through a Hash Table

Problem

You want to perform a specific action on each element of a hash table.

Solution

The most concise way is arguably MAPHASH. (But there are others; see below.) Let's start with this hash table that associates fictional characters with their first appearances in print:

```
* (defparameter *h* (make-hash-table))
*H*
* (loop for (key value) in '((superman 1938)
                             (donald-duck 1934)
```

```
                                  (batman 1939)) do
        (setf (gethash key *h*) value))
NIL
```

If you now wanted to know which of these is the "oldest," you could do this:

```
* (let ((min 2015) oldest)
    (maphash (lambda (hero year)
               (when (< year min)
                 (setf min year
                       oldest hero)))
             *h*)
    oldest)
DONALD-DUCK
```

How It Works

MAPHASH is called with a hash table and a function. This function will always be called once for each key/value pair in the hash table. And it'll be called with two arguments: the key and the value. This is the functional way of doing it and one where you usually won't need to type a lot.

A slightly more complicated but also more powerful way to iterate through a hash table is provided by the macro WITH-HASH-TABLE-ITERATOR. It is used to define a *local macro*, which on each invocation returns three values: the key and the value for each entry, as in MAPHASH, but first a generalized boolean that is true as long as entries are returned.

With WITH-HASH-TABLE-ITERATOR, our example from above could have been written like so:

```
(let ((min 2015) oldest)
  (with-hash-table-iterator (next-hero *h*)
    (loop
     (multiple-value-bind (not-done hero year)
         (next-hero)
       (unless not-done
         (return oldest))
       (when (< year min)
         (setf min year
               oldest hero))))))
```

Let's dissect this. We have provided a name (the symbol NEXT-HERO) as the first argument to WITH-HASH-TABLE-ITERATOR. As long as we're within the body of the

WITH-HASH-TABLE-ITERATOR form, each invocation of (NEXT-HERO) will now deliver one key/value pair of *H*, with the guarantee (as with MAPHASH) that each key/value pair will occur exactly once. As soon as NEXT-HERO runs out of entries, the first return value (called NOT-DONE in our example) will be NIL. (We could now continue to call NEXT-HERO, but we would always get the same result.)

Although WITH-HASH-TABLE-ITERATOR is often a bit more cumbersome to use than MAPHASH, it is strictly more powerful. The standard shows how you could write MAPHASH yourself using WITH-HASH-TABLE-ITERATOR:

```
(defun my-maphash (function hash-table)
  (with-hash-table-iterator (next-entry hash-table)
    (loop (multiple-value-bind (more key value)
              (next-entry)
            (unless more (return nil))
            (funcall function key value)))))
```

But you can't implement WITH-HASH-TABLE-ITERATOR using MAPHASH. Suppose you wanted to write a function to look up a key for a specific value.[7] Once you've found such a key, you are done, so you won't need to look at all the remaining key/value pairs. With WITH-HASH-TABLE-ITERATOR, you could do it like so:

```
(defun hero-from (this-year)
  (with-hash-table-iterator (next-hero *h*)
    (loop
      (multiple-value-bind (not-done hero year)
          (next-hero)
        (unless not-done
          (return nil))
        (when (= year this-year)
          ;; skip the rest, we're done
          (return hero))))))
```

But there's no way to do that with MAPHASH; it will trudge on and apply whatever search function you use to all remaining key/value pairs.[8]

The third way to iterate through a hash table is with the so-called "extended" LOOP form. This combines the power of WITH-HASH-TABLE-ITERATOR with the conciseness of MAPHASH, but uses, well, LOOP, which some Lispers love and some hate. (See Chapter 7.) If using LOOP is OK for you, you can rewrite our example like so:

```
(loop with min = 2015 and oldest
      for hero being the hash-keys of *h*
```

[7]But see footnote 2.

[8]Unless, of course, you use a *non-local exit* like THROW.

```
    using (hash-value year)
  when (< year min)
    do (setf min year
             oldest hero)
  finally (return oldest))
```

Here, HERO is obviously bound to each of the hash keys in turn. If you only need the keys, you only need the BEING THE HASH-KEYS clause, but you can add the USING clause if you also want to bind the value belonging to the key on each iteration.[9]

You could have exchanged the roles of keys and values as well:

```
(loop with min = 2015 and oldest
      for year being the hash-values of *h*
        using (hash-key hero)
      when (< year min)
        do (setf min year
                 oldest hero)
      finally (return oldest))
```

(And again, you could have left out the USING clause.)

Don't Rely on Any Order!

What all these iteration constructs have in common (typical for hash tables in general, not only in COMMON LISP) is that you can't rely on any order. You can be sure that you'll have a chance to visit each key/value pair exactly once, but you'll never know which one comes first, which comes second, and so on.[10] This means that with our hash table from above, the result of evaluating

```
(loop for hero being the hash-keys of *h*
      collect hero)
```

could be (BATMAN SUPERMAN DONALD-DUCK), or (SUPERMAN DONALD-DUCK BATMAN), or one of the other four permutations of this list.

[9] You could have written FOR YEAR = (GETHASH HERO *H*) instead, but that would most likely be pretty inefficient compared to what LOOP does. (Look at the macro expansion—it will almost certainly use WITH-HASH-TABLE-ITERATOR internally.)

[10] You can't even be sure to get the same order again if you immediately repeat an iteration although that's probably a reasonable assumption for most implementations.

Don't Modify While You're Iterating!

The general rule for iteration also holds for hash tables. You are not allowed to add or remove hash tables while you're in the middle of an iteration through the hash table (no matter which of the three variants described above you use). The only exception is that you may change (or even remove) the *current* key/value pair. So, this would be OK:

```
(loop for hero being the hash-keys of *h*
        using (hash-value year)
      when (< year 1935)
        do (remhash hero *h*))
```

But this would *not* be OK:

```
;; don't do that!
(loop for hero being the hash-keys of *h*
        using (hash-value year)
      when (eql hero 'batman)
        do (setf (gethash 'robin *h*) (1+ year)))
```

Can't This Be More Concise, Please?

One sometimes wonders why the standard doesn't have something similar to DOLIST to iterate through a hash table; something that is not functional like MAPHASH and not as chatty as the other two variants. Luckily, it's very easy to write such a macro:

```
(defmacro dohash ((key-name value-name hash-table) &body body)
  (let ((next (gensym "NEXT"))
        (more (gensym "MORE")))
    `(with-hash-table-iterator (,next ,hash-table)
       (loop (multiple-value-bind (,more ,key-name ,value-name)
                 (,next)
               (unless ,more (return nil))
               ,@body)))))
```

You can now use it like so:

```
* (dohash (hero year *h*)
    (format t "~A: ~A~%" year hero))
;; order might be different -- see above
1934: DONALD-DUCK
1938: SUPERMAN
```

```
1939: BATMAN
NIL
```

Finally, the ITERATE library (see Recipe 7-14) also has a nice idiom to iterate through hash tables:

```
* (iter (for (hero year) in-hashtable *h*)
        (format t "~A: ~A~%" year hero))
1938: SUPERMAN
1934: DONALD-DUCK
1939: BATMAN
NIL
```

6-5. Understanding Hash Table Tests and Defining Your Own

Problem

If you're new to hash tables, you might be tempted to modify the example from Recipe 6-1 a bit and you could be surprised by the result:

```
* (defparameter *h* (make-hash-table))
*H*
* (setf (gethash "Batman" *h*) "Gotham City")
"Gotham City"
* (gethash "Batman" *h*)
NIL
NIL
```

Why didn't we get `"Gotham City"` as the answer here?

If, on the other hand, you're a more experienced Lisp programmer, you might wonder if and how it's possible to use test functions other than `EQ`, `EQL`, `EQUAL`, and `EQUALP`.

Both questions will be answered in this recipe.

Solution

The reason that we didn't get `"Gotham City"` above is that each hash table comes with a *hash test* function, which is used to check if two keys are equal; specifically, if the key you provide to `GETHASH` or `REMHASH` is the same as one of the keys already present in the hash table. The default hash test is `EQL`, and as you'll know (or see

Recipe 3-4), you can't use EQL to compare strings. The problem is easily solved by providing a fitting hash test:

```
* (defparameter *h* (make-hash-table :test 'equal))
*H*
* (setf (gethash "Batman" *h*) "Gotham City")
"Gotham City"
* (gethash "Batman" *h*)
"Gotham City"
T
```

The functions you can use as hash tests are EQ, EQL, EQUAL, and EQUALP and the natural question at this point might be: "Can't I use arbitrary hash tests? This is COMMON LISP after all!"

The short answer is that you can't, but read on...

How It Works

Although probably not permitted if you adhere to a strict formal interpretation of the standard,[11] many COMMON LISP implementations will allow you to define hash tables employing hash tests other than the four standard ones listed above. But to fully understand how this works, we'll have to first dive a bit deeper into the inner workings of hash tables.

The standard doesn't prescribe a specific implementation strategy, but it is probably safe to assume that it's basically like this: for each key, its *hash*[12] is computed by means of a *hash function* (which is not to be confused with the *hash test*). A hash function must be a function in the mathematical sense in that it must always return the same value for the same input.[13] Also, any two objects that are identical according to the hash test must have the same hash—that's the whole point of hashes. (We also want hash functions to be reasonably fast. But that probably goes without saying.)

The hash usually is a non-negative *fixnum* (see Recipe 4-2). To each hash belongs a so-called *bucket*, where the corresponding key/value pairs are stored. This will probably become clearer through an example, so let's start with the following hash table:

```
* (defparameter *h* (make-hash-table :test 'equal))
*H*
* (loop for (key value) in '(("Superman" 1938)
```

[11]But see section 18.1.2.4!

[12]That's where the name *hash table* comes from, obviously.

[13]This has the interesting consequence that you can't utilize something like the memory address of an object to compute a hash as this address might change due to garbage collection.

```
                          ("Donald Duck" 1934)
                          ("Batman" 1939)) do
      (setf (gethash key *h*) value))
NIL
```

Let's assume we have a pretty simplistic hash function that uses as a hash the character code (see Recipe 3-1) of the first character of a key. The internal representation of *H* would then look like so:

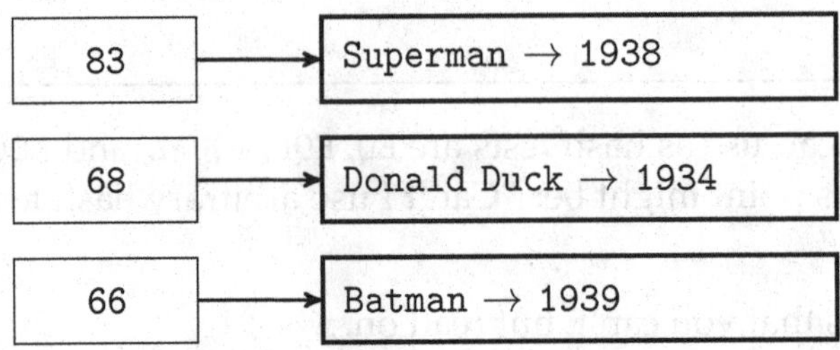

For example, the character code of #\S is 83, and so the key/value pair of "Superman" and 1938 will end up in the bucket, which hangs off the number 83.

If we now add the following value

```
(setf (gethash "Daisy Duck" *h*) 1940)
```

this entry's key will have the same hash (68) as that of Donald Duck, so that we'll now have two pairs in the corresponding bucket:[14]

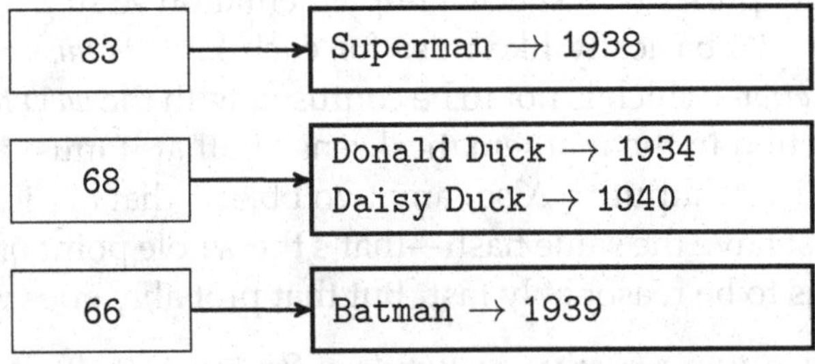

Buckets are usually implemented as small data structures with linear access characteristics, which means that the performance of a hash table will get worse as more entries end up in the same bucket. (In our example, if we add ten more entries where the key starts with #\D, the 68 bucket will already hold a dozen entries, and looking up a nonexistent key starting with #\D will entail iterating through all twelve of them first.)

That's why you want hash functions that provide a uniform distribution of hashes; you want the probability of collisions to be as low as possible.

[14] In computer science parlance, this is a *collision*.

Now, as long as we're using the four standard hash tests, we don't really have to care about this, as we can hopefully trust the implementation to provide good hash functions. However, if you want to use custom hash tests, implementations will typically ask you to provide a corresponding hash function as well. That's why you need at least a basic understanding of the purpose of hash functions and how they should behave.

Let's finally go through an (implementation-specific)[15] example of how a hash table with a custom hash test can be defined. (We'll use LISPWORKS here, but it should work just the same in SBCL.) Let's assume we want to go through the contents of lots of books and compute how often each character occurs. Once we've read a character CHAR, we want to increment its counter:[16]

```
(incf (gethash char hash-table 0))
```

But we want to ignore case. We could, of course, replace the statement above with

```
(incf (gethash (char-downcase char) hash-table 0))
```

and be done with it, but for the sake of this example, let's assume we want a case insensitive hash table where both

```
(incf (gethash #\z hash-table 0))
```

and

```
(incf (gethash #\Z hash-table 0))
```

will have the same effect. This means we can't use one of the standard hash tests; we want CHAR-EQUAL (see Recipe 3-4) instead.

In this case, we could just use the character code of the downcased (or upcased) character as its hash. That would meet all requirements. The code is a non-negative integer (and will even be a fixnum on all reasonable implementations). It is easy to compute. And if we downcase the characters first, then two characters which are considered equal by the hash test will have the same hash code.

So, the definition of our hash table would look like this:

```
(make-hash-table :test 'char-equal
                 :hash-function (lambda (char)
                                  (char-code
                                   (char-downcase char))))
```

[15]The library CL-CUSTOM-HASH-TABLE purports to provide a portability layer for this.
[16]See page 142 for an explanation of this technique.

Note that coming up with a good hash function for your custom hash test might require some thought. In the worst case, your hash function will put all entries into just a few buckets and the performance characteristics of your hash table won't be any different from those of a list, which would render the whole point of using a hash table futile.

What Is SXHASH For?

The standard mentions a function SXHASH in the chapter about hash tables. But if you read carefully, you'll notice that it wasn't made for hash tables but rather for situations where the (standard) hash tables are insufficient. The intention of SXHASH is to provide some kind of "basic" hash function that could be used with EQUAL or "finer" hash tests. You might want to consider using SXHASH as an ingredient in case you ever need to write your own hash function.

6-6. Controlling Hash Table Growth

Problem

You know the hash tables you are going to work with will be very large and you're wondering whether you can optimize them for this.

Solution

Let's start with the remark that this is essentially an optimization recipe and could thus be as well a part of Chapter 17. If you don't understand some of the concepts mentioned here (like "consing" or the TIME function), have a look at this chapter first. Also, as with all optimization topics, this is probably something you shouldn't worry about unless you really, really need to.

Instead of giving you a solution, I'll show you the results of a little experiment[17] that is admittedly unscientific but should nevertheless demonstrate what this recipe is about:

```
* (defparameter *h* (make-hash-table))
*H*
* (hash-table-count *h*)
0
* (time (loop for n below 1000000 do (setf (gethash n *h*) n)))
```

[17]Much of what you're seeing in this recipe is implementation-specific, but in its essence, it should still apply to other Lisp compilers as well. (Also, the output, which is from SBCL 1.2.9 on a 64-bit Linux system, has been edited a bit to reduce clutter.)

```
Evaluation took:
  0.300019 seconds of total run time (0.284018 user, 0.016001 system)
  805,907,956 processor cycles
  83,833,376 bytes consed
NIL
* (hash-table-count *h*)
1000000
* (clrhash *h*)
#<HASH-TABLE :TEST EQL :COUNT 0 {10038B5C13}>
* (hash-table-count *h*)
0
* (time (loop for n below 1000000 do (setf (gethash n *h*) n)))
Evaluation took:
  0.172011 seconds of total run time (0.172011 user, 0.000000 system)
  461,093,456 processor cycles
  0 bytes consed
NIL
```

We created a hash table and filled it with one million key/value pairs. Then we removed all these pairs and filled the hash table once again with the same entries. What you probably didn't expect is that the second run was significantly faster (it took less than 60 percent of the time), which seems mostly due to the fact that the first invocation involved lots of consing while for the second one there was no consing at all.

We'll explain below why this is so and how you can use this behavior to your advantage.

How It Works

Although the standard doesn't tell implementors how hash tables have to work "under the hood," it mentions the concept of the *size* of a hash table that is not to be confused with the number of entries. Rather, the *size* is supposed to be the maximal number of entries the hash table can accommodate before it has to grow and thus achieve a larger size.

Here we have the session from above again, but with some additional input and output that was suppressed when we showed it the first time:

```
* (defparameter *h* (make-hash-table))
*H*
* (hash-table-count *h*)
0
* (hash-table-size *h*)
```

```
16
* (hash-table-rehash-size *h*)
1.5
* (hash-table-rehash-threshold *h*)
1.0
* (time (loop for n below 1000000 do (setf (gethash n *h*) n)))
Evaluation took:
  0.300019 seconds of total run time (0.284018 user, 0.016001 system)
  805,907,956 processor cycles
  83,833,376 bytes consed
NIL
* (hash-table-count *h*)
1000000
* (hash-table-size *h*)
1048576
* (clrhash *h*)
#<HASH-TABLE :TEST EQL :COUNT 0 {10038B5C13}>
* (hash-table-count *h*)
0
* (hash-table-size *h*)
1048576
* (time (loop for n below 1000000 do (setf (gethash n *h*) n)))
Evaluation took:
  0.172011 seconds of total run time (0.172011 user, 0.000000 system)
  461,093,456 processor cycles
  0 bytes consed
NIL
```

The most important point is that after the call to `CLRHASH`, the table has no more entries but its size is still 1,048,576, as it was directly before the hash table was cleared. Initially, the size was only 16, though, which means that it had to be enlarged no later than when we tried to insert the 17th key.

The parameters shown above also reveal how exactly the process of growing the hash table is supposed to work. The hash table is enlarged whenever its *occupancy level* (the number of entries divided by its size) reaches the *rehash threshold*, which is always a number between 0 and 1. As the threshold in this case was `1.0`, the hash table was first enlarged after the 16th entry was added. Had it been `0.75` instead, it would already have been enlarged after the 12th entry.

By how much the table is enlarged is controlled by the *rehash size*. In our case it is `1.5`, which means that the size should be multiplied by this factor.[18] So, the next size

[18]This parameter can also be an integer, in which case this number is *added* to the current size each time the hash table has to grow. That'd mean linear instead of exponential growth.

after 16 would be 24, which would be followed by 36, and so on. To get from 16 to (at least) one million by multiplying by 1.5 in each step, we would need

$$\log_{1.5} \frac{1000000}{16} \approx 27.4$$

steps, which would mean that the compiler had to create (and later throw away) 27 intermediate hash tables before the loop was finished.[19]

So, if you know in advance how large (approximately) your hash table will be in the end, you can provide this as a hint, which will very likely have positive effects:

```
* (defparameter *h* (make-hash-table :size 1000000))
*H*
* (time (loop for n below 1000000 do (setf (gethash n *h*) n)))
Evaluation took:
  0.172011 seconds of total run time (0.172011 user, 0.000000 system)
  461,830,145 processor cycles
  0 bytes consed
NIL
```

Likewise, you can use keyword arguments to create hash tables with different rehash thresholds and rehash sizes, if you expect a certain growth pattern and you want to fine-tune your hash tables for that.

As a final remark it has to be said that your implementation is free to ignore all the parameters mentioned in this recipe and to grow and shrink the hash table in a completely different way (or not at all). Although this might sound disappointing at first, it's actually a good thing as it means that implementors are free to pursue whichever strategy they deem best. And the best hash table implementation is probably one that "just works" without the need to screw around with low-level details.

6-7. Getting Rid of Hash Table Entries Automatically

Problem

Sometimes the only reference you still have to an object is a hash table entry (or only its key or value) and you might want this entry to vanish automatically if it is "no longer needed."

To demonstrate the problem and the solution, we concoct a little example (which admittedly isn't totally realistic but should be good enough to drive the point home).

[19] It turns out this is not what is actually happening. SBCL will multiply by 1.5, but then round to the next power of two; so if we start with 16, we're effectively multiplying by 2 in each step. Still, there are quite a few hash tables that have to be created, only to be thrown away microseconds later.

We have a couple of WORKER objects that are managed in a "database" *WORKERS*. Workers can have a "buffer" associated with them and this association is maintained by a hash table *BUFFER-HASH*. We use the following demo code:

```
(defclass worker ()
  ((id :initarg :id)))

(defparameter *workers* ())

(defparameter *buffer-hash* (make-hash-table))

(defun add-worker (id &optional with-buffer-p)
  (let ((new-worker (make-instance 'worker :id id)))
    (push new-worker *workers*)
    (when with-buffer-p
      (setf (gethash new-worker *buffer-hash*)
            (make-array 1024)))
    new-worker))
```

We now create some workers, and some of them will get buffers:

```
CL-USER 1 > (dotimes (i 10)
              (add-worker i (oddp i)))
NIL
CL-USER 2 > (list (length *workers*)
                  (hash-table-count *buffer-hash*))
(10 5)
```

Some time later, one of the workers is retired:

```
CL-USER 3 > (pop *workers*)
#<WORKER 21F1168F>
CL-USER 4 > (list (length *workers*)
                  (hash-table-count *buffer-hash*))
(9 5)
```

Although the buffer for this worker is no longer needed, it is still there (as a value of one hash table entry) and won't go away unless we manually remove it with REMHASH (see Recipe 6-3).

Solution

The solution (in LISPWORKS in this case) would be to replace the line

```
(defparameter *buffer-hash* (make-hash-table))
```

from above with this one:

```
(defparameter *buffer-hash* (make-hash-table :weak-kind :key))
```

If you do this, then the result of evaluating

```
(list (length *workers*)
      (hash-table-count *buffer-hash*))
```

after removing the worker will eventually[20] be `(9 4)`.

How It Works

A hash table entry (a key/value pair) is technically a reference to the key *and* to the value. So, as long as the entry exists, the Lisp garbage collector can remove neither the key nor the value. As there are sometimes situations similar to the one described above, where you want hash table entries to go away if they are the only remnants of objects that aren't used anywhere else anymore, many Lisps have extended the traditional hash table concept and offer so-called "weak" hash tables.

The syntax to create[21] weak hash tables might differ a bit among implementations,[22] but the general concept is similar. You can usually select between several or all of the following choices:

- Hash table entries will become eligible for garbage collection once their keys are no longer referenced from outside the hash table.
- Hash table entries will become eligible for garbage collection once their values are no longer referenced from outside the hash table.
- Hash table entries will become eligible for garbage collection once their keys *and* their values are no longer referenced from outside the hash table.
- Hash table entries will become eligible for garbage collection once their keys *or* their values are no longer referenced from outside the hash table.
- Hash table entries will never become eligible for garbarge collection. (This is the standard behavior of non-weak hash tables.)

[20] As this will be a result of garbage collection, it is kind of unpredictable when it will actually happen. For the sake of this experiment, you might want to give your Lisp a helping hand by invoking the garbage collector explicitly (see Recipe 22-10).

[21] In some Lisps you can even make a hash table weak *after* it has been created.

[22] For an attempt to unify this, check out the TRIVIAL-GARBAGE library (see also Recipe 22-10).

As this is about garbage collection, you can't usually pinpoint the exact moment the hash entries will really vanish. You can just be sure that they will be collected once the GC thinks it is time for a spring-cleaning.

Note that in some implementations, arrays can also be "weak." Check your Lisp's documentation to find out more.

6-8. Representing Maps As Association Lists

Problem

You need an ad hoc way to associate keys with values, which is more lightweight than hash tables. (And which, by the way, has some other advantages as well; see below.)

Solution

Use *alists*:

```
* (defparameter *a* (list (cons 'superman 'metropolis)
                          (cons 'batman 'gotham-city)))
*A*
* (assoc 'batman *a*)
(BATMAN . GOTHAM-CITY)
* (cdr (assoc 'batman *a*))
GOTHAM-CITY
* (assoc 'donald-duck *a*)
NIL
* (push (cons 'donald-duck 'duckburg) *a*)
;; output edited to fit paper width
((DONALD-DUCK . DUCKBURG)
 (SUPERMAN . METROPOLIS)
 (BATMAN . GOTHAM-CITY))
* (assoc 'donald-duck *a*)
(DONALD-DUCK . DUCKBURG)
;; "Entenhausen" is Duckburg's name in Germany...
* (push (cons 'donald-duck 'entenhausen) *a*)
((DONALD-DUCK . ENTENHAUSEN)
 (DONALD-DUCK . DUCKBURG)
 (SUPERMAN . METROPOLIS)
 (BATMAN . GOTHAM-CITY))
* (assoc 'donald-duck *a*)
```

```
(DONALD-DUCK . ENTENHAUSEN)
* (progn (pop *a*) (pop *a*) *a*)
((SUPERMAN . METROPOLIS)
 (BATMAN . GOTHAM-CITY))
* (setf *a* (acons 'donald-duck 'entenhausen *a*))
((DONALD-DUCK . ENTENHAUSEN)
 (SUPERMAN . METROPOLIS)
 (BATMAN . GOTHAM-CITY))
```

How It Works

Association lists (usually called "alists" in the Lisp world) are (like hash tables) a variant of the abstract data type called *associative array* or *map*. Like hash tables, they are collections of key/value pairs. In alists, the key value pairs are simply conses (see Recipe 2-1) with the key being the car and the value being the cdr of the cons, and the collection is just a list of these conses.[23] (If you call a cons an *ordered pair* and view a list as a *set* (see Recipe 6-10), an alist comes pretty close to the set-theoretical construction of a *map* or *function*.)

If we use the "cons cell notation" introduced in Recipe 2-1, (the start of) an alist looks like this:

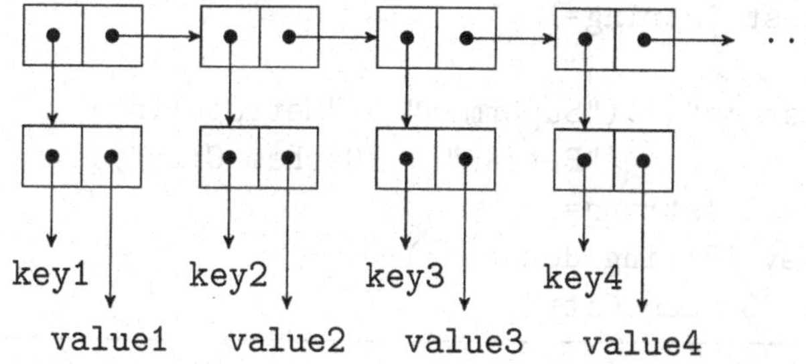

Here the cons cells in the first row make up the list structure, while the cons cells in the second row hold the key/value pairs. The keys and values hanging off of these cons cells can, of course, be any kind of Lisp object; although we only use symbols, numbers, and strings in our examples.

Given this specification, you should already be able to write your own alist implementation using just the primitive COMMON LISP functions for conses and lists; but

[23] A fundamental difference between hash tables and alists in COMMON LISP is how the *identity* of the data structure is provided. A hash table is represented as an object, and even if the data within the hash table changes, this object always stays the same. An alist, on the other hand, is represented by a cons cell. If you, for example, add an entry using `ACONS`, then you don't modify the old alist, but instead you create a *new* one; that is, a new cons cell.

In other words, if someone was holding a reference to the alist, then they wouldn't "notice" that you prepended a new association. This wouldn't happen to someone holding a reference to a hash table. (But see also page 162 for why this isn't always an advantage.)

luckily there are several built-in functions that will make your life easier:

- ASSOC will search an alist sequentially, looking for a key, and will return the first matching key/value pair.

  As the example above shows, alists can have several key/value pairs with the same key, and ASSOC will simply give you the first entry.

- ASSOC accepts a :TEST keyword argument, that will be used to determine if the search key and one of the keys in the alist are the same:

```
* (assoc "Batman" '(("Superman" . "Metropolis")
                    ("Batman" . "Gotham City")))
NIL
* (assoc "Batman" '(("Superman" . "Metropolis")
                    ("Batman" . "Gotham City"))
         :test 'string=)
("Batman" . "Gotham City")
```

- ASSOC also accepts a :KEY argument to specify a function to apply to the keys prior to searching:

```
* (assoc "batman" '(("Superman" . "Metropolis")
                    ("Batman" . "Gotham City"))
         :test 'string=)
NIL
* (assoc "batman" '(("Superman" . "Metropolis")
                    ("Batman" . "Gotham City"))
         :test 'string=
         :key 'string-downcase)
("Batman" . "Gotham City")
```

  (As you will have noticed, ASSOC essentially does nothing FIND couldn't do.)

- There's a variant ASSOC-IF to search for keys satisfying certain criteria:

```
* (assoc-if 'oddp '((2 . "two")
                    (4 . "four")
                    (3 . "three")
                    (5 . "five")))
(3 . "three")
```

- To add a new entry to an alist you can use PUSH or construct the new alist directly using CONS:

```
(setf *a* (cons (cons 'lois-lane 'metropolis) *a*))
```

As this is quite often done with alists, there's a shortcut ACONS which is demonstrated above.

- Another shortcut is PAIRLIS,[24] which will construct an alist by matching keys with values:[25]

```
* (pairlis (list "Batman" "Superman" "Donald Duck")
           (list "Gotham City" "Metropolis" "Duckburg"))
(("Donald Duck" . "Duckburg")
 ("Superman" . "Metropolis")
 ("Batman" . "Gotham City"))
```

  PAIRLIS can also be used to prepend several entries at once to an existing alist by providing this alist as an optional third argument.

- And if you want to search by values instead of keys (or switch the position of keys and values) there's RASSOC (of which there's also an -IF variant):

```
* (rassoc "Metropolis" '(("Superman" . "Metropolis")
                         ("Batman" . "Gotham City"))
          :test 'string=)
("Superman" . "Metropolis")
```

- If you want to copy a whole alist, use COPY-ALIST.

Finally, to remove a key/value pair from an alist, use any of the list manipulation functions described in Chapters 2 or 7.

Combining Lookup and Manipulation

If Batman were to move to New York City, you could write

```
(setf (cdr (assoc 'batman *a*)) 'new-york-city)
```

to update your alist. Be aware, though, that this is not consistent with how (SETF GETHASH) works because, for example,

```
(setf (cdr (assoc 'spider-man *a*)) 'new-york-city)
```

won't add a *new* entry to the alist if SPIDER-MAN isn't already a key but instead signal an error.

[24] And please don't ask why this is not called "PAIRLIST"...

[25] Note the order of the result which tells us something about how this function is likely implemented in this particular implementation. This order is not mandated by the standard, though.

Some Lisps offer convenience functions for such tasks. In LISPWORKS you can do it like this, for example:

```
(setf (sys:cdr-assoc 'spider-man *a*) 'new-york-city)
```

(Recipe 10-8 shows how you can add this functionality to any Lisp.)

Why Would Anybody Prefer Alists over Hash Tables?

At first glance, everything that can be done with alists can also be done with hash tables. And obviously the main disadvantage of an alist is that looking up something in it will take longer the more entries you have (because in the worst case, you have to iterate through the whole list); whereas in hash tables, lookup times are constant (at least as long as the buckets are more or less uniformly utilized; see Recipe 6-5). So, why alists?

There are actually several reasons why alists might be a better solution than hash tables in some situations:

- Unlike hash tables, alists can be ordered, so you can use them for tasks that hash tables aren't capable of.[26]
- Alists have a human-readable printed representation.
- Alists can be easily serialized and de-serialized (see Recipe 14-13).
- Not all COMMON LISP hash table implementations offer customizable tests (see Recipe 6-5), but alists do. (And even if your Lisp has custom hash tests, with alists you don't need to bother with hash functions.)
- Because of `RASSOC`, keys and values in alists are essentially interchangeable; whereas in hash tables, keys and values play very different roles.
- As Lisps are naturally optimized for operations involving conses, working with alists might actually be faster than working with hash tables, as long as the number of keys is small enough.
- Finally, by prepending a new cons with an *existing* key to an alist and later removing it again (like with a stack; see Recipe 2-9), you can temporarily *shadow* the old value associated with the key. (Whereas in a hash table you would destroy the existing association.) This makes alists a natural implementation technique for things like environments.

[26]Or you could arrange an alist in such a way that entries that are looked up often come first.

6-9. Representing Maps As Property Lists

Problem

You want to understand and use property lists.

Solution

Let's revisit the example from Recipe 6-8 and now do it with property lists:

```
* (defparameter *l* (list 'superman 'metropolis
                           'batman 'gotham-city))
*L*
* (getf *l* 'batman)
GOTHAM-CITY
* (getf *l* 'donald-duck)
NIL
* (getf *l* 'donald-duck 'nirvana)
NIRVANA
* (setf *l* (list* 'donald-duck 'duckburg *l*))
;; output edited to fit paper width
(DONALD-DUCK DUCKBURG
 SUPERMAN METROPOLIS
 BATMAN GOTHAM-CITY)
* (getf *l* 'donald-duck)
DUCKBURG
* (setf *l* (list* 'donald-duck 'entenhausen *l*))
(DONALD-DUCK ENTENHAUSEN
 DONALD-DUCK DUCKBURG
 SUPERMAN METROPOLIS
 BATMAN GOTHAM-CITY)
* (getf *l* 'donald-duck)
ENTENHAUSEN
* (remf *l* 'donald-duck)
T
* *l*
(DONALD-DUCK DUCKBURG
 SUPERMAN METROPOLIS
 BATMAN GOTHAM-CITY)
* (setf (getf *l* 'donald-duck) 'entenhausen)
ENTENHAUSEN
* *l*
(DONALD-DUCK ENTENHAUSEN
```

```
 SUPERMAN METROPOLIS
 BATMAN GOTHAM-CITY)
* (get-properties *l* '(batman superman))
SUPERMAN
METROPOLIS
(SUPERMAN METROPOLIS BATMAN GOTHAM-CITY)
```

How It Works

Property lists (or *plists* for short) are somewhat similar to alists, albeit a bit less flexible. Even if you never use alists for your own data, plists are important because they appear in lambda lists in the form of keyword arguments (see, for example, Recipe 2-11.)

Plists also arrange key/value pairs in a list, but in this case it is a flat list (which means that it must have an even number of elements). The structure thus looks like this:

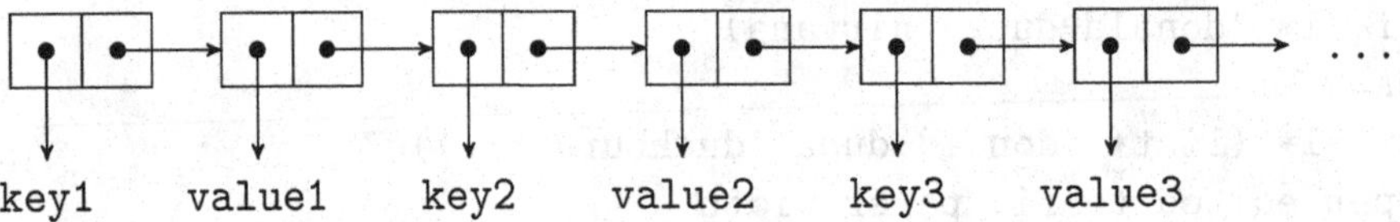

Plists are probably best explained by listing how they differ from alists:

- The equivalent of ASSOC is GETF, except that it returns only the value and not the key/value pair.
- You can't specify a test function; it is always EQ. That essentially makes symbols the only reasonable choice for keys in plists.
- You can provide a default value for GETF as with GETHASH (see Recipe 6-2).
- GETF can be used with SETF to change the value of a key/value pair.
- ASSOC-IF and RASSOC have no equivalent in the plist world.
- There's a special function REMF to remove a key/value pair.

All of these differences can be witnessed in the example above.

The one additional plist function that needs a special explanation is GET-PROPERTIES. It is used to look up several keys at once, which are provided as a list. As seen in the example, it returns three values: the first key found, the corresponding value, and the part of the plist starting with the key/value pair that was returned. The idea is that you use this function in a loop, like the following, in order to avoid repeated list traversals:

```
CL-USER 1 > (defparameter *l*
              (loop for symbol in '(:a :b :c :d :e :f :g :h :i :j :k)
                    ;; use ASCII code as value
                    for code = (char-code
                                (char (symbol-name symbol) 0))
                    collect symbol
                    collect code))
*L*
CL-USER 2 > *l*
(:A 65 :B 66 :C 67 :D 68 :E 69 :F 70 :G 71 :H 72 :I 73 :J 74 :K 75)
CL-USER 3 > (let ((plist *l*) key value)
              (loop
               (multiple-value-setq (key value plist)
                   (get-properties plist '(:f :j :a)))
               ;; leave loop if nothing was found
               (unless key (return))
               ;; skip key/value pair which was found
               (setf plist (cddr plist))
               ;; do something with the data
               (print (list key value))))
(:A 65)
(:F 70)
(:J 74)
NIL
```

When to Prefer Plists over Alists

We already discussed the main technical differences between plists and alists above. As they are otherwise very similar, plists have more or less the same relation to hash tables as alists; see page 162. But are there situations where plists would be a better choice than alists? At least two come to mind:

- Plists are arguably even more human-readable then alists because they have "less structure." They can be a good choice for things like configuration files.
- With plists, you can very easily switch from data to code, as in

  ```
  (apply #'some-function my-plist)
  ```

  or something similar. That's very elegant and Lisp-y.

The Plist of a Symbol

Every symbol in COMMON LISP has a plist associated with it, which essentially works like any other plist but can be accessed and modified with special functions like SYMBOL-PLIST, GET, and REMPROP. It is usually a bad idea to hang information off of a symbol because symbols are global. You might have a perfectly good reason to do it anyway, but in that case, I'll have to refer you to the HyperSpec for more information.

6-10. Working with Sets

Problem

You want to work with sets (in the mathematical sense).

Solution

COMMON LISP has several built-in functions that can treat lists as sets:

```
;; primes below 24
* (defparameter *p* (list 2 3 5 7 11 13 17 19 23))
*P*
;; odd numbers below 24
* (defparameter *o* (list 1 3 5 7 9 11 13 15 17 19 21 23))
*O*
* (union *p* *o*)
;; order could be different in your Lisp
(21 15 9 1 2 3 5 7 11 13 17 19 23)
* (intersection *p* *o*)
;; same here...
(23 19 17 13 11 7 5 3)
* (set-difference *p* *o*)
(2)
* (set-difference *o* *p*)
(21 15 9 1)
* (set-exclusive-or *p* *o*)
(21 15 9 1 2)
* (subsetp *o* *p*)
NIL
* (subsetp '(11 23) *p*)
T
* (adjoin 2 *p*)
```

```
(2 3 5 7 11 13 17 19 23)
* (adjoin 29 *p*)
(29 2 3 5 7 11 13 17 19 23)
* (member 29 *p*)
NIL
* (member 17 *p*)
(17 19 23)
```

How It Works

COMMON LISP provides several standard functions that can be used to work with lists *as if they were sets*, although lists aren't a perfect match for sets. We should probably start by listing (no pun intended) the two crucial differences between lists and sets:

- Sets aren't ordered, whereas lists are.

  For example, (1 2 3) and (1 3 2) are different lists, even if compared by EQUAL, but they represent the *same* set.

  As a consequence, you should never expect from any of the set-related functions mentioned in this recipe that it preserves the order within its arguments.

- An object is either an element of a set or it isn't, which means that no object can appear *twice* in a set.

  For example, (1 2 2) and (1 2) are different lists, even if compared by EQUAL, but they represent the *same* set.

As you can see from the example above, you have the following correlation between the mathematical operators and relations (on the left) and their COMMON LISP counterparts:

Name	Symbol	Lisp Function
Union	$\cup$	UNION
Intersection	$\cap$	INTERSECTION
Symmetric difference	$\triangle$	SET-EXCLUSIVE-OR
Relative complement[27]	$\setminus$	SET-DIFFERENCE
Subset	$\subseteq$	SUBSETP
Element	$\in$	MEMBER

ADJOIN is used to add a new element to a set[28] (and, as you could see above, does

[27] Also called *set-theoretic difference*.

[28] There's no set-theoretical notation for this.

nothing if this element is already present). You could also use PUSHNEW as an alternative.[29]

MEMBER returns NIL if its first argument is not a member of the second one, but in the opposite case it returns the part of the list that starts with the element found (which in some situations might be more helpful than just returning T). You can, of course, also use functions like FIND or FIND-IF with sets.

All of these functions will accept :KEY and :TEST arguments like many other COMMON LISP functions. You can, for example, use them to decide when exactly two elements of a set are considered to be the same:

```
* (set-difference '("Groucho" "Chico" "Harpo") '("Groucho"))
;; default test is EQL, as usual
("Harpo" "Chico" "Groucho")
* (set-difference '("Groucho" "Chico" "Harpo") '("Groucho")
                  :test 'string=)
("Harpo" "Chico")
```

What is curiously missing in the standard library is a function to check if two sets are equal; not as lists (where you could use EQUAL), but really as sets in the sense that they have the same elements. It is easy to write such a function, though. Probably the most elegant way is to use the fact that sets A and B are identical, if and only if their symmetric difference $A \triangle B$ is the empty set $\emptyset$:

```
* (defun set-equal (a b)
    (null (set-exclusive-or a b)))
SET-EQUAL
* (set-equal '(1 2 2 3) '(3 3 1 1 2))
T
```

Have a look at the ALEXANDRIA library (see Recipe 18-4) for a more sophisticated version of SET-EQUAL.

As we've learned by now, the set functions don't care whether an element appears twice (or even more often) in a "set." Still, you might want to clean up your sets. Remember that you can use REMOVE-DUPLICATES for that.

While this way of representing sets as lists is very convenient, it can become a performance problem if your sets are too large.[30] We'll therefore look at two other ways to represent sets.

[29]But you should, of course, be aware that PUSHNEW is a macro that modifies a *place* (see Recipe 10-8), whereas ADJOIN is a "pure" function.

[30]When would they be too large? That, of course, depends on your application (see Recipe 17-2).

Representing Sets As Hash Tables

The concept of a set is essentially a *binary* one in the sense that an object is either an element of a set or not. That's why you could also represent sets as hash tables where the keys are the elements. Set membership could either be decided by the mere fact that a key is present (the second return value of GETHASH; see Recipe 6-1) or by the corresponding value, which should be true.[31]

If we opted for the second variant, then, for example, testing whether X is an element of S would simply be (GETHASH X S), and adding Y to the set S would be nothing more than (SETF (GETHASH Y S) T).

As an example, let's implement union and intersection for this scenario:[32]

```
(defun hash-set-union (a b)
  (let ((result (make-hash-table)))
    (loop for key being the hash-keys of a
          do (setf (gethash key result) t))
    (loop for key being the hash-keys of b
          do (setf (gethash key result) t))
    result))

(defun hash-set-intersection (a b)
  (let ((result (make-hash-table)))
    (loop for key being the hash-keys of a
          when (gethash key b)
            do (setf (gethash key result) t))
    result))
```

The obvious advantage of this approach is that testing for membership and element removal is far more efficient for large sets. On the other hand, for operations like union and intersection, we still need to "walk" through the whole set. For small sets, sets as lists are certainly a more lightweight approach. (Compare with the discussion in Recipe 6-8.)

Representing Sets As Bit Patterns

The idea from the last subsection can be taken even further if we replace the values *true* (set member) and *false* (not a set member) with *one* and *zero*. A set is then simply a binary number. This works great if only a few objects are eligible for being members of sets at all, so that you can count them, that is, assign a number to each of

[31] Note that we're describing two *different* potential implementations here, although they would have very similar characteristics.

[32] Both of these functions assume that keys are only present for set members and that all values are T.

them. A set is then simply an integer and the nth object is an element of this set *iff* the nth bit of the integer is set.

You'll probably remember from math class that there's a close relation between set-theoretic operations and logical connectives:

Set theory	Propositional logic
$A \cup B$	$\alpha \vee \beta$
$A \cap B$	$\alpha \wedge \beta$
$A \setminus B$	$\alpha \wedge \neg\beta$
$A \triangle B$	$\alpha \veebar \beta$

This leads to a straightforward implementation where, for example, union would be done with LOGIOR, intersection with LOGAND, and so on. (And set equality would just be =.)

Here are some examples where the members are simply the numbers 0, 1, 2, ... themselves:[33]

```
;; *A* is the set {0,1,3}
* (defparameter *a* #b1011)
*A*
;; *B* is the set {0,3,4}
* (defparameter *b* #b11001)
*B*
* (setf *print-base* 2)
10
;; union
* (logior *a* *b*)
11011
;; intersection
* (logand *a* *b*)
1001
;; remove element 1 from set *A*
* (setf (ldb (byte 1 1) *a*) 0)
0
* *a*
1001
```

The advantage would be super-fast operation compared to the other two set representations that we discussed. The disadvantage is that this requires a bit of effort, and as I already said, only works if there's a relatively small class of member "candidates." (At least you're not constrained by some limit like 32 or 64, because the relevant functions all work with *bignums*; see Recipe 4-1.)

[33]For the binary representation used in this example, see Recipe 4-4.

7. Sequences and Iteration

Lists (see Chapter 2) and vectors (see Chapter 5) have in common that you can traverse them sequentially. That's why they are subsumed under the type `SEQUENCE` in COMMON LISP. There are a lot of functions in the standard that work on sequences, which is to say that they accept lists as well as vectors as arguments. (And also strings, see Chapter 3, because those are vectors, too.) We'll discuss most of them in this chapter. (And see also Recipe 3-7.)

Sequences are also intimately related to iteration, which is the other major topic of this chapter. We are not going to discuss the basics of iteration because we're assuming that you already have some experience with `DO`, `DOTIMES`, `LOOP`, and friends.[1] But maybe we can present some techniques or idioms that you weren't aware of so far.

As you'll probably know, `LOOP` is a pretty controversial part of the COMMON LISP standard—some love it and some hate it. There are two alternatives to `LOOP` that have been around for a long time; and both can claim with a certain eligibility to be more elegant and more "Lisp-y" than `LOOP`. If you're mainly writing open source software and want to cooperate with as many COMMON LISP hackers as possible, then your best bet is probably to stick with `LOOP` because everyone knows it and has it available. If, on the other hand, you're working alone or within a small group, you might want to have a look at Recipes 7-14 and 7-15 to meet two interesting alternatives to `LOOP`.

You will also find recipes concerned with iteration in other chapters (see for example Recipes 1-7 and 6-4).

7-1. Filtering a Sequence

Problem

Many languages offer some way of "filtering" a sequence; that is, of selecting elements of the sequence based on certain criteria. You want to do that as well.

[1]If not, *Practical Common Lisp* has a good, if somewhat brief, introduction to the `LOOP` macro in its chapter 22. See `http://www.gigamonkeys.com/book/loop-for-black-belts.html`.

Solution

This is very easy to do once you've realized that the corresponding function is *not* called "FILTER" in COMMON LISP. Here we filter all symbols out of a list of various objects:

```
CL-USER> (remove-if-not 'symbolp '(:foo 42 #\a bar "string" quux))
(:FOO BAR QUUX)
```

In other words, we *remove* everything that is *not* a symbol.

How It Works

The "basic" function behind this functionality is actually REMOVE, which removes all occurrences of an element from a sequence.

```
CL-USER> (remove #\a "Aardvark")
"Ardvrk"
CL-USER> (remove #\a "Aardvark" :test 'char-equal)
"rdvrk"
```

As you can see here, many sequence functions accept a :TEST keyword argument. The function supplied thusly (which defaults to EQL; see Recipe 10-1) is used to compare the first argument to each element of the second argument. That's why in the first case the uppercase character wasn't removed and in the second it was.

REMOVE's "siblings" are REMOVE-IF and REMOVE-IF-NOT, which remove something from a sequence if it fulfills (or doesn't fulfill) a certain criterion.[2]

By the way, if you look up these functions in the HyperSpec, you'll find out that REMOVE-IF-NOT (like some other functions or keyword arguments) is "deprecated." Don't worry. Each implementation has this function; the chances that there'll be a new COMMON LISP standard tomorrow which'll ultimately *remove* (pun intended) these functions is pretty slim...

7-2. Searching a Sequence

Problem

You want to find an element in a sequence or a sub-sequence of a sequence.

[2]The family also has some black sheep the names of which start with "DELETE." You should avoid them unless you really need them (see page 534).

Solution

Use FIND or SEARCH:

```
CL-USER> (find #\c "abcde")
#\c
CL-USER> (find #\C "abcde")
NIL
CL-USER> (find #\C "abcde" :test 'char-equal)
#\c
CL-USER> (search "bcd" "abcde")
1
CL-USER> (search "bdc" "abcde")
NIL
```

And there are various variants and alternatives explained below.

How It Works

A variant of FIND is FIND-IF (and also FIND-IF-NOT), which doesn't search for a specific object but rather checks whether some element of the sequence satisfies a test:

```
CL-USER> (find-if 'plusp '(-3 -13/17 -4.5 0 42))
42
```

If you replace the word "FIND" with "POSITION" in these three functions, then the same search is performed, but the position where it was found is returned instead of the element itself:

```
CL-USER> (position #\c "abcde")
2
CL-USER> (position #\x "abcde")
NIL
CL-USER> (position-if 'plusp '(-3 -13/17 -4.5 0 42))
4
```

Note that POSITION is better suited to test *if* an element belongs to a sequence than FIND (because the latter can return NIL even if it found something):

```
CL-USER> (find nil (list nil))
NIL
CL-USER> (position nil (list nil))
0
CL-USER> (find nil (list 42))
```

```
NIL
CL-USER> (position nil (list 42))
NIL
```

Like other sequence functions, FIND, POSITION, and so on can also be asked to start searching from the end of the sequence:

```
CL-USER> (position #\a "Zappa")
1
CL-USER> (position #\a "Zappa" :from-end t)
4
```

Interestingly, most of these functions[3] aren't really *required* to traverse the sequence in the opposite direction;[4] they just have to return a result that would be the same *if* they had done it. The paper *Processing List Elements in Reverse Order*[5] by Irène Durand and Robert Strandh has a nice take on the :FROM-END keyword argument.

For lists, there's also MEMBER (see Recipe 6-10), which returns the whole sublist starting with the element found, which sometimes is exactly what you need:

```
CL-USER> (find :d (list :a :b :c :d :e))
:D
CL-USER> (member :d (list :a :b :c :d :e))
(:D :E)
```

SEARCH doesn't search for individual elements but for a whole subsequence. Like FIND and all other sequence functions it'll also accept a :TEST keyword parameter:[6]

```
CL-USER> (search '(:c :d) '(a b c d e))
NIL
CL-USER> (search '(:c :d) '(a b c d e) :test 'string=)
2
```

Finally, an interesting relative of SEARCH is MISMATCH, which compares two sequences element-wise and returns the position where they start to differ (or NIL if they don't differ at all):

```
CL-USER> (mismatch "amnesty" "amnesia")
5
CL-USER> (mismatch "and" "andante")
3
```

[3]One notable exception is COUNT.

[4]Consider what that would mean for lists (see Recipe 2-1).

[5]See http://metamodular.com/reverse-order.pdf.

[6]Recipe 1-9 explains why we can use STRING= to compare symbols.

```
CL-USER> (mismatch "and" "And" :test 'char-equal)
NIL
```

7-3. Sorting and Merging Sequences

Problem

You want to sort one sequence or you want to merge two (sorted) sequences into one sorted sequence.

Solution

COMMON LISP already has the standard functions `SORT` and `MERGE` that will do that for you; both are pretty flexible.

```
CL-USER> (sort (list 3 1 2 5 4) '<)
(1 2 3 4 5)
CL-USER> (merge 'list (list 2 4 8 16 32)
                      (list 3 5 7 11 13 17 19)
                 '<)
(2 3 4 5 7 8 11 13 16 17 19 32)
```

There are just a few things to look out for...

How It Works

Both operators want a predicate function that'll be used for comparison (which is the < in our preceding example). This function compares individual elements of the sequence(s). As you can use any function whatsoever as the predicate, there's no problem if you only need a specific part of your elements for the comparison:

```
CL-USER> (sort (list '(:three 3) '(:two 2) '(:four 4) '(:one 1))
               (lambda (pair-1 pair-2)
                 ;; we only use the second element of each pair
                 (< (second pair-1) (second pair-2))))
((:ONE 1) (:TWO 2) (:THREE 3) (:FOUR 4))
```

But it's often shorter and more convenient to specify a *key function* to pick the part of the element you're interested in:

```
CL-USER> (sort (list '(:three 3) '(:two 2) '(:four 4) '(:one 1))
               '<
               :key 'second)
((:ONE 1) (:TWO 2) (:THREE 3) (:FOUR 4))
```

What you'll have to keep in mind is that both operators are allowed to (and often will) *destructively modify* their arguments. The following is something that *can* happen (although your implementation might behave differently):

```
CL-USER> (defparameter *list* (list 1 2 3 4 5))
*LIST*
CL-USER> (sort *list* '>)
(5 4 3 2 1)
CL-USER> *list*
(2 1)                          ;; <-- oops...
```

For SORT, this means two things. First, you must *always* use its return value, so *this* would have been the correct idiom:

```
(setf *list* (sort *list* '>))
```

Second, if you're not the only one holding a reference to the sequence that is to be sorted, you must work on a copy of it:

```
(setf *list* (sort (copy-list *list*) '>))              ;; or COPY-SEQ
```

For MERGE, the same rules apply, and the second one applies to *both* arguments.

Finally, two remarks about the sorting behavior:

- MERGE is only really useful if the two sequences to be merged are already sorted by the same predicate.
- SORT has a "sibling" STABLE-SORT that guarantees that two elements that aren't comparable by the sorting predicate[7] never switch places. SORT doesn't make that guarantee:

```
CL-USER> (sort (vector '(:two-1 2) '(:two-2 2)
                       '(:one-1 1) '(:one-2 1))
               '< :key 'second)
;; one of four possible answers:
#((:ONE-2 1) (:ONE-1 1) (:TWO-2 2) (:TWO-1 2))
CL-USER> (stable-sort (vector '(:two-1 2) '(:two-2 2)
```

[7]That's the technical wording. If your predicate is a *strict total order*, like for example <, then this simply means that the two elements are equal.

```
                '(:one-1 1) '(:one-2 1))
          '< :key 'second)
;; only allowed answer:
#((:ONE-1 1) (:ONE-2 1) (:TWO-1 2) (:TWO-2 2))
```

7-4. Mixing Different Sequence Types

Problem

You want to use one of the standard sequence functions that accept more than one sequence as an argument with arguments of different types.

Solution

Just do it:

```
;; list meets string
CL-USER> (search '(#\b #\a #\r) "foobarbaz")
3
;; vector meets list
CL-USER> (mismatch #(f r u g a l) '(f r u n o b u l a x))
3
;; vector and list again
CL-USER> (map 'list '+ #(1 2 3) '(3 2 1))
(4 4 4)
```

How It Works

Not a big deal, but maybe something you never thought of: the standard sequence functions not only work with all sequence types, they also work fine, as we could witness above, if they have to deal with more than one sequence type at the same time. (Too bad there are only two, but see Recipe 7-13.)

7-5. Re-Using a Part of a Sequence

Problem

You want to perform some action only on a subsequence of some sequence (or you need the subsequence as an argument to a function) and you want to avoid creating a new sequence.

Solution

Suppose we want to count the number of occurrences of a character in some text:

```
CL-USER> (defparameter *text* "The thirty-three thieves thought
that they thrilled the throne throughout Thursday.")
*TEXT*
CL-USER> (count #\t *text* :test 'char-equal)
16
```

However, we're only interested in a part of the text; for example, some 40 characters in the middle. We could do it like so:

```
CL-USER> (count #\t (subseq *text* 11 51) :test 'char-equal)
8
```

Or we could do it like so:

```
CL-USER> (count #\t *text* :test 'char-equal :start 11 :end 51)
8
```

In both cases, the result is identical, but the second variant is more efficient. We'll explain why next. And also how you can sometimes avoid `SUBSEQ` even if you're dealing with a function that doesn't accept `:START` and `:END` keyword parameters.

How It Works

Most of the standard functions that operate on sequences accept `:START` and `:END` keyword parameters like the ones we used above. If they are not specified, then the function acts on the whole sequence, otherwise only on a certain subsequence of it.

But this is not only a convenience feature. In our first example, `SUBSEQ` created a *new* sequence (i.e. a new string) of length 40, which it then handed over to `COUNT`. This new string wasn't otherwise needed and immediately thrown away after `COUNT` was finished. That's a typical case of needless *consing*.[8]

If, on the other hand, `COUNT` is called with the keyword parameters, it doesn't create a new sequence, it just starts and stops at the right positions within the sequence.

But there are situations when you need to call functions that want sequences as arguments but don't provide these keyword parameters. Suppose we have a function

[8]See Recipe 17-6.

TEXT-ANALYSIS that wants a string as its only argument and then returns some interesting information about it. You have a large string *INPUT* but its text has a header and a footer that shouldn't be analyzed. Your only choice seems to be to start the analysis like so:

```
(text-analysis (subseq *input* 342 4080751))
```

However, there's a way to circumvent this using *displaced arrays* (see Recipe 5-8):

```
(defun shared-subseq (sequence start end)
  (make-array (- end start)
              :element-type (array-element-type sequence)
              :displaced-to sequence
              :displaced-index-offset start))
```

If you now call your function like so

```
(text-analysis (shared-subseq *input* 342 4080751))
```

no new string containing more than four million characters will be created. And TEXT-ANALYSIS won't notice the difference.

While SHARED-SUBSEQ itself is not a destructive function, its name should remind you that what it returns shares structure with its argument; and thus you shouldn't hand this return value over to destructive functions, lest they destroy the original sequence we're displacing to.

Of course, while this is a technique you should probably have heard about (and you have now), in many situations it can just mean premature optimization. Have a look at Recipe 17-2 before you use it extensively.

7-6. Repeating Some Values Cyclically

Problem

As part of an iteration, one variable's value is to be set cyclically from a certain set of values.

Solution

Create an endless list:

```
* (loop for x in '#1=(a b c . #1#)
        repeat 30
```

```
      collect x)
(A B C A B C A B C A B C A B C A B C A B C A B C A B C A B C)
```

How It Works

We use the #= syntax described in Recipe 8-6 to create a list that repeats the same three elements endlessly. This is how it looks in our "cons notation" from Recipe 2-1:

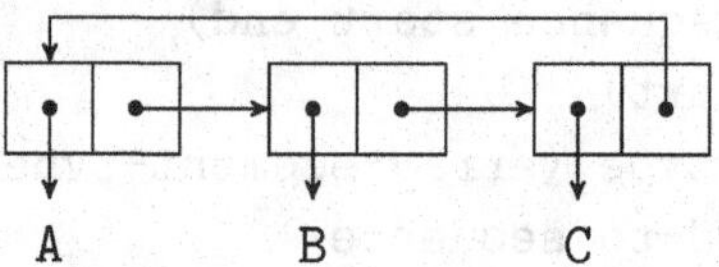

`LOOP` (or `DOLIST` if you prefer) marches dutifully through this list as if it were a finite, albeit pretty large list. Of course, you'll need some means to break out of your loop (that's the `REPEAT` part in the preceding example), or otherwise your iteration will never end.

You must also be careful with such *circular lists* for another reason: your Lisp might run into an endless loop when trying to print them. Try this:

```
* (defparameter *c* '#1=(a b c . #1#))
*C*
```

If you now type `*C*` into your listener (don't do it!), your Lisp will attempt to print the value of the variable `*C*` but won't know when to stop. Luckily, there's a global special variable called `*PRINT-CIRCLE*`, which if set to a true value instructs the Lisp printer to detect circularity and print it using the same syntax you'd use to enter it:

```
* (setf *print-circle* t)
T
* *c*
#1=(A B C . #1#)
```

`*PRINT-CIRCLE*` can also be useful to distinguish uninterned symbols.[9] These will usually look identical because only their names are printed:

```
* (setq *print-circle* nil)
NIL
* (let ((yo-1 (make-symbol "YO"))
        (yo-2 (make-symbol "YO")))
    (list yo-1 yo-2 yo-1))
(#:YO #:YO #:YO)
```

[9]See Recipe 1-3.

But with *PRINT-CIRCLE*, we can see what's really going on:

```
* (setq *print-circle* t)
T
* (let ((yo-1 (make-symbol "YO"))
        (yo-2 (make-symbol "YO")))
    (list yo-1 yo-2 yo-1))
(#1=#:YO #:YO #1#)
```

Alternatives

You don't have to use the #= syntax, by the way. It also works like this:

```
CL-USER> (setq *print-circle* t)
T
CL-USER> (defparameter *c* (list 'a 'b 'c))
*C*
CL-USER> (setf (cdr (last *c*)) *c*)
#1=(A B C . #1#)
```

And if you don't like the idea of an endless list at all, you can always exploit that modular arithmetic (see Recipe 4-3) describes circular repetitions. You could achieve the same effect as above with a bit more code like so:

```
(loop with values = '(a b c)
      for i below 30
      collect (nth (mod i 3) values))
```

Whether this is more or less elegant than the variant above is in the eye of the beholder.[10]

Finally, if you have a cycle of length two, then you're effectively switching between two values. A typical case is a flag that switches back and forth between *true* and *false*. This can be implemented very succinctly, like so:

```
CL-USER> (loop for flag = t then (not flag)
               repeat 10
               collect flag)
(T NIL T NIL T NIL T NIL T NIL)
```

[10]Depending on the length of the cycle the second variant may also be a bit less efficient because of the usage of NTH.

7-7. Counting Down

Problem

You want to use LOOP with some decreasing numerical value.

Solution

An aspect of LOOP that people often find confusing is that both of the following forms don't yield the result they expect, namely the list (5 4 3 2 1):

```
(loop for i from 5 to 1 collect i)

(loop for i from 5 to 1 by -1 collect i)
```

In both cases you'll either get NIL or an error is signaled.

This is one of the ways to make it work:

```
CL-USER> (loop for i downfrom 5 to 1 collect i)
(5 4 3 2 1)
```

How It Works

If you want to use LOOP's FROM/TO idiom to have a value that is decreasing, then one of the loop keywords must signal the downward direction. You must either use DOWNTO or ABOVE instead of TO or you must use DOWNFROM instead of FROM or both.[11] Also, the value used with BY—where we tried -1 above—must *always* be positive. It can't be used to denote the counting direction.

But why is that so? The answer is that LOOP is a macro that is expanded into code before it "knows" where counting is supposed to start and stop.[12] To demonstrate this, I macroexpanded the following simple usage of LOOP

```
(loop for i from a to b collect i)
```

[11]LOOP also understands the equivalent loop keywords UPFROM and UPTO, but they are rarely used because the default is to count upwards anyway.

[12]In our specific example it *could* have known (because 1 and 5 are constant values), but understandably LOOP doesn't make any special provisions for such "trivial" cases.

and then cleaned the result up a bit so that we can concentrate on the important parts.[13] This is what I got and I have marked the important part:

```
(block nil
  (let ((i a)
        (%limit% b)
        (%accumulator% nil))
    (tagbody
     %begin-loop%
      (when (> i %limit%)                          ;; <-------------------
        (go %end-loop%))
      (setq %accumulator% (cons i %accumulator%)
            i (+ i 1))
      (go %begin-loop%)
     %end-loop%
      (return-from nil
       (nreverse %accumulator%)))))
```

The test `(> I %LIMIT%)` is performed to check whether the loop should end. If you now replace `FROM` with `DOWNFROM`, the test will become `(< I %LIMIT%)`.[14] `LOOP` wants to know at macro expansion time, which of the two tests it should use; and that's why you need to help it by using the right loop keywords.

If you want to write a loop where both directions are possible, you'll have to use an idiom like so:

```
(defun test (start end step)
  (loop for i = start then (+ i step)
        until (= i end)
        collect i))
```

However, be aware that due to the terminating condition used here the outcome is not the same as before and ugly things can happen:

```
CL-USER> (test 1 5 1)
(1 2 3 4)
CL-USER> (test 5 1 -1)
(5 4 3 2)                          ;; not (5 4 3 2 1)
CL-USER> (test 1 5 .3)             ;; <- ATTENTION, WILL LOOP FOREVER
```

[13]This is based on CLISP's `LOOP`. You might see something completely different in your Lisp, but the essence will be the same.

I've taken the liberty to mark internal variables (which in the original macro expansion are uninterned symbols) with percent signs so that they stand out.

[14]And `(+ I 1)` will become `(- I 1)`.

7-8. Iterating over "Chunks" of a List

Problem

You want to iterate over a list and on each pass perform some operation on two or more consecutive elements.

Solution

Use ON together with LOOP's destructuring capabilities.

For example, for a function similar to GET-PROPERTIES (see Recipe 6-9), except that it returns all values at once, you could proceed like this:

```
CL-USER> (defun get-all-properties (plist keys)
           (loop for (key value) on plist by #'cddr
                 when (member key keys)
                   collect value))
GET-ALL-PROPERTIES
CL-USER> (get-all-properties
          '(:one 1 :two 2 :three 3 :four 4 :five 5 :six 6 :seven 7)
          '(:one :five :two))
(1 2 5)
```

How It Works

This is pretty simple; you just have to know that it's possible. One thing is that the ON loop keyword repeatedly gives you the *whole* list (while IN gives you its first element):

```
CL-USER> (loop for thing on '(1 2 3 4)
               do (print thing))
(1 2 3 4)
(2 3 4)
(3 4)
(4)
NIL      ;; return value
```

This is done until (ATOM THING) becomes true.[15]

[15]See Recipe 2-1 for ATOM.

The list is traversed by repeated application of the function supplied to the `BY` loop keyword, which by default is `CDR` but can be anything:

```
CL-USER> (loop for thing on '(1 2 3 4) by #'cddr
               do (print thing))
(1 2 3 4)
(3 4)
NIL      ;; return value
```

And we can *destructure* what we get. This is not quite as powerful as `DESTRUCTURING-BIND` (see Recipe 2-11), but suffices to dissect arbitrary list structures:

```
CL-USER> (loop for thing on '(1 2 3 4) by #'cddr
               for (first second . rest) = thing
               do (print (list first second rest)))
(1 2 (3 4))
(3 4 NIL)
NIL      ;; return value
```

We now pack the first two lines into one to get rid of the intermediate variable `THING`. Also, `LOOP` allows us to use `NIL` for variables like `REST`, which we never use:

```
CL-USER> (loop for (first second . nil) on '(1 2 3 4) by #'cddr
               do (print (list first second)))
(1 2)
(3 4)
NIL      ;; return value
```

And if such a `NIL` is at the end of a destructuring pattern, we can even remove it completely. We thus end up with the technique we've used above:

```
CL-USER> (loop for (first second) on '(1 2 3 4) by #'cddr
               do (print (list first second)))
(1 2)
(3 4)
NIL      ;; return value
```

Finally, you can also cut variable-sized pieces from the cake with a bit more work:[16]

```
CL-USER> (loop for data = (list 1 2 3 4 5 6) then (nthcdr size data)
               for size in '(2 0 3 1)
               collect (subseq data 0 size))
((1 2) NIL (3 4 5) (6))
```

[16]For real code, you probably want to check that you still have enough of `DATA` left before calling `SUBSEQ`.

(And note how this fails to work if you change the order of the first two clauses.)

7-9. Closing over Iteration Variables

Problem

You want to create closures from within a loop (not necessarily done with the LOOP macro).

Solution

Quick quiz question: Which outcome do you expect from this form?

```
(mapcar 'funcall (loop for i below 10
                       collect (lambda () i)))
```

If your answer wasn't correct (see below), you should probably continue with this recipe. If it *was* correct, then what would your answer have been for this form?

```
(let (closures)
  (dotimes (i 10)
    (push (lambda () i) closures))
  (mapcar 'funcall (reverse closures)))
```

In this case it's not as clear-cut as you might think...

How It Works

The answer in the first case, as you can easily confirm by evaluating it in your Lisp, is a list of ten tens. It happens quite often that someone new to the concept of closures expects the outcome (0 1 2 3 4 5 6 7 8 9) here.

It is true, that the first closure is *created* while I has the value 0, the second one is created while its value is 1, and so on. But the closures don't close over the *value* but over the *binding*: LOOP creates a binding for the lexical variable I and assigns a new value to it on each iteration. And all ten closures close over this *same* binding and "follow" it.[17] That's why they must all return the same value when we use them. And that's also why they don't return 9 but 10, because this is the value I had when the loop was finally terminated.

[17]See also Recipe 10-4.

If you really wanted each closure to return the value of I at the time of its creation you need to create a new binding on each iteration and close over that:

```
CL-USER > (mapcar 'funcall
                  (loop for i below 10
                        collect (let ((j i))           ;; new binding
                                  (lambda () j))))
(0 1 2 3 4 5 6 7 8 9)
```

Now, what about the DOTIMES form? On six different Lisps I had on my hard disk the result also always consisted of ten tens. The funny thing, though, is that other than in the LOOP case, this is not mandated by the standard. Instead it says that DOTIMES *may* establish a *new* binding of I on *each* iteration.[18] So, although it seems to be a rare edge case, if you're intending to write portable and future-proof code, you shouldn't rely on DOTIMES using only one binding throughout the whole iteration—even if all current Lisps do it like that.

7-10. "Extending" Short Sequences in Iterations

Problem

When iterating over several sequences in parallel, you want to loop until the *longest* sequence is exhausted.

Solution

LOOP is defined to stop an iteration once the shortest list is exhausted:[19]

```
CL-USER> (loop for a in '(A B C D E F)
               for b in '(:A :B :C :D)
               collect (list a b))
((A :A) (B :B) (C :C) (D :D))
```

But you can "extend" the shorter list by as many NILs as needed like so:

```
CL-USER> (loop for a in '(A B C D E F)
               for b% = '(:A :B :C :D) then (cdr b%)
               for b = (car b%)
```

[18]And the same for DOLIST.

[19]And the same holds for all sequence functions that can work on more than one sequence (see for example Recipe 7-12).

```
                    collect (list a b))
((A :A) (B :B) (C :C) (D :D) (E NIL) (F NIL))
```

How It Works

We use a helper variable B% that iterates over the tail of the shorter list (as if with ON) and employ the fact that both (CDR NIL) and (CAR NIL) are defined to return NIL.

You can, of course, use other default values than NIL:

```
CL-USER> (loop for a in '(A B C D E F)
               for b% = '(:A :B :C :D) then (cdr b%)
               for b = (if b% (car b%) 42)
               collect (list a b))
((A :A) (B :B) (C :C) (D :D) (E 42) (F 42))
```

And the same can be done with arrays, but it's a bit unwieldy compared to the list solution:

```
(loop with b% = #(:A :B :C :D)
      with len = (length b%)
      for a across #(A B C D E F)
      for i from 0
      for b = (and (< i len) (aref b% i))
      collect (list a b))
```

7-11. Breaking out of LOOP

Problem

In a LOOP form, you want to stop iterating depending on some condition.[20]

Solution

There are several different ways to do it. We'll investigate them based on the following simple example where we iterate through a string and collect its vowels:

```
CL-USER> (loop for char across "counterrevolutionaries"
               when (find char "aeiou")
```

[20]Related to what you would do with break in a for loop in C or JAVA.

```
                    collect char)
(#\o #\u #\e #\e #\o #\u #\i #\o #\a #\i #\e)
```

Now suppose we want to stop collecting once we have seen at least five vowels. Let's introduce a counter:[21]

```
CL-USER> (loop with counter = 0
               for char across "counterrevolutionaries"
               until (= counter 5)
               when (find char "aeiou")
                 collect char
                 and do (incf counter))
(#\o #\u #\e #\e #\o)
```

Here we use UNTIL, which is one of LOOP's standard clauses, to terminate an iteration based on a test.[22] But maybe you need to leave the loop based on some conditional clause like WHEN. In that case, you can use RETURN. But in order to return something you need to be able to name it, so we now need to collect INTO something:

```
CL-USER> (loop with counter = 0
               for char across "counterrevolutionaries"
               when (find char "aeiou")
                 collect char into result                 ;; note INTO here
                 and do (incf counter)
               when (= counter 5)
                 return result)
(#\o #\u #\e #\e #\o)
```

We only need to check the counter if it actually was incremented, so let's change the code again:

```
CL-USER> (loop with counter = 0
               for char across "counterrevolutionaries"
               when (find char "aeiou")
                 collect char into result
                 and do (incf counter)
                        (when (= counter 5)
                          (return result)))
(#\o #\u #\e #\e #\o)
```

The final tweak now is to return a string instead of a list:

[21] Note that the AND is necessary. Without it, the counter would be incremented for each character and not only for each vowel.

[22] The other one is WHILE and in a way you can also add THEREIS, ALWAYS, and NEVER.

```
CL-USER> (loop with counter = 0
               for char across "counterrevolutionaries"
               when (find char "aeiou")
                 collect char into result
                 and do (incf counter)
                        (when (= counter 5)
                          (return (coerce result 'string))))
"oueeo"
```

But if you now replace "counterrevolutionaries" with "dandelion" (which has only four vowels), you will get NIL. You could fix this like so:

```
CL-USER> (loop with counter = 0
               for char across "dandelion"
               when (find char "aeiou")
                 collect char into result
                 and do (incf counter)
                        (when (= counter 5)
                          (return (coerce result 'string)))
               finally (return (coerce result 'string)))
"aeio"
```

But this is kind of ugly as the same code is repeated twice in different places. The better solution is this:

```
CL-USER> (loop with counter = 0
               for char across "dandelion"
               when (find char "aeiou")
                 collect char into result
                 and do (incf counter)
                        (when (= counter 5)
                          (loop-finish))              ;; <-- changed
               finally (return (coerce result 'string)))
"aeio"
```

How It Works

There are three things about LOOP worth noting here:

- Once we name something we collect into (in our case the list RESULT), it isn't returned automatically anymore.

- The LOOP clause RETURN is just an abbreviation for DO (RETURN ...). Both work because the loop is implicitly enclosed in a block named NIL.
- LOOP-FINISH is a local macro that can be used anywhere inside a loop to "jump" to the loop's *epilogue*; that is, the forms that will be executed after the loop has finished.

  If you exit the loop with RETURN, the epilogue will *not* be executed:

```
CL-USER> (loop for i in '(3 7 8 1)
               do (print i)
               when (evenp i)
                 return nil
               finally (print :done))
3
7
8
NIL
CL-USER> (loop for i in '(3 7 8 1)
               do (print i)
               when (evenp i)
                 do (loop-finish)
               finally (print :done))
3
7
8
:DONE       ;; <- that's the difference
NIL
```

7-12. Making Sense of the MAP... Zoo

Problem

You are wondering why there are *nine* different standard functions with names starting with "MAP" and would like to know what the differences are.

Solution

For one of these nine, MAPHASH, the name reveals what it is for. You'll find more about it in Recipe 6-4, in the chapter about hash tables.

The two functions where the name is really just MAP or MAP-INTO are the more recent sequence variants of Lisp's mapping functions. They are discussed at the end of this recipe.

The remaining majority of the "MAP family" is comprised of six functions (having made-up words as names) which all act on lists exclusively. They can be categorized by what they do with their input and how they construct their output:

	List of Return Values	*Concatenates* Return Values	*No Output*
processes *elements*	MAPCAR	MAPCAN	MAPC
processes *tails*	MAPLIST	MAPCON	MAPL

How It Works

All of these six operators work on lists, and for all of them, the first argument is a function[23] f that is followed by one or more lists. All six operators traverse these lists (in the sense of applying CDR successively) in parallel until the shortest one is exhausted. The difference between the first row and the second row is that the operators in the first row apply f to the *elements* of the lists in turn while the ones in the second row apply f to each *tail*; it's like the difference between LOOP's IN and ON.[24] For example:

```
CL-USER> (mapcar 'length '((1) (2) (3) (4)))
(1 1 1 1)
CL-USER> (maplist 'length '((1) (2) (3) (4)))
(4 3 2 1)
```

Now for the differences between the columns. The operators in the first column create a list where the elements are the return values of the applications of f. The operators in the second column, however, create a list by *concatenating* (using NCONC) the return values (so they'd better be lists). This is like the difference between LOOP's COLLECT and NCONC. For example:

```
CL-USER> (mapcar 'list '(1 2 3 4) '(:one :two :three :four))
((1 :ONE) (2 :TWO) (3 :THREE) (4 :FOUR))
CL-USER> (mapcan 'list '(1 2 3 4) '(:one :two :three :four))
(1 :ONE 2 :TWO 3 :THREE 4 :FOUR)
```

Finally, the operators in the *third* column just return their second argument, which is as if they didn't return anything at all. They call f solely for its side effects. This is like using LOOP only with DO.

[23] Actually a *function designator*, see Recipe 8-5.

[24] See Recipe 7-8.

```
CL-USER> (defparameter *counter* 0)
*COUNTER*
CL-USER> (mapc (lambda (x)
                 (incf *counter* x))
               '(1 2 3 4 5 6 7 8 9 10))
(1 2 3 4 5 6 7 8 9 10)
CL-USER> *counter*
55
CL-USER> (setf *counter* 0)
0
CL-USER> (mapl (lambda (x)
                 (incf *counter* (length x)))  ;; note the difference
               '(1 2 3 4 5 6 7 8 9 10))
(1 2 3 4 5 6 7 8 9 10)
CL-USER> *counter*
55
```

And while we are talking about LOOP, here's how these six operators could be implemented with it (using two lists each for this example):

`(mapcar f list-1 list-2)`	`(loop for x-1 in list-1`
	`      for x-2 in list-2`
	`      collect (funcall f x-1 x-2))`

`(mapcan f list-1 list-2)`	`(loop for x-1 on list-1`
	`      for x-2 on list-2`
	`      collect (funcall f x-1 x-2))`

`(maplist f list-1 list-2)`	`(loop for x-1 in list-1`
	`      for x-2 in list-2`
	`      nconc (funcall f x-1 x-2))`

`(mapcon f list-1 list-2)`	`(loop for x-1 on list-1`
	`      for x-2 on list-2`
	`      nconc (funcall f x-1 x-2))`

`(mapc f list-1 list-2)`	`(loop for x-1 in list-1`
	`      for x-2 in list-2`
	`      do (funcall f x-1 x-2))`

`(mapl f list-1 list-2)`	`(loop for x-1 on list-1`
	`      for x-2 on list-2`
	`      do (funcall f x-1 x-2))`

Now, can I tell you where these strange names come from and can I provide you with a cool mnemonic for them? I'm afraid the answer is *no* in both cases.[25] I guess we'll have to accept them as a part of Lisp folklore.

The Sequence Variants

`MAP` is in a way like `MAPCAR`, except that it is a "generic" sequence function;[26] its arguments can not only be lists but also vectors (or other sequences; see Recipe 7-13) or a mix thereof (see Recipe 7-4). As the result type can also be of any sequence type, `MAP` needs an additional argument (which is the first one) to denote this type:[27]

```
CL-USER> (map 'list '1+ '(0 1 2 3 4))
(1 2 3 4 5)
CL-USER> (map 'vector '1+ '(0 1 2 3 4))
#(1 2 3 4 5)
```

`MAP-INTO` is like `MAP` except that you supply it with a container where the results are to be stored.[28] The mapping will simply stop if the container is too short (or leave unused places within the container untouched if it's too long):

```
CL-USER> (map-into (make-list 4 :initial-element '-)
                   '1+ '(0 1 2 3 4))
(1 2 3 4)
CL-USER> (map-into (make-array 6 :initial-element '-)
                   '1+ '(0 1 2 3 4))
#(1 2 3 4 5 -)
```

Finally, `MAP-INTO` is the only operator discussed in this recipe that doesn't actually need a sequence to "work on." Try this:

```
(map-into (make-list 3) 'get-internal-run-time)
```

7-13. Defining Your Own Sequence Types

Problem

You'd like to have something similar to JAVA's `Collection` or `Iterable` in COMMON LISP; that is, a way to create your own sequence implementations which work with

---

[25]OK, `MAPCAR` and `MAPLIST` make kind of sense, but the others...

[26]Not *generic* in the CLOS sense, mind you.

[27]And if this first argument is `NIL`, `MAP` works only for the side effects like `MAPC`.

[28]In other words, the container will be *destructively modified*.

the standard sequence functions.

Solution

This is currently only supported in SBCL and ABCL. We'll have a brief look at an incomplete (!) example to just give you an idea what it's about.

The idea for this example is to view (text) files as sequences of characters.[29] We want to be able to treat them like ordinary lists of characters or like strings. For that, compile and load the following code (in SBCL):

```
(defclass file-sequence (sequence standard-object)
  ((path :initarg :path)))

(defmethod sb-sequence:length ((sequence file-sequence))
  (with-open-file (in (slot-value sequence 'path))
    (file-length in)))

(defmethod sb-sequence:elt ((sequence file-sequence) index)
  ;; silly example, see below
  (with-open-file (in (slot-value sequence 'path))
    (file-position in index)
    (read-char in)))
```

You can now do things like these:

```
;; results from a Linux system
CL-USER> (defparameter *passwd* (make-instance 'file-sequence
                                               :path "/etc/passwd"))
*PASSWD*
CL-USER> (length *passwd*)
1924
CL-USER> (search "bash" *passwd*)
27
CL-USER> (subseq (coerce *passwd* 'list) 27 31)
(#\b #\a #\s #\h)
```

Given our code, it is probably not surprising that `LENGTH` works, but note that the standard functions `SEARCH` and `COERCE` also immediately accepted a `FILE-SEQUENCE` object as a fully-fledged sequence.

[29]If you need something like that, you might want to have a look at Recipes 7-14 and 14-4 for a more realistic approach.

How It Works

As COMMON LISP is in many other areas one of the most malleable programming languages one can imagine, it is kind of strange that the functionality it offers for sequences is restricted to the standard types `LIST` and `VECTOR`[30] and can't be deployed by user-defined sequence classes. Christophe Rhodes succinctly describes the situation (including the problems implementors are confronted with if they try to change it) in his paper *User-extensible sequences in Common Lisp*.[31] Being one of the SBCL maintainers, he has also implemented his proposal from that paper in SBCL. Unfortunately, the only other Lisp so far to pick up the torch has been ABCL.

The example above is, of course, just a quick demonstration that doesn't care about error checking or efficiency. (It would be really, really dumb to open and close the file for each individual character.) However, we can at least glean the basics of SBCL's user-extensible sequences from it:

- To create your own sequence class, you define one that inherits from `SEQUENCE`. As `SEQUENCE` is a *system class* (see Recipe 13-3), you'll also have to inherit from `STANDARD-OBJECT` so that your new class behaves like a normal user-defined CLOS class.
- You now have to implement a couple of methods (as you would have to if you implemented a JAVA interface). There are five methods you *must* implement.[32]
- You don't have to implement other methods, but you can do it if the default implementations turn out to be inefficient for your sequence class.

You'll have to look up the rest in the SBCL manual where extensible sequences are fully documented.

7-14. Iterating with iterate

Problem

You don't like `LOOP` and you're looking for a replacement.

[30] And, at least in theory, additional sequence types offered by the implementation.

[31] Available online at `http://www.doc.gold.ac.uk/~mas01cr/papers/ilc2007/sequences-20070301.pdf`.

[32] We implemented just two of them and we could only get away with that because we refrained from using certain sequence functions for our demonstration.

Solution

A LOOP replacement that many people like is the venerable ITERATE by Jonathan Amsterdam. ITERATE comes with extensive documentation so we'll only provide some examples here that are mainly intended to showcase the differences between ITERATE and LOOP.[33]

After loading ITERATE with QUICKLISP (see Recipe 18-2), evaluate the following form (so that the example code below gets a little less chatty):

```
(use-package :iter)
```

(If you've already used LOOP in the same image, you might run into a couple of harmless name conflicts; see Recipe 1-4.)

First, ITERATE uses mostly the same loop keywords as LOOP or at least similar ones, so the basic stuff should look and feel quite familiar:

```
CL-USER> (iter (for i from 1 to 5)
               (collect (* i i)))
(1 4 9 16 25)
```

This already explains why some people call it "LOOP with parentheses."

The next example shows that accumulation constructs like COLLECT or APPENDING can appear anywhere and will "just work;" whereas in LOOP, they must be in clearly specified places. (So, to clarify, the CASE form below is the vanilla CASE and not a special ITERATE clause. You can use any Lisp form there and nest the accumulation as deeply as you wish.)

```
CL-USER> (iter (for thing in '(:one :two :three))
               (case thing
                 (:one (collect 1))
                 (:two (appending (list 2 2)))
                 (:three (collect 3)
                         (appending (list 3 3)))))
(1 2 2 3 3 3)
```

This is not impossible in LOOP, but would require more work and be quite ugly.

Now consider the following LOOP form:

```
CL-USER> (loop for i in '(2 5 11 23)
               while (< i 17)
```

[33]In case you're thinking that the comparison is biased toward ITERATE: I'm always using LOOP for my daily work for the reasons described in the introduction to this chapter. But I nevertheless think that ITERATE is superior to LOOP in almost every area. Too bad it's not in the standard…

```
                   for j = (print i)
                   collect (list j j))
2
5
11
23  ;; <-- some Lisps will print this, some won't
((2 2) (5 5) (11 11))
```

The intention should be quite clear; we want the loop to terminate once I isn't less than 17 anymore and we placed the J assignment *behind* the test so that it will only happen if we're still iterating.[34] Unfortunately, this is not legal LOOP syntax because the WHILE clause belongs to the loop *body* and all FOR clauses have to appear *before* the body. Some Lisps will warn you about this and some even might refuse to accept this form, but the most serious problem probably is that different Lisps will execute different code. (In our example, some will print 23 and some won't.)

In ITERATE, on the other hand, there are no such restrictions regarding the order of clauses and the outcome is defined, which in such cases often allows you to write your code more naturally:

```
CL-USER> (iter (for i in '(2 5 11 23))
               (while (< i 17))
               (for j = (print i))
               (collect (list j j)))
2
5
11
((2 2) (5 5) (11 11))
```

ITERATE also has so-called "finders" that LOOP doesn't have at all. For example, to estimate where the minimum of $x^2 - 4x + 1$ is between -5 and 5, we just need this:

```
CL-USER> (iter (for x from -5 to 5 by 1/100)
               (finding x minimizing (1+ (* x (- x 4)))))
2
```

Another feature of ITERATE that LOOP is missing is the presence of *generators*. You can replace FOR with GENERATE, which means that the variable is not automatically assigned on each iteration, but rather whenever you use NEXT:

```
CL-USER> (iter (for x in '(:foo foo 42 :bar #\a :quux "string"))
               (generate y in '(a b c))
               (when (keywordp x)
```

[34]Imagine, instead of PRINT, an expensive computation or something that'll signal an error if I is too large. Or simply something with a side effect like PRINT itself.

```
                 (collect (cons x (next y)))))
((:FOO . A) (:BAR . B) (:QUUX . C))
```

Finally, here's ITERATE looping through a file.

```
;; on a Linux system:
CL-USER> (iter (for c in-file "/etc/passwd" using 'read-char)
               (repeat 4)
               (collect c into result)
               (finally (return (coerce result 'string))))
"root"
```

There's also a nice syntax for hash table iterations (see end of Recipe 6-4), a general syntax for sequences that works for lists as well as vectors, and so on.

How It Works

ITERATE boasts that it has (at least) the following advantages over LOOP:[35]

- It feels more "Lisp-y" and also *looks* more Lisp-like, as it obvious how to indent ITERATE forms—as opposed to LOOP forms.
- It can do all the things LOOP can do and more. And it can usually do them in a more elegant and concise way.
- It is extensible.

As for the first two points, my take is that they are correct. LOOP has given up idiomatic Lisp syntax in favor of its own sub-language, which no IDE I'm aware of can indent correctly and which for more complex constructs is hard to parse, even for an experienced Lisper. And LOOP makes some things very easy, while it makes other things needlessly hard or impossible. In both areas it is easily beaten by ITERATE. (Although, of course, you still have a new sublanguage that you need to get used to.)

There's no "official" way to extend LOOP in the sense of adding your own iteration clauses for your own data structures. However, many of the major Lisp implementations were initially based on an MIT version of the LOOP macro,[36] and because of this common heritage it is possible to "hack" them in more or less the same way. If you really want to try your luck at this, have a look at the CLSQL source code

[35]See also `https://common-lisp.net/project/iterate/doc/Differences-Between-Iterate-and-Loop.html`. For a very detailed comparison see Sabra Crolleton's article at `https://sites.google.com/site/sabraonthehill/loop-v-iter`.

[36]If you're into historical studies, you can have a look at it at `https://www.cs.cmu.edu/afs/cs/project/ai-repository/ai/lang/lisp/code/iter/loop/mit/0.html`.

(see page 667) to see how it's done.[37] But be aware that you'll be using undocumented functionality and unexported symbols, which is not a good basis for stable, forward-looking code.

It's, of course, easier for ITERATE to offer extensibility, as there's only one implementation of it. We'll close this recipe with a simple example of how this is done; you just write a certain class of macros:

While ITERATE has a general ACCUMULATING clause, there's no built-in facility to construct a string from individual characters. But we can create it ourselves, like so:[38]

```
(defmacro-clause (collect-char char)
  `(accumulating ,char by (lambda (next-char array)
                            (vector-push-extend next-char array)
                            array)
                 initial-value (make-array 0 :adjustable t
                                             :fill-pointer t
                                             :element-type
                                               'character)))
```

With this new clause, our file example from above can be reduced to three lines:

```
CL-USER> (iter (for c in-file "/etc/passwd" using 'read-char)
               (repeat 4)
               (collect-char c))
"root"
```

7-15. Iterating with series

Problem

You want a more "functional" approach to iteration.

Solution

Try the SERIES library. It offers ways to perform iteration that are considerably different from the built-in COMMON LISP constructs and also from ITERATE (see Recipe 7-14).

After loading SERIES using QUICKLISP (see Recipe 18-2), you can, for example, do something like this to compute the first ten primes:

[37]Or look here: http://users.actrix.co.nz/mycroft/db/.

[38]See Chapter 5 for VECTOR-PUSH-EXTEND, fill pointers, adjustable arrays, and so on.

```
CL-USER> (use-package :series)
T
CL-USER> (defun primep (n)
           (zerop
             (collect-length
               (choose-if (lambda (d)
                            (zerop (mod n d)))
                          (scan-range :from 2 :upto (sqrt n))))))
PRIMEP
CL-USER> (defun all-primes ()
           (choose-if 'primep (scan-range :from 2)))
ALL-PRIMES
CL-USER> (subseries (all-primes) 0 10)
#Z(2 3 5 7 11 13 17 19 23 29)
```

This is certainly not the most efficient way of doing it, but arguably a pretty elegant one. It will be explained below.

How It Works

The SERIES library, written by Richard C. Waters, is something that was considered by the committee working on the COMMON LISP standard but eventually lost to LOOP. But at least it found its way into *CLtL2* (see page 296) where you can still find its documentation. There it is claimed that "at least 90 percent of the loops programmers typically write can be replaced by SERIES expressions that are much easier to understand and modify, and just as efficient."

I'm not in a position to confirm or refute this, but I think that SERIES offers something interesting that is worth studying, if only for the pleasure of seeing a different approach to an old problem.

What the Example Does

We can't explain all of SERIES in one recipe, but we can step through our example from above to highlight some of its concepts:

- A *series* is an abstract object representing a sequence[39] of values.
- Series can be generated in many different ways. A very simple one is to specify a range of integers, as we did in PRIMEP for the sequence $2, 3, 4, \ldots, \lfloor\sqrt{n}\rfloor$ using SCAN-RANGE.

[39]In the usual sense of the word, not in the sense of COMMON LISP's *sequences*.

- Many of the functions from the SERIES library accept series as arguments and also return series. CHOOSE-IF, for example, *filters*[40] a series based on a certain predicate. In our example, it generates a series of all divisors of n that aren't greater than $\sqrt{n}$.
- COLLECT-LENGTH, on the other hand, is one of the functions that produce non-series output based on series input. (It just returns the length of the series.)
- So, PRIMEP returns a true value if n doesn't have any divisors between 2 and $\sqrt{n}$.
- ALL-PRIMES is interesting because it returns a series of *all* primes; that is, an *infinite* series.[41] This is possible because values of series are only computed if needed.

  (If you know CLOJURE, you will be reminded of its *lazy sequences*; something SERIES apparently already had in the 1980s.)
- Finally, SUBSERIES is to series what SUBSEQ is to COMMON LISP sequences. Evaluating the last form of the example causes SERIES to compute the first ten values of the infinite series returned by ALL-PRIMES.

Here's the example from Recipe 7-11 using SERIES:

```
CL-USER> (collect 'string
          (subseries (choose-if (lambda (char)
                                  (find char "aeiou"))
                                (scan "counterrevolutionaries"))
                     0 5))
"oueeo"
```

[40]See Recipe 7-1.

[41]That's why you shouldn't evaluate the form (ALL-PRIMES) in your REPL! (Unless you have set *PRINT-LENGTH*—see Recipe 9-1—to some sensible value.)

8. The Lisp Reader

Whatever you enter into your computer (whether interactively or via a file containing source code) has to be parsed first. The part of your Lisp system that consumes characters one by one and tries to make sense of them is called the *Lisp reader*. Its behavior is clearly specified (as is pretty much everything in COMMON LISP), but it also is configurable (as is pretty much everything in COMMON LISP) so that you can bend it to your will.

The ability to create *domain-specific languages* perfectly tailored to your problem is often praised (and rightly so) as one of the "unique selling propositions" of COMMON LISP. The fact that you can intercept the parser at such a low level and thus modify the syntax can be an integral part of this process, and some hackers have done cool (and also sometimes crazy) stuff that way.[1] We'll have a closer look at such modifications in the recipes at the end of this chapter, starting with Recipe 8-7, which should probably be read in sequence.

Be aware, though, that you can use these techniques to alter the syntax to a point where what you can type and how it is interpreted can hardly be called "Lisp" anymore. *Maybe* this is what you need, but it will very likely make your code hard to read and maintain.

Finally, let's not forget that not only can you *modify* the parser, you can also simply *use* it; even that is something pretty valuable and it will be discussed in some of the recipes here.

(See also Recipe 1-8 in Chapter 1.)

8-1. Employing the Lisp Reader for Your Own Code

Problem

You want to parse input that has Lisp syntax or at least a pretty similar syntax.

[1]For a very elaborate example, see XMLISP at `http://agentsheets.com/lisp/XMLisp/`.
You might also want to check out the `#I` infix reader macro by Mark Kantrowitz, the `#U` reader macro in the PURI libary, or CL-INTERPOL.

Solution

Use READ. This function can parse anything your REPL can parse:

```
CL-USER 1 > (with-input-from-string
                 (in "(#\\a \"foo\" #c(3 4) 4/5)")
               (read in))
(#\a "foo" #C(3 4) 4/5)
```

Or, if you're reading from a string (like above), use the shortcut READ-FROM-STRING. But be also aware of the dangers of untrusted input:

```
CL-USER 2 > (read-from-string "(nIL .3141d1 #.(print 42) foo)")
42              ;; <- this was printed, it is not the return value!
(NIL 3.141D0 42 FOO)
30
CL-USER 3 > (intern "FOO")
FOO
:INTERNAL
```

See more below.

How It Works

Every compiler or interpreter needs a parser to convert the source code it is supposed to execute into a fitting internal representation. But once this has been done and your program is running, you rarely have access to this parser anymore. From the point of view of, say, a typical C++ program, the parsing process is part of its history and otherwise inaccessible. Not so in COMMON LISP. Here, the part of the system that parses user input is encapsulated in a single function called READ that any Lisp program can call at any time.

READ reads characters from a character stream (see Chapter 14) until it has completely read one object and then returns this object (as opposed to its textual representation it consumed from the stream). READ understands everything you could also type into your REPL or write in a COMMON LISP source code file. In the examples above, the things recognized included characters, complex numbers, floating-point numbers, symbols, and lists. But really everything will work.

READ-FROM-STRING is just a convenience function that makes reading from strings easier; you don't have to explicitly create a stream from the string (see Recipe 14-7) as we did in the first example. The function is also capable (using keyword arguments) of starting to read somewhere in the middle of a string. As it also returns the position in the string where it stopped reading, you can combine these two features to read from a string piecemeal:[2]

```
(let ((input "84/2 #c(23 0)"))
  (multiple-value-bind (part-1 position)
      (read-from-string input)
    (list part-1 (read-from-string input t nil :start position))))
```

This form should return the list (42 23) because we remembered the second return value (POSITION) from the first call to (READ-FROM-STRING) and used it as a keyword argument to the second call, so that the second call started reading behind the "84/2" part.[3]

Why READ Is Potentially Dangerous

The potential caveat with READ is that it is in a way too powerful and you can't selectively turn certain features on or off (or at least not without considerable effort—see more on this shortly). If you're reading data from someone you don't trust, they have many chances to attack you in one way or the other if you use READ to parse their stuff. One possibility is to use the #. syntax to execute *arbitrary* COMMON LISP code. (We did this in the example when we printed 42.) This is explained in Recipe 8-3 and there you'll also learn how to turn this feature off.

Nevertheless, there are other things an attacker could do; they can feed you lots of symbols that your reader must *intern*[4] (also demonstrated in the example with the symbol FOO), or they can give you things like huge lists to parse, which might occupy the Lisp reader for a long time and/or stress your garbage collector. The bottom line is that you should be careful with READ simply because it can do so much.

What READ Doesn't Do

If you enter the following form

```
(read-from-string "(+ 40 2)")
```

and you are surprised that the form doesn't return 42, then you are confusing the reader with the REPL. If you enter (+ 40 2) into your REPL, it will first *read* the character sequence and convert it into a list and it will then *evaluate* this list, which

[2]In case you're wondering why we had to write T NIL before :START, this is explained later in this recipe.

[3]Note how the fraction was automatically canceled and the complex number converted into an integer. See Chapter 4 for more about this.

[4]See Chapter 1.

entails calling the function +. But the Lisp reader (which is what's behind READ and READ-FROM-STRING) is only concerned with the first part of this, *not* with the evaluation. If you are really interested in the sum, you should try something like this:

```
(eval (read-from-string "(+ 40 2)"))
```

The Optional Arguments to READ

READ accepts up to four (!) optional arguments, which is considered bad style nowadays but is the way it is for historical reasons.[5] You can specify the stream you want to read from (which by default is *STANDARD-INPUT*), and you can specify what to do if READ reaches the end of a file: it can signal an error or return a default value instead.

The last optional argument is called RECURSIVE-P and should be set to a true value if you're calling READ from something like your own reader macro function (see Recipe 8-9), but to NIL if you call it as a stand-alone function (see also footnote 32).

Go Wild!

Of course, you can also use the Lisp reader (and thus READ) to parse things that are quite different from Lisp code. If you can live with the basic syntax for symbols and numbers, everything else can be changed. (See Recipe 8-8 and those that follow for the whole story.)

8-2. Troubleshooting Literal Object Notation

Problem

Literal notation for compound objects is convenient but can lead to subtle problems that are pretty common as well as hard to detect. This recipe explains what's happening behind the scenes.

Solution

The following example (arguably somewhat contrived) illustrates this. Consider this function:

[5] For READ-FROM-STRING it is even worse because it mixes optional with keyword arguments which is something you should never ever do. This is certainly one of those things that would be different if COMMON LISP were a greenfield project.

```
(defun count-1-2-3 (list)
  (let ((counters '(:one 0 :two 0 :three 0)))
    (dolist (item list)
      (incf (getf counters item)))
    counters))
```

The idea is that COUNT-1-2-3, given a list where the elements are the keywords :ONE, :TWO, and :THREE, will return a property list (see Recipe 6-9) with a tally for these elements. So,

```
(count-1-2-3 (list :one :three :three :one :one :one))
```

will *probably* return (:ONE 4 :TWO 0 :THREE 2) in most implementations—meaning four :ONEs, no :TWOs, and two :THREEs—but you can't rely on this. (See below.)

And if you now try

```
(count-1-2-3 (list :two :two))
```

the value returned will very likely *not* be (:ONE 0 :TWO 2 :THREE 0), as you might have expected. It *could* be (:ONE 4 :TWO 2 :THREE 2), but technically it could be anything, or your Lisp image could crash or whatever. Why is that?

How It Works

COMMON LISP, like many other programming languages, has a literal syntax not only for simple, immediate objects like numbers, symbols, and characters, but also for things like list and arrays. Some of them are introduced in various recipes in this book.

"Literal" in this case means that instead of, say, instructing you compiler to create an array using the function MAKE-ARRAY, you simply write down the contents of the array (using a special syntax described in Recipe 8-4).

While such "shortcuts" are often handy, they can be dangerous as well and are one of the most frequent causes for hard-to-detect bugs. The conceptual picture to have in mind here is that a literal object appearing somewhere in your code is constructed "on the spot" while the compiler is reading your source code and is stored right there (i.e., in its internal representation of the code). If you were to modify such an object (as does COUNT-1-2-3 with the literal list '(:ONE 0 :TWO 0 :THREE 0)), then you would modify the code!

That's why the standard explicitly bans the modification of literal objects. Or rather it says that "the consequences are undefined," which in a way is even worse. Your compiler doesn't need to warn you or prevent you from doing it, but might later do *very* strange things...

How could we have avoided this? In this particular case, we could simply replace the form `'(:ONE 0 :TWO 0 :THREE 0)` with `(LIST :ONE 0 :TWO 0 :THREE 0)`. As a consequence, your Lisp would now, on each call to `COUNT-1-2-3`, construct a *fresh* list, and you wouldn't have to care about what happened during earlier calls.

So, only ever use literal notation for *constant* ("read-only") objects; that is, for things that will never change during the entire lifetime of your program.[6]

This Also Applies to Strings!

What we said above applies to lists (as in our example), but also to arrays and other objects. And note that strings are technically also arrays. Watch this:

```
CL-USER 1 > (defun oldest-marx-brother () "Chico")
OLDEST-MARX-BROTHER
CL-USER 2 > (setf (subseq (oldest-marx-brother) 0 4) "Harp")
"Harp"
;; what follows is technically undefined behavior!
CL-USER 3 > (oldest-marx-brother)
"Harpo"
```

So, again, never modify literal objects!

8-3. Evaluating Forms at Read Time

Problem

You want to insert a constant value into your source code, but you don't want to write it down. (Maybe it's something that's too tedious to write down or it's the result of a longer computation.)

Solution

Use the `#.` notation. The form following the dot will be evaluated and the result of this evaluation will *replace* `#.` and the form.

[6]This is, of course, not an issue with *immediate* objects like numbers and characters because they aren't comprised of constituents that can be changed. (While technically a rational number—see Recipe 4-5—has a numerator and a denominator, there's no portable way to, say, modify the denominator of 2/3 so that it suddenly is 2/7 instead.)

If, for example, the constant PI were not already defined and you wanted to write a function to compute the area of a circle, you *could* write this:

```
(defun area (radius)
  (* 3.141592653589793D0
     radius radius))
```

But it would arguably be more elegant (and more obvious to readers of your code) to write this:

```
(defun area (radius)
  (* (* 4 (atan 1d0))
     radius radius))
```

Except that in the second version, your computer has to compute (* 4 (ATAN 1D0)) each and every time the function AREA is called.[7] But you can have your cake and eat it too. It looks like so:

```
(defun area (radius)
  (* #.(* 4 (atan 1d0))
     radius radius))
```

The function AREA is now indistinguishable from the one defined in the first version.

How It Works

The form following the dot can be any form that the compiler is able to evaluate.[8] To give a more interesting example: although COMMON LISP doesn't have a syntax for literal hash tables, you can insert hash tables (even with certain entries already being set) directly into your source code, like so:

```
#.(let ((h (make-hash-table)))
    (setf (gethash 42 h) t)
    h)
```

(But see also the section titled "Alternatives" below.)

[7] Well, unless you have a sufficiently clever compiler that recognizes that this is a constant value. But bear with me for the sake of this example.

[8] Really *any* form, no matter how complicated. You could even, say, read and process a whole file of data and use this syntax to insert the results into your source code before it is compiled.

What to Look Out For

The important point here is that the form following `#.` is evaluated at *read time* and thus *before* the expression it is part of is compiled. This implies that whatever is needed for the aforementioned evaluation must already be known to the compiler once it encounters the `#.` part. If you split the preceding example into two parts, like this

```
(defun compute-pi ()
  (* 4 (atan 1d0)))
(defun area (radius)
  (* #.(compute-pi) radius radius))
```

then `AREA` can only be read (and thus compiled) if `COMPUTE-PI` is already defined and can be called to produce a result. Likewise, if `COMPUTE-PI` were to compute π using a costly series approximation, then it'd better already be *compiled* when `AREA`'s definition is read.

By the way, this whole machinery can be disabled by setting the value of the global special variable `*READ-EVAL*` to `NIL`.[9] (In this case, if the compiler encounters `#.` somewhere in your code, it'll signal an error.) This is something you definitely should do if you ever want to apply the Lisp reader to data supplied by untrusted sources.[10]

Finally, whatever you insert into your source code this way is technically a literal value, so the warnings from Recipe 8-2 apply here as well.

Alternatives

There are various ways to achieve something similar. One is to use the `DEFCONSTANT` macro, which arguably would have been the better solution for our somewhat contrived `PI` example. Another one is to use `LOAD-TIME-VALUE` (see Recipe 10-5). Finally, you might also want to consider `EVAL-WHEN`, described in chapter 20 of *Practical Common Lisp*. But note that none of these variants is doing *exactly* the same as `#.` because the value in question is computed at different times. Only with `#.` is it computed at *read time*.

To give you another example, suppose the following function is called each time your program starts up:

```
(defun banner ()
  (format t "Version 4.2. Compiled at Lisp universal time ~A.~%"
```

[9] This, by the way, can also have an effect on how objects are *printed*. See page 235 and the HyperSpec dictionary entry for `*PRINT-READABLY*`.

[10] But that is rarely, if ever, a good idea anyway! See also Recipe 8-1.

```
  #.(get-universal-time)))
```

It will always show a "timestamp" reflecting the time when it was compiled (or, to be more exact, when the compiler read the function definition).[11] When the file containing this function is compiled anew, the message will change automatically. This is something that can only be done with the #. syntax.

8-4. Embedding Literal Arrays into Your Code

Problem

You want to describe an array together with its contents in your source code.

Solution

Use the #(syntax for simple (see Recipe 5-2) vectors:

```
CL-USER 1 > (defparameter *a* #(1 2 4 8 16))
*A*
CL-USER 2 > (aref *a* 3)
8
CL-USER 3 > *a*
#(1 2 4 8 16)
```

And use the #*n*A(syntax for arrays:

```
CL-USER 4 > (defparameter *a* #2A((1 2 4 8) (1 3 9 27)))
*A*
CL-USER 5 > (aref *a* 1 3)
27
CL-USER 6 > *a*
#2A((1 2 4 8) (1 3 9 27))
```

How It Works

The literal syntax for vectors is just like the literal syntax for lists, except that instead of '(you start with #(. You can only create *simple* vectors this way because there's no syntax to specify fill pointers (see Recipe 5-6) or other things. This, of course, implies that once you've created a vector this way, its length is fixed. You can, however,

[11]See Recipe 22-9 for GET-UNIVERSAL-TIME.

specify a length that is different from the number of elements you provide, but only if it's greater than the number of elements you have. In such a case, the last specified element will be used to fill the vector:

```
CL-USER 1 > #4(1 2 3)
#(1 2 3 3)
```

The syntax for arbitrary arrays is slightly more complicated. You add the character A to the vector syntax and this time there *must* be a number behind the sharpsign. This number is the *rank* (see Recipe 5-1) of the array. What follows is then interpreted exactly as if it were the value of the :INITIAL-CONTENTS argument (see Recipe 5-4) to MAKE-ARRAY. Note the different outcomes below, where the inputs differ *only* in rank:

```
CL-USER 1 > #2A((1 2 4 8) (1 3 9 27))
#2A((1 2 4 8) (1 3 9 27))
CL-USER 2 > (aref * 1 1)
3
CL-USER 3 > #1A((1 2 4 8) (1 3 9 27))
#((1 2 4 8) (1 3 9 27))
CL-USER 4 > (aref * 1)
(1 3 9 27)
CL-USER 5 > #0A((1 2 4 8) (1 3 9 27))
#0A((1 2 4 8) (1 3 9 27))
CL-USER 6 > (aref *)
((1 2 4 8) (1 3 9 27))
```

The last one is an array of rank zero, which is further explained in Recipe 5-3.

Again, there's no way to specify fill pointers or other array amenities as described in Chapter 5.

The Usual Warning

Please read Recipe 8-2 if you haven't done so already. Don't mistake the literal vector/array notation as a shortcut for a call to MAKE-ARRAY. Again, never modify literal objects!

8-5. Understanding the Different Ways to Refer to a Function

Problem

If you want to refer to a function by name, you can prepend a simple quote to the name or a sharpsign followed by a quote. You want to know if there's a difference and if so, what it is.

Solution

There is indeed a big difference:

```
* (defun foo (x) (+ x 42))
FOO
* (flet ((foo (x) (1+ x)))
    (list (funcall 'foo 0) (funcall #'foo 0)))
(42 1)
* (funcall #'foo 0)
42
```

This clearly shows that `'` and `#'` mean entirely different things, and also that `#'` seems to change its meaning depending on the context. Read on for an explanation of what's happening.

How It Works

It is actually not the Lisp reader that makes the difference here, but for most people, the potential confusion manifests itself as the distinction between `'` and `#'`. That's why this recipe ended up in the chapter about syntax.

There are lots of functions in the standard, which—like `FUNCALL`—accept as one of their arguments a so-called *function designator*. This can be either the function itself or its *name*. As for the function itself, you will certainly know that functions are first-class objects in COMMON LISP and can be passed around like numbers, lists, or any other kind of object. And names are, of course, symbols, so that, for example, the function defined with `DEFUN` in the preceding example has as its name the symbol `FOO`.

But how do you get the actual function (as an object), given its name? That's what (the special operator) `FUNCTION` is for; it accepts as its only argument a symbol[12] and

[12]It'll also accept *lambda expressions*, but you'll probably never need that.

returns the function named by this symbol. #' is just syntactical sugar; #'FOO is a convenient abbreviation for (FUNCTION FOO), just like 'FOO is an abbreviation for (QUOTE FOO).

The tricky part in the example above is where this name is looked up if there are several competing function definitions using the same name. Except that it's not really tricky; it's a *lexical* lookup where the innermost lexical definition (by means of FLET or LABELS[13]) "wins" if there is one. Otherwise (that's the third form in our example), the global function with the same name is used—if there is one, of course.

If, on the other hand, you're using a symbol as a function designator, local functions are ignored, and the name will always refer to a global function definition.

8-6. Repeating Something You Already Typed

Problem

You need to repeat exactly the same form that already appears somewhere else in your code.

Solution

The Lisp reader offers a facility to "record" forms and "replay" them later. Here's a toy example:

```
(+ #1=21 #1#)
```

The result will be 42, although you obviously typed 21 only once and there are no variables involved.

How It Works

An important mantra of programming is "DRY"—*Don't Repeat Yourself.* Whenever you catch yourself typing the same thing again and again, you should consider rolling whatever you're doing into a function or macro. But sometimes this won't do, or a function would be too much overhead. An example would be a DO loop where one of your variables is supposed to be set from a function call on each iteration.

[13]With the caveat that MACROLET is also relevant here. If you were to nest a MACROLET inside the body of a LABELS or FLET, and if you'd use the same name for a local macro as for a local function defined in an enclosing form, you wouldn't be able to access the function anymore.

If your variable is X and your function is PREPARE-AND-COMPUTE-THE-NEXT-VALUE, then your loop will start like this:[14]

```
(do ((x (prepare-and-compute-the-next-value)
        (prepare-and-compute-the-next-value))
     ;; more
```

However, you could achieve the same effect (resulting in exactly the same code) like so:

```
(do ((x #42=(prepare-and-compute-the-next-value) #42#)
     ;; more
```

The #42= part instructs the compiler to read the form following the equals sign and to remember it with the number (42 in this case) you specified. If it later sees #42# (which can happen more than once), this is *as if* you had typed the form it remembered again.

This will always work provided that the Lisp reader hasn't already finished reading the outermost form containing the #*n*= part before it encounters the reference. So, this will work:

```
(defun foo ()
  (let ((a (list #2='foo))
        (b (list #2# #2#)))
    (append a b)))
```

The reference is within a different form than the definition, but the reader won't "forget" the definition before it has read the whole DEFUN form. It won't work to have a definition like this immediately following FOO's definition, though:

```
(defun bar ()
  (list #2# 'bar))
```

A clever way to employ this syntax is to construct endless lists:

```
(let ((a '#1=(10 . #1#)))
  (nth 42 a))
```

The cool thing here is that the reader allows us to play this game: at the point where it encounters the #1# reference, the #1= isn't even finished. Still, the effect is as if you had written

```
(let ((a '(10 . (10 . (10 . (10 . (10 . (10 . (10 . ;; ad infinitum
```

[14]With LOOP, you'd just write (LOOP FOR X = (PREPARE-AND-COMPUTE-THE-NEXT-VALUE) ...).

instead.[15]

In Recipe 14-13 and on page 180 you can see how the Lisp printer can utilize this syntax in useful ways.

They Don't Only Look Identical, They Are Identical!

The syntax described in this recipe is not only about what the reader *sees*. Technically, it constructs an object whenever it reads a form and it will remember this *object* (as opposed to just the sequence of symbols). So, compare these two experiments:

```
CL-USER 1 > (let ((a '(1 2 3))
                  (b '(1 2 3)))
              (list (equal a b) (eq a b)))
;; result is implementation-dependent
(T NIL)
CL-USER 2 > (let ((a #1='(1 2 3))
                  (b #1#))
              (list (equal a b) (eq a b)))
(T T)
```

The two lists in the first example are literal constants, but they are two *different* literal constants in most implementations; as demonstrated by `EQ` returning `NIL` above.[16] In the second example, the compiler will—for `#1#`—really substitute the literal value it already used. This is subtly different from just typing the same form twice and it is potentially dangerous (although only in conjunction with literal values, which are dangerous to begin with; see Recipe 8-2).

8-7. Safely Experimenting with Readtables

Problem

You want to experiment with the syntax of your Lisp, but you want an escape hatch as well.

Solution

To change the syntax, you modify the *current readtable*, which is stored in the vari-

[15] See also Recipe 7-6.

[16] Although the compiler is allowed to *coalesce* them (see chapter 3 of the HyperSpec) which would mean that the first form *could* return `(T T)`.

able *READTABLE*. Luckily, you can use COPY-READTABLE to work on a copy of the standard readtable if you're afraid of clobbering it. You can even get back to normal Lisp syntax if you didn't make a copy.

How It Works

Everything that *can* be changed syntax-wise (but see below) is stored in an opaque object of type READTABLE. Whenever the Lisp reader reads something, it interprets it according to the *current* readtable, which is stored in the global special variable *READTABLE*. All functions that modify the syntax (examples will follow in subsequent recipes) modify a readtable and by default they modify the current readtable.

Modifying the readtable is potentially dangerous; in the worst case you might paint yourself into a corner where you can't enter anything meaningful anymore. You might therefore be tempted to follow a typical Lisp idiom and try something like

```
(let ((*readtable* (my-new-readtable)))
  ;; experiment with new readtable
  )
```

where MY-NEW-READTABLE would be a function returning a new, modified readtable, and the body of the LET would contain forms using your new syntax.

But while it is true that *READTABLE* will be back to its normal, unchanged self after the LET has been evaluated, the switch to your new readtable will have no effect whatsoever on the forms in the body of the LET, as they will have already been read before execution starts.[17]

If you really want to try out syntax modifications interactively, the right idiom is something like this:

```
CL-USER 1 > (setf *readtable* (copy-readtable))
#<READTABLE 200AD00F>
;; now change the current readtable
;; and afterward enter forms to try out your new syntax
CL-USER 42 > (setf *readtable* (copy-readtable nil))
#<READTABLE 200B4D77>
```

This first form sets *READTABLE* to a copy of the current readtable, so any modifications you'll subsequently perform will be performed on the copy and not on the original readtable. COPY-READTABLE can make a copy of any readtable, but if it is

[17]The only way to perform tests this way would be with calls to functions like READ or READ-FROM-STRING in the LET body (see Recipe 8-1).

called with no arguments as above, the default is to use the current readtable; that is, `(COPY-READTABLE)` is equivalent to `(COPY-READTABLE *READTABLE*)`.[18]

But the argument to `COPY-READTABLE` can also be `NIL`,[19] which stands for the standard readtable—the one that's described by, you guessed it, the standard. This is required to always work; that is, you can clobber the *initial* readtable (which is in effect when you start your Lisp image), but the *standard* readtable can always be restored like this.[20]

Temporarily Switching to Standard IO Syntax

There's also a helpful macro called `WITH-STANDARD-IO-SYNTAX`. It evaluates its body with all global special variables which affect reading and printing (all variables with names starting with "`*READ`" or "`*PRINT`" as well as `*PACKAGE*`) reset to their defaults as defined by the standard. Here's a simple example:[21]

```
(with-input-from-string (in "10 10")
  (let ((*read-base* 16))
    (list (read in)
          (with-standard-io-syntax
            (read in)))))
```

When `READ` is called the first time, the Lisp reader expects to read hexadecimal numbers and thus interprets `10` as the (decimal) number `16`. But the second call to `READ` is wrapped with `WITH-STANDARD-IO-SYNTAX` and thus the second occurrence of `10` is read as a decimal.

A typical usage of this macro would be the serialization and de-serialization of data using the Lisp printer and reader (i.e., using functions like `PRINT` and `READ`). If you use `WITH-STANDARD-IO-SYNTAX` for serialization as well as for de-serialization later, you can be sure that you won't inadvertently use slightly different syntaxes for the two complimentary tasks.

By the way, if your implementation has other variables that control reading and/or printing, it is required by the standard to reset these to standard values as well if inside `WITH-STANDARD-IO-SYNTAX`. (And for some implementations, this macro can cause significant overhead, which might be an issue if you "switch back and forth" pretty often.)

---

[18]Unless, that is, you've done something very devious like changing the syntax of `*`.

[19]Technically, the argument is a *readtable designator*—similar to the function designators mentioned in Recipe 8-5. But that's a bit of a mouthful for such a simple concept.

[20]So, if you're just trying out things, you won't even need the first call to `COPY-READTABLE`.

[21]See Recipe 4-4 for more about `*READ-BASE*`.

8-8. Changing the Syntax Type of a Character

Problem

You want to change the syntax of one or more characters.

Solution

Use SET-SYNTAX-FROM-CHAR. Here's an example that makes the dollar sign another comment character like the semicolon:

```
* 'ab$c
AB$C
* (set-syntax-from-char #\$ #\;)
T
* 'ab$c
AB
;; see Recipe 8-7
* (setf *readtable* (copy-readtable))
;; implementation-dependent output
#<READTABLE 402001D193>
```

For a more useful example, see Recipe 3-12.

How It Works

To fully understand what's happening here, we have to make sense of what exactly the (Lisp) reader does when it reads what we typed (no matter if it reads from console input, from a file with Lisp code, or from any other character stream). It essentially reads the input, character by character, and builds internal objects out of it by grouping characters together. Some of the most basic internal objects that it builds are numbers and symbols, and these are represented as so-called *tokens*, sequences of characters. For example, if the reader encounters the input

```
foo
```

(i.e., the three letters `f`, `o`, and `o`) it views them as one token and interprets this token as the name of a symbol. Likewise, if its input is

```
1.s-4
```

it "sees" a token consisting of five characters denoting a floating-point number.

But how does it know where the token starts and where it ends? That's where *syntax types* come in. Each character has a specific syntax type (we'll discuss all of them in the next section) and for each character it reads, the reader decides what to do next depending on this syntax type. In the `FOO` example, the three letters are of syntax type *constituent* and the reader simply collects those until a character of another syntax type comes by; for example, whitespace or a comment sign. Only afterward does it combine the constituents seen so far to form a token. (And it then decides whether it has seen a symbol or a number—which is something we won't bother with now.)

The Six Syntax Types

So, what are these syntax types? We'll now list all of them and explain what they are for:[22]

constituent: Most characters (in particular all decimal digits and all letters of the Latin alphabet) are of this type. They are used when constructing tokens as described above. Collection of token constituents typically ends when a character of another syntax type is encountered (unless this character is an *escape* character).

whitespace: These characters—like the space character (ASCII Code 32), horizontal tabs (ASCII Code 9), or linefeeds (ASCII Code 10)—are simply skipped[23] when reading. But as their syntax type is *not* that of constituents, they serve to end token collection.

single escape: The only single escape character in the standard syntax is the backslash. When a single escape character is read while a token is constructed, the *next* character is interpreted as if it were a constituent character from the Latin alphabet, no matter what its actual syntax type might be:[24]

```
* (set-syntax-from-char #\$ #\\)
T
* 'a\$b$\c
A$B\\C
;; see Recipe 8-7
```

[22]We list six here. The standard, in section 2.1.4, also lists a syntax type *invalid*, but it mentions no character that actually has this syntax type, and from the wording in other sections, one can infer that *invalid* is merely a constituent trait. (Constituent traits are explained at the end of this recipe.)

[23]But see Recipe 8-11.

[24]You might have noticed a small detail in this example: when the symbol is printed after it has been read, the backslash is used as the escape character; although you might think the dollar sign could have been used as well.

And even if you change the syntax of the backslash character so that it *isn't* an escape character anymore, it will still be used as an escape character in output. This is because the Lisp printer will—if it tries to make its output *readable* (see Recipe 14-13)—assume the standard readtable (see Recipe 8-7) to be present.

```
* (setf *readtable* (copy-readtable))
;; implementation-dependent output
#<READTABLE 402001D193>
```

Here we made the dollar sign another single escape character and then constructed a symbol where we first (after the a) escaped the dollar sign with a backslash and then (after the b) the backslash with the dollar sign.

multiple escape: Like a single escape character, a multiple escape character can appear while a token is constructed. Its effect is that *all* characters following it up to the next escape character[25] will become alphabetic constituents of the token, no matter what syntax type they actually have:

```
* (set-syntax-from-char #\$ #\|)
T
* 'a$"()$c
A\"\(\)C
* 'a|"()$c
A\"\(\)C
;; see Recipe 8-7
* (setf *readtable* (copy-readtable))
;; implementation-dependent output
#<READTABLE 402001D193>
```

Here we made the dollar sign another multiple escape character and used it to escape three characters (the double quote character, followed by a pair of parentheses). Note how in the second version, one multiple escape character is used to end the "escape sequence" started by *another* multiple escape character.

terminating macro character: A macro character always has a *reader macro function* associated with it, which is called when such a character is read. As such a function can more or less do anything it wants, macro characters deserve their own recipe, which follows this one. Standard characters of this syntax type are, for example, double quote, parentheses, and commas.

non-terminating macro character: This is like a *terminating* macro character, except that while within a token it becomes a simple constituent (i.e., its reader macro function is *not* called). The only standard character of this type is sharpsign. This means that you can type something like `'f#o` to construct a symbol with the name `"F#O"`. This wouldn't work if, say, you'd use double quote instead of sharpsign.

[25] At this point, you might be wondering if I really wanted to say: "up to the next *multiple* escape character" and you're kind of right. However, even between multiple escape characters, single escape characters are still special. That's so you can type strange stuff like `'a|()\|()|b`—in case you ever need it...

How to Actually Change the Syntax Type

While these syntax types are all clearly defined, there's no direct way to ask for a character's syntax type nor is there a way to set its syntax type explicitly.[26] What you *can* do, though, is copy the syntax type of another character using the function SET-SYNTAX-FROM-CHAR. That's what we did in the examples above. In its full form, this function accepts two more arguments: the readtable to modify and the readtable to copy the syntax from. This last argument can be a *readtable designator* (see Recipe 8-7) and can thus be NIL in particular to denote the *standard* readtable.[27]

Our initial example looked like this:

```
* (set-syntax-from-char #\$ #\;)
```

This will not work as expected if you've already meddled with the readtable and the semicolon doesn't have its usual syntax anymore. What will always work is this:

```
* (set-syntax-from-char #\$ #\; *readtable* nil)
```

SET-SYNTAX-FROM-CHAR not only copies the syntax type of a character, in the case of macro characters it also copies reader macro functions and dispatch tables (see more in Recipes 8-9 and 8-10).

Some Things Never Change

By modifying the readtable, you can alter the behavior of COMMON LISP to a point where people will have difficulties recognizing it as a Lisp, or even as a programming language. However, there's one thing you can't change and that's the so-called *constituent trait* of a character. This is used by the reader to determine whether a token it just read is a symbol or a number, and if it is a number, what kind of number it is. These constituent traits are "hard-wired" into COMMON LISP, which means that, for example, you can make a semicolon a constituent character, but you won't be able to convince your Lisp to treat it (like the slash) as a *ratio marker* to separate numerators from denominators in rational numbers.

[26]Except, in a way, for macro characters. See the following recipes.

[27]So, if you have figure 2-7 of the HyperSpec handy, you'll always find a character to copy from if you need a specific syntax type.

8-9. Creating Your Own Reader Macros

Problem

You want to create your own reader macro for a specific task.

Solution

As an example, let's create a (very rough) syntax for literal hash tables using braces (which are simply constituents—see Recipe 8-8—in standard syntax):[28]

```
CL-USER 1 > (defun brace-reader (stream char)
              (declare (ignore char))
              (let ((hash (make-hash-table)))
                (loop for (key value)
                          on (read-delimited-list #\} stream t)
                          by #'cddr
                        do (setf (gethash key hash) value))
                hash))
BRACE-READER
CL-USER 2 > (set-macro-character #\{ 'brace-reader)
T
CL-USER 3 > (set-macro-character #\} (get-macro-character #\) nil))
T
CL-USER 4 > {:two 2 :five 5}
;; implementation-dependent output
#<EQL Hash Table{2} 40201BF823>
CL-USER 5 > (gethash :five *)
5
T
```

This is, of course, a very cheap example because it only creates EQL hash tables and it doesn't care about errors (like if you have an odd number of elements between the braces). Its only purpose is to illustrate the idea of a reader macro function.

How It Works

There's actually a lot of stuff happening here, so let's take things one by one:

We mentioned in Recipe 8-8 that the way numbers are interpreted (and distinguished from symbols) is something we can't change. But apart from that, there's no fixed

[28]See Recipe 16-11 for the meaning of *.

syntax for things like lists, strings, characters, comments, or other things. This is all actually realized with *reader macro functions*[29] (which are associated with macro characters) and can thus be changed at will.

We also already know that SET-SYNTAX-FROM-CHAR copies these reader macro functions. Thus the simplest way to set a reader macro function for a character is to use this function. We actually did that when we made the dollar sign a comment character on page 219. (So, there's no syntax type "comment character"—the semicolon is just a macro character that reads and throws away whatever follows it, up to the next line.) You could do the same for, say, double quote:

```
CL-USER 1 > (set-syntax-from-char #\! #\")
T
CL-USER 2 > !Hello World!
"Hello World"
```

But note that in both cases, it wasn't perfectly clear that this would work because we don't have access to the reader macro functions we copied. In a way we're just lucky that the reader macro function for double quote (which we copied) doesn't look for another occurrence of double quote to end the string, but rather for the character that triggered it.[30]

What Reader Macro Functions Do

So, the Lisp reader reads characters from a stream and constructs objects while it's doing that. Once it encounters a macro character, it hands it over to this character's reader macro function; and this function does the same: it reads characters from the stream and eventually terminates and gives an object back to the reader, which now is in control again (but will be further down the stream, where the reader macro function left off). That's why the first argument to a reader macro function is this very stream. Its second argument is the character that invoked it[31] and that was already consumed. This should explain the overall structure of the function BRACE-READER in our example.

BRACE-READER, in turn, calls the convenience function READ-DELIMITED-LIST which

[29]Unfortunately, we'll have to cope with this three-word construct throughout because technically a *reader macro* is something different.

[30]The standard itself mentions that this won't work as expected if you wanted to replace parentheses with, say, brackets. You might think it would suffice to copy the reader macro function from the open parenthesis, but it'll look for a closing *parenthesis* and not for a closing *bracket*. So you'll have to roll your own reader macro function instead of copying one—which is what this recipe is mainly about.

[31]This character can often be ignored, as in our example, but it might make sense to actually use it in the case of several macro characters sharing the same code. That's the reason our double quote example worked.

reads and constructs objects from the stream until it comes across a specific character (the closing brace in this case) and then returns all of these objects as a list.[32]

Note that to perform its task, READ-DELIMITED-LIST will, of course, call READ which in turn might call our reader macro function again recursively. This means that an input like

```
{:two 2 :inner-hash {:one 1 :foo 'foo}}
```

will actually work (creating an "outer" hash table with two keys and an "inner" hash table being one of the values of the "outer" one).

To associate BRACE-READER with the open brace character, we used the function SET-MACRO-CHARACTER. This function does two things: it changes the syntax of its first argument so that it becomes a macro character and it also sets the reader macro function for the character. (There's also an optional third argument to distinguish between *terminating* and *non-terminating* macro characters; see Recipe 8-8.)

At this point, we're mostly done. The one remaining issue is that so far the closing brace is a constituent character. This would mean that

```
{:two 2 :five 5 }
```

would work as expected while

```
{:two 2 :five 5}
```

wouldn't (because the reader, while inside a call to READ called from READ-DELIMITED-LIST, would interpret the two-character sequence 5} as *one* token).

So we have to change the syntax of the character #\} as well. There are several ways to do this, but a particularly elegant way is to make it a macro character and copy the reader macro function of the closing parenthesis. This function isn't usually called (the reader macro function of the opening parenthesis will have consumed the closing parenthesis already), but when it *is* called, it signals an error, which we simply reuse.[33]

We could have achieved this with SET-SYNTAX-FROM-CHAR, but we've used the example as an excuse to introduce GET-MACRO-CHARACTER, which, as you might have guessed, returns the reader macro function of a macro character.[34]

[32]The third argument to READ-DELIMITED-LIST is T, meaning that the function is not called as a standalone function but rather as part of a process involving the Lisp reader. In short, you should always call it like this from reader macro functions. The subtle details are explained in section 23.1.3.2 of the standard.

[33]Well, the error message might talk about a "parenthesis," while we'd rather see the word "brace" there, but let's leave it at that.

[34]And its second argument is again a readtable designator; see Recipe 8-7.

8-10. Working with Dispatching Macro Characters

Problem

You want to create (or modify) a dispatching macro character like the sharpsign (#) character.[35]

Solution

As a silly example, let's concoct a syntax extension where something starting with #? and ending with ? acts like the double quote syntax for strings but with the added "benefit" that you can use an *infix* argument to remove all characters with the corresponding character code from the string:

```
CL-USER 1 > (defparameter *string-reader*
              (get-macro-character #\" nil))
*STRING-READER*
CL-USER 2 > (set-dispatch-macro-character
             #\# #\?
             (lambda (stream sub-char infix)
               (let ((string
                       (funcall *string-reader* stream sub-char)))
                 (cond (infix (remove (code-char infix) string))
                       (t string)))))
;; output is implementation-dependent
#<anonymous interpreted function 223D12AA>
CL-USER 3 > #?abc?
"abc"
CL-USER 4 > (char-code #\a)
97
CL-USER 5 > #97?abcacba?
"bccb"
```

Note how in the beginning we "borrow" the reader macro function for double quote. This is explained in Recipe 8-9. The rest of what's happening here is explained below.

[35]This sign is called *sharpsign* in the COMMON LISP standard, but today we distinguish between the musical symbol and the one used in technical disciplines, which is usually called *number sign* or *hash sign*. I'm nevertheless using *sharpsign* throughout in order to be in accordance with the HyperSpec.

How It Works

There are only so many characters available that are suitable as macro characters[36] and you might be tempted to be thrifty with them when making changes to the syntax. That's what *dispatching* macro characters are for: they give you a chance to cram lots of different tasks into one macro character, which then *dispatches* to various other characters. And there's also the added benefit of automatic parsing of infix parameters; keep reading.

The only dispatching macro character in standard COMMON LISP is sharpsign and it is used for many different things, many of which are described in this book; see, for example, the literal array notation (Recipe 8-4) or complex numbers (Recipe 4-8).

So, how does it work? A dispatching macro character owns a *dispatch table*, which for every valid *sub-character*, tells it what to do (by means of a function). If, for example, something starts with `#A`, then the sharpsign is the dispatching macro character and `A` is the sub-character. The dispatch table associates `A` with a function responsible for implementing the syntax—literal array syntax in this case. But a bit more is actually happening: dispatching macro characters can also deal with decimal numbers between the dispatching character and the sub-character.[37] These numbers (called *infixes*) are parsed and handed over to the function of the sub-character, so (as you know from Recipe 8-4) you can also start with `#3A` (in this case meaning an array with rank 3).

To establish a character as a dispatching macro character, you call the function `MAKE-DISPATCH-MACRO-CHARACTER`.[38] It changes the character's syntax type (see Recipe 8-8) accordingly and provides it with an empty dispatch table. Or rather with a dispatch table giving meaningful error messages for characters that aren't yet known to be sub-characters: if you evaluate

```
(make-dispatch-macro-character #\!)
```

and then immediately afterward type `!a`, you get an error message. (And depending on your Lisp, you might see this message as soon as you type the `a`.)

In our example, there was no need to call `MAKE-DISPATCH-MACRO-CHARACTER`, as sharpsign is already a dispatching macro character in standard COMMON LISP, so we just added a new sub-character.

To establish a new sub-character for an existing dispatching macro character, you call `SET-DISPATCH-MACRO-CHARACTER`, as we did above. The function you have to provide is different from a reader macro function in two respects. First, its second

[36]Of course, with Unicode there are *lots* of different characters. But there probably aren't many that are convenient to type and at the same time not something you'd rather have as a constituent character.

[37]That's why decimal digits obviously don't make sense as sub-characters.

[38]You could also do this with `SET-SYNTAX-FROM-CHAR` (see Recipe 8-8), but that's rarely a good idea, because that would copy the entire dispatch table of the character you copied the syntax from.

argument is not the dispatching macro character but the sub-character (which, of course, makes sense). And second, it receives a third argument that is either the infix parameter mentioned above or NIL, if there is none.

8-11. Preserving Whitespace

Problem

You want to implement your own syntax using READ, but for your purposes, white-space can be significant while for READ it never is.

Solution

Use READ-PRESERVING-WHITESPACE instead of READ.

The point where the following two forms differ is marked by a comment:[39]

```
CL-USER 1 > (with-input-from-string (in "42  23")
              (read in)                                    ;; <--
              (list (read-char in)
                    (read-char in)))
(#\Space #\2)
CL-USER 2 > (with-input-from-string (in "42  23")
              (read-preserving-whitespace in)              ;; <--
              (list (read-char in)
                    (read-char in)))
(#\Space #\Space)
```

First, READ parsed the number 42. The space following the number was used to signal the end of the object. As it has syntax type whitespace (see Recipe 8-8), it serves no other purpose in standard COMMON LISP syntax and was thus discarded.

READ-PRESERVING-WHITESPACE is different in that it keeps the space. (It actually calls UNREAD-CHAR to put it back on the stream.)

How It Works

Whitespace is sometimes needed in COMMON LISP syntax, but only as a delimiter between tokens. As it serves no other purpose, it is thrown away by the Lisp reader

[39]There are two spaces between the numbers 42 and 23.

directly after it has been read. In particular, the reader doesn't care how much whitespace there is between objects and what characters the whitespace is composed of (which could be spaces, horizontal tabs, linefeeds, and so on).

If you have modified the syntax and need to know more about the spatial structure of whitespace between objects,[40] you should use the function READ-PRESERVING-WHITESPACE. It acts exactly like READ, except that it always leaves whitespace intact after reading an object.

You can also preserve whitespace if you're using READ-FROM-STRING. In this case, it's done with the :PRESERVE-WHITESPACE keyword parameter:

```
? (read-from-string "424242 ")
424242
7
? (read-from-string "424242 " t nil :preserve-whitespace t)
424242
6
```

Here the difference is in the second return value, which is 7 for READ and 6 for READ-PRESERVING-WHITESPACE.

[40]The dictionary entry for READ-PRESERVING-WHITESPACE has a good example for such a modification.

9. Printing

In languages like C++ or JAVA, it is possible to, say, write a huge GUI program without ever thinking about the printed representation of the objects (numbers, strings, arrays, etc.) that you're working with. This is quite different in COMMON LISP, where due to how one typically works when developing something, you're constantly seeing those objects being printed in the REPL.

This is why we're devoting a chapter to printing (while Chapter 8 deals with "the other half" of the REPL's front end). We'll cover the low-level building blocks like WRITE, as well as high-level facilities like the pretty printer. (The pretty printer is the subject of the last four recipes, starting with 9-9. If you've never worked with it before, you might want to read them in order.)

And then there's the notorious FORMAT function. *Practical Common Lisp*'s chapter 18[1] is modestly called "A Few FORMAT Recipes," but it really tells you pretty much everything you need to know about FORMAT for most tasks. In our treatment of FORMAT here, we'll thus assume that you have at least a working knowledge of it and we'll only discuss a few features that may not be so familiar to everyone.

9-1. Using the Printing Primitives

Problem

You want to understand the basic building blocks of the Lisp printer.

Solution

The "atomic" operation of the Lisp reader (see Chapter 8) is READ, which reads (the textual representation of) one *object* from a stream. Its counterpart is the function WRITE[2] which writes one object to a stream (by default to standard output):

```
CL-USER> (write 42)
42                                ;; <- printed to *STANDARD-OUTPUT*
```

[1]Available online at http://www.gigamonkeys.com/book/a-few-format-recipes.html.

[2]The corresponding directive for FORMAT would be "~W".

```
42                                        ;; <- return value
```

READ and WRITE are both integral parts of the REPL. However, WRITE is in a sense a lot more complex than READ because its behavior can be modified by 16 (!) keyword parameters and 15 global special variables. We'll try to make sense of this below.

How It Works

One of the keyword parameters of WRITE is :STREAM and it does what you expect:[3]

```
CL-USER> (with-output-to-string (out)
           (write 42 :stream out))
"42"
```

All the other 15 keyword parameters are paired with a special variable of the same name (but with "PRINT-" in front and asterisks around it), so, for example, the keyword parameter :CIRCLE is paired with the variable *PRINT-CIRCLE*, and so on. (These variables are called *printer control variables*.)

What WRITE will do depends on the values of the 15 special variables. And the effect of providing one of the keyword arguments is that the corresponding special variable will be bound to this argument during the call to WRITE (whereas otherwise, it'll remain unchanged). If, say, the value of *PRINT-BASE* (see Recipe 4-4) is currently 10, then while (WRITE *FOO*) is executed, *PRINT-BASE* will be bound to 10. But *PRINT-BASE* will be bound to 16 during the execution of (WRITE *FOO* :BASE 16):[4]

```
CL-USER> *print-base*
10
CL-USER> (write 42)
42
42
CL-USER> (write 42 :base 16)
2A
42
```

Now let's go through those 15 variables. We'll see that it's not as intimidating as it sounds:

[3]See Recipe 14-7 for WITH-OUTPUT-TO-STRING.

[4]In case you're wondering why the variables have to be (re-)bound at all, consider that—like READ—WRITE might call itself recursively, either directly or indirectly through calls of, say, PRINT-OBJECT (see Recipe 9-8).

See Recipe 10-3 for how keyword parameters like these can be implemented.

- `*PRINT-BASE*` and `*PRINT-RADIX*` control how integers are printed. This is explained in detail in Recipe 4-4.
- `*PRINT-CASE*` controls how symbols are printed (see Recipe 1-8).
- `*PRINT-GENSYM*` controls how uninterned symbols (see Recipe 1-2) are printed. If its value is `NIL`, they'll lose the "`#:`" prefix:

```
CL-USER> *print-gensym*
T
CL-USER> (write (gensym "FOO") :gensym nil)
FOO847
#:FOO847
```

- If `*PRINT-CIRCLE*` is true, then the printer is supposed to detect circularity (see more on page 180).
- Arrays are usually printed as shown in Chapter 5, but if `*PRINT-ARRAY*` is `NIL`, then they are shown in a special (implementation-dependent) way so that they can be identified, but their contents aren't shown (and they thus can't be read back in).[5]

```
CL-USER> *print-array*
T
CL-USER> (write #(1 2 3) :array nil)
#<(SIMPLE-VECTOR 3) {1005686F6F}>
#(1 2 3)
```

  Strings (see Chapter 3)—although they are also arrays—are not affected by this variable.

- `*PRINT-LEVEL*` and `*PRINT-LENGTH*` together control how structures built out of conses[6] (see Chapter 2) are printed. They are both initially set to `NIL`, which means that there are no limits. If `*PRINT-LENGTH*` is an integer, then it determines how much of a list will be printed before the rest will only be hinted at by dots:

```
CL-USER> *print-length*
NIL
CL-USER> (dolist (len '(nil 0 1 2 3 4 5))
           (write '(1 2 3 4 5) :length len)
           (terpri))
(1 2 3 4 5)
(...)
```

[5]See also `PRINT-UNREADABLE-OBJECT` on page 247.

[6]But not only those. See below.

```
(1 ...)
(1 2 ...)
(1 2 3 ...)
(1 2 3 4 ...)
(1 2 3 4 5)
NIL
```

This also applies to nested lists:

```
CL-USER> (write '(:foo (1 2 3 4 5)) :length 2)
(:FOO (1 2 ...))
(:FOO (1 2 3 4 5))
```

PRINT-LEVEL, on the other hand, determines how much—in terms of *depth*—of a nested cons structure (see Recipe 2-8) will be shown before the rest will be hinted at by a sharpsign:

```
CL-USER> *print-level*
NIL
CL-USER> (dolist (lev '(nil 0 1 2 3 4 5))
           (write '(1 (2) (2 (3)) (2 (3 (4))) (2 (3 (4 (5)))))
                  :level lev)
           (terpri))
(1 (2) (2 (3)) (2 (3 (4))) (2 (3 (4 (5)))))
#
(1 # # # #)
(1 (2) (2 #) (2 #) (2 #))
(1 (2) (2 (3)) (2 (3 #)) (2 (3 #)))
(1 (2) (2 (3)) (2 (3 (4))) (2 (3 (4 #))))
(1 (2) (2 (3)) (2 (3 (4))) (2 (3 (4 (5)))))
```

Note that above the list itself is at level 0 while, for example, its first element 1 is at level 1, and so on. The rule is that an object that is at level *n* is printed if *PRINT-LEVEL* has the value *n*, but *only* if it doesn't have components (which would by definition be at a higher level):

```
CL-USER> (write 42 :level 0)
42
42
CL-USER> (write '(42) :level 0)
#
(42)
```

Both variables also affect other objects printed in "list-like syntax:"

```
CL-USER> (write #(1 2 3) :length 2)
#(1 2 ...)
#(1 2 3)
CL-USER> (defstruct foo a b)
FOO
CL-USER> (write (make-foo) :length 1)
#S(FOO :A NIL ...)
#S(FOO :A NIL :B NIL)
```

- The variables *PRINT-LINES*, *PRINT-MISER-WIDTH*, *PRINT-RIGHT-MARGIN*, and *PRINT-PPRINT-DISPATCH* are only relevant to the pretty printer which in turn is "switched on" by *PRINT-PRETTY* (see Recipe 9-9).

Printing Objects So That They Can Be Read Back in Again

There are two variables that we haven't covered so far, as they deserve their own subsection: *PRINT-ESCAPE* and *PRINT-READABLY*.

For several types of objects, *PRINT-ESCAPE* determines whether they are printed in such a way that they can be read back in again.[7] If its value is NIL, then the necessary escape characters won't be printed, otherwise they will:

```
CL-USER> *print-escape*
T
CL-USER> (write #\X :escape nil)
X
#\X
CL-USER> (write :x :escape nil)
X
:X
CL-USER> (write "X" :escape nil)
X
"X"
CL-USER> (write #p"X" :escape nil)
X
#P"X"
```

Up to this point, we have seen a lot of printer control variables that can affect whether objects are printed in a reader-compatible way; not only *PRINT-ESCAPE*, but also

[7]To be more precise, whether an *attempt* to do that is made. Also, when we say that *they* can be read back in, the intended meaning is that the object read is EQUAL (see Recipe 10-1) to the one that was printed.

PRINT-ARRAY, *PRINT-GENSYM*, *PRINT-LENGTH*, and *PRINT-LEVEL*.[8]

PRINT-READABLY is kind of a "meta variable," which if set to a true value has two effects:[9]

A) During printing the variables just mentioned will all be treated *as if* they had been set to print readably. (So, *PRINT-LENGTH* will, for example, be treated as if its value were NIL.)

B) If an attempt is made to print an object that can't be printed readably, an error is signaled.

For example:

```
CL-USER> (setq *print-length* 2)
2
CL-USER> '(1 2 3)
(1 2 ...)
CL-USER> (setq *print-readably* t)
T
CL-USER> '(1 2 3)
(1 2 3)
CL-USER> *print-length*
2
```

Now, what happens if you type (MAKE-HASH-TABLE) at this point? It depends. Some implementations signal an error, whereas others are able to print the hash table in a readable way (see also page 428.)

Shortcuts

Because some settings are fairly common, there are several shortcuts available:

Shortcut	Equivalent to
(PRINC <obj>)	(WRITE <obj> :ESCAPE NIL :READABLY NIL)
(PRIN1 <obj>)	(WRITE <obj> :ESCAPE T)
(PRINT <obj>)	(PROGN (TERPRI) (PRIN1 <obj>) (WRITE-CHAR #\Space))
(PPRINT <obj>)	(PROGN (TERPRI) (WRITE <obj> :ESCAPE T :PRETTY T))

As a rule of thumb, PRINC should be used to generate output for humans, whereas PRIN1's output is intended for the Lisp reader. PRINT and PPRINT (see Recipe 9-9) are

[8] And also the pretty printer variable *PRINT-LINES*.

[9] And in addition, the outcome is also affected by the value of *READ-EVAL* (see Recipe 8-3). Look up the details in the standard.

variants of PRIN1; they only differ in how whitespace is arranged between objects.

All of these shortcut functions accept a second optional argument which is used as the :STREAM keyword argument to WRITE.

9-2. Printing to and into Strings

Problem

You want to generate (formatted) output that ends up in a string. Or maybe you want such output to appear within an *existing* string.

Solution

There are various ways to do that. Let's look at some examples first and then discuss the details below (where we'll also see how to "cheat" our output into another string):

```
CL-USER> (list (write-to-string 42)
               (format nil "~A" 42)
               (with-output-to-string (out)
                 (format out "~A" 42)))
("42" "42" "42")
```

How It Works

If you want your output to end up as a string, there are essentially three ways of doing it, which were demonstrated above:

- You can use NIL as the destination of FORMAT. While FORMAT usually sends its output *to* the destination and *returns* NIL, in this case it sends its output to a newly created string and returns that.
- You can use a *string stream* which can be used anywhere where a stream can be used but collects the output into a string that you can eventually obtain. This is explained in Recipe 14-7.
- The low-level printing functions WRITE, PRINC, and PRIN1 (see Recipe 9-1) have variants in which their names end with "-TO-STRING" and that return their output as a string.

What all the examples have in common so far is that they create a *new* string for their output. But you can also use *existing* strings. And there are again two ways to do that:

One way is with string streams. Recipe 14-7 shows that a string stream can be created from an existing string if it has a *fill pointer*.[10] This means that if your existing stream has a fill pointer, you can use a combination of WITH-OUTPUT-TO-STRING and moving the fill pointer to generate output anywhere in your string:

```
CL-USER> (defparameter *s*
           (make-array 25
                       :element-type 'character
                       :fill-pointer t
                       :initial-contents "Here please: __.  Thanks!"))
*S*
CL-USER> *s*
"Here please: __.  Thanks!"
CL-USER> (setf (fill-pointer *s*) 13)
13
CL-USER> *s*
"Here please: "
CL-USER> (with-output-to-string (out *s*)
           (princ 42 out))
42
CL-USER> *s*
"Here please: 42"
CL-USER> (setf (fill-pointer *s*) 25)
25
CL-USER> *s*
"Here please: 42.  Thanks!"
```

And there's even a nice shortcut for this where you don't need to create an intermediate string stream: FORMAT accepts a string with a fill pointer as its destination and treats it as if a string stream were wrapped around it:

```
;; continued from above
CL-USER> (setf (fill-pointer *s*) 13)
13
CL-USER> (format *s* "~D" 23)
NIL
CL-USER> (setf (fill-pointer *s*) 25)
25
CL-USER> *s*
```

[10]See Recipe 5-6 for information about fill pointers.

```
"Here please: 23.  Thanks!"
```

Now, that is all fine and dandy, but what if the string you want to write to doesn't have a fill pointer? Even that problem can be overcome: just create *another* string *with* a fill pointer that is *displaced*[11] to the original string:[12]

```
CL-USER> (defparameter *s* (copy-seq "Here please: __.  Thanks!"))
*S*
CL-USER> (let ((s (make-array (length *s*)
                              :element-type 'character
                              :fill-pointer 13
                              :displaced-to *s*)))
           (format s "~D" 42))
NIL
CL-USER> *s*
"Here please: 42.  Thanks!"
```

9-3. Printing NIL As a List

Problem

NIL is both a symbol as well as one way of representing the empty list. Depending on the context it can sometimes make sense to print it as () instead of NIL.

Solution

FORMAT can do that:

```
CL-USER> (format nil "~A" nil)
"NIL"
CL-USER> (format nil "~:A" nil)
"()"
```

How It Works

With the "~A" directive (and also with "~S"), FORMAT prints NIL as () if the colon modifier is used. However, this unfortunately does not work with *nested* occurrences

[11] See Recipe 5-8.

[12] Depending on the version, you might have to use a different element type on LISPWORKS. See the section about character and string types in the *Internationalization* chapter of their documentation.

of NIL:

```
CL-USER> (format nil "~:A" '(()))
"(NIL)"
```

Likewise, there's no portable way to convince the Lisp printer (see Recipe 9-1) to print NIL as (). Although 22.1.3.3 of the standard says that NIL *might* be printed as () when *PRINT-PRETTY* is true and printer escaping is enabled, the implementations I tried all insisted on printing NIL.

9-4. Extending FORMAT Control Strings Over More Than One Line

Problem

You have a complicated FORMAT control string that you'd rather distribute over several lines for legibility, but you don't want to introduce arbitrary line breaks into the output.

Solution

Just add a tilde to each input line break that you don't want to be an output line break:

```
CL-USER> (format nil "~A
~A" 42 23)
"42
23"
CL-USER> (format nil "~A~
~A" 42 23)
"4223"
```

How It Works

That's not a trick but it's actually a FORMAT directive, namely a tilde followed by a newline character. This directive is also "clever" enough to ignore any whitespace following the newline:

```
CL-USER> (format nil "~A~
                      ~A" 42 23)
"4223"
```

If you don't want that, you have to tell it using the colon modifier:

```
CL-USER> (format nil "~A~:
                      ~A" 42 23)
"42                   23"
```

9-5. Using Functions As FORMAT Controls

Problem

A function wants a format control as an argument and you want to use your own (custom) formatting function instead.

Solution

There are several functions in the standard[13] and also in open source libraries which want as arguments a *format control* and some *format arguments* that are supposed to be fed to FORMAT.

As an example, let's construct a simple case of such a function:

```
(defun my-report (fmt-ctrl &rest fmt-args)
  (with-output-to-string (out)
    (format out "Report: ")
    (apply #'format out fmt-ctrl fmt-args)))
```

The *format control* that's typically expected is a string that would also be suitable as the second argument to FORMAT:

```
(my-report "All was ~A today." :fine)
```

However, a format control can also be a function as returned by FORMATTER:

```
(let ((fmt-ctrl (formatter "All was ~A today.")))
  (my-report fmt-ctrl :ok))
```

And it can even be an arbitrary function as long as it follows certain argument conventions:

```
(let ((fmt-ctrl (lambda (stream adjective)
                  (write-string "All was " stream)
```

[13]For example Y-OR-N-P, BREAK, or ERROR.

```
                (princ adjective stream)
                (write-string " today." stream))))
  (my-report fmt-ctrl 'cool))
```

How It Works

Sometimes, providing a string as a format control doesn't seem to be the right thing. The string might be too complicated and look like line noise, or you might encounter performance problems,[14] or you might even run into a situation where FORMAT isn't powerful enough. (Although the latter is hard to imagine; see specifically Recipe 9-6. Let's say you *think* FORMAT isn't powerful enough.)

That's what the macro FORMATTER is for; its only argument is a format control string that it transforms into a function. This function accepts a stream as its first argument, and it "does to the stream and its other arguments what FORMAT would have done," so to say.

For example, the return value of

```
(formatter "~A")
```

will *essentially*[15] be a function that does this:

```
(lambda (stream arg)
  (princ arg stream))
```

As an aside and for educational purposes, you might want to use DISASSEMBLE (see Recipe 17-12) to see what your compiler does if it encounters a constant format control string. For example, both LISPWORKS and SBCL compile a function like

```
(defun foo (arg)
  (format t "~A" arg))
```

essentially as if it had been written like so in the first place:[16]

```
(defun foo (arg)
  (princ arg))
```

[14]Because the format control string has to be parsed and interpreted anew by FORMAT each time the function is called.

[15]Not exactly, though, but the differences will only become apparent once you provide too many or too few arguments to this function (see footnote 17).

[16]This probably means that they have a *compiler macro* for FORMAT, which comes into effect if the format control is a constant string and does the equivalent of converting (FORMAT T "~A" ARG) into (FORMAT T (FORMATTER "~A") ARG) (see Recipe 17-9).

But back to FORMATTER. Its output—the function it returns—is acceptable as a second argument to FORMAT; that is, it *is* a format control. What's less obvious, but clearly specified in the standard, is that *any* function that treats its arguments in the same way[17] is a valid format control. And that's what we took advantage of in our example. This can also be combined with recursive processing of format controls (see Recipe 9-7).

9-6. Creating Your Own FORMAT Directives

Problem

You want your own FORMAT directives in addition to "~A", "~D", "~[", and friends.

Solution

It's not really possible to add new directives or to change what existing directives do. But there's a way out. The "~/" directive allows you to call arbitrary functions of your choosing from within a FORMAT control.

We'll start with a simple example here and will then use a more realistic one below. The idea is that you first create a function that'll accept a stream and a second argument and that'll write something to the stream based on that second argument. Here's a function which simply doubles whatever it receives:

```
CL-USER> (defun twice (stream arg &rest other-args)
           (declare (ignore other-args))
           (format stream "~A~:*~A" arg))
TWICE
CL-USER> (twice *standard-output* 42)
4242
NIL
```

Don't worry about OTHER-ARGS for now, we'll talk about that later.

Here's how we can use the new function from FORMAT:

```
CL-USER> (format nil "~A~/twice/~A"  #\b #\o #\t)
"boot"
```

So, the "~/" directive works like this: whatever follows the slash is used, up to the next slash and after upcasing, as the name of a function to call. This function is

[17] Roughly, the first argument is the stream and the following arguments should be processed in order with the unused ones returned, if any. See the HyperSpec entry for FORMATTER for details.

then applied to the argument corresponding to the directive (which here was the character #\o).

But "real" directives can also receive *modifiers* and *parameters*, right? Read on...

How It Works

For our "real" example, let's first create a new package:[18]

```
CL-USER> (defpackage :iso-8601 (:export :date))
#<PACKAGE "ISO-8601">
```

Now define the following function which is supposed to write an ISO 8601 representation of a universal time[19] to a stream:

```
(defun iso-8601:date (stream universal-time
                             colon-p at-sign-p &rest params)
  (multiple-value-bind (sec min hour date mon year day dst zone)
      (decode-universal-time universal-time (first params))
    (declare (ignore day dst))
    (format stream "~4,'0D-~2,'0D-~2,'0D" year mon date)
    (unless colon-p
      (format stream "T~2,'0D:~2,'0D:~2,'0D" hour min sec)
      (when at-sign-p
        (multiple-value-bind (quo rem)
            (truncate zone)
          (format stream "~:[+~;-~]~2,'0D:~2,'0D"
                  (minusp quo) (abs quo)
                  (floor (abs (* rem 60)))))))))
```

In case you don't understand what the directives in this function do, this would be a good time to brush up your FORMAT-fu (see this chapter's introduction.) We'll briefly summarize what's important:

- The function has four required arguments of which we already know the first two; the stream to write to and the one argument corresponding to the directive.
- The other two arguments are, as their names suggest, booleans for whether the colon and/or the at-sign modifiers were used with the "~/" directive that called the function.
- Likewise, all the following arguments to the function, if any, correspond to the parameters given to the directive.

[18]See Chapter 1.

[19]See Chapter 22.

- If the colon modifier is used, we print the time, otherwise we only print the date.
- If in addition to that, the at-sign modifier is used, we also print the time zone.
- We accept the time zone as the first (and only) parameter for the directive, and if it's present, we use it in the call to DECODE-UNIVERSAL-TIME.

Let's make sure the function works as expected:

```
CL-USER> (loop with time = (get-universal-time)
               for fmt-ctl in '("~/iso-8601:date/"
                                "~@/iso-8601:date/"
                                "~:/iso-8601:date/"
                                "~5@/iso-8601:date/"
                                "~-3/iso-8601:date/")
                 collect (format nil fmt-ctl time))
;; output edited for legibility
("2015-08-28T13:00:07"
 "2015-08-28T13:00:07-01:00"
 "2015-08-28"
 "2015-08-28T06:00:07+05:00"
 "2015-08-28T14:00:07")
```

We also see now that we can use package-qualified symbol names between the slashes. To be precise, the function name between the slashes can be any sequence of characters except for a slash. And the first colon (or double-colon) encountered is used as the package marker.

So, with "~/", you can extend FORMAT in almost arbitrary ways, except that you can't create "directives," which can consume a variable number of arguments or which "jump around" in the list of arguments.

For more customization, see Recipes 9-5 and 9-7.

9-7. Recursive Processing of FORMAT Controls

Problem

A part of a larger FORMAT control is only known at run time.

Solution

You can use the "~?" directive for that. This works as if the directive itself had been replaced with its argument (which must be a format control). In the simplest version this looks like so:

```
CL-USER> (format nil "X~?Y" "~%" nil)
"X
Y"
```

Here the "~?" was replaced by the "~%" directive, which eventually produced a line break.

Note that we needed the final NIL there. This is because, other than "~%", directives usually consume arguments; so "~?" always wants two arguments and the second one should be a list that will become the list of arguments for the substitute format control fragment. Here's a more elaborate example:

```
CL-USER> (format nil "X~?~A" "~A~A" '(Y Z) :W)
"XYZW"
```

How It Works

That's all there is to this directive, except for the fact that you can alternatively let the inserted control fragment work on the original list of arguments by using the at-sign modifier. Compare this one to the previous example:

```
CL-USER> (format nil "X~@?~A" "~A~A" :Y :Z :W)
"XYZW"
```

This can also be nested:

```
CL-USER> (format nil "X~@?~A" "~A~@?" :Y "~A~A" :Z :W :V)
"XZYWV"
```

You just have to make sure to not confuse yourself too much with too many levels of recursion...

Finally, the format control can also be a function, as we have seen in Recipe 9-5:

```
CL-USER> (let ((fmt (formatter "~A~@?")))
           (format nil "X~@?~A" fmt :Y "~A~A" :Z :W :V))
"XYZWV"
```

9-8. Controlling How Your Own Objects Are Printed

Problem

You have created your own class of CLOS objects and want them to have a specific appearance when printed.

Solution

If you define your own CLOS class (see Chapter 13), the instances of this class are usually printed in a certain way that is implementation-dependent but usually very similar across different Lisps:

```
CL-USER> (defclass foo () ((bar :initarg :bar)))
#<STANDARD-CLASS FOO>
CL-USER> (make-instance 'foo)
#<FOO {10063FE7A3}>
```

What you'll get is the name of the class (which is `FOO` here) and some unique identifier (so that two different objects can be distinguished) wrapped with angle brackets.

The opening angle bracket is actually a *sub-character* of the *dispatching macro character* sharpsign (see Recipe 8-10) and its only job is to signal an error in case you want to read something that starts with these two characters. Try this and you'll get an error:

```
(read-from-string (prin1-to-string (make-instance 'foo)))
```

"Behind the scenes," the implementation uses `WRITE` (see Recipe 9-1) to print your object which in turn calls the generic function `PRINT-OBJECT`. There is a predefined method of `PRINT-OBJECT` for standard objects, but the whole point of this generic function, of course, is that you can specialize it for your own objects if you want.

Let's start with a method that does exactly what we had before:

```
(defmethod print-object ((object foo) stream)
  (print-unreadable-object (object stream :type t :identity t)))
```

Here we're using the convenience macro `PRINT-UNREADABLE-OBJECT` which creates the typical `#<...>` output we've already seen:

```
CL-USER> (make-instance 'foo)
#<FOO {10041F92A3}>
```

Experiment with using `NIL` for the `:TYPE` or the `:IDENTITY` keyword argument or for both to see how this affects the output.

Now for something a bit more interesting. Let's expose the contents of the BAR slot when printing a FOO object:

```
(defmethod print-object ((object foo) stream)
  (print-unreadable-object (object stream :type t :identity t)
    (format stream "(BAR: ~S)" (slot-value object 'bar))))
```

It should now look like so:

```
CL-USER> (make-instance 'foo :bar 42)
#<FOO (BAR: 42) {10047A37A3}>
```

But you can essentially do whatever you want in your own printing method (see Recipe 2-10 for another example.)

How It Works

Specializing PRINT-OBJECT for you own classes is a bit like implementing your own toString method in JAVA; you get to control the textual representation of your objects. (Which is a good thing. You should generally write PRINT-OBJECT methods for all classes you define, because that will help a lot when you're debugging your code and inspecting your data.)

For something a bit more interesting let's try this:

```
CL-USER> (defvar *last-id* 0)
*LAST-ID*
CL-USER> (defclass tag ()
           ((name :initarg :name
                  :reader name)
            (contents :initarg :contents
                      :initform "" :reader contents)
            (id :initform (incf *last-id*)
                :reader id)))
#<STANDARD-CLASS TAG>
CL-USER> (defmethod print-object ((tag tag) stream)
           (format stream "<~A id='~A'>~A</~3:*~A>"
                   (name tag) (id tag) (contents tag)))
#<STANDARD-METHOD PRINT-OBJECT (TAG T) {1005D27563}>
CL-USER> (make-instance 'tag :name 'foo)
<FOO id='1'></FOO>
CL-USER> (make-instance 'tag :name 'bar :contents *)
<BAR id='2'><FOO id='1'></FOO></BAR>
```

This demonstrated two things:

- Of course, you don't have to use the PRINT-UNREADABLE-OBJECT macro. You just have to write something meaningful to the stream.
- When our PRINT-OBJECT method printed the second object, it called itself recursively to print the first one.[20]

However, our method from above is slightly wrong because it doesn't observe the settings of certain special variables, which are explained in Recipe 9-1. Consider this:

```
CL-USER> (setq *print-readably* t)
NIL
CL-USER> (make-instance 'tag :name 'baz)
<BAZ id='3'></BAZ>
```

We should get an error message here because what was printed is clearly not readable. But it would have been the job of the method to signal the error. That's one of the things PRINT-UNREADABLE-OBJECT does automatically; and if you don't use it, you must implement it yourself.[21]

The alternative in this case would, of course, have been to print the objects in a readable way to begin with. You should try that as an exercise.

By the way, your Lisp also uses PRINT-OBJECT internally whenever it prints built-in objects like numbers, lists, and so forth. It might be tempting to redefine such a method, and this will indeed work in some Lisps. But there's no way to make this work in a portable way.[22] The situation is different for pretty printing, though (see Recipe 9-12).

9-9. Controlling the Pretty Printer

Problem

You want to control how structured data is printed, for example, in the REPL.

Solution

The pretty printer is switched on and off using the *printer control variable*[23] *PRINT-PRETTY*, and a shortcut for switching it on temporarily is the function PPRINT.

[20]Technically, due to the "~A" directive, it was as if PRINC (see Recipe 9-1) had been called for the CONTENTS slot, which in turn is a shortcut for WRITE with certain parameters. And WRITE eventually called PRINT-OBJECT.

[21]For other printer control variables you need to observe, see the HyperSpec entry for PRINT-OBJECT.

[22]See #19 of 11.1.2.1.2 in the standard for why this is so.

[23]See Recipe 9-1.

Three other printer control variables specifically influence the "active area" of the pretty printer. They are `*PRINT-MISER-WIDTH*`, `*PRINT-RIGHT-MARGIN*`, and `*PRINT-LINES*`, and their impact can be outlined like so:[24]

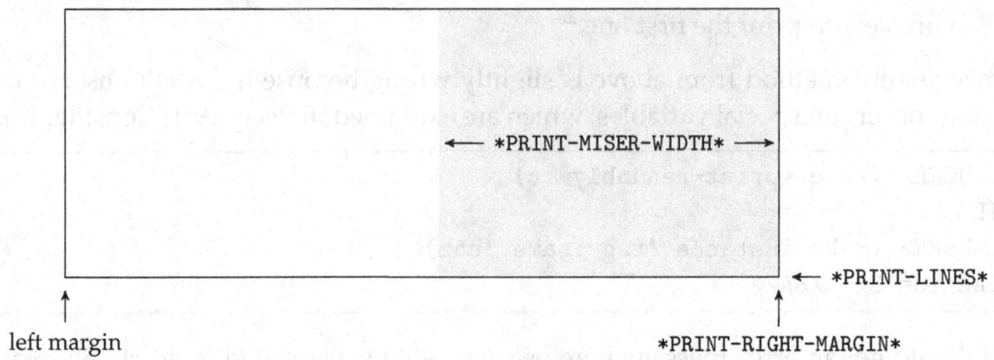

How It Works

As I already said in this chapter's introduction, the printer is of particular importance in Lisp because you work with it all the time in the REPL. This becomes especially relevant once you're looking at larger nested data structures. It is the job of the *pretty printer* to help you with this. (And its name is a bit misleading, as whether its output is really *pretty* is, of course, subjective. It is rather trying to *structure* the output within given constraints.)

To make this a bit more concrete, let's work with *Calkin-Wilf trees*, which we'll create using this recursive function:[25]

```
(defun calkin-wilf (value levels)
  (if (zerop levels)
    value
    (let* ((numerator (numerator value))
           (denominator (denominator value))
           (sum (+ numerator denominator)))
      (list value
            (calkin-wilf (/ numerator sum) (1- levels))
            (calkin-wilf (/ sum denominator) (1- levels))))))
```

Let's see what this function gives us:[26]

[24] As a side note, the first two and other things in the description of the pretty printer are measured in units of *ems*; that is, the standard actually meant this to work with variable-width fonts as well. In this chapter, I will assume that the fonts have fixed width, though.

[25] You don't need to care about what this function does, as we'll only use it to generate some nested S-expressions (see also page 652).

[26] The following results are from SBCL. Implementations have some leeway with respect to pretty printing and thus your mileage may vary.

```
CL-USER> (setq *print-pretty* nil)
NIL
CL-USER> (calkin-wilf 1 4)
(1 (1/2 (1/3 (1/4 1/5 5/4) (4/3 4/7 7/3)) (3/2 (3/5 3/8 8/5) ...
```

Note that we first set `*PRINT-PRETTY*` to `NIL` because the standard doesn't define its initial value. (And indeed, in some Lisps it's `T` on startup and in others it's `NIL`.)

What you'll typically see is something like above where the dots mean that this list is actually longer. This is not very helpful as it doesn't reveal the structure of the data. This is better:[27]

```
CL-USER> (let ((*print-right-margin* 30)
               (*print-miser-width* nil))
           (pprint (calkin-wilf 1 4)))
;; 456789012345678901234567890 <- the first 30 columns
(1
 (1/2
  (1/3 (1/4 1/5 5/4)
   (4/3 4/7 7/3))
  (3/2 (3/5 3/8 8/5)
   (5/2 5/7 7/2)))
 (2
  (2/3 (2/5 2/7 7/5)
   (5/3 5/8 8/3))
  (3 (3/4 3/7 7/4)
   (4 4/5 5))))
; No value
```

We did two things here. One was that we "switched on" pretty printing by temporarily setting `*PRINT-PRETTY*` to a true value. (This is what `PPRINT` does.) The second change is that we asked the pretty printer to not use more than 30 columns if possible. (The other variable we'll come to in a minute.) It was thus forced to insert line breaks. And as a consequence, it indented the list elements in such a way as to reveal their tree structure.

Most Lisps will also be able to pretty-print Lisp code in a specific way. Try, for example,

```
(let ((*print-right-margin* 30)
      (*print-miser-width* nil))
  (pprint '(defun fac (n) (if (zerop n) 0 (* n (fac (1- n)))))))
```

[27]In order to save dead trees, I've removed some empty lines from the output although I realize that this isn't the best idea in a recipe about the details of pretty printing. My apologies.

and compare this with what you get if you replace PPRINT with just PRINT.

Now for the "miser width." Enter the following function to generate some fake code we can play with:

```
(defun fake-code (level)
  (if (zerop level)
    '(do-something)
    `(when (test ,level) ,(fake-code (1- level)))))
```

Then try this:

```
CL-USER> (let ((*print-right-margin* 30)
               (*print-miser-width* nil))
           (pprint (fake-code 8)))
;; 4567890123456789012345678 90 <- the first 30 columns
(WHEN (TEST 8)
  (WHEN (TEST 7)
    (WHEN (TEST 6)
      (WHEN (TEST 5)
        (WHEN (TEST 4)
          (WHEN (TEST 3)
            (WHEN (TEST 2)
              (WHEN (TEST 1)
                (DO-SOMETHING)))))))))
; No value
```

And now this:

```
CL-USER> (let ((*print-right-margin* 30)
               (*print-miser-width* 20))      ;; <-- what we changed
           (pprint (fake-code 8)))
;; 456789012345678901234567890 <- the first 30 columns
(WHEN (TEST 8)
  (WHEN (TEST 7)
    (WHEN (TEST 6)
      (WHEN (TEST 5)
        (WHEN (TEST 4)
          (WHEN                        ;; <-- output differs
           (TEST 3)
           (WHEN
            (TEST 2)
            (WHEN
             (TEST 1)
             (DO-SOMETHING))))))))))
```

```
; No value
```

What we see here is that SBCL initially indents the code by two columns for each new WHEN. However, a value of 20 for *PRINT-MISER-WIDTH* means: "Once you're at a point where you have only 20 columns or less left to the right margin, become parsimonious with space." And so at that point, it switches to a one-column indentation scheme and inserts more line breaks to save horizontal space. (It switches to *miser style* printing.)

The last printer control variable relevant to pretty printing that we're going to look at in this recipe is *PRINT-LINES*. When printing large structures, you typically want to restrict the output. We've already seen (in Recipe 9-1) how this can be achieved with *PRINT-LEVEL* and *PRINT-LENGTH*. A third way to do it is to restrict the number of lines to print:

```
CL-USER> (let ((*print-right-margin* 30)
               (*print-miser-width* nil)
               (*print-lines* 5))
           (pprint (fake-code 8)))
(WHEN (TEST 8)
  (WHEN (TEST 7)
    (WHEN (TEST 6)
      (WHEN (TEST 5)
        (WHEN (TEST 4) ..)))))
; No value
```

Note that an ellipsis consisting of two dots is printed at the end. This is not only meant for humans, but it also makes sure that the Lisp reader (see Chapter 8) can't read this back in without signaling an error.

9-10. Printing Long Lists

Problem

You want to print long lists of objects (presumably from FORMAT) and want to control how they are printed if there's too much data to fit into one line.

Solution

The standard offers a choice of three different functions for this task. You can call them directly, but all three are designed so that they can also be used with the "~/"

directive we encountered in Recipe 9-6. Here's what they do:[28]

```
CL-USER> (let ((*print-pretty* t)
               (*print-right-margin* 40)
               (*print-miser-width* nil)
               (list (make-list 10 :initial-element :foo)))
           (format t "fill: ~/pprint-fill/
~:*lin:  ~/pprint-linear/
~:*tab:  ~7/pprint-tabular/" list)
           ;; increase margin
           (setq *print-right-margin* 60)
           (format t "~&~%lin:  ~/pprint-linear/" list))
;; 4567890123456789012345678901234567890 <- the first 40 columns
fill: :FOO :FOO :FOO :FOO :FOO :FOO
      :FOO :FOO :FOO :FOO
lin:  :FOO
      :FOO
      :FOO
      :FOO
      :FOO
      :FOO
      :FOO
      :FOO
      :FOO
      :FOO
tab:  :FOO   :FOO   :FOO   :FOO   :FOO
      :FOO   :FOO   :FOO   :FOO   :FOO

lin:  :FOO :FOO :FOO :FOO :FOO :FOO :FOO :FOO :FOO :FOO
NIL
```

How It Works

It should be pretty clear from the example what these three functions do (*if* pretty printing is enabled):

- PPRINT-FILL prints as much as possible without extending beyond the right margin, then starts a new line.
- PPRINT-LINEAR either fits everything into one line (if possible) or uses one line per element.

[28]For *PRINT-RIGHT-MARGIN* and other printer control variables used here, see Recipe 9-9.

- PPRINT-TABULAR uses a fixed size per element (seven columns in our example), but is otherwise like PPRINT-FILL.
- All three reuse the indentation they started from when beginning a new line.

We can also use these functions to have a first look at how the pretty printer works internally:

(i) Output is conceptually grouped into *logical blocks*, which, as the name suggests, are meant to comprise objects that belong together into one entity. Logical blocks can be nested.

(ii) At various points *conditional newlines* can be inserted. One effect of them is that the pretty printer decides, based on the available amount of horizontal space, whether to emit a newline at this point.

(iii) The other effect of conditional newlines is that they, together with logical blocks, divide the whole output into *sections*, which are the components the pretty printer actually deals with; its main goal is to either fit whole sections into one line, or if that's not possible, to split them at conditional newline positions.

(iv) The output as a whole is also considered a logical block and a section.

(v) The pretty printer automatically keeps track of indentation within a logical block and between sections, but this can be influenced by the programmer.

To develop an understanding of how these parts interact, let's look at how the functions above might be implemented. We want our list from above to be divided into sections, like so:[29]

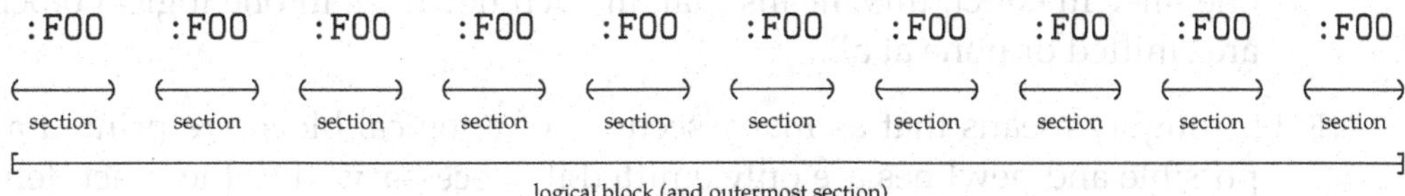

And this is done by inserting conditional newlines between the sections.

So, a *simplified*[30] implementation of PPRINT-FILL could look like this:

```
(defun my-pprint-fill (*standard-output* list)
  (pprint-logical-block (*standard-output* list)
    (pprint-exit-if-list-exhausted)
    (loop (write (pprint-pop))
          (pprint-exit-if-list-exhausted)
```

[29] Sections can not only nest but also overlap as we'll see in later recipes. This example just demonstrates the simplest case.

[30] Not only simplified but *wrong* because its lambda list is too short. But bear with me for this example.

```
        (write-char #\Space)
        (pprint-newline :fill))))
```

Here we already see most of the building blocks of writing code for the pretty printer:

- PPRINT-LOGICAL-BLOCK is a macro that wraps a logical block around its body and (usually, but not necessarily) works on a *list* of objects to print.[31] It also sets up the following two *local macros*.
- PPRINT-EXIT-IF-LIST-EXHAUSTED exits once the list we're working on is empty. The effect would seem similar to something like

  ```
  (unless list (return-from pprint-fill))
  ```

  but this convenience macro actually does a bit more (like keeping track of indentation, and so on).
- PPRINT-POP delivers the next object from the list. Again, one could think

  ```
  (pop list)
  ```

  would be just as well, but PPRINT-POP also observes printer control variables like *PRINT-LENGTH* and does other things behind the scenes.
- The function PPRINT-NEWLINE inserts a conditional newline. Its required argument must be one of the following keywords:

  :LINEAR means to insert a newline if the *containing* section can't be printed on one line. In effect, this means that all such newlines in one logical block are emitted or none at all.

  :FILL roughly means that as many sections of a logical block are printed as possible and newlines are only emitted if "necessary." For the exact definition, consult the HyperSpec.

  :MISER means the same as :LINEAR, but only while *miser style* (see Recipe 9-9) is in effect.

  :MANDATORY unconditionally emits a newline (and thus might affect other conditional newlines, as it can prevent sections from being printed on one line).

So, PPRINT-LINEAR could be implemented exactly like PPRINT-FILL, except with :LINEAR as the argument to PPRINT-NEWLINE.[32]

[31]For an example of using this macro with a non-list, see the next recipe.

[32]PPRINT-TABULAR is usually implemented in terms of another primitive called PPRINT-TAB, which we won't discuss here.

Finally, PPRINT-LOGICAL-BLOCK also accepts keyword parameters for *prefixes* and *suffixes*,[33] for example:

```
CL-USER> (let ((*print-pretty* t)
               (*print-right-margin* 5))
           (pprint-logical-block (*standard-output* '(:foo :foo)
                                  :prefix "<" :suffix ">")
             (pprint-exit-if-list-exhausted)
             (loop (write (pprint-pop))
                   (pprint-exit-if-list-exhausted)
                   (write-char #\Space)
                   (pprint-newline :fill))))
<:FOO
 :FOO>
NIL
CL-USER> (let ((*print-pretty* t)
               (*print-right-margin* 5))
           (pprint-logical-block (*standard-output* '(:foo :foo)
                                  :per-line-prefix ";;; ")
             (pprint-exit-if-list-exhausted)
             (loop (write (pprint-pop))
                   (pprint-exit-if-list-exhausted)
                   (write-char #\Space)
                   (pprint-newline :fill))))
;;; :FOO
;;; :FOO
NIL
```

9-11. Pretty-Printing Compound Objects

Problem

You want to create a textual representation of a compound object that reflects its structure.

Solution

We are going to demonstrate how this can be done with a more elaborate example. You should already know the pretty printer functions explained in Recipe 9-10.

[33] And the three list-printing functions that this recipe is about use this feature to optionally wrap parentheses around the list they print.

First, we create this class:

```
(defclass tag ()
  ((name :initarg :name
         :reader name)
   (attributes :initarg :attributes
               :initform nil
               :reader attributes)
   (body :initarg :body
         :initform nil
         :reader body)))
```

And without further ado, here's a function to pretty-print objects of this class, which we'll look at in detail below:[34]

```
(defun pprint-tag (*standard-output* tag)
  (pprint-logical-block (*standard-output* nil)
    (write-char #\<)
    (write-string (name tag))
    (pprint-logical-block (*standard-output* (attributes tag))
      (pprint-exit-if-list-exhausted)
      (loop (write-char #\Space)
            (destructuring-bind (name value)
                (pprint-pop)
              (write-string name)
              (write-char #\=)
              (write-string value)
              (pprint-exit-if-list-exhausted)
              (pprint-newline :fill))))
    (write-char #\>)
    (when (body tag)
      (pprint-indent :block 2)
      (pprint-newline :linear)
      (pprint-logical-block (*standard-output* (body tag))
        (pprint-exit-if-list-exhausted)
        (loop (pprint-tag *standard-output* (pprint-pop))
              (pprint-exit-if-list-exhausted)
              (pprint-newline :fill))))
    (pprint-indent :block 0)
    (pprint-newline :linear)
    (write-string "</")
    (write-string (name tag))
```

[34]Note how we bind the special variable `*STANDARD-OUTPUT*` here by using it as a function parameter. See Recipes 10-3 and 14-1 for more.

```
    (write-char #\>)))
```

(Don't worry if this looks complicated and intimidating. We'll eventually see a much shorter version of this function.)

If you now try this function with a TAG object like this one

```
(let ((inner-1 (make-instance 'tag
                              :name "INNER1"
                              :attributes '(("id" "1"))))
      (inner-2 (make-instance 'tag :name "INNER2")))
  (make-instance 'tag :name "OUTER"
                      :attributes '(("id" "42")
                                    ("alt" "23"))
                      :body (list inner-1 inner-2)))
```

and with various different settings for the right margin (as we did in other recipes), you will see outputs like these:

```
<OUTER id=42 alt=23><INNER1 id=1></INNER1><INNER2></INNER2></OUTER>

<OUTER id=42 alt=23>
  <INNER1 id=1></INNER1><INNER2></INNER2>
</OUTER>

<OUTER id=42 alt=23>
  <INNER1 id=1></INNER1>
  <INNER2></INNER2>
</OUTER>

<OUTER id=42 alt=23>
  <INNER1 id=1>
  </INNER1>
  <INNER2></INNER2>
</OUTER>

<OUTER id=42
       alt=23>
  <INNER1 id=1>
  </INNER1>
  <INNER2>
  </INNER2>
</OUTER>
```

How It Works

Our function PPRINT-TAG demonstrates the two missing pieces of the pretty printer puzzle that we didn't already discuss in Recipe 9-10; nested logical blocks and indentation.

Indentation is fairly simple. The function PPRINT-INDENT is used to specify indentation either relative to the logical block we're in (as we did here) or to the current position (using :CURRENT instead of :BLOCK). The value can also be negative, although the printer won't move to the left of the outermost margin. Also, indentation settings will only have an effect within a logical block and, of course, only after (and *if*) a newline was emitted.

As for nested logical blocks, let's have a look at our example and mark the logical blocks as well as the conditional newlines our function introduced:

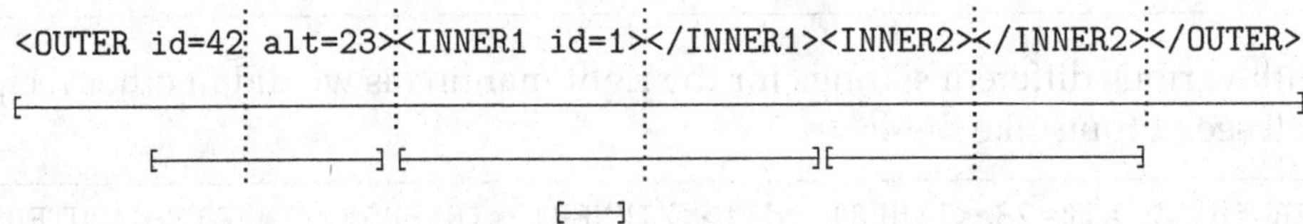

We said on page 255 that conditional newlines divide the output into *sections*, but we didn't say what this means in the presence of nested logical blocks. Here are the sections corresponding to the picture above:

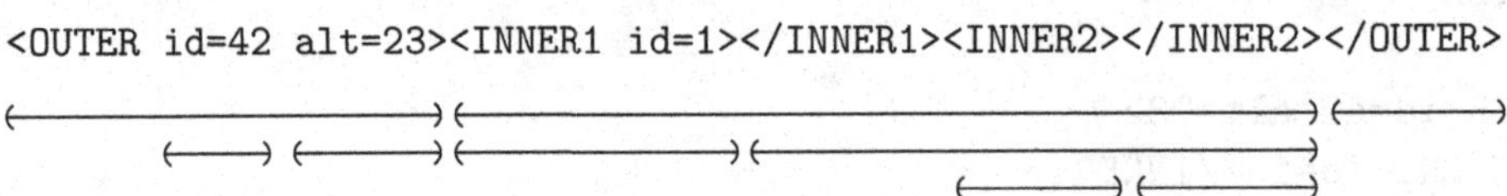

So, the whole truth is that conditional newlines divide logical blocks into sections, but the rightmost section of each logical block extends up to the next newline in the *containing* block. For example, while the *logical block* for the attributes id=42 alt=23 ends with the character 3, the last *section* of this block includes the next character (which is >) as well.

The pretty printer will now try its best to print each section on one line. And if that's not possible, it'll only ever break up sections at positions where there were conditional newlines. This should explain the results we saw on page 259.

Using the Pretty Printer from FORMAT

We promised that our function PPRINT-TAG could be a lot shorter. That's indeed easy as long as you're feeling comfortable with FORMAT's "line noise." Each of the pretty printer functions and macros we've used has a corresponding FORMAT directive:[35]

[35]You can also specify the *prefixes* and *suffixes* of a logical block this way. See the HyperSpec for details.

Function/Macro	Directive(s)
(PPRINT-LOGICAL-BLOCK ...)	~< ... ~:>
(PPRINT-NEWLINE :LINEAR)	~_
(PPRINT-NEWLINE :FILL)	~:_
(PPRINT-NEWLINE :MISER)	~@_
(PPRINT-NEWLINE :MANDATORY)	~:@_
(PPRINT-INDENT :BLOCK *n*)	~*n*I
(PPRINT-INDENT :CURRENT *n*)	~*n*:I

Which means that we can translate our function from above into a (pretty convoluted) format control string, like so:

```
(defun pprint-tag (*standard-output* tag &rest other-args)
  (declare (ignore other-args))
  (format t "~@<<~A~<~^~@{ ~A=~A~^~:_~}~:>>~
~@[~2I~_~<~^~@{~/PPRINT-TAG/~^~:_~}~:>~]~0I~_</~3:*~A>~:>"
          (name tag)
          (mapcan 'copy-list (attributes tag))
          (body tag)))
```

Some notes:

- The logical block directive usually wants one argument that must be a list. But like with "~{" (iteration), you can use the at-sign modifier to use up all remaining arguments. That's what we do above for the first block.
- The format control is not a verbatim translation of our function and that's not even always possible. One relevant difference is that a logical block always needs an argument in FORMAT, whereas in code we can, as we did above, use NIL as the argument (and then simply not use PPRINT-POP).
- It is important that the closing "~:>" directive contains the colon as shown because otherwise this means something completely different (justification) which doesn't mix with pretty printing.

This final example packed about all there is to know about FORMAT and pretty printing into one string. Maybe your head is spinning now. Luckily, the pretty printer is one of the few areas where the standard actually offers a whole slew of useful examples. You might want to look at its section 22.2.22.

9-12. Modifying the Pretty Printer

Problem

You want to change the way the pretty printer prints certain objects.

Solution

This is easy. Assuming our definitions from Recipe 9-11, we can simply do this:

```
(set-pprint-dispatch 'tag 'pprint-tag)
```

If you now use PPRINT to print a TAG object, you should see the representation from that recipe; whereas with PRINT (and assuming *PRINT-PRETTY* is NIL), you should see the normal CLOS object representation:

```
CL-USER> (setq *print-pretty* nil)
NIL
CL-USER> (write (make-instance 'tag :name "FOO") :pretty t)
<FOO></FOO>
#<TAG {1005439743}>
```

How It Works

As you can influence how objects are usually printed (see Recipe 9-8), you can also intervene in the pretty-printing process. The way you do it is different, though—you have more fine-grained control even over built-in objects.

During pretty-printing (i.e., when *PRINT-PRETTY* is true), the Lisp printer first consults its *pretty print dispatch table*, which is a table that associates *types* (see Recipe 13-1) with printing functions. If the object to be printed matches one[36] of the type specifiers, the corresponding function is used. Only if no matching type was found will the pretty printer fall back to calling PRINT-OBJECT (see Recipe 9-8).

So, to implement pretty printing for your own objects, you can either hook them into the pretty print dispatch table with SET-PPRINT-DISPATCH as we did above or write your own PRINT-OBJECT method, which does different things based on whether *PRINT-PRETTY* is true or not.

But you can also use type specifiers for built-in objects. Let's say you want to represent (real) numbers between 0 and 1 as percentages:

[36]If more than one type specifier matches, selection is performed by *priority* but we won't go into that here.

```
CL-USER> (set-pprint-dispatch '(real 0 1)
                              (lambda (stream number)
                                (format stream "~,2F%"
                                        (* 100 number))))
NIL
CL-USER> (pprint (list 1/3 .3333 3333D-4))
(33.33% 33.33% 33.33%)
; No value
```

This also explains how pretty printing of code (see page 251) is likely implemented. As type specifiers are fairly flexible, you can use a type like `(CONS (MEMBER DEFUN))` for the dispatch table.[37]

There are some similarities between pretty print dispatch tables and readtables (see Recipe 8-7). The *current* table is in `*PRINT-PPRINT-DISPATCH*` and you can copy such a table or get a copy of the initial table using the function `COPY-PPRINT-DISPATCH`. It is advisable, although not as critical as with readtables, to work on a *copy* of the current pretty print dispatch table and only install it as the current table once you're sure it does what you want.

[37]See page 35.

10. Evaluation, Compilation, Control Flow

To be honest, I couldn't find a better title for this chapter. It's kind of a hodgepodge of various subjects, although many of them would probably indeed fit into the chapter called *Evaluation and Compilation* in the COMMON LISP standard.

However, I think that specifically Recipes 10-8 and 10-9 deserve your attention as they provide fairly detailed treatments of topics which are rarely, if ever, covered in COMMON LISP books.

10-1. Comparing Arbitrary Lisp Objects

Problem

You're confused by `EQ`, `EQL`, `EQUAL`, and `EQUALP`. Which one are you supposed to use when?

Solution

It is actually not as complicated as it seems. If you just need a few simple rules of thumb, here they are:

I) When comparing objects of the same type, use the equality predicate(s) made for that type.[1]

II) For a general test of whether two arbitrary objects are the *same*, use `EQL`.

III) *Don't* use `EQ`![2]

IV) `EQUAL` and `EQUALP` will only be helpful in rare cases.

If you want more information, read on...

[1]See Recipe 3-4 for strings and characters. For numbers, you can and should always use = and you only need to be careful if you're comparing rationals with floating-point numbers (see Recipe 4-10), which is questionable style anyway.

[2]Yeah, other Lispers might give you different advice. But, hey, whose book is this? Also, rules are there to be broken once you've understood them...

How It Works

The COMMON LISP standard distinguishes between two objects being the *same* object or being *identical*.[3] Two objects are *identical* if their *internal representations* are indistinguishable, but that's an implementation detail that a COMMON LISP programmer should never rely on.[4]

`EQ` checks for this kind of identity and is thus a low-level technical predicate that should usually be avoided. A good mental model, although maybe not totally accurate, is that `EQ` simply compares the two machine words representing its two arguments.[5] In the case of two different compound objects (like two lists), you will have two different pointers regardless of the contents of the objects, so they are not `EQ`; which is OK because they really are two different things. But you might, say, have two `CHARACTER` objects that both *mean* the *same* letter, but that for technical reasons can't be stored as "immediate objects" and will thus be reported as *not* being `EQ`. (And the same thing can happen with numbers; see specifically page 112.)

`EQL`, on the other hand, tests for *semantic* identity; that is, it checks whether two "primitive" objects *denote* the same thing. In short, `EQL` does the right thing for symbols, characters, and numbers no matter how they are represented internally. In all cases where `EQL` returns `NIL`, `EQ` will also return `NIL`, which means that whenever `EQ` would "work," you could just as well use `EQL`.

And don't be tempted to replace `EQL` with `EQ` for performance reasons. If you think you have enough information to be sure that `EQ` is safe to use, then tell the compiler about it (see Recipe 17-5) and let it decide whether `EQ` is OK and will actually make your program faster.

Comparing State

For compound objects, there isn't such a thing as a perfect solution. That's why in a language like JAVA, you are encouraged to implement your own `equals` methods for your own classes. The idea is that `equals` compares *state* (and only you can really know how it should do this), whereas == compares *identity*.

COMMON LISP has `EQUAL`, `EQUALP`, and also `TREE-EQUAL`, which all work by recursing into compound structures but they do it in different ways:

- `TREE-EQUAL` views its two arguments as *trees* built out of *conses* (see Recipe 2-8) and descends into these trees using `CAR` and `CDR`. Whenever it encounters two *atoms* (i.e. non-conses, see page 35) it compares them with a user-specified test:

[3]Being always very careful with the wording, they are actually a bit pickier. Two objects can be the *same* object with respect to some specific predicate and if there's no predicate mentioned, then `EQL` is implied. Whereas *identical* means "the *same* under the predicate `EQ`."

[4]If you want a comparison, it is as if a C programmer would rely on `int` always being 16 bits wide.

[5]It is roughly equivalent to what == does in JAVA.

```
CL-USER > (eql '(a (b c) (3/4 (d) e))
               '(a (b c) (3/4 (d) e)))
NIL
CL-USER > (tree-equal '(a (b c) (3/4 (d) e))
                      '(a (b c) (3/4 (d) e))
                      :test 'eq)
NIL
CL-USER > (tree-equal '(a (b c) (3/4 (d) e))
                      (list 'a '(b c) (list 3/4 '(d) 'e))
                      :test 'eql)
T
CL-USER > (tree-equal '(a (b c) (3/4 (d) e))
                      '(a (b c) (3/4 (d)))
                      :test 'eql)
NIL
```

The first test yields `NIL` because the two trees *look* identical but are different objects. The second test could, in theory, yield `T` in some implementations, but if you see `NIL`, it's because of the `(EQ 3/4 3/4)` test (see above). The third test must always return `T` because both trees have the same structure and the same leaves, while the fourth test must always yield `NIL` because the trees don't have the same structure.

- `EQUAL` descends into conses like `TREE-EQUAL` but uses different tests for different objects. It also recurses into strings and bit vectors, but *not* into arbitrary arrays nor into other compound objects, like hash tables or structures. Simple objects (symbols, numbers, characters) are compared by `EQL`. (Sound complicated? It is...) Some examples:

```
CL-USER > (equal '(1 #\a a) (list 1 #\a 'a))
T
CL-USER > (equal '(1 #\a a) (list 1 #\A 'a))
NIL
CL-USER > (eql "abc" "abc")
NIL
CL-USER > (equal "abc" "abc")
T
CL-USER > (equal "abc"
                 (make-array 3
                             :element-type 'character
                             :initial-contents
                               (list #\a #\b #\c)))
T
CL-USER > (equal (make-array 3
```

```
                          :element-type 'fixnum
                          :initial-contents (list 1 2 3))
               (make-array 3
                          :element-type 'fixnum
                          :initial-contents (list 1 2 3)))
NIL
CL-USER > (equal "abc" "Abc")
NIL
```

EQUAL can also compare the contents of pathnames (see Chapter 15) but leaves some of the details to the implementation so that, for example, on Windows the result of

```
(equal #p"Test" #p"test")
```

is T for LISPWORKS and NIL for SBCL (which both make sense, kind of).

- EQUALP is more "lenient" than EQUAL. It always yields T if EQUAL yields T, but it also ignores case in strings and descends intos arbitrary arrays, hash tables, or structures:

```
CL-USER > (equalp "abc" "Abc")
T
CL-USER > (equalp (make-array 3
                          :element-type 'fixnum
                          :initial-contents (list 1 2 3))
               (make-array 3
                          :element-type 'fixnum
                          :initial-contents (list 1 2 3)))
T
CL-USER > (flet ((test-hash ()
                 (let ((hash (make-hash-table)))
                   (setf (gethash 42 hash) 'foo)
                   hash)))
            (list (equal (test-hash) (test-hash))
                  (equalp (test-hash) (test-hash))))
(NIL T)
```

If you're interested in even more details, you'll have to look it up in the standard.

As you can see, EQUAL and EQUALP both have very specific ideas about when compound objects should be considered as representing the "same" thing. This might perfectly coincide with what you're doing, but more often than not, you'll probably have to write your own predicates for equality testing.

One thing these four predicates are obviously good for, though, is that you can use them as test functions for hash tables (see Chapter 6). If, say, your keys are strings, then you can use `EQUAL` or `EQUALP` as hash tests instead of writing your own (see Recipe 6-5).

Constants

If in SBCL your source file contains a form like this

```
(defconstant +list+ '(1 2 3))
```

and you compile and load the file, you'll get an error message that claims that the constant `+LIST+` "is being redefined (from `(1 2 3)` to `(1 2 3)`)."

At first sight, this doesn't seem to make much sense (although it does). The SBCL maintainers themselves call this an *idiosyncrasy* and explain it in their manual.[6]

The gist of it is that the SBCL compiler evaluates the form twice (at compile time and again at load time) and as a result you'll have two *different* lists that only look identical but aren't the *same* anymore (under `EQL`). You have thus (involuntary) redefined a value that was supposed to be constant. Most other Lisps silently ignore this. For SBCL, see their manual for a workaround; or you might want to use the `DEFINE-CONSTANT` macro of the ALEXANDRIA library.[7]

But if the standard apparently didn't *want* things like lists to be the values of constant variables, this should at least make us think a bit—even if our Lisp doesn't complain like SBCL. Only use constants other than numbers, characters, or symbols if you never rely on their object identity anywhere!

10-2. Using Constant Variables as Keys in CASE Macros

Problem

To increase readability and maintainability, you want to use constant variables in a `CASE` macro, but apparently this is not possible.

Solution

Suppose you are receiving small integer values from some source that are to be interpreted as commands. Parts of your code would look like so:

---

[6]See `http://www.sbcl.org/manual/#Defining-Constants`.

[7]See Recipe 18-4.

```
(case input
  (0 (stop-processing))
  (1 (accelerate))
  (2 (turn-left))
  (3 (turn-right)))
```

As the numbers are rather arbitrary, you have defined constants to name them:

```
(defconstant +stop-command+ 0)
(defconstant +speed-up-command+ 1)
(defconstant +left-command+ 2)
(defconstant +right-command+ 3)
```

So you want to write your code like this instead:

```
(case input
  (+stop-command+ (stop-processing))
  (+speed-up-command+ (accelerate))
  (+left-command+ (turn-left))
  (+right-command+ (turn-right)))
```

Except that this doesn't work. The individual alternatives are never called...
The right way to do it is like so:

```
(case input
  (#.+stop-command+ (stop-processing))
  (#.+speed-up-command+ (accelerate))
  (#.+left-command+ (turn-left))
  (#.+right-command+ (turn-right)))
```

How It Works

The keys of a `CASE` (or `CCASE` or `ECASE`) form are not evaluated. As keys are supposed to be compared by `EQL` (see Recipe 10-1), only numbers, characters, and symbols can be meaningful keys anyway, and they can be distinguished by their syntax. In a `CASE` statement like

```
(case whatever
  (42 (do-something))
  (#\Z (do-something-else))
  (foo (do-something)))
```

it is obvious that 42 is a number, #\Z is a character, and FOO is a symbol.

But this doesn't leave any room for variables; if we have a key like +STOP-COMMAND+ above, it is interpreted as the *symbol* and not as the constant variable named by the symbol.

The solution is to use the #. reader syntax (see Recipe 8-3), which inserts the values of the constant variables instead. The only thing you have to watch out for is that the constants have to be defined before they are used this way.

10-3. Using Arbitrary Variable Names for Keyword Parameters

Problem

You want to have a lambda list where a keyword parameter and the corresponding variable don't have the same name.

Solution

The typical usage of keyword parameters looks like so:

```
CL-USER> (defun foo (&key (arg 23))
           (list arg))
FOO
CL-USER> (foo :arg 42)
(42)
CL-USER> (foo)
(23)
```

Here we specify the parameter name ARG and as a result, we must use the symbol :ARG from the KEYWORD package to introduce the argument when we call FOO.

But sometimes this might not be what you want. You might, for example, want to bind a special variable but use a different (maybe shorter) name for the parameter (akin to how this is done with WRITE; see Recipe 9-1). This is also possible:

```
CL-USER> (defun bar (&key ((:arg argument) 23))
           (list argument))
BAR
CL-USER> (bar :arg 42)
(42)
```

```
CL-USER> (bar)
(23)
```

Here we still need to use :ARG when calling the function, but within the function, the argument will be bound to the variable ARGUMENT and *not* to ARG.

To simulate WRITE's behavior, we'd do this:

```
CL-USER> (defun quux (&key ((:stream *standard-output*)
                                 *standard-output*))
           (princ 42))
QUUX
CL-USER> (quux)
42
42
CL-USER> (with-output-to-string (out)
           (quux :stream out))
"42"
```

(Note that the first *STANDARD-OUTPUT* in the lambda list is the name of the variable, while the second one is the default value.)

How It Works

The typical usage of keyword parameters (as in FOO above) is just a shortcut. We use a symbol and the keyword symbol with the same name will become the *keyword name*[8] used when matching arguments, while the symbol itself will become the name of the variable in the function. The long version (as in BAR) specifies both separately.

Keyword Names Don't Have to Be Keywords

And we can actually use any symbol as a keyword name, not only keywords:

```
CL-USER> (defun baz (&key ((foo bar) 42))
           (list bar))
BAZ
CL-USER> (baz 'foo 23)
(23)
```

This also demonstrates why we usually don't do that: we now have to *quote* the symbols.

[8]That's the term used in the standard. As we will soon see, this doesn't necessarily imply that this is a *keyword* in the sense of being a symbol from the KEYWORD package.

Keyword Dames Don't Have to Be Constant

And while we're at it, the keyword names don't have to be constant when *calling* a function with keyword arguments. Consider this example:

```
CL-USER> (defun color (&key (red 0.0) (green 0.0) (blue 0.0))
           (list red green blue))
COLOR
CL-USER> (color :red 0.3 :blue 0.4)
(0.3 0.0 0.4)
CL-USER> (defun pure-color (which value)
           (color which value))
PURE-COLOR
CL-USER> (pure-color :red 0.7)
(0.7 0.0 0.0)
CL-USER> (pure-color :green 0.1)
(0.0 0.1 0.0)
```

The function PURE-COLOR calls COLOR as

```
(color which value)
```

with no "apparent" keyword name. But it works!

10-4. Creating "Static Local Variables," Like in C

Problem

You want variables that are local to a function, but that will keep their values between different calls to it.

Solution

In a language like C, you can declare a function-local variable as "static," like so:

```
#include <stdio.h>

void count() {
  static int counter = 0;
  counter++;
  printf("%d\n", counter);
}
```

This means that space for the variable is allocated only once (as opposed to per function call), and it also means that the initialization of `counter` with the value `0` only happens once (the first time `count` is called).[9] So, if you call this function three times in a row, it will first print `1`, then `2`, and then `3`.

In COMMON LISP, you can achieve almost the same effect with a *lexical closure*:

```
(let ((counter 0))
  (defun my-count ()
    (print (incf counter))))
```

How It Works

We're assuming that you know what a *lexical closure* is and how closures are used in COMMON LISP.[10] What maybe isn't so clear is that closures can not only be used with anonymous functions created in and returned from a specific lexical environment (which is the typical example to introduce closures), but that they work perfectly fine with named functions defined with `DEFUN` (or `DEFMETHOD`) as well, as you'll see if you try out our `MY-COUNT` from above.

One of the nice things about such closed-over variables is that they can only be accessed by the functions defined within their scope, so, for example, nobody can accidentally read or modify the value of `COUNTER`. This can only be done by calling `MY-COUNT`.

You can also define several functions closing over the same lexical variable(s). Here's an example:

```
(let ((counter 0))
  (defun reset-counter ()
    (setf counter 0))

  (defun my-count ()
    (print (incf counter))))
```

You'd thus have a defined way of resetting `COUNTER` without exposing it:

```
CL-USER> (my-count)
1
1
CL-USER> (my-count)
2
2
```

[9] In JAVA, a similar concept would be that of a *static member variable*.

[10] If not, you might want to read chapter 6 of *Practical Common Lisp*.

```
CL-USER> (my-count)
3
3
CL-USER> (reset-counter)
0
CL-USER> (my-count)
1
1
```

One subtle difference between C and the COMMON LISP code is that in C the variable is initialized the first time it is called, while the way we did it here, the Lisp variable is initialized when the function definition is loaded. This might be relevant if the initialization process is complicated, but there are, of course, ways to postpone initialization if necessary.[11]

DEFUN isn't treated specially as a *top-level form*,[12] so as far as the compiler is concerned, a DEFUN as above is like any other DEFUN. You might have problems with your IDE, however, because the editor or facilities to find definitions of functions might expect that a definition always start with "(DEFUN ..." in the leftmost column.

Also, while this is convenient, it is not thread-safe per se. If you're expecting that MY-COUNT might be called from different threads at the same time, you will have to modify it accordingly (see Chapter 11).

10-5. "Preponing" the Computation of Values

Problem

You want to execute some computation before a program starts, but only once compilation and loading of the program has finished.

Solution

In many situations, the special operator LOAD-TIME-VALUE is what you need. We'll use a minimal example to demonstrate its effects:

We create a file foo.lisp with the following contents, but for now, we neither load it nor compile it:

[11] You could, for example, bind the variable to NIL when the function is defined and in MY-COUNT check if it's still NIL.

[12] See 3.2.3.1 of the standard.

```
(defun test ()
  (print (load-time-value (get-internal-real-time))))
```

Now for the test:[13]

```
CL-USER> (get-internal-real-time)
48983
CL-USER> (compile-file "foo.lisp")
;; some output elided
#P"/tmp/foo.fasl"
NIL
NIL
CL-USER> (get-internal-real-time)
69045                                      ;; <- point in time A
CL-USER> (load **)
T
CL-USER> (get-internal-real-time)
78764                                      ;; <- point in time B
CL-USER> (test)
74396                                      ;; <- between A and B
74396
CL-USER> (get-internal-real-time)
86876
CL-USER> (test)
74396                                      ;; <- same as above
74396
```

The following are the important things to note here:

- TEST always produces the same output whenever it's called.
- The time returned by TEST is the time when the file was *loaded*, not when it was *compiled*.

How It Works

There are only about two dozen *special operators* in COMMON LISP[14] for things you couldn't do yourself with functions or macros. LOAD-TIME-VALUE is one of them.

The way this operator works is that when a file is compiled it leaves a "gap" in the file in the place where the LOAD-TIME-VALUE form was. If the compiled FASL file is then subsequently loaded, this gap is filled with the results of evaluating the form

[13]GET-INTERNAL-REAL-TIME is explained in Recipe 22-8.

[14]Although implementations are technically not required to adhere to this.

enclosed by LOAD-TIME-VALUE. The idea is that you want this value to be ready once the file has been loaded, but that computing it at compilation time already might be too early (for example, because some supporting functions or data structures don't exist yet).

This operator is mainly intended to be used with COMPILE-FILE, so it doesn't make much sense to contemplate how exactly it'll behave in other situations, except that you can expect the behavior to be reasonable.[15] Here's an example with an implementation that distinguishes between interpreted and compiled code:

```
CL-USER > (get-internal-real-time)
7036706                                   ;; <- point in time C
CL-USER > (defun test-2 ()
            (print (load-time-value (get-internal-real-time))))
TEST-2
CL-USER > (get-internal-real-time)
7050980                                   ;; <- point in time D
CL-USER > (test-2)
7054381                                   ;; <- after D
7054381
CL-USER > (test-2)
7055692                                   ;; <- later, NOT the same as before
7055692
CL-USER > (get-internal-real-time)
7062790                                   ;; <- point in time E
CL-USER > (compile 'test-2)
TEST-2
NIL
NIL
CL-USER > (get-internal-real-time)
7071510                                   ;; <-point in time F
CL-USER > (test-2)
7067782                                   ;; <- between E and F
7067782
CL-USER > (test-2)
7067782                                   ;; <- same as above
7067782
```

One thing to take care of is that something like this (compare with Recipe 10-4) will *not* work:

```
(let ((counter 0))
  (defun test ()
```

[15] Of course, the behavior is meticulously described in the standard.

```
    (print (load-time-value (format nil "~B" counter)))))
```

The reason is that when the "gap" is filled, this happens in a so-called "null lexical environment," which means that at that moment the compiler doesn't "know" about the closed-over variable COUNTER.

For a typical use of LOAD-TIME-VALUE see Recipe 17-9.

(According to some dictionaries, "prepone" is a relatively new English word that probably originated in India or Pakistan. Even if you've never heard it before, its meaning as the opposite of "postpone" should be pretty obvious.)

10-6. Modifying the Behavior of Functions You Don't Have the Source Of

Problem

You're working with Lisp code that you only have in compiled form (as a "FASL" file or as part of your *image*; see page 429 and Recipe 16-1), but want to change how it behaves, nevertheless.

Solution

Note first that this is no problem if the function you're interested in is a *generic function*, as in this case, you can just use the so-called *auxiliary* methods of the *standard method combination* to alter the function's conduct.[16]

But what about plain functions? Let's say you know that you'll only ever feed real numbers to COMMON LISP's SQRT function and that you want it to return NIL if its argument is negative (instead of returning a complex number). In LISPWORKS, for example, you'd do it like this:

```
(defadvice (sqrt no-complex-roots :around)
    (real)
  (if (minusp real)
    nil
    (call-next-advice real)))                    ;; <- call original SQRT
```

You can now test the new behavior of SQRT:

[16]This is explained in chapter 16 of *Practical Common Lisp*, which is also available online at http://www.gigamonkeys.com/book/object-reorientation-generic-functions.html.

```
CL-USER 1 > (sqrt 3d0)
1.7320508075688772D0
CL-USER 2 > (sqrt -3d0)
NIL
```

To restore SQRT's old behavior, we need the name we used above:

```
CL-USER 3 > (remove-advice 'sqrt 'no-complex-roots)
T
CL-USER 4 > (sqrt -3d0)
#C(0.0D0 1.7320508075688772D0)
```

How It Works

The ability to "advise" functions already existed in various Lisp dialects that predated COMMON LISP,[17] but it didn't make it into the COMMON LISP standard.[18] Some Lisps have it, some don't. As of July 2015, at least ALLEGROCL, CMUCL, CLOZURECL, and LISPWORKS had some kind of advice facility, but all had slightly different semantics and wildly different names; search their manuals for words like *advice*, *advise*, or *fwrapper*.

Similar to what can be done with generic functions, you can usually attach various pieces of code to an existing function that are run *before* or *after* or *instead* of ("*around*") the original function. Also, different pieces of advice can be combined and arranged in different orders.

Lisps that have advice facilities will generally also allow you to advise macros (and not only functions). Here's a hack to make the output of TIME (see page 513) a bit shorter:

```
CL-USER 5 > (time (loop repeat 2000 sum most-positive-fixnum))
Timing the evaluation of (LOOP REPEAT 2000 SUM MOST-POSITIVE-FIXNUM)

User time    =        0.015
System time  =        0.000
Elapsed time =        0.016
Allocation   = 1571724 bytes
0 Page faults
Calls to %EVAL    42027
1073741822000
CL-USER 6 > (defadvice (time keep-it-short :around)
```

[17]And it has, by the way, also been a part of GNU Emacs since 1994.

[18]Or rather only in the form of the *auxiliary* methods mentioned above.

```
               (form env)
             `(let* (result
                     (output
                      (with-output-to-string (*trace-output*)
                        (setf result ,(call-next-advice form env)))))
                (format *trace-output* "~A"
                        (subseq output (search "User time" output)))
                result))
T
CL-USER 7 > (time (loop repeat 2000 sum most-positive-fixnum))
User time    =        0.015
System time  =        0.000
Elapsed time =        0.016
Allocation   = 2049596 bytes
0 Page faults
Calls to %EVAL    42027
1073741822000
```

(Note how we're writing a macro ourselves, which is given the form to expand and the environment; see Recipe 10-9.)

10-7. Swapping the Values of Variables (or Places)

Problem

You want to exchange the values of two variables.

Solution

Use ROTATEF.

If your variables are called A and B, then do it like so:

```
(rotatef a b)
```

But ROTATEF can do a lot more. Read on...

How It Works

If you want to swap the values of two variables in C, you have to do it with pointers, like on page 600. If you want to implement this yourself in COMMON LISP, you have to write a macro and it'll probably look like so:

```
(defmacro swap (var-1 var-2)
  (let ((temp (gensym)))
    `(let ((,temp ,var-1))
       (setf ,var-1 ,var-2
             ,var-2 ,temp)
       (values))))
```

Let's try this:

```
CL-USER > (defparameter *a* 42)
*A*
CL-USER > (defparameter *b* 23)
*B*
CL-USER > (swap *a* *b*)
CL-USER > (list *a* *b*)
(23 42)
```

Because of the power of SETF,[19] your macro will also work for situations you might not have foreseen:

```
CL-USER > (let ((list (list 23 42)))
            (swap (first list) (second list))
            list)
(42 23)
```

But for more sophisticated situations your macro is not quite correct:

```
CL-USER > (let ((list (list 23 42)))
            (swap (nth (print 0) list) (second list))
            list)
0
0
(42 23)
```

This demonstrates that the form that accessed the first element of the list was evaluated twice, which is something a macro shouldn't do.

Now look at this:

```
CL-USER > (let ((list (list 23 42)))
            (rotatef (nth (print 0) list) (second list))
            list)
```

[19]See Recipe 10-8.

```
0
(42 23)
```

ROTATEF does the right thing. And it can do more as its name reveals; it generalizes the swapping of two values to a rotation of an arbitrary number of values:

```
CL-USER > (let ((arr (make-array 4 :initial-contents (list 1 2 3 4)))
                (list (list 10 20 30))
                (var 42))
            (print (list arr list var))
            (rotatef (aref arr 0)
                     (elt list 2)
                     var
                     (second list))
            (list arr list var))
(#(1 2 3 4) (10 20 30) 42)
(#(30 2 3 4) (10 1 42) 20)
```

To see how this is a cyclical permutation, look at the following picture:

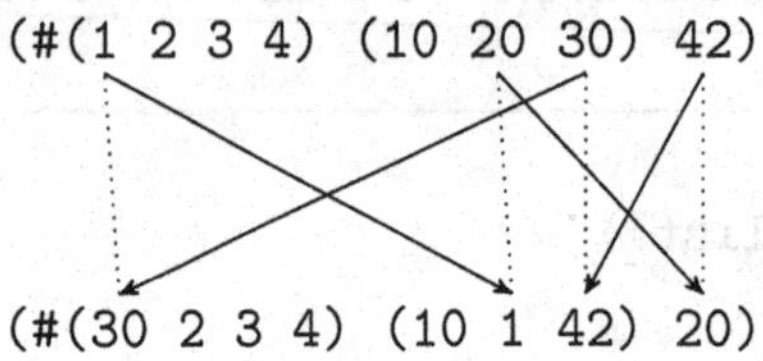

A variant of ROTATEF is SHIFTF, which does almost the same job but doesn't "close the cycle:"

```
CL-USER > (let ((arr (make-array 4 :initial-contents (list 1 2 3 4)))
                (list (list 10 20 30))
                (var 42))
            (print (list arr list var))
            (print (shiftf (aref arr 0)
                           (elt list 2)
                           var
                           (second list)))
            (list arr list var))
(#(1 2 3 4) (10 20 30) 42)
1
(#(30 2 3 4) (10 20 42) 20)
```

The effect looks like this (and the 1 that "leaves the picture" is the return value of the SHIFTF form):

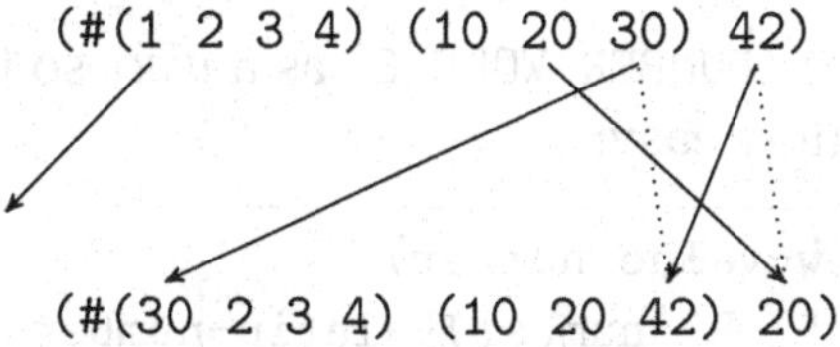

If you are interested in how you could implement something like this yourself, have a look at Recipe 10-8.

10-8. Creating Your Own Update Forms for "Places"

Problem

In your code, you are using some kind of *reader* form that you want to be able to *write to* with SETF as if it were a variable, similar to what can be done with standard accessors like AREF or GETHASH.

Solution

There are several ways to do this, which we'll look at ordered by increasing complexity. Let's start with an example for the easiest case. Suppose you have a "database" of Latin number words that is unfortunately indexed by Roman numerals. You write a convenience function NUMBER-WORD[20] that'll give you the word corresponding to a Lisp integer:

```
CL-USER > (defparameter *latin-numbers*
            (make-hash-table :test 'equal))
*LATIN-NUMBERS*
CL-USER > (setf (gethash "II" *latin-numbers*) "duo"
                (gethash "III" *latin-numbers*) "tres"
                (gethash "VI" *latin-numbers*) "sex")
"sex"
CL-USER > (defun number-word (number)
            (gethash (format nil "~@R" number) *latin-numbers*))
NUMBER-WORD
CL-USER > (number-word 3)
```

[20]See Recipe 4-4 for an explanation of the "~@R" part.

```
"tres"
T
```

Now you want to be able to use something like (NUMBER-WORD 3) as a *place* so that you can update your database. This is surprisingly easy:

```
CL-USER > (defun (setf number-word) (new-value number)
            (setf (gethash (format nil "~@R" number) *latin-numbers*)
                  new-value))
(SETF NUMBER-WORD)
CL-USER > (setf (number-word 9) "novem")
"novem"
CL-USER > (number-word 9)
"novem"
T
```

The most surprising fact, if you've never seen this, probably is what follows directly after the symbol DEFUN: a function's *name* cannot only be a symbol but also a list of the form (SETF *name*), where *name* is a symbol.

If a *setf function* is defined like this, it can have a lambda list like any other function (including &OPTIONAL, &KEY, and &REST parts), the only difference is that the *new value* must be the first parameter. The rest of the parameters will be used for the *place* form. Such setf functions can even be generic functions,[21] and they also work with FUNCALL or APPLY; see for example page 119.

Setf functions must always return the new value. In this case, it is automatic because (SETF GETHASH) does it for us.

Below we will look at situations where this approach won't suffice and we'll have to use macros instead.

How It Works

COMMON LISP defines the concept of a *generalized reference*, which means that a certain form (called a *place*) can be written to as if it were a variable by using SETF.[22] A typical example is AREF, where the form (AREF ARR 4 2) returns a certain element of the array ARR, while you can change this element with SETF like so:

```
(setf (aref arr 4 2) new-value)
```

[21] In other words, this also works with DEFGENERIC and DEFMETHOD.

[22] See more in chapter 6 of *Practical Common Lisp* which is at http://www.gigamonkeys.com/book/variables.html.

True to COMMON LISP's promise of being the programmable programming language, you can create your own places and define how they can be updated with SETF. The preceding example showed the easiest way to do it by simply using DEFUN, but it is not always the most concise one and sometimes it is not possible. We'll now discuss the alternatives.

Using DEFSETF

DEFSETF is a convenience macro; it is helpful if you already have a function which does the work of updating your place. So, let's assume we hadn't already written the setf function in our example above.[23] Instead, we have a function that does the same work but isn't a setf function:

```
CL-USER > (defun set-number-word (number new-value)
            (setf (gethash (format nil "~@R" number) *latin-numbers*)
                  new-value))
SET-NUMBER-WORD
```

In this case, defining the setf function is as simple as this:

```
CL-USER > (defsetf number-word set-number-word)
NUMBER-WORD
CL-USER > (setf (number-word 7) "septem")
"septem"
CL-USER > (number-word 7)
"septem"
T
```

While that's certainly convenient, there are two catches. One is that the parameter for the new value must be the last one, so this will only work with lambda lists that only have required parameters. The second is that you now have defined a macro and not a function. In the first example, you had a function object you could refer to with #'(SETF NUMBER-WORD), but this is not the case here.

DEFSETF also has a so-called "long form," where you provide a macro instead of a function, but it is what the standard calls a "function-like macro" and you can't do the things with it that DEFINE-SETF-EXPANDER (see next) can do.

[23]If you want to follow along, ask your IDE to *undefine* (see Recipe 16-9) the function (SETF NUMBER-WORD) or start a new image and define only the hash table and the NUMBER-WORD function.

Using DEFINE-SETF-EXPANDER

This is the most complex but also the most powerful way to do it. And because of the inherent complexity, we'll approach it with a series of examples, some of which will be *partly broken on purpose* so that we can gradually see why this macro is as complicated as it is.

(Note: If you've never written a macro before, this is not for you. You should read the relevant chapters of *Practical Common Lisp* first.)

Let's do something similar to our NUMBER-WORD example from above, but with the role of strings and numbers reversed (and even a tad simpler):[24]

```
(defparameter *english-numbers* (make-hash-table :test 'equal))

(setf (gethash "one" *english-numbers*) 1
      (gethash "two" *english-numbers*) 2
      (gethash "fifteen" *english-numbers*) 15)

(defun word-number (word)
  (values (gethash word *english-numbers*)))
```

Without further ado, we could now do this:

```
(define-setf-expander word-number (word)
  (let ((new-value-var (gensym)))
    (values nil
            nil
            `(,new-value-var)
            `(setf (gethash ,word *english-numbers*) ,new-value-var)
            `(word-number ,word))))
```

Let's try it:

```
CL-USER > (word-number "one")
1
CL-USER > (word-number "eight")
NIL
CL-USER > (setf (word-number "eight") 8)
8
CL-USER > (word-number "eight")
8
```

[24]We wrapped the output of GETHASH with VALUES to get rid of the second return value, but that is only for cosmetic reasons.

So, what did we do? We defined a *setf expander*, the job of which is to return a *setf expansion*. And that in turn is, as you can see, a collection of five values. We'll ignore the first two values for now (they are `NIL` above) and look at the other three:

(iii) The third value is the name of a variable, which the compiler will use to deliver the new value to us. (That's what `NEW-VALUE` was in our setf function at the beginning of the recipe.) As we'll need a name that's guaranteed to be new, we use `GENSYM` (see Recipe 1-2) as usual.

Note that this variable name is wrapped in a list. That's because this is supposed to also work with multiple values (see page 293).

(iv) The fourth value is the actual form that will be executed to perform the update on our *place*. This is essentially what the bodies of our setf functions did so far. This form must also return the new value.

(v) While the fourth value is a form to *update* (i.e., write) the place, the fifth value is a form to *access* (i.e., read) it. For now, let's not worry why we might need this. (Or see footnote 26 if you can't wait.)

`SETF` is supposed to also work in more complicated settings, so how about this?[25]

```
CL-USER > (word-number "fifteen")
15
CL-USER > (setf (ldb (byte 1 0) (word-number "fifteen")) 0)
0
CL-USER > (word-number "fifteen")
14
```

Now our translation table is wrong, but otherwise it worked as expected, right? Nope:

```
CL-USER > (setf (ldb (byte 1 0) (word-number (print "fifteen"))) 0)
"fifteen"
"fifteen"
0
```

`"fifteen"` was printed twice, so obviously the form `(PRINT "fifteen")` was evaluated twice.[26] And that is never a good sign for a macro and it should be avoided at all costs.

The right way to define our setf expander would have been like so:

[25] For `LDB` and `BYTE` see chapter 24 of *Practical Common Lisp*.

[26] This also shows, by the way, that somewhere during the evaluation of this form both our update *and* our access form were used. Have a look at a possible setf expansion of `LDB` in the dictionary entry for `DEFINE-SETF-EXPANDER` if you're wondering why this is so.

```
(define-setf-expander word-number (word)
  (let ((word-var (gensym))                                   ;; <- new
        (new-value-var (gensym)))
    (values `(,word-var)                                      ;; <- new
            `(,word)                                          ;; <- new
            `(,new-value-var)
            `(setf (gethash ,word-var                         ;; <- changed
                            *english-numbers*)
                   ,new-value-var)
            `(word-number ,word-var))))                       ;; <- changed
```

Now:

```
CL-USER > (word-number "fifteen")
14
CL-USER > (setf (ldb (byte 1 0) (word-number (print "fifteen"))) 1)
"fifteen"
1
CL-USER > (word-number "fifteen")
15
```

This gives us a chance to explain the first two values of the setf expansion:

(i) The first value is a list of variable names for temporary variables.

(ii) The second value is a list of forms (with as many forms as there were names in the first list). Before anything else is done, each variable name will be bound to the result of evaluating the corresponding form.

In this corrected version, `WORD` is only evaluated once and whenever its value is needed, we use `WORD-VAR` instead.

OK, but we could still have done all of this with setf functions. So why all the effort?

At the end of Recipe 6-8, we mentioned a function "`CDR-ASSOC`" for the typical combination of `ASSOC` and `CDR`. Writing this function is, of course, easy:

```
CL-USER > (defparameter *alist*
            (list (cons 'donald-duck 'duckburg)
                  (cons 'superman 'metropolis)
                  (cons 'batman 'gotham-city)))
*ALIST*
CL-USER > (defun cdr-assoc (item alist)
            (cdr (assoc item alist)))
MY-CDR-ASSOC
CL-USER > (cdr-assoc 'batman *alist*)
```

```
GOTHAM-CITY
```

But we can't write a suitable `(SETF CDR-ASSOC)` with a setf *function* if we also want to be able to *add* conses to the alist. That would mean we'd have to modify the *place* represented by the second argument to `CDR-ASSOC`; with setf functions (or even with the macros generated with `DEFSETF`), it would have been evaluated.

Our first attempt at solving this is to construct our setf expander like so:

```
(define-setf-expander cdr-assoc (item alist)
  (let ((item-var (gensym))
        (cons-found (gensym))
        (alist-var (gensym))
        (new-value-var (gensym)))
    (values '(,item-var ,alist-var ,cons-found)
            '(,item ,alist (assoc ,item-var ,alist-var))
            '(,new-value-var)
            '(cond (,cons-found
                     (setf (cdr ,cons-found) ,new-value-var))
                    (t
                     (setf ,alist (acons ,item-var ,new-value-var
                                         ,alist-var))
                     ,new-value-var))
            '(cdr ,cons-found))))
```

(Note how we use `ITEM-VAR` in the form for `CONS-FOUND`. The bindings described by the first and second value of the setf expansion will be performed in sequence as with `LET*`.)

This seems to work:

```
CL-USER > (cdr-assoc 'donald-duck *alist*)
DUCKBURG
CL-USER > (setf (cdr-assoc 'donald-duck *alist*) 'entenhausen)
ENTENHAUSEN
CL-USER > (cdr-assoc 'donald-duck *alist*)
ENTENHAUSEN
CL-USER > (setf (cdr-assoc 'spider-man *alist*) 'new-york-city)
NEW-YORK-CITY
CL-USER > (cdr-assoc 'spider-man *alist*)
NEW-YORK-CITY
```

But how about a more complicated setting?

```
CL-USER > (defparameter *container* (list :whatever *alist*))
*CONTAINER*
```

```
CL-USER > (cdr-assoc 'daredevil (nth 1 *container*))
NIL
CL-USER > (setf (cdr-assoc 'daredevil (nth (print 1) *container*))
                'new-york-city)
1
1
NEW-YORK-CITY
CL-USER > (cdr-assoc 'daredevil (nth 1 *container*))
NEW-YORK-CITY
```

So, our setf expansion *kind of* does the right thing, but although we took care to evaluate the ALIST parameter only once, we again see a double evaluation. And we can't replace (SETF ,ALIST ...) with (SETF ,ALIST-VAR ...), because then we'll only update our internal variable and not the original place we're interested in. Bummer...

The solution is to realize that there are *two* setf expansions at work here: our own and that of (SETF NTH). With DEFINE-SETF-EXPANDER, we can instruct the compiler to sort the mess out and arrange all setf expanders into a complicated but efficient choreography that we don't have to care about. This is the final form:

```
(define-setf-expander cdr-assoc (item alist &environment env)
  (multiple-value-bind (temp-vars temp-forms store-vars
                        setter-form getter-form)
      (get-setf-expansion alist env)
    (let ((item-var (gensym))
          (cons-found (gensym))
          (new-value-var (gensym)))
      (values `(,@temp-vars ,item-var ,cons-found)
              `(,@temp-forms ,item (assoc ,item-var ,getter-form))
              `(,new-value-var)
              `(cond (,cons-found
                      (setf (cdr ,cons-found) ,new-value-var))
                     (t
                      (let ((,(first store-vars)
                              (acons ,item-var ,new-value-var
                                     ,getter-form)))
                        ,setter-form
                        ,new-value-var)))
              `(cdr ,cons-found)))))
```

Here we prepare for the fact that the ALIST parameter is itself a *place* and ask for *its* setf expansion.[27] (Even if it's "just" a variable, it'll have one.) We then use this

[27]Note the use of the environment parameter (see Recipe 10-9).

information when appropriate:

- Whenever we need the value of the `ALIST` parameter, we call its access form (which we've called `GETTER-FORM` here).
- When binding our temporary variables, we also bind the temporary variables of the "inner" setf expansion (here called `TEMP-VARS`). If we hadn't done that (or if we hadn't done it first), we could have run into a problem when using `GETTER-FORM` later because this form might need these temporary variables.
- When we eventually update the *place* `ALIST`, we don't use `SETF` as before, but instead call the corresponding update form which we've called `SETTER-FORM`.

  For that to succeed we first have to store the new value in the corresponding variable (the counterpart to our `NEW-VALUE-VAR`), which is the first name in `STORE-VARS`.

Yes, this is quite a mouthful, but it enables the compiler to generate efficient code even in heavily nested `SETF`s and it gives us almost unlimited power to create arbitrary setf expanders.[28]

As an exercise, you might want to look at macros like `ROTATEF` and `SHIFTF` (see Recipe 10-7) and implement them yourself using `DEFINE-SETF-EXPANDER`. Also, the `MACROEXPAND` function will be a very helpful tool to debug your own setf expanders.

So, Which One Do I Use?

I'd say you should define setf functions with `DEFUN` or `DEFMETHOD` whenever possible, because this'll give you function objects and method dispatch, if needed. And if you come to a point where functions won't suffice, use `DEFINE-SETF-EXPANDER`.

`DEFSETF` is of limited utility because it can't do things the `DEFUN` version can't also do. It is most likely in the standard for historical reasons.[29]

Using `DEFINE-MODIFY-MACRO`

`DEFINE-MODIFY-MACRO` is a relatively simple macro that you can use to define macros that modify *places* in a way similar to what `INCF` does. (Macros like these traditionally have an "`F`" at the end of their name.)

---

[28]In case you're still somewhat unsure about how this macro should be used, its HyperSpec dictionary entry also contains some examples. And one more is following on page 293.

[29]See `http://www.lispworks.com/documentation/HyperSpec/Issues/iss174_w.htm`. Before function names like `(SETF FOO)` were allowed, the only way to write setf accessors was with macros and for that `DEFSETF` was the more convenient variant. It probably was left in for backward compatibility.

It may look like a pure convenience macro, but we'll see that it can again help us to avoid multiple evaluations.

The equivalent of

```
(incf a k)
```

would in C be

```
a += k;
```

In C, you can also write

```
a >>= k;
```

which in COMMON LISP would be

```
(setf a (ash a -k))
```

How would you write something like "ASHF" so that you have this shorter form?

```
(ashf a -k)
```

You could try to write the macro yourself:

```
(defmacro ashf (integer-place count)
  `(setf ,integer-place (ash ,integer-place ,count)))
```

Let's test it:

```
CL-USER > (defparameter *x* 8)
*X*
CL-USER > (ashf *x* -1)
4
CL-USER > *x*
4
CL-USER > (defparameter *arr* (make-array 10 :initial-element 16))
*ARR*
CL-USER > (ashf (aref *arr* (print 1)) -1)
1
1
8
CL-USER > (aref *arr* 1)
8
```

It's like above. Our macro does the job, but it is not quite correct because it again suffers from double evaluation. We could fix this ourselves using DEFINE-SETF-EXPANDER, but that would involve quite a lot of work.

The easier way to do it is like so:

```
(define-modify-macro ashf (count) ash)
```

This will make sure that ASHF does the right thing without double evaluation (try it). Note that we have to specify a lambda list *without* the first argument (which must be the place to modify).

Multiple-Valued Places

Places can also consist of multiple values. We're going to extend our superhero database from above to demonstrate this:

```
(defparameter *superheroes*
  (list (list 'superman 'clark-kent 'metropolis)
        (list 'batman 'bruce-wayne 'gotham-city)))

(defun superhero-info (hero database)
  (let ((entry (assoc hero database)))
    (values (second entry)
            (third entry))))
```

This can now be used like so:

```
CL-USER > (superhero-info 'superman *superheroes*)
CLARK-KENT
METROPOLIS
```

If we want to have a setf expander matching this, it has to look like so:

```
(define-setf-expander superhero-info (hero database
                                      &environment env)
  (multiple-value-bind (temp-vars temp-forms store-vars
                        setter-form getter-form)
      (get-setf-expansion database env)
    (let ((hero-var (gensym))
          (entry-found (gensym))
          (new-value-vars (list (gensym) (gensym))))
      (values `(,@temp-vars ,hero-var ,entry-found)
              `(,@temp-forms ,hero (assoc ,hero-var ,getter-form))
              `,new-value-vars
              `(cond (,entry-found
```

```
                    (setf (cdr ,entry-found)
                          (list ,@new-value-vars)))
                   (t
                    (let ((,(first store-vars)
                           (cons (list ,hero-var ,@new-value-vars)
                                 ,getter-form)))
                      ,setter-form
                      (values ,@new-value-vars))))
              `(values-list (rest ,entry-found)))))
```

And it can be utilized like this:

```
CL-USER > (superhero-info 'spider-man *superheroes*)
NIL
NIL
CL-USER > (setf (superhero-info 'spider-man *superheroes*)
                (values 'peter-parker 'new-york-city))
PETER-PARKER
NEW-YORK-CITY
CL-USER > (superhero-info 'spider-man *superheroes*)
PETER-PARKER
NEW-YORK-CITY
```

The relevant change here is that we now have a list `NEW-VALUE-VARS` of two variables instead of the one variable we previously had. Everything else works pretty much as before.

10-9. Working with Environments

Problem

So-called *"environments"* can potentially be very helpful for the macros that you are writing. Unfortunately, the standard treats environments as black boxes and many implementations almost conceal them.

So, what are environments and how can you use them to your advantage?

Solution

Let's start with the first question and use an example to demonstrate what environments are for. (We'll use SBCL throughout this recipe. If you try to reproduce this with another Lisp, you might get slightly different results, although the general ideas are the same.)

Recipe 17-9 has a compiler macro that makes a decision based upon whether the argument to a function is constant or not. For our investigations, a simplified macro will do:

```
(defmacro do-something (input)
  (if (constantp input)
    `(do-something-at-load-time ,input)
    `(do-something-at-run-time ,input)))

(defun do-something-at-load-time (input)
  (declare (ignore input))
  'did-something-at-load-time)

(defun do-something-at-run-time (input)
  (declare (ignore input))
  'will-do-something-at-run-time)
```

Let's try this:

```
CL-USER> (do-something 42)
DID-SOMETHING-AT-LOAD-TIME
CL-USER> (defconstant +foo+ 42)
+FOO+
CL-USER> (do-something +foo+)
DID-SOMETHING-AT-LOAD-TIME
CL-USER> (let ((foo 42))
           (do-something foo))
WILL-DO-SOMETHING-AT-RUN-TIME
CL-USER> (symbol-macrolet ((foo +foo+))
           (do-something foo))
WILL-DO-SOMETHING-AT-RUN-TIME
```

This all seems fine, except for the last form. FOO is just a symbol macro (see Recipe 1-5) that expands to the constant variable +FOO+; so why can't the compiler "see" that it is constant?

The reason is that we were sloppy when writing our macro. We should have written it like so:

```
(defmacro do-something (input &environment env)        ;; <- added env
  (if (constantp input env)                            ;; <- used it
    `(do-something-at-load-time ,input)
    `(do-something-at-run-time ,input)))
```

Now it works as expected:

```
CL-USER> (symbol-macrolet ((foo +foo+))
           (do-something foo))
DID-SOMETHING-AT-LOAD-TIME
```

But why? Keep reading.

How It Works

Every macro may optionally have a so-called *environment* parameter prefixed by &ENVIRONMENT in its lambda list. And we have seen that a function like CONSTANTP accepts an environment object as an optional argument. (We've also seen environment objects in use on page 290.) But this is already all the standard allows us to do with environment objects; we can receive them and then pass them on without looking at them.

So, why could SBCL recognize that FOO was just a "local name" for the constant variable +FOO+? Because this information was contained in the environment object ENV.[30] Which leads to the question what information can be found in an environment.[31]

The full answer can be found in section 3.1.1 of the standard, but it also depends on how much of this your implementation is willing to reveal (and what additional information it might provide). Roughly, you can expect to be able to suck this information out of an environment object:

- Bindings that are currently in effect (dynamic and lexical variables, local and global functions, and so on).
- Declarations[32] and proclamations that are currently in effect. This might include type information and optimization settings.
- Information about active handlers and restarts, and so forth. (See what Chapter 12 has to say about the *dynamic environment*.)

Once we know that there's potentially useful information in these environment objects, the next question, of course, is: how do we get at it? Part of the answer is Guy Steele's book *Common Lisp the Language, 2nd Edition*[33] (Digital Press, 1990; fondly

[30]Note that according to the standard it is implementation-dependent whether the expansion of a symbol macro is stored in the environment; which means that this example might not work the same with other Lisps.

[31]We'll use the terms *environment* and *environment object* interchangeably from now on, although technically there is a difference. An *environment object* is something like what was bound to ENV in our example, while there are usually several *environments* that are active at any given point in the execution of a program. The *environment object* can be used to query these *environments*.

[32]See, for example, Recipe 17-3.

[33]Available online at http://www.cs.cmu.edu/Groups/AI/html/cltl/cltl2.html.

called "*CLtL2*"), which was released before the ANSI standard was finalized; it describes some language features that didn't make it into the standard. One of these features is a description of environment access (section 8.5), and luckily those implementations that expose their environment objects mostly follow the specification of *CLtL2*. In particular, as of July 2015:

- ALLEGROCL has arguably the best support for environment access, which includes very detailed documentation.
- LISPWORKS implements most of what's in *CLtL2* and briefly documents the individual functions as part of its HCL package.
- Environment access for the open source implementations CMUCL, SBCL, and CLOZURECL is available; and there's the library INTROSPECT-ENVIRONMENT (installable with QUICKLISP; see Recipe 18-2) that provides a unified interface for all three (and maybe even some more once you read this).

Let's look at two examples of how we can utilize environment information. For the first example, we assume that we've implemented two algorithms to solve a problem; one is an exact solution, the other usually delivers only approximations but is much faster. For our tests, we'll use these two stubs that will help us distinguish which function was called:

```
(defun quick-approximation (arg)
  (declare (ignore arg))
  0)

(defun slow-and-exact (arg)
  (declare (ignore arg))
  1)
```

We now write a compiler macro (see Recipe 17-9) that is supposed to decide which of the two will be used based on the SPEED optimize quality currently in effect (see Recipe 17-3) and we do it like so:

```
(define-compiler-macro slow-and-exact (&whole form &environment env
                                                input)
  (if (eql 3
           (second
            (assoc 'speed
                   (introspect-environment:declaration-information
                    'optimize env))))
      `(quick-approximation ,input)
      form))
```

DECLARATION-INFORMATION is one of the functions described in *CLtL2* and it is used here to query for OPTIMIZE declarations. The result will be a list like this:

```
((SPEED 1) (SPACE 1) (SAFETY 3) (DEBUG 2) ...
```

We then use ASSOC (see Recipe 6-8) and SECOND to get at the specific information we need. To try this, compile the following two functions:[34]

```
(defun test-1 (input-list)
  (loop for input in input-list
        sum (slow-and-exact input)))

(defun test-2 (input-list)
  (declare (optimize speed))
  (loop for input in input-list
        sum (slow-and-exact input)))
```

You should now see this in the REPL:

```
CL-USER> (test-1 (list 1 2 3))
3
CL-USER> (test-2 (list 1 2 3))
0
```

For the second example, let's assume we have a function COMPUTATION, of which we know that if its argument is a fixnum it'll always return a fixnum. We can again exploit this with a compiler macro:[35]

```
(define-compiler-macro computation (&whole form &environment env
                                    input)
  (if (eql 'fixnum
           (cdr
            (assoc 'type
                   (nth-value
                    2
                    (introspect-environment:variable-information
                     input env)))))
      `(locally (declare (notinline computation))
         (the fixnum (computation ,input)))
      form))
```

VARIABLE-INFORMATION is one of those *CLtL2* functions and it'll return three values (for example, information about whether the variable is lexically bound). We are

[34]And make sure to compile SLOW-AND-EXACT *after* the compiler macro was defined or else it won't have any effect.

[35]The NOTINLINE declaration is in there to prevent the compiler macro from being called again and again on the same form.

only interested in the third one, which among other things, informs us about declared types.

If you now compile these two functions

```
(defun test-1 (arg)
  (+ 42 (computation arg)))

(defun test-2 (arg)
  (declare (fixnum arg))
  (+ 42 (computation arg)))
```

and look at the generated code (see Recipe 17-12), you will see that `TEST-1` calls an internal function `GENERIC+` to perform the addition, while `TEST-2` does it directly in machine language.

10-10. Commenting Out Parts of Your Code

Problem

You want to completely hide parts of your code (as in "commenting out") or you want to hide or reveal them selectively based on the capabilities of the underlying Lisp system.

Solution

Let's start with hiding code unconditionally. If you (compile and) load the following file, then none of the four function definitions will have any effect (some Lisps might even complain that the file is empty):

```
;; (defun foo () 42)

#|
(defun bar () 43)

(defun baz () 44)
|#

#+(or)
(defun quux () 45)
```

This happens because we've used three different techniques:

- Everything following a semicolon up to the end of the line will be ignored.
- Everything following the two-character sequence `#|` will be ignored up to and including the (matching) two-character sequence `|#`.

  This is obviously meant for commenting out larger parts of your code.
- The (one) *form* following `#+(OR)` will be ignored for reasons that we'll explain next.

How It Works

The most interesting part of this is the third point above; the `#+` syntax, which is actually intended for *conditional* hiding or revealing of code. It works like this:

(i) Every COMMON LISP has a global special variable called `*FEATURES*`, which holds a list of symbols. These are typically keyword symbols, but they don't have to be.

(ii) Every Lisp's list of *features* will be different (that being the whole point), but a couple of things can be expected:

- One or more symbols identifying the vendor, like `:LISPWORKS`, `:SBCL`, or `:CLISP`.
- Sometimes also symbols identifying the version, like `:LISPWORKS6` or even `:LISPWORKS6.1`.
- Symbols identifying the underlying operating system or architecture, like `:LINUX` or `:X86`.
- Symbols denoting capabilities the Lisp might or might not have (maybe depending on how it was built or on the platform it runs on), like `:SB-THREAD` for versions of SBCL with multithreading or `:IEEE-FLOATING-POINT` (see Recipe 4-6).

(iii) User code and library code can modify this list and might add symbols to it. For example, once you've loaded the CFFI library, it has added `:CFFI` to `*FEATURES*`, but maybe also `CFFI-FEATURES:FLAT-NAMESPACE` (see Recipe 19-1).

(iv) If your Lisp reads something like

```
#+:foo (bar)
```

then it'll first read the *symbol* `:FOO` and check whether `:FOO` is in `*FEATURES*`. If it is, it will simply continue reading the `(BAR)` form. If it is *not*, it will *skip* that form.

(v) Symbols will be read as if the keyword package were the current package, so the above could also have been written like so:

```
#+foo (bar)
```

But the following would be different because it'd mean to look for the symbol CL-USER::FOO in *FEATURES*:

```
#+cl-user::foo (bar)
```

(vi) If the form following the #+ is to be ignored, it will be read in a special mode[36] so that the reader will find the end of the form without creating symbols, complaining about non-existent packages, and so on.

So, if you're on SBCL, then this

```
#+:lispworks (fli:register-module :thing-fish)
```

won't result in error messages, even if there is no package named "FLI" in your image.

(vii) Instead of a symbol, you can also have expressions behind #+ that are comprised of symbols and the logical connectives AND, OR, and NOT, with the usual meaning.

For example, this

```
#+(or cmucl (and sbcl (not os-windows))) (do-it)
```

would mean to skip the (DO-IT) form unless we are on CMUCL or on SBCL, but in the latter case, only if the OS isn't Microsoft Windows.

(viii) There's also #-, which is simply the opposite of #+. (So, if it weren't there, you could simulate it with NOT.)

As almost all of the features aren't standardized; you can't really rely on certain things. For example, what do you need to be sure you're on Mac OS X? Will :DARWIN be in *FEATURES* or :MACOS or something else? This question is addressed by the TRIVIAL-FEATURES library (installable with QUICKLISP; see Recipe 18-2), which tries to provide a unified list of features as far as things like the operating system or the architecture are concerned.

So, finally, how does #+(OR) work? It is just a clever trick relying on the fact that, in order to be logically consistent, the expression (OR) must always evaluate to NIL (try it), so this is as if you had written #+FOO with :FOO not being in your list of features. (Except that there's no symbol of which you can be absolutely sure that it's not in somebody's *FEATURES* somewhere.)

[36]Look up *READ-SUPPRESS* in the standard for details.

Some Notes About `;` and `#|`

The comment sequences, of course, only have an effect when the Lisp reader is not in a mode that ignores them. So, typing `'ab;c` into your REPL will result in the symbol `AB`, but typing `'|ab;c|` will create a symbol with the symbol name `"ab;c"`. Likewise, typing `"ho#|ho|#ho"` will give you the string `"ho#|ho|#ho"`.

Also, blocks enclosed between `#|` and `|#` can be nested, but you'll always need matching pairs.

And finally, after reading `#|`, the reader switches to a character-by-character reading mode (as opposed to its usual, form-based reading mode) so that in pathological cases, a `|#` that was formerly ignored (like above) will now be interpreted as the end of the comment. This is probably so rare that you'll never have to worry about it, but if you're interested in such things, have a look at section 2.4.8.19.1 of the standard.

How `;`, `#|`, and Others Are Implemented

In case you're curious, these character sequences do their work by means of *syntax types* and *reader macro functions*. (See Chapter 8 for more information about this.) Recipe 8-8, for example, shows you how you can add another character that works like the semicolon, while Recipe 8-10 explains how something like `#|` can be implemented.

11. Concurrency

Many Lisps have offered some means of providing multiple execution strands for quite some time. However, most of them originally implemented it themselves in that the Lisp image managed several "Lisp processes" and had full control over them.[1] Only in the last decade or so, parallel to multi-core machines becoming mainstream, did most of the major COMMON LISP implementations move to a new model where these "Lisp processes" became *threads* that could be distributed over several cores and were no longer scheduled by the Lisp system, but by the underlying operating system.

We will only discuss the latter kind[2] here, although most of the content will also apply to the "traditional" approach. And we will interchangeably use words like *threads* or *processes* (which is the traditional word used in the Lisp world) for the same thing because we'll only care about how this stuff works as viewed from the Lisp side of things.[3]

In other words, when we're talking about *multithreading* here, we don't differentiate between ways to implement it (multiple processors or only one, multiple cores per processor or not, etc.), we're just assuming that several strands of execution operate simultaneously (or *as if* simultaneously) without the Lisp programmer generally being able to influence the sequence of events or how they take turns.

Of course, multithreading isn't mentioned in the COMMON LISP standard, so everything we're talking about in this chapter is implementation-dependent. And even more so than in other areas not covered by the HyperSpec is it indispensable to consult your Lisp's documentation because in this case, small differences can have disastrous consequences; see for example Recipe 11-2.

We can't reasonably provide a comprehensive introduction to concurrent programming in a few recipes. Instead, we will do the following. The first four recipes will cover the basics in an implementation-independent way. This should give you enough information to write your first simple multithreaded programs.[4] But you're

[1] An approach often called *cooperative multitasking*, or sometimes *green threads*.

[2] Some Lisp vendors call this *symmetric multiprocessing* (SMP).

[3] There will be situations where you'll need to know more details about how Lisp "processes" are implemented; for example, if you're interacting with other, non-Lisp programs or if you're using shared libraries. (And then it might also make sense to distinguish OS *processes* from *threads*.) But that's beyond the scope of this chapter.

[4] And probably also enough rope to hang yourself. If you've never done anything like this before, then this chapter alone certainly won't teach you how to write parallel programs.

probably better off looking at more high-level approaches; we'll introduce one in Recipe 11-5. This will not render the previous recipes obsolete, though, because some basic knowledge, especially about the perils of concurrent programming, is necessary—even if you're using a library that provides a very abstract view of your problems.

(If, on the other hand, you are already intimately familiar with multithreading from using other programming languages, you might simply want to skip everything up to Recipe 11-5 and just skim the BORDEAUX THREADS documentation instead.)

11-1. Managing Lisp Processes

Problem

You want to run some Lisp code in a parallel "process."

Solution

For this and the following recipes, we'll use the BORDEAUX THREADS[5] library (available via QUICKLISP; see Recipe 18-2), which provides a compatibility layer so that our example code will run in many different Lisps.[6]

Let's play a bit:

```
CL-USER > (defparameter *counter* 0)
*COUNTER*
CL-USER > (defvar *thread*)
*THREAD*
CL-USER > (progn
            (setq *thread* (bt:make-thread (lambda ()
                                             (sleep 2)
                                             (incf *counter*))))
            (print *thread*)
            (sleep 1)
            *counter*)
```

[5]Note that BORDEAUX THREADS was always intended to be a *minimal* interface, so don't be mistaken in thinking that the functionality this library offers is all that you can expect from a typical Lisp implementation of multithreading. What you're seeing is rather the lowest common denominator. And in case you're wondering what the name means, it refers to the 1st European Lisp Symposium (ELS)—held in Bordeaux in 2008—where the API of this library was proposed by Daniel Barlow as a layered standard. The library was initially implemented by Greg Pfeil.

[6]The output you're seeing will still be implementation-dependent, though. The following lines, for example, show LISPWORKS output and on, say, SBCL you'd see `SB-THREAD:THREAD` instead of `MP:PROCESS`.

```
#<MP:PROCESS Name "Anonymous thread" Priority 85000000
             State "Running">
0
;; wait at least a second
CL-USER > *counter*
1
CL-USER > *thread*
#<MP:PROCESS Name "Anonymous thread" Priority 0
             State "Dead">
```

We started a separate thread, to increment the value of `*COUNTER*`,[7] but in order to see some effect, we let it first sleep for approximately two seconds. We then saw that after one second, the value of `*COUNTER*` was still `0`, but some time later it had changed to `1`. We also saw that the printed representation of the `*THREAD*` object changed. Let's dissect this a bit more.

How It Works

You should, of course, first check whether your Lisp supports multithreading.[8] The fact that the BORDEAUX THREADS library can be loaded doesn't necessarily imply that. But it should work if *after* successfully loading the library you see the keyword symbol `:THREAD-SUPPORT` in `*FEATURES*` (see Recipe 10-10). Alternatively, you can query the global special variable `BT:*SUPPORTS-THREADS-P*`.

If your Lisp has multithreading support, then at least one thread will already be running and you can check this by evaluating the following form:

```
(bt:current-thread)
```

This will usually show a thread that has "REPL" or "Listener" as part of its name. Typically, there will be even more threads, and you can get a list of them with `(BT:ALL-THREADS)`. In the Windows IDE of LISPWORKS, this gives me eight threads, whereas in SBCL run from within SLIME, I see seven threads. (Just to give you an idea that even if *you* don't use threads, there's a lot going on already.)

Now for our little example:

- When you call `BT:MAKE-THREAD`, two things happen:
  - The only required argument is a function of no arguments, which will be run immediately in a separate, newly created Lisp process.

[7]See Recipe 11-3 for more about special variables and multithreading.

[8]As of July 2015, CLISP, for example, doesn't have multithreading at all, while for some other Lisps, support for multithreading differs depending on the underlying platform.

  - An object representing this process is created and returned, which will typically be a CLOS object with an implementation-dependent class (and with the *type* BT:THREAD; see Recipe 13-2).

- In our example, the new thread was printed as "anonymous." That's because we didn't give it a name. You can do that with a keyword argument to BT:MAKE-THREAD. The name itself doesn't matter for the underlying implementation, but it is, of course, a good idea to name threads and to use different names for different threads.
- What happens if the function that a thread was initialized with returns? As we can see from the output, the thread changes its *state*; it used to be *running* (sometimes also called *active*) and then changed to *dead* (or *finished*). You can use BT:THREAD-ALIVE-P (see example below) to check if a thread is still running.[9]
- The return value of the function, if any, is discarded. In other words, you only run it for its side effects.

What if we want to stop a process before it finishes what it's doing? That's what BT:DESTROY-THREAD is for:

```
CL-USER > (defparameter *counter* 0)
*COUNTER*
CL-USER > (let ((thread (bt:make-thread (lambda ()
                                          (sleep 5)
                                          (incf *counter*)))))
            (print (bt:thread-alive-p thread))
            (sleep 1)
            (bt:destroy-thread thread)
            (sleep 1)
            (print (bt:thread-alive-p thread))
            (sleep 5)
            *counter*)
T                                      ;; <-- immediately
NIL                                    ;; <-- about two seconds later
0                                      ;; <-- even later
```

We see here that the thread wasn't able to finish what it was supposed to do because *COUNTER* still has the value 0 after more than five seconds. And that's, of course, because the thread isn't alive anymore, as we can see from the second line that was printed.

It's not as easy as it looks, though. First, destroying a thread like this can be dangerous unless you're absolutely sure it doesn't do anything where it shouldn't be

[9]There will usually be other states like *stopped* or *waiting*, but BORDEAUX THREADS provides no means to query for them.

interrupted. (Does it, for example, currently have exclusive access to important resources—like a lock, see Recipe 11-2—which it should better have a chance to release first?) This could be ameliorated by running *cleanup forms* (like in UNWIND-PROTECT; see Recipe 12-8) before a thread is destroyed; but BORDEAUX THREADS can make no guarantees that this'll happen in all supported implementations. Second, different Lisps use different means to destroy processes and you'll have to look at their documentation to figure out how exactly this is implemented. You can generally not assume that a thread is destroyed immediately (or at all) after BT:DESTROY-THREAD is executed.

As a rule of thumb, BT:DESTROY-THREAD should be avoided if possible; rather, you should implement a "cooperative" way to stop a thread. A typical technique would be that the thread checks some flag at regular intervals and stops doing whatever it's doing once this flag has been set:[10]

```
CL-USER > (defparameter *counter* 0)
*COUNTER*
CL-USER > (let* (please-stop          ;; the flag
                 (thread (bt:make-thread
                          (lambda ()
                            (loop repeat 5 do (sleep 1)
                                  when please-stop do (return)
                                  finally (incf *counter*))))))
            (print (bt:thread-alive-p thread))
            (sleep 1)
            (setf please-stop t)  ;; raise the flag
            (sleep 1)
            (print (bt:thread-alive-p thread))
            (sleep 5)
            *counter*)
T                                        ;; <-- immediately
NIL                                      ;; <-- about two seconds later
0                                        ;; <-- even later
```

Escape Hatches

What do you do if you're experimenting with threads and one of them "runs amok" and threatens to clog your Lisp? It is a good idea to familiarize yourself with your IDE before that happens to figure out what can be done in such a case. As long as you have at least full control over your REPL, you should be able to identify the offending thread and destroy it using the commands described above. In more serious

[10]There are better ways to do this; see, for example, the end of Recipe 11-4.

situations, it might be helpful to use a graphical IDE like the one from LISPWORKS where you have tools like *process browsers* available.

You might, for example, want to try this (replace 4 with the number of cores that you have available, or try even higher numbers)

```
(loop repeat 4 do (bt:make-thread (lambda () (loop))))
```

and then see how to get out of this mess.

Threads Are Expensive

Our examples so far were atypical in that we started threads for simple, short-lived functions. Usually, threads execute long-running computations or endless loops waiting for some kind of event to act on. While what `BT:MAKE-THREAD` returns is, in a way, "just another Lisp object," it will be the result of a complex negotiation between your Lisp and the operating system; it should be considered an expensive resource not to be used and immediately thrown away like a simple cons cell.[11]

If you think you have a problem where *lots* of short-lived threads[12] would be the natural solution, you should search for "lightweight thread" implementations for COMMON LISP.

11-2. Accessing Shared Resources Concurrently

Problem

In your program, several threads want to modify the same object, potentially at the same time. Or one thread wants to read an object that another thread is modifying.

Solution

To see why this is a problem at all, let's start with a demonstration of what can happen. We're using BORDEAUX THREADS again (see Recipe 11-1).

Compile and load the following code:

```
(defparameter *counter* 0)

(defun test ()
```

[11]Some Lisps even automatically assume that threads are always long-lived and thus put them into high GC generations so that they won't be garbage-collected automatically.

[12]Think of something like ERLANG, where you could easily juggle with thousands of *processes*.

```
  (loop repeat 100
        do (bt:make-thread
             (lambda ()
               (loop repeat 100000 do (incf *counter*))
               (loop repeat 100000 do (decf *counter*))))))
```

Now run (TEST), make sure that all threads have finished (using BT:ALL-THREADS), and then look at the value of *COUNTER*. The value *should* be 0 because each thread increments the value as often as it decrements it. But it very likely *isn't* 0; at least it never was when I tested with various Lisps and on various machines.[13]

We'll discuss below what the reason for this behavior was. (And we'll even see cases where, other than here, only one thread modifies an object and we still get inconsistent results.) But we'll first try one solution to this problem:

```
(defparameter *counter* 0)

(defparameter *lock* (bt:make-lock))

(defun test ()
  (loop repeat 100
        do (bt:make-thread
             (lambda ()
               (loop repeat 100000 do (bt:with-lock-held (*lock*)
                                        (incf *counter*)))
               (loop repeat 100000 do (bt:with-lock-held (*lock*)
                                        (decf *counter*)))))))
```

If you now run (TEST) again, you might have to wait considerably longer until all threads have finished, but in the end, the value of *COUNTER* will definitely be 0.

How It Works

Let's try to understand why the original code didn't produce the expected outcome.[14] The form (INCF *COUNTER*) will likely be expanded (see Recipe 10-8) to something like this:

```
(setq *counter* (+ 1 *counter*))
```

[13]Should you always consistently see 0, rest assured that it'll be moderately easy to construct a similar example where your Lisp will "fail" as well.

[14]This is, by the way, something that's not likely to happen with cooperative multitasking (see the introduction to this chapter).

We'll now "translate" this to instructions for a simplified imaginary CPU. (In other words, this is definitely *not* what's really happening but should suffice to get the idea across.) The variable `*COUNTER*` represents some RAM address and for the operation above, three steps will be performed in our machine:

(I) The first step is to transfer the current value of `*COUNTER*` (let's say it is `42`) from memory to the CPU (in our case, into a register we'll call `R1`).

The pictures will show the state of the machine *after* the corresponding operation:

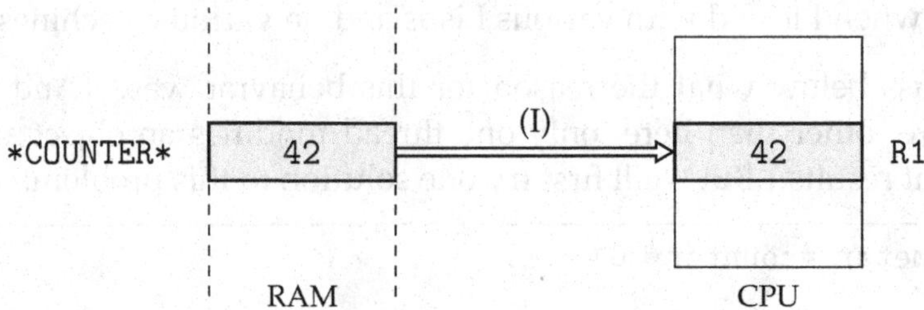

(II) In the second step, the CPU will perform the addition and increment the value of register `R1` by one.

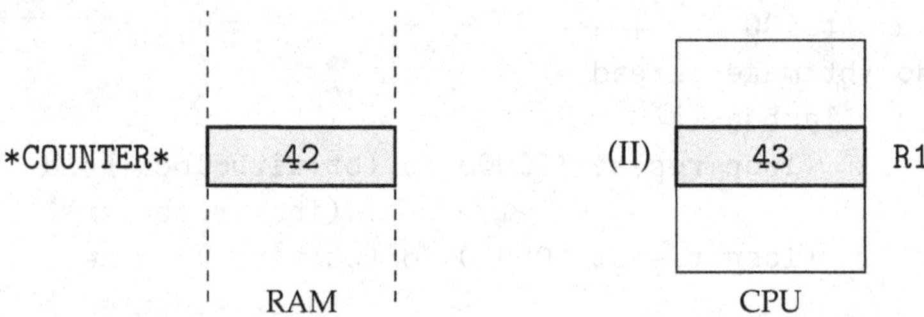

(III) In the final step, the contents of `R1` will be written back to the same RAM location they originally came from.

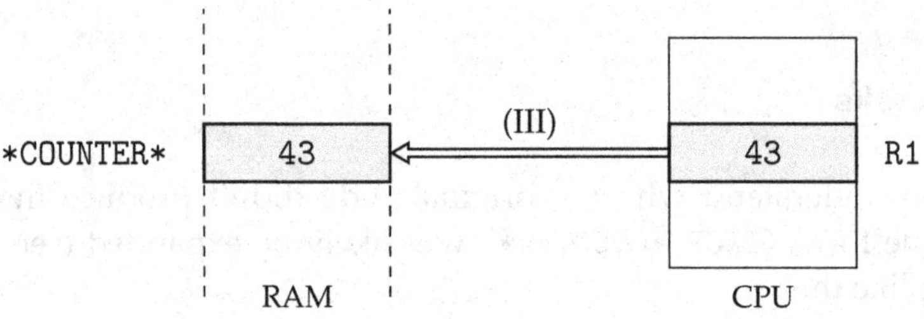

Now let's assume two threads are running this code. The first thread performs steps (I) and (II) but is then interrupted and can only execute its step (III) *after* the other thread had a chance to perform its three steps, which we'll call (I′) to (III′) here. This'll end up like so:[15]

[15]The first thread is on the left side, the second one on the right. We have depicted each thread with its own CPU, but that doesn't imply that each thread has its own core or processor. It suffices that the operating system arranges for each thread to "think" it has exclusive access to a CPU.

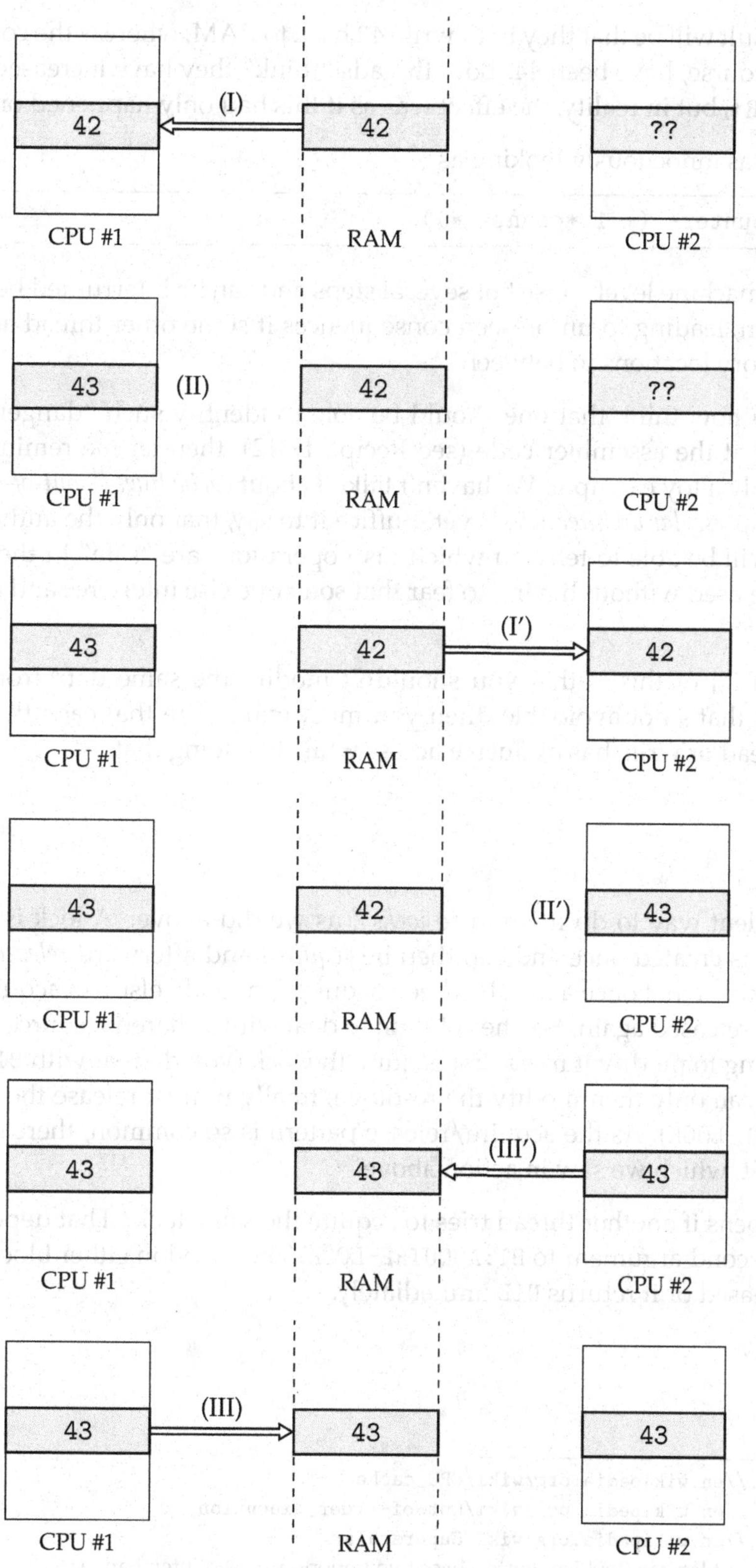
(I)
42
42
??
CPU #1
RAM
CPU #2
43
(II)
42
??
CPU #1
RAM
CPU #2
43
42
(I′)
42
CPU #1
RAM
CPU #2
43
42
(II′)
43
CPU #1
RAM
CPU #2
43
43
(III′)
43
CPU #1
RAM
CPU #2
43
(III)
43
43
CPU #1
RAM
CPU #2

And the result will be that they both write 43 back to RAM, whereas the correct result would, of course, have been 44. Both threads "think" they have increased the value of *COUNTER*, but in reality, the effect was as if this had only happened once.

Something as innocuously looking as

```
(setq *counter* (+ 1 *counter*))
```

will at the machine level consist of several steps and can be interrupted between any two of them, leading to unforeseen consequences if some other thread accesses the same memory locations in between.

And if you now think that one should be able to identify such "dangerous" parts by looking at the assembler code (see Recipe 17-12), then let me remind you that this was only a toy example. We haven't talked about *cache lines*,[16] *out-of-order execution*,[17] or *superscalar architectures*[18] yet. Suffice it to say, that only the authors of your compiler will be able to tell you which Lisp operations are "safe" in the sense that they can be used without having to fear that someone else interferes and adulterates the result.

The gist of all of this is that you shouldn't modify the same data from different threads. If that's not avoidable, then you must make sure that each thread that is trying to read or write has exclusive access while it's doing that.

Locks

One prevalent way to do it is to use *locks*[19] as we did above. A lock is an opaque object that is created once and can then be *acquired* and afterward *released*. The important point is that once a lock has been acquired, nobody else can acquire it before it has been released again. So, the solution to deal with a shared resource is that each thread trying to modify it must first acquire the lock (you do that with BT:ACQUIRE-LOCK) and can only then modify the resource; finally it must release the lock (using BT:RELEASE-LOCK). As the acquire/release pattern is so common, there's a "WITH-" macro for it, which we saw in action above.

What happens if another thread tries to acquire the same lock? That depends on the optional second argument to BT:ACQUIRE-LOCK. The function either blocks until the lock is released or it returns NIL immediately.

[16]See https://en.wikipedia.org/wiki/CPU_cache.
[17]See https://en.wikipedia.org/wiki/Out-of-order_execution.
[18]See https://en.wikipedia.org/wiki/Superscalar.
[19]Or *mutexes*. At least in the Lisp world, these two notions are used interchangeably.

Atomic Operations

Locks are a good solution to prevent problems like above, but as you'll know, there ain't no such thing as a free lunch; acquiring and releasing locks costs time, as we could witness. It would thus be nice if at least some operations were *atomic* in the sense that they can't be inadvertently interrupted. And indeed, most multithreaded Lisp implementations provide such operations, but these aren't part of BORDEAUX THREADS, as they differ between compilers and platforms. You'll have to look them up in the documentation.

In LISPWORKS, we could, for example, solve our initial problem with atomic operations and without locks, like so:[20]

```
(defun test ()
  (loop repeat 100
        do (bt:make-thread
            (lambda ()
              (loop repeat 100000
                    do (sys:atomic-incf *counter*))
              (loop repeat 100000
                    do (sys:atomic-decf *counter*))))))
```

A typical example where you want an atomic (or "thread-safe") operation is hash table access (see Chapter 6). You want to be sure that something like

```
(setf (gethash key my-hash-table) new-value)
```

isn't interrupted in the middle of what it's doing;[21] that is, you want that other threads see `MY-HASH-TABLE` either as it was *before* or *after* your update, but *not* in some intermediate state. Most multithreading-capable Lisps will provide something like this, but maybe you'll have to enable it when creating the hash table. In SBCL you would, for example, use the `:SYNCHRONIZED` keyword, like so:[22]

```
(make-hash-table :synchronized t)
```

In LISPWORKS, on the other hand, hash tables are thread-safe by default, but you can disable this (for efficiency reasons) like so:

```
(make-hash-table :single-thread t)
```

[20]In SBCL you can do almost the same thing with `SB-EXT:ATOMIC-INCF`, `SB-EXT:ATOMIC-DECF`, and a bit more work. According to their documentation, this interface is still experimental and subject to change, though. (As of July 2015.)

[21]Which could lead to disastrous consequences. Even if one thread is only reading from a hash table and another one is writing, then if the writer is interrupted at the wrong time, the reader may be in a situation where what it is trying to access isn't even a proper hash table anymore.

[22]This feature is currently also marked as "experimental" in the SBCL manual.

As usual, check your Lisp's documentation really carefully. Terms like "thread-safe" might mean different things in different Lisps. Also, that a single operation on a hash table is atomic doesn't guarantee atomicity *between* access operations; and even something seemingly simple like `(INCF (GETHASH ...))` expands into *two* access operations.[23]

The same caution should be applied to arrays (see below) and other compound data structures.

More Problems

I'll show two more typical problems with concurrent access that are different from what we had before. That'll hopefully make clear how problematic mutable data structures can be once more than one thread is involved.

The first example can be reproduced with LISPWORKS and might "work" with other Lisps.[24] Compile and load this code:

```
(defparameter *a*
  (make-array 1000 :element-type '(signed-byte 4)
                   :initial-element 0))

(defun writer (i)
  (loop repeat 100000 do
        (loop repeat 4 do (incf (aref *a* i)))
        (loop repeat 4 do (decf (aref *a* i)))))
```

This doesn't seem too fancy. The array element `(AREF *A* I)` will oscillate between `0` and `4` when `WRITER` is called.

Now try this:

```
(mapc 'bt:make-thread
      (list (lambda () (writer 0))
            (lambda () (writer 1))))
```

One thread will constantly modify the first array element while the other thread will do the same with the second element. Other than in our first example, no two threads access the *same value* at the same time. Still, if you try this a couple of times, you will very likely either get an error message, or at the end, the first two array elements won't be `0` as expected. So, what's the problem?

[23]See for example the `HCL:MODIFY-HASH` function in LISPWORKS.

[24]Which is not to say that this is a bug in LISPWORKS. They explicitly mention in their documentation that this specific type of array isn't thread-safe.

Due to its element type (see Recipe 5-9), the array needs only four bits per element and so they are arranged in such a way that two elements fit into one octet. Here's how the start of the array looks if the first two elements are 1 and 3:

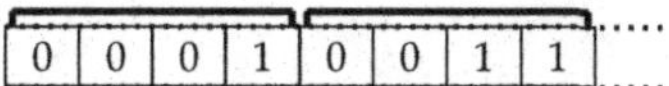

Let's assume the first thread is about to increase the first array element and the second thread wants to decrease the second element at the same time. The correct outcome would, of course, be this:

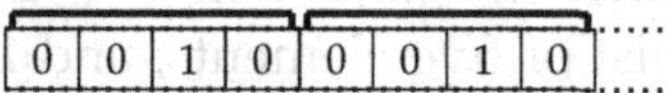

But due to the underlying hardware, the Lisp system will always have to transfer one octet (i.e., *two* adjacent array elements) at a time from memory to the CPU or vice versa.

What *could* thus happen is this: both threads have pulled one octet (comprising two array elements) into their respective CPUs.[25] The first thread has increased the value of the first element while the second thread has decreased the value of the second element. It now looks like so (with the changed bits marked gray):

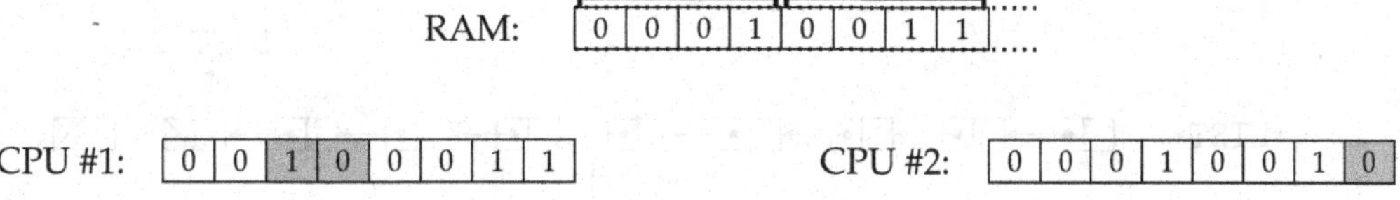

Now both threads will transfer the whole octet back to RAM. Whoever does it last "wins," but in both cases the result is wrong...

This was a case where two threads modified the same compound data structure, although they did *not* work on the same data. The next example will show a situation where only one thread is making modifications while another thread is just reading. Even that can lead to subtle problems:

```
(defparameter *list* (make-list 10))

(defun swap ()
  (let ((last-2 (last *list* 2))
        (new-tail (make-list 5)))
    (setf (cdr (nthcdr 4 *list*)) new-tail
          (cdr last-2) nil)))

(defun writer ()
  (loop repeat 1000000
```

[25] Again, you don't really need more than one core to see this error. It can also happen with two threads running on one core as the operating system will arrange things to happen *as if* each thread had its own CPU.

```
      do (swap)))

(defparameter *results* nil)

(defun reader ()
  (loop repeat 1000000
        do (pushnew (length *list*) *results*)))
```

Let's first examine what the function SWAP is doing.[26] *LIST* is a list of ten elements, NEW-TAIL is another—new—list of five elements, and LAST-2 is a "pointer" to the end of *LIST*.

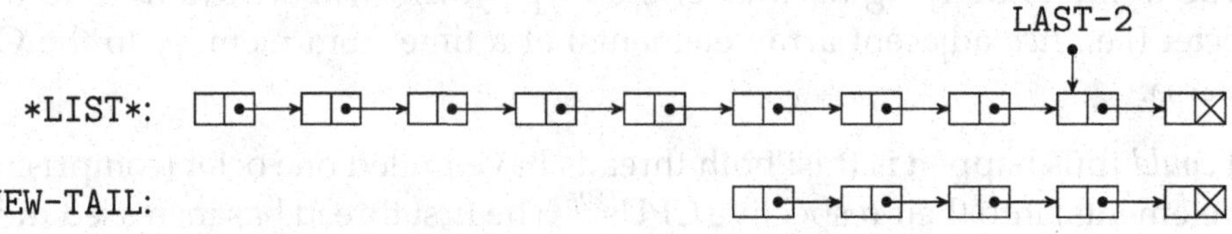

Now the function "redirects" one connection in *LIST* so that it gets a new tail. Afterward, it "cuts off" the old tail of *LIST* at the end:

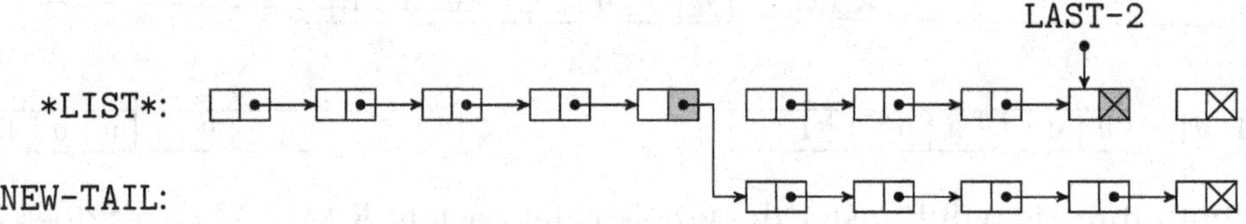

However, before and after this operation, *LIST* is always a list with ten elements, so if everything happened "in the right order," then READER would always push 10 onto *RESULTS*, so that in the end we would expect the value of *RESULTS* to be (10).

But if you try this

```
(mapc 'bt:make-thread '(writer reader))
```

then there's a good chance that *RESULTS* will be (9 10) in the end.

The reason, of course, is that in order to compute its length, READER has to walk through the whole list, element by element (see page 34). If both threads run in parallel long enough, then it's almost inevitable that at some point READER will end up in what was once the second half of *LIST*; but that has just been shortened by one. It will thus conclude that *LIST* comprises only nine elements.

[26]See also Chapter 2.

11-3. Using Special Variables in Concurrent Programs

Problem

You want to use special variables[27] in a multithreaded application, but you're unsure about how they will work there.

Solution

We're going to answer the question by going through a couple of experiments. We'll use BORDEAUX THREADS, as in Recipe 11-1.[28]

```
CL-USER> (defparameter *foo* 42)
*FOO*
CL-USER> (defparameter *results* nil)
*RESULTS*
CL-USER> (bt:make-thread (lambda () (push *foo* *results*)))
#<SB-THREAD:THREAD "Anonymous thread" RUNNING {1005433413}>
CL-USER> *results*
(42)
CL-USER> (let ((*foo* :yo))
           (bt:make-thread (lambda () (push *foo* *results*))))
#<SB-THREAD:THREAD "Anonymous thread" RUNNING {100554AE33}>
CL-USER> *results*
(42 42)
```

We have a global special variable `*FOO*` and when we start the first thread, we see that it can access its value (and that it can modify the value of `*RESULTS*`). This is not very surprising, we've already seen this in previous recipes.

However, if we rebind `*FOO*` before starting a new thread, this thread doesn't pick up the new binding but uses the original binding instead. Hmm...

```
CL-USER> (defparameter *foo* 42)
*FOO*
CL-USER> (defparameter *results* nil)
*RESULTS*
CL-USER> (map nil 'bt:make-thread
              (list (lambda ()
                      (let ((*foo* 1))
```

[27] For this recipe, we're assuming that you know how special variables work in single-threaded COMMON LISP programs. Otherwise, you might want to have a look at *Practical Common Lisp*.

[28] The following was recorded with SBCL, but results should be similar on all multithreaded Lisps.

```
                        (sleep .1)
                        (push (cons 1 *foo*) *results*)))
                    (lambda ()
                      (let ((*foo* 2))
                        (sleep .1)
                        (push (cons 2 *foo*) *results*)))))
NIL
CL-USER> *results*
((2 . 2) (1 . 1))
```

This certainly wasn't a scientific test, but it *seems* that each thread is able to establish its own binding for `*FOO*` without interfering with other threads.

Finally, you might be wondering why we used `*RESULTS*` instead of just letting the threads print something. Let's see...

If you evaluate

```
(bt:make-thread (lambda () (print 42)))
```

in a console session, you will likely see the number 42 printed. Maybe you will even see it printed in the middle of the printed representation of the thread returned by `BT:MAKE-THREAD`. If you instead evaluate the same form in SLIME or the LispWorks IDE, you will *not* see the 42 printed in your REPL.

This somewhat surprising behavior is also related to special variables.

How It Works

Again, the standard doesn't say anything about multithreading. But in the case of global special variables all Common Lisp implementations agree on the same behavior:[29]

- The initial, *global* value of the variable (that would be 42 in our example) can be seen and modified by all threads.
- Special variables can be rebound as usual, but those bindings are always *per thread* and don't have any global effect.

  This is why the second thread we started above didn't "see" the `:YO` binding; this binding was only effective in the REPL thread.

So, special global variables are what one usually calls *thread-local storage*.[30] And this also explains why we don't see the output of our last example in an IDE like SLIME

[29]Because a different behavior would have strange consequences for many global variables defined by the standard.

[30]See `https://en.wikipedia.org/wiki/Thread-local_storage`.

(see Recipe 16-2). IDEs usually rebind *STANDARD-OUTPUT* for various reasons, and while we're in the SLIME REPL, this variable is bound to a stream, which sends it output to a certain Emacs buffer. However, the new thread we started doesn't pick up this binding, but uses the original value.[31]

You usually don't want two or more threads writing to the same stream concurrently, but if you want to send the output of one of your threads to the SLIME REPL for debugging purposes, you can, for example, do it like so:[32]

```
(bt:make-thread (lambda () (print 42 #.*standard-output*)))
```

This works because the value of *STANDARD-OUTPUT* will now be evaluated at *read time* and thus before the thread is created. Without the #. this would, of course, not work as expected, as that would be the same as simply not providing a second argument to PRINT.

Per-Thread Initial Bindings

But how do we furnish threads we create with initial bindings? The approach we tried with :YO above obviously didn't work. BORDEAUX THREADS provides a special variable BT:*DEFAULT-SPECIAL-BINDINGS* for this task. The value of this variable must be an alist (see Recipe 6-8), where the keys are the names of special variables and the values are forms that will be evaluated (as with EVAL) on thread creation. The thread will then start with the corresponding local bindings. In other words, we could have achieved what we wanted above, like so:

```
CL-USER > (defparameter *foo* 42)
*FOO*
CL-USER > (defparameter *results* nil)
*RESULTS*
CL-USER > (let ((bt:*default-special-bindings*
                 '((*foo* . :yo))))
            (bt:make-thread (lambda ()
                              (push *foo* *results*))))
#<SB-THREAD:THREAD "Anonymous thread" RUNNING {1004A6C3D3}>
CL-USER > *results*
(:YO)
```

Variables That Are Always Global

As you might have guessed, the machinery necessary to make special variables

[31]Have a look into the *inferior-lisp* buffer to see where the 42 ended up.

[32]For the #. syntax, see Recipe 8-3.

thread-local entails a performance penalty. It's fairly small and you usually won't have to worry about this. But if it becomes a problem, you should be aware that most implementations, for this reason, will allow you to declare that a special variable will never be rebound. (See for example `SB-EXT:DEFGLOBAL` in SBCL or `HCL:DEFGLOBAL-VARIABLE` and `HCL:DEFGLOBAL-PARAMETER` in LispWorks.)

11-4. Communicating with Other Threads

Problem

One of your threads needs to notify one or more other threads about some event.

Solution

We'll use Bordeaux Threads again for a portable solution (see Recipe 11-1).

For the sake of completeness, we'll first mention `BT:JOIN-THREAD`. The caller of this function will wait until its argument—a thread—has finished:[33]

```
CL-USER> (let* ((state :not-yet-started)
                (thread (bt:make-thread
                         (lambda ()
                           (sleep 3)
                           (setf state :finished)))))
           (bt:join-thread thread)
           state)
:FINISHED      ;; <- after three seconds
```

This is rarely what you want, though.[34] A more typical situation is that one thread waits for some kind of "event," performs some action once it has "received" this event, and then goes back to its waiting state again. In theory, you could do this like so:

```
(defparameter *new-result* nil)

(defun producer ()
  (dotimes (i 5)
    (setf *new-result* (* i i))
    (sleep 1))
  (setf *new-result* :done))
```

[33]Note that the function running in the thread we started closes over the lexical variable `STATE`.

[34]At least not as a means of communication. `BT:JOIN-THREAD` can, of course, be useful in other circumstances.

```
(defun consumer ()
  (setf *new-result* nil)
  (bt:make-thread 'producer)
  (loop
   (case *new-result*
     (:done (return))
     ((nil))
     (otherwise (print *new-result*)
                (setf *new-result* nil)))
   (sleep .001)))
```

If you now execute (CONSUMER), you will see the values 0, 1, 4, 9, and 16 printed in the REPL, with breaks of approximately one second between them.

The "producer" computes results at certain intervals; the "consumer" prints them. Both threads communicate via the global variable *NEW-RESULT*.[35] The problem with this approach is that CONSUMER does what is usually called *busy waiting* or *spinning*; it is wasting valuable CPU time by performing regular checks on *NEW-RESULT*.[36]

This is the better way to do it:

```
(defparameter *new-result* nil)

(defun producer (cv lock)
  (flet ((set-value-and-notify (new-value)
           (bt:with-lock-held (lock)
             (setf *new-result* new-value)
             (bt:condition-notify cv))))
    (dotimes (i 5)
      (set-value-and-notify (* i i))
      (sleep 1))
    (set-value-and-notify :done)))

(defun consumer ()
  (let ((cv (bt:make-condition-variable))
        (lock (bt:make-lock)))
    (bt:make-thread (lambda () (producer cv lock)))
    (loop
       (bt:with-lock-held (lock)
         (bt:condition-wait cv lock)
```

[35]They should use a lock (see Recipe 11-2), but we've left that out here for brevity.

[36]And there's no simple way out of this. Check more often and you waste even more CPU cycles. Check less often and you probably introduce unwanted latency into your system.

```
      (when (eql *new-result* :done)
        (return))
      (print *new-result*)))))
```

How It Works

We're using a so-called *condition variable* that must always be paired with a lock (see Recipe 11-2). The consumer calls BT:CONDITION-WAIT, which effectively means that it'll sleep without consuming any CPU cycles until it is woken up by the OS scheduler. This happens whenever another thread calls BT:CONDITION-NOTIFY. That's all. The lock and the internal implementation will make sure that this works in an efficient way, and we don't have to worry about the perils of shared resources.

But it might be worth it to have a closer look anyway:

- Both BT:CONDITION-WAIT and BT:CONDITION-NOTIFY can only be called by a thread that currently holds the associated lock.
- Once a thread calls BT:CONDITION-WAIT and it is put to sleep, the lock will automatically be released in an atomic way (see page 313).
- If a thread that was waiting is woken up again, it will automatically reacquire the lock. It is as if it had held the lock all the time and was only dreaming that it was gone...

Note that this mechanism will also work with several threads waiting for the same condition variable—so that you can implement something like a pool of "worker threads." (See, for example, page 325.)

Alternatives

We should emphasize, once again, that BORDEAUX THREADS only provides the lowest common denominator between several different COMMON LISP multithreading implementations. Individual Lisps will provide more and other mechanisms of inter-thread communication. You might want to search your Lisp's documentation for things like *barriers, semaphores, mailboxes,* and *timers,* for example.

11-5. Parallelizing Algorithms Without Threads and Locks

Problem

You want to utilize all cores of your CPU for computation-intensive tasks without wading knee-deep in the intricacies of concurrent programming.

Solution

You could, for example, use the LPARALLEL library (which can be installed with QUICKLISP; see Recipe 18-2). We'll introduce it by means of an example.

Let's start with some fake code to simulate a CPU-bound task:[37]

```
(defun seed ()
  (random 100000000))

(deftype von-neumann ()
  '(integer 0 99999999))

(defun middle-square (seed n)
  (declare (optimize speed)
           (type von-neumann seed)
           (fixnum n))
  (loop for i below n
        for val of-type von-neumann = seed
          then (mod (floor (* val val) 10000) 100000000)
        finally (return val)))
```

The function MIDDLE-SQUARE accepts an integer with up to eight decimal digits and computes an integer of at most the same length by repeatedly applying von Neumann's *middle square method*.[38] (But what it does is really irrelevant as long as it keeps the CPU busy.)

We will now do the following:

```
(defparameter *seeds*
  (coerce (loop repeat 40000 collect (seed)) 'vector))

(defparameter *repetitions*
  (coerce (loop repeat 40000 collect (random 100000)) 'vector))

(defun test ()
  (map 'vector 'middle-square *seeds* *repetitions*))
```

We create two vectors of 40000 random seed values and 40000 repetition counts. Each seed/repetition pair is then fed into MIDDLE-SQUARE to eventually produce a result vector. Running (TEST) should take a couple of seconds, even on a fast ma-

[37] For DEFTYPE, see Recipe 13-1, and for DECLARE, see Recipe 17-3. (The function MIDDLE-SQUARE is only optimized to avoid unnecessary consing, which would distort the results. My timings are from SBCL on a 64-bit Windows machine, but the exact numbers don't really matter anyway.)

[38] See https://en.wikipedia.org/wiki/Middle-square_method.

chine. (Of course, all the code in this example should be compiled, because it'll otherwise take a *really* long time.)

Now, add the following code (and replace the number 4 with the number of cores that your computer has):

```
(setf lparallel:*kernel* (lparallel:make-kernel 4))

(defun ptest ()
  (lparallel:pmap 'vector 'middle-square *seeds* *repetitions*))
```

EQUALP (see Recipe 10-1) will show you that TEST and PTEST compute exactly the same results. But PTEST should be significantly faster. On my machine with four cores, it is consistently faster by a factor of approximately 3.5.

How It Works

LPARALLEL by James M. Lawrence is a relatively new COMMON LISP concurrency library based on BORDEAUX THREADS (see Recipe 11-1), the aim of which is to abstract away most of the ugliness of multithreading without losing the benefits. Roughly, it offers three layered levels of abstraction:

(i) At the lowest level, you submit *tasks* via *channels* and your tasks can communicate via *queues*. This is not very far away from the basics we discussed in the previous recipes, but at least you are (mostly) relieved of chores like thread creation and synchronization.

(ii) At the next level, you model your algorithms in terms of *futures*, *promises*, and related concepts[39] from functional programming.

(iii) At the highest level, you either use what Lawrence calls *cognates*—various operators like LPARALLEL:PMAP which work exactly like their COMMON LISP counterparts, except that they offer automatic parallelization—or *ptrees* (of which more below).

In this recipe, we're only able to introduce some functionality of the highest level, but it is certainly a good idea to look at the other stuff as well. LPARALLEL comes with good documentation, so you shouldn't have problems finding your way around.

Even with the highest abstraction level, there'll still be some work for you left, of course:

- You must understand your problem well enough to identify those parts that can be computed independently of others. Only those can be swapped out to

[39] See https://en.wikipedia.org/wiki/Futures_and_promises.

separate threads.[40]

- If there are dependencies between individual parts of your algorithm, you might still be able to utilize LPARALLEL's high-level constructs (see, for example, the upcoming *ptrees* example), but this might become more involved.
- Although LPARALLEL will abstract away many details, you must nevertheless be aware of the pitfalls of shared mutable objects (see Recipe 11-2). The more functional your code is, the easier will it be to employ convenience operators like the aforementioned *cognates*.

What the Example Does

Before LPARALLEL will actually do something useful for you, it needs a *kernel*, which we define above using the function `LPARALLEL:MAKE-KERNEL`. This will start a couple of "worker threads," the number of which you determine with the required argument to this function. This is essentially the only situation in LPARALLEL where you are required to come into contact with the guts of multithreading. The worker threads will be started once and they'll then wait for work to be done.[41] If you're using the high-level operators, it is LPARALLEL's job to distribute the work among the workers, and you don't have to worry about them.

The *cognates* are functions or macros like the `LPARALLEL:PMAP` we've already seen. Apart from a "`P`" at the beginning, they have the same name as some COMMON LISP operator and will do the same thing as this operator, except that they will subdivide the work to be done into parts and perform these tasks in parallel. The only difference between the non-parallel code and the parallel code in our example was that we switched to `LPARALLEL:PMAP`, which does the same as `CL:MAP`. It couldn't get much easier...

But note that this parallelization entails what we said above: what you want to do must be amenable to such a division. It also means that you can't rely on order; `LPARALLEL:POR`, say, will have slightly different semantics than `CL:OR`. Both will return the result from the first form that doesn't evaluate to `NIL`, but they differ in what "*first*" means for them; for `CL:OR`, this is determined by going through the forms from left to right, whereas for `LPARALLEL:POR`, it depends on the order in which forms are executed—which in the presence of multithreading is non-deterministic.

[40]In our example, this was easy and obvious—no element of the result vector depended on anything else except for the two arguments used to compute it—because I created it that way.

[41]So that after creating a kernel, LPARALLEL will usually not start or destroy any threads (see page 308).

Fine-Tuning

There are essentially two knobs that you can use to adjust the behavior of LPARALLEL when trying to optimize CPU utilization. One is the number of worker threads; that is, the argument to `LPARALLEL:MAKE-KERNEL`. You probably want to set this to the number of cores your computer has.[42] The idea is that if LPARALLEL is able to distribute the work evenly, then all cores will be busy. Using more worker threads than cores will very likely not buy you anything, as time will be lost due to needless *context switches*.[43]

One might think that using $n-1$ worker threads on an n-core system might be a sensible choice, as one core will be used by LPARALLEL's scheduler, other Lisp threads (see page 305), and other programs running on your computer. But for a computation-intensive program, all this other activity will only be background noise and it typically won't force one core to operate at full capacity.

For n cores, the theoretical upper bound for the possible speed improvement for a fully parallelizable algorithm will be the factor n. In my experiments with the example above, the factor was 3.5 on a four-core CPU, which is already quite nice.

The second knob comes into play if not all parts of your algorithm need the same time. An operator like `LPARALLEL:PMAP` will typically subdivide the work into n parts, where n is the number of worker threads you configured when creating the kernel. But if one part requires considerably less time than others, then one thread will twiddle its thumbs while the others are still busy. In such cases it will be better to create more (and smaller) parts and assign new work to threads whenever they're done with their current job. You can do that with the `:PARTS` keyword argument for most cognates.

Ptrees

We will consider one more example in which the parallelization is not as simple as it was above. In this case, our computation will again be subdivided into parts, but some parts will depend on others. This is what *ptrees* in LPARALLEL are for.

Let's start with a well-known recursive algorithm without concurrency. We'll use a simple, unoptimized version of the *Karatsuba algorithm*[44] for multiplying large integers:

```
(defun mult (a b)
  ;; number of bits the larger factor has
  (let ((length (max (integer-length a) (integer-length b))))
```

[42] See Recipe 11-6.

[43] See `https://en.wikipedia.org/wiki/Context_switch`.

[44] See `http://mathworld.wolfram.com/KaratsubaMultiplication.html`.

```
  (when (< length 100000)
    ;; numbers are "small"
    (return-from mult (* a b)))
  (let* ((length/2 (floor length 2))          ;; half of the bits
         (mask (1- (ash 1 length/2)))         ;; bitmask for right half
         (a1 (ash a (- length/2)))            ;; left half of A
         (a2 (logand a mask))                 ;; right half of A
         (b1 (ash b (- length/2)))            ;; left half of B
         (b2 (logand b mask))                 ;; right half of B
         (a1*b1 (mult a1 b1))
         (a2*b2 (mult a2 b2))
         (prod3 (mult (+ a1 a2) (+ b1 b2))))
    (+ (ash a1*b1 (* 2 length/2))
       a2*b2
       (ash (+ prod3 (- a1*b1) (- a2*b2)) length/2)))))
```

The idea is that instead of multiplying A and B directly (to which we fall back if the numbers are "small" by some arbitrary measure), we split both factors into two parts (A1 and A2 for A and similarly for B) and compute three products, out of which we then combine the result. We rely on the fact that multiplication is considerably more expensive than addition. Computation of these three smaller products will again be performed by MULT, resulting in potentially more recursion.[45]

An example for much smaller numbers (and in decimal instead of binary) would be the product $4321 \cdot 5618$, where instead we compute

$$4321 \cdot 5618 = 43 \cdot 56 \cdot 10^4 + ((43+21) \cdot (56+18) - 43 \cdot 56 - 21 \cdot 18) \cdot 10^2 + 21 \cdot 18$$

and thus we only need three multiplications instead of four:[46]

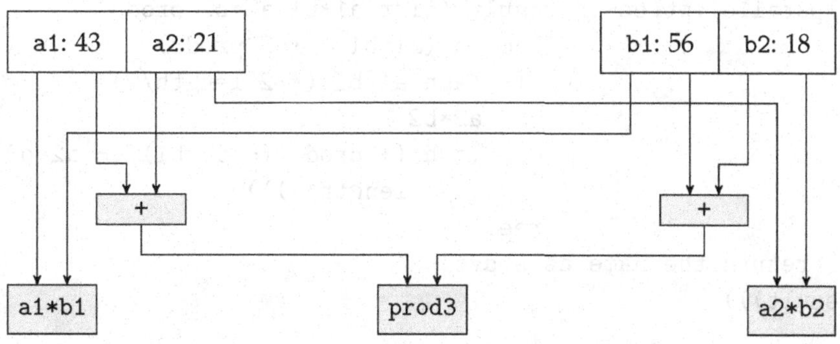

Parallelizing this algorithm is a bit more work than before, because partial results depend on other partial results, and thus the work can't be simply subdivided into

[45]This is a typical *divide and conquer* algorithm; see https://en.wikipedia.org/wiki/Divide_and_conquer_algorithms.

[46]Assuming that something like multiplication with 10^4 is a shift and thus cheap.

several parts that can be executed in any order. The solution is to use a *ptree*, which is meant to model such dependencies.

But the modified algorithm still looks very similar to the original one:

```
(defun pmult% (a b tree)
  (let ((length (max (integer-length a) (integer-length b))))
    (when (< length 100000)
      (let ((result (gensym)))
        ;; add function to ptree using name RESULT
        (lparallel:ptree-fn result ()
                            ;; this function has no dependencies
                            (lambda () (* a b))
                            tree)
        ;; return this name
        (return-from pmult% result)))
    (let* ((length/2 (floor length 2))
           (mask (1- (ash 1 length/2)))
           (a1 (ash a (- length/2)))
           (a2 (logand a mask))
           (b1 (ash b (- length/2)))
           (b2 (logand b mask))
           ;; the following three are now symbols instead of numbers
           (a1*b1 (pmult% a1 b1 tree))
           (a2*b2 (pmult% a2 b2 tree))
           (prod3 (pmult% (+ a1 a2) (+ b1 b2) tree))
           (result (gensym)))
      ;; add function to ptree using name RESULT and
      ;; tell lparallel which results this'll depend on
      (lparallel:ptree-fn result (list a1*b1 a2*b2 prod3)
                          (lambda (a1*b1 a2*b2 prod3)
                            (+ (ash a1*b1 (* 2 length/2))
                               a2*b2
                               (ash (+ prod3 (- a1*b1) (- a2*b2))
                                    length/2)))
                          tree)
      ;; return the name as above
      result)))

(defun pmult (a b)
  (let ((tree (lparallel:make-ptree)))
    (lparallel:call-ptree (pmult% a b tree) tree)))
```

The main function, PMULT, just creates a *ptree* and then calls the helper function,

PMULT%, which computes the dependencies. PMULT% now returns *symbols*[47] instead of numbers, which within the ptree are placeholders for work that still has to be done (or for future results). The function LPARALLEL:PTREE-FN associates such a symbol with other symbols that it depends on (i.e., other parts of the ptree, which have to be computed first) and with a function that will be called once its arguments are ready.

In the Karatsuba algorithm, each node has three children that it depends on. In that $4321 \cdot 5618$ example, the dependency tree, if broken down to single digits, would look like so:

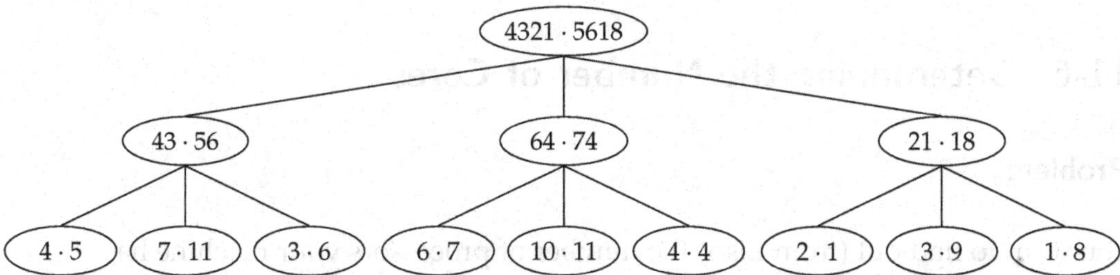

The whole computation is then started by calling LPARALLEL:CALL-PTREE, at which point LPARALLEL will take care to compute everything in the right order and parallelize as much as possible. So, this was harder than our first example, but still a lot easier and less error-prone than a "handmade" multithreaded solution.

To test the code, I used something like this:[48]

```
(setf lparallel:*kernel* (lparallel:make-kernel 4))

(defparameter *a* (random (expt 2 1000000)))
(defparameter *b* (random (expt 2 1000000)))
```

These are two numbers each of which uses up approximately one million bits (!) and we can now check how long multiplication takes with and without parallelization:

```
(time (defparameter *p1* (mult *a* *b*)))
(time (defparameter *p2* (pmult *a* *b*)))
```

On my machine, I get again an impressive speed-up of more than a factor of three; certainly worth the effort. And something that can easily be improved by just throwing better hardware at the problem.

Oh, yes, and the result is correct, too: `(= *p1* *p2* (* *a* *b*))` returns T.

[47]See Recipe 1-2 for GENSYM.

[48]On a four-core 64-bit Linux system with SBCL.

Alternatives

Lisp has traditionally been a language where programmers tried out lots of new things and never accepted that there should only be one way of doing something. It is therefore not surprising that there are quite a few different high-level approaches to concurrency, of which LPARALLEL is only one. You might want to have a look at http://www.cliki.net/concurrency as a starting point for several interesting alternatives.

11-6. Determining the Number of Cores

Problem

You want to find out (from Lisp) the number of processors your machine has.

Solution

You will very likely have to use the foreign function interface (see Chapter 19). Using the CFFI library, this would, for example, work on Linux and OS X like so:

```
(defconstant +sc-nprocessors-onln+ 84)

(cffi:defcfun "sysconf" :long
  (name :int))

(defun get-number-of-processors ()
  (sysconf +sc-nprocessors-onln+))
```

After this definition, you can evaluate (GET-NUMBER-OF-PROCESSORS).

How It Works

As we have seen in Recipe 11-5, it can be quite useful in concurrent programming to know the number of cores that are available. And if your program is intended to run on more than one machine, it would be helpful if you could figure this out dynamically at run time. Surprisingly, none of the multithreading-capable Lisps I've tried offers this information out of the box, although it is readily available from the underlying operating system.

The code above shows how to do it yourself using the FFI and the function `sysconf`. For Windows, it's a little bit more complicated, but also doable in a few lines of code:[49]

```
(cffi:defctype dword :unsigned-long)
(cffi:defctype word :unsigned-short)

(cffi:defcstruct processor-struct
  (processor-architecture word)
  (reserved word))

(cffi:defcunion oem-union
  (oem-ide dword)
  (processor-struct (:struct processor-struct)))

(cffi:defcstruct system-info
  (oem-info (:union oem-union))
  (page-size dword)
  (minimum-application-address :pointer)
  (maximum-application-address :pointer)
  (active-processor-mask (:pointer dword))
  (number-of-processors dword)
  (processor-type dword)
  (allocation-granularity dword)
  (processor-level word)
  (processor-revision word))

(cffi:defcfun ("GetSystemInfo" get-system-info) :void
  (data (:pointer (:struct system-info))))

(defun get-number-of-processors ()
  (cffi:with-foreign-object (info '(:struct system-info))
    (get-system-info info)
    (cffi:foreign-slot-value info '(:struct system-info)
                             'number-of-processors)))
```

Note that both code examples forgo error checking for brevity. You should add that for production code.

[49]This could, of course, be a lot shorter if we just used the right offset from the `INFO` pointer, but this way we have the "official" definition of the function.

12. Error Handling and Avoidance

Errors happen. There's no magic bullet that'll help you to avoid all errors your code could possibly ever encounter. But you can, of course, try to program defensively and anticipatory so that typical errors are noticed early and avoided before they can harm you. And you can be prepared to handle those errors that can't be avoided.

Many modern programming languages nowadays include facilities for *structured exception handling* and COMMON LISP is no exception (pun intended).[1] But it *is* different from many other languages in that it

(i) generalizes exceptions through its hierarchy of *conditions*,

(ii) doesn't necessarily unwind the stack if an exception occurs, and

(iii) offers *restarts* to programmatically continue "where the error happened."

As far as I know, *Practical Common Lisp* was the very first book to give these topics a thorough treatment.[2] I could now, as I did in other chapters, refer you to Peter's book for the basics. But in this case I'll make an exception (sorry, the pun again) and cover conditions, handlers, and restarts from the ground up. Not because I think Peter's explanation is lacking (to the contrary, I like it a lot!), but rather because I think it can't hurt if we have at least *two* books covering this. Why not read both?

12-1. Checking Types at Run Time

Problem

You want to be certain that an object has a certain type. Or you want to make a decision based on the type of an object.

---

[1]In fact, Lisp is not only not an exception but actually kind of a leader of the pack. See `https://en.wikipedia.org/wiki/Exception_handling#History`.

[2]Unless you count *CLtL2*. But it was obviously more written like a standards document and less like a textbook.

Solution

For an example, let's assume your program needs to take square roots and wants to make sure that its argument is a non-negative real number.[3] The easiest way to do this is with CHECK-TYPE:

```
(defun my-sqrt (x)
  (check-type x (real 0))
  (sqrt x))
```

If you now evaluate (MY-SQRT 9), all is fine. However, if you try (MY-SQRT -9), you'll get an error with a message like this one:

```
The value of X is -9, which is not of type (REAL 0).
```

Or something similar, like this:

```
The value -9 of X is not of type (REAL 0).
```

In any case, you will be able to *correct* this error by providing a different value for X. And there are alternatives to CHECK-TYPE. See more below. (And for another example, see Recipe 3-10.)

How It Works

While Lispers generally consider it a good thing that COMMON LISP is dynamically typed, you sometimes want to make sure that some object has a certain type; be it during testing or be it to provide meaningful error messages in case someone uses your code in a wrong way.

The CHECK-TYPE macro was made for that and does exactly what its name says; it *checks* whether its first argument has the *type* specified by its second argument. As you could see above, the first argument is evaluated and the second one—a *type specifier* (see Recipe 13-1)—isn't. If the first argument is *not* of the specified type, an error of type TYPE-ERROR is signaled. There is an escape hatch, though: a *restart* (see Recipe 12-6) is made available to give you the chance to provide a different value, interactively at the REPL or programmatically.

Three more things that aren't obvious from our little example:

- The first argument to CHECK-TYPE can't just be a variable—it can be any *place* (see Recipe 10-8); that is, anything that can be modified with SETF.[4]

[3] SQRT, of course, wouldn't care (see Recipe 4-8).

[4] On the other hand, that means you can't evaluate a form like (CHECK-TYPE 42 INTEGER) interactively in the REPL to check a type. For that, use TYPEP.

- The standard error message will just repeat the type specifier you provided. But you can change that with a third argument.
- `CHECK-TYPE` can, of course, appear anywhere in your code, not only at the beginning of a function's body.

So, let's redefine the function like so:

```
(defun my-sqrt (list)
  (check-type (first list) (real 0) "a non-negative real number")
  (sqrt (first list)))
```

And here, as an example, is an excerpt from a LISPWORKS session[5] where we used the new function:

```
CL-USER 1 > (defparameter *l* (list -9 :whatever))
*L*
CL-USER 2 > (my-sqrt *l*)
Error: The value -9 of (FIRST LIST) is not a non-negative real number.
  1 (continue) Supply a new value of (FIRST LIST).
  2 (abort) Return to level 0.
  3 Return to top loop level 0.
;; some output elided
CL-USER 3 : 1 > :c 1                    ;; selecting the first restart
Enter a form to be evaluated: 9         ;; we entered 9 here
3.0                                     ;; the return value of MY-SQRT
CL-USER 4 > *l*
(9 :WHATEVER)
```

Note the new error message and—more importantly—note that the value of `*L*` changed due to our correction!

Alternatives

In some Lisps, it will—depending on the safety settings—suffice to just *declare* (see Recipe 17-3) the type of a variable. For example, in SBCL the following definition

```
(defun my-sqrt (x)
  (declare (type (real 0) x))
  (sqrt x))
```

would also have the effect of signaling an error if `X` weren't a non-negative real (but there'd be no restart). However, this is not portable; that is, you can't rely on it to work the same in other Lisps.

[5]Where we're thrown into the *debugger* (see Recipe 16-3).

If you want to do different things based on an object's type, you can do that with TYPECASE, which works like CASE except that it tries different types until there's a match.[6] Or you can call the function TYPEP to test if an object is of a specific type. The difference between this function and the macros mentioned before it is that its type argument is evaluated so that you can decide at run time which types you want to check for. Examples for the usage of TYPECASE and TYPEP can be found in the first recipes of Chapter 13.

Finally, it is *not* a good idea to use TYPE-OF for programmatic type checks because what this function returns can differ between implementations (while still being conformant with the standard). Evaluating (TYPE-OF "foo"), for example, gave me four different results when tried with six different implementations.

(See also Recipe 13-3.)

12-2. Adding Assertions to Your Code

Problem

You want to add assertions to your code in order to make sure that you didn't make any mistakes.

Solution

As an example, let's assume you wrote a function to compute the *dot product*[7] of two sequences, but you aren't sure if this function is always called with compatible arguments. You could then insert a check for that, like so:

```
(defun dot-product (x y)
  (assert (and (typep x '(or list vector))
               (typep y '(or list vector))
               (= (length x) (length y)))
          (x y)
          "~S and ~S should have been sequences of the same length."
          x y)
  (reduce '+ (map 'list '* x y)))
```

Here's an example of using this function with CLOZURECL:

```
? (dot-product '(2 3 4) '(4))
> Error: (2 3 4) and (4) should have been sequences of the same ...
```

[6] And as CASE has "relatives" CCASE and ECASE, so does TYPECASE have CTYPECASE and ETYPECASE.

[7] See http://mathworld.wolfram.com/DotProduct.html.

```
;; some output elided
1 > :go                                   ;; selecting the CONTINUE restart
Type expressions to set places to, or nothing to leave them alone.
Value for X:                              ;; we just pressed "Return" here
Value for Y: #(4 3 2)                     ;; we entered a new value for Y
25                                        ;; the return value of DOT-PRODUCT
```

How It Works

Assertions are a well-known technique in software development[8] and it therefore isn't surprising that COMMON LISP has them. Anywhere in your program you can add something that in its simplest form looks just like

```
(assert <form>)
```

and the effect will be that at run time the form will be evaluated. If it returns a true value, the program will simply continue; if it returns NIL, the program will signal an error.

The other, optional, arguments to ASSERT are essentially "convenience" facilities to give you more control about what should happen in case of a failed assertion:

- The first optional argument is a list of *places* (see Recipe 10-8) that can be modified before the assertion is tried again. This is similar to the restart offered by the CHECK-TYPE macro discussed in Recipe 12-1.
- But even without this argument there's a CONTINUE restart (see page 355) that gives you the chance to make some modifications before retrying the assertion.
- The following optional arguments constitute a *condition designator* (page 343) that you can utilize to create a meaningful error message or a specific error condition.

As with CHECK-TYPE, ASSERT can appear anywhere in your code. A typical technique while testing the correctness of more complicated algorithms is, for example, to establish *loop invariants* and those would be good candidates for assertions.

And while we're talking about CHECK-TYPE, you might want to define something similar in terms of ASSERT as an exercise.[9]

[8]See https://en.wikipedia.org/wiki/Assertion_%28software_development%29.

[9]You'll find out that this is rather tricky if you want to mimic CHECK-TYPE's error messages and at the same time avoid double evaluation.

Disabling Assertions in "Production Code"

In languages like C and C++, assertions are often completely removed from the code for the "release" builds.[10] This is not something you can do with ASSERT out of the box, but you could add a modified version ASSERT* to your code

```
(defmacro assert* (test-form &rest other-args)
  (declare (ignorable test-form other-args))
  #-:release
  `(assert ,test-form ,@other-args))
```

and use it instead of ASSERT throughout. Once you're ready for a "release build," you can then do

```
(pushnew :release *features*)
```

and recompile *everything* (including ASSERT* itself).[11] (See Recipe 10-10 for *FEATURES* and the #- syntax.)

12-3. Defining Your Own Conditions

Problem

You want to create your own condition (or error) types.

Solution

That's what DEFINE-CONDITION is for:

```
(define-condition too-expensive (error)
  ((price :initarg :price
          :reader price))
  (:report (lambda (condition stream)
             (format stream "At ~A Euro~:P that's too expensive."
                     (price condition)))))
```

Once you've evaluated the form above, you can now create conditions of this type, print them, or signal (see Recipe 12-4) them:

[10]This is, of course, only meaningful if (a) the assertions were only ever meant to test for *programmer* errors and not for *user* errors and (b) removing the assertions doesn't alter the code's behavior; that is, if the code in the assertions doesn't have any inadvertent side effects.

[11]If you use ASDF (see Recipe 18-1), look up the :FORCE keyword argument for enforced recompilation of all files.

```
CL-USER> (make-condition 'too-expensive :price 42)
#<TOO-EXPENSIVE {100419ECA3}>
CL-USER> (format nil "~A" *)
"At 42 Euros that's too expensive."
CL-USER> (error **)
;; this will throw you into the debugger
```

And, most importantly, you can now use HANDLER-CASE or HANDLER-BIND to specifically handle errors of the type you just created (see Recipe 12-5).

How It Works

In any larger piece of software, it is important that you cannot only determine *that* an error occurred but that you can also figure out what *kind* of error you're dealing with. That's why object-oriented languages like C++, JAVA, or COMMON LISP provide a hierarchy of classes representing exceptional situations.

In COMMON LISP, the class CONDITION is at the top of this hierarchy and every instance of this class or one of its subclasses is called a *condition*. A condition is a generalization of an *error* in the sense that a condition describes *some* kind of exceptional situation, whereas errors are those exceptional situations that require (user or program) intervention.

The chart on the following page shows the hierarchy of condition types that's already defined by the standard. Your implementation will surely have added several others to it.

So, conditions are objects with—as we saw in our example—slots and inheritance,[12] but they are not *standard objects* (see Recipe 13-3) and they thus can't be treated like the CLOS objects you create yourself.[13] Specifically,

- You don't create condition *classes* with DEFCLASS. You create condition *types* with DEFINE-CONDITION. (But this macro mostly looks and feels like DEFCLASS.)
- You don't create conditions with MAKE-INSTANCE, you create them with MAKE-CONDITION. (And so you don't have the same freedom of influencing the creation process as described in Recipe 13-4.)
- You don't access the slots of a condition with SLOT-VALUE. You can only do it with readers and writers defined when creating the condition type.

[12]Even multiple inheritance, as witnessed for example by READER-ERROR or SIMPLE-WARNING.

[13]That's why the standard mostly talks about condition *types* instead of condition *classes*. However, you'll also find (for example in section 9.1) sentences like, "A hierarchy of condition *classes* is defined in COMMON LISP."

This is essentially a historical remnant. The condition system specification was retrofitted to coexist with CLOS when the standard was created.

The main purpose of conditions is then to be signaled (see Recipe 12-4) and to be handled (see Recipe 12-5).

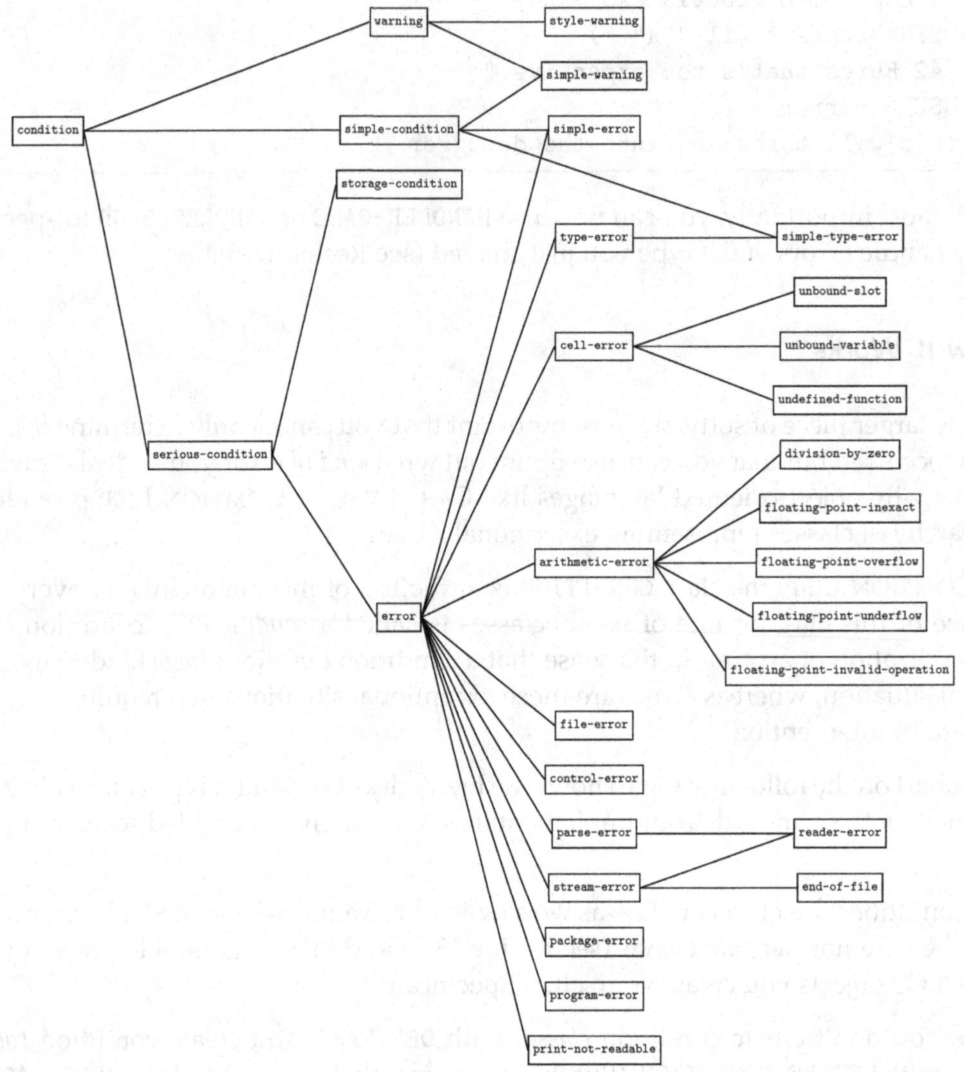

How Conditions Are Printed

Conditions are always printed in such a way that they can't be read back in. However, their printed representation differs depending on the setting of `*PRINT-ESCAPE*` (see Recipe 9-1). If its value is true, a condition looks very much like other "opaque" objects without a specific human-readable representation (like, say, hash tables or CLOS objects). If `*PRINT-ESCAPE*` is `NIL`, though, the *condition reporter* is used for printing. That's the function[14] we added with the `:REPORT` option in our example.

[14]The condition reporter can also be just a constant string.

This representation is also used if a condition throws you into the debugger, or if, say, you call WARN.

12-4. Signaling a Condition

Problem

You want to do the equivalent of what's often called *throwing an exception* in other languages.

Solution

In COMMON LISP the technical term is *signaling a condition* and the most basic function to do that is SIGNAL. The thing that's initially surprising is that if you "just" signal a condition, even an error, nothing happens:[15]

```
CL-USER 1 > (signal (make-condition 'error))
NIL
CL-USER 2 > (list (signal (make-condition 'error)) 42)
(NIL 42)
```

If you *want* something to happen, you have to use other functions to signal conditions (more below) or you have to establish *handlers*. Handlers are discussed in Recipe 12-5, but let's have a quick look at how the presence of a handler changes the behavior of the code above:

```
CL-USER 3 > (handler-case
                (list (signal (make-condition 'error)) 42)
              (error ()
                (list :foo :bar)))
(:FOO :BAR)
```

How It Works

We have seen how signaling a condition will only have an effect if an active handler is found. What if we want more "grave" consequences?

In that case, use ERROR instead of SIGNAL. For example, here's what would happen in the LISPWORKS REPL:

[15]For the creation of conditions and condition classes, see Recipe 12-3.

```
CL-USER 4 > (list (error (make-condition 'error)) 42)
Error: The condition #<ERROR 200CFFE8> occurred
  1 (abort) Return to level 0.
  2 Return to top loop level 0.
;; some output elided
CL-USER 5 : 1 > :a                          ;; selecting the "abort" option
CL-USER 6 >                                 ;; no return value
```

And here's what the same thing would look like with the handler from above:

```
CL-USER 7 > (handler-case
                (list (error (make-condition 'error)) 42)  ;; changed
              (error ()
                (list :foo :bar)))
(:FOO :BAR)
```

So, *with* a handler handling the condition, it makes no difference whether we use `SIGNAL` or `ERROR` to signal a condition. However, *without* the condition being handled, `SIGNAL` does nothing and just returns `NIL`, whereas `ERROR` throws us into the *debugger*.[16] And usually[17] the only way out will be to abort the current computation and not getting any result at all.

So, a simplified version of `ERROR` could be written like so:

```
(defun error (condition)
  (signal condition)
  (invoke-debugger condition))
```

If you want a chance to carry on with what you were doing after leaving the debugger, the easiest way to do that is to use `CERROR` instead of `ERROR`:

```
CL-USER 8 > (list (cerror "Proceed." (make-condition 'error)) 42)
Error: The condition #<ERROR 200A0D74> occurred
  1 (continue) Proceed.                ;; this is new
  2 (abort) Return to level 0.
  3 Return to top loop level 0.
;; some output elided
CL-USER 9 : 1 > :c                     ;; selecting the "continue" option
(NIL 42)                               ;; return value
```

`CERROR` takes an additional (first) argument—a *format control* (see Recipe 9-5) used for a text shown to the user—but is otherwise like `ERROR`; the one difference is that in

[16]Using `INVOKE-DEBUGGER`. See more in Recipe 16-3.

[17]Unless you've established at least one *restart* (see Recipe 12-6) around the `ERROR` form.

the debugger, you now have the choice to continue with the program by returning NIL. (Technically, CERROR offers a CONTINUE restart; see page 355.)

As with ERROR, it is probably a good idea to look at a simplified version of what CERROR actually does (although this might only make sense once you've read Recipe 12-6):

```
(defun cerror (format-control condition)
  (with-simple-restart
      (continue format-control condition)
    (error condition)))
```

The last standard function you can use to signal conditions is WARN, which does *not* throw you into the debugger, but will, as a side effect, apply the *condition reporter* (see page 340) to the *ERROR-OUTPUT* stream:

```
CL-USER 10 > (list (warn (make-condition 'warning)) 42)
WARNING: Condition WARNING was signalled.            ;; error output
(NIL 42)
```

Also, WARN only works with conditions of type WARNING.[18]

To summarize, here are the standard functions you can use to signal conditions:

Function	Invokes Debugger	Prints	Returns	Establishes Handler	All Conditions
SIGNAL			✓		✓
ERROR	✓				✓
CERROR	✓		maybe	✓	✓
WARN		✓	✓	✓	

Condition Designators

In all the examples so far we created a condition using MAKE-CONDITION and used that as the argument for SIGNAL and friends. However, these functions[19] will all accept *condition designators* as arguments, which means there are three ways to specify a condition:

(i) There's only one argument and it already is a condition, as seen above.

(ii) The arguments are the same that one would use for MAKE-CONDITION. So, for example,

```
(signal 'unbound-variable :name 'foo)
```

[18] And it establishes a handler that we'll discuss in Recipe 12-7.

[19] And also other functions and macros; see, for example, Recipe 12-2.

is just an abbreviation for

```
(signal (make-condition 'unbound-variable :name 'foo))
```

(iii) The arguments are the same as for FORMAT (except for the stream). This means that a condition of a certain default type is created where the default depends on the function called:

These two forms are equivalent (and the same for CERROR):

```
(error "~S and ~S don't match." :foo "FOO")

(error (make-condition 'simple-error              ;; <- default type
                       :format-control "~S and ~S don't match."
                       :format-arguments (list :foo "FOO")))
```

And these two are equivalent:

```
(warn "~S and ~S don't match." :foo "FOO")

(warn (make-condition 'simple-warning             ;; <- default type
                      :format-control "~S and ~S don't match."
                      :format-arguments (list :foo "FOO")))
```

(This third form of condition designators is actually the reason for the existence of the type SIMPLE-CONDITION.)

12-5. Handling Conditions

Problem

You want to "catch" an "exception" that was "thrown" somewhere in your code (to pick up the manner of speaking used at the beginning of Recipe 12-4).

Solution

We already saw this on page 341, but here's a more elaborate example:

```
CL-USER> (defun test (a b)
           (handler-case
               (/ a b)
             (type-error (condition)
               (format *error-output*
```

```
                         "Oops, ~S should have been of type ~A."
                         (type-error-datum condition)
                         (type-error-expected-type condition))
                 :no-meaningful-result)
               (division-by-zero ()
                 (format *error-output*
                         "This might create black holes!")
                 (values))))
TEST
CL-USER> (test 42 7)
6
CL-USER> (test 42 "23")
Oops, "23" should have been of type NUMBER.
:NO-MEANINGFUL-RESULT
CL-USER> (test 42 0)
This might create black holes!
; No value
```

It works like this: HANDLER-CASE executes exactly *one* form, which is (/ A B) in our example, and returns its value(s). Under "normal" circumstances, that's all there is to it.

The rest of the HANDLER-CASE form consists of so-called *error clauses* (of which we have two here), each starting with a *condition type*. If, during the execution of this form, a condition is signaled,[20] then these clauses are tried in order, and if the type of the signaled condition matches one of the error clause types, the code within that clause is executed. The code can have access to the condition (as in the first clause) or it can do without it (as in the second form). In any case, what the body of the clause returns will then be what HANDLER-CASE returns.

If no matching clause can be found, it is as if there had been no HANDLER-CASE around the form at all. To demonstrate this, try the following:

```
(test most-positive-double-float least-positive-double-float)
```

This could signal a FLOATING-POINT-OVERFLOW error[21] and throw you into the debugger, as this is neither a division by zero nor a type error.

But there's something *much* more interesting than HANDLER-CASE and that's HANDLER-BIND. Read on...

[20]To be picky, *and* if that condition is not already handled *within* the form.

[21]But it doesn't have to. See https://en.wikipedia.org/wiki/IEEE_754-1985#Positive_and_negative_infinity.

How It Works

What in other languages might be called *catching an exception* is in COMMON LISP *handling a condition*. And HANDLER-CASE essentially mimics what similar code in JAVA or C++ would do.

To understand the much more powerful HANDLER-BIND, let's change our code from above a bit:

```
CL-USER> (defparameter *special* :old)
*SPECIAL*
CL-USER> (defun div (x y)
           (let ((*special* :new))
             (catch 'catch-tag
               (/ x y))))
DIV
CL-USER> (defun test (a b)
           (handler-case
               (div a b)
             (type-error (condition)
               (format *error-output*
                       "Oops, ~S should have been of type ~A."
                       (type-error-datum condition)
                       (type-error-expected-type condition))
               *special*)
             (division-by-zero ()
               (format *error-output*
                       "This might create black holes!")
               (throw 'catch-tag -1))))
TEST
```

If we now try (TEST 10 2), things are, of course, like before. However:

```
CL-USER> (test 100 "NaN")
Oops, "NaN" should have been of type NUMBER.
:OLD
```

The result is :OLD, which is the initial value of the special variable *SPECIAL*, and *not* the symbol :NEW that this variable was bound to when the error was signaled. Even worse, if you try this

```
(test 42 0)
```

you'll end up in the debugger with a *control error* informing you that the catch tag CATCH-TAG doesn't exist.

At this point it is helpful to have a look at the *call stack* (see page 510) and extend it a bit. In its simplest form, we know of three frames resulting from function calls; TEST was called, which called DIV, which in turn called /. So, the stack (growing from bottom to top) looked like this when the error occurred:

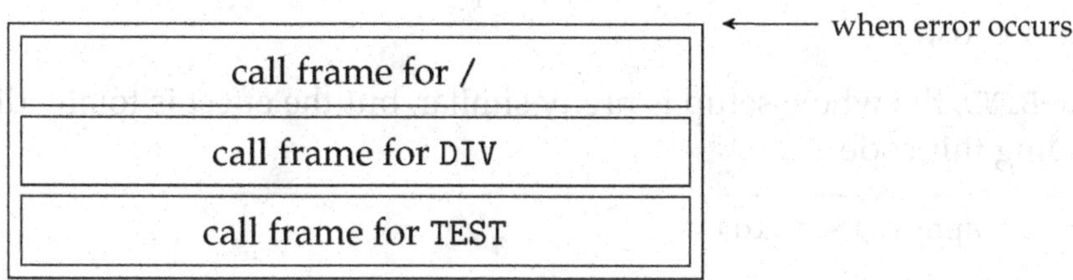

It is, however, more helpful to envisage[22] some additional frames there:

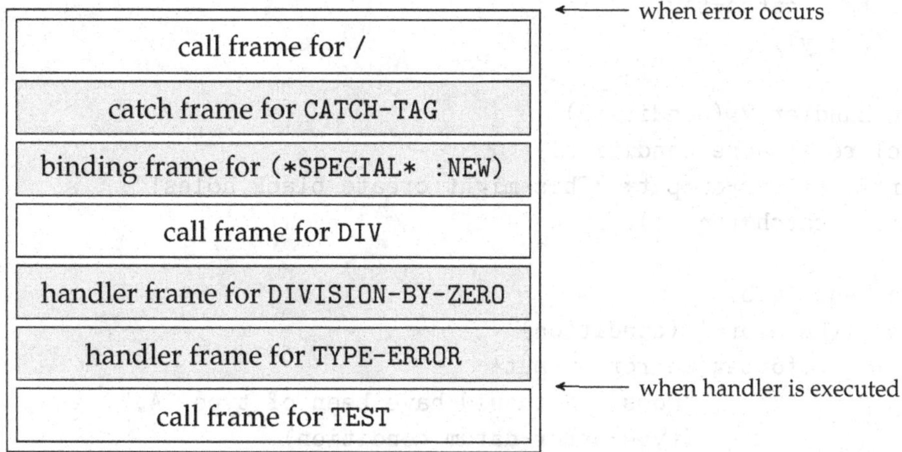

Binding the special variable to the value :NEW resulted in a *binding frame* being put on the stack. (So, looking up the value of such a variable is like going down the stack until the "youngest" binding frame for it is found.) Establishing the catch tag CATCH-TAG put a corresponding *catch frame* on the stack. (Again, once THROW is called, it is as if the Lisp system went down the stack to find the "youngest" catch frame with a matching name.) And, finally, the HANDLER-CASE caused *handler frames* to be put on the stack.

This ordered collection of stack frames below the current position is what is called the *dynamic environment* in COMMON LISP; in addition to function call information, it contains bindings of special variables, catch tags, and handlers. (And also *restarts* and UNWIND-PROTECT frames; see Recipes 12-6 and 12-8.)

[22]It doesn't matter whether your implementation really does it this way. *Conceptually* it'll work like this more or less. But implementations might by default "hide" some stack frames from you to not clutter up backtraces. If you want to understand how your Lisp implements facilities like catch tags or special variable bindings, you might thus need to convince it to "unhide" those frames. For example, look at the documentation for DBG:*PRINT-BINDING-FRAMES*, DBG:*PRINT-CATCH-FRAMES*, DBG:*PRINT-HANDLER-FRAMES*, and DBG:*PRINT-RESTART-FRAMES* in LISPWORKS.

Now, when the error is signaled from within the / function, the system goes down the stack looking for the first handler frame with a matching condition type. Once it has been found, the dynamic environment is *unwound*, which means the actual *handler* is called in the dynamic environment that existed at the entrance of the HANDLER-CASE form; see the lower arrow in the picture. In particular, the catch frame and the binding frame are lost.

With HANDLER-BIND, the whole setup is pretty similar, but the effect is totally different. After loading this code

```
(defparameter *special* :old)

(defun div (x y)
  (let ((*special* :new))
    (catch 'catch-tag
      (/ x y))))

(defun handler-2 (condition)
  (declare (ignore condition))
  (format *error-output* "This might create black holes!")
  (throw 'catch-tag -1))

(defun test (a b)
  (flet ((handler-1 (condition)
           (format *error-output*
                   "Oops, ~S should have been of type ~A."
                   (type-error-datum condition)
                   (type-error-expected-type condition))
           (return-from test *special*)))
    (handler-bind ((type-error #'handler-1)
                   (division-by-zero #'handler-2))
      (div a b))))
```

you will see these results:

```
CL-USER> (test 100 "NaN")
Oops, "NaN" should have been of type NUMBER.
:NEW
CL-USER> (test 42 0)
This might create black holes!
-1
```

The main difference between HANDLER-BIND and HANDLER-CASE is that the handlers of HANDLER-BIND are run *before* the dynamic environment is unwound. For example, in the situation above, the binding of *SPECIAL* to :NEW and the catch tag CATCH-

TAG, which were visible when the error occurred, are still there for HANDLER-1 and HANDLER-2 to deploy.

Here are some less important, technical differences:

- In the HANDLER-BIND form, the handlers come first, followed by the *body* to execute; whereas in HANDLER-CASE, the *form* to execute comes first, followed by the handlers.
- This implies that HANDLER-BIND can wrap handlers around more than one form.
- Where in HANDLER-CASE, the handlers (i.e., their bodies) are integrated into the form, HANDLER-BIND just wants function designators (of functions that accept one argument, namely the condition).

While the above is all more or less obvious from just looking at the HANDLER-BIND form, there's one point that isn't visible but nevertheless pretty important. What is a handler actually supposed to do? The handler function can essentially do anything it wants, but as long as it returns normally (like a typical Lisp function would), it is—from the viewpoint of the Lisp system—*declining* to handle the condition, which in turn means the Lisp will continue searching for another handler. Only if the handler leaves the dynamic environment (if in standard parlance it performs a *non-local exit*) will what it did be considered as *handling* the condition. This is what, for example, HANDLER-1 does by invoking RETURN-FROM.

It might be a good exercise to implement a HANDLER-CASE macro in terms of HANDLER-BIND. The HyperSpec entry for HANDLER-CASE shows an example of how one could tackle this.

Ignoring Errors

In general, it is obviously not a good idea to ignore errors because the whole point of errors is that they should *not* be ignored but some action should be taken. But sometimes you want to do exactly that because maybe you already know that errors are expected and you can't do anything about them anyway.

With what we have learned so far, it is easy to do that:

```
(handler-case
    (progn
      ;; code where errors will be ignored
      )
  (error ()))
```

This will usually just execute the code in the PROGN form. Should an error be signaled within this form, though, execution is aborted and NIL is returned.

The standard even offers a shortcut for this, which does yet a bit more. It's a macro called IGNORE-ERRORS, which in case of an error returns NIL (as above), but as a second return value, also the condition that was signaled:[23]

```
CL-USER> (ignore-errors (parse-integer "42"))
42
2
CL-USER> (ignore-errors (parse-integer "fourty-two"))
NIL
#<SB-INT:SIMPLE-PARSE-ERROR "junk in string ~S" {100541CB33}>
```

(See also Recipe 12-7.)

12-6. Providing and Using Restarts

Problem

You are anticipating certain kinds of errors in your code and you want to provide means of "fixing" them, either interactively or programmatically.

Solution

As an example, let's create a function that just returns the ratio of two numbers as a string showing the corresponding percentage. However, we only want to do that for ratios between zero and one. And in case someone enters wrong values, we want to give them a chance to correct their input. Let's start with a somewhat "naïve" version, which we'll improve later:[24]

```
(define-condition not-a-percentage (error)
    ((dividend :initarg :dividend
               :reader dividend)
     (divisor :initarg :divisor
              :reader divisor))
  (:report (lambda (condition stream)
             (format stream
                     "The quotient ~A/~A is not between 0 and 1."
                     (dividend condition) (divisor condition)))))


(defun percentage (a b)
  (restart-case
```

[23]See Recipe 4-9 for PARSE-INTEGER.

[24]For DEFINE-CONDITION, see Recipe 12-3; for the function ERROR, see Recipe 12-4.

```
      (let ((ratio (/ a b)))
        (unless (typep ratio '(real 0 1))
          (error 'not-a-percentage :dividend a :divisor b))
        (format nil "~,2F%" (* 100 ratio)))
    (use-other-values (new-a new-b)
      :report "Use two other values instead."
      :interactive (lambda ()
                     (flet ((get-value (name)
                              (format t "~&Enter new value for ~A: "
                                      name)
                              (read)))
                       (list (get-value 'a) (get-value 'b))))
      (format nil "~,2F%" (* 100 (/ new-a new-b))))))
```

So, the actual code of our function is the LET form, which computes the ratio, signals an error if it's outside of the accepted range, and otherwise returns the percentage string. But the interesting part for this recipe is the RESTART-CASE wrapped around it. If we leave out the optional stuff, the meat of it looks like so:

```
(restart-case
    ;; [restartable form here]
  (use-other-values (new-a new-b)
    (format nil "~,2F%" (* 100 (/ new-a new-b)))))
```

The effect is that a *restart* with the name USE-OTHER-VALUES is *established*, which works *as if* we had defined this function

```
(lambda (new-a new-b)
  (format nil "~,2F%" (* 100 (/ new-a new-b))))
```

to be *temporarily* available under that name in case of an emergency.[25]

One possible "user" of this restart is the debugger; that is, the restart can be deployed interactively like so:[26]

```
CL-USER 1 > (percentage 3 7)
"42.86%"
CL-USER 2 > (percentage 4 2)
Error: The quotient 4/2 is not between 0 and 1.
  1 (continue) Use two other values instead.         ;; "our" restart
  2 (abort) Return to level 0.
  3 Return to top loop level 0.
```

[25]Except that this function can't be called with FUNCALL or APPLY but only with INVOKE-RESTART, as we'll see soon.

[26]This is how it looks in the LISPWORKS REPL, but it should work more or less the same in any Lisp.

```
;; some output elided
CL-USER 3 : 1 > :c 1                              ;; select it
Enter new value for A: 21                         ;; we entered 21
Enter new value for B: 50                         ;; we entered 50
"42.00%"
```

Once the error is signaled (and not handled; see Recipe 12-5), the debugger kicks in and presents us with a list of available restarts. Two of these are the ones that are always there and which we've seen very often already. The first one, however, is the restart we established; and it is presented using the :REPORT information we provided.[27] If we select this restart, our :INTERACTIVE function from above is run; and it is expected to return a *list* of values that will be used with the aforementioned "emergency function" as if it had been called with APPLY. What this function eventually returns will then be the return value of the RESTART-CASE form.

What we have so far has one flaw, though. If we invoke the restart and provide values for NEW-A and NEW-B, which are *again* wrong, then this will neither be noticed nor will we get another chance to correct it. The canonical way to use restarts therefore is to embed them into some kind of looping construct so that, in theory, there's an infinite sequence of available retries. In our example, that can be easily achieved, like so:[28]

```
(defun percentage (a b)
  (restart-case
      (let ((ratio (/ a b)))
        (unless (typep ratio '(real 0 1))
          (error 'not-a-percentage :dividend a :divisor b))
        (format nil "~,2F%" (* 100 ratio)))
    (use-other-values (new-a new-b)
      :report "Use two other values instead."
      :interactive (lambda ()
                     (flet ((get-value (name)
                              (format t "~&Enter new value for ~A: "
                                      name)
                              (read)))
                       (list (get-value 'a) (get-value 'b))))
      (percentage new-a new-b))))                        ;; <-- changed
```

The emergency function[29] now simply calls PERCENTAGE again and so another restart

[27]As with DEFINE-CONDITION, this can not only be a string but also a function.

[28]The recursive approach shown here will have the effect that you can have "nested" errors with "unnecessary" stack frames. An alternative approach without recursion is shown in the example on page 354.

[29]My apologies for using an ad hoc term here, but there's no official name for this function. (The term *restart function,* which suggests itself, is already used for something else; see page 355.)

is established, the check is performed again, and so on.

But restarts can also be invoked programmatically with the function INVOKE-RESTART. This is typically done from within a condition handler and counts as a *non-local exit* (see page 349):

```
(handler-bind ((not-a-percentage
                (lambda (condition)
                  (declare (ignore condition))
                  (invoke-restart 'use-other-values 1 10))))
  (percentage 4 2))
```

The code above will try to call PERCENTAGE with the arguments 4 and 2, but this will result in a NOT-A-PERCENTAGE error, which will trigger the handler established by HANDLER-BIND. The handler then calls, via INVOKE-RESTART, our emergency function with the arguments 1 and 10. (So the return value of the whole form should be "10.00%". Try it!)

How It Works

When we say that a restart is *established*, what we actually mean is that—if we pick up our mental image from page 347—a *restart frame* is put on the stack. In our example above this would look like so in the moment the error is signaled:

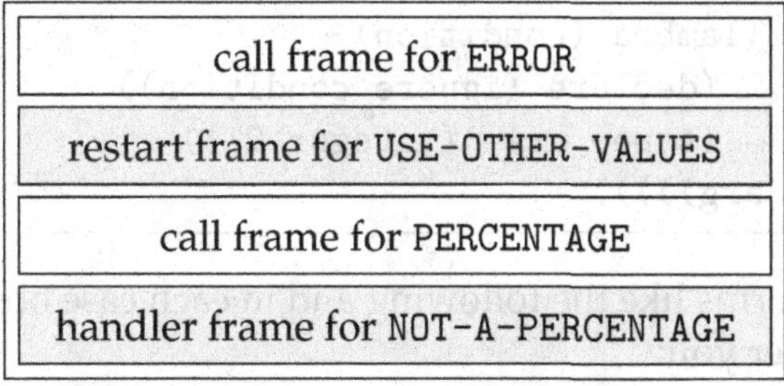

The form (INVOKE-RESTART 'USE-OTHER-VALUES 1 10) is actually a shortcut for

```
(invoke-restart (find-restart 'use-other-values) 1 10)
```

and FIND-RESTART will go down the stack looking for a restart frame with the corresponding name. This should also demonstrate quite clearly why we need HANDLER-BIND while HANDLER-CASE won't work in this case. See Recipe 12-5.

(There's also a RESTART-BIND macro that is technically more general than RESTART-CASE, but which in my experience you'll rarely, if ever, need. The main difference is that RESTART-BIND will not by itself perform a non-local exit.)

Visible Restarts

Here's a more complicated example that not only shows that you can use RESTART-CASE to establish more than one restart at once, but which also demonstrates that not all restarts are always *visible*:

```
(defun divide-by-three (arg)
  (loop (restart-case
            (let ((type-error (make-condition 'type-error
                                              :expected-type 'integer
                                              :datum arg)))
              (with-condition-restarts
                  type-error (list (find-restart 'parse-string))
                (cond ((stringp arg) (error type-error))
                      ((zerop (mod arg 3)) (return (/ arg 3)))
                      (t (error "Not divisible by three.")))))
          (parse-string ()
            (setf arg (parse-integer arg)))
          (increase-value ()
            :test (lambda (condition)
                    (declare (ignore condition))
                    (typep arg 'integer))
            (incf arg))
          (decrease-value ()
            :test (lambda (condition)
                    (declare (ignore condition))
                    (typep arg '(integer 2)))
            (decf arg)))))
```

You should first try forms like the following and in each case observe which restarts the debugger will offer you:

```
(divide-by-three 2)
(divide-by-three 1)
(divide-by-three "3")
```

You will see that, depending on your input, one or two of the three restarts will be available, but never all three of them. In the case of INCREASE-VALUE and DECREASE-VALUE the reason is the :TEST argument we provided, which is a predicate that accepts a condition as its only argument. Only if this predicate returns a true value will the restart be considered *visible*, so, for example, DECREASE-VALUE is only visible if ARG is an integer and greater than 1.

For the PARSE-STRING restart, we used the WITH-CONDITION-RESTARTS macro, which *associates* one or more restarts with a condition.[30] This is the same as if the restart's :TEST function would compare its argument with this specific condition.

At this point, you're probably wondering where the condition argument to the :TEST predicate comes from. It is provided by FIND-RESTART, which accepts it as a second (optional) argument. So, handlers can actively look for restarts applicable to "their" conditions. (And restart tests should be prepared to be called with the condition argument NIL.)

For even more sophisticated ways of selecting a restart, look up the function COMPUTE-RESTARTS in the HyperSpec.

Predefined Restarts

The standard defines five restarts which are available in certain situations:

```
abort
continue
muffle-warning
store-value
use-value
```

The first two you'll have encountered in the debugger already. For the third one, see Recipe 12-7. The other two can pop up in certain situations, which you'll find described in the HyperSpec. (For example, STORE-VALUE is used with CHECK-TYPE;[31] see Recipe 12-1.)

What these five have in common is that for each of them there's a function of the same name which is just a shortcut for finding and invoking the corresponding restart, so, for example, USE-VALUE is probably implemented like so:

```
(defun use-value (new-value &optional condition)
  (let ((restart (find-restart 'use-value condition)))
    (when restart
      (invoke-restart restart new-value))))
```

Here's an example of how such a *restart function* is supposed to be used. With this code[32]

```
(define-condition too-many-iterations (error)
  ())
```

[30] This is rarely used. A more typical usage is to deploy this macro implicitly. See the HyperSpec entry for RESTART-CASE.

[31] And it would be a good exercise to implement the CHECK-TYPE macro yourself, with restarts and all.

[32] See https://en.wikipedia.org/wiki/Collatz_conjecture.

```
(defun collatz (start &optional (max 10))
  (let ((count 0)
        (value start))
    (loop (incf count)
          (setf value (if (evenp value)
                          (/ value 2)
                          (1+ (* 3 value))))
          (when (= value 1)
            (return))
          (when (>= count max)
            (cerror "Continue trying?" 'too-many-iterations)
            (setf max (* 2 max))))
    (format t "Reached end after ~A iterations." count)))
```

you can effectively disable the function's "safety net," like so:

```
CL-USER> (handler-bind ((too-many-iterations #'continue))
           (collatz 6171))
Reached end after 261 iterations.
NIL
```

12-7. Getting Rid of Warning Messages

Problem

You are distracted by certain warnings and want to get rid of them.

Solution

The function `WARN` (see page 343) has the side effect[33] of printing something to `*ERROR-OUTPUT*`. But it also establishes the standard restart (see page 355) `MUFFLE-WARNING` so that you can prevent the printing from happening by using the restart function of the same name:[34]

```
CL-USER> (defun my-expt (base power)
           (unless (and (typep power 'integer)
                        (typep base '(or rational
                                         (complex rational))))
```

[33]One could even argue that this is its main purpose, as the signaling of the warning will have no effect in the absence of handlers for it.

[34]See page 88 for a discussion of the math involved here.

```
            (warn "Result may have round-off errors."))
        (expt base power))
MY-EXPT
CL-USER> (my-expt 10 (log 1/4 10))
WARNING: Result may have round-off errors.
0.25000003
CL-USER> (handler-bind ((warning #'muffle-warning))
           (my-expt 10 (log 1/4 10)))
0.25000003
```

How It Works

Of course, what we said on page 349 applies here as well: warnings should generally *not* be ignored. But if you really want to, you now know how to do it.

Having said that, warnings that are prone to annoying people most are those emitted by compilers. There are usually better ways to muffle these. For example, in SBCL you can use the non-standard declaration `SB-EXT:MUFFLE-CONDITIONS` to selectively muffle compiler diagnostics. Other Lisps will likely have different means of controlling their compiler's verbosity.

12-8. Protecting Code from Non-Local Exits

Problem

Your code ends in some kind of "epilogue" that has to be executed no matter what happens. In particular, you want this part of your code to be run even if an error has occurred previously. (This would be similar to what a `finally` block does in JAVA.)

Solution

Here's an example that "models" a refrigerator with some eggs in it:[35]

```
(defclass fridge ()
  ((door-open-p :initform nil
                :accessor door-open-p)
   (eggs :initform 10
         :accessor eggs)))
```

[35]Everything you need to know about conditions, handlers, and restarts to fully understand this example is explained in previous recipes of this chapter. Refrigerators are discussed in the chapter about household appliances.

```
(define-condition fridge-error (error)
  ((fridge :initarg :fridge
           :reader fridge)))

(define-condition no-eggs (fridge-error) ())

(defmethod open-door ((fridge fridge))
  (setf (door-open-p fridge) t))

(defmethod close-door ((fridge fridge))
  (setf (door-open-p fridge) nil))

(defmethod remove-egg ((fridge fridge))
  (unless (plusp (eggs fridge))
    (error 'no-eggs :fridge fridge))
  (decf (eggs fridge)))

(defmethod get-some-eggs ((fridge fridge) n)
  (open-door fridge)
  (loop repeat n do (remove-egg fridge))
  (close-door fridge)
  ;; return number of eggs left
  (eggs fridge))
```

It is, of course, important to always close the door after removing something from the fridge, and that's what GET-SOME-EGGS does. However, something like this can now happen:

```
CL-USER> (defparameter *fridge* (make-instance 'fridge))
*FRIDGE*
CL-USER> (door-open-p *fridge*)
NIL
CL-USER> (get-some-eggs *fridge* 7)
3
CL-USER> (door-open-p *fridge*)
NIL
CL-USER> (handler-bind ((no-eggs #'abort))
           (get-some-eggs *fridge* 4))
;; no return value because of ABORT restart
CL-USER> (door-open-p *fridge*)
T
```

When we tried to remove the eleventh, non-existent egg, an error was signaled, and as a result, the door was left open because the CLOSE-DOOR form of GET-SOME-EGGS wasn't executed anymore. Here's how to fix this. Redefine GET-SOME-EGGS like so:

```
(defmethod get-some-eggs ((fridge fridge) n)
  (open-door fridge)
  (unwind-protect
      (loop repeat n do (remove-egg fridge))
    (close-door fridge))
  (eggs fridge))
```

And now let's refill the fridge and try again:

```
;; continued from above
CL-USER> (setf (eggs *fridge*) 4)
4
CL-USER> (close-door *fridge*)
NIL
CL-USER> (handler-bind ((no-eggs #'abort))
           (get-some-eggs *fridge* 7))
CL-USER> (door-open-p *fridge*)
NIL
```

We still didn't get the eggs. But at least this time the fridge was closed!

How It Works

To understand what UNWIND-PROTECT does (and where its name comes from), it is helpful to look at the stack again, as we did on pages 347 and 353. This is how it'll look for our second version of GET-SOME-EGGS at the moment the error occurs:[36]

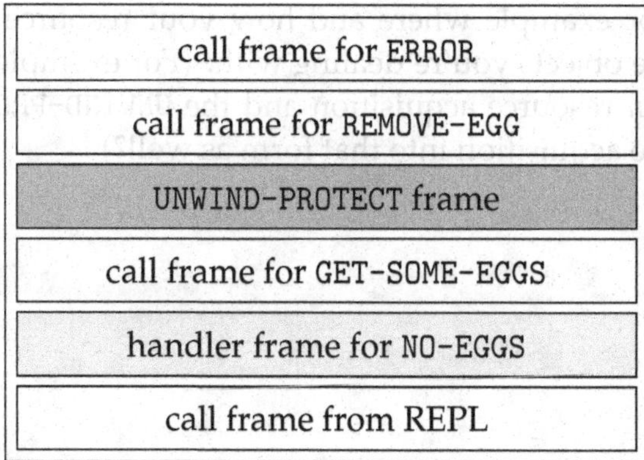

[36] Again, some implementations will really do it like this and some won't. The underlying mechanism, however, will be the same nevertheless.

The relevant frame for this recipe is the UNWIND-PROTECT frame. Remember that when the error happens and we're using the ABORT restart, the *dynamic environment* is unwound (see page 348). This happens *as if* the Lisp was walking the stack all the way down to the REPL. However, on its way down, it encounters the UNWIND-PROTECT frame and will execute its *cleanup forms*[37] before unwinding further.

The dynamic environment will be unwound anyway, either when the function exits normally or by a *non-local exit* (see page 349), which can be due to an error but also due to something like THROW, GO, or RETURN-FROM. But no matter how and why the unwinding happens, there's no way to get past the UNWIND-PROTECT frame without the cleanup forms being executed first.

"WITH-" Macros

Not only refrigerators need to be closed. There are many resources that need to be taken care of in one way or the other after they have been used. That's why our usage of UNWIND-PROTECT is a pretty common idiom that you can, for example, find in WITH-OPEN-FILE and in many "WITH-" macros that you'll find in open source libraries. If you need to do something like this yourself, you should roughly follow this general pattern:

```
(defmacro with-resource ((var &rest args) &body body)
  `(let ((,var (acquire-resource ,@args)))
     (unwind-protect
         (progn ,@body)
       (release-resource ,var))))
```

The crucial detail here is that RELEASE-RESOURCE is a cleanup form and thus guaranteed to be executed.

Other details, like for example where and how your resource is acquired, will of course depend on the objects you're dealing with. (For example, what if something can go wrong *between* resource acquisition and the UNWIND-PROTECT form? Maybe it's better to move the acquisition into that form as well?)

[37]That's only the CLOSE-DOOR form in our example.

13. Objects, Classes, Types

I often meet people (and this even includes some of my computer science colleagues) who are surprised to hear that COMMON LISP is "object-oriented" at all. If you are reading this book, you most likely don't belong in this group, but still, just knowing that something exists and having utilized it successfully are two very different pairs of shoes.

In chapters 16 and 17 of *Practical Common Lisp*,[1] Peter Seibel explains how COMMON LISP's object system (usually called "CLOS") works and also how COMMON LISP compares to other object-oriented languages, in terms of functionality as well as from a historical perspective. Peter does that much better than I could ever do and I urge you to read at least these two chapters if you've never worked with CLOS before.

If you're coming from a static, SIMULA-inspired OO language like C++ or JAVA, then CLOS will feel different and might require some getting used to. It might be a good idea to go through the source code of some open source libraries first. A lot of them use CLOS and are worth studying.

Some of the recipes in this chapter are about what one could call "advanced" features of CLOS.[2] They are not necessarily meant as something you must absolutely know, but rather to give you a feeling of what's possible in case you might need or want it one day.

And some recipes are concerned with *types*. While types aren't a part of CLOS, there's a close relation between types and classes (see specifically Recipe 13-2) and it is thus appropriate for types to make an appearance here.

13-1. Defining Types

Problem

You want to define your own types.

[1]Available online at `http://www.gigamonkeys.com/book/object-reorientation-generic-functions.html` and `http://www.gigamonkeys.com/book/object-reorientation-classes.html`.

[2]Or call them "esoteric" if you feel like it. One man's meat is another man's poison.

Solution

This is something you can do with the DEFTYPE macro. Here are some examples; they will be explained in detail below:

```
CL-USER> (deftype zahl (&optional from to)
           `(integer ,from ,to))
ZAHL
CL-USER> (deftype small-prime ()
           '(member 2 3 5 7 11 13 17 19))
SMALL-PRIME
CL-USER> (defun test (x)
           (typecase x
             ((not zahl) :not-an-integer)
             ((zahl * 1) :primes-are-greater-than-one)
             (small-prime :definitely-prime)
             (otherwise :could-be-prime)))
TEST
CL-USER> (mapcar 'test '(two 23.0 -10 17 15485863))
(:NOT-AN-INTEGER
 :NOT-AN-INTEGER
 :PRIMES-ARE-GREATER-THAN-ONE
 :DEFINITELY-PRIME
 :COULD-BE-PRIME)
CL-USER> (defun has-simple-name (symbol)
           (let ((name (symbol-name symbol)))
             (and (< (length name) 5)
                  (every (lambda (char)
                           (char-not-greaterp #\a char #\z))
                         name))))
HAS-SIMPLE-NAME
CL-USER> (deftype simple-symbol ()
           '(and symbol (satisfies has-simple-name)))
SIMPLE-SYMBOL
CL-USER> (mapcar (lambda (thing)
                   (typep thing 'simple-symbol))
                 (list "foo" 'foo 'foobar 'x42 '|qUUx|))
(NIL T NIL NIL T)
```

How It Works

COMMON LISP is "strongly typed" in the sense that each datum has a type that can be queried at run time. The language will use type information routinely (for example, if you call a built-in function like +), but you can also utilize this type information yourself with functions like TYPEP and TYPE-OF or macros like TYPECASE or CHECK-TYPE (see Recipe 12-1) or with declarations (see Recipe 17-5).

For objects like symbols, lists, or characters, which are discussed in various other chapters of this book, there are built-in types named by symbols, like SYMBOL, LIST, or CHARACTER. These are called *type specifiers*. But there are also *compound type specifiers* and *derived types*.

Compound Type Specifiers

- A type specifier can be a symbol like INTEGER but also a list starting with a symbol like so:

  ```
  (integer 0 42)
  ```

  The items following the initial symbol provide additional information to restrict the set of objects belonging to the type. In this particular example the items 0 and 42 mean that only integers between 0 and 42 (i.e. only 43 different numbers) belong to this type.[3]

- There are no further restrictions about the number and types of these so-called *subsidiary items*. Above we had two that were both numbers; here we have only one, which is itself a type specifier:

  ```
  (complex integer)
  ```

  This would be the type of all *Gaussian integers*.[4]

  And here

  ```
  (array double-float (2 2))
  ```

  we have an item that is a list. (This is the type of all arrays with exactly two rows of two double floats.)

- Subsidiary items can often be replaced with the symbol *, which means "unspecified:"

  ```
  (double-float 0d0 1d0)
  (double-float * 1d0)
  (double-float 0d0 *)
  ```

[3]Equivalent type specifiers for this example would be (MOD 43) or (INTEGER 0 (43)).

[4]See https://en.wikipedia.org/wiki/Gaussian_integer.

Here the first type denotes all elements of the closed interval[5] $[0, 1]$ as long as they can be represented as COMMON LISP double floats (see Recipe 4-6), while the second and third type would correspond to the intervals $(-\infty, 1]$ and $[0, \infty)$.

- If one or more items at the end are unspecified, they can simply be left out:

```
(double-float 0d0)
```

The above would thus be an abbreviation for (DOUBLE-FLOAT 0D0 *).

- And if all items are unspecified, you can replace the list with its first symbol:

```
double-float
```

This is the same type as (DOUBLE-FLOAT), which in turn is the same type as (DOUBLE-FLOAT * *).

- Type specifiers can be combined with the logical connectives AND, OR, and NOT to define intersections, unions, and complements of types:

```
(and (integer 0 1000000)
     fixnum)
```

This type represents all non-negative integers that are not greater than one million, and that are at the same time fixnums (which *in theory* could mean that the type could comprise significantly less than one million numbers; see Recipe 4-2).

```
(or (single-float 0s0 1s0)
    (double-float 0d0 1d0))
```

This type represents numbers in the interval $[0, 1]$, no matter whether they are single or double floats.

```
(and real
     (not (or short-float
              single-float)))
```

This would be the type of all Lisp reals that are either exact or have at least double precision.

- Compound type specifiers can also start with MEMBER, which means that an object is of the specified type if it is the same (see Recipe 10-1) as one of the objects listed after MEMBER:

[5] See https://en.wikipedia.org/wiki/Interval_%28mathematics%29.

```
(member 40 41 42)
```

That would be equivalent to (INTEGER 40 42).

- The most general type specifier starts with SATISFIES. In this case, you provide a predicate that is used to test whether an object is of the type or not:

```
(and (satisfies integerp)
     (satisfies minusp))
```

The preceding would be equivalent to the type (INTEGER * -1).

Derived Types

A *derived type* is roughly a type you define with DEFTYPE.[6] This macro is similar to DEFUN in that you define a function that is called whenever your new type is used, and the job of which is to return a type specifier.

The simplest example would be something like this:

```
(deftype zahl () 'integer)
```

This defines ZAHL[7] as a synonym for INTEGER, and no matter how it is implemented internally, it works like this: whenever the symbol ZAHL is used as a type specifier somewhere, a function is called, which returns the symbol INTEGER, which is then used instead of ZAHL. In other words, this is as if you had written

```
(defun zahl () 'integer)
```

and the result of evaluating (ZAHL) would be used.

An example with subsidiary items would look like so

```
(deftype zahl (from to)
  `(integer ,from ,to))
```

Now a type specifier like (ZAHL 0 42) would be replaced with (INTEGER 0 42).[8] Unfortunately, something like (ZAHL 0) wouldn't work, nor would ZAHL.

Luckily, optional and keyword parameters are treated differently in DEFTYPE; the default is the symbol * and not NIL as usual. So, this works as expected:

[6] I wrote "roughly" because in principle an implementation could decide to provide other means of doing this.

[7] See https://en.wikipedia.org/wiki/Integer.

[8] Again note how this is as if you had written a function ZAHL accepting the parameters FROM and TO.

```
(deftype zahl (&optional from to)
  `(integer ,from ,to))
```

And, yes, you can also use &KEY and &REST and so on to create arbitrarily complex type specifiers; for example:

```
(deftype my-number (&key from to (exactp t))
  `(,(if exactp 'rational 'real) ,from ,to))
```

13-2. Using Classes As Types

Problem

You want to use macros like TYPECASE and CHECK-TYPE with your classes or define new types based on them.

Solution

This is easy. Whenever you define a class, you automatically also define a *type* of the same name.

```
CL-USER 1 > (defclass foo () ())
#<STANDARD-CLASS FOO 200A55E3>
CL-USER 2 > (defparameter *f* (make-instance 'foo))
*F*
CL-USER 3 > (typep *f* 'foo)
T
CL-USER 4 > (defun test (x)
              (typecase x
                (number (1+ x))
                (foo :foo)
                (otherwise nil)))
TEST
CL-USER 5 > (mapcar 'test (list 42 *f* "foo"))
(43 :FOO NIL)
CL-USER 6 > (deftype bar () '(or foo number))
BAR
CL-USER 7 > (subtypep 'foo 'bar)
T
T
CL-USER 8 > (typep 23 'bar)
```

```
T
CL-USER 9 > (typep *f* 'bar)
T
```

How It Works

The simple rule of thumb regarding the relation of classes and types in COMMON LISP is that every class is also a type, but not every type is a class.

As every class is a type, in our example we could immediately use the *type* FOO, which came into being as a "twin" of the *class* FOO. We also used FOO to define a new type BAR.

But BAR is *not* a class. Even if we had written

```
(deftype quux () 'foo)
```

then QUUX would have acted as a synonym for the *type* FOO but *not* for the class FOO; that is, you could not have used QUUX in place of FOO in method definitions or when instantiating objects (see end of Recipe 13-3).

13-3. Writing Methods for Built-In Classes

Problem

You want to write a generic function that specializes on built-in data types, like numbers or strings.

Solution

Just do it!

For an example, let's suppose you've written an implementation of the gamma function[9] that uses its Taylor series to approximate its values. This is reasonably fast and accurate but will produce results like 5.999991410072404D0 for (GAMMA 4); whereas you know that for positive integers, you could use the factorial function for an exact result (which would be 6 in this case). This is how GAMMA could look like:

```
(defmethod gamma ((x number))
  ;; Taylor series approximation
  ;; see for example http://rosettacode.org/wiki/Gamma_function
```

[9]See https://en.wikipedia.org/wiki/Gamma_function.

```
)

(defmethod gamma ((n integer))
  (if (plusp n)
    ;; compute factorial of (1- N) if N is a positive integer
    (loop for i from 1 to (1- n)
          for result = 1 then (* result i)
          finally (return result))
    ;; otherwise use method above
    (call-next-method)))
```

And as we've now used the factorial function (a recursive version of which must, by some age-old rule, appear in every Lisp book) let's implement it as a generic function for another example:

```
(defgeneric factorial (n)
  (:method ((n (eql 0))) 1)
  (:method ((n integer)) (* n (factorial (1- n)))))
```

How It Works

On the one hand, every Lisp *datum*—everything you can stuff into a variable—is by definition an *object* in COMMON LISP and you can use CLASS-OF to figure out which class it belongs to. In that respect, COMMON LISP is object-oriented all the way down.[10]

On the other hand, there are a couple of restrictions regarding the so-called *system classes*.[11] While things like numbers, strings, or lists have a class, these classes can't be subclassed, you can't create an instance of them using MAKE-INSTANCE, and so on. But you *can* use them as parameter specializers as we did above.

In our example, we used the fact that not only there are system classes like NUMBER (encompassing all numerical types, including rationals and complex numbers; see Chapter 4), but also there are relations between these classes prescribed by the standard; for example, that INTEGER must be a subclass (although not a direct one) of

[10]And arguably more so than, say, C++ or JAVA, which have *primitive* built-in types the "instances" of which aren't objects in the OOP sense.

[11]Technically, it is like this: if you define your own class FOO using (DEFCLASS FOO () ()), then for an instance A of FOO, the result of (CLASS-OF (CLASS-OF A)) (the *metaclass* of the object A) will be the class STANDARD-CLASS; and thus FOO is what the HyperSpec calls a *standard class*. The result of (CLASS-OF (CLASS-OF 42)) will, on the other hand, very likely be the class BUILT-IN-CLASS, which makes the class of 42 (which is FIXNUM) a so-called *built-in class*.

However, an implementation is allowed to deviate from this and implement, say, FIXNUM as a standard class. But when writing portable programs, you can't rely on this, as FIXNUM will still be a *system class* in the sense that your program must treat it as if it *could* be a built-in class.

NUMBER. This entails that for an argument like 42, the method which computes the factorial of (1- 42) will be called, whereas for an argument like -23, we can use CALL-NEXT-METHOD to "fall back" to the approximation method.

Note that parameter specializers must (unless they are EQL specializers) be *symbols* naming *classes*; you can't use types nor can you use more complicated expressions. This will *not* work because the parameter specializer is not a symbol:

```
;; will signal an error:
(defmethod gamma ((n (integer 1 *)))
  (loop for i from 1 to (1- n)
        for result = 1 then (* result i)
        finally (return result)))
```

And this will not work because the parameter specializer names a type that is not a class:

```
;; this is fine:
(deftype positive-integer () '(integer 1 *))

;; but this will signal an error:
(defmethod gamma ((n positive-integer))
  (loop for i from 1 to (1- n)
        for result = 1 then (* result i)
        finally (return result)))
```

(See also Recipe 13-2.)

13-4. Providing Constructors for Your Classes

Problem

You want constructors for your classes similar to how it's done in JAVA or C++.

Solution

CLOS doesn't have constructors per se. You can either write your own "constructors" (i.e., create a function like MAKE-FOO for your FOO class and advise users to employ this function instead of MAKE-INSTANCE), or you can hook into the CLOS object creation process at various levels. We'll show a simple example here and then we'll discuss the whole process in detail below.

Let's say we have a class which is defined like so:

```
(defclass foo ()
  ((key :reader key)))

(defun make-key (secret)
  (format nil "~A-~A" secret (random 100)))
```

When creating a FOO object, the user is supposed to supply a "secret" that will then be used to set the KEY slot using the MAKE-KEY function you wrote.

This can be done by defining a suitable after method for INITIALIZE-INSTANCE:

```
(defmethod initialize-instance :after ((new-object foo)
                                       &key secret)
  (setf (slot-value new-object 'key) (make-key secret)))
```

The key will now be created automatically:

```
CL-USER> (make-instance 'foo :secret "confidential")
#<FOO {10031B6C33}>
CL-USER> (key *)
"confidential-42"
```

How It Works

The constructors you can write in other languages are generally more expressive than what can be done with MAKE-INSTANCE because you can have essentially arbitrary argument lists. So, in cases where it doesn't suffice to provide initialization arguments matching slots of your class, an easy way out is to write your own "constructor functions." An example would be something like this:

```
CL-USER> (defclass bar ()
           ((range :initarg :range
                   :reader range)))
#<STANDARD-CLASS BAR>
CL-USER> (defun make-bar (begin end)
           (make-instance 'bar
                          :range (loop for i from begin to end
                                       collect i)))
MAKE-BAR
CL-USER> (make-bar 3 10)
#<BAR {100392E9F3}>
CL-USER> (range *)
```

```
(3 4 5 6 7 8 9 10)
```

This could have been done using MAKE-INSTANCE alone and we'll show it in a minute. Whether you find this version more elegant or the one below is your call.

The process of creating a new CLOS object is divided into several steps each of which can be customized so that you have a pretty large degree of freedom:

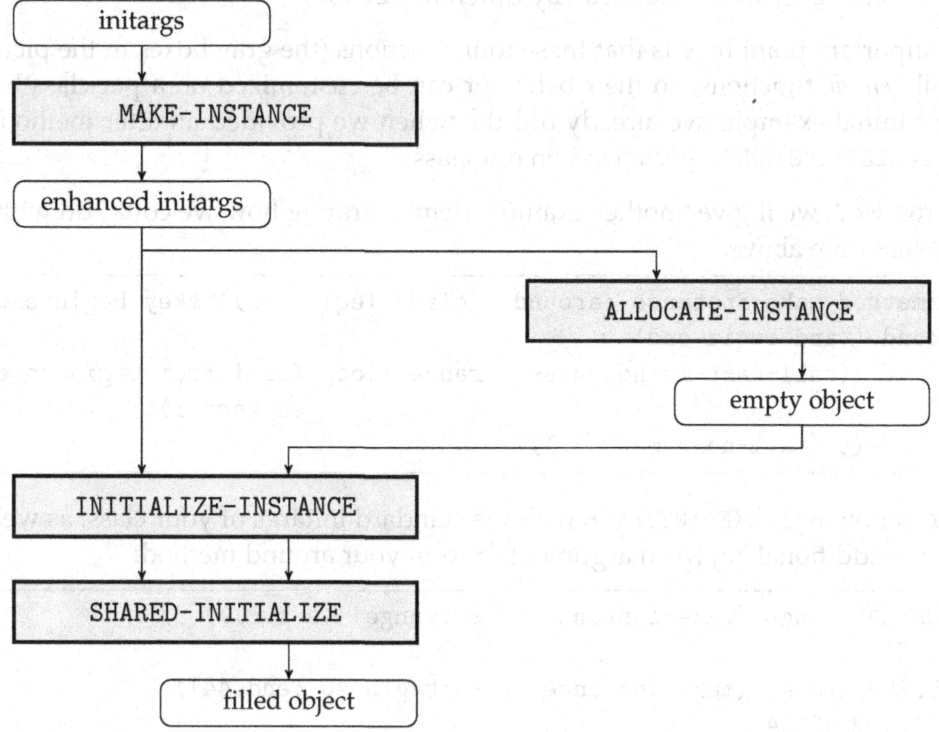

It works like this:

(i) When classes are defined, the slot options :INITARG and :INITFORM as well as the class option :DEFAULT-INITARGS can be used to control which slot values can be supplied when creating an instance of the class and what the defaults are. This is explained in detail in *Practical Common Lisp*.

(ii) To actually create an instance, the function MAKE-INSTANCE is called (usually with keyword arguments matching the symbols declared with :INITARG).

(iii) The default method for MAKE-INSTANCE checks the arguments it received and optionally provides defaults; see (i). All functions called by MAKE-INSTANCE will receive this "enhanced" set of initialization arguments.

(iv) MAKE-INSTANCE then calls ALLOCATE-INSTANCE, the job of which is to return a new "empty" (in the sense that all slots are unbound) object of the requested class.

(v) This empty object is then handed over to INITIALIZE-INSTANCE, which is responsible for filling the slots.

(vi) The default method for INITIALIZE-INSTANCE does nothing except for calling SHARED-INITIALIZE to do the actual work. The reason for this indirection is that the former function is only called for *new* objects while the latter is also used in other circumstances (see, for example, Recipe 13-8) and thus provides functionality that is "shared" by different callers.

The important point here is that these four functions (the gray boxes in the picture) are all *generic* functions, so their behavior can be customized on a per-class basis. In our initial example, we already did this when we provided an after method for INITIALIZE-INSTANCE specialized on our class.

As promised, we'll give another example demonstrating how we could do without MAKE-BAR from above:

```
(defmethod make-instance :around ((class (eql 'bar)) &key begin end)
  (cond ((and begin end)
         (call-next-method class :range (loop for i from begin to end
                                              collect i)))
        (t (call-next-method))))
```

You can now use MAKE-INSTANCE with the standard initargs of your class, as well as with the additional keyword arguments[12] from your around method:

```
CL-USER> (range (make-instance 'bar :range '(a b c)))
(A B C)
CL-USER> (range (make-instance 'bar :begin 40 :end 44))
(40 41 42 43 44)
```

13-5. Marking Slots As "Private"

Problem

You want to have "private" slots similar to private class members in JAVA or C++.

[12]If you look at the HyperSpec entry for MAKE-INSTANCE, you'll see that this generic function was defined with &ALLOW-OTHER-KEYS in its lambda list, so it is OK to add keywords like we did. This is the case for the other three functions as well.

Solution

The short answer is that there are no private slots in CLOS; there are only conventions.

You can emphasize the fact that a slot should not be accessed directly by providing readers and writers for it and you can reinforce this message using the package system, but that's about it.

How It Works

The philosophy of COMMON LISP is one of openness and this also applies to CLOS. Whereas many object-oriented languages provide various levels of access like "private" or "protected" for class members, in CLOS, all slots of a class are equal in this regard. Once you know the name[13] of a slot (and COMMON LISP's introspection tools—see Chapter 16—will make it easy for you to find out), you can get and set its value using the function `SLOT-VALUE`.

But there are some general rules regarding slot access that are agreed upon by pretty much everyone in the COMMON LISP community:

- If readers and/or writers are defined for a slot, you should use those instead of `SLOT-VALUE`. Specifically, if a reader is defined and there's no writer, that should be viewed as a sign that the slot is meant to be read-only.
- If the class is defined in a package and a slot's name is not exported from that package (see Recipe 1-1), you shouldn't use it. (This, of course, not only applies to slot names. It's a general rule that you should avoid using unexported symbols of other packages.)
- The best solution, of course, would be documentation. If the class you want to use comes with good documentation, then it should explain how the class is supposed to be used, and what's OK and what's not.

If you're really, really concerned about someone accidentally accessing slots they shouldn't access, you can use the MOP:[14]

```
(defclass foo ()
  ((bar)))

(defmethod (setf closer-mop:slot-value-using-class) :after
    (new-value (class standard-class) (object foo) slot)
```

[13]This is actually where you *could* do crazy things like using uninterned symbols (see Recipe 1-2) to name slots, but that would be very bad style and I won't show you how to do it.

[14]See Recipe 13-11, which also explains the `CLOSER-MOP:` package prefix in this example.

```
  (when (eql (closer-mop:slot-definition-name slot) 'bar)
    (print (list :bar-changed-to new-value))))
```

If you now try something like

```
(setf (slot-value (make-instance 'foo) 'bar) 42)
```

you should see the corresponding message printed. This should give you an idea how to "guard" slot access.

As with most things MOP, this example, which I ran in SBCL, is not fully portable. In LISPWORKS, for example, you must explicitly define your class with the option `(:OPTIMIZE-SLOT-ACCESS NIL)` in order for this to work. Also, the fourth argument won't be a *slot definition metaobject* but rather the slot's name, which is more convenient, but not how it should be done according to the MOP spec.

13-6. Changing the Argument Precedence Order

Problem

The standard way in which CLOS sorts applicable methods doesn't match your problem domain and you want to change it.

Solution

We're going to concoct an example that is complex enough to demonstrate the problem, yet simple enough to fit onto a page. Let's suppose you have, in your graphics program, classes for scalars, vectors, and matrices:

```
(defclass geometry-object () ())
(defclass scalar (geometry-object) ())
(defclass vec (geometry-object) ())
(defclass matrix (geometry-object) ())
```

You now want to write a very general generic function that can multiply any two of your geometry objects as long as the operation makes sense. You have already written very fast routines for anything involving vectors—maybe something that utilizes SIMD instructions. So, because all of your objects can be multiplied with vectors and vectors can be multiplied with matrices, you start with this:

```
(defmethod mult ((factor1 geometry-object) (factor2 vec))
  :use-fast-simd-routines)
```

```
(defmethod mult ((factor1 vec) (factor2 matrix))
  :use-fast-simd-routines)
```

Also, you can multiply all of your objects with scalars and as they all provide a similar interface to iterate through all entries, your next method definition looks like so:

```
(defmethod mult ((factor1 scalar) (factor2 geometry-object))
  :iterate-through-all-entries)
```

And finally there's the multiplication of two matrices, which involves two nested iterations:

```
(defmethod mult ((factor1 matrix) (factor2 matrix))
  :double-iteration)
```

This is all fine, except that you will see the following result:

```
CL-USER > (mult (make-instance 'scalar) (make-instance 'vec))
:ITERATE-THROUGH-ALL-ENTRIES
```

The fast SIMD routines could have been used here, but instead CLOS selects the method that iterates through all entries one by one.

You eventually realize that you could fix this by changing the order of the arguments to MULT, but that's not really an option as it would be out of sync with the way such multiplications are usually written.

The more elegant solution is to do it like so:

```
(defgeneric mult (factor-1 factor-2)
  (:argument-precedence-order factor-2 factor-1))
```

How It Works

Let's dissect what's happening here. We have three classes, which would amount to nine possible combinations of factors, of which we only need seven.[15] We wrote four methods to cover these seven cases:[16]

	SCALAR	VEC	MATRIX
SCALAR	(SCALAR *)	(SCALAR *) or (* VEC)	(SCALAR *)
VEC		(* VEC)	(VEC MATRIX)
MATRIX		(* VEC)	(MATRIX MATRIX)

[15]We don't have methods for vector times scalar and for matrix times scalar.

[16]We're using * instead of GEOMETRY-OBJECT in order to save space.

We notice that our "fast method" covers three cases (the whole second column) and the "iteration method" also covers three cases (the first row). There's one case where they overlap.

When we now evaluate

```
(mult (make-instance 'scalar) (make-instance 'vec))
```

then CLOS first computes all *applicable methods*. In this case, that'd be two methods, as we already saw in the table above.

The next step then is to *sort* the applicable methods (if there's more than one) and this is by default done by going through the individual parameters in the order they are defined in the lambda list and by comparing by specificity. In this case, the first parameter of the "fast method" is specialized on GEOMETRY-OBJECT and the first parameter of the "iteration method" is specialized on the subclass SCALAR, which is clearly more specific. So, the latter method comes first and is the one executed by the standard method combination.

Which is not what we want. As I already said, this could be ameliorated by changing the lambda list. But that is sometimes, as in this case, not desirable for stylistic reasons; or sometimes it's not even possible (think of setf methods; see Recipe 10-8). In those cases, you can keep your lambda list and ask CLOS to use a different order when sorting applicable methods, as we did in the example above.

13-7. Automatically Initializing Slots on First Usage

Problem

You know how to automatically initialize a slot's value using :INITFORM, but you want the initialization to happen when the slot is first used, not when the object is created (perhaps because initialization is expensive and not always needed).

Solution

We'll first show how this is done and then we'll explain the underlying mechanism.[17]

```
CL-USER> (defclass foo ()
           ((first-access :reader first-access)))
#<STANDARD-CLASS FOO>
CL-USER> (defparameter *foo* (make-instance 'foo))
*FOO*
```

[17]See Recipe 22-9 for GET-UNIVERSAL-TIME.

```
CL-USER> (defmethod slot-unbound (class (object foo)
                                   (slot-name (eql 'first-access)))
           (setf (slot-value object 'first-access)
                 (get-universal-time)))
#<STANDARD-METHOD SLOT-UNBOUND (T FOO (EQL FIRST-ACCESS)) ...
CL-USER> (get-universal-time)
3646741042
CL-USER> (first-access *foo*)
3646741051
CL-USER> (get-universal-time)
3646741056
CL-USER> (first-access *foo*)
3646741051
```

How It Works

This is actually pretty simple. Whenever you're attempting to read the value of an unbound slot of a CLOS object, the function SLOT-UNBOUND is called, which by default signals an error. But as almost everything in CLOS this is customizable because SLOT-UNBOUND is a generic function.

In our example, we specialized it by creating a method for our specific class and the one slot we're interested in. Obviously, the method will be called at most once for each object and slot.

And note that this would have worked just as well even if we hadn't use the reader FIRST-ACCESS but had instead used SLOT-VALUE to access the slot directly.

13-8. Changing and Redefining Classes on the Fly

Problem

You want to change the class of an existing object. Or you want to redefine an existing class but in such a way that all existing instances of that class "survive" the change.

Solution

Let's first see what the default behavior is if an object switches classes:[18]

[18]This is SBCL and the output has been edited for brevity. What exactly DESCRIBE prints might look slightly different in other Lisps, but the gist of it will be the same.

```
CL-USER> (defclass foo ()
           ((a :initarg :a)
            (b :initarg :b)
            (c :initarg :c)))
#<STANDARD-CLASS FOO>
CL-USER> (defparameter *object* (make-instance 'foo :a 1 :b 2))
*OBJECT*
CL-USER> (describe *object*)
#<FOO {10045DD053}>
  [standard-object]
Slots with :INSTANCE allocation:
  A  = 1
  B  = 2
  C  = #<unbound slot>
CL-USER> (defclass bar ()
           ((b :initarg :b)
            (c :initarg :c)
            (d :initarg :d)))
#<STANDARD-CLASS BAR>
CL-USER> (change-class *object* 'bar)
#<BAR {10045DD053}>
CL-USER> (describe *object*)
#<BAR {10045DD053}>
  [standard-object]
Slots with :INSTANCE allocation:
  B  = 2
  C  = #<unbound slot>
  D  = #<unbound slot>
```

What happens can be represented graphically, like so:

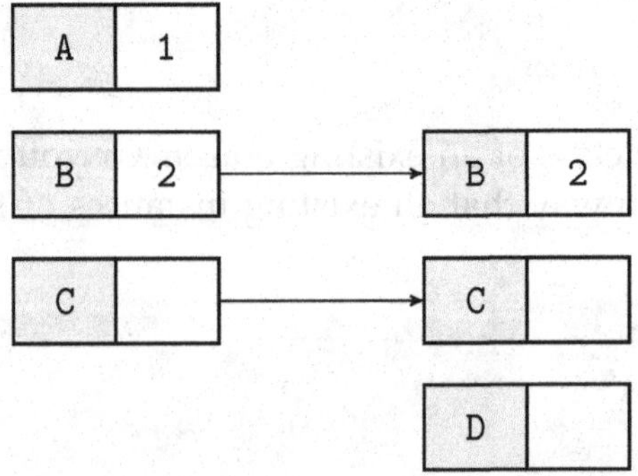

Whenever slots in the old and the new class have the same name, they are unchanged; the B slot keeps the value 2, while the C slot remains unbound. Slots like the one named A, which don't have a counterpart in the new class, simply vanish; while new slots in the new class, like the one named D, are unbound.

However, CHANGE-CLASS will accept additional arguments, which will be interpreted like initargs for the new class, so we could have done it like so:

```
;; continued from above with same class definitions
CL-USER> (defparameter *object* (make-instance 'foo :a 1 :b 2))
*OBJECT*
CL-USER> (change-class *object* 'bar :c 3 :d 4)
#<BAR {100565C9C3}>
CL-USER> (describe *object*)
#<BAR {100565C9C3}>
  [standard-object]
Slots with :INSTANCE allocation:
  B  = 2
  C  = 3
  D  = 4
```

Here we used the initargs to not only initialize the new D slot but to also "overwrite" the value of the C slot.

So, after what happened above, SHARED-INITIALIZE[19] is called with the arguments that the caller of CHANGE-CLASS provided to modify the object accordingly. The picture should therefore rather look like so:

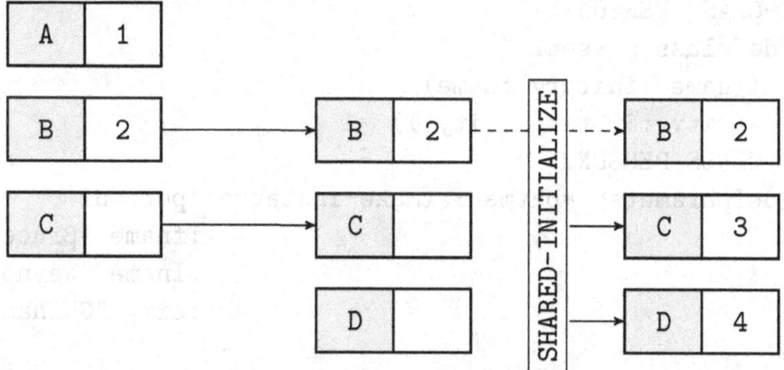

But this can be customized even further, as we'll see below. And we'll also discuss how modifying the class will affect the objects.

How It Works

If you've ever talked to experienced Lispers, you've probably heard "war stories" of huge and complex systems to which substantial modifications were applied while

[19]See Recipe 13-4.

they kept running and without interrupting the services they provided. Although this sometimes has to be taken with a grain of salt, it is in fact true that many COMMON LISP features were designed from the ground up to be dynamic in the sense that they can be changed at run time. This includes CLOS, where an object can change from one class to another, and where classes can be modified, although they already have objects "hanging off" of them.[20] (Note that in all the examples of this recipe, the objects of course keep their *identity*; see Recipe 10-1.)

Objects Changing Their Class

We've already seen above what happens if we assign a different class to an object. But that wasn't the whole truth. In the second step, the function `SHARED-INITIALIZE` is actually called by the function `UPDATE-INSTANCE-FOR-DIFFERENT-CLASS`, which, as you might have expected, is a generic function and can thus be specialized. What we've observed by now was only the default behavior.

For a slightly more interesting example, let's suppose that we have a class for persons, which has slots for first and last name, and another class where the full name is stored:

```
CL-USER> (defclass person1 ()
           ((fname :initarg :fname)
            (lname :initarg :lname)
            (city :initarg :city)))
#<STANDARD-CLASS PERSON1>
CL-USER> (defclass person2 ()
           ((name :initarg :name)
            (city :initarg :city)))
#<STANDARD-CLASS PERSON2>
CL-USER> (defparameter *batman* (make-instance 'person1
                                                :fname "Bruce"
                                                :lname "Wayne"
                                                :city "Gotham City"))
*BATMAN*
CL-USER> (describe *batman*)
#<PERSON1 {1003683273}>
  [standard-object]
Slots with :INSTANCE allocation:
  FNAME  = "Bruce"
  LNAME  = "Wayne"
  CITY   = "Gotham City"
```

[20] See, for example, `https://www.snellman.net/blog/archive/2015-07-27-use-cases-for-change-class-in-common-lisp/` for a more detailed discussion on why this sometimes is a very useful feature.

By defining a method, we can now automate the process of switching from the PERSON1 class to the PERSON2 class:

```
CL-USER> (defmethod update-instance-for-different-class
             ((old person1) (new person2) &key)
           (setf (slot-value new 'name)
                 (format nil "~A ~A"
                         (slot-value old 'fname)
                         (slot-value old 'lname))))
#<STANDARD-METHOD UPDATE-INSTANCE-FOR-DIFFERENT-CLASS ...
CL-USER> (change-class *batman* 'person2)
#<PERSON2 {1003683273}>
CL-USER> (describe *batman*)
#<PERSON2 {1003683273}>
  [standard-object]
Slots with :INSTANCE allocation:
  NAME  = "Bruce Wayne"
  CITY  = "Gotham City"
```

(Note that the city was kept automatically, as before.)

Redefining Classes

Now let's see what happens to objects if the definition of their class changes:

```
CL-USER> (defclass foo ()
           ((a :initarg :a)
            (b :initarg :b)
            (c :initarg :c)))
#<STANDARD-CLASS FOO>
CL-USER> (defparameter *object* (make-instance 'foo :a 1 :b 2))
*OBJECT*
CL-USER> (describe *object*)
#<FOO {10048620E3}>
  [standard-object]
Slots with :INSTANCE allocation:
  A  = 1
  B  = 2
  C  = #<unbound slot>
CL-USER> (defclass foo ()                          ;; <-- same class
           ((b :initarg :b)
            (c :initarg :c)
            (d :initarg :d)))                      ;; <-- new slot
#<STANDARD-CLASS FOO>
```

```
CL-USER> (describe *object*)
#<FOO {10048620E3}>
  [standard-object]
Slots with :INSTANCE allocation:
  B  = 2
  C  = #<unbound slot>
  D  = #<unbound slot>
```

Obviously, this is almost identical to what we've seen before; some existing slots are discarded, some new slots are created, some are kept. And as you might have expected, there's again a way to customize this. The generic function in this case is called UPDATE-INSTANCE-FOR-REDEFINED-CLASS and the only relevant difference is that there's, of course, only one class to specialize on and that it receives as arguments information about added and deleted slots.

Our person example from above would now look like so:

```
CL-USER> (defclass person ()
           ((fname :initarg :fname)
            (lname :initarg :lname)
            (city :initarg :city)))
#<STANDARD-CLASS PERSON>
CL-USER> (defparameter *batman* (make-instance 'person
                                                 :fname "Bruce"
                                                 :lname "Wayne"
                                                 :city "Gotham City"))
*BATMAN*
CL-USER> (describe *batman*)
#<PERSON {10051DBA13}>
  [standard-object]
Slots with :INSTANCE allocation:
  FNAME  = "Bruce"
  LNAME  = "Wayne"
  CITY   = "Gotham City"
CL-USER> (defclass person ()                                ;; <-- same class
           ((name :initarg :name)
            (city :initarg :city)))
#<STANDARD-CLASS PERSON>
CL-USER> (defmethod update-instance-for-redefined-class
             ((object person) added deleted plist &key)
           (declare (ignore added deleted))
           (setf (slot-value object 'name)
                 (format nil "~A ~A"
                         (getf plist 'fname)
                         (getf plist 'lname))))
```

```
#<STANDARD-METHOD UPDATE-INSTANCE-FOR-REDEFINED-CLASS ...
CL-USER> (describe *batman*)
#<PERSON {10051DBA13}>
  [standard-object]
Slots with :INSTANCE allocation:
  NAME  = "Bruce Wayne"
  CITY  = "Gotham City"
```

The slight difficulty here is that in our method, we don't have an "old" object, so how are we going to access the discarded slot values? That's what the PLIST argument is for; it's a plist (see Recipe 6-9), which gives us exactly this information. In our case, it would have looked like so:

```
(FNAME "Bruce" LNAME "Wayne")
```

One last thing worth noting is that in our example, we first changed the class definition and only afterward defined the method. SBCL was "lazy" in this case in that it only really modified the object once we accessed it with DESCRIBE. This is not something you can rely on, though.

13-9. Making Your Objects Externalizable

Problem

You need to enable your Lisp system to reconstruct instances of your classes so that the compiler can "dump" them to a FASL file. This is usually the case if these instances appear as (literal) constants in your code.

Solution

For a simple example, enter this class definition into your REPL:

```
(defclass point ()
  ((x :initarg :x
      :reader x)
   (y :initarg :y
      :reader y)))
```

And after that, create a file with these contents

```
(defmethod distance ((p1 point) (p2 point))
  (sqrt (+ (expt (- (x p1) (x p2)) 2)
           (expt (- (y p1) (y p2)) 2))))
```

```
(defmethod distance-from-origin ((p point))
  (distance #.(make-instance 'point :x 0 :y 0) p))
```

and apply COMPILE-FILE to it. You will get some kind of error message from your compiler to the extent that it doesn't know how to "dump" a POINT object. It might even give you a hint how to fix this problem by mentioning MAKE-LOAD-FORM.

The solution would be to enter this into the REPL:[21]

```
(defmethod make-load-form ((p point) &optional environment)
  (declare (ignore environment))
  `(make-instance 'point :x ,(x p) :y ,(y p)))
```

If you now try COMPILE-FILE again, it'll work.

How It Works

The reason for the error above is the #. form (see Recipe 8-3), which is supposed to insert a literal POINT object into your code. COMPILE-FILE's job is to transform your source code into a binary file (a FASL file; see page 429), which can be read by LOAD. And thus the POINT object (the "origin" in our function) also needs to be represented as part of the FASL file so that LOAD can reconstruct it. (The object needs to be *externalizable*.)

But the compiler doesn't know how to do it, so we have to help it. And we do that by providing a *form* that will be put into the FASL file as a placeholder for the object and that will be evaluated to construct the object when the file is loaded.

At this point, you might be wondering what the problem is. Wasn't it obvious what we did? After all, we just re-created the object by filling the slots with the "right" values. And indeed, in many cases, it's a simple as that. There's even a shortcut for this; we could have written our MAKE-LOAD-FORM method from above like so:[22]

```
(defmethod make-load-form ((p point) &optional environment)
  (declare (ignore environment))
  (make-load-form-saving-slots p :slot-names '(x y)))
```

But something like this isn't done by default because the compiler doesn't know how our objects "work." Maybe they have slots that aren't initialized but computed; maybe objects aren't always created anew but first looked up in a database; maybe each creation of an object is registered somewhere; and so on. These are all things

[21]See Recipe 10-9 for the ENVIRONMENT parameter.

[22]OK, it's not really shorter in this particular case, but for more complex objects it will be.

that only the creator of the class can know, and that's why he or she is responsible for the load form as well.

Now let's see what MAKE-LOAD-FORM-SAVING-SLOTS gave us:

```
;; continued from above
CL-USER> (make-load-form (make-instance 'point :x 0 :y 0))
(ALLOCATE-INSTANCE (FIND-CLASS 'POINT))
(PROGN
 (SETF (SLOT-VALUE #<POINT {1002DB7C73}> 'X) '0)
 (SETF (SLOT-VALUE #<POINT {1002DB7C73}> 'Y) '0))
```

This is the output from SBCL and the output from other Lisps will differ, but the important part to note is that *two* forms were returned and this is what you can also do yourself if writing a method for MAKE-LOAD-FORM; the first form is meant to *create* the object[23] while the second form will be used to *initialize* it. The second form isn't necessarily executed immediately after the first form which will come in handy if the first form references other literal objects which might need to be reconstructed in complicated ways themselves. See the HyperSpec for more details (including a useful example).

This, by the way, is not only necessary for standard CLOS objects, but also for structures (created with DEFSTRUCT) and conditions.

13-10. Using and Defining Non-Standard Method Combinations

Problem

For your code, the standard method combination isn't the best fit.

Solution

For an example, let's model the symmetries of various classes of quadrilaterals. We'll start with our class hierarchy:

```
(defclass quadrilateral () ())
(defclass kite (quadrilateral) ())
(defclass parallelogram (quadrilateral) ())
(defclass trapezoid (quadrilateral) ())
(defclass rhombus (kite parallelogram) ())
```

[23]See Recipe 13-4 for ALLOCATE-INSTANCE.

```
(defclass rectangle (parallelogram trapezoid) ())
(defclass square (rectangle rhombus) ())
```

A graphical representation would look like so:

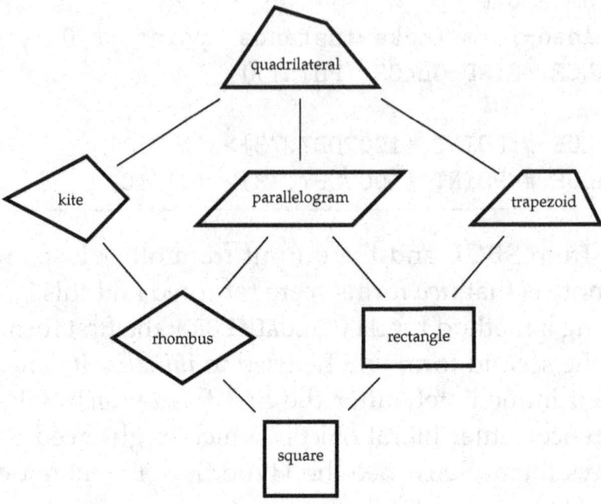

And we now define a generic function SYMMETRIES and its methods like so:[24]

```
(defgeneric symmetries (shape)
  (:method-combination append))

(defmethod symmetries append ((shape quadrilateral))
  '(:identity))
(defmethod symmetries append ((shape kite))
  '(:reflection-horizontal))
(defmethod symmetries append ((shape parallelogram))
  '(:rotation-180-degrees))
(defmethod symmetries append ((shape rhombus))
  '(:reflection-vertical))
(defmethod symmetries append ((shape rectangle))
  '(:reflection-vertical :reflection-horizontal))
(defmethod symmetries append ((shape square))
  '(:rotation-90-degrees :rotation-270-degrees
    :reflection-diagonal-1 :reflection-diagonal-2))
```

As you can see, for each shape, we only listed those symmetries that aren't already present in more general shapes. The method combination we're using will ensure that we'll eventually see all symmetries:

[24]Note that we need the *method qualifier* APPEND in *each* of the method definitions.

```
CL-USER> (symmetries (make-instance 'rectangle))
;; output edited to fit page width
(:REFLECTION-VERTICAL :REFLECTION-HORIZONTAL
 :ROTATION-180-DEGREES :IDENTITY)
CL-USER> (symmetries (make-instance 'rhombus))
(:REFLECTION-VERTICAL :REFLECTION-HORIZONTAL
 :ROTATION-180-DEGREES :IDENTITY)
```

(For example, the method specialized on RECTANGLE only returns two reflections but by also being a parallelogram and a quadrilateral, the rectangle "inherits" a rotation and the identity, and so the generic function returns a list of four symmetries.)

How It Works

Peter Seibel claims that 99 percent of the time, the standard method combination will be exactly what you want. I won't argue with that, but even if his estimate is completely accurate, there will be cases where you'd like something else. In many other object-oriented languages, you don't have a choice in how methods are selected, and that doesn't prevent people from writing great programs. But in COMMON LISP, you have, and if using a different method combination will make your program easier to read and reason about, you should do it.

So, what's happening if we evaluate the following form?

```
(symmetries (make-instance 'rhombus))
```

As with the standard method combination, CLOS will first compute all *applicable* methods; see Recipe 13-6. In the case of the rhombus, there are four of them; the one for rhombi, but also the methods specialized on kites, parallelograms, and on general quadrilaterals. The *standard* method combination would now sort these by specificity and then execute only the most specific one (the one for rhombi).

But we used the APPEND method combination, which executes *all* applicable methods and combines their results using the function APPEND. That's why we got the result we saw above which was computed like so:

```
(append '(:reflection-vertical)    ;; from RHOMBUS
        '(:reflection-horizontal) ;; from KITE
        '(:rotation-180-degrees)  ;; from PARALLELOGRAM
        '(:identity))             ;; from QUADRILATERAL
```

It doesn't matter in our case, but one might be concerned about the order of the results. Why, for example, is :IDENTITY the last one? That's because the most specific methods are executed first.[25] We could have gotten the reverse order by defining the generic function like so:

```
(defgeneric symmetries (shape)
  (:method-combination append :most-specific-last))
```

`APPEND` is one of the so-called *simple built-in method combination types* and there are several others that are all listed in section 7.6.6.4 of the standard. What they all have in common is that all applicable methods are computed and then some operation (in our case, `APPEND`) is applied to them.

Rolling Your Own

One simple method combination type that's not built-in is `UNION`, which is a good thing because it gives us a chance to demonstrate how you can define your own method combinations.

It turns out that `APPEND` isn't really the best fit, as we get this:

```
CL-USER> (symmetries (make-instance 'square))
(:ROTATION-90-DEGREES :ROTATION-270-DEGREES
 :REFLECTION-DIAGONAL-1 :REFLECTION-DIAGONAL-2
 :REFLECTION-VERTICAL :REFLECTION-HORIZONTAL                    ;; <---
 :REFLECTION-VERTICAL :REFLECTION-HORIZONTAL                    ;; <---
 :ROTATION-180-DEGREES :IDENTITY)
```

The square inherits the horizontal reflection from the kite, but also from the rectangle, and so both of them are present in the result; but we'd rather avoid duplicates.

One way to solve this would be to add an around method:[26]

```
(defmethod symmetries :around ((shape quadrilateral))
  (remove-duplicates (call-next-method)))
```

But let's not do it because we wanted an excuse to create our own method combination. We can have it like so:[27]

```
(defun set-union (&rest sets)
  (reduce 'union sets))
```

[25] `KITE` comes before `PARALLELOGRAM` because that's how we arranged the superclasses when we defined the `RHOMBUS` class.

[26] With the simple built-in method combination types you can't have before and after methods, but you can have around methods like here.

[27] We can't simply use `UNION` because this function only accepts two sets as arguments. Also, the standard wouldn't allow us to name a method combination `UNION` anyway.

```
(define-method-combination set-union)
```

Here the *name* of the new method combination is the symbol SET-UNION and the *operation* to perform is the function SET-UNION that we just defined. Because the names coincide, we could use the short form, which is an abbreviation for this:

```
(define-method-combination set-union :operation set-union)
```

The generic function is now defined as before except that we replace all occurrences of APPEND with SET-UNION:[28]

```
(defgeneric symmetries (shape)
  (:method-combination set-union))

(defmethod symmetries set-union ((shape quadrilateral))
  '(:identity))
(defmethod symmetries set-union ((shape kite))
  '(:reflection-horizontal))
(defmethod symmetries set-union ((shape parallelogram))
  '(:rotation-180-degrees))
(defmethod symmetries set-union ((shape rhombus))
  '(:reflection-vertical))
(defmethod symmetries set-union ((shape rectangle))
  '(:reflection-vertical :reflection-horizontal))
(defmethod symmetries set-union ((shape square))
  '(:rotation-90-degrees :rotation-270-degrees
    :reflection-diagonal-1 :reflection-diagonal-2))
```

(SYMMETRIES (MAKE-INSTANCE 'SQUARE)) will then return a set of only eight elements, as expected.

Arbitrarily Complex Method Combinations

This was actually the so-called "short form" of DEFINE-METHOD-COMBINATION. With the "long form," you can create method combinations as complex and strange as you like. We can't do full justice to it in a page or two, but we'll at least show an example to give you an idea of what's possible.

As there is already a simple built-in method combination type called + that computes the sum of the results of all applicable methods, we'll implement something similar

[28]Depending on your implementation you might need to evaluate (FMAKUNBOUND 'SYMMETRIES) first because some Lisps don't like it if you change the method combination of an existing generic function. See also Recipe 16-9.

that computes a *weighted sum* where each method can specify its own weight factor:[29]

```
(defun number-qualifier-p (method-qualifiers)
  (and (numberp (first method-qualifiers))
       (null (rest method-qualifiers))))

(define-method-combination weighted-sum
    (&optional (initial-value 0))
    ((instead-methods (:instead))
     (sum-methods number-qualifier-p))
  (cond (instead-methods `(call-method ,(first instead-methods)
                                        ,(rest instead-methods)))
        (t `(let ((sum ,initial-value))
              ,@(loop for method in sum-methods
                      collect `(incf sum
                                     (* ,(first
                                          (method-qualifiers method))
                                        (call-method ,method))))
              sum))))
```

So, what have we done here?

- Our methods must have exactly one *method qualifier*. For the standard method combination these are keywords like `:AROUND` or `:AFTER`. In our case, a method qualifier is either the keyword `:INSTEAD` or the list of method qualifiers passes the test `NUMBER-QUALIFER-P`, so only a single number is allowed.
- `DEFINE-METHOD-COMBINATION` automatically groups all applicable methods for us according to this specification (and sorts them as usual). It will also signal an error if we try to sneak in a method using a wrong combination of method qualifiers.[30]
- We allow for an optional parameter `INITIAL-VALUE`, which will be added to the computed sum. This is similar to the optional `:MOST-SPECIFIC-LAST` argument we saw above.
- If there are methods marked with `:INSTEAD`, no sum will be computed and only the most specific of these methods will be executed. Note that we do this using `CALL-METHOD` (which exists solely for this purpose) and provide the *other* methods as a second argument. This is so that the method's code can use `CALL-NEXT-METHOD`.

Let's try it:

[29]This is without error checking. You should, for example, call the function `METHOD-COMBINATION-ERROR` in case there are no methods at all.

[30]There are other ways to differentiate by method qualifiers that we don't show here.

```
(defgeneric foo (number)
  (:method-combination weighted-sum 42))

(defmethod foo 2 ((x real)) x)
(defmethod foo 10 ((x rational)) x)
(defmethod foo :instead ((x fixnum)) x)
```

This should give you results like these:

```
CL-USER> (foo 10.0)
62.0
CL-USER> (foo 1/2)
48
CL-USER> (foo 23)
23
```

There's only one applicable method for the argument `10.0`. This number is multiplied by 2 (that's the factor of the method) and of course 42 is added, so we get 62. In the second case, there are two applicable methods; the one we already had and one for rational numbers with a factor of 10. The result is $42 + 2 \cdot \frac{1}{2} + 10 \cdot \frac{1}{2} = 48$. Finally, for the fixnum 23, there's an "instead method" that overrides the weighted sum and so 23 is simply returned.

As I said, there's a lot more you can do with `DEFINE-METHOD-COMBINATION`. You might want to study its HyperSpec entry, which also contains several helpful examples.

One thing to keep in mind, though, is that this is a part of COMMON LISP that sometimes feels a bit more static than the rest of the language. Specifically, you should not expect the forms returned by your method combinations to be computed each time a generic function is called. This would be horribly inefficient, and thus implementations will *cache* these forms and only recompute them when a generic function is changed.[31] If you want more "dynamic" behavior, you'll have to use the MOP (see Recipe 13-11).

13-11. Extending and Modifying CLOS

Problem

You want to do things with CLOS that it usually can't do.

[31]In other words, you can't even expect an existing generic function to pick up changes to a method combination that are performed after it has been defined.

Solution

The solution is to utilize the so-called *Metaobject Protocol* (usually abbreviated as *MOP*). Before proceeding, you should first load the CLOSER TO MOP library (via QUICKLISP; see Recipe 18-2).

We'll show a toy example to demonstrate the basic idea (which we'll explain below). In our example, we want certain classes to automatically log object creation. Compile and load the following code:

```
(defclass logged-class (standard-class)
  ((creation-log :initform nil
                 :accessor creation-log)))

(defmethod closer-mop:validate-superclass
    ((class logged-class)
     (superclass standard-class))
  t)

(defmethod make-instance :around ((class logged-class) &key)
  (let ((new-object (call-next-method)))
    (push (format nil "~A created at ~A."
                  new-object (get-universal-time))
          (creation-log class))
    new-object))
```

To try out our new *metaclass*, we can do something like this:

```
CL-USER> (defclass foo () () (:metaclass logged-class))
#<LOGGED-CLASS FOO>
CL-USER> (make-instance 'foo)
#<FOO {1005674923}>
CL-USER> (make-instance 'foo)
#<FOO {10056799B3}>
CL-USER> (creation-log (class-of *))
("#<FOO {10056799B3}> created at 3646720679."
 "#<FOO {1005674923}> created at 3646720677.")
CL-USER> (defclass bar () () (:metaclass logged-class))
#<LOGGED-CLASS BAR>
CL-USER> (make-instance 'bar)
#<BAR {10057F4683}>
CL-USER> (creation-log (class-of *))
("#<BAR {10057F4683}> created at 3646720715.")
```

How It Works

Like Gray streams (see Recipe 14-14) and environment access (see Recipe 10-9), the MOP is a *de facto* standard in the sense that it's not part of the ANSI standard, but most implementations (more or less) adhere to it by following a specific document.[32] The document in this case is the 1991 book *The Art of the Metaobject Protocol* (fondly called *AMOP*) by Gregor Kiczales, Jim des Rivieres, and Daniel G. Bobrow (MIT Press).[33]

The basic idea of the MOP is that the inner workings of CLOS (what happens if a class or a method is defined, what happens if a generic function is invoked, and so on) are themselves implemented in CLOS[34] and exposed to the user in such a way that their behavior can be modified. As Kiczales et al. say in *AMOP*:

> Languages that incorporate metaobject protocols blur the distinction between language designer and language user. [...] The [...] approach [...] is based on the idea that one can and should "open languages up," allowing users to adjust the design and implementation to suit their particular needs. In other words, users are encouraged to participate in the language design process.

So, the MOP offers a whole slew of flexibility that otherwise wouldn't exist in CLOS (which in itself is already rather flexible); but it also elevates object-oriented programming to a level where you act as a kind of a "language designer" with all the complexity that this task entails.[35]

What the example does

As I already said, the idea is that CLOS is implemented in terms of CLOS. Specifically, the class of an object is itself an object of some class, which is called the *metaclass* of the first object:

```
CL-USER> (defclass quux () ())
#<STANDARD-CLASS QUUX>
CL-USER> (make-instance 'quux)
#<QUUX {1005DBDBD3}>
CL-USER> (class-of *)
```

[32] It's a bit more convoluted actually, as some parts of the MOP indeed made it into the standard.

[33] The specification part of the book is available online at `http://www.alu.org/mop/dictionary.html`, but the whole book is still worth reading.

[34] As you'll probably know, this *Münchhausenesque* idea of dragging yourself out of the swamp by your own hair is called *meta-circularity*. See `https://en.wikipedia.org/wiki/Meta-circular_evaluator` for more information.

[35] Of course, one could argue that one of the key ideas of the *programmable programming language* COMMON LISP is that you (re-)design it until it fits your problem domain. In this sense, the MOP is just a natural extension of these ideas.

```
#<STANDARD-CLASS QUUX>                       ;; class of QUUX object
CL-USER> (class-of *)
#<STANDARD-CLASS STANDARD-CLASS>             ;; metaclass of QUUX object
```

If you define a class using DEFCLASS as above, then the metaclass will be STANDARD-CLASS. Much of the functionality of CLOS (some of which was detailed in earlier recipes) is realized using generic functions that take a class argument and are specialized on STANDARD-CLASS.

In our initial example, we subclassed STANDARD-CLASS with the intention of making LOGGED-CLASS a valid metaclass. That is, a LOGGED-CLASS class object contains the same information a STANDARD-CLASS class object has, but also has an additional slot CREATION-LOG. We can now use this new class as a metaclass by using the :METACLASS class option, as in our definitions of the classes FOO and BAR. The only small detail that is missing is the VALIDATE-SUPERCLASS method.[36]

We're now adding a new around method to the standard generic function MAKE-INSTANCE (see Recipe 13-4), which is specialized on our new metaclass, so only objects with this metaclass will be affected by the change. And then we see this in action with our example classes FOO and BAR—whenever a new instance is created, a corresponding entry is added to the list in the CREATION-LOG slot.

Of course, you could have implemented something very similar like so:

```
(defclass foo ()
  ((creation-log :initform nil
                 :accessor creation-log
                 :allocation :class)))      ;; <-- this is new

(defmethod make-instance :around
    ((class (eql 'foo)) &key)              ;; <-- one specific class
  (let ((new-object (call-next-method)))
    (push (format nil "~A created at ~A."
                  new-object (get-universal-time))
          (creation-log new-object))        ;; <-- hangs off class
    new-object))
```

However, the crucial difference is that you'd have to do the same thing again for BAR and for every other class that you wanted "logged," whereas with the MOP approach you do it only once.

[36]This is necessary because when we define the class FOO, we don't provide an explicit *superclass*, so the superclass defaults depending on the *metaclass* LOGGED-CLASS which in turn inherits from STANDARD-CLASS. The effect is that the superclass of FOO will be STANDARD-OBJECT. But FOO and STANDARD-OBJECT have different metaclasses and the MOP doesn't "know" if this is OK, so we have to tell it.

The only "obvious" MOP functionality we used was `VALIDATE-SUPERCLASS`. The abilities to specify a metaclass with `DEFCLASS` and to specialize `MAKE-INSTANCE` on the metaclass are, in a way, aspects of the MOP which made it into the standard.

For "real" MOP stuff, you are on implementation-specific territory. The CLOSER TO MOP library we used provides a thin compatibility layer that tries to paper over the cracks, but this is not always possible. (It comes with a file `features.txt` that contains a detailed list of how different Lisps interpret the MOP.)

The *AMOP* book has more than 300 pages, so a recipe like this can't really do justice to the MOP. For example, generic functions and methods are also implemented as objects, and like with metaclasses, you can replace them with your own implementations. If you're interested in exploring more of this, good examples for non-trivial application of the MOP are the CLSQL and BKNR.DATASTORE libraries (see Recipes 21-2 and 21-3). You might also want to browse the web site of Pascal Costanza,[37] the author of CLOSER TO MOP, where you'll find MOP-related papers and code.

[37]See `http://www.p-cos.net/`.

14. I/O: Streams and Files

Communication between COMMON LISP and the "world outside" is usually performed via *streams*, whether you are interacting with files, with network connections, or with your IDE. These streams, which can be *character streams* (for textual data of all kinds) or *binary streams* (to transfer bits in chunks of *bytes*), are conceptually easy to use but still remarkably flexible and they are ultimately also used by the Lisp reader (see Chapter 8) and the Lisp printer (see Chapter 9). This chapter is about the various ways you can use, adapt, and combine streams and it ends with a recipe that demonstrates how you can create your own stream classes for almost every task you can imagine.

(See also Recipe 3-3.)

14-1. Redirecting Streams

Problem

You want to (temporarily) "redirect" `*STANDARD-INPUT*` or `*STANDARD-OUTPUT*` to another stream.[1]

Solution

Simply enclose the part of your code where the redirection should take place in a `LET` form, where you bind `*STANDARD-INPUT*` or `*STANDARD-OUTPUT*` (or both) to another stream.

```
CL-USER 1 > (defun foo (n)
              (make-list n :initial-element (read)))
FOO
CL-USER 2 > (with-input-from-string (stream "42")
              (let ((*standard-input* stream))
                (foo 3)))
(42 42 42)
CL-USER 3 > (let ((apropos-result
```

[1]This is in a way similar to *I/O redirection* on Unix, but there are also significant differences.

```
                    (with-output-to-string (stream)
                      (let ((*standard-output* stream))
                        (apropos 'foo))))
                      apropos-result)
;; output is implementation-dependent
"CLOS::FOO-METHOD-COMBINATION-ARGUMENTS (defined)
:ATK-ROLE-FOOTER, value: :ATK-ROLE-FOOTER
SYSTEM::FOO
DBG::|internal-flet-name-for-FOO|
FOO (defined)"
```

We write a small test function `FOO` that reads from `*STANDARD-INPUT*` and does something with the object read. Then we show how we can redirect `*STANDARD-INPUT*` to a *string stream*[2] such that we can use `FOO` with this string stream, although it wasn't written with anything other than `*STANDARD-INPUT*` in mind.[3] Likewise, we redirect `*STANDARD-OUTPUT*` to a string stream to capture the output of `APROPOS`, although the built-in `APROPOS` function (see Recipe 16-8) will always write to `*STANDARD-OUTPUT*`.

How It Works

What we're using here isn't a special feature of COMMON LISP streams but rather the *dynamic scope* of dynamic ("special") variable bindings.[4] It works because `*STANDARD-INPUT*` and `*STANDARD-OUTPUT*` (as well as the other stream variables defined by the COMMON LISP standard; see Recipe 16-10) are special variables.

Other Ways to Do It

The COMMON LISP forms that start with "`WITH-`" and accept a variable name as one of their arguments, establish a binding like `LET`. In other words, we could have written the preceding examples shorter, like so:[5]

```
CL-USER 1 > (with-input-from-string (*standard-input* "42")
              (foo 3))
(42 42 42)
CL-USER 2 > (with-output-to-string (*standard-output*)
              (apropos 'foo))
;; again - output is implementation-dependent
```

[2]See Recipe 14-7.

[3]Note that `READ` (see Recipe 8-1) can, of course, read data from any stream but if used with no arguments, like here, will read from `*STANDARD-INPUT*`.

[4]See chapter 6 of *Practical Common Lisp* (`http://www.gigamonkeys.com/book/variables.html`).

[5]See also Recipe 14-7.

```
"CLOS::FOO-METHOD-COMBINATION-ARGUMENTS (defined)
:ATK-ROLE-FOOTER, value: :ATK-ROLE-FOOTER
SYSTEM::FOO
DBG::|internal-flet-name-for-FOO|
FOO (defined)"
```

Many other CL variables are special variables and can thus temporarily be set to another value:[6]

```
CL-USER 1 > (let ((*print-base* 2))
              (print 10))
1010
10
```

Note how the number 10 is printed by PRINT as 1010 (i.e. as a binary number) because when PRINT is invoked, *PRINT-BASE* is set to 2. The 10 *returned* by this form, however, is printed by the REPL as a decimal number because the binding for *PRINT-BASE* has already been disestablished at this point.

Synonym Streams

You might have noticed that up until now we've been talking about changing the bindings of variables; we haven't actually redirected streams. To do that, you can use COMMON LISP's *synonym streams*, which associate a stream with a dynamic variable:

```
CL-USER 1 > (let ((result
                    (with-output-to-string (stream)
                      (let ((my-standard-output
                              (make-synonym-stream
                               '*standard-output*)))
                        (print 42 my-standard-output)
                        (let ((*standard-output* stream))
                          (print 43 my-standard-output))
                        (print 44 my-standard-output)))))
              result)

42
44
"
43 "
```

[6]See Recipe 4-4 for *PRINT-BASE*.

By temporarily binding `*STANDARD-OUTPUT*` to another value, we changed the behavior of `MY-STANDARD-OUTPUT`, which is a "virtual" stream associated with the *symbol* (not the *stream*) `*STANDARD-OUTPUT*`. In other words, if you're sending something to `MY-STANDARD-OUTPUT`, the *current* value of the variable `*STANDARD-OUTPUT*` will be used (and not the stream that this variable was bound to when `MY-STANDARD-OUTPUT` was created).

If you're wondering why and when you might want to use synonym streams instead of the technique described above, see the end of Recipe 14-5. For a typical usage of synonym streams, see page 499.

14-2. Flushing an Output Stream

Problem

You are sending output to a stream but the output doesn't arrive immediately because the stream is buffered.

Solution

Use `FORCE-OUTPUT` or `FINISH-OUTPUT`:

```
* (progn
   (write-char #\.)
   (sleep 2)
   (write-char #\.)
   (values))
  ..
* (progn
   (write-char #\.)
   (force-output)
   (sleep 2)
   (write-char #\.)
   (values))
  ..
```

You won't see a difference in print (or did you?), but if you try this in the REPL, it's very likely that in the first example you'll see both dots after two seconds; whereas in the second example you'll see the first dot immediately and the next one after two seconds. (But note that what you'll actually see is implementation-dependent.)

How It Works

Lisp output streams are usually "buffered;" that is, output sent to the stream isn't sent immediately to the underlying physical "device" (file, terminal, socket, etc.) character by character, but rather in larger chunks whenever the system deems it appropriate. There are situations when you want to surpass this and want to "see" the output immediately, usually when there are time lags between portions of your output and you want the user to see that something is happening.

There are two standard functions that you can use to "flush" (i.e., empty) a stream's buffer: `FORCE-OUTPUT` and `FINISH-OUTPUT`. The only difference between these two functions is that `FINISH-OUTPUT` waits until the buffer is really empty before it returns, whereas `FORCE-OUTPUT` just initiates the emptying of the buffer and returns immediately. (This implies that it cannot report any errors that may occur when writing to the stream.)

The (optional) argument to these functions can be any output stream. If no argument is given (as in the preceding example), the functions work on `*STANDARD-OUTPUT*`.

The standard doesn't provide a means to make an output stream unconditionally unbuffered. If you really need such a thing, you must invent your own streams to do that (see Recipe 14-14 for details).

Note that stream buffering is a means to increase the performance of I/O; that is, it's generally a good thing to have. You should only flush a stream when you really think it's necessary.[7]

14-3. Determining the Size of a File

Problem

You want to know how big a file is.

Solution

Use the standard function `FILE-LENGTH` like so:

```
(with-open-file (in "C:/Windows/winhlp32.exe"
                    :element-type '(unsigned-byte 8))
  (file-length in))
```

[7]One situation where it could make sense to call `FINISH-OUTPUT` is before closing a stream. On some implementations, errors occurring when the stream is flushed implicitly due to `CLOSE` might not be reported (but will be reported if you flush explicitly).

How It Works

FILE-LENGTH returns the length (or size) of a file. Note that FILE-LENGTH's single argument has to be a *stream*,[8] not a pathname; that is, you have to OPEN a file before you can determine its length.

The length returned by FILE-LENGTH is measured in units of the stream's element type if you're doing binary I/O. If, say, your element type is (SIGNED-BYTE 16) and your file is 200 octets (8-bit bytes) long, don't be surprised if the function FILE-LENGTH will correctly report a length of 100.

For character streams, you can assume (given the current COMMON LISP implementations) that the length will be measured in octets no matter how the characters are encoded.[9] This should be pretty much what you'd expect if you come from another language, like C, PERL, or JAVA, but might be surprising if you expected the number of *characters* (see Recipe 3-3).

14-4. Reading a Whole File at Once

Problem

You want to read the complete contents of a file into memory at once.

Solution

First, check if your implementation doesn't already have special support for this task. Or use a library function (see below).

To do this yourself in portable COMMON LISP, use FILE-LENGTH and READ-SEQUENCE. Here's an example session with LISPWORKS on Linux, but the function FILE-AT-ONCE shown here should work with any COMMON LISP:

```
CL-USER 1 > (defun file-at-once (filespec &rest open-args)
              (with-open-stream (stream (apply #'open filespec
                                               open-args))
                (let* ((buffer
                        (make-array (file-length stream)
                                    :element-type
                                    (stream-element-type stream)
                                    :fill-pointer t))
```

[8] And, of course, it can't be any stream, but the stream has to be associated with a file.

[9] This means that even without the :ELEMENT-TYPE part, our code from above should have yielded the same result.

```
                        (position (read-sequence buffer stream)))
                   (setf (fill-pointer buffer) position)
                   buffer)))
FILE-AT-ONCE
CL-USER 2 > (defun number-of-users ()
               (count #\Newline
                     (file-at-once "/etc/passwd"
                                   :element-type 'character)))
NUMBER-OF-USERS
CL-USER 3 > (number-of-users)
42
;; LispWorks-specific:
CL-USER 4 > (subseq (hcl:file-string "/etc/passwd") 0 4)
"root"
```

To illustrate how to slurp a whole file, we wrote a function FILE-AT-ONCE that accepts a pathname designator and keyword arguments like OPEN; in fact, the arguments to FILE-AT-ONCE are directly handed over to OPEN to open the stream. After we've opened the stream, we can ask for the file's length and use this information to create a vector that will hold the file's contents. The last line shows that LISPWORKS comes with a function that already does what we want. Check your Lisp's documentation to see if it offers something similar.

For bonus points, try to implement the setf function (SETF FILE-AT-ONCE) (see Recipe 10-8).

How It Works

The crucial function here is READ-SEQUENCE.[10] Given a stream and an existing buffer, this function will destructively modify the buffer by replacing its elements with elements read from the stream. This is most likely the fastest portable way to read large amounts of data from a stream, even if you don't want to read a whole file at once. Note that READ-SEQUENCE accepts :START and :END keyword parameters, so you can modify just a part of the sequence if you want. And don't ignore that the function is called READ-SEQUENCE, not "READ-VECTOR;" that is, you can also use a list as its target.[11]

READ-SEQUENCE returns the index of the first element that was not updated, which we store in the variable POSITION. READ-SEQUENCE's counterpart is WRITE-SEQUENCE, which can write a whole sequence (or a part of it) to a stream.

The other function worth mentioning is FILE-LENGTH, which is discussed in detail

[10]See also Recipe 14-10

[11]Try it. Replace MAKE-ARRAY with MAKE-LIST in our example above.

in Recipe 14-3. Note that the string returned by FILE-AT-ONCE (if we're reading a character file) can be shorter than the number of octets reported by FILE-LENGTH; there are several character encodings, like UTF-8, which (can) use more than one octet per character.[12] That's why we use a fill pointer (see Recipe 5-6) in our function above.

Our FILE-AT-ONCE doesn't do any error checking, although the macro WITH-OPEN-STREAM makes sure that the stream is closed if anything goes wrong.[13] For a "real-world" function, you'd want to check that OPEN does in fact return a stream and not NIL.

Alternatives

Your implementation might already have such a function. LISPWORKS, for example, has HCL:FILE-STRING, while ALLEGROCL has EXCL:FILE-CONTENTS. Or use the ALEXANDRIA library (see Recipe 18-4) which offers the functions READ-FILE-INTO-BYTE-VECTOR and READ-FILE-INTO-STRING.

Also, there are, of course, alternatives to reading a whole file into memory. You can, for example, read a text file line by line with READ-LINE,[14] or character by character with READ-CHAR. Or you can use READ-SEQUENCE to read a "chunk" of the file and process it before you read the next one.

14-5. Sending Data to Two Streams in Parallel

Problem

You have two or more files or streams to which you want to send the same output.

Solution

Use *broadcast streams*:

```
CL-USER 1 > (with-open-file (stream-1 "/tmp/foo1" :direction :output)
              (with-open-file (stream-2 "/tmp/foo2"
                                        :direction :output)
                (let ((out (make-broadcast-stream stream-1 stream-2)))
                  (format out "This line goes to foo1 and foo2~%")
                  (format stream-1 "Only foo1~%")
```

[12]Or see the example with #\Newline in Recipe 14-12.
[13]Using UNWIND-PROTECT; see Recipe 12-8.
[14]See Recipe 14-9.

```
                    (format stream-2 "Only foo2~%")
                    (format out "Again both files~%"))))
;; see explanation below for FILE-AT-ONCE
CL-USER 2 > (file-at-once "/tmp/foo1")
"This line goes to foo1 and foo2
Only foo1
Again both files
"
CL-USER 3 > (file-at-once "/tmp/foo2")
"This line goes to foo1 and foo2
Only foo2
Again both files
"
```

We open two output streams to different files `foo1` and `foo2`. We then combine these streams into one broadcast stream and write a line to both streams at once. Then we send a line that only goes to `foo1` and a line that only goes to `foo2`. Finally, we send a closing line, which again goes to both files. Afterward, we use `FILE-AT-ONCE` from Recipe 14-4 to check the files we just created.

How It Works

COMMON LISP has the concept of a *broadcast stream*—a virtual output stream which sends data to all the streams associated with it in parallel. Such a stream is created with `MAKE-BROADCAST-STREAM`, which takes any number of arguments: these are the streams to be associated with the broadcast stream. The conceptual picture behind our first example is that the broadcast stream `OUT` works like a distributor for the streams `STREAM-1` and `STREAM-2`; whatever is sent to `OUT` is immediately broadcast to `STREAM-1` and `STREAM-2`:

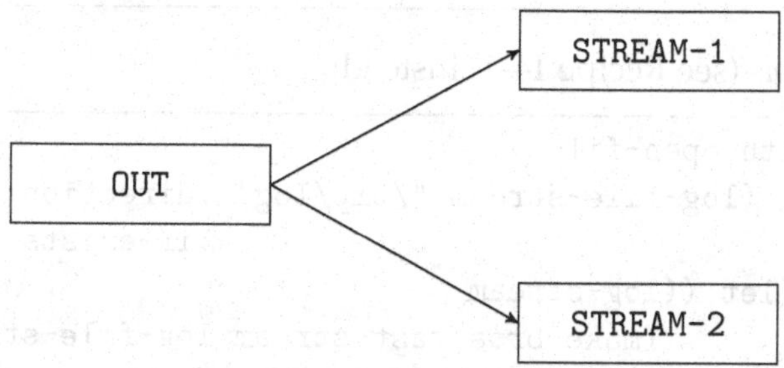

That the function that creates broadcast streams accepts a variable number of arguments means that you're not limited to two streams being attached to a broadcast stream; you could have three, 42, one (albeit that seems a bit pointless), or none at all (see Recipe 14-6).

A typical application of this is error logging, where you might want to send error messages to *ERROR-OUTPUT* but also log them to a file: open an error log file and create a broadcast stream which sends data to this log file and also to *ERROR-OUTPUT*.

You can at any time query a broadcast stream with the function BROADCAST-STREAM-STREAMS to get a list of the streams that it sends output to.

Synonym Streams

The arguments to MAKE-BROADCAST-STREAM are streams, not variables, so if you "redirect" one of these streams using the technique described in Recipe 14-1, the broadcast stream will still write to the original stream:

```
CL-USER 1 > (with-open-file
                (log-file-stream "/tmp/log" :direction :output)
              (let ((log-stream
                     (make-broadcast-stream log-file-stream
                                            *error-output*)))
                (format log-stream "An error occurred~%")
                (with-open-file (*error-output* "/tmp/log2"
                                                :direction :output)
                  (format log-stream "Another error occurred~%"))
                (format log-stream "Zounds! Again an error!~%")))
An error occurred
Another error occurred
Zounds! Again an error!
NIL
;; see above for FILE-AT-ONCE
CL-USER 2 > (file-at-once "/tmp/log2")
""
```

Use *synonym streams* (see Recipe 14-1) instead:

```
CL-USER 1 > (with-open-file
                (log-file-stream "/tmp/log" :direction :output
                                            :if-exists :supersede)
              (let ((log-stream
                     (make-broadcast-stream log-file-stream
                                            (make-synonym-stream
                                             '*error-output*))))
                (format log-stream "An error occurred~%")
                (with-open-file
                    (*error-output* "/tmp/log2" :direction :output
                                                :if-exists :supersede)
```

```
              (format log-stream "Another error occurred~%"))
            (format log-stream "Zounds! Again an error!~%")))
An error occurred
Zounds! Again an error!
NIL
;; see above for FILE-AT-ONCE
CL-USER 2 > (file-at-once "/tmp/log2")
"Another error occurred
"
```

14-6. Sending Data to "/dev/null"

Problem

You want to redirect output to "nowhere." In other words, you want it to disappear.

Solution

Use *broadcast streams*, introduced in Recipe 14-5. Specifically, use MAKE-BROADCAST-STREAM without an argument:

```
CL-USER(1): (defun print-some-stuff ()
              (dotimes (i 10) (format t "~R~%" i)))
PRINT-SOME-STUFF
CL-USER(2): (print-some-stuff)
zero
one
two
three
four
five
six
seven
eight
nine
NIL
CL-USER(3): (let ((*standard-output* (make-broadcast-stream)))
              (print-some-stuff))
NIL
```

Here we create a little function that prints a couple of lines, and then we redirect (see Recipe 14-1) *STANDARD-OUTPUT* to the result of calling MAKE-BROADCAST-STREAM without an argument. The printed output of our function disappears completely.

How It Works

Most users of Unix-like system will be familiar with /dev/null, which is a special device you can use to send data to Nirvana; for example, in JAVA, you might use something like this:[15]

```
PrintStream nps
  = new PrintStream(new FileOutputStream("/dev/null"));
System.setOut(nps);
```

COMMON LISP offers a similar[16] feature: just employ a broadcast stream that "broadcasts" to no streams at all. See Recipe 14-5 for more information about broadcast streams.

14-7. Pretending a String Is a Stream

Problem

You want to read data from a string instead of a file or stream. Or you want to output your data to a string instead of a file or stream.

Solution

Use *string streams*:

```
* (with-input-from-string (s "(41 42 43)")
    (second (read s)))
42
* (with-input-from-string (s "(41 42 43)" :start 4 :end 5)
    (read s))
4
* (with-output-to-string (s)
    (write-string "Look: " s)
```

[15]Use "NUL:" on Windows.

[16]This is similar but not identical. Writing to something like /dev/null is a system-level feature, while what we're doing here works at the language level. You could also, from within COMMON LISP, really open a stream to /dev/null, but it'd be slower.

```
  (princ (list 1 2 3) s))
"Look: (1 2 3)"
* (let ((string (make-array 0 :element-type 'character
                              :fill-pointer t
                              :adjustable t)))
    (vector-push-extend #\[ string)
    (with-output-to-string (s string)
      (write-string "Look: " s)
      (princ (list 1 2 3) s))
    (vector-push-extend #\] string)
    string)
"[Look: (1 2 3)]"
```

We use the convenience macros `WITH-INPUT-FROM-STRING` and `WITH-OUTPUT-TO-STRING` to create streams (called `S` here) that last while the macro's body is executed. The stream in `WITH-INPUT-FROM-STRING` gets its input from the second argument. The second example shows that we can use `:START` and `:END` keyword arguments so that only a part of the string is used as the stream's source.

In the third example, we use `WITH-OUTPUT-TO-STRING` with only one argument. In this case, the macro will create an "anonymous" string for us, which'll collect the output sent to the string stream. It'll be returned as the result of the whole macro. In the fourth example, we provide `WITH-OUTPUT-TO-STRING` with a string that we've created ourselves. It must have a fill pointer and it must be *actually adjustable* (see Recipe 5-7).[17] Now this particular string will be used as the sink of the string stream and the macro will return the result(s) of its last form.

How It Works

I/O usually means that you associate a stream with a file or your terminal and then send data to that stream or read it from there. But there are cases where you want to work with strings instead. Like, you might want to send test data to a function that is designed to read from a stream, or you want to capture the output of a function that writes to `*STANDARD-OUTPUT*` in a string for post-processing.

Luckily, COMMON LISP has *string streams*, which are streams created from strings that, for all practical purposes, behave like "normal" streams.[18] String streams can be input or output streams but not both. Input string streams get their data from a string that you provide when creating the stream, whereas output string streams use an adjustable string with a fill pointer as their data sink.

[17] To be more precise, it only has to be adjustable if you're trying to write past the end of the string.

[18] If you've already worked with JAVA's `StringWriter` and `StringReader`, you're used to this idea.

The examples above show how to use the two macros provided by COMMON LISP that provide convenient means to handle string streams.

More Details

The `WITH-INPUT-FROM-STRING` macro also accepts an `:INDEX` keyword argument. This argument should be a *place*[19] in which the macro will save the index into the string of the first character that was *not* read. The following example shows how to use this feature:

```
* (loop with ptr = 0
        with eof = (gensym)
        for from = ptr
        for object = (with-input-from-string
                         (s "41  42 43" :start ptr :index ptr)
                       (read s nil eof))
        until (eq object eof)
        do (format t "~A-~A: ~A~%" from ptr object)
        finally (return (values)))
0-3: 41
3-7: 42
7-9: 43
```

Instead of the "WITH-" macros, you can also use more low-level facilities that directly create and access string streams:

```
* (let* ((s (make-string-input-stream "41 42 43"))
         (a (read s))
         (b (read s)))
    (list a b (read s)))
(41 42 43)
* (let ((s (make-string-output-stream)))
    (write-string "Look: " s)
    (princ (list 1 2 3) s)
    (format t "1: ~S~%" (get-output-stream-string s))
    (write-string "More..." s)
    (format t "2: ~S~%" (get-output-stream-string s)))
1: "Look: (1 2 3)"
2: "More..."
NIL
```

[19] See Recipe 10-8.

Note how the second call to GET-OUTPUT-STREAM-STRING only returns what has been written to S since the previous call.

If you are looking for something similar (using in-memory data structures as feeds or sinks of streams) for binary data, that's not part of the standard. But you can do it yourself (see Recipe 14-14) or use the *in-memory streams* provided by the FLEXI-STREAMS library.

(See also Recipe 9-2.)

14-8. Concatenating Streams

Problem

You want to concatenate streams; that is, you want to read from one stream until you reach its end and then you want to immediately continue with the next stream without the reading function noticing a difference.

Solution

Use MAKE-CONCATENATED-STREAM. Here we have an example with string streams (see Recipe 14-7), but this will work with all input streams.

```
* (read-line
   (make-concatenated-stream
    (make-string-input-stream "Duc")
    (make-string-input-stream "k So")
    (make-string-input-stream "up")))
"Duck Soup"
```

How It Works

It's as simple as it looks. Pass as many input streams to MAKE-CONCATENATED-STREAM as you like, and they'll all be read from, one after another; that is, you'll read from the first until it reaches EOF, and then, without an error being signaled and without any intervention from the reading function, input will come from the second stream, and so on.

As I said, this is done in such a way that the reading function won't need to worry about it. But it can, of course, figure out if it's working on a concatenated stream by checking if its class or type (see Recipe 13-2) is CONCATENATED-STREAM and it can also access the individual streams using the function CONCATENATED-STREAM-STREAMS.

14-9. Processing Text Files Line by Line

Problem

You want to read and process data in a text file line by line (as for example most Unix shell utilities do).

Solution

Use the built-in functions WRITE-LINE and READ-LINE. Here's an example:

```
CL-USER(1): (with-open-file (out "/tmp/foo.txt"
                                 :direction :output)
              (write-line "First line" out)
              (write-line "Second line" out)
              (write-line "The third line" out :start 4 :end 9)
              (write-string "Last line, without Newline" out))
"Last line, without Newline"
CL-USER(2): (with-open-file (in "/tmp/foo.txt")
              (loop for (line no-nl-p)
                      = (multiple-value-list (read-line in nil nil))
                    while line
                    do (format t "~S~:[ <newline at end>~;~]~%"
                               line no-nl-p)))
"First line" <newline at end>
"Second line" <newline at end>
"third" <newline at end>
"Last line, without Newline"
NIL
```

How It Works

There's not much to say about these functions. WRITE-STRING will write a string to an output stream (*STANDARD-OUTPUT* by default) and will accept :START and :END keyword arguments if you only want to write part of the string. WRITE-LINE does the same, but will always append a newline afterward.

READ-LINE reads from a stream (*STANDARD-INPUT* by default) until it encounters either a newline or the end of the stream. It will return the string read *without* the newline if there was one. READ-LINE returns a second value, which is true if the string wasn't terminated by a newline. Like all of COMMON LISP's functions that read from a stream, READ-LINE accepts optional arguments to control its behavior in case it's at the end of the stream. The default behavior is to signal an error (see below), but you can change this to return a certain value instead; we chose `NIL` in our example, which allows us to write "`WHILE LINE`" to control when the loop has to end.

What Happens at the End of a Line?

One thing to note is that the `#\Newline` character in COMMON LISP is an abstraction. While you're working with Lisp streams, it is one character (usually, but not necessarily represented as the ASCII linefeed character), but when you communicate with the "world outside" (files, streams), it is converted from and to the end-of-line marker corresponding to your operating system. If, for example, you're working with Windows, `WRITE-LINE` will emit two characters (Carriage Return, ASCII 13, and Linefeed, ASCII 10) at the end of the line, and `READ-LINE` will treat these two octets together as an indicator for the end of a line. Likewise, `(WRITE-CHAR #\Newline)` is equivalent to this:

```
(progn
  (write-char #\Return)
  (write-char #\Linefeed))
```

The intention of this behavior is that Lisp programs are portable between different operating systems as long as you don't cross boundaries. However, you might have to be careful if you're dealing with text files that were created with another operating system. Most Lisps offer means to control a stream's behavior with respect to `#\Newline`, usually by implementation-dependent *external formats* (see more about this in Recipe 3-3).

Following is a simple example for ALLEGROCL. Check your vendor's documentation for details.

```
CL-USER(4): (with-open-file (out "/tmp/foo.txt"
                                 :direction :output
                                 :if-exists :supersede
                                 :external-format '(:e-crlf :latin1))
              (write-line "First line" out)
              (write-line "Second line" out)
              (write-line "The third line" out :start 4 :end 9)
              (write-string "Last line, without Newline" out))
"Last line, without Newline"
CL-USER(5): (with-open-file (in "/tmp/foo.txt")
              (loop for line = (read-line in nil)
                    while line
                    do (format t "~S~%"
```

```
                                        (char line (1- (length line)))))
#\Return
#\Return
#\Return
#\e
NIL
CL-USER(6): (with-open-file (in "/tmp/foo.txt"
                                 :external-format '(:e-crlf :latin1))
              (loop for line = (read-line in nil)
                    while line
                    do (format t "~S~%"
                               (char line (1- (length line))))))
#\e
#\e
#\d
#\e
NIL
```

This was executed on a Linux system, which uses a single linefeed character to separate lines. We create the file `foo.txt` with Windows-like line endings by using the (ALLEGROCL-specific) "composed external format" `:E-CRLF`. The file `foo.txt` now behaves as if it was created by a Windows program. In particular, if we use `READ-LINE` with the default (Unix) external format, the last character for each line except the last one is `#\Return` (which is ASCII 13).

What Happens at the End of the File?

Sometimes there might be valid reasons to do something special in case the end of the stream is encountered, be it just to increase the readability of your code. This can, of course, be done by accepting the default `EOF` behavior of `READ-LINE` and handling the error (see Recipe 12-4) that is signaled:

```
CL-USER(3): (handler-case
              (with-open-file (in "/tmp/foo.txt")
                (loop for line = (read-line in)
                      do (format t "~S~%" line)))
              (end-of-file ()
                (format t "-->END OF FILE HERE<--~%")))
"First line
"Second line
"third
"Last line, without Newline"
-->END OF FILE HERE<--
```

```
NIL
```

If you want more control of text I/O, you can work on a character-by-character basis: look up the standard functions `READ-CHAR` and `WRITE-CHAR` in the HyperSpec. You can even go one level deeper and read and write octets[20] (use a stream element type of `(UNSIGNED-BYTE 8)`) with `READ-BYTE` and `WRITE-BYTE`, converting them from and to characters using your own function for character encoding.

14-10. Working with Binary Data

Problem

You want to read or write binary data with a fixed record size.

Solution

Use *binary streams*; that is, those created with an integral element type:

```
CL-USER(1): (with-open-file (out "/tmp/data"
                                 :direction :output
                                 :element-type '(signed-byte 16))
              (dolist (byte '(28483 27503 28514 27503))
                (write-byte byte out)))
NIL
CL-USER(2): (with-open-file (in "/tmp/data"
                                :element-type '(signed-byte 16))
              (loop for byte = (read-byte in nil)
                    while byte
                    collect byte))
(28483 27503 28514 27503)
;; the following results are implementation-dependent
CL-USER(3): (with-open-file (in "/tmp/data"
                                :element-type '(signed-byte 32))
              (loop for byte = (read-byte in nil)
                    while byte
                    collect byte))
(1802465091 1802465122)
CL-USER(4): (+ 28483 (* 65536 27503))
1802465091
CL-USER(5): (with-open-file (in "/tmp/data"
```

[20] See also Recipe 14-10.

```
                                  :element-type '(unsigned-byte 8))
             (loop for byte = (read-byte in nil)
                   while byte
                   collect byte))
(67 111 111 107 98 111 111 107)
CL-USER(6): (+ 67 (* 256 111))
28483
CL-USER(7): (with-open-file (in "/tmp/data")
             (read-line in))
"Cookbook"
T
```

We write some binary data to the file /tmp/data and read it back in with the same element type. The subsequent examples show implementation-dependent results; we read the data with *different* element types and thus get an idea of how it's laid out on disk. We even read the file as a character stream in order to show how the 8-bit bytes correspond to characters.

How It Works

Any stream opened (with OPEN or WITH-OPEN-FILE) with an element type that is not (a subset of) CHARACTER is a "binary stream." Its element type is a finite subset of INTEGER, and each element written to or read from the stream (called a "byte") has to belong to this subset. The basic I/O operations for binary streams are READ-BYTE and WRITE-BYTE.

Reading or Writing Several Bytes at Once

Instead of READ-BYTE and WRITE-BYTE, you can also use READ-SEQUENCE and WRITE-SEQUENCE to read and write larger amounts of binary data. These operations might be significantly faster than their byte-oriented counterparts when the sequences are long enough.[21]

```
CL-USER(8): (with-open-file (out "/tmp/data"
                                  :direction :output
                                  :if-exists :supersede
                                  :element-type '(signed-byte 16))
             (write-sequence '(100 200 300 400 500 600 700) out
                             :start 2 :end 6))
(100 200 300 400 500 600 700)
CL-USER(9): (with-open-file (in "/tmp/data"
```

[21]These two functions can also be used with character streams. See Recipe 14-4 for an example.

```
                        :element-type '(signed-byte 16))
        (let ((result (make-array 8 :initial-element 0)))
          (read-sequence result in :start 3 :end 7)
          result))
#(0 0 0 300 400 500 600 0)
```

You Might Get Bigger Chunks Than You Asked For

The element type doesn't have to be (SIGNED-BYTE x) or (UNSIGNED-BYTE y). As I said above, any type which is a finite subset of INTEGER is allowed; so you could, for example, use types like (MOD 32) or (INTEGER -27 101). The following example (which is implementation-dependent) shows that choosing a very small subset doesn't necessarily save disk space:

```
CL-USER(10): (with-open-file (out "/tmp/data"
                                  :direction :output
                                  :if-exists :supersede
                                  :element-type '(mod 16))
               (dotimes (i 16)
                 (write-byte i out)))
NIL
CL-USER(11): (let ((*print-length* nil))
               (with-open-file (in "/tmp/data"
                                   :element-type '(mod 16))
                 (print (loop for byte = (read-byte in nil)
                              while byte
                              collect byte)))
               (values))
(0 1 2 3 4 5 6 7 8 9 10 11 12 13 14 15)
CL-USER(12): (let ((*print-length* nil))
               (with-open-file (in "/tmp/data"
                                   :element-type '(unsigned-byte 8))
                 (print (loop for byte = (read-byte in nil)
                              while byte
                              collect byte)))
               (values))
(0 1 2 3 4 5 6 7 8 9 10 11 12 13 14 15)
```

This is because implementations are allowed to "upgrade" the element type of a binary stream. That's the same mechanism that's described on page 133 in the chapter about arrays and it is probably safe to assume that most Lisps nowadays will upgrade to *octets* (i.e., (UNSIGNED-BYTE 8) in Lisp parlance) or multiples thereof, because that's the "chunk size" of the underlying operating system.[22] You can query the "real" element of the stream you created with STREAM-ELEMENT-TYPE.

So, although convenient, this kind of binary I/O cannot be used as a general mechanism to exchange data between *different* Lisp implementations, because the way the data is sent to and read from the stream is implementation-dependent. However, if you use "standard-sized" integers (8-bit, 16-bit, 32-bit), you might be lucky if your Lisps are on the same OS.

Also, restricting the set of integers that can be written to the stream doesn't necessarily catch errors. The ANSI standard doesn't require implementations to signal an error if you write data that the stream wasn't made for:

```
;; some Lisps will signal an error, some won't:
CL-USER(11): (with-open-file (out "/tmp/data"
                                  :direction :output
                                  :if-exists :supersede
                                  :element-type '(mod 16))
               (write-byte 16 out))
NIL
```

14-11. Reading "Foreign" Binary Data

Problem

You want to read binary data from a file that was written by another program (in another programming language).

Solution

The BINARY-TYPES library might be helpful. But maybe you have to get your hands dirty and decode the data on your own.

Let's suppose the data that we want to read was written with this C program (which was compiled with GCC on a Linux x86-64 machine):

```
#include <stdio.h>

struct foo {
  char tag;
  unsigned short x0;
```

[22]Should you ever need to be able to read or write bytes of arbitrary sizes (possibly at the cost of speed), have a look at the ODD-STREAMS library.

```
  unsigned short y0;
  long size;
};

int main (int argc, char* argv[]) {
  static struct foo foo1 = {'x', 12, 24, -666};
  static struct foo foo2 = {'A', 42, 1, 1234567810};

  FILE* out = fopen("/tmp/data", "w");

  fwrite(&foo1, sizeof(struct foo), 1, out);
  fwrite(&foo2, sizeof(struct foo), 1, out);

  fclose(out);
}
```

If you use a hex editor, the file `/tmp/data` will now look similar to this:

78	00	0C	00	18	00	00	00	66	FD	FF	FF	FF	FF	FF	FF
41	00	2A	00	01	00	00	00	82	02	96	49	00	00	00	00

We're only interested in the gray parts. The rest is padding[23] added by the C compiler and the amount of padding is specific to the compiler used.

Then, after loading the BINARY-TYPES library,[24] we can read the data like this:

```
* (rename-package :binary-types :bt)
#<PACKAGE "BT">
* (bt:define-binary-class data-point ()
    ((tag
      :accessor tag
      :binary-type bt:char8)
     ;; see remark about padding above
     (padding-1
      :binary-type 1)
     (x0
      :accessor x0
      :binary-type bt:u16)
     (y0
      :accessor y0
      :binary-type bt:u16)
     ;; see above
```

[23]See `http://en.wikipedia.org/wiki/Data_structure_alignment`.

[24]Which can be done with QUICKLISP; see Recipe 18-2.

```
      (padding-2
       :binary-type 2)
      (size
       :accessor size
       :binary-type bt:s32)
      ;; so that size is 16 octets
      (padding-3
       :binary-type 4)))
DATA-POINT
* (defmethod print-object ((data-point data-point) stream)
    (print-unreadable-object (data-point stream :type t)
      (with-accessors ((tag tag)
                       (x0 x0)
                       (y0 y0)
                       (size size))
          data-point
        (format stream "Tag: ~S, " tag)
        (format stream "X0: ~S, " x0)
        (format stream "Y0: ~S, " y0)
        (format stream "Size: ~S" size))))
#<STANDARD-METHOD PRINT-OBJECT (DATA-POINT T) {1005B008E3}>
* (let ((bt:*endian* :little-endian))
    (bt:with-binary-file (in "/tmp/data")
      (values (bt:read-binary 'data-point in)
              (bt:read-binary 'data-point in))))
#<DATA-POINT Tag: #\x, X0: 12, Y0: 24, Size: -666>
#<DATA-POINT Tag: #\A, X0: 42, Y0: 1, Size: 1234567810>
```

Of course, our own PRINT-OBJECT method[25] isn't really necessary; we just use it so we can easily show the important parts of the objects that were read in. But this example illustrates how the BINARY-TYPES library can help us to avoid some of the tedious work needed to make sense of binary data. Basically, we just define a class that mimics the C struct used to write the data and then use the provided BT:READ-BINARY function to read objects of this class. This is all pretty simple, except that we need to know how exactly the individual parts of the struct are aligned in memory by the C compiler. (That's what the PADDING-*n* slots are for.)

How It Works

Reading arbitrary binary data from a stream is certainly a non-trivial task. It amounts to reading the data, octet by octet (or whatever the smallest unit written by the file's creator is), and decoding it based on your knowledge about it.

[25] See Recipe 9-8.

The BINARY-TYPES library by Frode Vatvedt Fjeld can help us here in that it predefines typical data units and provides ways to build compound objects out of these, which can be read in and automatically converted to Lisp data. Unfortunately, it can't read your mind, so you still have to feed it with enough information about how your input is formatted so that it can find its way through the file.

If you're reading structured binary data written by, say, a C, PASCAL, or FORTRAN program, the trickiest bit is to get the data layout right. This starts with the "endianness" of the platform that the data was generated on, but that's only half of the story. You will need to know the compiler that was used better than your loved ones, because only then will you be able to predict where it "padded" the data to get the "alignment" it liked most (see the remark about the padding slots in our example above). If in doubt, you'll have to peek at the data with a hex editor. Good luck...

Floating-Point Values

As of this writing, the BINARY-TYPES library doesn't support floating-point types. If you have to read floating-point data, then currently your best bet seems to be the IEEE-FLOATS library by Marijn Haverbeke. Here's an example. In this case, our data was written with this C program:

```
#include <stdio.h>

int main (int argc, char* argv[]) {
  double x = 42.5E9;
  double y = -.89E-12;

  FILE* out = fopen("/tmp/data", "w");

  fwrite(&x, sizeof(x), 1, out);
  fwrite(&y, sizeof(y), 1, out);

  fclose(out);
}
```

On the Lisp side you could now read the data like so:

```
* (with-open-file (in "/tmp/data" :element-type '(unsigned-byte 64))
    (loop repeat 2
          collect (ieee-floats:decode-float64 (read-byte in))))
(4.25d10 -8.9d-13)
```

But be aware of possible issues with endianness.[26]

[26]See http://en.wikipedia.org/wiki/Endianness#Floating-point_and_endianness.

As an alternative, you could use your Lisp's foreign function interface (see Chapter 19) and read, for example, a double float by reading four octets at a time and storing two of them into an `unsigned int` array of size two. Then you'd coerce a pointer to this array to a pointer to a `double float` and read what the pointer points to.[27]

14-12. Using Random Access I/O

Problem

You want to read data from the middle of a file without having to read everything in front of that item.

Solution

Use `FILE-POSITION`:

```
CL-USER(1): (with-open-file (out "/tmp/data"
                                 :direction :output
                                 :element-type '(signed-byte 32))
              (loop for i below 1000
                    do (write-byte (* i i) out)))
NIL
CL-USER(2): (with-open-file (in "/tmp/data"
                                :element-type '(signed-byte 32))
              (file-position in 333)
              (values (read-byte in)
                      (file-position in)))
110889
334
CL-USER(3): (* 333 333)
110889
CL-USER(4): (with-open-file (out "/tmp/data.txt" :direction :output)
              (write-string
               "Now, fair Hippolyta, our nuptial hour
Draws on apace; four happy days bring in
Another moon: but, O, methinks, how slow
This old moon wanes! she lingers my desires,
Like to a step-dame or a dowager
Long withering out a young man revenue." out))
```

[27] Sounds kind of ugly and pretty C-like, but might be necessary if you're dealing with data where the layout is implicitly specified by a foreign language (as opposed to clearly defined).

```
"Now, fair Hippolyta, our nuptial hour
Draws on apace; four happy days bring in
Another moon: but, O, methinks, how slow
This old moon wanes! she lingers my desires,
Like to a step-dame or a dowager
Long withering out a young man revenue."
CL-USER(5): (with-open-file (in "/tmp/data.txt")
              (file-position in 190)
              (let ((string (make-string 7)))
                (read-sequence string in)
                (values string (file-position in))))
"dowager"
197
```

In the first example, we write 1000 pieces of data (see Recipe 14-10) and we open the file we've just written for reading. We then move forward to position 333[28] within the file and read one byte. We verify that what've read is really the square of 333, as expected.

In the next example, we write a piece of text[29] to a file, open it for reading, and, after moving beyond the 190th character, we read exactly seven characters; see Recipe 14-10 for more about READ-SEQUENCE. After reading the string, we call FILE-POSITION again to confirm that we're now at position 197.

How It Works

The ANSI standard defines the function FILE-POSITION, which can be used to move to an arbitrary position within a stream. It can also be used to query a stream as to where it is currently positioned.

The optional second argument to FILE-POSITION, the *file position designator*, can be either a positive integer, as in the examples above, or it can be one of the keywords :START or :END (obviously meaning the start or end of the file):

```
CL-USER(6): (with-open-file (out "/tmp/data.txt"
                                 :direction :output
                                 :if-exists :supersede)
              (write-string
                "The present day sysadmin refuses to die." out))
"The present day sysadmin refuses to die."
;; see Recipe 14-4 for FILE-AT-ONCE
CL-USER(7): (file-at-once "/tmp/data.txt")
```

[28] As usual, positions start at 0.

[29] Where's that from?

```
"The present day sysadmin refuses to die."
CL-USER(8): (with-open-file (out "/tmp/data.txt"
                                  :direction :output
                                  :if-exists :overwrite)
              (file-position out 16)
              (write-string "composer" out)
              (file-position out :end)
              (write-string " (Edgar Varese)" out))
" (Edgar Varese)"
CL-USER(9): (file-at-once "/tmp/data.txt")
"The present day composer refuses to die. (Edgar Varese)"
```

Note the `:IF-EXISTS` keyword argument `:OVERWRITE` that we used in the second call to `OPEN`. This is necessary so that we can actually write "in the middle" of some existing file.

With this in mind, it is fairly easy to, say, write a portable function that accepts *negative* "file position designators" for binary streams:

```
(defun file-position* (stream &optional (pos nil pos-provided-p))
  (cond ((not pos-provided-p)
         (file-position stream))
        ((and (integerp pos) (< pos 0))
         (file-position stream (+ (file-length stream) pos)))
        (t (file-position stream pos))))
```

Note that this function lacks production-quality error checking. It's just here for illustration purposes.

Different Characters May Have Different Lengths

For binary streams, the unit by which the position within the file is measured is clearly defined by the standard (one unit equals one *byte*, as defined by the stream's element type), yet it is up to the implementation to determine how this is done for character streams. For most current Lisps, you can be pretty sure that the unit is octets (8-bit bytes), though, as with `FILE-LENGTH` (see Recipe 14-4).

This implies that depending on the stream's external format (see Recipe 3-3), file position n will not necessarily be the position in front of the nth character.

Here's an example where the file `test.txt` was created with a Windows program; that is, it uses CRLF line terminators:

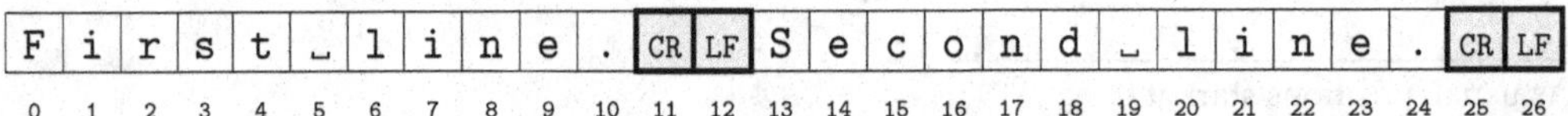

Now let's try the following:

```
;; external format is specific to AllegroCL
CL-USER(10): (with-open-file (in "/tmp/test.txt"
                                  :external-format '(:e-crlf :latin1))
               (loop for line = (read-line in nil)
                     while line
                     collect line))
("First line." "Second line.")
CL-USER(11): (with-open-file (in "/tmp/test.txt"
                                  :external-format '(:e-crlf :latin1))
               (let ((line (read-line in)))
                 (values (length line)
                         (file-position in))))
11
13
```

The first line that we read has eleven characters and there was a newline character, so we expect the stream to be at position 12. It is, however, at position 13 because the newline was created by consuming two octets, Carriage Return (ASCII 13) and Linefeed (ASCII 10). This implies that for variable-length file encodings like UTF-8 (see Recipe 3-3), there is no "random access" using `FILE-POSITION`, as you'll risk landing in the middle of a character. The only reasonable way to use `FILE-POSITION` with such encodings is to only use arguments that were returned from previous calls to `FILE-POSITION` at "safe" positions.

14-13. Serializing Lisp Objects

Problem

You want to store arbitrary Lisp data in a file and later read it back in.

Solution

Use `PRINT` and `READ`:[30]

```
CL-USER(1): (with-open-file (out "/tmp/store" :direction :output)
              (print #\x out)
              (print 42 out)
              (print 'foo out)
              (print (* 2 pi) out)
```

[30]See Recipe 14-4 for `FILE-AT-ONCE`.

```
              (print "Zoot Allures" out)
              (print (loop for i below 10 collect i) out))
(0 1 2 3 4 5 6 7 8 9)
CL-USER(2): (with-open-file (in "/tmp/store")
              (loop with eof = (gensym)
                    for object = (read in nil eof)
                    until (eq object eof)
                    collect object))
(#\x 42 FOO 6.283185307179586d0 "Zoot Allures"
     (0 1 2 3 4 5 6 7 8 9))
CL-USER(3): (file-at-once "/tmp/store")
"
#\\x
42
FOO
6.283185307179586d0
\"Zoot Allures\"
(0 1 2 3 4 5 6 7 8 9) "
```

Pretty self-explanatory, isn't it? We opened a file for output, PRINTed a couple of objects to the resulting stream, and then we read the file back in. The objects were returned as expected. Furthermore, we looked at the file's contents (see Recipe 14-4) and saw that they are also readable by humans. Read on for more details; but for a more elaborate solution, you might also want to look at Recipe 21-1.

How It Works

The standard function PRINT cannot only print arbitrary Lisp objects, it can print them in such a way that they can be read in again by READ. This comes in very handy when you want to somehow persist data that isn't structured in a way that would fit in, say, an RDBMS or a binary file (see Recipes 21-2 and 14-10). Note that you can also use this technique to send data over a network stream to another Lisp instance. So, it's not only about *storing* but also *sharing* data with minimal effort.

If you define your own CLOS classes, you have to take care about a useful way to print them yourself by defining a suitable PRINT-OBJECT method; see Recipe 9-8.[31]

The approach sketched above is helpful and easy to use if you want to persist relatively small amounts of heterogeneous, unstructured data. If you are trying to store data units that are all of the same kind, or if you're dealing with large batches of

[31]Structures defined by DEFSTRUCT will usually be printed in a default way such that they can be read back in (but only, of course, if the corresponding structure type is defined before the object is read). But you can override this behavior and use your own print methods for your structures; see the HyperSpec's dictionary entry for DEFSTRUCT.

data, you should look at other techniques or consider using a database. Have a look at Chapter 21.

Shared Structure

One thing to watch out for is shared structure (see Recipe 2-7). Naïvely printing data to a stream will usually not take care of preserving this. Here's a simple example:

```
CL-USER(4): (defun circle-test ()
              (let* ((a (list 1 2 3))
                     (b (cons 0 a)))
                (with-open-file
                    (out "/tmp/store" :direction :output
                                      :if-exists :supersede)
                  (print (list a b) out))
                (with-open-file (in "/tmp/store")
                  (let* ((c (read in))
                         (a% (first c))
                         (b% (second c)))
                    (format t "Read ~S and ~S~%" a% b%)
                    (values (eq a (cdr b))
                            (eq a% (cdr b%)))))))
CIRCLE-TEST
CL-USER(5): (circle-test)
Read (1 2 3) and (0 1 2 3)
T
NIL
```

Our little test function creates two lists, A and B, where the CDR of B is A. We write them to a file and read them back in. Now the resulting lists A% and B% have the same elements, but they don't share structure anymore.

Luckily, the COMMON LISP standard defines the #n# notation (see Recipe 8-6) and your Lisp can automatically take care of using this notation if you instruct it to do so by setting the special variable *PRINT-CIRCLE* (see also page 180) to a *true* value:

```
;; continued from above
CL-USER(6): (let ((*print-circle* t))
              (circle-test))
Read #1=(1 2 3) and (0 . #1#)
T
T
```

Be aware, though, that the printer will only preserve shared structure within *one* object. Had we replaced the statement (PRINT (LIST A B) OUT) with the two statements (PRINT A OUT) and (PRINT B OUT), the effect would have been the same with and without *PRINT-CIRCLE* set to T.

Is It Readable?

Also, there are some Lisp objects that can't be printed to a stream, such as functions or (in many Lisp implementations) hash tables. If you want to make sure that you don't unintentionally print data that can't be read in again, use the special variable *PRINT-READABLY*. If it is set to a *true* value, your Lisp is supposed to try to print objects readably, or signal an error if it can't.[32]

```
;; not all implementations will signal an error here
CL-USER(7): (let ((*print-readably* t))
              (print (make-hash-table)))

Error: Unable to print #<EQL hash-table with 0 entries
       @ #x7169020a> readably and *PRINT-READABLY* is true.
  [condition type: PRINT-NOT-READABLE]
```

If you want to print such objects anyway, you'll either have to play with the Lisp reader (see example in Recipe 8-9) or you may get away with using the #. read syntax (see Recipe 8-3). As an example of the latter, here's a toy implementation[33] of a function that serializes a hash table to a stream so that it can be read back in with READ:

```
(defun print-eql-hash-table (hash-table
                             &optional (stream *standard-output*))
  (format stream "#.")
  (pprint `(let ((new-hash-table (make-hash-table)))
             ,@(loop for key being the hash-keys of hash-table
                     using (hash-value value)
                     collect `(setf (gethash ',key new-hash-table)
                                    ',value))
             new-hash-table)
          stream))
```

(This is not a lot of code, but it uses several techniques that you might want to look up in other chapters. Looping through a hash table is, for example, explained in

[32]See also Recipe 9-1.

[33]As the name says, this function only works with EQL hash tables. It has several other design flaws as well and it should not be used in production code. The only reason for its existence is to get the general idea across.

Recipe 6-4, while the syntax using backquotes, commas, and at-signs is explained in Recipe 2-4.)

To test it, you might want to do something like this:

```
* (defparameter *h* (make-hash-table))
*H*
* (setf (gethash 13 *h*) 42)
42
* (setf (gethash 'foo *h*) 'bar)
BAR
* (print-equal-hash-table *h*)
#.
(LET ((NEW-HASH-TABLE (MAKE-HASH-TABLE)))
  (SETF (GETHASH '13 NEW-HASH-TABLE) '42)
  (SETF (GETHASH 'FOO NEW-HASH-TABLE) 'BAR)
  NEW-HASH-TABLE)
* (defparameter *h2* (read-from-string
                      (with-output-to-string (out)
                        (print-equal-hash-table *h* out))))
```

H2 should now be a "copy" of *H*.

Can This Be Done Faster, Please?

COMMON LISP implementations usually use a specific binary format to store compiled code, which is traditionally referred to as "FASL" (for *fast loading*). As the name suggests, the intention is that FASL files load faster than text files with source code, as the Lisp system can skip the parsing part when reading such a file.

If you are using the techniques described in this recipe to serialize Lisp data, you might want to check if your Lisp offers facilities to "dump" data in the same FASL format it uses internally. (With LISPWORKS, for example, you should start by searching for `HCL:DUMP-FORM`, `HCL:LOAD-DATA-FILE`, and similar functions in their documentation.) Depending on your data, this could considerably speed up loading.

Be aware, though, that you cannot expect that data dumped in this manner can be read by a different Lisp implementation. There might even be incompatibilities between the FASL formats used by the same Lisp on different operating systems or between different releases of the same Lisp.

(See also Recipe 13-9.)

What About JSON or Other Formats?

The way of serializing data that we described here is, of course, a very Lisp-y way of doing it, because it utilizes the Lisp reader and printer and is used to read and write COMMON LISP data structures. However, most basic data structures are very similar across different programming languages, so it might also make sense to serialize your data in a format that can be used by those other languages. A popular example is JSON, and we describe how to use it in Recipe 19-11.

14-14. Customizing Stream Behavior

Problem

You want to have your own streams that work with all standard functions (like `FORMAT`, `READ`, `WRITE-SEQUENCE`, and so on) but have a somewhat different behavior. Maybe you want to read from a source that is neither a file nor a string, or you want to perform some form of transformation on the data before it is sent to some network, or whatever.

Solution

Use *Gray streams* (if your Lisp has them).

As a simple example, let's create a stream that can read bytes from a *vector* (see Recipe 5-2).[34] We first load the TRIVIAL-GRAY-STREAMS library via QUICKLISP (see Recipe 18-2). We then create a class that inherits from `FUNDAMENTAL-BINARY-INPUT-STREAM` and define a method `STREAM-READ-BYTE` for this class:

```
CL-USER 1 > (ql:quickload "trivial-gray-streams")
;; some output elided
("trivial-gray-streams")
CL-USER 2 > (use-package :trivial-gray-streams)
T
CL-USER 3 > (defclass my-vector-stream
                          (fundamental-binary-input-stream)
              ((vector :initarg :vector)
               (index :initform 0)))
#<STANDARD-CLASS MY-VECTOR-STREAM 200F5727>
CL-USER 4 > (defmethod stream-read-byte ((stream my-vector-stream))
              (with-slots (index vector) stream
```

[34] A much more elaborate version of this behavior is exhibited by the *in-memory streams* found in the FLEXI-STREAMS library; see Recipe 3-3.

```
                ;; return one byte or the keyword :EOF
                (cond ((< index (length vector))
                       (prog1 (aref vector index)
                         ;; move "position within stream"
                         (incf index)))
                      (t :eof))))
#<STANDARD-METHOD STREAM-READ-BYTE NIL (MY-VECTOR-STREAM) ...
```

If we don't have more specific needs, this is already all there is to it. We can now use our new stream class:

```
CL-USER 5 > (defparameter *in*
              (make-instance 'my-vector-stream
                             :vector #(42 43 44 45 46 47)))
*IN*
CL-USER 6 > (list
             (read-byte *in*)
             (let ((list (make-list 3)))
               (read-sequence list *in*)
               list)
             (read-byte *in*)
             (streamp *in*)
             (open-stream-p *in*))
(42 (43 44 45) 46 T T)
CL-USER 7 > (progn
              (read-byte *in*)
              (read-byte *in*))
Error: End of file while reading stream #<MY-VECTOR-STREAM ...
;; etc.
```

Note that a lot of stuff is already taken care of for us: READ-SEQUENCE, for example, works as expected, although we only implemented a replacement for READ-BYTE.[35] We also get a reasonable error once our vector has been fully consumed, although our code didn't signal it.

For another example, this time with output instead of input, and with a character stream instead of a binary stream, let's create a silly stream class to duplicate every character except for linefeeds before sending it to *STANDARD-OUTPUT*. We start with the same two forms as above and then proceed as follows:

```
CL-USER 3 > (defclass my-dupe-stream
                (fundamental-character-output-stream)
              ())
```

[35] But we can—let's say we're concerned about performance—implement our own version of READ-SEQUENCE. See below.

```
#<STANDARD-CLASS MY-DUPE-STREAM 20100647>
CL-USER 4 > (defmethod stream-write-char
                ((stream my-dupe-stream) char)
              (write-char char)
              (unless (char-equal char #\Newline)
                (write-char char)))
#<STANDARD-METHOD STREAM-WRITE-CHAR NIL (MY-DUPE-STREAM T) ...
CL-USER 5 > (defparameter *out* (make-instance 'my-dupe-stream))
*OUT*
CL-USER 6 > (print 42 *out*)
4422
42
CL-USER 7 > (format *out* "~R~%" 42)
ffoorrttyy--ttwwoo
NIL
CL-USER 8 > (write-string "cooeeing" *out*)
ccoooooeeeeiinngg
"cooeeing"
```

The same pattern here. We only implemented a replacement for WRITE-CHAR and immediately stuff like FORMAT or PRINT also worked.

How It Works

Streams in COMMON LISP are instances of CLOS classes (see Chapter 13), but there aren't many stream classes defined in the standard, and the functions that use streams for input or output (and there are *lots* of them as witnessed, for example, by this chapter and Chapters 8 and 9) aren't generic, unfortunately. Which means you can't simply, say, subclass one of these classes and write your own methods to modify their behavior.

There was a proposal to add several generic functions (often with the same name as the corresponding standard function, but beginning with "STREAM-") to be used by the existing I/O functions so that programmers would be able to write their own stream implementations, but unfortunately, it didn't make it into the final COMMON LISP standard. The good news is that pretty much all vendors implemented this proposal nevertheless, so that we can nowadays almost use it as if it were a standard feature.

But implementations differ in how they name the package that their Gray streams are in (for obvious reasons, they can't live in the COMMON-LISP package) and sometimes also in other minor details. That's what the library TRIVIAL-GRAY-STREAMS is for—to paper over these cracks. It won't magically give you Gray streams if your Lisp doesn't have them, it just provides a thin layer atop them so that you have a unified means to use them independently of any specific implementation.

As you can see in our example, Gray streams can be backed by a "real" stream, but they don't have to. You can essentially do whatever you want. The Gray streams generic functions are designed in such a way that you can usually get away with defining only very few methods (we had only one per class above) and let the rest be done by default fallback methods.[36] But you can tweak a lot more if you want. See the original proposal[37] for a list of the generic functions that can be specialized. (Most implementations even provide a few more. Have a look at the LISPWORKS documentation[38] for a pretty extensive Gray streams implementation.)

Note that you could implement string streams (see Recipe 14-7) yourself with Gray streams. This might even be a good exercise to become acquainted with Gray streams. A good tutorial is the chapter *User Defined Streams* of the LISPWORKS user guide. And you might also want to look at the source code of the FLEXI-STREAMS (see Recipe 3-3) and CHUNGA (used for instance by DRAKMA, see Recipe 18-7) libraries for examples of non-trivial Gray stream code with extensive documentation.

Finally, Gray streams are named after David Gray, who made the proposal mentioned above. So, even if you're from the United Kingdom, you shouldn't call them "Grey streams."

[36]But you should probably implement more than the required minimum or your Gray streams could end up being pretty slow compared to "normal" streams. As usual, there's a price you have to pay for flexibility and if speed is important, you might want to profile (see Recipe 17-2) your Gray streams or check for vendor-specific alternatives, like, for example, ALLEGROCL's "simple streams."

[37]To be found at `http://www.nhplace.com/kent/CL/Issues/stream-definition-by-user.html`.

[38]The part about Gray streams is at `http://www.lispworks.com/documentation/lw70/LW/html/lw-175.htm`.

15. Pathnames, Files, Directories

COMMON LISP uses so-called *pathnames* as a pretty elaborate way of dealing with files and directories. This is at least partly due to the diversity of file systems a COMMON LISP implementation could encounter at the time the standard was conceived.[1] While the result is, on the one hand, remarkably flexible, it might, on the other hand, seem pretty arcane and convoluted to someone who only ever had to deal with file systems on Windows or on Unix-like operating systems.

Also, the price you have to pay for this flexibility is that implementations have some leeway in interpreting certain features, the consequence being that there are some things that you probably think *should* be obvious but aren't. That's why this chapter pretty mentions implementation-specific functionality and asks you to look up how things are supposed to work in your Lisp.

Luckily, Peter Seibel was already concerned about this when he wrote *Practical Common Lisp* and created some code to paper over the most crucial cracks. This code has been turned into a library, which we'll discuss in Recipe 15-10. Some other recipes will refer to this library as well.

It is assumed that you understand the basics of pathnames; at least you should know what a `PATHNAME` object is, which components it has, and what *pathname merging* means. This is explained, for example, in chapter 14 of *Practical Common Lisp*.[2]

15-1. Getting and Setting the Current Directory

Problem

You want to know (or change) your Lisp's "current working directory."

[1]There were systems where a "directory" wasn't necessarily an object that could be named and accessed, for example. It also wasn't uncommon that one single Lisp image had access to different file systems with different semantics at the same time.

[2]See `http://www.gigamonkeys.com/book/files-and-file-io.html` in case you don't have the book.

Solution

Use *DEFAULT-PATHNAME-DEFAULTS* (and also check if your Lisp hasn't added some homegrown stuff).

```
CL-USER(1): *default-pathname-defaults*
;; result is implementation-dependent
#p"/tmp/"
CL-USER(2): (probe-file "passwd")
NIL
CL-USER(3): (let ((*default-pathname-defaults* #p"/etc/"))
              (probe-file "passwd"))
#p"/etc/passwd"
```

We check if the file passwd exists[3] and get a negative result. This result is to be interpreted relative to the "current directory" *DEFAULT-PATHNAME-DEFAULTS* which at the moment is #p"/tmp/". If we temporarily[4] set *DEFAULT-PATHNAME-DEFAULTS* to #p"/etc/", the result is *true* (at least on a Unix-like system).

How It Works

Operating systems like Unix and Windows have a notion of a "current" or "working" directory, which is usually initially set to the directory an application is started from and is used as a default base for relative pathnames.

The COMMON LISP equivalent to this is the special variable *DEFAULT-PATHNAME-DEFAULTS*, which is a pathname that is merged in as the default whenever a standard function accepts a pathname argument and gets one where not all components are specified (i.e., non-NIL). On startup, this variable should be set to a value corresponding to the directory that you started your Lisp from. However, this is not only about directories. Rather, *DEFAULT-PATHNAME-DEFAULTS* can be seen as a "template" that can fill in other components as well; for example, the type component:

```
CL-USER(1): (with-open-file (out "/tmp/foo.txt"
                                 :direction :output
                                 :if-exists :supersede)
              (write-string "42" out))
"42"
CL-USER(2): (probe-file #p"foo")
NIL
CL-USER(3): (let ((*default-pathname-defaults* #p"/tmp/whatever.txt"))
```

[3]See Recipe 15-2 for PROBE-FILE.

[4]See Recipe 14-1.

```
            (probe-file #p"foo"))
#p"/tmp/foo.txt"
```

If there are components that you don't want to be filled, you can provide the value :UNSPECIFIC instead of NIL:

```
;; continued from above
CL-USER(4): (pathname-type #p"foo")
NIL
CL-USER(5): (let ((*default-pathname-defaults* #p"/tmp/whatever.txt"))
              (probe-file (make-pathname :name "foo"
                                         :type :unspecific)))
NIL
```

Shortcuts and Deviations

From within SLIME, you can manipulate *DEFAULT-PATHNAME-DEFAULTS* using so-called "shortcuts" that are invoked by typing a comma at the REPL prompt. With these shortcuts, you also have a stack of old values, so that you can "push" and "pop" working directories at your discretion.[5]

Unfortunately, not all COMMON LISP implementations follow the standard's suggestion that *DEFAULT-PATHNAME-DEFAULTS* should be set to a meaningful value when your Lisp image starts up. Some of them always start with #p"" or some other value that is not very helpful.

Also, some Lisps inherit the notion of "the current directory" from the operating system and let it live in parallel (or sometimes even in disagreement) with *DEFAULT-PATHNAME-DEFAULTS*.[6] So, if in doubt, you have to check your Lisp's documentation.

15-2. Testing Whether a File Exists

Problem

You want to find out if a file is present in your file system.

[5]See https://www.common-lisp.net/project/slime/doc/html/Shortcuts.html. And in the ALLEGROCL REPL, you have similar convenience operators, like :CD, :PUSHD, and :POPD.

[6]For example, LISPWORKS has the functions HCL:GET-WORKING-DIRECTORY and HCL:CHANGE-DIRECTORY, which are not related to *DEFAULT-PATHNAME-DEFAULTS*.

Solution

Use PROBE-FILE:[7]

```
CL-USER(1): (probe-file "/tmp/foo")
NIL
CL-USER(2): (with-open-file (s "/tmp/foo" :direction :output)
              (write-string "bla" s))
"bla"
CL-USER(3): (probe-file "/tmp/foo")
#p"/tmp/foo"
CL-USER(4): (ensure-directories-exist
              (make-pathname :directory '(:absolute "tmp" "bar")))
#p"/tmp/bar/"
T
CL-USER(5): (probe-file *)
#p"/tmp/bar/"
```

These examples were executed on a Linux machine. The first form checked whether the file denoted by "/tmp/foo" was there. (It wasn't, the answer was NIL.) We then created the file and tried again; and this time we got a *true* return value; namely the file's pathname. The last example shows that, in spite of its name, PROBE-FILE works with files as well as directories. (At least in this implementation; see more below.)

How It Works

PROBE-FILE accepts a pathname, a string denoting a pathname, or a stream as its only argument, and returns false (i.e., NIL) if there is no such file. If the file exists, the function PROBE-FILE returns the file's *truename* (see Recipe 15-12), which can subsequently be used to work with the file.

PROBE-FILE doesn't accept a *wild* pathname as its argument; that is, you can only check for one specific file. If you want to check for the existence of several files at once, use DIRECTORY (see Recipe 15-4):[8]

```
;; continued from above
CL-USER(6): (directory "/tmp/foo*")
(#p"/tmp/foo")
CL-USER(7): (with-open-file (s "/tmp/foo2" :direction :output)
              (write-string "bla" s))
"bla"
```

[7]See Recipe 15-3 for ENSURE-DIRECTORIES-EXIST.

[8]Note that the wild pathspec "/tmp/foo*" in our example isn't portable between all COMMON LISP implementations.

```
CL-USER(8): (directory "/tmp/foo*")
(#p"/tmp/foo" #p"/tmp/foo2")
```

In this example, we first check for all files in the /tmp/ directory with a name starting with "foo" and get a one-element list as our result. Then we create a new file /tmp/foo2 and call DIRECTORY again.

Note that OPEN (and thus WITH-OPEN-FILE) accepts the keyword arguments :IF-EXISTS and :IF-DOES-NOT-EXIST, which means that in many cases, you don't have to use PROBE-FILE explicitly but you can instruct OPEN what to do if a file doesn't exist, although you expected it to (or vice versa).

What About Directories?

This function is intended to check for the existence of *files*, not directories. It just so happens that on the file systems most popular today, directories can sometimes be treated like files; but that doesn't mean PROBE-FILE must accept pathnames that name directories. At least one Lisp implementation (CLISP) doesn't (but provides a function EXT:PROBE-DIRECTORY instead). You might want to look at the function FAD:DIRECTORY-EXISTS-P of the CL-FAD library (see Recipe 15-10) for a portable solution.

15-3. Creating a Directory

Problem

You want to create one or more directories.

Solution

Use the function ENSURE-DIRECTORIES-EXIST:

```
CL-USER(1): (ensure-directories-exist "/tmp/foo/bar/")
"/tmp/foo/bar/"
T
CL-USER(2): (ensure-directories-exist "/tmp/foo/bar/baz/frob"
                                      :verbose t)
;; ensure-directories-exist: creating /tmp/foo/bar/baz/frob
;; Directory /tmp/foo/bar/baz/ does not exist, will create.
"/tmp/foo/bar/baz/frob"
T
CL-USER(3): (ensure-directories-exist "/tmp/foo/bar/baz/frob"
```

```
                                           :verbose t)
"/tmp/foo/bar/baz/frob"
NIL
CL-USER(4): (ensure-directories-exist "/tmp/foo/bar/baz/frob/"
                                           :verbose t)
;; ensure-directories-exist: creating /tmp/foo/bar/baz/frob/
;; Directory /tmp/foo/bar/baz/frob/ does not exist, will create.
"/tmp/foo/bar/baz/frob/"
T
;; this will only work on AllegroCL
CL-USER(5): (excl:make-directory "/tmp/bar" #o700)
T
```

These examples were executed on a Linux machine. The first example made sure that all the directories `/tmp/`, `/tmp/foo/`, and `/tmp/foo/bar/` existed. The second return value was `T`, which means that at least one directory was actually created. The second example created another directory, `/tmp/foo/bar/baz/`, but it did *not* create `/tmp/foo/bar/baz/frob/` as you might have expected (see the upcoming "What Might Go Wrong" section). The third example did not create anything, and thus the second return value was `NIL`. The fourth example created the directory `/tmp/foo/bar/baz/frob/`. The last example finally used an implementation-specific function to create the directory `/tmp/bar/` with specific access permissions.

Note that what we did in the second case and the fourth case isn't strictly portable (see below).

How It Works

This function is a bit different from what you might know from other languages. You don't explicitly specify a directory, but instead you specify a pathname (most likely one of a file you want to create) and ask your Lisp to make sure that *all* directories needed to make this pathname valid on your system are created. So this function will, if necessary, create several directories at once, similar to the the Unix `mkdir` command when invoked with the `-p` option.[9]

You can supply the `:VERBOSE` keyword argument, which, when true, asks the implementation to print information about what it's doing to `*STANDARD-OUTPUT*`. What you'll actually see then (and whether you'll see something at all) is at your Lisp's discretion.

The function will return two values: its first argument and a boolean that is true if

[9]JAVA's `File` class has a `mkdirs` method that is similar to `ENSURE-DIRECTORIES-EXIST`. However, you don't have a direct way to specify "Please create the directories I need before I can create this particular file,"—you always specify directories.

any directory has actually been created. The fact that this function returns its first argument as its primary value makes it possible to use it as an "intermediate" step within other operations. A typical idiom for this looks like this:

```
(with-open-file (stream (ensure-directories-exist pathname)
                        :direction :output)
  ;; do something
  )
```

Implementation-Specific Alternatives

Every implementation will most likely offer means for a more straightforward approach; for example, ALLEGROCL has `EXCL:MAKE-DIRECTORY`, CLISP has `EXT:MAKE-DIR`, and so on. Check your Lisp's documentation about what is there and what exactly these functions are doing. This will also depend on the underlying operating system. And in some cases, you obviously *must* resort to implementation-specific functionality; for example, if you want to specify the mode bits for a Unix file system.[10]

What Might Go Wrong

`ENSURE-DIRECTORIES-EXIST` will behave differently depending on whether the first argument denotes a directory[11] or a file (see examples 3 and 4 above). The "solution" shown here to append a slash to the pathname string is specific to the namestring syntax, but you can always use pathnames instead of namestrings, and you can provide a dummy filename to be fully portable; that is, you could instead have written:

```
(ensure-directories-exist (make-pathname :directory
                                          '(:absolute "tmp"
                                                      "foo"
                                                      "bar"
                                                      "baz"
                                                      "frob")
                                          :name "dummy"))
```

Also note that the outcome of this function, of course, depends on the access rights you have on your machine; that is, you might not be allowed to create the directory you wanted to have. An error of type `FILE-ERROR` should be signaled in this case.

[10]On CMUCL and SBCL, the function `ENSURE-DIRECTORIES-EXIST` has a non-standard keyword parameter `:MODE` for this purpose.

[11]Strictly speaking, you are not even allowed to provide a directory as the first argument. It just so happens that on the systems you're most likely to come across (Unix, Windows, Mac OS), this will likely work.

15-4. Finding Files Matching a Pattern

Problem

You want to get a list of all files in a directory that match a certain pattern.

Solution

Use the standard function DIRECTORY. But beware of implementation-specific issues.

What follows is an example session on Linux with ALLEGROCL. The /tmp/foo/ directory contains the following six files:

```
a.txt
b.txt
c.txt
a.lisp
bar.lisp
baz.lisp
```

We'll see various ways to list all or some of these files. Note that all examples except for the first three use an implementation-specific namestring syntax; see below.

```
CL-USER(1): (directory
             (make-pathname :name :wild :type :wild
                            :directory '(:absolute "tmp" "foo")))
(#p"/tmp/foo/a.txt" #p"/tmp/foo/b.txt" #p"/tmp/foo/c.txt"
 #p"/tmp/foo/a.lisp" #p"/tmp/foo/bar.lisp"
 #p"/tmp/foo/baz.lisp")
CL-USER(2): (directory
             (make-pathname :name :wild :type "lisp"
                            :directory '(:absolute "tmp" "foo")))
(#p"/tmp/foo/a.lisp" #p"/tmp/foo/bar.lisp"
 #p"/tmp/foo/baz.lisp")
CL-USER(3): (directory
             (make-pathname :name "a" :type :wild
                            :directory '(:absolute "tmp" "foo")))
(#p"/tmp/foo/a.txt" #p"/tmp/foo/a.lisp")
CL-USER(4): (directory "/tmp/foo/*.lisp")
(#p"/tmp/foo/a.lisp" #p"/tmp/foo/bar.lisp"
 #p"/tmp/foo/baz.lisp")
CL-USER(5): (directory "/tmp/foo/a.*")
(#p"/tmp/foo/a.txt" #p"/tmp/foo/a.lisp")
CL-USER(6): (directory "/tmp/foo/*")
```

```
(#p"/tmp/foo/a.txt" #p"/tmp/foo/b.txt" #p"/tmp/foo/c.txt"
 #p"/tmp/foo/a.lisp" #p"/tmp/foo/bar.lisp"
 #p"/tmp/foo/baz.lisp")
CL-USER(7): (directory "/tmp/foo/*.*")
(#p"/tmp/foo/a.txt" #p"/tmp/foo/b.txt" #p"/tmp/foo/c.txt"
 #p"/tmp/foo/a.lisp" #p"/tmp/foo/bar.lisp"
 #p"/tmp/foo/baz.lisp")
CL-USER(8): (directory "/tmp/foo/ba*.lisp")
(#p"/tmp/foo/bar.lisp" #p"/tmp/foo/baz.lisp")
CL-USER(9): (directory (make-pathname :name "ba*" :type :wild
                                      :directory "/tmp/foo/"))
(#p"/tmp/foo/bar.lisp" #p"/tmp/foo/baz.lisp")
CL-USER(10): (directory (make-pathname :name "ba?" :type :wild
                                       :directory "/tmp/foo/"))
(#p"/tmp/foo/bar.lisp" #p"/tmp/foo/baz.lisp")
CL-USER(11): (directory (make-pathname :name "*b*" :type :wild
                                       :directory "/tmp/foo/"))
(#p"/tmp/foo/b.txt" #p"/tmp/foo/bar.lisp"
 #p"/tmp/foo/baz.lisp")
CL-USER(12): (directory "/tmp/foo/b*.lisp")
(#p"/tmp/foo/bar.lisp" #p"/tmp/foo/baz.lisp")
CL-USER(13): (directory "/tmp/foo/b*.*")
(#p"/tmp/foo/b.txt" #p"/tmp/foo/bar.lisp"
 #p"/tmp/foo/baz.lisp")
CL-USER(14): (directory "/tmp/foo/b??.lisp")
(#p"/tmp/foo/bar.lisp" #p"/tmp/foo/baz.lisp")
```

How It Works

Sometimes you want to search a given directory for files matching a pattern. This operation is supported by the standard function `DIRECTORY`. `DIRECTORY` will accept a pathname as its argument that contains one or more components that are the keyword `:WILD`. It will return a list of all filenames that "match" this pathname such that the "non-wild" parts are equal to the ones in this pathname, and the "wild" parts can be anything.

Furthermore, an implementation can extend the concept of "wild" pathnames by allowing specific characters within filenames to act as "wildcard" characters. These will usually be the same characters that are also used by the operating system; so on a Unix or a Windows system, you can expect the asterisk (*) and the question mark (?) to be special, meaning "zero or more arbitrary characters" or "one arbitrary character," respectively.[12] Examples 4 to 14 above show instances of this syntax.

[12] Note that the meaning of * is slightly different on Unix and Windows.

Read the documentation of your Lisp system for details.

The directory component of a pathname is somewhat special in that it itself is structured (its internal representation usually is a list) and each of its parts can be wild or not. This offers a whole slew of other possibilities to make a pathname wild. Suppose that you have these files:

```
/tmp/foo/bar1/baz/frob1
/tmp/foo/bar2/baz/frob2
/tmp/foo/frob3
```

Then you can, for example, try the following ways to list (some of) these files:[13]

```
;; continued from above
CL-USER(15): (directory
               (make-pathname :directory
                              '(:absolute "tmp" "foo" :wild "baz")
                              :name :wild :type :wild))
(#p"/tmp/foo/bar1/baz/frob1" #p"/tmp/foo/bar2/baz/frob2")
CL-USER(16): (directory
               (make-pathname :directory
                              '(:absolute "tmp" "foo" :wild "baz")
                              :name "frob*" :type :wild))
(#p"/tmp/foo/bar1/baz/frob1" #p"/tmp/foo/bar2/baz/frob2")
CL-USER(17): (directory
               (make-pathname :directory
                              '(:absolute "tmp" "foo" :wild :wild)
                              :name "frob*" :type :wild))
(#p"/tmp/foo/bar1/baz/frob1" #p"/tmp/foo/bar2/baz/frob2")
CL-USER(18): (directory "/tmp/foo/*/baz/*")
(#p"/tmp/foo/bar1/baz/frob1" #p"/tmp/foo/bar2/baz/frob2")
CL-USER(19): (directory "/tmp/foo/*/baz/frob*")
(#p"/tmp/foo/bar1/baz/frob1" #p"/tmp/foo/bar2/baz/frob2")
CL-USER(20): (directory "/tmp/foo/*/*/frob*")
(#p"/tmp/foo/bar1/baz/frob1" #p"/tmp/foo/bar2/baz/frob2")
CL-USER(21): (directory "/tmp/foo/bar*/baz/frob*")
NIL
```

Furthermore, the ANSI standard allows Lisp implementations to accept the keyword `:WILD-INFERIORS` as part of a directory component meaning "any number of directory levels:"

```
;; continued from above
```

[13] It is specific to ALLEGROCL that the result is `NIL` in the last case. All other Lisps I've tried return the same list of two files in *all* cases.

```
CL-USER(22): (directory
               (make-pathname :directory
                              '(:absolute "tmp" "foo" :wild-inferiors)
                              :name "frob*" :type :wild))
(#p"/tmp/foo/frob3" #p"/tmp/foo/bar1/baz/frob1"
 #p"/tmp/foo/bar2/baz/frob2")
```

Note that `#p"/tmp/foo/frob3"` was part of the result; that is, "any number" can also mean *zero*. Check your Lisp implementation if it supports `:WILD-INFERIORS`.[14]

The ANSI standard specifically allows Lisp implementations to accept additional keywords to the `DIRECTORY` function; some vendors actually provide additional functionality this way, so you'll have to look that up in the documentation that comes with your Lisp.[15]

Note that almost everything here is implementation-dependent. Some things differ depending on the underlying operating system, but unfortunately even on the same OS, two COMMON LISP implementations might return different results although both are ANSI-compliant. You will need to try things out and/or consult your Lisp's documentation.[16]

The function `FAD:LIST-DIRECTORY` of the CL-FAD library (see Recipe 15-10) isn't as flexible as `DIRECTORY` but will, in most "typical" cases, be more predictable across different implementations and file systems.

15-5. Splitting a Filename into its Component Parts

Problem

You want to extract a file's name and/or its enclosing directory from its full pathname.

Solution

Use `FILE-NAMESTRING` and `DIRECTORY-NAMESTRING`:

---

[14]Some Lisps (notably CLISP) might not understand `:WILD-INFERIORS` per se but will accept a namestring syntax like `"/tmp/foo/**/frob*"` instead. On the other hand, most Lisps that understand `:WILD-INFERIORS` will also accept `**` in namestrings.

[15]One example is ALLEGROCL's `:DIRECTORIES-ARE-FILES`. Another example is how Lisps treat symbolic links in directory listings; see Recipe 15-12.

[16]One major source of irritation is if and how your Lisp's `DIRECTORY` function will return directories as well as files.

```
CL-USER(1): (defun split-pathspec (pathspec)
              (values (directory-namestring pathspec)
                      (file-namestring pathspec)))
SPLIT-PATHSPEC
CL-USER(2): (split-pathspec #p"/etc/passwd")
"/etc/"
"passwd"
CL-USER(3): (split-pathspec #p"/usr/local/lib/")
"/usr/local/lib/"
NIL
CL-USER(4): (split-pathspec #p"/usr/lib/libc.so")
"/usr/lib/"
"libc.so"
CL-USER(5): (probe-file #p"foo.doc")
NIL
CL-USER(6): (split-pathspec #p"foo.doc")
"./"
"foo.doc"
```

How It Works

Sometimes COMMON LISP's abstract pathname calculus isn't enough and you want to have access to the (OS-specific) strings that are used to access files. The standard defines the convenience functions `FILE-NAMESTRING` and `DIRECTORY-NAMESTRING`, which are somewhat similar to the GNU shell utilities `basename` and `dirname`. The last example above shows that they also work on non-existent files.

As in the third example, the results of `FILE-NAMESTRING` and `DIRECTORY-NAMESTRING` are not always strings but can also be `NIL`. Other Lisp implementations might return the empty string instead.

You will probably know that there's also `NAMESTRING`, which will return the *full* string representation of a pathname. So, for example, on a Windows system, the call `(namestring "/WINDOWS/winhlp32.exe")` might return something like `"C:\\WINDOWS\\winhlp32.exe"`.

And, of course, you can access the individual components of a pathname object and get more fine-grained results, like the pathname's type:

```
CL-USER(7): (pathname-type #p"libc.so")
"so"
```

But maybe this is not always what you want (and implementation-dependent):

```
CL-USER(8): (pathname-type #p"foo.tar.gz")
"gz"
CL-USER(9): (pathname-type #p".bashrc")
NIL
CL-USER(10): (pathname-type #p"foo.")
""
```

The problem here is that operating systems like Unix or Windows don't really have the concept of a file's "type," so Lisp's abstract division of "name" and "type" is helpful in the context of compiling Lisp source files, but maybe not so meaningful in other cases. Depending on your needs, it might be useful to further dissect the result of FILE-NAMESTRING with other means like; for example, with regular expressions (see Recipe 18-6).

15-6. Renaming a File

Problem

You want to rename (or "move") a file.

Solution

Use RENAME-FILE:

```
CL-USER(1): (ensure-directories-exist "/tmp/foo/dummy.txt")
"/tmp/foo/dummy.txt"
T
CL-USER(2): (directory "/tmp/foo/*.*")
NIL
CL-USER(3): (with-open-file (s "/tmp/foo/a.txt" :direction :output))
NIL
CL-USER(4): (directory "/tmp/foo/*.*")
(#p"/tmp/foo/a.txt")
CL-USER(5): (rename-file "/tmp/foo/a.txt" "/tmp/foo/b.txt")
#p"/tmp/foo/b.txt"
#p"/tmp/foo/a.txt"
#p"/tmp/foo/b.txt"
CL-USER(6): (directory "/tmp/foo/*.*")
(#p"/tmp/foo/b.txt")
CL-USER(7): (rename-file "/tmp/foo/b.txt" "c.txt")
#p"/tmp/foo/c.txt"
```

```
#p"/tmp/foo/b.txt"
#p"/tmp/foo/c.txt"
CL-USER(8): (directory "/tmp/foo/*.*")
(#p"/tmp/foo/c.txt")
CL-USER(9): (rename-file "/tmp/foo/c.txt" "d")
#p"/tmp/foo/d.txt"
#p"/tmp/foo/c.txt"
#p"/tmp/foo/d.txt"
CL-USER(10): (directory "/tmp/foo/*.*")
(#p"/tmp/foo/d.txt")
CL-USER(11): (rename-file "/tmp/foo/d.txt"
                          (make-pathname :type "lisp"))
#p"/tmp/foo/d.lisp"
#p"/tmp/foo/d.txt"
#p"/tmp/foo/d.lisp"
CL-USER(12): (directory "/tmp/foo/*.*")
(#p"/tmp/foo/d.lisp")
```

Here we first make sure that a directory `/tmp/foo/` exists, and then we look into it to see that it's empty. We create an empty file `a.txt` in this directory, and then rename it in turn to `b.txt`, `c.txt`, `d.txt`, and `d.lisp`, using various "shortcuts" described below.

How It Works

The standard function `RENAME-FILE` will rename a file for you as you would expect. However, it does a bit more, and depending on your standpoint, you might call its behavior either clever or strange. If its second argument has unsupplied components, it will fill them in by merging the new name with the old one.[17] You can see this in action in several places above. When we first rename the file `/tmp/foo/b.txt`, we provide the new name as `"c.txt"`, not as `"/tmp/foo/c.txt"`; the directory is merged in from the old name. This is probably what you'd expect. But in the next example, we just provide the new name `"d"` and the resulting file is *not* `/tmp/foo/d` but rather `/tmp/foo/d.txt`, because `"d"` results in a pathname with an empty `:TYPE` component; and so this component is filled in from the old name, where it was `"txt"`. The same happens in the last example, where we provide a pathname with a type but an empty name component.

[17] For that, it actually calls the function `MERGE-PATHNAMES`, which is explained in *Practical Common Lisp*.

Implementation-Specific Alternatives

Most Lisp implementations will provide some means of "raw" renaming, which directly uses the functions provided by the operating system interface. Here's an example for ALLEGROCL:

```
CL-USER(1): (directory "/tmp/foo/*.*")
(#p"/tmp/foo/a.txt")
CL-USER(2): (excl.osi:rename "/tmp/foo/a.txt" "/tmp/foo/b")
T
CL-USER(3): (directory "/tmp/foo/*.*")
(#p"/tmp/foo/b")
```

Note that in this case, the new file is actually called "b", not "b.txt". On CMUCL, for example, the corresponding function is called UNIX:UNIX-RENAME, while on SBCL the name is SB-UNIX:UNIX-RENAME.

Don't Expect "Move" Behavior!

Many people are surprised the first time that they use RENAME-FILE with relative directories because they expect RENAME-FILE to behave like their operating system; but it doesn't. Here's an example:

Suppose you are in a Linux or Unix shell (the behavior is similar for Windows) and have cd'd into the /tmp/ directory, which has two subdirectories: foo and bar. bar is empty and foo contains the file a.txt. You want to move this file from foo into bar and rename it as b.txt:

```
edi@bird:/tmp > ls foo/ bar/
bar/:

foo/:
a.txt
edi@bird:/tmp > mv foo/a.txt bar/b.txt
edi@bird:/tmp > ls foo/ bar/
bar/:
b.txt

foo/:
```

Now suppose that in the same situation you had started ALLEGROCL from /tmp/ and then tried to do the same thing:

```
CL-USER(1): (rename-file "foo/a.txt" "bar/b.txt")
Error: renaming "/tmp/foo/a.txt" resulted in error (code 2):
```

```
      No such file or directory.
  [condition type: FILE-ERROR]
```

Why that? Well, as I said above, RENAME-FILE will construct the new name with the help of MERGE-PATHNAMES. And as the directory component of "bar/b.txt" is a relative directory, by the rules of pathname merging, it will be *appended* to the directory component of "foo/a.txt"; that is, RENAME-FILE will try to rename /tmp/foo/a.txt to /tmp/foo/bar/b.txt.

What can you do to get what you want? You can either make sure that the new filename doesn't contain a relative directory in its directory component (i.e., you construct the correct absolute directory yourself) or you can use one of the "raw" functions described above.[18]

15-7. Deleting a File

Problem

You want to delete one or more files.

Solution

Use DELETE-FILE, maybe in conjunction with DIRECTORY.

```
CL-USER(1): (probe-file "foo.lisp")
#p"/tmp/foo.lisp"
CL-USER(2): (delete-file "foo.lisp")
T
CL-USER(3): (probe-file "foo.lisp")
NIL
```

That was easy. We used PROBE-FILE (see Recipe 15-2) to confirm that a file foo.lisp existed and then subsequently deleted it. PROBE-FILE returns NIL afterward, as expected.

How It Works

The ANSI standard provides a function DELETE-FILE, which can be used portably to delete one file. It returns T if it succeeds; it signals an error otherwise.

[18]Interestingly, ALLEGROCL has a function EXCL:RENAME-FILE-RAW that works like RENAME-FILE, except for the fact that it mimics Unix/Windows when resolving relative directory components.

DELETE-FILE is not required to accept wild pathnames as arguments, and in most implementations it doesn't. Of course, you can use MAPC to delete a list of files,[19] but you must be careful if you use MAPC together with DIRECTORY (see Recipe 15-4) and a wild pathname. The list returned by DIRECTORY might include directories.

A saner approach would look more like this:

```
;; this example will only work with AllegroCL
CL-USER(4): (defun delete-files (pathspec)
              (dolist (pathname (directory pathspec))
                (unless (excl:file-directory-p pathname)
                  (delete-file pathname))))
DELETE-FILES
CL-USER(5): (directory #p"bar*" :directories-are-files nil)
(#p"/tmp/bar/" #p"/tmp/bar.lisp" #p"/tmp/bar.fasl"
              #p"/tmp/bar.err")
CL-USER(6): (delete-files #p"bar*")
NIL
CL-USER(7): (directory #p"bar*" :directories-are-files nil)
(#p"/tmp/bar/")
```

As you will have noticed, our DELETE-FILES uses implementation-specific functions and this is why it's not in the standard. You need to know whether the results returned by DIRECTORY are files or directories, and that's not portable (see Recipes 15-4 and 15-10 for more details).

Some Lisps also provide direct access to underlying OS functionality, like the Unix system call unlink(2), if you need it.

What Does "Success" Mean Anyway?

The standard says that DELETE-FILE returns T on success, but it doesn't define what "success" means. In particular, it is up to the implementation what it'll do if the file that should be deleted doesn't exist. In most implementations, this will result in an error.[20]

As with most functions that accept a pathname as an argument, DELETE-FILE actually accepts a *pathname designator*, which can also be an open stream. So, you could be tempted to do something like this:

```
CL-USER(8): (probe-file #p"foo.txt")
NIL
```

[19]As in (MAPC #'DELETE-FILE '(#p"foo.txt" #p"foo.lisp"))

[20]It would seem intuitive to return NIL in this case, but you can't actually do this if you adhere to the standard, word for word...

```
CL-USER(9): (with-open-file (out #p"foo.txt" :direction :output)
              (values (probe-file #p"foo.txt")
                      (probe-file out)
                      (progn (delete-file out)
                             (probe-file #p"foo.txt"))))
#p"/tmp/foo.txt"
#p"/tmp/foo.txt"
NIL
```

However, the result of this little experiment is implementation-dependent and you shouldn't expect it to work with other Lisps. For example, there's no reason to assume that at the time DELETE-FILE is called, a file corresponding to the stream OUT has already been created in the file system; so you might get an error instead.

In most Lisps, DELETE-FILE won't delete directories, only files; see Recipe 15-8 if you want to delete directories. Also note that the outcome of this function, of course, depends on the access rights you have on your machine; that is, you might not be allowed to delete the file you wanted to delete.

15-8. Deleting a Directory

Problem

You want to delete a directory.

Solution

You should first check whether the directory is empty. If it is, chances are good that an implementation-dependent solution will be available.

```
;; example for AllegroCL
CL-USER(1): (directory "/tmp/foo/*.*")
NIL
CL-USER(2): (excl:delete-directory "/tmp/foo")
T
CL-USER(3): (directory "/tmp/bar/*.*")
(#p"/tmp/bar/frob.txt")
CL-USER(4): (excl:delete-directory "/tmp/bar")
Error: Could not remove directory: Directory not empty.
  [condition type: FILE-ERROR]
```

Here we first check whether `/tmp/foo` is empty[21] and then use an ALLEGROCL-specific function to delete it. Then we look at `/tmp/bar/` and find out that this directory contains a file. The attempt to delete this directory fails.

How It Works

The ANSI standard doesn't contain a function to delete a directory, so you have to find out whether your implementation provides a function for this task. Most do and it's usually called something like `DELETE-DIRECTORY`, `DELETE-DIR`, or (on some Unix systems) `RMDIR`.

As with most other programming languages the directory is usually (but not necessarily) required to be empty before it can be deleted. If you want to remove a directory with all of its contents you may either find a vendor-supplied function that does that (for example, ALLEGROCL's `EXCL:DELETE-DIRECTORY-AND-FILES`) or you can use `FAD:DELETE-DIRECTORY-AND-FILES` from the CL-FAD library.[22] (But first carefully read how symbolic links are treated by this function.)

15-9. Copying a File

Problem

You want to copy a whole file programmatically (instead of using methods supplied by your operating system).

Solution

That's pretty easy. You can do it with this little function:

```
(defun copy-file (from to)
  (let* ((element-type '(unsigned-byte 8))
         (buffer (make-array 8192 :element-type element-type)))
    (with-open-file (in from :element-type element-type)
      (with-open-file (out to :element-type element-type
                              :direction :output
                              :if-exists :supersede)
        (loop (let ((position (read-sequence buffer in)))
```

[21] This is implementation-specific, although it uses a standardized function. If `/tmp/foo/` is not empty but contains only directories, then some implementations will return `NIL` as a result of evaluating `(DIRECTORY "/tmp/foo/*.*")`.

[22] See Recipe 15-10.

```
          (when (zerop position)
            (return))
          (write-sequence buffer out :end position)))
    (pathname out)))))
```

How It Works

This is essentially how you'd write it in any other language as well. You open both files as binary files and then use a *buffer* to transfer larger "chunks" from one file into the other. There are several hidden assumptions in this code, of course. One is that *octets* (8-bit bytes) are a meaningful element type for binary streams. While this will almost certainly be the case on Windows, Mac OS, or Linux, the HyperSpec has nothing to say about this.[23] Another one is that 8192 octets is a good size for the buffer. Why not more or less? (Answer: It's pretty arbitrary but a power of two probably makes sense. Experiment yourself if you are concerned about efficiency.)

Also, be warned that the keyword `:SUPERSEDE` in our code means that an existing file named by the pathname `TO` is unceremoniously overwritten. If this is not what you want, do change it! The `(PATHNAME OUT)` at the end is not really needed. It just makes sure we have a defined return value.

A slightly more elaborate version of our `COPY-FILE` function from above, which also takes some implementation idiosyncrasies into account, can be found (under the same name) in the CL-FAD library; see Recipe 15-10.

15-10. Processing the Contents of a Directory Recursively

Problem

You want to do something to all files in a directory and its sub-directories. (And sub-sub-directories and so on...)

This would be similar to things you could do with the Unix `find` command.

Solution

Use the function `FAD:WALK-DIRECTORY` of the CL-FAD library.[24] For example, with the following code I can count how many `.tex` and `.sty` files I have in my local TEX installation on my Windows laptop:

[23] And how could it? Maybe you're reading this book, which you found at a flea market, in 2030 and you're laughing about the idea of octets.

[24] Available via QUICKLISP; see Recipe 18-2.

```
(let ((tex-counter 0)
      (sty-counter 0))
  (fad:walk-directory "C:/Users/edi/Documents/MiKTeX/"
                      (lambda (pathname)
                        (let ((type (pathname-type pathname)))
                          (cond ((string-equal type "tex")
                                 (incf tex-counter))
                                ((string-equal type "sty")
                                 (incf sty-counter))))))
  (list tex-counter sty-counter))
```

How It Works

There are several recipes in this chapter where I had to refer to implementation-specific behavior (see the chapter's introduction for why this is so), and "walking" a directory is a perfect example for something that simply can't be done portably (in the sense that it'll work in every Lisp with every file system).

I could now write a subrecipe to show you how to do this in SBCL, and another one for LispWorks, and another one for ClozureCL, and so on. But that would be a pretty tedious exercise.

The CL-FAD Library

Peter Seibel already faced this problem when writing *Practical Common Lisp* and thus devised some code that works consistently and predictably in a couple of major Lisps on the three "big" operating systems. This code was later cast into a little library and then extended by community volunteers to work with pretty much every Common Lisp available today. This is still not strictly *portable* code in the theoretical sense that it should yield identical results on every conforming implementation, but it is probably as practically portable as it gets.

`FAD:WALK-DIRECTORY` is one of the central functions of this library and takes as its argument a *pathname designator* (essentially a string or a pathname) naming a directory and a function of one argument, which will then be applied recursively to all files in the directory and its sub-directories.

`FAD:WALK-DIRECTORY` also accepts several keyword arguments. `:TEST`, for example, can be used to provide a test function that will allow you to control which files will be handed over to the main function. If in the example from above I only wanted to count `.tex` files, I could also do it like so:

```
(let ((tex-counter 0))
  (fad:walk-directory "C:/Users/edi/Documents/MiKTeX"
                      (lambda (pathname)
                        (declare (ignore pathname))
                        (incf tex-counter))
                      :test (lambda (pathname)
                              (string-equal (pathname-type pathname)
                                            "tex")))
  tex-counter)
```

The other keywords control how exactly FAD:WALK-DIRECTORY will traverse the file tree.

CL-FAD also offers FAD:LIST-DIRECTORY (see Recipe 15-4), FAD:DIRECTORY-EXISTS-P (see Recipe 15-2), FAD:COPY-FILE (see Recipe 15-9), FAD:DELETE-DIRECTORY-AND-FILES (see Recipe 15-8), various convenience functions to manipulate pathnames, and a facility for temporary files (see its documentation for more information).

15-11. Getting the Pathname a Stream Is Associated With

Problem

You are working on a file stream—a stream that was created with OPEN or WITH-OPEN-FILE—and want to know which file it writes to or reads from.

Solution

Use the function PATHNAME:

```
CL-USER(1): (with-open-file (in "/etc/passwd")
              (pathname in))
#p"/etc/passwd"
CL-USER(2): (let ((in (open "/etc/passwd")))
              (close in)
              (pathname in))
#p"/etc/passwd"
CL-USER(3): (pathname *standard-output*)
Error: There is no filename associated with stream
       #<TERMINAL-SIMPLE-STREAM [initial terminal io] fd 0/1 @
         #x7119b9e2>
  [condition type: STREAM-ERROR]
```

(As the last example shows, this, of course, only makes sense for streams that *are* associated with a file.)

How It Works

A stream created with `OPEN` or `WITH-OPEN-FILE` is "associated" with a file; that is, it either reads from this file or writes to it. Sometimes you are given such a stream from another function and you want to know which file you're actually working on. You might have expected that there's a function like "`FILE-STREAM-PATHNAME`" to get at this information, but it's even easier. The standard function `PATHNAME` will accept a file stream as its argument and will return the corresponding filename. The stream may even already be closed at the time we call `PATHNAME`.

`PATHNAME` will return a pathname object that can be used to refer to the file that the stream is associated with. It is *not* required to return the *same* object that was used to create the file, though. For example, version 1.2.12 of SBCL behaves like this:

```
* (let ((pathname (pathname "/etc/passwd")))
    (with-open-file (in pathname)
      (eq pathname (pathname in))))
NIL
```

15-12. Dealing with Symbolic Links

Problem

You want to resolve a symbolic link in your file system.

Solution

This is an example that was performed on a Linux system:

```
edi@nanook:/tmp$ rm -f foo* bar* quux*
edi@nanook:/tmp$ echo "Waka/Jawaka" > foo.txt
edi@nanook:/tmp$ ln -s foo.txt bar.txt
edi@nanook:/tmp$ ln -s bar.txt quux.txt
edi@nanook:/tmp$ cat quux.txt
Waka/Jawaka
```

We now have a small text file, `foo.txt`, and a symbolic link, `bar.txt`, pointing to the same file. Furthermore, we have a symbolic link, `quux.txt`, which points to `bar.txt` and thus indirectly also to the original `foo.txt`. Now in SBCL:

```
* (pathname "/tmp/foo.txt")
#P"/tmp/foo.txt"
* (pathname "/tmp/bar.txt")
#P"/tmp/bar.txt"
* (truename "/tmp/bar.txt")
#P"/tmp/foo.txt"
* (probe-file "/tmp/quux.txt")
#P"/tmp/foo.txt"
```

How It Works

File systems based on concepts from the Unix world know the idea of a *symbolic link* (or *symlink* for short), which "looks" like a file but is rather kind of a pointer to another file (or even a pointer to a pointer, and so on). The standard offers the function `TRUENAME` which is meant to return the "canonical name" of a file; and it even mentions symlinks as an example of what the intended meaning of such a canonical name is. So you can be very confident that all COMMON LISP implementations on platforms like Linux, FreeBSD, or OS X will *resolve* symlinks when asked for the *truename* of a file; that is, they will follow symbolic links until they finally reach the real thing.[25]

There are also several other file-related standard functions, like `PROBE-FILE` (see example above) or `DIRECTORY`, that are required to return truenames. The corresponding entries in the HyperSpec will tell you which are and which aren't.

On Windows, the situation is a bit more complicated. There, the most obvious candidates for symlinks are the so-called "desktop shortcuts," but these probably don't qualify as they are something managed by Windows Explorer and *not* by the underlying file system.[26] Windows indeed *has* symlinks (at least with the NTFS file system), which can be created with the `mklink` command. You'll have to experiment or to look up your documentation to find out how your Lisp will deal with symbolic links on Windows. (ASDF, for example, can resolve desktop shortcuts,[27] so why should your Lisp not be able to do it?)

---

[25]Be aware that due to *hard links*, it is possible that there ain't no such thing as *the* canonical name. But you will definitely get a filename that is not a symlink.

[26]They will show up with the `.lnk` extension in directory listings.

[27]See more at `https://common-lisp.net/project/asdf/asdf/Configuring-ASDF-to-find-your-systems-_002d_002d_002d-old-style.html`.

What If I Want the Symlinks?

Sometimes you may wish to be able to distinguish symlinks from what they're pointing to. For this, many implementations have added an additional keyword argument to the `DIRECTORY` function (see Recipe 15-4). Here's how it's done in SBCL:

```
;; continued from above
* (directory "/tmp/*.txt")
(#P"/tmp/foo.txt")
* (directory "/tmp/*.txt" :resolve-symlinks nil)
(#P"/tmp/bar.txt" #P"/tmp/foo.txt" #P"/tmp/quux.txt")
```

You see that by default the three `.txt` "files" in the directory are treated as if they were only one because two of them are symlinks. But with `:RESOLVE-SYMLINKS` set to `NIL`, all three files will be listed. On CLOZURECL, the corresponding keyword argument is `:FOLLOW-LINKS`. On LISPWORKS, you should check the `:LINK-TRANSPARENCY` keyword argument.

15-13. Navigating a Directory Tree

Problem

You want to know what the equivalent of `..` (two dots) would be in COMMON LISP's pathname syntax; that is, you want to know how to go "up" one or more directories from where you are.

Solution

The short answer is that in namestrings the sequence `..` will very likely work as expected in any current Lisp implementation. There are some caveats, though. Also, there's an interesting tidbit on how directories can be specified, which (depending on your implementation) might make directory navigation a bit more flexible.

Let's create a simple directory structure with a symlink (see also Recipe 15-12) on Linux:

```
edi@nanook:~$ cd /tmp
edi@nanook:/tmp$ rm -rf foo quux
edi@nanook:/tmp$ mkdir -p foo/bar
edi@nanook:/tmp$ ln -s foo/bar quux
edi@nanook:/tmp$ ls -l /tmp/quux/..
```

```
total 4
drwxr-xr-x 2 edi edi 4096 2015-05-27 21:44 bar
```

We now have a directory bar inside a directory foo, and a symlink quux that "points to" (or acts like) bar but is at the same level as foo:

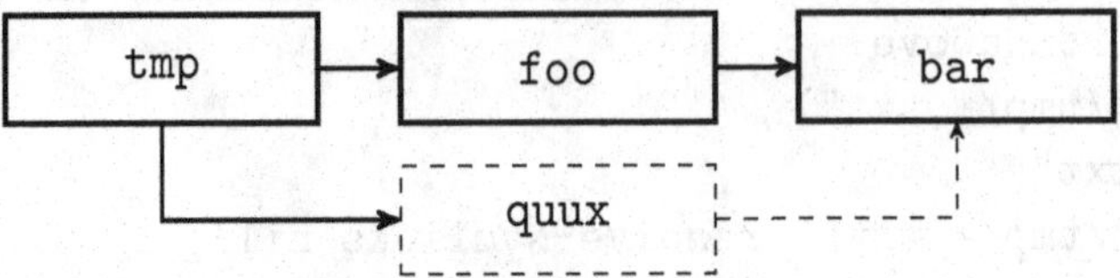

The outcome of ls at the end shows us that a path such as /tmp/quux/.. is interpreted *semantically*, which means something like:

(i) Go to directory /tmp.

(ii) From there, go to directory quux (which turns out to be foo/bar because of the symlink).

(iii) From there, go one level *up* (so that we are finally in foo).

Now, if you use a namestring in COMMON LISP, you will most likely see something like this:

```
CL-USER 1 > (truename "/tmp/quux/..")
#P"/tmp/foo/"
```

(One would hope that namestrings work essentially like those of the host operating system.)

You can also get the same behavior with a PATHNAME object:

```
CL-USER 2 > (truename
             (make-pathname :directory
                            (list :absolute "tmp" "quux" :up)))
#P"/tmp/foo/"
```

However, there's an alternative and it looks like so:

```
CL-USER 3 > (truename
             (make-pathname :directory
                            (list :absolute "tmp" "quux" :back)))
#P"/tmp/"
```

How It Works

While `:UP` in a directory component list is interpreted semantically (as `..` is by the shell in our example), `:BACK` is interpreted *syntactically* in the sense of "remove the last item of the list." (So in this case, the presence of `:BACK` resulted in the removal of `"quux"`.) In other words, for `:UP` to be meaningful, the Lisp system actually has to look at the current contents of the file system; whereas the meaning of `:BACK` can already be resolved at pathname creation time. This can be a useful distinction in case you're creating pathnames programmatically.

As usual (see the introduction to this chapter), this behavior is implementation-dependent. For our example above, we used LISPWORKS. Although the standard recommends this behavior, at the time that this book was written, at least one implementation treated `:UP` and `:BACK` as if they meant the same thing. So, as always, you'll have to check yourself.

15-14. Figuring Out (Source) File Locations Programmatically

Problem

You want to programmatically find out where in the file system a file is located; for example, if you're writing code that will be executed on a machine that is different from the one where it was written.

Solution

Use `*LOAD-PATHNAME*` or `*COMPILE-FILE-PATHNAME*`, or one of the two variants where the "`-PATHNAME*`" ending is replaced with "`-TRUENAME*`." But make sure that you understand *when* these values are actually available (see below).

How It Works

The standard specifies the special variables mentioned above, which can be used to answer our question; albeit they might be a bit tricky to use.

`*LOAD-PATHNAME*` is the pathname that is used when `LOAD` is executed, but only *while* `LOAD` is executed. If you evaluate `*LOAD-PATHNAME*` in the REPL, you'll get `NIL` as an answer, which is the value of this variable while `LOAD` is *not* executed.

So, as an experiment create a file called `foo.lisp` with nothing but the form

```
(defparameter *foo* *load-pathname*)
```

in it and then LOAD this file from your REPL *without* compiling it first. The value of *FOO* should now be the pathname you gave to LOAD although *LOAD-PATHNAME* has "forgotten" this information in the meantime; that is, it is back to its initial value NIL.

However, now try

```
(load (compile-file "foo.lisp"))
```

instead. If you check *FOO* again, it will, of course, have a different value; namely, the pathname of the compiled ("FASL") file that was loaded by LOAD.

If you're interested in the pathname of the source file, you'll have to use *COMPILE-FILE-PATHNAME* instead, so add the form

```
(defparameter *bar* *compile-file-pathname*)
```

to foo.lisp, then *delete* the FASL file and then from the REPL LOAD foo.lisp again. *BAR* will be NIL, as you might have expected, because there was no compilation.[28]

So, let's try

```
(load (compile-file "foo.lisp"))
```

again. After that, *BAR* still has the value NIL! Are you surprised? Well, this is so because the DEFPARAMETER form is only evaluated when the (compiled) file is loaded, at which time *COMPILE-FILE-PATHNAME* is already back to NIL.

How can we fix that? One way is to replace the contents of foo.lisp with this:[29]

```
(defparameter *foo* *load-pathname*)
(eval-when (:compile-toplevel)
  (defparameter *bar* *compile-file-pathname*))
```

This will ensure that the value of *BAR* is set at the right time.[30]

Sometimes you might prefer *LOAD-TRUENAME* and *COMPILE-FILE-TRUENAME* to *LOAD-PATHNAME* and *COMPILE-FILE-PATHNAME*, respectively, because the first two

[28]Even if your Lisp compiles everything by default, like CLOZURECL, there was no *file compilation*.

[29]See chapter 20 of *Practical Common Lisp* for EVAL-WHEN.

[30]An alternative would have been to write (DEFPARAMETER *BAR* #.*COMPILE-FILE-PATHNAME*) (see Recipe 8-3) instead of using EVAL-WHEN. The compiler will insert the pathname as a literal value at *read time*, which, of course, happens during file compilation, as it has to read the code before it can compile it. The value of *BAR* still won't be set before the FASL file is eventually loaded, but at that time, the literal value created earlier is used.

values will capture the arguments provided to the corresponding functions and *not* necessarily the physical locations of the actual files. (The arguments could, for example, have been logical pathnames; see Recipe 15-15.)

15-15. Understanding Logical Pathnames

Problem

You want to define pathnames that work consistently across wildly different file systems. (Or maybe you just want to understand the way an open source library, the source of which you're reading, uses logical pathnames.)

Solution

Before you begin to use logical pathnames, you first have to decide what your "logical" (or "virtual" if you like) file system will look like. Your logical file system will have a hierarchical structure with nested directories, like what you're used to from Windows or Unix-like platforms. And it will have filenames with name and type parts.[31] It *won't* have hosts and devices, though, and probably the most severe restriction is that you can only use uppercase letters, digits, and hyphens to name directories and files.

Let's assume thatyou have a very simple structure where you have two root directories: SOURCE (for your COMMON LISP, and, say, JAVASCRIPT source files) and RESOURCES (for images, movies, databases, whatever). A small part of your logical structure might look like this at some point in time:

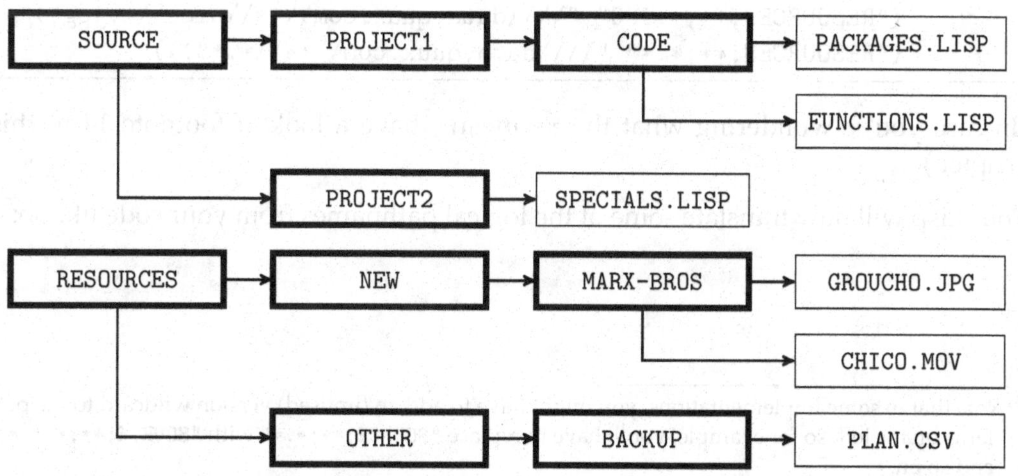

[31]It can also have versions, but that won't make a lot of sense unless the underlying physical system you want to map to also has versioned files.

(Here, boxes with thicker borders denote directories and an arrow means "is part of" or "resides in.")

Now, in your code, you'd consistently use only logical pathnames to refer to these files, so the picture of Groucho Marx would be

```
"STUFF:RESOURCES;NEW;MARX-BROS;GROUCHO.JPG"
```

and the directory containing `FUNCTIONS.LISP` would be accessed with this string:

```
"STUFF:SOURCE;PROJECT1;CODE"
```

(These are namestrings for logical pathnames, the syntax of which will be explained further down below.)

The `"STUFF:"` part is your logical pathname *host* (of which you can have several). Like the logical pathnames themselves, this is also just a virtual entity (in a way, it's the name of the universe that the picture above lives in), and it comes to life by providing *translations* for it. Because the logical pathnames might be all fine and dandy, but so far, your Lisp wouldn't know how to map your "virtual files" to real-world bits on a hard disk, in case you're calling functions like `OPEN` or `RENAME-FILE`.

So, let's provide translations to a Windows file system. We want the `SOURCE` directory and all of its contents to be situated on drive `D:` in the `Dev` directory, but we want the `RESOURCES` directory to reside on a network drive reachable as `\\data.quux.com`. Furthermore, for whatever reason, we want JPGs to live in their own `pics` subdirectory next to where they would end up without this extra rule. This is done like so:[32]

```
(setf (logical-pathname-translations "STUFF")
      '(("SOURCE;**;*.*" "D:\\Dev\\**\\*.*")
        ("RESOURCES;**;*.JPG" "\\\\data.quux.com\\**\\pics\\*.jpg")
        ("RESOURCES;**;*.*" "\\\\data.quux.com\\**\\*.*")))
```

(In case you're wondering what the `**` means, have a look at footnote 14 in this chapter.)

Your Lisp will now translate some of the logical pathnames from your code like so:[33]

---

[32]Note that in some implementations, you might have to add an (unused) version wildcard to the patterns on the left, so for example, you'll have to replace `"SOURCE;**;*.*"` with `"SOURCE;**;*.*.*"`, and so on.

[33]You can check yourself with `TRANSLATE-LOGICAL-PATHNAME`, but be aware that the results on the right side are partly implementation-dependent; for example, the fact that you get lowercase letters throughout. More about this below.

Logical Pathname Namestring	Physical Pathname
"STUFF:SOURCE;PROJECT1;CODE;PACKAGES.LISP"	#P"D:\\Dev\\project1\\code\\packages.lisp"
"STUFF:SOURCE;PROJECT2;SPECIALS.LISP"	#P"D:\\Dev\\project2\\specials.lisp"
"STUFF:RESOURCES;NEW;MARX-BROS;GROUCHO.JPG"	#P"\\\\data.quux.com\\new\\marx-bros\\pics\\groucho.jpg"
"STUFF:RESOURCES;NEW;MARX-BROS;CHICO.MOV"	#P"\\\\data.quux.com\\new\\marx-bros\\chico.mov"
"STUFF:RESOURCES;OTHER;BACKUP;PLAN.CSV"	#P"\\\\data.quux.com\\other\\backup\\plan.csv"

Later, maybe you want to port your program to a Linux machine. You want the source directory to live in `/usr/local/lisp` and the resources to be in a subdirectory of your home directory. In addition, every resource that has on its path a directory called `BACKUP` is supposed to go into `/mnt/bak`, preserving its directory structure, except for the `BACKUP` part. Luckily, you don't have to change anything except for the pathname translations, which will now look like so:

```
(setf (logical-pathname-translations "STUFF")
      '(("SOURCE;**;*.*" "/usr/local/lisp/**/*.*")
        ("RESOURCES;**;BACKUP;**;*.*" "/mnt/bak/**/**/*.*")
        ("RESOURCES;**;*.*" "~/data/**/*.*")))
```

And this is the result:

Logical Pathname Namestring	Physical Pathname
"STUFF:SOURCE;PROJECT1;CODE;PACKAGES.LISP"	#P"/usr/local/lisp/project1/code/packages.lisp"
"STUFF:SOURCE;PROJECT2;SPECIALS.LISP"	#P"/usr/local/lisp/project2/specials.lisp"
"STUFF:RESOURCES;NEW;MARX-BROS;GROUCHO.JPG"	#P"~/data/new/marx-bros/groucho.jpg"
"STUFF:RESOURCES;NEW;MARX-BROS;CHICO.MOV"	#P"~/data/new/marx-bros/chico.mov"
"STUFF:RESOURCES;OTHER;BACKUP;PLAN.CSV"	#P"/mnt/bak/other/plan.csv"

How It Works

To pick up a word that was already used in the introduction to this chapter, the so-called *logical pathnames* of COMMON LISP might seem arcane to you. And in a way this is true, they *are* arcane because they attempt to solve a problem that largely doesn't exist anymore and do so with a somewhat baroque and cryptic syntax. It is probably fine if you completely ignore logical pathnames for your own code, as long as you don't run into the problems they purport to solve. (But see the end of this recipe.) Some people are still using them, though, and some even have to because they have to support legacy systems. At some point, you might be in a situation where you need to understand logical pathnames; this recipe tries to at least give you some starting points. (It certainly isn't long enough to discuss all the gory details and it would be hard to justify spending much more time on them in a book like this.)

One should probably start by explaining what logical pathnames are *not*. They are *not* a general facility to map arbitrary pathname abstractions to "real" (or "physical" in COMMON LISP parlance) filenames at the programmer's discretion. And logical pathname translations are *not* meant to be applied to user-supplied filenames—as in "Please select a file to save the picture you've drawn."[34]

Rather, logical pathnames describe a fairly restricted subset of the set of all possible pathnames and a way of mapping these "few" pathnames to as many different file systems as possible. The main (and intended) use case for logical pathnames is to ease the portability of build instructions for (Lisp) programs. Their promise is that if you stick to clearly specified logical pathnames throughout in a large system, porting it (or at least those parts where you refrain from using physical pathnames) to a totally different file system is just a matter of changing the logical pathname translations.

The restrictions you have to deal with were already mentioned in the example. No devices, no hosts, and only a very minimal set of allowed characters. If you can adhere to that (which should be no problem if you are in full control of the names of your files), you can map these logical pathnames to physical pathnames by means of translations, as shown above. You select a name for your host[35] (in our case, it was "STUFF") and provide an alist (see Recipe 6-8) consisting of pathname pairs. Whenever your Lisp encounters a logical pathname, it will try to find a match against this list using PATHNAME-MATCH-P, and for the first match (which means that order matters!) it will use TRANSLATE-PATHNAME to create a new pathname. So, a simplified version of this process would look like so:

```
(defun translate-logical-pathname (pathname rules)
  (let ((rule (assoc pathname rules :test #'pathname-match-p)))
    (unless rule (error "No translation rule for ~A" pathname))
    (translate-pathname pathname (first rule) (second rule))))
```

The main difference between this little function and what's really happening is that the result is allowed to be another logical pathname (maybe for another logical pathname host), in which case the translation process starts again—until you finally end up with a physical pathname.

I won't go into the details of PATHNAME-MATCH-P and TRANSLATE-PATHNAME (consult the HyperSpec if you're curious) except for saying that it's essentially a simple pattern matching and substitution process with the familiar pathname wildcards. And like always, how the process works is implementation-dependent (for example, whether wildcard characters within strings are allowed; see Recipe 15-4); but

[34]To quote from the corresponding X3J13 issue: "It is not a goal of logical pathnames to be able to represent all possible filenames. Their goal is rather to represent just enough filenames to be useful for storing software. Real pathnames, in contrast, need to provide a uniform interface to all possible filenames, including names and naming conventions that are not under the control of COMMON LISP."

[35]You can pick anything except for "SYS", which is reserved.

you shouldn't be worried about that because the whole point of logical pathnames is that you can delegate this stuff to your (or somebody else's) Lisp system.

What Exactly Are Logical Pathnames?

At this point you might be wondering how the system decides if a pathname is logical. The answer is simple: a pathname is logical if its host component has translations associated with it, either by you or by your implementation. So, in our example above, we've made "STUFF" a logical pathname host and every pathname with this host is now a logical pathname.

Other than that, logical pathnames have the same structure as physical pathnames. They also have their own namestring syntax, which was purposefully designed to stand off from most conceivable physical namestring syntaxes. We've used such namestrings above already and it should be obvious that they consist of the host's name, followed by a colon, followed by directories separated by semicolons, followed by the file, with name and type separated by a dot:

```
HOST:DIRECTORY1;DIRECTORY2;DIRECTORY3;FILENAME.TYPE
```

One thing that needs getting used to is that relative paths start with an extra semicolon (otherwise, they're absolute):

```
HOST:;DIRECTORY1;DIRECTORY2;DIRECTORY3;FILENAME.TYPE
```

So, Maybe Logical Pathnames Aren't Totally Useless...

If you made it up to this point, you might still be wondering if you'll ever use logical pathnames in your own code. Here's one idea: as you will have noticed after reading this chapter, pathnames are complicated and you're very often at the mercy of your implementation. And this is by design and makes sense as, for example, a backslash in a namestring has to be interpreted differently on Windows and Unix; or Windows has drive letters and OS X hasn't; and most Lisps on Linux will probably understand "~/", while on Windows they probably won't.

If you have full control over the pathnames in your application (i.e., if there's no "user intervention"), then you can decide to use logical pathnames throughout and only care about the underlying file system in one place. Except that you won't really have to care that much at all as long as your "virtual" files are mapped in some consistent way.

This is even more of an advantage if you're writing open source code that aims to support various Lisps on various platforms. Just write your code using logical pathnames and ask prospective users of your code to provide meaningful logical pathname translations for their own implementation. Once they've done this, the pathname-related part of your code will "just work" and you won't even need to have access to their Lisps. (For an example of how logical pathnames are used in the "real world," see page 488.)

16. Developing and Debugging

The Lisps that were dominant at the time when COMMON LISP was created, already had impressive interactive debugging facilities, and so the standard codified that every Lisp should have them. Thus, no matter which implementation you're using (as long as it conforms to the ANSI standard), your Lisp has to have a debugger, a tracer, an inspector, and several other features discussed in this chapter.[1] While offering these features is in a way easy due to COMMON LISP's image-based nature (see Recipe 16-1), many of the currently popular open source Lisps are quite Spartan compared to their forebears and offer only relatively raw text-based versions of the aforementioned tools.

That's why you want some kind of IDE wrapped around your Lisp and thus many parts of this chapter will refer to SLIME (see Recipe 16-2) in one way or the other. While I think that SLIME is a great piece of software and an important part of the COMMON LISP ecosystem, I personally prefer the LISPWORKS IDE,[2] which I think has more to offer in terms of integration and features. But the best solution that works for virtually every COMMON LISP implementation currently in use[3] is certainly SLIME, and therefore it is the obvious choice for a book like this (as it already was for *Practical Common Lisp*).

16-1. Embracing Lisp's Image-Based Development Style

Problem

You are coming from another programming language and you are unsure about how development in COMMON LISP is typically performed.

Solution

The main idea of developing in COMMON LISP is that the whole system is one "image" that you continuously modify until it fits your needs. And this image will be

[1]It could even offer a *resident editor*. If you're curious, enter (ED) in your implementation.

[2]I'm certainly biased because I've been a customer of LISPWORKS for more than a decade now. But the argument works both ways; their IDE is one of the reasons I'm using LISPWORKS...

[3]And also, by the way, for several SCHEME implementations. Some people have even connected SLIME to CLOJURE, GOO, or JAVASCRIPT.

the final result (as opposed to, say, a binary executable compiled from source files).

You will still work with text source files, but you should not view them as the output of one tool (the editor) that is fed into another tool (the preprocessor, the compiler, or the interpreter), but rather as keeping track of what you did to modify the image and how to repeat that.

How It Works

If you're familiar with other Lisp-like languages or with SMALLTALK or FORTH, you will immediately understand the idea of "image-based" development. If, on the other hand, you've only used more "mainstream" languages, you might need to adapt a bit and maybe even "unlearn" some habits you're used to.

As with pretty much every other language, programming in Lisp evolves around text files that contain source code. The main difference between Lisp and most languages that can trace their ancestry back to FORTRAN and ALGOL is that with the latter family of languages, usually the eventual goal is to produce a program by "executing" the source code[4] in some other process. And if your program doesn't do what it's supposed to do, you go back to your editor, make changes, execute it again, and test again, and so forth.

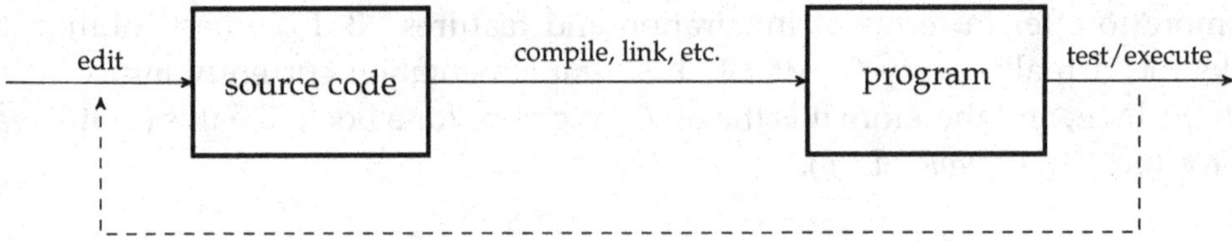

In theory, you could do the same in Lisp,[5] but that would be a very bad idea. The "natural" way of working in COMMON LISP is based on the idea that once your system starts up you are in an *image*, which is the collection of all Lisp objects in RAM.[6] And developing then means *modifying* this image—for example, by adding functions or altering the values of variables—until it does what you want.

Even if you don't use an IDE and just start your Lisp from the console, you're always in the REPL (the "**R**ead-**E**val-**P**rint **L**oop") where you continuously enter forms to be evaluated. This has two effects:

- Each form *returns* something which means that you can query the state of the

[4]I've tried to avoid talking about compilation here because, although there certainly are important differences between interpreted and compiled languages, the *modus operandi* during development is typically pretty similar.

[5]You could for example edit your Lisp code with whichever editor you prefer and then from time to time invoke `make` to create an executable from it (as in Recipe 22-4). Don't do that!

[6]You might want to think of a big "structured" memory dump comprising the whole *state* of your Lisp system.

image at any time, and, for example, find out the value of a variable or test whether a function does what it's supposed to do.

- Many forms also have *side effects* that modify the image. A `DEFUN` form, for example, returns a function name but it also adds a new function to the Lisp image or alters an existing function.

There is no division into separate tools like preprocessors, compilers, assemblers, linkers, and so on. And in a certain sense there isn't even a "program" (although we certainly also use that term in the Lisp world), there's just this one image that you're working *in* and *on* all the time.

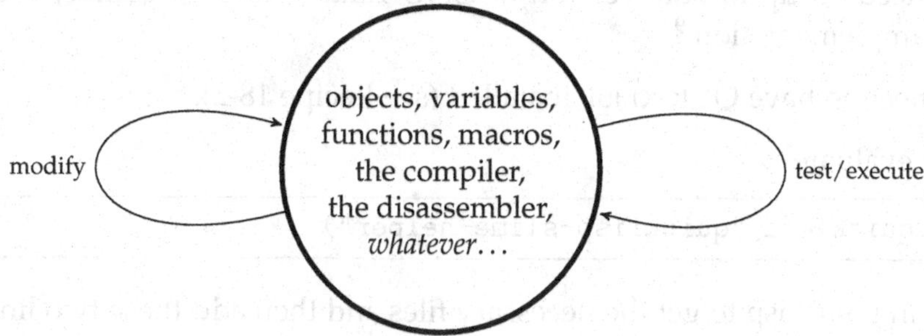

The Role of the Source Code

In *theory*, you could fire up your Lisp, enter stuff into the REPL until you're content with what you've achieved, and then save (see page 687) the image. At a later date, you could then start with that image and modify it further or just use it.

In *practice*, though, this would be at least inconvenient if not outright fatuitous. It'd be hard or impossible to figure out what exactly you did that led to the current (maybe erroneous) state of the image and it'd be impossible to share your code with others unless they'd be willing to replace their image with yours.

That's why, of course, even with image-based development, you will be using text files containing source code—usually containing the *side effect* code that modifies the image, like `DEFUN`s, `DEFMACRO`s, `DEFVAR`s, and so on. `LOAD`ing these files[7] is then essentially like replaying what you did to the image to bring it into a certain state.

16-2. Deciding Which IDE to Use

Problem

You're wondering if you can keep the IDE you know and love from *<insert other*

[7]You will typically first *compile* them and then load the FASL files (see page 429), but compilation is orthogonal to what we're discussing here.

language here>. (Or whether what some people say is true: that you *must* use Emacs.)

Solution

The short answer is that if you're serious about COMMON LISP, your best bets are: to use Emacs with SLIME or to use an (Emacs-based) IDE that came with your Lisp. See below for the rationale.

To install SLIME, if you haven't done so already, follow these steps:

(i) You need an up-to-date version of GNU Emacs[8] and, of course, a COMMON LISP implementation.[9]

(ii) You need to have QUICKLISP installed (see Recipe 18-2).

(iii) Now evaluate

```
(ql:quickload "quicklisp-slime-helper")
```

once in your Lisp to get the necessary files and then add these two lines

```
(load (expand-file-name "~/quicklisp/slime-helper.el"))
(setq inferior-lisp-program "sbcl")
```

to your `~/.emacs` file.

(Replace `"sbcl"` with whatever is needed to start the Lisp implementation of your choice.)

You should now be all set, and the next time you start Emacs, SLIME should be available. You start your Lisp from Emacs with *M-x slime*.[10]

Other recipes in this chapter discuss various aspects of SLIME, but don't provide a thorough introduction. Have a look at the manual, which is quite good. There are also various tutorials to be found on the Internet. If you are new to SLIME, make sure to familiarize yourself with at least the basic functionality, like `slime-compile-defun` (usually bound to *C-c C-c*) or `slime-compile-and-load-file` (usually on *C-c C-k*), and then read the rest of this chapter.

[8]See `https://www.gnu.org/software/emacs/`. XEmacs is not supported by SLIME.

[9]This won't work with the free trial version of LISPWORKS, but with LISPWORKS you should probably use their IDE instead of SLIME anyway.

[10]Here and in other parts of the chapter we use the Emacs notation for entering commands.

How It Works

To become really productive in COMMON LISP, you absolutely need at least two features in your editor/IDE:

- Good editing support for COMMON LISP's S-expression syntax.

  You want editor commands like `forward-sexp`, `backward-sexp`, `kill-sexp`, `transpose-sexps`, `up-list`, `down-list`, and so on.[11] You want automatic and correct indentation of Lisp code, and you want your editor to recognize code that is commented out (see Recipe 10-10), and so forth.

  COMMON LISP code is organized in S-expressions and only incidentally divided into lines in text files. If you catch yourself writing non-idiomatic code like so

```
;; YIKES!!!
(defun fac (n)
  (cond ((zerop n)
          1
         )
         (t
          (* n (fac (1- n)))
         )
  )
)
```

  "because it's easier to edit," then you're doing something substantially wrong and you won't have a lot of fun with Lisp in the long run. (Not to mention that the other kids won't play with you because your code is so ugly.)

  While the basic syntax of Lisp is simple, it can become tricky to some extent (see, for example, Chapter 8), and providing editor support for it is no mean feat. Very few editors are really good at this. Emacs is.

- Facilities for interactive, image-based (see Recipe 16-1) development.

  You want the ability to selectively evaluate or expand arbitrary forms in your source files and to look up definitions. You want convenient integration with all the introspective and diagnostic tools available in your Lisp (some of which are described in other recipes of this chapter). You want to be able to compile and load files with one keystroke. You want means to undo changes that you've made to your image. And most of all, as the state of the *image* is constantly changing, you want your IDE to be on top of that all the time.[12]

[11]If you don't know these commands, look them up in Emacs and memorize their keybindings.

[12]Examples would be symbol completion and display of argument lists. IDEs for static languages have to implement this by constantly compiling the code in the background while in COMMON LISP this

An IDE that is very good for the edit-compile-debug development style described on page 470 isn't necessarily well suited for Lisp. What typically works well in COMMON LISP is either an IDE that is actually a part of the Lisp image, like the LISPWORKS IDE, or one that maintains a permanent communication with it. For the latter variant, SLIME—an Emacs mode originally written by Luke Gorrie and Helmut Eller—currently seems to be the only viable option.[13]

A Brief History of Emacs (As Seen from Lisp)

Emacs is not one single program but a whole family of text editors with a shared history and similar features. The first "EMACS" was created in the 1970s by Richard Stallman and Guy Steele. It was a set of macros for the TECO editor, which ran only on the PDP-10 computer with the ITS operating system. (As TECO was, in a sense, also a programming language, it is probably fair to say that this first-ever version of Emacs was coded in a language that is now extinct.)

The second Emacs was "EINE," written shortly thereafter by Dan Weinreb. It ran on Lisp Machines and was thus implemented in one of the precursors of COMMON LISP. Many Emacs variants have since been implemented in many different Lisp dialects.

The most widely used Emacs nowadays is GNU Emacs, also initially written by Stallman. It is implemented in a mixture of C and EMACS LISP.[14]

Of the Emacs versions that were implemented in COMMON LISP, the most popular nowadays is HEMLOCK. It was originally integrated with CMUCL, but it is now also available for other open source Lisps as a portable library loadable with QUICKLISP (see Recipe 18-2). In addition to that, HEMLOCK is a part of the (Mac-only) IDE of CLOZURECL and a progenitor of the editor of the LISPWORKS IDE.

So, there's no way to avoid Emacs. Whether you're using HEMLOCK, the IDEs of CLOZURECL, or LISPWORKS, or even the now-ancient FRED editor of MACINTOSH COMMON LISP, you're using Emacs. This is unfortunate if you've never worked with Emacs before, as you'll now not only have to become acquainted with a new programming language, but also need to learn a new editor. The only consolation is that after some time of extensive usage, you'll have forgotten the initial woes—like driving a bicycle or a car quickly becomes second nature, but initially might seem complex and intractable.

---

information is always readily available in the image. The IDE just has to query for it.

[13]When SLIME starts your Lisp, it will ask it to start up a server (called SWANK) and will then talk to it over TCP/IP.

[14]A Lisp dialect which is only used inside of Emacs and which differs significantly from COMMON LISP. See `https://en.wikipedia.org/wiki/Emacs_Lisp`.

Alternatives (?)

If you absolutely despise Emacs, or youlove another IDE or editor so much that you don't want to abandon it, then it *might* make sense to look for COMMON LISP support elsewhere. For example, there is something called "SLIME for Vim,"[15] and with a bit of effort, you'll also find things like Lisp plug-ins for ECLIPSE, a stand-alone Windows IDE, and so on. Alas, what most of these efforts seem to have in common is that after a somewhat budding start, they don't gain a lot of traction and then eventually peter out.

If you want a solution that will likely still be around and maintained in a couple of years, and which has enough users to get you help in case you're stuck, you should stick with the options described earlier.

16-3. Debugging with the Debugger

Problem

You want to efficiently use the debugger you're landing in when an error occurs.

Solution

We'll use the following code for this recipe, which you should compile and load first:[16]

```
(defparameter *quux* 42)

(defun foo (x)
  (let ((*quux* 23))
    (bar (1- x) *quux*)))

(defun bar (a b)
  (declare (optimize debug))
  (let ((c (* b b)))
    (catch 'tag
      (baz c a))))

(defun baz (v w)
  (/ v w))
```

[15]See `http://www.vim.org/scripts/script.php?script_id=2531`.

[16]See Recipe 17-3 for `DECLARE`.

If you now evaluate (FOO 1) in the SLIME REPL, an Emacs window will pop up and show something like this:[17]

```
arithmetic error DIVISION-BY-ZERO signalled
Operation was /, operands (529 0).
   [Condition of type DIVISION-BY-ZERO]

Restarts:
 0: [RETRY] Retry SLIME REPL evaluation request.
 1: [*ABORT] Return to SLIME's top level.
 2: [ABORT] abort thread (#<THREAD "repl-thread" RUNNING {1003C40033}>)

Backtrace:
  0: (SB-KERNEL::INTEGER-/-INTEGER 529 0)
  1: (BAZ 529 0)
  2: (BAR 0 23)
  3: (FOO 1)
  4: (SB-INT:SIMPLE-EVAL-IN-LEXENV (FOO 1) #<NULL-LEXENV>)
  5: (EVAL (FOO 1))
 --more--
```

The Emacs mode line shows that you're now in a new mode (called SLDB), which is a unified front end for your Lisp's debugger wrapped around it by SLIME. You're seeing the *condition* (see Recipe 12-3) that was responsible for entering the debugger, the available *restarts* (see Recipe 12-6), and the *backtrace*; that is, the *call stack* (see page 510).

The idea is that you should now be able to operate mainly with one-key shortcuts. Most of the content in the buffer can be "activated" by navigating to it with the cursor keys and pressing *Return*. You can, for example, use this feature to *inspect* (see Recipe 16-7) the condition or to invoke one of the restarts.

For now, move to the (green) stack frames and press *Return* on each of them. The backtrace part of your SLDB buffer should now look like what is shown on the next page.

If we look at the stack frame for BAR, we see the two arguments, A and B, as well as the lexical variable C, together with their values. We also see that a catch tag TAG was established here. However, in the two other functions, the compiler has removed some information so that the names of the arguments are no longer available. We get more information for the BAR frame because, in this case, we specifically asked for it.[18] (Without the declaration, we wouldn't even see a lexical variable there because the compiler would have optimized it away.)

[17]We're using SBCL for this example. If you're using another Lisp, things will surely look different.

[18]Note that in SLIME you can use slime-compile-defun (see page 472) with a *prefix argument* to achieve the same effect without an explicit declaration.

```
Backtrace:
  0: (SB-KERNEL::INTEGER-/-INTEGER 529 0)
  1: (BAZ 529 0)
      Locals:
        SB-DEBUG::ARG-0 = 529
        SB-DEBUG::ARG-1 = 0
  2: (BAR 0 23)
      Locals:
        A = 0
        B = 23
        C = 0
      Catch-tags:
        TAG
  3: (FOO 1)
      Locals:
        SB-DEBUG::ARG-0 = 1
  4: (SB-INT:SIMPLE-EVAL-IN-LEXENV (FOO 1) #<NULL-LEXENV>)
  5: (EVAL (FOO 1))
  --more--
```

So, what we see in the debugger depends on the *optimization qualities* we compiled with. But it also depends on the Lisp we're using. For example:

- SBCL showed the catch tag in the stack frame for BAR. Other Lisps might show it in a separate frame or not at all.
- SBCL didn't show that we bound *QUUX* in FOO. Other Lisps might do that, either in the FOO frame or in a separate frame.
- Your Lisp might decide to optimize some functions away (see Recipe 17-11). For example, CLOZURECL and LISPWORKS won't show BAZ in the backtrace.
- Some Lisps will offer more restarts.
- Stack frames might look very different in other Lisps to begin with.

Anyway, you should now experiment a bit with the debugger and learn what backtraces will look like in the Lisp of your choice and how you can influence the amount of information they provide. Most importantly, you should learn all the things you can do from within the debugger. As long as you're in SLDB, you'll see a menu of the same name, which shows the commands available together with their one-key shortcuts. Try this: navigate to the BAR frame, type *:* (which is the shortcut for `sldb-eval-in-frame`) and enter `(THROW 'TAG 42)`. This should end your SLDB session and put you back into the REPL.

How It Works

A debugger in COMMON LISP is not a favor you have to thank your implementation for; it's a feature demanded by the standard, so every Lisp has to have it.[19] Here's the essence of the debugger's main job:

- In case of an error that wasn't handled, give the user the chance to invoke one of the *active restarts* (see Recipe 12-6) interactively.
- For this to work, the debugger has to maintain the *dynamic environment* (see page 347) of the time when the error was signaled.
- The debugger should preferably also offer additional restarts, as far as they make sense in the current situation.
- Allow the user to inspect and change the environment.

Metaphorically speaking, in case of an error, the debugger "brings time to a stop" and allows you to "modify the past" before continuing, or alternatively to "select a different future." Although often the most important feature is not that you can continue in some way but rather that you can rummage around and inspect the "history" that led to the error in order to find out what exactly went wrong.

Entering the Debugger Intentionally

There are various ways to bring you into the debugger

(i) The most direct way is to call the function INVOKE-DEBUGGER with a *condition* (see Recipe 12-3) as its only argument, for example like so:

```
(invoke-debugger
 (make-condition 'type-error :expected-type 'fixnum :datum 42.0))
```

(ii) The most typical way is that a condition is signaled using ERROR or CERROR (see Recipe 12-4) and not handled:

```
(error 'type-error :expected-type 'fixnum :datum 42.0)
```

(iii) You can set the global special variable *BREAK-ON-SIGNALS* to a *type specifier* (see Recipe 13-1), and each signaling of a condition that matches this type will *immediately* throw you into the debugger—no matter whether the condition would have been handled or whether the function signaling the condition would later have invoked the debugger anyway.

Try, for example, one of the two forms below:

[19] Although, while the HyperSpec prescribes when and how the debugger has to be entered, it doesn't specify what exactly the debugger should be able to do.

```
(let ((*break-on-signals* 'type-error))
  (signal 'type-error :expected-type 'fixnum :datum 42.0))

(let ((*break-on-signals* 'arithmetic-error))
  (ignore-errors
    (error 'division-by-zero
           :operands (list 42 0) :operation '/)))
```

Note that in both cases the debugger would *not* have been invoked without the outer LET.[20]

(iv) BREAK uses its arguments like FORMAT to print a message and then immediately enters the debugger. It works very similar to CERROR, except that it bypasses *DEBUGGER-HOOK* (see below).

(The latter two are meant for debugging and shouldn't appear in production code.)

Finally, there's a global special variable *DEBUGGER-HOOK*, which you can use to execute code *before* the debugger is entered, or even to bypass the debugger completely:[21]

```
CL-USER> (catch 'tag
           (let ((*debugger-hook*
                  (lambda (condition old-debugger-hook)
                    (declare (ignore old-debugger-hook))
                    (format *error-output*
                            "Condition ~S was suppressed.~%"
                            condition)
                    (throw 'tag 42))))
             (error "Some error.")))
Condition #<SIMPLE-ERROR "Some error." {1004513453}> was suppressed.
42
```

(Now try the same with ERROR replaced with BREAK.)

Without SLIME

If you work without an IDE like SLIME, which wraps an interface around the debugger (or if from within SLDB you type *B* for sldb-break-with-default-debugger), you will land in the "raw" debugger. This is typically hinted at by a slightly modi-

[20]Which demonstrates another reason (see page 349) why you usually shouldn't ignore errors: it will make debugging harder.

[21]So you could replace it with your own custom debugger like SLIME does.

fied prompt that shows *that* you are in the debugger and *at what level* you are. While, for example, the typical prompt on LISPWORKS might be

```
CL-USER 42 >
```

the debugger prompt will then be this:

```
CL-USER 43 : 1 >
```

And if *in* the debugger you manage to do something that again invokes the debugger (recursively), you'll see this (note the "2" there):

```
CL-USER 44 : 2 >
```

Such a debugger works essentially like a normal REPL with a couple of special shortcut commands available (that usually are keywords); many Lisps offer for example `:A` (for "abort") to exit the debugger and go one level "up."

In the debugger you can usually get a list of all available debugger commands with `:?` or `:H` or just `?`.

Bypassing SLDB can sometimes make sense because it can't possibly offer all the amenities individual debuggers might have. While SLDB is a good and convenient choice for most typical cases, you should also familiarize yourself with your Lisp's "native" debugger.

Logging Backtraces

It should be obvious from this recipe that in case of an error, the backtrace contains a lot of useful information. And this is not only the case during interactive debugging, but will also be true for unattended applications. It is thus a good idea to log the backtrace somewhere, even if the program can recover from an error.

All implementations can do this somehow, but the way to do it is different in each. The library TRIVIAL-BACKTRACE provides a portable wrapper around this functionality. Here's a simple example of how it can be used:

```
(block my-block
  (handler-bind
      ((error
         (lambda (condition)
           (return-from my-block
             (trivial-backtrace:print-backtrace condition
                                                 :output nil)))))
    (foo 1)))
```

16-4. Tracing Functions

Problem

In a complex part of your program, you lost track of which function is called when.

Solution

You can *trace* individual functions. If a function is traced, then your implementation will inform you whenever this function is called and it'll tell you which arguments it received. You'll also see what the function eventually returns. Let's use these simple Hofstadter sequences[22] as an example:

```
(defun female (n)
  (cond ((zerop n) 1)
        (t (- n (male (female (1- n)))))))

(defun male (n)
  (cond ((zerop n) 0)
        (t (- n (female (male (1- n)))))))
```

Let's trace the function MALE and see what we get:[23]

```
CL-USER> (trace male)
(MALE)
CL-USER> (male 3)
  0: (MALE 3)
    1: (MALE 2)
      2: (MALE 1)
        3: (MALE 0)
        3: MALE returned 0
      2: MALE returned 0
    1: MALE returned 1
    1: (MALE 1)
      2: (MALE 0)
      2: MALE returned 0
    1: MALE returned 0
  0: MALE returned 2
2
```

[22]See https://en.wikipedia.org/wiki/Hofstadter_sequence.

[23]Output from SBCL. As usual, your results may look slightly different in other Lisps.

We eventually see the return value 2 of the form (MALE 3) but before that, we see that (MALE 2) is called, which in turn calls (MALE 1), and so on. While this follows immediately from the definition of the function MALE, it is maybe not so obvious why the value of (MALE 2) is 1 or why, after (MALE 2) has returned, (MALE 1) is also called from within (MALE 3).[24] Let's also trace FEMALE and try again:

```
;; continued from above
CL-USER> (trace female)
(FEMALE)
CL-USER> (male 3)
  0: (MALE 3)
    1: (MALE 2)
      2: (MALE 1)
        3: (MALE 0)
        3: MALE returned 0
        3: (FEMALE 0)
        3: FEMALE returned 1
      2: MALE returned 0
      2: (FEMALE 0)
      2: FEMALE returned 1
    1: MALE returned 1
    1: (FEMALE 1)
      2: (FEMALE 0)
      2: FEMALE returned 1
      2: (MALE 1)
        3: (MALE 0)
        3: MALE returned 0
        3: (FEMALE 0)
        3: FEMALE returned 1
      2: MALE returned 0
    1: FEMALE returned 1
  0: MALE returned 2
2
```

This should now give us a pretty clear picture of what exactly happens when we evaluate (MALE 3).

Finally, let's turn tracing off again:

```
;; continued from above
CL-USER> (trace)            ;; which functions are currently traced
(FEMALE MALE)
CL-USER> (untrace male)     ;; stop tracing MALE
```

[24]The indentation and the prefixes in front of the forms are obviously meant to convey the function call hierarchy.

```
T
CL-USER> (trace)                    ;; check again
(FEMALE)
CL-USER> (untrace)                  ;; untrace ALL functions
T
CL-USER> (trace)                    ;; check again
NIL
CL-USER> (female 42)
26
```

How It Works

Each COMMON LISP implementation is required by the standard to offer the macros TRACE and UNTRACE with the functionality demonstrated above. But apart from fulfilling these minimal requirements, individual Lisps will typically offer a lot more, although what exactly you'll get is, as usual, implementation-dependent:

- Only trace a function call if a specified test succeeds before the function is called (or after it is called or both).
- Enter the debugger whenever a traced function is entered (or when it returns).
- Step (see Recipe 16-5) a function instead of tracing it.
- Only trace function calls that are invoked from within a certain other function.
- When tracing, perform some custom task instead of (or in addition to) printing the function's arguments and return values.
- Only trace in certain specified threads (see Chapter 11).
- Trace only individual methods instead of a whole generic function.
- Report allocation or show backtraces together with the usual tracing information.

You'll have to consult your manual to learn which of these features your Lisp has and which syntax you'll need to use them.

(See also Recipe 16-10.)

Graphical Tracing

The output of the tracer can be pretty overwhelming at times. In more complex scenarios, a graphical interface to it might be helpful. The LISPWORKS IDE has a particularly neat tool for that, where you're shown a tree representation of the traced function calls with nodes that can be inspected and the ability to expand and collapse parts of the tree.

SLIME offers something similar, albeit not as posh, through its "Trace Dialog." To use it, you can, for example, move your cursor to the definitions of `MALE` and `FEMALE` and press *C-c M-t* (for `slime-trace-dialog-toggle-trace`) on each of the function names. Then evaluate something like `(FEMALE 4)` and afterward press *C-c T* (for `slime-trace-dialog`). See the SLIME manual for more information.

Note that this SLIME feature works *in parallel* to your Lisp's "native" tracer, so that the standard macros `TRACE` and `UNTRACE` have no effect on what's traced in this dialog.

16-5. Stepping Through Your Code

Problem

While debugging some code, you want to execute a function "step by step" in order to see what exactly it does and where things go wrong.

Solution

We'll briefly demonstrate stepping in SBCL. (We'll first do this in a session started from the console, but we'll later see that stepping from within SLIME doesn't make much of a difference in this case.)

We start with the following code, which you should compile and load. Note that a *declaration* (see Recipe 17-3) with a suitable `DEBUG` optimize quality is necessary, or otherwise we won't be able to step at all.

```
(defun foo (a)
  (declare (optimize debug))
  (let* ((b (random 5))
         (c (expt a b)))
    (- c a)))
```

Let's now step through one evaluation of `(FOO 3)`. We marked where something was entered by us; the rest was printed by SBCL:[25]

[25]As is typical with text-based COMMON LISP tools, you can enter something like `:?` or `?` to get a list of available stepper commands. We only used `:STEP` here, but typically you'll also have commands available to skip certain forms or to make changes.

```
* (step (foo 3))                                  ;; we entered this
; Evaluating call:
;   (FOO 3)
; With arguments:
;   3
1] :step                                          ;; we entered this
; Evaluating call:
;   (RANDOM 5)
; With arguments:
;   5
1] :step                                          ;; we entered this
; (RANDOM 5) => 4
; Evaluating call:
;   (EXPT A B)
; With arguments:
;   3
;   4
1] :step                                          ;; we entered this
; (EXPT A B) => 81
; Evaluating call:
;   (- C A)
; With unknown arguments
0] :step                                          ;; we entered this
; (FOO 3) => 78
78
```

If you do the same in SLIME, you're put into SLDB (see page 476) with additional restarts for stepping. SLIME will also try to show you where in the source code you are while stepping through it. Try it...

How It Works

Each COMMON LISP implementation has to provide the macro STEP, but—like with INSPECT (see Recipe 16-7), for example—what it actually does varies wildly. The *intention* is that you should be able to "single-step" through the evaluation of a form. But it obviously depends on the compiler[26] what a "step" actually is.

In our example, we saw how individual forms were evaluated and computation was always halted between these forms. We sometimes saw information about the arguments and the results, but not always. (During evaluation of the (- C A) form,

[26] And not only on the compiler but often (see above) also on the compilation settings. It is usually advisable to compile code you want to step through with high DEBUG settings.

the compiler didn't know the values of `A` and `C`.) It would also be quite easy to create code where SBCL's stepper would not be helpful at all.

That's because implementing a useful stepper is hard. It is pretty obvious what to do for interpreted code, but for compiled code to be "steppable," it usually has to be *instrumented* somehow; which means that code that is good for the stepper is very different from the code normally created by the compiler. The standard therefore allows Lisps to treat `STEP` as if it were just a synonym for `PROGN` (which is what CLOZURECL currently does, for example).

The two "big" commercial implementations (ALLEGROCL and LISPWORKS) both have very sophisticated and convenient graphical stepper tools integrated into their IDEs. But in most other Lisps, support for stepping is currently unfortunately rather bleak or non-existent.

16-6. Acquiring Information About Functions, Macros, and Variables

Problem

You need information about parts of your image that you didn't write yourself (or maybe about parts you lost track of because you wrote them some time ago).

(This recipe is about things typically defined in source code. For how to get detailed information on arbitrary Lisp objects, see Recipe 16-7.)

Solution

In such cases, what you will need is *documentation* or the *source code* (which might contain inline documentation, for example).

The standard makes sure that you can attach documentation to every function, macro, variable, class definition, and so on. And there's a standard function `DOCUMENTATION` to access this documentation.

So that we have an example for this recipe, put the following code in a file, and then compile and load it:[27]

```
(defvar foo 42
  "A variable with the same name as the function FOO.")

(defun foo (x y)
```

[27]It would be unidiomatic to name a special variable like so and we're doing it only so that we have two different objects with the same name.

```
  "Computes the BAR of X and Y and binds FOO."
  (let ((foo 23))
    (bar x y)))

(defun bar (a b)
  "Computes FLOOR after switching the arguments."
  (floor b a))
```

In the REPL, you can now do something like this:

```
CL-USER> (documentation 'foo 'function)
"Computes the BAR of X and Y and binds FOO."
CL-USER> (documentation 'foo 'variable)
"A variable with the same name as the function FOO."
```

But this won't necessarily work for standard functions or variables. Also, a good implementation will be able to provide much more information and a good IDE will make it easier to get at this information (see below).

How It Works

Let's switch to SLIME (see Recipe 16-2) to see the functionality a Lisp IDE typically offers. Some of this is not covered by the standard, but the necessary information is available in practically every Lisp implementation.

Assuming you have the code from above loaded, type this (and only this) into the SLIME REPL

```
(bar
```

so that the cursor is right behind the last character. You now have available, for example, one of these actions:

- Invoke the command `slime-documentation` (not bound to a key by default) to see the function's documentation string, and some additional information, in a separate buffer.
- Type *M-.* (for `slime-edit-definition`) to jump to where `BAR` was defined. You can now see the source code, and as a part of it, also the docstring.[28]

  If you try this with `FOO` instead of `BAR`, SLIME will offer you the choice of editing either the function's or the variable's definition.

[28]Which probably is the reason that `slime-documentation` isn't used that often and doesn't have a default key binding. Be aware, though, that it is technically possible to us `(SETF DOCUMENTATION)` to add a docstring to a function without this string being visible anywhere near the function's definition.

Of course, for this to work, the compiler has to *know* where the object you are examining was defined. This is generally not a problem for your own code (if your definitions came from a file and weren't executed in the REPL, that is), but typically won't work for standard functions or macros. However, with some open source Lisps, you can do that. For example, with SBCL, I downloaded the source tarball matching the version I'm currently using, unpacked it into the `/opt/` directory of my Linux machine, resulting in a directory `/opt/sbcl-1.2.13/`, and then added this to SBCL's init file (see Recipe 22-5):[29]

```
(setf (logical-pathname-translations "SYS")
      '(("SYS:SRC;**;*.*.*"
         #p"/opt/sbcl-1.2.13/src/**/*.*")
        ("SYS:CONTRIB;**;*.*.*"
         #p"/opt/sbcl-1.2.13/contrib/**/*.*")))
```

I can now, for example, type *M-.* while the cursor is on `TRANSLATE-LOGICAL-PATHNAME` and see how this function is implemented in SBCL.

- Type the *Space* key and the function's argument list will be shown in the echo area. This is a helpful feature if you, for example, forgot the exact order of arguments or the available keyword arguments for a function (assuming the function's author used meaningful names for these parameters).

  This not only works for functions, but also for macros, classes, conditions, and so forth. For example, type

  ```
  (make-condition 'type-error
  ```

  followed by the *Space* key.

Accessing the HyperSpec

While the HyperSpec provides meticulous information about standard functions, variables, macros, and so on, not all of this is typically available as part of your image. But SLIME can help you with that. For example, type

```
(multiple-value-bind
```

into the REPL[30] and then type *C-c C-d h* (for `slime-hyperspec-lookup`). This should open your web browser and show the HyperSpec dictionary entry for `MULTIPLE-VALUE-BIND`. There's also `hyperspec-lookup-format` to look up *format directives* (see

[29]These are translations for *logical pathnames*; see Recipe 15-15.

[30]If you really typed the whole name into the REPL, you still need to familiarize yourself more with SLIME. You should have typed instead something like "`(m-v-b`" followed by the *Tab* key (for `slime-indent-and-complete-symbol`).

Chapter 9) and `hyperspec-lookup-reader-macro` to look up *reader macros* (see Chapter 8).

One tiny flaw is that there'll be an Internet connection for each lookup. But you can customize this function (see its documentation) and use a local copy (see page XXIV) of the HyperSpec instead.

You also might want to check out the redirect service at `http://l1sp.org/` (brought to you by Zach Beane of QUICKLISP fame), which covers the HyperSpec and various other sources of COMMON LISP information.

Cross-Reference Information

SLIME can also provide extensive *cross-reference* information. To see what this means, type

```
(bar
```

and then *C-c C-w c* (for `slime-who-calls`) to be offered a list of source locations where the function `BAR` is called. (In this case, it's only called from within `FOO`.) Likewise, you could type

```
foo
```

and then *C-c C-w b* (for `slime-who-binds`) to see that the *function* `FOO` binds the *variable* `FOO`.

There's more like this. Type *C-h a* (for `apropos-command`) and then enter

```
slime.*\(who\|calle\)
```

to see all the cross-reference commands that SLIME offers.

16-7. Inspecting and Modifying (Compound) Objects

Problem

You want detailed information about a Lisp object, specifically about its constituents, and maybe you also want to modify it.

(See Recipe 16-6 for how to get information about things like functions or classes, which are typically *defined* in *source code*.)

Solution

The standard offers two functions for this task. The first one is DESCRIBE:[31]

```
CL-USER> (describe (make-condition 'type-error
                                   :expected-type 'string
                                   :datum #\X))
#<TYPE-ERROR expected-type: STRING datum: #\X>
  [condition]
Slots with :INSTANCE allocation:
  DATUM          = #\X
  EXPECTED-TYPE  = STRING
; No value
CL-USER> (describe (let ((hash-table (make-hash-table)))
                     (setf (gethash 42 hash-table) 23)
                     hash-table))
#<HASH-TABLE :TEST EQL :COUNT 1 {100495E4D3}>
  [hash-table]
Occupancy: 0.1
Rehash-threshold: 1.0
Rehash-size: 1.5
Size: 16
Synchronized: no
; No value
```

The other, more powerful, function is INSPECT, which we'll discuss below.

How It Works

The job of DESCRIBE is to print *information* about its argument, which can be any Lisp object, to *STANDARD-OUTPUT* (or to another stream provided as its second argument). The information should be as useful and detailed as possible without overwhelming you, but what exactly you'll get depends very much on your implementation.[32]

DESCRIBE is deliberately non-interactive because there's another function to provide information, which is by definition interactive; that's INSPECT. The purpose of the *inspector* started by INSPECT is that you can see a fixed set of information about an object, and that you can also "dig down" into it (which specifically makes sense for

[31]Output, which is obviously implementation-dependent, is from SBCL with a couple of empty lines removed.

[32]Except for your own CLOS objects where you can influence DESCRIBE's output with your own DESCRIBE-OBJECT method similar to what you can do with PRINT-OBJECT (see Recipe 9-8).

compound objects like lists, arrays, hash tables, structures, CLOS objects, etc.) and modify it.

The text-based inspectors offered by most Lisps work a bit similarly to text-based debuggers (see Recipe 16-3). You are in a special mode where you still have some kind of REPL, but with additional (shortcut) commands. And as with the debuggers, you can usually use something like `:?` or `?` to ask for help.

As an example, let's briefly look at an inspector session in LispWorks:[33]

```
CL-USER 1 > (defparameter *thing*
              (vector :lp (list 20 "Hotels") 1971))
*THING*
CL-USER 2 > (inspect *thing*)                            ;; (I)
;; some output elided
#(:LP (20 "Hotels") 1971) is a (SIMPLE-VECTOR 3)
0      :LP
1      (20 "Hotels")
2      1971
CL-USER 3 : Inspect 1 > 1                                ;; (II)
(20 "Hotels") is a LIST
0      20
1      "Hotels"
CL-USER 4 : Inspect 2 > (list $ $$)                      ;; (III)
((20 "Hotels") #(:LP (20 "Hotels") 1971))
CL-USER 5 : Inspect 2 > (setf (first $) 200)             ;; (IV)
200
CL-USER 6 : Inspect 2 > 1                                ;; (V)
"Hotels" is a SIMPLE-BASE-STRING
0      #\H
1      #\o
2      #\t
3      #\e
4      #\l
5      #\s
CL-USER 7 : Inspect 3 > :s 0 #\M                         ;; (VI)
CL-USER 8 : Inspect 3 > :q                               ;; (VII)
"Motels"
CL-USER 9 > *thing*
#(:LP (200 "Motels") 1971)                               ;; (VIII)
```

[33]Inspectors vary wildly between different implementations, so probably none of what you're seeing here will work exactly like this in another Lisp. You'll have to consult the documentation.

Also, LispWorks has a second, graphical inspector, which is very nice but it obviously wouldn't make much sense to demonstrate it here.

And here's a bit of explanation:

(I) We start the inspector. The *vector* `*THING*` has three elements, which the inspector displays as three *slots* with numbers. The prompt then shows that we're in the inspector.

(II) By entering the number `1`, we tell it that we want to go "one level deeper;" that is, start an inspector recursively for the contents of the second slot. The next prompt will show the new level.

(III) The variables `$`, `$$`, and `$$$` work like `*` and friends (see Recipe 16-11), except that they keep track of the last three inspected objects.

(IV) We can evaluate arbitrary Lisp forms and modify the inspected object.

(V) We again select one of the slots to "dig deeper."

(VI) To change the value of one of the current slots, we use a special inspector command (instead of a standard Lisp form).

(VII) We leave the inspector.

(VIII) We have actually modified the object we inspected.

The SLIME Inspector

SLIME has its own inspector, which has an Emacs-based "graphical user interface." To enter it, you either press *C-c I* (for `slime-inspect`) and enter an expression, the value of which will be inspected, or you right-click the *presentation* (see also page 501) of an object and select *Inspect* from the menu you'll get. (Note that a typical way of entering the inspector also is via the debugger.)

You are now in a special mode with several one-key shortcuts which is similar to SLDB (see page 476) and should be pretty self-explanatory once you've understood what the basic job of an inspector is. Again, you should familiarize yourself with this tool, as you'll likely use it fairly often in the future.

16-8. Browsing Your Lisp Image

Problem

You want to use a function but you don't remember its name.

Solution

The standard function APROPOS can help you with that:[34]

```
? (apropos "odd")
 CCL::%BIGNUM-ODDP, Def: FUNCTION
X8632::FULLTAG-ODD-FIXNUM,  Value: 4
X8664::FULLTAG-ODD-FIXNUM,  Value: 8
  CCL::ODD-KEYS-ERROR, Def: FUNCTION
      :ODD-KEYWORDS,  Value: :ODD-KEYWORDS
  CCL::ODDEXP
       ODDP, Def: FUNCTION
 CCL::$XODDSETQ,  Value: 17
? (apropos :odd :cl)
ODDP, Def: FUNCTION
? (apropos-list "odd" :cl)
(ODDP)
```

How It Works

APROPOS will print a list of all symbols that contain, ignoring case, a given substring. As we could see above, the output will usually provide a bit of additional information about the symbol, although that's at your Lisp's discretion. The second example shows that we can restrict the output to the symbols accessible in a specific package and that the first argument is a *string designator* (see Recipe 1-9).

APROPOS-LIST answers the same question as APROPOS, but instead of printing it, it'll give you a list of the symbols found for further processing.

So, if you remember at least a part of a function's or a variable's name or if, say, you suspect that your image should have a macro with "tensor" in its name, this standard function will help you.

Alternatives

The function PPCRE:REGEX-APROPOS of the CL-PPCRE library (see Recipe 18-6) accepts *regular expressions* instead of just substrings, so you can do things like this:

```
? (ppcre:regex-apropos "lo.*lo.*la" :cl)
LOAD-LOGICAL-PATHNAME-TRANSLATIONS [compiled function]
```

[34]The output is obviously implementation-dependent. In this particular case, it's from CLOZURECL.

SLIME has its own replacement for APROPOS, which is quite nice. You invoke it with *C-c C-d a* (for slime-apropos) and as a result, you'll get the list of symbols in a buffer where you can press *Return* on each of them for more information.

Finally, the LISPWORKS IDE has a graphical "Apropos Dialog" and several so-called "browsers," which are tools to find things like symbols, classes, or methods in various other ways.

16-9. "Undoing" Definitions

Problem

You want to "undefine" something that you have defined, like a function, a macro, a variable, a class, a condition, and so forth.

Solution

The standard offers some rudimentary functionality to "undo" definitions:[35]

- Use FMAKUNBOUND to remove the association between a function and its name:

```
? (defun my-add (x) (+ x x))
MY-ADD
? (fmakunbound 'my-add)
MY-ADD
? (my-add 3)
> Error: Undefined function MY-ADD called with arguments (3) .
;; etc.
```

  Note that the *function* itself might still be there, though:

```
? (defun my-add (x) (+ x x))
MY-ADD
? (defparameter my-add-fn #'my-add)
MY-ADD-FN
? (fmakunbound 'my-add)
MY-ADD
? (funcall my-add-fn 21)
42
```

[35]The output shown below is from CLOZURECL, but the results should be the same in any Lisp.

- Use MAKUNBOUND to make a symbol unbound:[36]

```
? (defvar *foo* 42)
*FOO*
? (makunbound '*foo*)
*FOO*
? *foo*
> Error: Unbound variable: *FOO*
;; etc.
```

- You can use REMOVE-METHOD to remove a method from a generic function. Consider the following definitions:

```
(defmethod my-length ((x list))
  (length x))

(defmethod my-length ((x symbol))
  (length (symbol-name x)))
```

This will implicitly generate a *generic function* called MY-LENGTH, which you can completely undefine using FMAKUNBOUND. But if you only want to, say, remove the first method, you have to proceed like so:

```
? (find-method #'my-length nil '(list))
#<STANDARD-METHOD MY-LENGTH (LIST)>
? (remove-method #'my-length *)
#<STANDARD-GENERIC-FUNCTION MY-LENGTH #x302000FC15AF>
? (my-length 'foo)
3
? (my-length '(f o o))
> Error: There is no applicable method for the generic function:
>           #<STANDARD-GENERIC-FUNCTION MY-LENGTH #x302000FC15AF>
>         when called with arguments:
>           ((F O O))
;; etc.
```

So, you first have to *find* the method—given its generic function, a list of its specializer arguments, and a list of its qualifiers (that's the NIL part above)—and you can then remove it. This is obviously a bit unwieldy compared to what we had to do for functions.

- You can remove the association between a class and its name using (SETF FIND-CLASS):

[36]So, FMAKUNBOUND modifies the *function cell* of a symbol while MAKUNBOUND modifies its *value cell*; see Chapter 1.

```
? (defclass my-class ()
    ((a :initform 42 :reader a)))
#<STANDARD-CLASS MY-CLASS>
? (defvar *a* (make-instance 'my-class))
*A*
? (find-class 'my-class)
#<STANDARD-CLASS MY-CLASS>
? (setf (find-class 'my-class) nil)
NIL
? (make-instance 'my-class)
> Error: Class named MY-CLASS not found.
;; etc.
```

However, the class will still be there and it will still "work." You can even continue creating new objects of this class:

```
;; continued from above
? *a*
#<An instance of #<STANDARD-CLASS MY-CLASS> #x302000F1102D>
? (class-of *)
#<STANDARD-CLASS MY-CLASS>
? (a *a*)
42
? (make-instance **)
#<An instance of #<STANDARD-CLASS MY-CLASS> #x302000F0264D>
```

You might also want to look up the functions `BOUNDP` and `FBOUNDP` in the HyperSpec.

How It Works

We have seen above that some of the definitions were not *completely* undone in a sense we might have envisioned. For that, you'll need the help of your implementation. We'll use LISPWORKS as an example here because it provides comprehensive and convenient undefinition support for pretty much everything:

In its IDE, navigate to a definition and invoke the editor command *Undefine*.[37] You can also invoke it with a prefix argument to ask it to show you what it *would* do to undo your definition. I've done that for a couple of cases below; each definition is followed by its own "undefinition," as inserted by the LISPWORKS editor:

```
(defvar *foo* 42)
;; (PROGN
```

[37] As of September 2015 SLIME doesn't have a comparable feature as general as this one.

```
;;   (SYSTEM::UNPROCLAIM '(SPECIAL *FOO*))
;;   (MAKUNBOUND '*FOO*))

(defun my-add (x) (+ x x))
;; (WHEN-LET (SYSTEM::REAL-SPEC (DSPEC:DSPEC-DEFINED-P '#'MY-ADD))
;;   (EVAL (DSPEC:DSPEC-UNDEFINER SYSTEM::REAL-SPEC)))

(defmethod my-length ((x list))
  (length x))
;; (CLOS::UNDEFMETHOD MY-LENGTH (LIST))

(define-condition my-error (error) ())
;; (CLOS::UNDEFCLASS MY-ERROR)

(defclass my-class ()
  ((a :initform 42 :reader a)))
;; (CLOS::UNDEFCLASS MY-CLASS)
```

Check your documentation for the equivalent forms in your Lisp.

16-10. Distinguishing Your IDE's Streams

Problem

Your program's output doesn't end up where it was supposed to end up. (And where exactly does its input come from?)

Solution

In addition to the well-known *STANDARD-OUTPUT* and *STANDARD-INPUT*, there are several more streams defined by the standard. Here's a little experiment to show some of them in action:

```
CL-USER> (defun foo (x) x)
FOO
CL-USER> (trace foo)
NIL
CL-USER> (with-output-to-string (*standard-output*)
           (with-input-from-string (*standard-input*
                                      (format nil "n~%"))
             (print (y-or-n-p "Do You Like My New Car?"))
             (foo 42)
```

```
          (warn "Achtung!")
          (print (read))))
Do You Like My New Car? (y or n)  y                        ;; I typed this

0> Calling (FOO 42)
<0 FOO returned 42
; Warning: Achtung!
; While executing: #<Anonymous Function #x3020012D74AF>, ...
"
T
N "
```

So, although we *redirected* (see Recipe 14-1) standard output and standard input, the following things happened:

(i) The question of the `Y-OR-N-P` form was shown in the REPL and the answer was read from the keyboard.

(ii) The output of tracing (see Recipe 16-4) `FOO` was shown in the REPL.

(iii) The warning (see Recipe 12-4) was shown in the REPL.

The only output that was actually redirected was that of the two calls to `PRINT`. `READ` read the character `#\n` from the string stream because it apparently wasn't used as input by `Y-OR-NO-P`.

The reason for this behavior is that all the functions we used by default operate on different streams. See below.

How It Works

The standard defines seven streams for various purposes:

Stream	I/O	Usage
`*standard-input*`	I	normal input, default for `READ` etc.
`*standard-output*`	O	normal output, default for `WRITE` etc.
`*error-output*`	O	for warnings and error messages
`*trace-output*`	O	for tracing (see Recipe 16-4)
`*query-io*`	I/O	for user interaction like `Y-OR-NO-P`
`*debug-io*`	I/O	for debugging (see Recipe 16-3)
`*terminal-io*`	I/O	implementation-dependent (see below)

For most of these streams, their names already explain what they're for quite clearly. And it should now be obvious why the redirections in our example "didn't work;"

we simply redirected the wrong streams.

What exactly `*TERMINAL-IO*` is will certainly differ from Lisp to Lisp and from OS to OS, but in a console session (outside of SLIME), it is not uncommon to see something like this:[38]

```
CL-USER 1 > (list *standard-output* *standard-input*)
(#<Synonym stream to *TERMINAL-IO*>
 #<Synonym stream to *TERMINAL-IO*>)
```

In fact, in a console session *all* of the streams listed above will probably be "the same stream" initially. The situation might become more complicated in IDEs (see Recipe 16-2) because they will usually redirect some of these streams.

You might also want to read what Recipe 11-3 has to say about the interaction between multithreading, IDEs, and the standard streams.

16-11. Utilizing the REPL's Memory

Problem

During interactive development, you want to reuse the return value(s) of the last form you evaluated or the form itself.

Solution

Your Lisp is required to keep track of the recent history of your interaction with the REPL in a couple of global special variables:

```
CL-USER> (floor 42 4)
10
2
CL-USER> :foo
:FOO
CL-USER> (parse-integer "42  ")
42
4
CL-USER> (list * ** *** / // /// + ++ +++ -)
;; output edited for legibility
(42 :FOO 10                                             ;; * ** ***
 (42 4) (:FOO) (10 2)                                   ;; / // ///
```

[38]See page 399 for *synonym streams*.

```
(PARSE-INTEGER "42  ") :FOO (FLOOR 42 4)                    ;; + ++ +++
(LIST * ** *** / // /// + ++ +++ -))                        ;; -
```

How It Works

It's pretty easy (once you realize that things like * or / are "just symbols" in COMMON LISP and can thus be variables). Whenever you evaluate a form in the REPL, the return value is stored in the variable *.

** and *** then work together with *, like the top of a *stack* (see Recipe 2-9). When the *next* form is evaluated, its return value is stored in *, but only *after* the previous value of * went into **. Before that, the previous value of ** was transferred to ***. (That variable, finally, just loses its old value.)

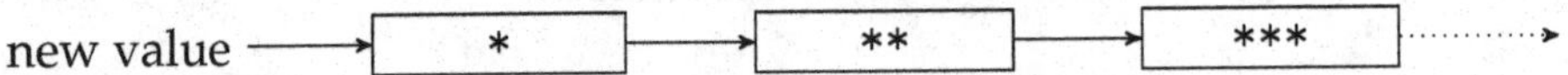

If you're dealing with forms that return multiple values (like FLOOR or PARSE-INTEGER above), * only keeps track of the first one. However, / will keep a *list* of all values returned (and there's a stack like with *).

While * and / take care of *output*, + remembers your *input*; that is, the actual *form* you entered. Finally, - is the form that is *currently* evaluated.

* and friends are probably the most helpful of these variables, as you can, for example, use them for iterative computations with intermediate results, akin to what you'd do with an RPN calculator. As a silly example, let's compute $x^2 + 5x - 3$ for $x = -\frac{3}{4}$:

```
CL-USER> -3/4
-3/4
CL-USER> (* 5 *)
-15/4
CL-USER> (* ** **)
9/16
CL-USER> (+ * ** -3)
-99/16
```

IDE History Features

Whereas * and / are often quite useful,[39] + is clumsy at best if you want to evaluate the last form or something similar again. Luckily, every self-respecting Lisp IDE

[39]But see the comment on page 707 about the interaction of these variables with the garbage collector.

(see Recipe 16-2) will offer a feature like SLIME's *M-p* (for `slime-repl-previous-input`), which you can use to bring back to the REPL prompt all the forms you previously entered so that you can evaluate them again (or edit them before doing that).[40]

And you can simply navigate the REPL buffer, go to a form you previously entered, maybe edit it, and then press *Return* to evaluate it again.

As a generalization of COMMON LISP's `*`, `**`, and `***`, you might also want to read what the SLIME manual has to say about *presentations*, an idea SLIME borrowed from the Lisp Machines.

16-12. Recording Your Work

Problem

You want to keep a "protocol" of what you did in the REPL.

Solution

That's what the standard function `DRIBBLE` is for:[41]

```
CL-USER 1 > (handler-case
                (delete-file "/tmp/my-dribble")
              (file-error ()))
NIL
CL-USER 2 > (dribble "/tmp/my-dribble")
;; some output elided
CL-USER 3 > (+ 40 2)
42
CL-USER 4 > (print *)
42
42
CL-USER 5 > (dribble)
; Closed dribble to "/tmp/my-dribble"
CL-USER 6 > (with-open-file (in "/tmp/my-dribble")
              (loop for line = (read-line in nil)
                    while line
                    do (format t "DRIBBLE: ~A~%" line)))
DRIBBLE: CL-USER 3 > (+ 40 2)
DRIBBLE: 42
```

[40] And if for some reason you have to work from the console, you should at least consider using something like `rlwrap`.

[41] Output from a LISPWORKS session with a couple of empty lines removed for brevity.

```
DRIBBLE: CL-USER 4 > (print *)
DRIBBLE: 42
DRIBBLE: 42
DRIBBLE: CL-USER 5 > (dribble)
NIL
```

The first form just makes sure that we start with an empty file (see Recipe 15-7) and we don't get an error message in case the file doesn't exist (see Recipe 12-5). The DRIBBLE form then opens the file and somehow arranges (see Recipes 14-1 and 14-5) that all I/O going through *STANDARD-INPUT* and *STANDARD-OUTPUT*[42] is written to that file. This is done until we call DRIBBLE again without an argument.

How It Works

So much for the theory. In practice, though, this is one of the areas where the SLIME approach isn't such a good fit. In some Lisps, at least from within SLIME, DRIBBLE either doesn't work at all or only with certain restrictions.

[42]But see Recipe 16-10.

17. Optimization

When I was younger, I learned somewhere the *Three Golden Rules of Optimization*. They are as follows:

I. Don't do it!

II. Don't do it!

III. Only for experts: Don't do it (yet).

I still think this is the most important advice you can give concerning optimization. Way too many people spend way too much time optimizing code although they shouldn't—or at least they're optimizing in all the wrong places. And optimization is not only useless work 99% of the time, it also usually makes the code harder to read and maintain and can introduce bugs.

So, in a way you shouldn't read this chapter at all. Or only if you you're absolutely sure that you really, really need it. And then you should start with Recipes 17-1 and 17-2 and maybe reconsider...

Nevertheless, this chapter is one of the longest of the book. This doesn't mean that I just ate my words from the previous paragraph. But optimization is a vast topic and it touches several complicated issues that have to be properly explained. Also, although lots of Lisp books were written in the 1980s and 1990s, there don't seem to be many that deal with optimization.[1] And if they do, the advice is probably outdated. So, hopefully, this long chapter helps to fill a void.

Also, although you can also optimize for *space*, this chapter is almost exclusively about optimizing for *speed* (which I gather is what most readers will be interested in). Space is rarely a problem these days, and if it is, you will most likely have to look at your data structures in a more general way that is not specific to Lisp. However, you might want to have a look at Recipe 17-14.

[1]One exception, which in my opinion is still worth reading, is Peter Norvig's *Paradigms of Aritificial Intelligence* (Morgan Kaufmann, 1992), often simply called *PAIP*.

17-1. Understanding the Importance of the Right Algorithms

Problem

You suspect that your program is too slow and you want to find out why.

Solution

The following function computes the sum of the numbers 1 to *n*:

```
(defun sum (n)
  (loop for i from 1 to n
        sum i))
```

Something like (sum 1000000000) will already take quite a while, and with some aggressive optimizations (of which more in the rest of this chapter), you might be able to speed it up maybe by a factor of two; for example, if you promise that all numbers involved in the computation will be fixnums (see Recipe 4-2). However, a much, much better "optimization" would be to use a different algorithm:[2]

```
(defun sum (n)
  (* 1/2 n (1+ n)))
```

How It Works

In case that seemed too banal, let's use a more interesting example. You are given a graph like this one:

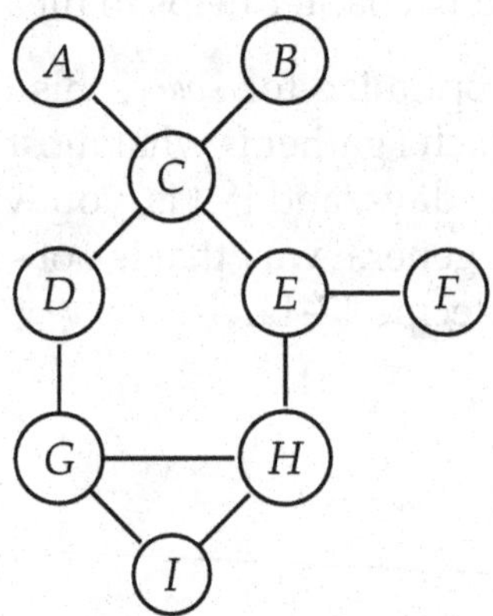

[2]You knew that, didn't you? See http://mathworld.wolfram.com/ArithmeticSeries.html.

Your job is to find a so-called *vertex cover* (a set of vertices such that each edge coincides with at least one of your selected vertices), which is as small as possible.[3] In this particular case, a possible solution would be $\{C, E, G, H\}$.

It is moderately easy to hack up a solution to this problem in a few lines that iterates through all sets of vertices in order of increasing size and stops once it has found a vertex cover. However, such a solution will have a time complexity worse than $\mathcal{O}(2^n)$ and cease to be usable once n (the number of vertices in your graph) exceeds a relatively small threshold.[4]

Now, as a true Lisper maybe in your first prototype you encoded the sets of vertices as lists and see some potential in using bit patterns instead (see Recipe 6-10). And indeed, you'll probably be able to speed up your code by a significant factor if you use a different representation and add some declarations in the right places. However, this won't change enough to really make a difference for larger n...

On the other hand, with a little bit of research, you'll find out that there are more sophisticated algorithms (although still quite easy to implement) for the same problem with a complexity of around $\mathcal{O}(1.7^n)$ or better. For, say, $n = 100$ that'd mean that such an algorithm could be more than a million times faster than your original one, no matter how much time you'd have spent optimizing it!

The point I'm trying to drive home here is that you should always think hard about algorithms (and data structures) first before getting your hands dirty with low-level optimizations. Optimization can (and often will) make code faster, but it will never turn bad code into good code!

17-2. Deciding If and Where to Optimize

Problem

You have read Recipe 17-1 and you *still* suspect that your program is too slow. You want to find out where it spends most of the time.

Solution

First, check if you have compiled your code. It may sound ridiculous, but my guess is that almost every Lisper with enough experience has, at least once in his career,

[3] This is a well-known problem from graph theory; see for example `http://mathworld.wolfram.com/VertexCover.html`.

[4] The *Landau notation*—the "$\mathcal{O}$"—used here is explained at `http://en.wikipedia.org/wiki/Big_O_notation`.

fretted about some "slow" code, only to find out after some tinkering that the code wasn't compiled.[5]

Once you're sure that interpreted code isn't the reason, you should start *measuring*. For this recipe, we'll use the following nonsense code,[6] the main purpose of which is to burn CPU cycles and to make it not too obvious where exactly this is happening:

```
(defpackage :foo
  (:use :cl)
  (:export :main))

(in-package :foo)

(defun foo-1 (n)
  (loop for i below (* 1000 n) maximize i))

(defun foo-2 (n)
  (loop for i below n sum i))

(defun foo-3 (n)
  (loop for i below n sum (foo-2 i)))

(defun bar-1 (n)
  (loop for i below n sum (foo-1 i)))

(defun bar-2 (n)
  (loop for i below n sum (foo-3 i)))

(defun baz-1 (n)
  (bar-2 (* 10 n)))

(defun baz-2 (n)
  (if (zerop n)
      (baz-1 1)
      (+ (bar-1 n) (baz-2 (1- n)))))

(defun main (n)
  (loop for i below n
        sum (+ (baz-1 i) (baz-2 i))))
```

[5]Of course, this doesn't apply to Lisp implementations that always compile their code like CLOZURECL or its ancestor MACINTOSH COMMON LISP.

[6]Many Lispers, including me, consider it good style to put `DEFPACKAGE` forms into separate files; see for example page 272 of *Practical Common Lisp*. I'm deviating from this here only for the sake of brevity.

Enter this code into a file, then compile (!) and load it. Now enter this into your REPL:

```
(time (foo:main 40))
```

We'll be using SBCL throughout the whole recipe.[7] On my 64-bit Linux machine, I see the following:

```
CL-USER> (time (foo:main 40))
Evaluation took:
  2.446 seconds of real time
  2.446628 seconds of total run time (2.446628 user, 0.000000 system)
  100.04% CPU
  5,855,347,068 processor cycles
  37,472 bytes consed
7958996320
```

This already gives you quite a bit of information (about which more below). But essentially, you now only have quantitative data about the overall behavior of your program or one specific function.

You want more fine-grained information. And for that, you should enlist the help of a *profiler*. Read on...

How It Works

As an application of the so-called *Pareto principle*, it is to be expected that in a typical program more than 80% of the execution time is spent in less than 20% of the code.[8] Which is to say that if you are serious about optimization, then your first task should be to find out where exactly these 20% are; that is, where your code spends most of its time. (Because optimizing the other 80% of your code will likely not buy you anything at all.)

That's what *profilers* are for; they are tools that monitor code while it's running and they can afterward deliver a report about which parts were employed and for how long. They usually come in two flavors.[9]

[7] Because it has two different built-in profilers which we can use to demonstrate two different approaches to profiling.

[8] And if you apply this estimate again on these 20%, then more than 64% of the execution time will concentrate on only 4% or less of your code.

[9] There are other profiling strategies (see `http://en.wikipedia.org/wiki/Profiling_%28computer_programming%29`), but I think statistical profiling and instrumentation (also called *deterministic profiling*) are dominant in COMMON LISP.

Instrumentation

The rough idea for the first type of profiler is as follows. Modify each function you're interested in in such a way that when the function is entered as well as when it returns you have a chance to intervene and do some bookkeeping. At the very least you can "look at a stopwatch" in both cases and thus figure out how long the function ran. You can also maintain a tally of how often the function was called. If FOO is such a function, then what's happening before and after FOO is executed will conceptually look like this:

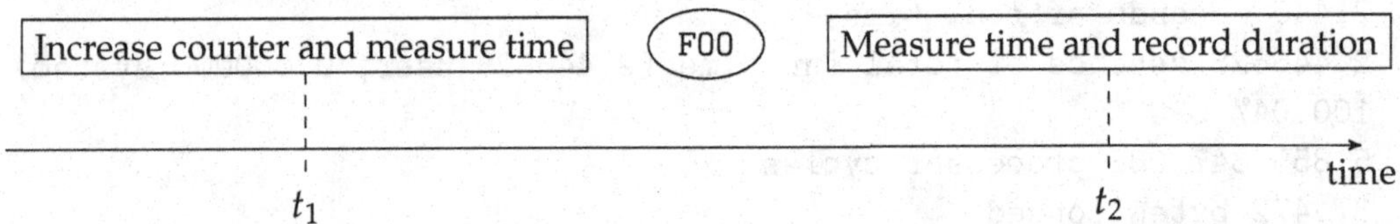

And after FOO has returned, we can make a note that the time it took was $t_2 - t_1$.

In theory, you could write such a profiler yourself in just a few lines. Peter Seibel demonstrated a very rudimentary draft in *Practical Common Lisp* and Peter Norvig already showed a more sophisticated approach in *Paradigms of Artificial Intelligence* in 1992. What these two (as well as related profilers[10]) are doing is called *instrumentation.*

Let's use this technique to investigate our code from above. First, we instrument it:

```
CL-USER> (profile "FOO")
; No value
CL-USER> (profile)
(FOO::FOO-3 FOO::BAR-2 FOO::FOO-1 FOO::FOO-2
 FOO::BAZ-1 FOO::BAZ-2 FOO::BAR-1 FOO:MAIN)
```

We called the macro PROFILE with the string "FOO" as its only argument, which means that we want all functions with names in the package named "FOO" to be instrumented. We then called PROFILE again without arguments and we were shown a list of all functions instrumented so far. We can also feed PROFILE several arguments at once or we can use symbols instead of strings to selectively name individual functions. So, we could have achieved the same effect like so:[11]

```
(profile foo::foo-3 foo::bar-2 foo::foo-1 foo::foo-2
         foo::baz-1 foo::baz-2 foo::bar-1 foo:main)
```

[10]There's a portable open source profiler available from http://www.cs.cmu.edu/afs/cs/project/ai-repository/ai/lang/lisp/code/tools/metering/0.html. It hasn't been maintained since 1994 but apparently it still works as intended in a couple of modern COMMON LISP implementations.

[11]Note that the symbols aren't evaluated and thus must not be quoted.

Now we actually run the (modified) code and afterward ask for a report:

```
CL-USER> (foo:main 40)
7958996320
CL-USER> (report)
measuring PROFILE overhead..done
  seconds  |     gc     | consed |    calls    |  sec/call  |  name
-------------------------------------------------------------------
     1.267 |      0.000 |      0 |      10,660 |   0.000119 | FOO::FOO-1
     1.071 |      0.000 |      0 |   1,024,900 |   0.000001 | FOO::FOO-2
     0.107 |      0.000 |      0 |       8,200 |   0.000013 | FOO::FOO-3
     0.003 |      0.000 |      0 |         780 |   0.000004 | FOO::BAR-1
     0.000 |      0.000 |      0 |          80 |   0.000000 | FOO::BAR-2
     0.000 |      0.000 |      0 |          80 |   0.000000 | FOO::BAZ-1
     0.000 |      0.000 |      0 |         820 |   0.000000 | FOO::BAZ-2
     0.000 |      0.000 |      0 |           1 |   0.000000 | FOO:MAIN
-------------------------------------------------------------------
     2.449 |      0.000 |      0 |   1,045,521 |            | Total

estimated total profiling overhead: 0.88 seconds
overhead estimation parameters:
  8.000001e-9s/call, 8.4399994e-7s total profiling,
  3.84e-7s internal profiling
; No value
```

Let's concentrate on the first, fourth, and last column. We now see very clearly what probably wasn't so obvious before, namely that `FOO-2` is the function that is called far more often than any other function, but that most of the time is spent while we're within function `FOO-1` (although it's "only" called about 10,000 times).

In a real-world situation, we would now already have a pretty good idea about which functions we should have a closer look at; and probably even more importantly, which functions we should *not* bother to optimize.

Let's not forget to restore our code to its original form:[12]

```
CL-USER> (unprofile "FOO")
; No value
CL-USER> (profile)
NIL
```

This is already very helpful, but it also has some disadvantages. One is that you have to actively modify (and later un-modify) your code. Another one is that you'll only

[12]There's also **RESET** to reset all counters and all the timing information. If you don't reset, you'll get cumulative results if you repeatedly execute code.

get data about code you *can* modify, so, for example, not about standard or internal functions. And finally, the modification of the code might in some cases adulterate your results. (See the output above about profiling *overhead*.)

Statistical Profiling

That's why some Lisp implementations also come with a built-in *statistical profiler*. To understand what they are doing, we have to briefly contemplate the role of the *call stack*. Whenever a function is called, the Lisp system puts some information on this stack, which includes, among other things, function parameters, local variables, and the address to return to once the function is finished. All this information together is called a *stack frame* and it stays on the stack as long as the function is executing and is removed once it's finished.[13]

So, when in our toy code `MAIN` is called, a `MAIN` stack frame is created. Then from within `MAIN` the function `BAZ-1` is called, so we have a stack frame for `BAZ-1` on top of the previous one (because `MAIN` hasn't finished yet). `BAZ-1` calls `BAR-2`, which results in another stack frame, and so on. At a certain point in time, the stack could look like this (with the most recent stack frame at the top):[14]

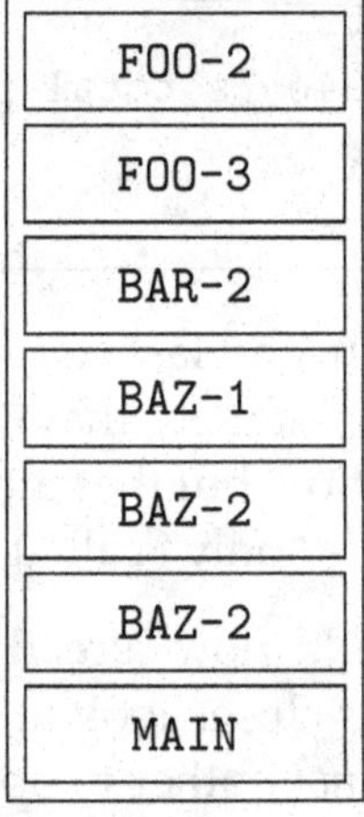

A statistical profiler now just takes "snapshots" of the call stack at regular intervals and records what it has seen.[15] All functions that are on the call stack are currently executing, so if a function is seen very often during those snapshots, it does a lot of work. On the other hand, only the function on the top of the stack is actually doing

[13]A Lisp system might typically pack more data into a stack frame. See what Chapter 16 has to say about the *dynamic environment*

[14]Note that `BAZ-2` appears twice because it called itself recursively.

[15]Which makes it obvious that while it's moderately easy to write a deterministic profiler in portable COMMON LISP, a statistical profiler can only be implemented with intimate knowledge of the inner workings of a specific Lisp.

something, while the other functions on the stack are technically executing but are really only waiting for the function they called.

Let's see how our code looks from this point of view:

```
CL-USER> (require :sb-sprof)
("SB-SPROF")
CL-USER> (sb-sprof:with-profiling (:report :flat)
           (foo:main 40))

Number of samples:   244
Sample interval:     0.01 seconds
Total sampling time: 2.44 seconds
Number of cycles:    0
Sampled threads:
 #<SB-THREAD:THREAD "repl-thread" RUNNING {1003B18033}>

           Self        Total        Cumul
  Nr  Count     %  Count     %  Count     %  Calls  Function
------------------------------------------------------------------------
   1     86  35.2     86  35.2     86  35.2      -  SB-VM::GENERIC-+
   2     83  34.0     83  34.0    169  69.3      -  FOO::FOO-1
   3     73  29.9     73  29.9    242  99.2      -  FOO::FOO-2
   4      2   0.8    118  48.4    244 100.0      -  FOO::FOO-3
   5      0   0.0    244 100.0    244 100.0      -  FOO:MAIN
;; lots of lines elided
  29      0   0.0    126  51.6    244 100.0      -  FOO::BAR-1
  30      0   0.0    126  51.6    244 100.0      -  FOO::BAZ-2
  31      0   0.0    118  48.4    244 100.0      -  FOO::BAR-2
------------------------------------------------------------------------
          0   0.0                                   elsewhere
#<SB-SPROF::CALL-GRAPH 244 samples {10039B9E93}>
```

The call to `REQUIRE` was necessary because the statistical profiler isn't loaded by default. The rest is very easy: we just wrap the code to be profiled with `SB-SPROF:WITH-PROFILING` and tell this macro that we want a (certain kind of) report.[16]

What we're interested in here is mainly the column titled "Self," which counts how often the specific function was actually on top of the stack during the 244 snapshots that were taken. As with instrumentation, we see that `FOO-1` is the most "expensive" of our functions, but as a bonus, we see that most of the time our code is actually performing addition. And this is information deterministic profiling can't give us be-

[16]There are a lot more optional arguments (for example how often snapshots are taken or that you want to repeat executing the same code until enough snapshots have been taken), but you'll have to look them up in the documentation.

cause it's about an internal function (`SB-VM::GENERIC-+`) that can't be instrumented.

But if you try this yourself and see the many lines I removed from the output (which came mostly from SLIME), you see one of the disadvantages of a statistical profiler. Because it blindly snapshots stack frames very frequently, it usually collects a lot more information than you actually need. It will sometimes require quite an amount of fine-tuning before you can see the forest for the trees.

Some Things Cannot Be Profiled

Also, be aware that some things can't be profiled. For one, macros can't be profiled because they are expanded during compilation and are gone once the profiler kicks in. A more subtle issue is that compilers sometimes transform code. An example from the LISPWORKS manual is that a form like

```
(member 'x '(x y z) :test #'eq)
```

will be transformed to the internal variant

```
(sys:memq 'x '(x y z))
```

during compilation so you'll never see calls to `MEMBER` in the profiler's output although this might be the most important bottleneck of your application.

Also, it usually doesn't make a lot of sense to profile interpreted code[17] because the profiler will then most of the time be busy profiling the interpreter.

Where to Go From Here

This recipe can only give you a brief glimpse into the abilities of profilers. It was hopefully general enough to be applicable to other COMMON LISP implementations, but you will definitely need to study your Lisp's documentation to learn about all the options you have. One important area that we haven't covered is for example the difference between the interactive profiling we've seen so far and programmatic control of profiling.[18] We also haven't talked about profiling in the presence of multithreaded programs.

And, finally, some Lisps (like LISPWORKS) offer graphical user interfaces to their profilers, which can make it much easier to see what is important and what is not.

[17] And why would you want that in the first place?

[18] In SBCL that would be `SB-SPROF:START-PROFILING` and `SB-SPROF:STOP-PROFILING`.

A Warning About Empirical Data

There's a nice quote from Donald Knuth that goes like this: "Beware of bugs in the above code; I have only proved it correct, not tried it." That's a bit tongue-in-cheek, of course, and it certainly also applies the other way around. In our case, it means that results gleaned from profiling (and especially in the case of statistical profiling) are always only empirical data and shouldn't be mistaken for a mathematical proof. Just because you *believe* you've profiled enough "typical" use cases doesn't mean you really have. And on top of it, it very likely doesn't mean you've tested the worst case. As is almost always the case, you still have to do the thinking yourself.

What Does `TIME` Do?

Although profilers aren't mentioned in the standard, the macro `TIME` that we used for a very crude measurement is required to be present in any COMMON LISP. However, the standard doesn't say much else about it[19] except that it should print information about (at least) "elapsed real time, machine run time, and storage management statistics." And we saw (right at the beginning of this recipe) that it did exactly that.

Try it on your Lisp to see which information you'll get and look at its documentation to find out if maybe there's similar functionality to get at even more information. (For example, LISPWORKS has `HCL:EXTENDED-TIME` which provides a more detailed breakdown of GC activity.)

CPUs Can Deceive You

The CPUs in today's computers are highly complex beasts and very few people (I am certainly not among them) have a full grasp of their performance characteristics. Because of all the optimizations they apply automatically "under the hood," it is sometimes hard to figure out what really happened due to the changes *you* made.

Here's a simple example to illustrate this point, done with SBCL 1.2.12 on a 64-bit Linux system with, according to `/proc/cpuinfo`, a "Quad-Core AMD Opteron(tm) Processor 1385." I started with a fresh image, and compiled and loaded a file with the following contents (see Recipe 17-3 for the meaning of the `DECLARE` form):[20]

```
(in-package :cl-user)

(defvar *l*
  (loop repeat 10000000
```

[19]Because obviously it can't. This is probably one of the most implementation-dependent parts of all of standard COMMON LISP.

[20]During compilation, you will see some chatter ("notes") from the compiler you don't need to care about. More about that in later recipes of this chapter.

```
         collect (random 1d0)))

(defun test-1 ()
  (let ((result 0))
    (map nil (lambda (x)
               (incf result (* 2d0 x))) *l*)
    result))

(defun test-2 ()
  (declare (optimize speed))
  (let ((result 0))
    (map nil (lambda (x)
               (incf result (* 2d0 x))) *l*)
    result))
```

Now I did the following:

```
* (time (test-1))
;; output abbreviated
Evaluation took:
  1.442 seconds of real time
  3,891,046,437 processor cycles
9998625.76219841d0
* (time (test-2))
Evaluation took:
  0.485 seconds of real time
  1,309,117,234 processor cycles
9998625.76219841d0
```

At this point, you're excused to think, "Wow, isn't that great? I asked the compiler to make the function faster and it was immediately sped up by a factor of almost three!"

`test-1`: 1.442 seconds

`test-2`: 0.485 seconds

Except that this is what happened next:

```
* (time (test-1))
Evaluation took:
  0.508 seconds of real time
  1,372,856,056 processor cycles
9998625.76219841d0
```

```
test-1: 1.442 seconds
```

```
test-2: 0.485 seconds
```

```
test-1: 0.508 seconds
```

Huh?!? Why's that? Well, it seems the first run of TEST-1 was used by my machine to "warm up the cache" and only the results seen afterward are really comparable. The lesson to be learned here is that superficial timing results are a dangerous trap to fall into. Real optimizations are hard to achieve and usually require a detailed analysis.

17-3. Asking the Compiler to Optimize

Problem

You want some functions to be faster and you're wondering whether your compiler can't take care of this itself.

Solution

Try *declarations* with *optimize qualities*. Here's a simple example:

```
(in-package :cl-user)

(defconstant +max+ 10000000)

(defvar *a*
  (make-array +max+ :initial-contents (loop repeat +max+
                                            collect (random 1d0))))

(defun test-1 ()
  (loop for i below +max+
        sum (aref *a* i)))

(defun test-2 ()
  (declare (optimize (safety 0)))
  (loop for i below +max+
        sum (aref *a* i)))
```

If I compile and load a file with this code (using SBCL 1.2.12 on a 64-bit Linux system), a careful analysis (see Recipe 17-2) seems to suggest that (TEST-2 +MAX+) is about 5% faster than `(TEST-1 +MAX+)`. Statistical profiling shows that the function that occupies rank 3 of those found most often on top of the call stack has the nice name

```
SB-KERNEL:HAIRY-DATA-VECTOR-REF/CHECK-BOUNDS
```

in `TEST-1`, while in `TEST-2` we find

```
SB-KERNEL:HAIRY-DATA-VECTOR-REF
```

instead. So, we asked (see below) the compiler to be more lenient as far as safety is concerned and it removed code for array bounds checking, which in turn resulted in a slight increase in speed.

But you know that there ain't no such thing as a free lunch, so here's the price we have to pay: if you call `(TEST-1 (1+ +MAX+))`, you'll rightly get an error message about an invalid array index. If you call `(TEST-2 (1+ +MAX+))`, you won't. Instead, several different bad things can happen: you'll silently get a wrong result, you'll get a completely unrelated error message much later, your Lisp image will blow up with a segmentation violation, and so on...

How It Works

If you've worked with GCC (the GNU Compiler Collection), you'll know that it has a wealth of command-line options[21] that can be used to optimize your code. The most enjoyable part about this is that you don't have to change your code; you just tell your compiler to work a bit harder and longer (and maybe reduce the debuggability of your program), and you'll usually get something that's automatically a bit faster.

COMMON LISP doesn't have as many compilation switches as GCC, but the general principle is the same: you can tell the compiler, even on a per-function basis, if, say, debuggability is important to you or if you'd rather sacrifice it for raw speed.

This is done via so-called *optimize qualities*, which are communicated to the compiler via a *declaration*; usually, but not necessarily so, at the beginning of a function.

The standard defines these five optimize qualities

```
compilation-speed
debug
safety
space
speed
```

[21]See `https://gcc.gnu.org/onlinedocs/gcc/Optimize-Options.html`.

and most of them mean what you expect. (The only one that's maybe not clear is `space`, which according to the HyperSpec is "*both* code size *and* run-time space.")

All of these qualities can have integer values between 0 (programmer doesn't care) and 3 (extremely important) where 1 is defined to be the "neutral" value.[22]

The standard doesn't say anything else about these qualities. Specifically, it doesn't even say what their defaults are.[23] And it obviously can't say what an implementation is supposed to do given a specific setting.[24] You are at the mercy of your Lisp's documentation here.

Your best option in the absence of comprehensive documentation is to experiment. One helpful rule of thumb is that optimize qualities often work best in *combination*. If one quality is very important to you, it will usually have a much more noticeable effect (or any effect at all) if you not only increase this quality to 3, but also decrease one or two other qualities. For example, `(speed 3)` typically won't make your code a lot faster if `safety` and `debug` are also at 3. Actually, it is my experience, that cranking up just the `speed` dial without doing anything else rarely buys you anything at all (because the compilers usually do quite a good job even without you explicitly asking for it).

Implementation-Defined Optimize Qualities

The standard explicitly allows implementations to add their own optimize qualities. Examples would include CMUCL's `EXTENSIONS:INHIBIT-WARNINGS` or for LISPWORKS `SYS:INTERRUPTABLE`, `HCL:FIXNUM-SAFETY`, and `FLOAT`.

Can I Have This Global, Please?

Declarations established with `DECLARE` have lexical scope; they typically apply to a function or even only to a part of a function. A question that often comes up is how one can make them global. And a sound reply would be: "Don't do that!"

For one, you rarely need to optimize more than a handful of your functions (see Recipe 17-2), so why would you want to give up safety and debuggability in the rest of your code? Secondly, although a compiler switch in GCC has global effects, it is "forgotten" as soon as the compiler has done its job. In Lisp, on the other hand,

[22]And as a shortcut you can omit the 3. So, `debug` is equivalent to `(debug 3)`.

[23]If you can access your Lisps environment objects (see Recipe 10-9), you can figure out the default settings with some effort.

[24]Well, there's one exception. Code with the optimize quality `(safety 3)` is called *safe code* and there are places in the standard where it says how safe code must behave.

global declarations can "spill over" into your *image* (see Recipe 16-1) and may "taint" other code, which wasn't supposed to be affected by your declarations.[25]

If you really, really think you need global declarations, have a look at PROCLAIM and DECLAIM.[26]

Compilers Aren't Wizards

There are only so many things that a compiler can optimize. Even with the help of type hints (see Recipe 17-5) it is to be expected that lots of functions won't gain any additional speed at all from excessive optimization declarations. If there were some magic that could make any program twice as fast without effort, you would have heard of it by now...

17-4. Obtaining Optimization Hints from the Compiler

Problem

You have identified (see Recipe 17-2) a function that could need some optimization, but you don't know where to start.

Solution

There's a good chance your compiler can help you. Here's an example using SBCL. If you compile a file containing this function

```
(defun array-sum (array)
  (loop for i below (length array)
        sum (aref array i)))
```

SBCL will just dutifully compile it. However, if you let the compiler know (see Recipe 17-3) that you're particularly interested in speed by changing the source code like so

```
(defun array-sum (array)
  (declare (optimize speed))    ; <-- THIS LINE WAS ADDED
  (loop for i below (length array)
        sum (aref array i)))
```

[25]To be more precise, according to the standard a declaration made with PROCLAIM is "always in force unless locally shadowed" while for a declaration made with DECLAIM it is "unspecified whether or not the compile-time side effects [...] persist."

[26]See also page 528.

a whole bunch of notes will scroll by, of which we'll show only a small part here:

```
; in: DEFUN ARRAY-SUM
;     (LENGTH ARRAY)
;
; note: unable to
;   optimize
; due to type uncertainty:
;   The first argument is a SEQUENCE, not a (SIMPLE-ARRAY * (*)).
;
; note: unable to
;   optimize
; due to type uncertainty:
;   The first argument is a SEQUENCE, not a VECTOR.

;     (AREF ARRAY I)
; ==>
;   (SB-KERNEL:HAIRY-DATA-VECTOR-REF/CHECK-BOUNDS ARRAY SB-INT:INDEX)
;
; note: unable to
;   optimize
; because:
;   Upgraded element type of array is not known at compile time.

;     (LOOP FOR I BELOW (LENGTH ARRAY)
;           SUM (AREF ARRAY I))
; --> BLOCK LET SB-LOOP::WITH-SUM-COUNT LET SB-LOOP::LOOP-BODY ...
; ==>
;   (+ #:LOOP-SUM-1 (AREF ARRAY I))
;
; note: forced to do GENERIC-+ (cost 10)
;       unable to do inline float arithmetic (cost 2) because:
;       The first argument is a NUMBER, not a DOUBLE-FLOAT.
;       The second argument is a T, not a DOUBLE-FLOAT.
;
; and so on...
```

You'll have to learn to read these notes and to separate the wheat from the chaff, but essentially the compiler will—whenever it sees a chance to *potentially* optimize some aspect of your function—explain what it did and why it couldn't choose a better (i.e., faster) alternative. (Usually, this will be because it is unsure about types; see Recipe 17-5.)

How It Works

Many COMMON LISP compilers can provide diagnostic information to aid the programmer in code optimization.

The PYTHON compiler (no relation to the much younger programming language of the same name) of CMUCL—variants of which are also used by SBCL and SCIENEER COMMON LISP—is, for example, (in)famous for its chattiness. You only have to tell it that you intend to optimize a function and it will promptly answer with a list of messages enumerating what could be done to further this goal.

This is usually a back-and-forth between you and the compiler because those proposals are about things the compiler can't optimize by itself as it lacks information. This information has to be provided by you, but, of course, only if it is true. For example, a lot of the notes for the function above evolve around the fact that the addition (the `SUM` part of the loop) could be made much faster if the compiler knew that the numbers were all of the same type, for example, of type `DOUBLE-FLOAT`. But if you're planning to use this function for arrays with mixed contents, you *can't* provide this information; it would simply be wrong. Don't ever be tempted to lie to the compiler!

Having said that, the good part about this approach is that you'll get hints specific to the compiler you are using. While a book like this can only give very general advice about optimization, which might have no (or even adverse) effect for your particular Lisp, the compiler should know exactly what will be helpful and what not. (Note that the PYTHON compiler even assigns "cost" values to give you an idea *how* helpful a change would be.)

Let's briefly look at two other implementations that are also quite good at providing useful optimization information:

LISPWORKS has a declaration called `:EXPLAIN` to which several options can be added to control which diagnostic messages you'd like to see. If we wanted about the same information SBCL gave us above, we'd use the declaration like so:

```
(defun array-sum (array)
  (declare (:explain :types))  ;; <- for LispWorks or AllegroCL
  (loop for i below (length array)
        sum (aref array i)))
```

Compiling `ARRAY-SUM` would then result in even more messages than we got above. We show only an excerpt of less than 20% here:

```
;;- -> Examining a call to + with arguments
;;-    an anonymous variable with type NUMBER
;;-    an anonymous variable with type T
;;- <- replaced by SYSTEM:|+2| (types matched)
;;- -- failed to replace by SYSTEM:+$FIXNUM-NOOV (types did not match)
```

```
;;- -- failed to replace by SYSTEM::+$FIXNUM-ONLY (types did not match)
;;- -- failed to replace by SYSTEM::+$FIXNUM-NOCHECK (types did not match)
;;- -- failed to replace by SYSTEM::+$DOUBLE$DOUBLE (types did not match)
;;- -- failed to replace by SYSTEM::+$SINGLE$SINGLE (types did not match)
;;- -- failed to replace by SYSTEM::+$SHORT$SHORT (types did not match)
;;- -- failed to replace by SYSTEM:+$FIXNUM (types did not match)
;;- -- failed to replace by SYSTEM::+$DOUBLE$SINGLE (types did not match)
;;- -- failed to replace by SYSTEM::+$SINGLE$DOUBLE (types did not match)
;;- <- no further choices, but call will now be to SYSTEM:|+2|
;;- -> Examining a call to SYSTEM:|+2| with arguments
;;-    an anonymous variable with type NUMBER
;;-    an anonymous variable with type T
;;- -- failed to replace by SYSTEM:+$FIXNUM-NOOV (types did not match)
;;- -- failed to replace by SYSTEM::+$FIXNUM-ONLY (types did not match)
;;- -- failed to replace by SYSTEM::+$FIXNUM-NOCHECK (types did not match)
;;- -- failed to replace by SYSTEM::+$DOUBLE$DOUBLE (types did not match)
;;- -- failed to replace by SYSTEM::+$SINGLE$SINGLE (types did not match)
;;- -- failed to replace by SYSTEM::+$SHORT$SHORT (types did not match)
;;- -- failed to replace by SYSTEM:+$FIXNUM (types did not match)
;;- -- failed to replace by SYSTEM::+$DOUBLE$SINGLE (types did not match)
;;- -- failed to replace by SYSTEM::+$SINGLE$DOUBLE (types did not match)
;;- <- no further choices, so call will still be to SYSTEM:|+2|
```

You get the idea...

Instead of information about :TYPES, you can also ask about variables, function calls, boxing (see page 525), and so forth. Have a look at the LISPWORKS documentation.

ALLEGROCL uses almost the same syntax. With the same code as above, we'd get the following diagnostic output (slightly edited to fit the page width):

```
;Tgen1:Examined a call to LENGTH with arguments:
;Targ2:  symeval ARRAY type T
;Tres1:   which returns a value in fixnum range
         of type (INTEGER 0 1152921504606846974)
;Tgen1:Examined a call to >=_2OP with arguments:
;Targ2:  symeval I type in fixnum range (INTEGER 0 1152921504606846974)
;Targ2:  symeval LOOP-LIMIT-1154 type
         in fixnum range (INTEGER 0 1152921504606846974)
;Tres1:   which returns a value of type T
;Tgen1:Examined a call to AREF with arguments:
;Targ2:  symeval ARRAY type T
;Targ2:  symeval I type in fixnum range (INTEGER 0 1152921504606846974)
;Tres1:   which returns a value of type T
;Tgen1:Examined a call to +_2OP with arguments:
;Targ2:  symeval LOOP-SUM-1155 type NUMBER
;Tinf1:     VARIABLE-information: LEXICAL: ((TYPE NUMBER))
;Targ1:  call to AREF
 type T
;Tres1:   which returns a value of type NUMBER
```

```
;Tgen1:Examined a call to +_2OP with arguments:
;Targ2:  symeval I type in fixnum range (INTEGER 1 1152921504606846973)
;Targ3:  constant 1 type in fixnum range (INTEGER 1 1)
;Tres1:   which returns a value in fixnum range
          of type (INTEGER 2 1152921504606846974)
```

17-5. Helping the Compiler by Providing Type Information

Problem

You know that certain values in your program will always be of a specific type[27] and you want to use this information to increase your program's speed (or maybe to catch errors).

Solution

We'll use SBCL to go through a serious of examples where we write and test several variants of the same function. As usual, your mileage may vary with other Lisps, but the general concepts should be applicable.

We start with this stupid way of multiplying a number by 100,000,000:

```
(defun foo-1 (x)
  (let ((result 0))
    (dotimes (i 100000000)
      (incf result x))
    result))
```

We compile this function, time it (see Recipe 17-2), and decide that it wouldn't hurt if it were faster. We ask the compiler for help (see Recipe 17-4) and it complains (among other things) that it can't optimize the addition (the `INCF`) because it is unsure about the types of the arguments.

So, let's assume we know that `X` will only ever be of type `DOUBLE-FLOAT`. We thus change the code like so:

```
(defun foo-2 (x)
  (declare (double-float x))                          ;; <-- added
  (let ((result 0d0))                                 ;; <-- changed
    (dotimes (i 100000000)
```

[27]See Recipe 13-1.

```
    (incf result x))
  result))
```

(Note that we changed the initial value of RESULT because we want "pure" DOUBLE-FLOAT arithmetic.)

Disassembling the code (see Recipe 17-12) will show us that this indeed resulted in different machine code and FOO-2 feels a tad faster than FOO-1, but not as much as we expected.

Maybe this is because we didn't tell the compiler that we were interested in speed? Let's try this:

```
(defun foo-3 (x)
  (declare (optimize speed)                              ;; <-- added
           (double-float x))
  (let ((result 0d0))
    (dotimes (i 100000000)
      (incf result x))
    result))
```

No, still no significant speed increase, but the compiler tells us (again, see Recipe 17-4) that it is still unsure about the types. This is actually a point where, in theory, we already provided enough information, but the compiler isn't smart enough[28] to use it:

As RESULT is initially of type DOUBLE-FLOAT and will only ever be modified by adding another variable of type DOUBLE-FLOAT to it, it is obvious (to us humans) that RESULT will never change its type. It is apparently not that obvious to the compiler, though, and thus we'll help it:

```
(defun foo-4 (x)
  (declare (optimize speed)
           (double-float x))
  (let ((result 0d0))
    (declare (double-float result))                      ;; <-- added
    (dotimes (i 100000000)
      (incf result x))
    result))
```

If we now try out FOO-4, we'll see that it really is *a lot* faster than the previous versions—by more than a factor of ten on my machine. Not bad...

[28]To be fair, SBCL's compiler is actually pretty smart at deriving type information. The particular case we're seeing here is mentioned in their documentation and might as well be fixed when you read this.

And there's actually an added benefit. If we enter

```
(foo-4 42)
```

then SBCL will rightly complain that 42 is not of type DOUBLE-FLOAT, so we not only made the function significantly faster, we also gained what people who champion statically typed languages call "type safety" for this function.

However, as in *The Fisherman and His Wife*[29] we're becoming greedy now, thinking that we don't need these pesky type checks and might gain some extra speed if we get rid of them:

```
(defun foo-5 (x)
  (declare (optimize speed (safety 0))                    ;; <-- added
           (double-float x))
  (let ((result 0d0))
    (declare (double-float result))
    (dotimes (i 100000000)
      (incf result x))
    result))
```

It turns out this doesn't make our function faster at all. However, there might be pretty dire consequences in case we make a mistake. If we enter

```
(foo-5 42)
```

we'll end up with a memory fault and we might have ruined the whole Lisp image...

How It Works

Missing static type information is probably *the* main reason why unoptimized compiled COMMON LISP programs are usually not as fast as, say, C or C++ programs.[30] The cool thing about COMMON LISP on the other hand is that you can *optionally* provide type information in strategic places and thus, in critical parts of your code, reach (almost) the speed of statically typed languages; without giving up the general freedom of a strongly, but dynamically typed language.

Let's dissect what exactly makes dynamic typing inherently slower so that we can better understand how to optimize this if needed. There are two "culprits," namely *generic operations*[31] and *boxing*.

[29] See https://en.wikipedia.org/wiki/The_Fisherman_and_His_Wife.

[30] The fact that COMMON LISP is not statically typed is, of course, something that most Lispers generally consider a good thing, mind you!

[31] These are not (necessarily) the same as *generic functions* in the CLOS sense.

Generic Operations

If a C compiler encounters an expression like

```
x + y
```

then it'll know exactly the types of x and y and can usually compile the expression directly to machine code; on X86, maybe one or two movl and then one addl.[32]

If, on the other hand, a COMMON LISP compiler is confronted with the form

```
(+ x y)
```

it generally knows nothing about the types of X and Y because at run time (when the code is already compiled) they can have any value whatsoever.

That's why, without further information, this form will be compiled into a call to an internal function,[33] which

- will first check if its arguments are numbers (so that a meaningful error can be signaled if they're not)
- and will then go through several cases until it finds a specialized function it can apply (like one for adding two fixnums or another one for adding two complex numbers), possibly after converting one of the arguments to a different type first.

All this has to happen at run time, obviously.

This not only applies to arithmetic, but also to other operations; consider something like LENGTH, which can be applied to lists, vectors, or strings.[34]

Boxing

And that's not all. The way values are stored has to fulfill two conflicting requirements:

- Values should preferably be compatible with the machine's word sizes so that machine instructions can be applied to them.
- Values must carry type information so that the Lisp system can figure out their types at run time.

[32]And even if x and y have different types, that is no significant complication as the compiler will just add another machine code instruction like, say, cvtsi2ss.

[33]Often called GENERIC-+ or something like that; see for example page 512.

[34]Strings are also vectors but might have their own internal representation.

Let's take values of type `SINGLE-FLOAT` on a 32-bit architecture as an example. On the one hand, they'd better use 32 bits so that the CPU's arithmetic operations for single floats can be applied to them. On the other hand, if you need a whole word (32 bits) for the numerical value, where do you store the type information? How can the Lisp system know that the 32-bit sequence

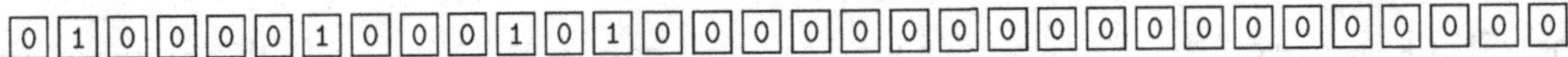

is the float `42.0F0` and not the integer `1109917696` or the address `#x42280000`? It can't. Which is why (except for a few so-called *immediate* types, see for example Recipe 4-2) most Lisp values are *boxed*. The simplified version is that the Lisp value `42.0F0` will be stored as a "typed pointer" (itself a 32-bit word) that points to another 32-bit word holding the actual value, the bit sequence shown above.[35] So, conceptually it looks like this:

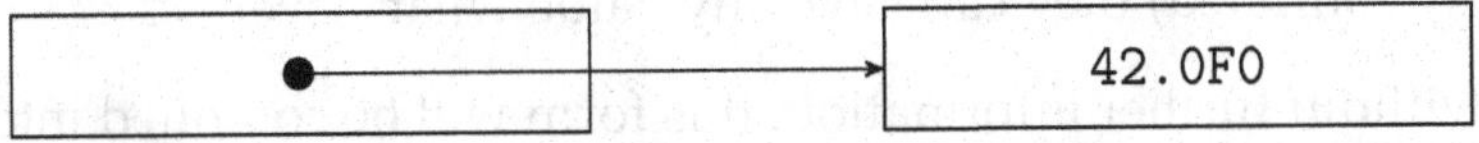

The pointer on the left is the "box" that "wraps" the floating-point number on the right.

If we now go back to our "generic" addition routine from above, it not only has to go through all the cases. Once it has figured out that it has to add two single floats, it has to do the following (or something similar, depending on the machine architecture):

- "Unbox" one of two floats; that is, follow the pointer and put the number pointed to into a machine register.
- Add the second float by using a machine instruction with an indirect reference (which is also "unboxing").
- "Box" the result; that is, store the sum somewhere and return a pointer to this number.

Surprisingly, and thanks to super-fast modern CPUs and clever COMMON LISP implementation techniques, this is still almost always "fast enough." But hopefully, this discussion also made it clear why, if we need it, the right type information can have such dramatic effects as in our example above.

How to Declare Types

As we've seen in the example, we inform the Lisp system about the types of variables with a `DECLARE` form. An example using the full syntax looks like this:

[35]How does the Lisp system know the type from the pointer? That doesn't need to concern us here, but one strategy is that different areas of the *heap* (see page 532) are reserved for different types.

```
(declare (type double-float x y z)
         (type (simple-array (unsigned-byte 8) (*)) buffer))
```

This shows that you can have more than one type declaration in one DECLARE[36] and that one type declaration can be applied to several variables at once. We also see that types can be quite complex as for the array BUFFER above. If a type can be described with a single symbol,[37] you can also use an abbreviated form (which we did above) like so:

```
(declare (double-float x y z))
```

A type declaration is a promise from you (the programmer) to the compiler that a variable will *always* have the declared type. If you're lying, then you'll have to live with the consequences; see above.

The Scope of Type Declarations

Declarations can appear at the beginning of many forms (a full list can be found in the HyperSpec entry for DECLARE) and have lexical scope. They usually appear right after a variable is introduced, but they don't have to. There's even a special operator called LOCALLY the sole purpose of which is to curtail the scope of declarations. You can, for example, use it like so:[38]

```
(defun foo (a)
  (cond ((typep a 'fixnum)
         (locally
           (declare (fixnum a))
           ;; do something
           ))
        ((integerp a)
         (locally
           (declare (integer a))
           ;; do something else
           ))
        (t
```

[36]Although you could also have a sequence of several DECLARE forms instead.

[37]In other words, if you don't need a *compound type specifier*; see page 363.

[38]You might be wondering if the mythical *sufficiently smart compiler* couldn't figure this out by itself. After all, for example the first LOCALLY is in the clause of the COND form where we already "know" that A is a fixnum. Well, but we don't know what else will happen in the ";; do something" part of the code. *Maybe* there'd be already enough information for a very clever compiler so that we wouldn't need to declare anything, but that would certainly depend on the code.

```
;; do the default stuff
)))
```

As special variables are global, you sometimes also need to be able to make global type declarations. For that, use DECLAIM like so:

```
(defparameter *global-counter* 0)
(declaim (fixnum *global-counter*))
```

(And see the remarks about global declarations on page 517.)

Declaring the Return Type of Forms

Let's say you have written a function FOO which accepts two numerical arguments and always returns values of type SINGLE-FLOAT. If the form (FOO 3 4.2) appears in your program, there's no way to indicate the information that its value is a single float to the compiler using the TYPE declarations we've seen so far. That's what FTYPE is for. The corresponding declaration for FOO would look like this:

```
(declare (ftype (function (number number) single-float) foo))
```

You can be even more specific and restrict a return type declaration to a single form (for example, in cases where the return type is not always the same but you know it in a particular situation). If, say, you compute the sum of the variables A and B and you know that this this sum will always be a fixnum, you can tell the compiler like so:

```
(the fixnum (+ a b))
```

In both cases you can also use the *type specifier* VALUES in case of forms or functions returning multiple values, for example:

```
(the (values integer integer) (floor m n))
```

Type Inference

In theory, just a few type declarations in the right places would be enough and the compiler would then infer the rest. Some statically typed languages like ML are well known for their ability to infer types and at least some of this should be possible in a dynamically typed language like COMMON LISP. And indeed, some implementations are pretty good at this. The PYTHON compiler (see page 520) in particular has a reputation of being the best in this area.

But our example demonstrated that even this compiler sometimes needs a nudge in practice when in theory this shouldn't be necessary. So, don't just rely on your compiler being smart, but let it tell you (see Recipe 17-4) if it needs more information.

Pitfalls

One problem is that the type information you provide could simply be wrong. As our example above shows, this can have very serious consequences. Although COMMON LISP programs are generally very "safe," inaccurate type information can make them behave like C programs running amok with wrong pointer arithmetic.

A common pitfall in connection with type declarations is the assumption that just because two numbers are of the same type, their sum, difference, or product must also be of this type. This is for floats, but it is wrong for fixnums (see Recipe 4-2) and can lead to subtle errors.

Finally, there's an aesthetic reason not to overuse type declarations: they tend to make beautiful code ugly...

17-6. Reducing "Consing"

Problem

You have figured out that your program is slow because it uses too much memory. (Or maybe you only *think* that this is a problem...)

Solution

There is no single "solution" to this problem; there's only a variety of strategies that you can try.

As usual, we'll start with a simple example:

```
(defun matching-p (edges)
  (let ((hash (make-hash-table)))
    (loop for (vertex-1 vertex-2) in edges
          when (or (gethash vertex-1 hash)
                   (gethash vertex-2 hash))
          do (return-from matching-p nil)
          else do (setf (gethash vertex-1 hash) t
                        (gethash vertex-2 hash) t))
    t))
```

This is a brute-force approach to testing whether a set of edges of a graph is a *matching*—a set of edges without common vertices.[39]

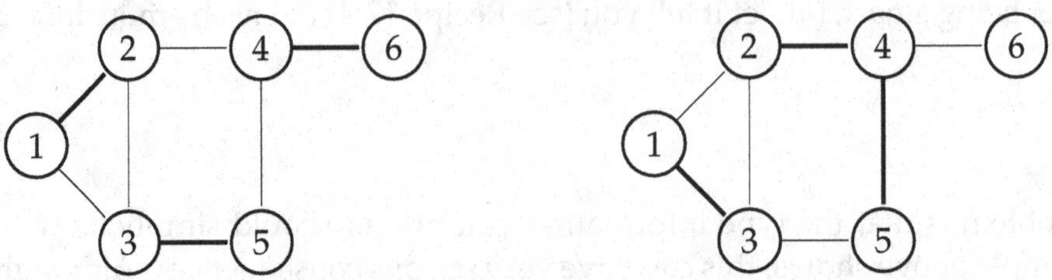

In the picture on the left, the set of thick edges is $\{\{1,2\},\{3,5\},\{4,6\}\}$ and it is a matching. In our program we'll represent it[40] as the list `((1 2) (3 5) (4 6))`. The set of thick edges on the right is $\{\{1,3\},\{2,4\},\{4,5\}\}$, which is *not* a matching as two of the edges coincide with the vertex 4.

To stress test our function, we create a large edge set where `MATCHING-P` will have to go through the whole list until it finally figures out that it wasn't a matching:

```
(defparameter *edges*
  (cons (list 99999 100000)
        (loop for i below 100000 by 2
              collect (list i (1+ i)))))
```

As a graph, this would look like so, with 99999 being the only vertex touched by two edges:

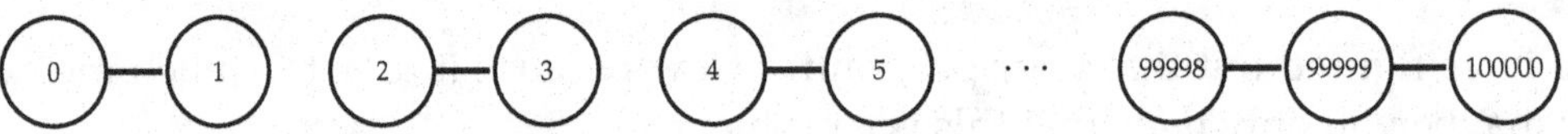

If you run `(MATCHING-P *EDGES*)` one hundred times under `TIME` (see Recipe 17-2), you will see a large amount of allocation. (In my tests, I had more than 300 million octets, which were created due to the test.)

The reason for the allocation is pretty obvious in this case. For each run, we create a new hash table. More importantly, for each edge we test we potentially create two new key/value pairs in this hash table.

Now, if this where part of a larger program (for example, to find a *maximum matching*), it would be very likely that a) `MATCHING-P` would be called a lot and b) we would be working on the same graph all the time, so that there'd only be a relatively small set of vertices. Thus, we could rewrite the function like so:[41]

```
(let ((hash (make-hash-table)))      ;; <-- now outside of the function
  (defun matching-p (edges)
```

[39]See `http://mathworld.wolfram.com/Matching.html`. There are better ways to test this than with brute force. But bear with me for the sake of this example.

[40]See also Recipe 6-10.

[41]See also Recipe 10-4.

```
    ;; the following initialization loop is new
    (loop for vertex being the hash-keys of hash
          do (setf (gethash vertex hash) nil))
    ;; the rest is exactly as above
    (loop for (vertex-1 vertex-2) in edges
          when (or (gethash vertex-1 hash)
                   (gethash vertex-2 hash))
          do (return-from matching-p nil)
          else do (setf (gethash vertex-1 hash) t
                        (gethash vertex-2 hash) t))
    t))
```

It now closes over a hash table which it reuses each time it is called. There's the additional work involved of initializing the hash table each time the function starts,[42] but at least in my tests this function was still about four times as fast as the earlier version, because it didn't allocate any memory at all.[43]

How It Works

COMMON LISP has, like JAVA, automatic memory management through garbage collection (GC).[44] This is usually a good thing as it relieves you of the burden of manual memory management as in C++ (which also comes with various ways to introduce subtle bugs that simply can't happen in Lisp or JAVA).

GC can be troublesome, though, if too much of the running time of your program is spent in memory management. And it can be an issue if the GC kicks in and causes stalls in your program's execution.[45]

As memory management is a feature that makes your code easier to write, read, and maintain, you should only ever worry about it if it really causes problems. Tools like those introduced in Recipe 17-2 will also give you memory allocation statistics, but the mere fact that your code acquires and releases large amounts of memory shouldn't bother you too much. Modern GCs are very good and many pieces of advice of old-time Lispers about *consing* (see below) should nowadays be taken with a grain of salt.

---

[42]And note well that we don't use `CLRHASH` here; we want to keep the existing key/value pairs.

[43]But see also Recipe 6-6.

[44]See Recipe 22-10.

[45]Whether this is really a problem, especially on a multithreaded system where the GC could, in theory, do its work while other code is running essentially unimpeded is an implementation question, of course. If you're convinced that your GC is making your life harder than it should be, you should consider trying another Lisp; see Recipe 17-15.

"Consing" and the Heap

Having said that, if your program really suffers from the fact that too much data is allocated, the first step in attacking such problems should be a basic understanding of what's going on behind the scenes.

Your Lisp system has reserved (probably already when it started up) a large amount of RAM[46] where it will maintain your program's data. This is usually called the *heap*. Now, whenever your program creates a data structure, a part of the heap will be reserved for it and the variable(s) "holding" the data will "point" to it.

As an example, let's consider a part of our program that looks like this:

```
(let* ((a (cons 42 23))
       (b "foo")
       (c (cons b a)))
  ;; more code here
```

The Lisp runtime will first create the cons cell with the two numbers on the heap and `A` will be a "pointer" to it. There'll also be the string `"foo"` somewhere else on the heap and `B` will point to it. Finally, another cons cell will be created on the heap which itself will point to the two previous locations (and `C` will hold a reference to this second cons cell). Conceptually, we now have this:

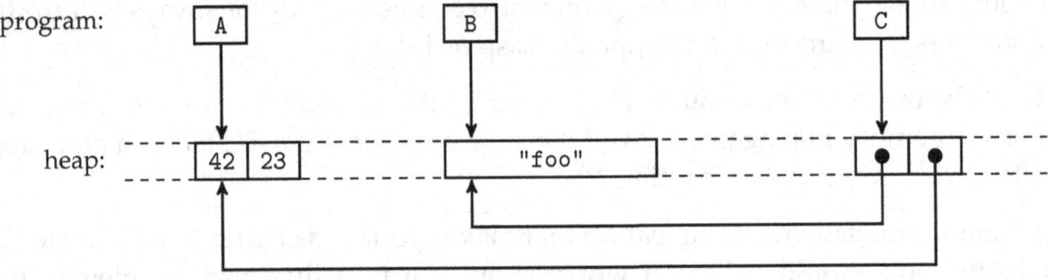

At the end of the `LET*`, the three variables `A`, `B`, and `C` will be out of scope, but maybe the value of `C` will have been stored in some variable `X` which is still "alive." We would then have this situation:

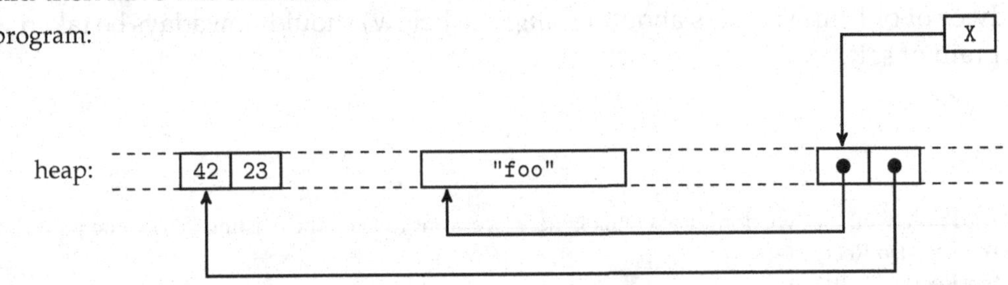

[46]Which will likely be divided into smaller parts depending on the GC strategy, but that doesn't need to bother us.

From time to time, the garbage collector will now (at its own discretion) scan the heap, searching for data structures that can't be reached from the program anymore. Those structures will be considered "garbage" and can be "reclaimed," meaning that the space they occupied can be given to other candidates. (In the second picture, there's, for example, no *direct* arrow from the program to the string `"foo"` anymore, but it can still be reached indirectly via `X`, so it is not yet garbage.)

The moral of the story for us is that each piece of data that lives on the heap requires work; it first needs to be allocated and later it needs to be scanned and eventually be reclaimed.

Allocation of data on the heap is, by the way, affectionately called "consing" by Lispers—which can be understood as a shortcut for "construction" but also as a reference to `CONS` (see Recipe 2-1), which was traditionally *the* function that caused allocation. So, if an experienced Lisper says that a function "conses," they usually mean that it allocates (too much) memory.

There are ways to avoid consing altogether by creating data structures on the stack instead. This is explained in Recipe 17-7.

Reusing Data Structures

One obvious solution to avoid consing is to reuse data structures. This is what we did in our example. The first version of our function created a new hash table each time and threw it away, thus handing it over to the GC. The second version keeps hold of a single hash table that is never reclaimed. This can be very useful at times, but there's no general rule for when you should reuse data structures. It depends on your algorithms and your knowledge about what is required and when.

A more elaborate variation of this theme is *pooling* where you not only keep one object but a whole bunch of them out of reach of the GC. Other parts of the program will then call specific functions to acquire a resource from the pool or give it back once they are no longer needed. But did you notice what I just described here? This is essentially giving up automatic memory management in favor of your own homegrown and probably crude manual memory management! That's very rarely a good idea.[47] (In the olden days, people actually devised schemes to reuse *cons cells*, but that seems rather ridiculous today.)

Also, even if it turns out that data structure reuse is beneficial for your program, be aware of problems that can arise from multithreading. For example, our second version of `MATCHING-P` from above will cease to work correctly if two threads call it at the same time (because they will both work on the *same* hash table; see Recipe 11-2). The first version, albeit slower, will do fine.

[47]Pooling can be useful in other cases, though. It is typically used when the resources require a significant amount of initialization, but can then be reused relatively cheaply. See, for example, the `DEFRESOURCE` macro from *PAIP* at `http://norvig.com/paip/auxfns.lisp`.

(For another "reuse" technique, see Recipe 7-5.)

Destructive Functions

Many functions offered by the standard come in two versions; a normal version and a "destructive" one. The destructive one is often distinguished by an "`N`" (as in `NSET-DIFFERENCE` as opposed to `SET-DIFFERENCE`), but not necessarily so (there's also, say, `DELETE-DUPLICATES` versus `REMOVE-DUPLICATES`). I've rarely mentioned these versions explicitly in other chapters as in my opinion they are more dangerous than useful, but I'll mention them here for the sake of completeness.

The idea of destructive functions (and you could of course also write destructive functions yourself; see for example Recipe 2-6) is that they modify one of their arguments and return the modified object instead of creating a fresh one. This will typically make the life of the GC a bit easier,[48] but as I said, it's dangerous. Both aspects of destructive functions can be seen in this example:

Create a file with the following contents, and then compile and load it:

```
(defparameter *l* (loop for i below 20 collect i))

(defun foo-1 (list n)
  (let ((dummy list))
    (dotimes (i n)
      (setf dummy (reverse dummy)))
    dummy))

(defun foo-2 (list n)
  (let ((dummy list))
    (dotimes (i n)
      (setf dummy (nreverse dummy)))        ;; <-- note the "N" here
    dummy))
```

Now, in the REPL:

```
* *l*
(0 1 2 3 4 5 6 7 8 9 10 11 12 13 14 15 16 17 18 19)
* (time (foo-1 *l* 99999999))
;; output edited for brevity
Evaluation took:
  17.912 seconds of real time
  32,000,023,728 bytes consed
```

[48]Although this isn't necessarily always the case. There may even be cases where, depending on the GC implementation, destructive functions are actually slower.

```
(19 18 17 16 15 14 13 12 11 10 9 8 7 6 5 4 3 2 1 0)
* *l*
(0 1 2 3 4 5 6 7 8 9 10 11 12 13 14 15 16 17 18 19)
* (time (foo-2 *l* 99999999))
Evaluation took:
  9.085 seconds of real time
  0 bytes consed
(19 18 17 16 15 14 13 12 11 10 9 8 7 6 5 4 3 2 1 0)
* *l*
(0)
```

That's obviously a huge difference in performance. (And the one and only reason is that FOO-2 didn't utilize the heap; while FOO-1 created almost 100 million intermediate lists with 20 elements only to throw them away immediately.) But also note that after the call to FOO-2, the value in *L* is no longer usable; it is neither the original list nor the reversed one!

If anything, destructive functions go completely against the grain of functional programming. Not that COMMON LISP is a functional programming language per se, but functions that don't modify their arguments and always return the same output given the same input are definitely easier to debug and maintain than others and should thus dominate even in programs written in an imperative (procedural) style. Each destructive function is a potential source of hidden errors. (Or to put it differently, by replacing 100 million calls to REVERSE with 100 million calls to NREVERSE, we were able to save less than ten seconds. So, if your program calls REVERSE 1000 times per second, you can expect to save one millisecond or less. Is that really worth the trouble?)

By the way, if you haven't used COMMON LISP's destructive functions before, keep in mind that, although they modify their arguments, you still want their *return value*. As you've just seen above, if you want to reverse the list *L*, you should *not* do something like

```
(nreverse *l*)
```

but evaluate

```
(setf *l* (nreverse *l*))
```

instead.

"Hidden" Consing

If you've worked with a garbage-collected language before, you might expect allocation for compound objects but not for "primitive" types. Be aware, though, that in a typical COMMON LISP implementation all numerical types except for fixnums are either compound objects (like bignums, rationals, or complex numbers) or otherwise need to be boxed[49] (like floating-point numbers).

For example, evaluating the form

```
(loop for i below 100000 sum (/ 1 (expt 1.0001d0 i)))
```

will on the 32-bit version of LISPWORKS 6.1 allocate more than 150 million (!) octets although there's "only" arithmetic going on.

So, "hidden" consing because of boxed values can (in certain situations) be problematic for efficiency. But this can almost always be solved with the techniques described in Recipe 17-3. If the compiler, for example, knows that all numbers involved in a calculation are double floats, it doesn't have to box and unbox them between calls to arithmetic functions.

(See also Recipe 17-14.)

"Tuning" the Garbage Collector

Sometimes the key to making the memory management usage of your program more efficient is not to avoid it altogether but to adapt the garbage collector's behavior to your allocation patterns. This is complicated stuff and requires a good knowledge of GC in general and of the GC techniques[50] used by your Lisp in particular. It thus is beyond the scope of this book, but it should at least be noted that a good COMMON LISP implementation will have something to say about this in its documentation and will likely provide several ways to fine-tune the GC's parameters.

17-7. Using the Stack Instead of the Heap

Problem

You have figured out that your program is slow because it uses too much memory, but you are not happy with (or can't use) the techniques described in Recipe 17-6.

Solution

A solution that sometimes works is to not use the heap at all: use the stack instead!

Let's try one of our toy examples:

[49] See page 525.

[50] See `https://en.wikipedia.org/wiki/Tracing_garbage_collection`.

```
(defun do-something (pair)
  (+ (first pair) (* 2 (second pair))))

(defun foo (list-1 list-2)
  (loop for a in list-1
        for b in list-2
        sum (do-something (list a b))))

;; does the same as FOO
(defun bar (list-1 list-2)
  (loop for a in list-1
        for b in list-2
        sum (let ((x (list a b)))
              (declare (dynamic-extent x))
              (do-something x))))

;; random test data
(defvar *l-1* (loop for i below 1000000
                    collect (random 100)))

(defvar *l-2* (loop for i below 1000000
                    collect (random 100)))
```

DO-SOMETHING is some nonsense function that I made up that wants a two-element list as its only argument. FOO is supposed to walk through two lists in parallel, combining each pair of neighboring elements into one list, which is then handed over to DO-SOMETHING.

As DO-SOMETHING needs a *list*, FOO has no choice but to create such a list for each pair of elements, so it seems perfectly clear that we *must* "cons:"

```
CL-USER 1 > (time (foo *l-1* *l-2*))
Timing the evaluation of (FOO *L-1* *L-2*)
User time    =        0.078
System time  =        0.046
Elapsed time =        0.062
Allocation   = 24000000 bytes
0 Page faults
148472425
```

And indeed, we consed 24 million "useless" octets to compute this sum.[51]

[51]Results on LispWorks. If you can't reproduce this, be aware that I actually wrapped the debugging macro SYS:WITH-OTHER-THREADS-DISABLED around the call to TIME. This is advisable if you want

Now, in theory, we could create one cons and reuse it (see Recipe 17-6) for all calls to DO-SOMETHING. But that would result in code so ugly that I didn't even bother to try.

Luckily, BAR employs a better alternative:

```
CL-USER 13 > (time (bar *l-1* *l-2*))
Timing the evaluation of (BAR *L-1* *L-2*)
User time    =         0.031
System time  =         0.000
Elapsed time =         0.031
Allocation   = 0 bytes
0 Page faults
148472425
```

No consing at all! How did it do that?!?

How It Works

To understand what's happening we have to talk about the call stack again.[52]

To say that C doesn't do any memory management at all is a bit unfair. Consider this simple (and stupid) function:

```
int foo(int n) {
  int x, y;

  x = n * n;
  y = x + x;

  return y;
}
```

The way it is written, we need two temporary variables, x and y, which means space has to be allocated for two integers somewhere. But C won't reserve space on the heap;[53] it will use the call stack instead.[54]

---

to measure GC behavior without interference from IDE threads.

[52]If you've never heard of this stack—also called *execution stack*—before, you might want to read the brief explanation on page 510.

[53]There *is* a heap in C, but you have to take care of it yourself using functions from the malloc/free family.

[54]Well, for a simple function like this it will probably put the values into registers. (And to be completely honest, a good C compiler will probably figure out that it doesn't need x and y at all and transform the code.) But that's a detail that isn't of much interest for us here. A COMMON LISP compiler will likewise utilize registers if that's possible, but *conceptually* we can imagine that they both simply use the stack.

Remember that I said on page 510 that on each function call, a *stack frame* is put on the stack; it contains information like the function's arguments, the return address, *and local variables*. While we imagined stack frames as opaque boxes in Recipe 17-2, let's now draw them with a bit more detail. The frame for our C function above will essentially look like so:

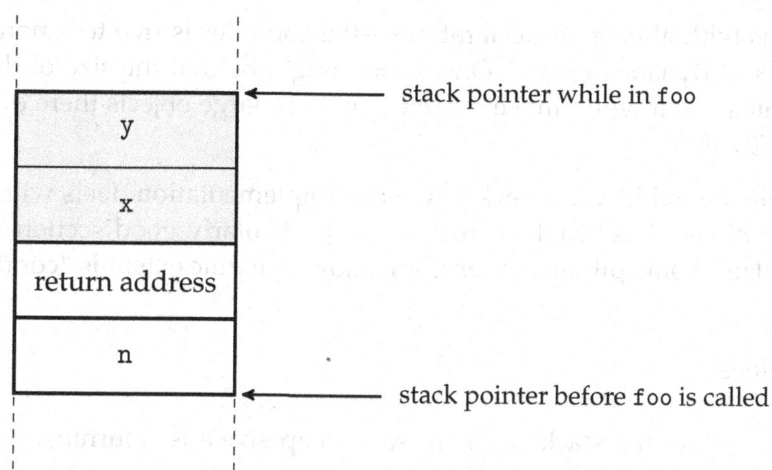

The gray area is the part that is occupied by local variables and, as this is just some part of the machine's RAM, it is completely irrelevant for the function whether these variables live on the stack or in some other place called *heap*. But the coolest thing is that we get "allocation" and "garbage collection" for free. The space is "allocated" by incrementing the stack pointer and it is "freed" by decrementing the stack pointer. Using ten local variables isn't more expensive than using only one; it's always just one movement of a pointer.

The reason why `BAR` in our example didn't cons (as opposed to `FOO`) was that all the small lists we created lived their short life on the stack.

But why didn't the compiler do that by itself in `FOO` already? Because it didn't know what would happen with these lists! The variable `X` in `BAR` has *lexical scope*, which means that you can't refer to it outside of the `LET`. But the *values* bound to this variable—and this applies to the lists created in `FOO` as well—have *indefinite extent*. The function `DO-SOMETHING` could collect all arguments it receives in a global list and we would, of course, expect these values to persist even after execution of `BAR` has ended. Which means that the stack is generally *not* a good place for such values as it is an ephemeral place that is constantly in flux; values on the stack left over from functions that are done will immediately be overwritten by stack frames of other functions.

So, couldn't the mythical *sufficiently smart compiler* figure out, by peeking at `DO-SOMETHING`, that in this particular case no special care was necessary? Nope, because COMMON LISP is a dynamic language and you can redefine `DO-SOMETHING` after `FOO` has been compiled. The only way for the compiler to be sure that the values in `X` can be safely allocated on the stack is by telling it that they will only have *dynamic extent*, meaning that they will no longer be used anywhere once the LET in BAR is finished. As with type declarations (see Recipe 17-5), this is a promise that you're giving to the compiler—and you'd better not lie. From the description above, it should be obvious what could happen...

Note that—as with almost all declarations—the compiler is free to ignore your information about dynamic extent. One reason might be that the size of the stack is typically limited, so it won't make sense to put very large objects there even if they have dynamic extent.

(It is probably a good idea to check how your implementation deals with dynamic extent declarations. The SBCL manual has a particularly good section about this that also explains some pitfalls; for example, how dynamic extent is "contagious.")

Multiple Values

Another area where the stack can help save heap space is returning values from functions. Here's an example:

```
(defun three-1 ()
  (list (random 100)
        (random 100)
        (random 100)))

(defun three-2 ()
  (values (random 100)
          (random 100)
          (random 100)))

;; just to make results comparable
(defvar *r* (make-random-state t))

(defun test-1 (n)
  (setf *random-state* (make-random-state *r*))
  (let ((result 0))
    (dotimes (i n result)
      (destructuring-bind (x y z)
          (three-1)
        (incf result (min x y z))))))

(defun test-2 (n)
  (setf *random-state* (make-random-state *r*))
  (let ((result 0))
```

```
    (dotimes (i n result)
      (multiple-value-bind (x y z)
          (three-2)
        (incf result (min x y z))))))
```

If you put the code above in a file, and then compile and load it, you should see results similar to these:

```
CL-USER 1 > (time (test-1 1000000))
Timing the evaluation of (TEST-1 1000000)
User time    =        0.795
System time  =        0.405
Elapsed time =        0.405
Allocation   = 36000256 bytes
0 Page faults
24489330
CL-USER 2 > (time (test-2 1000000))
Timing the evaluation of (TEST-2 1000000)
User time    =        0.280
System time  =        0.000
Elapsed time =        0.281
Allocation   = 256 bytes
0 Page faults
24489330
```

(The second version doesn't cons. The 256 bytes you're seeing are from the new RANDOM-STATE object.)

If you're coming from a language where functions can only ever return one thing, then you are used to the idea of packaging several objects into some kind of container (in Lisp a list would be the obvious choice) in order to return them all. But in COMMON LISP, a function can also return multiple values.[55] Although there's no difference semantically, the technical difference is that multiple values will be passed via the stack and thus there's no need to allocate a container for them on the heap.

Finally, nothing that we've said about the stack here is mandated by the COMMON LISP standard. An implementation doesn't even need to have something like a call stack. But rest assured that every implementation available today has one and this is unlikely to change in the near future.

[55]See chapter 20 of *Practical Common Lisp* which can be found online at `http://www.gigamonkeys.com/book/the-special-operators.html`.

17-8. Optimizing Recursive Functions

Problem

You're wondering whether recursive functions will be compiled into optimal code.

Solution

If you were to implement COMMON LISP's `MEMBER` yourself, one (simplified) version could look like so:

```
(defun member* (elt list)
  (cond ((null list) nil)
        ((eql (first list) elt) list)
        (t (member* elt (rest list)))))
```

Try this in your Lisp and then call it with a large list where the element to be found isn't present:

```
(member* 42 (make-list 10000000 :initial-element 41))
```

If that works without problems, it's pretty likely that you don't have to worry at all. If you get an error message, read on.

How It Works

In functional programming languages, the preferred style of repeating computations is usually *recursion*; the technique of functions calling themselves again with changed arguments. COMMON LISP is not a functional programming language per se, but it is perfectly OK to (mostly) use it as if it were. However, while languages like SCHEME come with certain guarantees about how recursion should be implemented, at least the COMMON LISP standard makes no such promises.

The relevant notion here is *tail call optimization* (TCO) or *tail call elimination*. If you call your function as `(MEMBER* 42 '(1 2 3 4))`, the execution stack[56] will look something like what we see on the left in the following picture.[57] After comparing `1` with `42`, the function now calls itself as `(MEMBER* 42 '(2 3 4))`, which in an unoptimized implementation, will result in a stack as shown in the right part of the picture:

---

[56]See more about the stack in Recipe 17-7.

[57]Of course, the whole list `(1 2 3 4)` won't be on the stack, but rather a pointer to it.

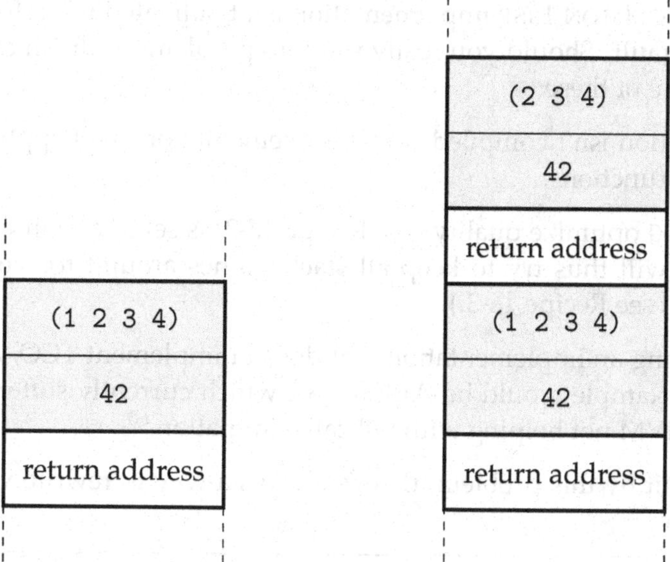

A compiler performing TCO will notice that once the second call to `MEMBER*` returns, the first call will also immediately return[58] without doing anything else because the second call to `MEMBER*` was a *tail call*; that is, it was the last thing `MEMBER*` did. Thus, the optimizing compiler will *not* add a second stack frame as above but rather *replace* the stack frame of the first function call with the stack frame of the second call:[59]

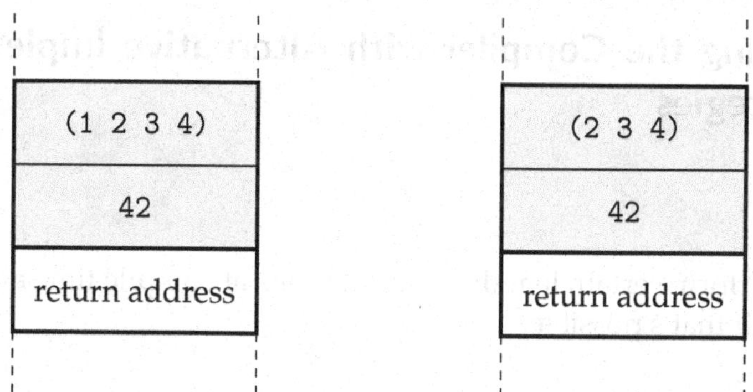

One way to observe the effects of TCO is to look at the output of the disassembler (see Recipe 17-12). On X86, a function call would usually appear as `call` but would be replaced by a `jmp` instruction in case of tail call elimination.

Without the elimination of tail calls, the stack will grow with each call, and that's why you might see an error message (about a "stack overflow") if too many frames accumulate on the stack.

---

[58] Well, we haven't explained how the return values of the functions are transferred, but that makes no difference for our discussion here.

[59] You will have noticed by now that this technique can be used whenever a function call is the last thing that happens in a function. It doesn't necessarily have to call *itself*, but can as well call any other function.

Now, while a COMMON LISP implementation isn't obligated to perform TCO, most will do it by default. Should you really run into problems with tail calls, the reason will likely be one of these:

- Your function isn't compiled. Most implementations will apply TCO only for compiled functions.
- Your `DEBUG` optimize quality (see Recipe 17-3) is set to a high value. (And the compiler will thus try to keep all stack frames around for you to inspect if necessary; see Recipe 16-3.)
- You're using an implementation that doesn't implement TCO. As of this writing, one example would be ABCL 1.3.2 which currently suffers from the underlying JVM not helping with tail call elimination.[60]

If you're ever hit by this problem, there's always a way to rewrite your code in an imperative style:[61]

```
(defun member* (elt list)
  (loop for rest on list
        when (eql (first rest) elt)
        do (return rest)))
```

17-9. Helping the Compiler with Alternative Implementation Strategies

Problem

You want to perform certain lengthy computations at compile time already (instead of at run time) if that's possible.

Solution

You can do that with *compiler macros*.

Let's assume that as part of a computer graphics program, you have a function `APPLY-TRANSFORM` that applies a (homogeneous) matrix to a vector and returns the resulting vector. As affine transformations are often described as a sequence of simpler transformations, your `APPLY-TRANSFORM` is actually a generic function with two

[60]See for example `http://www.drdobbs.com/jvm/tail-call-optimization-and-java/240167044`.

[61]At least in theory. You can always rewrite your code as a set of instructions for a Turing machine, which doesn't even have such thing as a function call. In practice, some programming languages will make conversion of recursion to iteration deliberately hard or even impossible.

methods; one where the transformation is a matrix and one where the transformation is a list (of matrices) that will first have to be converted to a single matrix.

In order not to blow up this example with technical details, let's simply "implement" our matrices and vectors as numbers. The code could then look like so:

```
(defmethod apply-transform ((transform number) vector)
  (* transform vector))

(defmethod apply-transform ((transforms list) vector)
  (apply-transform (compound-transform transforms) vector))

(defun compound-transform (transforms)
  (let ((compound-transform 1))
    (dolist (transform transforms)
      (setf compound-transform (* transform compound-transform)))
    compound-transform))
```

You would now probably be reluctant to write something like

```
(apply-transform '(1 2 3 4 5) vector)
```

in a tight loop as it would mean that for each call the product of the five numbers would have to be computed although you could compute it once manually and write

```
(apply-transform 120 vector)
```

instead. (Remember that in our "real" example, these are matrices and you might prefer the first version because it's easier to read or maintain.)

As the next paragraph will explain, compiler macros can automatically transform the first to the second version.

How It Works

According to the standard, compiler macros "exist for the purpose of trading compile-time speed for run-time speed," so this is a typical example of when they are appropriate. The idea is that in addition to your normal function definition you write a *compiler macro function*, which can replace, during compilation,[62] a function call with an alternative implementation under certain circumstances.

The compiler macro for our example would look like so:

[62]Technically, it is also possible that this happens with interpreted code, but the standard explicitly discourages implementations from doing so.

```
(define-compiler-macro apply-transform (&whole form &environment env
                                        transform vector)
  (cond ((and (constantp transform env) (listp transform))
         `(apply-transform (load-time-value
                            (compound-transform ,transform))
                           ,vector))
        (t form)))
```

The following are the main points:

- A compiler macro has the same name as the function the call to which it can potentially replace.
- If the compiler macro decides not to transform the function call, it must return the entire form. (This is what happens in the (T FORM) part of the code above.)
- The compiler macro should thus have a lambda list beginning with &WHOLE so that one of its variables is bound to the form.
- The lambda list of the compiler macro is otherwise identical[63] to that of its corresponding function (except for the &ENVIRONMENT part, which is explained in Recipe 10-9).

In this particular example we check if the first argument to APPLY-TRANSFORM is constant (i.e., if its value is known at compile time) and a list and in this case arrange for the compound transformation to be computed and inserted into the compiled code when it is loaded. (For LOAD-TIME-VALUE, see Recipe 10-5.)

You can observe the effects of the compiler macro like so:[64]

```
CL-USER 1 > (trace compound-transform)
(COMPOUND-TRANSFORM)
CL-USER 2 > (defun foo (vector)
              (apply-transform '(1 2 3 4 5) vector))
FOO
CL-USER 3 > (foo 10)
0 COMPOUND-TRANSFORM > ...
  >> TRANSFORMS : (1 2 3 4 5)
0 COMPOUND-TRANSFORM < ...
  << VALUE-0 : 120
1200
CL-USER 4 > (compile 'foo)
```

[63]The compiler will arrange for automatic destructuring of optional and keyword arguments even if the form is a FUNCALL.

[64]Unless your Lisp (like, for example, CLOZURECL) always compiles your code immediately. In that case, only the part after the call to COMPILE is relevant. (See Recipe 16-4 for TRACE.)

```
0 COMPOUND-TRANSFORM > ...
  >> TRANSFORMS : (1 2 3 4 5)
0 COMPOUND-TRANSFORM < ...
  << VALUE-0 : 120
FOO
NIL
NIL
CL-USER 5 > (foo 10)
1200
```

This shows that the call to COMPOUND-TRANSFORM is performed during compilation and that after the function FOO has been compiled, further calls to FOO don't result in further calls to COMPOUND-TRANSFORM anymore.

It is possible, although unlikely, that you don't see these effects. A COMMON LISP implementation doesn't have to expand compiler macros. Still, if it doesn't in a case like this, you should probably ask your vendor why...

See Recipe 10-9 for another example of a compiler macro and see page 553 for a possible reason why a compiler macro might not be expanded.

17-10. Avoiding Repeated Computations

Problem

You have a function that, on the one hand, might involve lengthy computations, and on the other hand, will often be called with the same arguments.

Solution

We'll use the well-known Fibonacci sequence as an example:[65]

```
(defun fib (n)
  (if (<= n 1)
    1
    (+ (fib (- n 2)) (fib (- n 1)))))
```

Computing the value like this requires quite some time, though:

[65] As the Fibonacci sequence is defined by a linear recurrence with constant coefficients, it has a closed-form solution (which in this particular case is the formula named after de Moivre and Binet), so Recipe 17-1 applies here. Still, the Fibonacci function is *the* standard example for memoization because it is so small and demonstrates the advantages of memoization so well.

```
CL-USER 1 > (time (fib 42))
Timing the evaluation of (FIB 42)
User time    =          4.305
System time  =          0.000
Elapsed time =          4.305
Allocation   = 0 bytes
0 Page faults
433494437
```

This is because we have a combinatorial explosion of function calls. If we just look at the beginning of what's happening, the call tree will look like this:

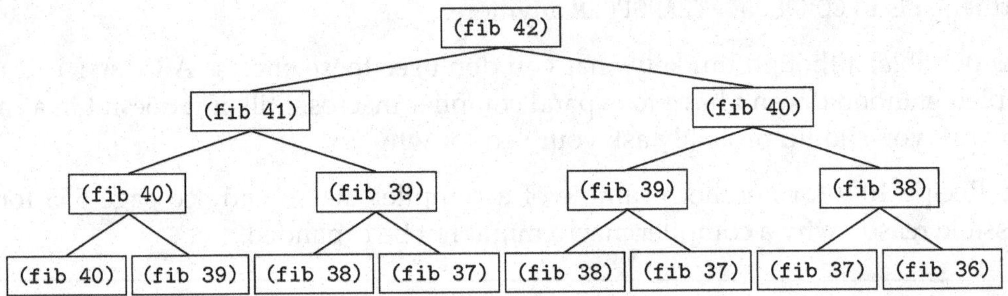

And it is immediately obvious that FIB is very often called with the same argument. For example, the picture already contains three (FIB 39) calls and one more is going to appear on the next level.

The way to overcome this problem is to store the values that have already been computed. For example, once we know the result of (FIB 39), we store it in a hash table (see Chapter 6) under the key 39, so that the next time we need (FIB 39), we don't have to compute it again but can just look it up. The modified function will look like this:[66]

```
(let ((hash (make-hash-table)))
  (defun fib* (n)
    (or (gethash n hash)
        (setf (gethash n hash)
              ;; below is the original algorithm
              (if (<= n 1)
                1
                (+ (fib* (- n 2)) (fib* (- n 1))))))))
```

If we now time this again, we see that the function became too fast to measure at this granularity:

```
CL-USER 2 > (time (fib* 42))
```

[66] See also Recipe 10-4.

```
Timing the evaluation of (FIB* 42)

User time    =       0.000
System time  =       0.000
Elapsed time =       0.000
Allocation   = 24 bytes
0 Page faults
433494437
```

How It Works

The technique of remembering function values so that you can later look them up is called *memoization*;[67] it has been around for quite some time, and it is certainly not specific to Lisp. However, Lisp macros make it especially easy to just "wrap" memoization around pretty much every function you like without changing it.[68]

So, instead of writing FIB* we could have installed the library FARE-MEMOIZATION[69] via QUICKLISP (see Recipe 18-2) and after evaluating the simple form

```
(fare-memoization:memoize 'fib)
```

a call like (FIB 42) from above would have been down to "0.000" seconds as well.

17-11. Avoiding Function Calls

Problem

You want to avoid function call overhead.

Solution

To demonstrate the difference that a function call can make, and how you can avoid it, I ran the following experiment on SBCL 1.2.12 on Windows. First, I compiled and loaded a file with the following contents:

```
(declaim (inline bar))                        ;; <- see (a) below
(defun bar (i)
  (declare (optimize speed)
```

[67]See https://en.wikipedia.org/wiki/Memoization.

[68]Exercise for the reader: Write your own simple memoization library in less than 20 lines of code.

[69]Or alternatively have a look at the FUNCTION-CACHE library.

```
          (double-float i))
  (let ((j (+ i 1d0)))
    (sqrt (+ (* i i) (* j j)))))
(declaim (notinline bar))                              ;; <- see (b) below

(defun foo-1 ()
  (declare (optimize speed))
  (let ((x 0d0)
        (i 1d0))
    (declare (double-float x))
    (loop
       (unless (< i 100000000d0)
         (return x))
       (incf x (the double-float (bar i)))
       (incf i 1d0))))

(defun foo-2 ()
  (declare (optimize speed)
           (inline bar))                               ;; <- see (c) below
  (let ((x 0d0)
        (i 1d0))
    (declare (double-float x))
    (loop
       (unless (< i 100000000d0)
         (return x))
       (incf x (bar i))                                ;; <- one declaration less
       (incf i 1d0))))
```

Note that the code already has enough declarations (see previous recipes) to make it as fast as possible. The only difference between FOO-1 and FOO-2 is that the first version calls BAR a hundred million times, whereas the second doesn't do that. This will be explained below.

Here are the results of my tests:

```
CL-USER> (time (foo-1))
Evaluation took:
  1.466 seconds of real time
  1.466410 seconds of total run time (1.466410 user, 0.000000 system)
  [ Run times consist of 0.263 seconds GC time,
    and 1.204 seconds non-GC time. ]
  100.00% CPU
  3,803,937,740 processor cycles
  3,200,024,576 bytes consed
7.071067811865478d15
```

```
CL-USER> (time (foo-2))
Evaluation took:
  0.436 seconds of real time
  0.436803 seconds of total run time (0.436803 user, 0.000000 system)
  100.23% CPU
  1,160,997,217 processor cycles
  0 bytes consed
7.071067811865478d15
```

You might want to disassemble (see Recipe 17-12) `FOO-1` and `FOO-2` to check that the first function contains a `call` to `BAR`, whereas the second one doesn't but is longer instead.

How It Works

Our discussions of the execution stack (see for example Recipes 17-2 and 17-7) should have given you a rough idea about what has to happen during a function call: arguments may have to be put on the stack, the machine code has to jump to some other location, maybe return values have to be retrieved from the stack, the machine code has to jump back to where it was called from, and the stack pointer has to be changed. An additional burden, which is specific to dynamically typed languages like Lisp, is that arguments and as return values have to be boxed (see page 525).

Under normal circumstances, this is still negligible and you shouldn't waste time thinking about it. But in tight loops with lots of repetitions, a function call can make all the difference. As in other languages, you can ask the compiler to *inline* the code of a function in specific places,[70] which means that the machine code won't contain a `call` to the function's code at these places, but instead the code itself will be inserted. The price you have to pay for this is that the size of the generated code will grow, as there'll be repetitions. But at least your source code won't grow considerably in size.

To inline code, you'll usually need some or all of the following three steps, which are all shown in the example above:

(a) For a function that is globally defined, use `DECLAIM` to notify your compiler that you might want to inline the function. In most COMMON LISP implementations this has to happen *before* the compiler sees the function itself so that it has a chance to record its code.

The `DECLAIM` has the additional effect that the function will now always be inlined whenever a call to it appears somewhere. (Or at least the compiler will assume that this is what you want.)

[70] And as, say, in C++ the compiler can decline to do that. This can for example be the case if the function to be inlined is too big.

(b) Optionally, *after* the global definition use DECLAIM again with NOTINLINE to tell the compiler that the function should only be inlined if you explicitly ask for it.[71]

(c) In specific places, use an INLINE declaration to inline the function.

For local functions (defined with FLET or LABELS) the last of the three steps will suffice. To continue our example from above with the same Lisp implementation, consider the following three variants of the same function:[72]

```
(defun foo-1 ()
  (flet ((bar (i)
           (sqrt (+ (* i i) (* i i)))))
    (loop for k below 42
          collect (bar k))))                                    ;; (A)

(defun foo-2 ()
  (flet ((bar (i)
           (sqrt (+ (* i i) (* i i)))))
    (loop for k below 42
          collect (+ (bar k) (bar (+ k 1))))))                  ;; (B)

(defun foo-3 ()
  (flet ((bar (i)
           (sqrt (+ (* i i) (* i i)))))
    (declare (inline bar))
    (loop for k below 42
          collect (+ (bar k) (bar (+ k 1))))))                  ;; (C)
```

Looking at the disassembly, one can observe the following:

(A) The compiler inlined BAR at its own discretion without us asking for it, obviously because there's only one call to BAR in the whole function.

(B) The compiler did *not* inline the two calls to BAR.

(C) The compiler did what we asked for and inlined both calls.

Note that whether the compiler inlines code or not might also depend on the value of the SPACE optimize quality (see Recipe 17-3). Check your Lisp's documentation for details.

---

[71]While the compiler can ignore INLINE declarations, it must obey NOTINLINE declarations.

[72]Results with other Lisps might lead to different results.

Alternatives That Aren't Really Alternatives

There are two "tempting" alternatives to inlining, which are both bad, but should probably be mentioned here just in case.

- One could "inline" source code instead of generated code by using copy-and-paste. That's a very bad idea because it destroys the modularity of your code. It will make it harder to read and maintain. (If you have three copies of the same code, then each change you make has to be applied three times.) Rather, use lots of small functions and follow the "DRY" mantra.[73]
- One could use macros instead of functions. Another bad idea. It will lead to uncontrollable code bloat, your "functions" won't be first-class objects of the language anymore (for example, they can't be `FUNCALL`'d), and it will make your code a lot harder to debug (because these macros will never appear in backtraces).

The `NOTINLINE` Declaration and Compiler Macros

Be aware that a `NOTINLINE` declaration has the additional (and somewhat surprising) effect that it prevents compiler macros (see Recipe 17-9) from being expanded!

17-12. Utilizing the Disassembler

Problem

You want to know which code the compiler eventually emits.

Solution

Use `DISASSEMBLE`.

As an example, let's consider these two functions, which will both compute a dot product of two-dimensional vectors:

```
(defun dot-product-1 (x-1 x-2 y-1 y-2)
  (+ (* x-1 y-1) (* x-2 y-2)))

(defun dot-product-2 (x-1 x-2 y-1 y-2)
  (declare (optimize (safety 2)
```

[73]See `https://en.wikipedia.org/wiki/Don%27t_repeat_yourself`.

```
                        (hcl:fixnum-safety 0)))
  (+ (* x-1 y-1) (* x-2 y-2)))
```

They both do the same, but in the second version we told the compiler (Recipe 17-5) that all computations will only ever involve fixnums[74] (see Recipe 4-2) and we asked it to believe us (see Recipe 17-3).

After compiling both functions with a 32-bit version of LISPWORKS on X86 we can now do the following:

```
CL-USER 1 > (disassemble 'dot-product-1)
;; output edited to fit page width
200B9FFA:
       0: 89E6           move  esi, esp
       2: 81CEFCFF0F00   or    esi, FFFFC
       8: 3966D0         cmp   [esi-30], esp
      11: 7355           jnb   L3
      13: 80FD04         cmpb  ch, 4
      16: 7550           jne   L3
      18: 55             push  ebp
      19: 89E5           move  ebp, esp
      21: 50             push  eax
      22: 50             push  eax
      23: 8B4510         move  eax, [ebp+10]
      26: 0B4508         or    eax, [ebp+8]
      29: A803           testb al, 3
      31: 7546           jne   L4
      33: 8B7D10         move  edi, [ebp+10]
      36: C1FF02         sar   edi, 2
      39: 89FE           move  esi, edi
      41: 0FAF7508       imul  esi, [ebp+8]
      45: 8975FC         move  [ebp-4], esi
      48: 7035           jo    4
L1:   50: 8B450C         move  eax, [ebp+C]
      53: 0B45F8         or    eax, [ebp-8]
      56: A803           testb al, 3
      58: 753B           jne   L5
      60: 8B7D0C         move  edi, [ebp+C]
      63: C1FF02         sar   edi, 2
      66: 89F8           move  eax, edi
      68: 0FAF45F8       imul  eax, [ebp-8]
      72: 702D           jo    L5
L2:   74: 8B5DFC         move  ebx, [ebp-4]
      77: 0BD8           or    ebx, eax
      79: F6C303         testb bl, 3
      82: 7530           jne   L6
      84: 8B7DFC         move  edi, [ebp-4]
```

[74]HCL:FIXNUM-SAFETY is a LISPWORKS-specific optimize quality which is essentially just a shortcut. We could have used various individual type declarations instead.

```
     87: 03F8          add   edi, eax
     89: 7029          jo    L6
     91: FD            std
     92: 89F8          move  eax, edi
     94: C9            leave
     95: C20C00        ret   C
L3:  98: E8613E0600    call  2011DEC2 ; #<Function RUNTIME:BAD-ARGS-OR-STACK>
L4: 103: FF7510        push  [ebp+10]
    106: 8B4508        move  eax, [ebp+8]
    109: E8C61E0600    call  2011BF32 ; #<Function SYSTEM::*%*$ANY-STUB>
    114: 8945FC        move  [ebp-4], eax
    117: EBBB          jmp   L1
L5: 119: FF750C        push  [ebp+C]
    122: 8B45F8        move  eax, [ebp-8]
    125: E8B61E0600    call  2011BF32 ; #<Function SYSTEM::*%*$ANY-STUB>
    130: EBC6          jmp   L2
L6: 132: 8B75FC        move  esi, [ebp-4]
    135: 897510        move  [ebp+10], esi
    138: C9            leave
    139: 8F442404      pop   [esp+4]
    143: 83C404        add   esp, 4
    146: E9E11D0600    jmp   2011BE72 ; #<Function SYSTEM::*%+$ANY-STUB>
    151: 90            nop
    152: 90            nop
    153: 90            nop
NIL
CL-USER 2 > (disassemble 'dot-product-2)
200B9E1A:
      0: 89E6          move  esi, esp
      2: 81CEFCFF0F00  or    esi, FFFFC
      8: 3966D0        cmp   [esi-30], esp
     11: 7327          jnb   L1
     13: 80FD04        cmpb  ch, 4
     16: 7522          jne   L1
     18: 55            push  ebp
     19: 89E5          move  ebp, esp
     21: 8B5D10        move  ebx, [ebp+10]
     24: 8B550C        move  edx, [ebp+C]
     27: 8B7D08        move  edi, [ebp+8]
     30: C1FF02        sar   edi, 2
     33: 0FAFFB        imul  edi, ebx
     36: 89C3          move  ebx, eax
     38: C1FB02        sar   ebx, 2
     41: 0FAFDA        imul  ebx, edx
     44: 8D041F        lea   eax, [edi+ebx]
     47: FD            std
     48: C9            leave
     49: C20C00        ret   C
L1:  52: E86F400600    call  2011DEC2 ; #<Function RUNTIME:BAD-ARGS-OR-STACK>
     57: 90            nop
```

```
NIL
```

How It Works

One feature of COMMON LISP that very few other compiled languages have is the presence of the function DISASSEMBLE in the standard; every implementation must be able to show you the code it generated for a specific function.[75]

If you're good at reading assembly code and well acquainted with your Lisp implementation, you can use this feature in a kind of dialogue with your compiler to mold a specific function until it exactly fits your requirements.

But even if you only have a very superficial understanding of machine code, a bit of familiarity with the output of your Lisp's disassembler can be beneficial. For example, if we look at the code from above, we immediately see that the second version is much shorter. This doesn't have to be an indicator of greater efficiency in itself, but it is probably a good sign. More importantly, we see that the first function contains several `call` instructions, which means function call overhead (see Recipe 17-11). The LISPWORKS compiler was also nice enough to tell us which internal functions are called here so that we can observe that in the second version these calls were replaced by simple arithmetic machine code instructions.

With more intimate knowledge of your CPU, you would also be able to spot indirect references that probably could be avoided, and so on.

17-13. Switching to Machine Code

Problem

You've checked (see Recipe 17-12) and there are critical parts in your code where you simply can't convince your compiler to generate the code you want.

Solution

Write these parts in C or assembler code and access them through your Lisp's foreign function interface (see Chapter 19).

[75]And some are very good at it. Have for example a look at the various options of ALLEGROCL's disassembler and note that it can even be coupled with a profiler!

How It Works

Even with ample type declarations (see Recipe 17-5), your Lisp compiler might, for various reasons, sometimes not be able to generate the best possible machine code. Or there might be low-level optimization techniques your compiler doesn't utilize.

This is where your last resort could be to generate this code in a different way; either with C, which arguably is the most elegant cross-platform "assembly language" available or—in a machine-dependent way—with a real assembler. In either case, you would then interface this code with your Lisp program via the foreign function interface (FFI) discussed in Chapter 19.

How much you'll gain from this will depend on your specific application, though. Don't forget that there might be some overhead when the "foreign" code is called as well as when it returns, so you'll only see a significant speed increase if there aren't too many FFI calls compared to the time spent in the "foreign" code.

Also, considerable speed improvements through C code are to be expected if you're working with integers that are small enough to fit into a machine register but too big to be fixnums[76] (see Recipe 4-2). For other code, the difference might not be as big as you expect. My own experience is that with a good compiler and enough effort, and with the exception just mentioned, one can usually generate Lisp code that is only between 20 and 40 percent slower than C. But sometimes you may need these 20 percent...

Inline Assembly Code

The Windows-only CORMAN LISP[77] has the unique (to my knowledge) feature that you can intersperse Lisp source code with assembly code. Unfortunately, it is otherwise not exactly the most ANSI-compliant COMMON LISP implementation and hasn't been maintained for a while.

The closest other Lisps come to inline assembly are probably SBCL's *virtual operations* (VOPs) which allow you to write assembly in S-expressions. Their main drawback is that there's almost no documentation for them, so you'll have to dig through the compiler's source code.

Lisps that compile to C (see page 560) might have the ability to inline C code. That's not assembly code, but it's pretty close (and more portable). (See Recipe 19-8 for an example.)

---

[76]But see Recipe 4-3.

[77]An implementation that used to be commercial but is now available under an MIT license at `https://github.com/sharplispers/cormanlisp/`.

17-14. Optimizing Array Access

Problem

You are working with large arrays, but although you've provided ample type information (see Recipe 17-5), the compiler doesn't generate the optimized code that you wished it would.

Solution

Use specialized arrays (see Recipe 5-9).

For an example, compile and load a file with the following code:

```
(defconstant +max+ 10000000)

(defvar *a*
  (let ((a (make-array +max+ :element-type 'double-float)))
    (dotimes (i +max+)
      (setf (aref a i) (random 1d0)))
    a))

(defun foo-1 (a)
  (let ((result 1d0))
    (declare (double-float result))
    (dotimes (i +max+)
      (incf result (the double-float (aref a i))))
    result))

(defun foo-2 (a)
  (declare (type (simple-array double-float (*)) a))
  (let ((result 1d0))
    (declare (double-float result))
    (dotimes (i +max+)
      (incf result (aref a i)))
    result))
```

On SBCL,[78] I get the following results:

```
* (time (foo-1 *a*))
Evaluation took:
```

[78]This was SBCL 1.2.12 on 64-bit Windows. With other Lisps, you might need slightly different optimize qualities (see Recipe 17-3), but the general point is the same.

```
  0.156 seconds of real time
  0.156001 seconds of total run time (0.156001 user, 0.000000 system)
  100.00% CPU
  457,821,372 processor cycles
  160,008,768 bytes consed
* (time (foo-2 *a*))
Evaluation took:
  0.031 seconds of real time
  0.015600 seconds of total run time (0.015600 user, 0.000000 system)
  51.61% CPU
  64,852,716 processor cycles
  0 bytes consed
```

How It Works

Because of their $\mathcal{O}(1)$ access characteristics, arrays (see Chapter 5) are often a good choice for fast algorithms. However, due to their flexibility and generality, array access in COMMON LISP isn't as fast as in statically typed languages, at least not out of the box.

At a first glance it seems that in FOO-1 above, we already provided enough type information for the compiler so that it should know we only want DOUBLE-FLOAT arithmetic. Still, the sheer amount of data consed looks fishy.

What's happening here is that the compiler doesn't know anything about the array A. That means the AREF form will end up being compiled into a call to some generic operation that can cope with any type of array and will at run time decide what to do; for example, whether the value retrieved from the array has to be unboxed (see page 525).

Sure, we wrapped the AREF in a THE (see page 528), but that only applies to the *result* of the AREF operation.

What comes to the rescue in FOO-2 is that we now inform the compiler that A is a particular kind of array where the elements are stored unboxed. (See Recipe 5-9 for the details.) This enables it to pull the numbers directly out of the array and presumably put them into a machine register immediately afterward.

(And note that in the second version of our function, we didn't need the THE anymore as the compiler now obviously knew what type to expect as a result of the AREF.)

Some Lisps offer their own variety of optimized array accessors. One example would be LISPWORKS's LW:TYPED-AREF. To be honest, I'm not really sure if I like this approach. While on the one hand you can create super-fast code with it, on the other hand it makes your code unportable. And what's probably worse, it forces you to *modify* your code (and on top of it in a rather ugly way), whereas in other cases you usually only have to add a few declarations in the right places to optimize your code.

17-15. Comparing Different Implementations

Problem

You've tried all recipes of this chapter, but you're still not happy with the speed of your program.

Solution

Try another COMMON LISP implementation.

How It Works

Although the number of different COMMON LISP implementations with their idiosyncrasies, and all the "implementation-dependent behavior" that crops up in a lot of places in this book may seem like a curse at times, it also has a good side: competition. Most of these Lisps are really *different* in that they employ a diverse array of compilation strategies. If you're not tied to a specific implementation for other reasons, it might be a good idea to give at least some of them a try if you seem stuck.

We'll try to give a quick (and certainly incomplete) survey of what to expect (as of mid-2015):

- Many implementations compile directly to the machine code of the underlying platform. This includes ALLEGROCL, LISPWORKS, CLOZURECL (and its ancestor MACINTOSH COMMON LISP), CORMAN LISP, and CMUCL and its "siblings" SBCL and SCIENEER COMMON LISP.

  Each of these compilers has different strengths and weaknesses and they will almost certainly create different machine code from the same Lisp source code.

- Some other Lisps compile to machine code but make a "detour" via C; that is, they compile the Lisp source code to C source code and then ask a C compiler (usually GCC) to generate machine code from that. This includes ECL, MANKAI COMMON LISP, and GCL, which are all descendants of KYOTO COMMON LISP.

  Although direct compilation to machine code seems to be a better strategy, it should not be underestimated how good C compilers are at optimization.

GCL, for example, has always been "good enough" to be the main implementation for demanding applications like MAXIMA or ACL2.

(See also Recipes 19-8 and 19-9.)

- CLISP compiles to an intermediate bytecode,[79] which is then executed by an interpreter.

  This might sound as if CLISP were, in terms of speed, hopeless compared to the Lisps listed above, but that's not necessarily true. For one, CLISP was always well known for its high-speed bignums and arbitrary-precision floating-point arithmetic (see also Chapter 4). For number crunching, it might be a better choice than the "native" Lisps. Also, recent versions of CLISP use GNU LIGHTNING for JIT compilation,[80] so it now kind of belongs to the "native" category as well.

- ABCL runs on the JVM;[81] that is, the generated code is JAVA bytecode.

  As with CLISP, one could argue that having an intermediate language should result in slower execution compared to machine code. But as with the "Kyoto descendants," one should keep in mind how good the underlying infrastructure is; which in this case consists not only of a highly optimized JIT compiler, but also of world-class garbage collectors.

  See also Recipes 19-10 and 20-3.

- Finally, there's the fairly new CLASP (see also Recipe 19-9), which uses yet another approach to compilation in that it targets the LLVM[82] ecosystem. What has been said above about some of the other Lisps which use "intermediate" compilation targets should apply here as well.

[79]See `https://en.wikipedia.org/wiki/Bytecode`.
[80]See `https://en.wikipedia.org/wiki/Just-in-time_compilation`.
[81]See `https://en.wikipedia.org/wiki/Java_virtual_machine`.
[82]See `http://llvm.org/`.

18. Libraries

There used to be a time, not so long ago, when people complained about the COMMON LISP library situation (and rightly so). It was perceived that—compared to more popular languages like, at that time, PERL—there weren't "enough" libraries available, and it was hard to find those that were. And, once you had found one, it was hard to install or it didn't play nicely with your specific implementation. Fortunately, those days are over and we now have an abundance of libraries, which are very easy to obtain and compatible with the prominent COMMON LISP compilers.

In this chapter, we'll see how a COMMON LISP library (or actually any larger program) is typically organized and how easy it is to load a library into your Lisp image.

The second half of the chapter will deal with some popular and useful libraries that didn't fit elsewhere. But note that almost all the other chapters also introduce open source libraries.

18-1. Organizing Your Code

Problem

You want to automate the process of compiling and loading a larger code base consisting of several files.

(Or maybe you just want to know how the large COMMON LISP library you just downloaded from the Internet is organized.)

Solution

Use ASDF to define a so-called "system." If, for example, your program consists of three files—`foo1.lisp`, `foo2.lisp`, and `bar.lisp`—that need to be loaded in this order, create a file `foo.asd` (a *system definition*) in the same folder as the other files with these contents:

```
(asdf:defsystem :foo
  :serial t
  :components ((:file "foo1")
```

```
            (:file "foo2")
            (:file "bar")))
```

Once ASDF knows about the existence of `foo.asd` (see below), you'll be able to load all three files at once, like so:

```
(asdf:require-system :foo)          ;; or use ASDF:LOAD-SYSTEM
```

This will not only load the files, it will compile them first, if necessary (i.e., if the source code has changed since the file was last compiled), and it will load them in the right order. It will also, for example, re-compile `bar.lisp` if `foo2.lisp` was updated.

How It Works

It is considered good practice to organize larger programs in a meaningful way by distributing the code over several files. But you don't want to compile and load all of these files manually each time you work with your code. That's what so-called *build automation tools* are for—programs like `make` or ANT.

ASDF (that's an acronym for "another system definition facility" and obviously a pun on how these keys are arranged on a typical QWERTY keyboard) is an open source build automation tool for COMMON LISP that was originally created in 2002 by Daniel Barlow. A couple of Lisps, like ALLEGROCL or LISPWORKS, already had (and still have) their own implementation-specific system definition facilities; there even was a portable open source solution called MK:DEFSYSTEM available at that time. Nevertheless, ASDF quickly gained mindshare and has since become the de facto standard. All libraries loadable by QUICKLISP (see Recipe 18-2) use ASDF, which nowadays comes pre-installed with all Lisps still in active development. So you can simply evaluate

```
(require :asdf)
```

and there it is.

ASDF has seen two major overhauls since its inception; it is at version 3 at the time of this writing, but most likely, you won't have to worry about version numbers because the developers always had backwards compatibility in mind.

Components

The most important job of a system definition is to list all the *components* that belong to a system. In most cases, these are source files like the three `.lisp` files in the example above, and you usually enumerate them in the form `(:FILE "foo")`. ASDF will automatically add ".lisp" at the end, and then look for the file in the directory where the system definition itself was located. You can make it look elsewhere by explicitly specifying the location of the file like so

```
(:file "foo" :pathname "src/foo.lisp")
```

where the pathname can be absolute or will otherwise be interpreted relative to the system definition file.

But even if you don't want to specify explicit pathnames for each file (which would certainly be tedious), you can organize your code in a neat hierarchical file structure. A component can also be a *module,* which as far as ASDF is concerned is simply a bunch of other components grouped together. Wherever a file would be acceptable as a component, a module is acceptable as well.[1] An example module could look like this:

```
(:module "quux"
 :components ((:file "symbols")
              (:file "util")
              (:file "algo")))
```

ASDF would now look for the module's files in a directory called quux relative to the system definition (or rather relative to where the parent of this module is located in the file system) but this can again be overridden with a `:PATHNAME` argument.

Dependencies

The *raison d'être* for a tool like ASDF is, of course, to keep track of *dependencies* in the sense of "this has to be done first before that can happen." That's why dependencies are the other main building block of a system definition. Let's suppose we have our code distributed over several files. The file `packages.lisp` contains package definitions and must be loaded prior to all other files. `specials.lisp` contains global special variables and constants that are used in `algo1.lisp` and `algo2.lisp` and `macros.lisp` contains (you guessed it) macros which are used in `algo1.lisp` but not in `algo2.lisp`. Finally, the file `api.lisp` contains the user-visible application code and relies on all other files being loaded first. One would now say that `algo1.lisp` *depends on* `macros.lisp`. The complete system of dependencies unfolds to what mathematicians call a *directed acyclic graph*[2] or *DAG*. Graphically, it'll look like this:

[1]Which implies that nobody is stopping you from nesting modules. So, components of a module could themselves be modules, which again could contain modules, and so on.

[2]It had better be acyclic, because otherwise, your system would never build!

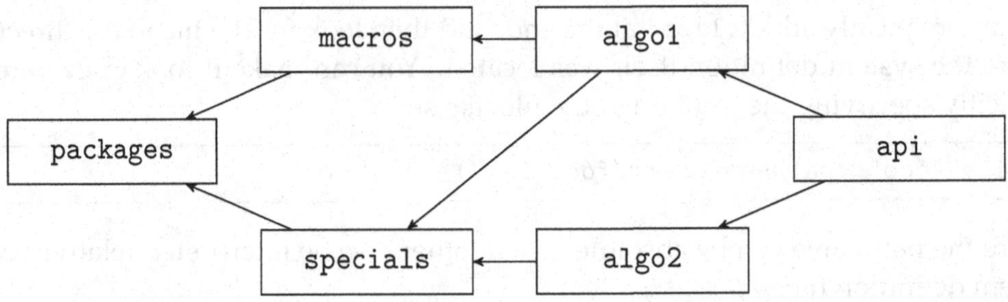

Here an arrow from *A* to *B* means that *A* depends on *B*. Such a graph (or rather the underlying relation) is implicitly understood to be *transitive*, which for example means that as `algo1.lisp` depends on `macros.lisp`, which in turn depends on `packages.lisp`, `algo1.lisp` depends on `packages.lisp` as well. ASDF will figure this out automatically so that you won't have to mention it explicitly.[3] It can be a bit of a nuisance to state all the dependencies of a system, but it will likely save you time in the long run. For example, if `macros.lisp` was changed, then `algo1.lisp` needs to be recompiled, but `algo2.lisp` doesn't. For larger systems, quite a lot of needless recompilation can be saved this way.[4]

The system definition corresponding to our example DAG would now look like this:

```
(asdf:defsystem :whatever
  :components ((:file "packages")
               (:file "specials" :depends-on ("packages"))
               (:file "macros" :depends-on ("packages"))
               (:file "algo1" :depends-on ("macros" "specials"))
               (:file "algo2" :depends-on ("specials"))
               (:file "api" :depends-on ("algo1" "algo2"))))
```

Essentially, all components should have a `:DEPENDS-ON` list of components that they directly (as opposed to transitively) depend on.

So what about the `:SERIAL` argument in our first example? This is merely a convenience feature for simple systems; it means that each component depends on the one listed directly before it.[5] The corresponding DAG would then look pretty boring:

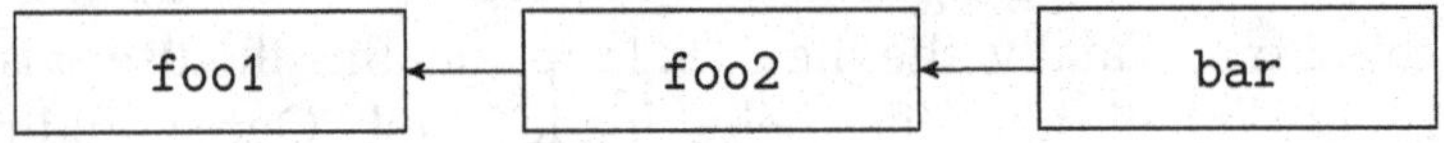

But not only can components depend on other components, whole systems can depend on other systems. If our first system with the three files used the DRAKMA

[3]One could argue that the relation is also *reflexive* in the sense that each file depends on itself; it must first be compiled before it can be loaded.

[4]But you can also introduce subtle errors if you forget to state some dependencies!

[5]Which also implies that in this case, the order of components in the system definition matters, while otherwise it doesn't.

library (see Recipe 18-7), and wouldn't work without it, we would modify the definition to look like so:[6]

```
(asdf:defsystem :foo
  :serial t
  :components ((:file "foo1")
               (:file "foo2")
               (:file "bar"))
  :depends-on (:drakma))
```

ASDF would then take care of compiling and loading DRAKMA first before starting to work on `foo1.lisp`; provided it knows where on your hard drive DRAKMA is. For that, see the next section.

It might be worth mentioning that `ASDF:REQUIRE-SYSTEM` and `ASDF:LOAD-SYSTEM` are meant to be used interactively from your REPL. As a general rule, they should *never* appear in your source code. Instead, dependencies should always be expressed in system definitions (like the dependency on DRAKMA in the example above).

How Does ASDF Find System Definitions?

In order for ASDF to find a system so that it can be loaded, it must find its `.asd` file. But where exactly does it look?

First, there's a special variable `ASDF:*CENTRAL-REGISTRY*` containing a list of directory pathnames. ASDF will search all directories in this list for files ending in `.asd`. So, there are essentially two ways to make a new system known to ASDF using this mechanism. You either add the pathname of the directory where your `.asd` file is to this list[7] or you create a (symbolic) link to your `.asd` file in a directory that's already in this list.

This is the "traditional" way of doing it, which has remained unchanged since ASDF saw the light of day. Newer versions of ASDF added more flexibility, but arguably also more complexity. You can put all your system definitions into subdirectories of[8]

```
~/.common-lisp/
```

[6]You're scratching your head because the files are named by strings and the DRAKMA system is named by a symbol? Read Recipe 1-9.

[7]Make sure that it really denotes a *directory*. A typical error is to forget the slash at the end.

[8]Or `~/.local/share/common-lisp/source/` for older versions of ASDF.

Here ~ means your home directory on Unix-like systems, as usual. But it is more complicated on Windows. At the time of this writing, your best bet is to look at the output of the (unexported) function `ASDF::DEFAULT-SOURCE-REGISTRY` to find out where ASDF looks by default on your particular machine.

or you can use so-called *configurations*. These are described in detail in the ASDF manual

But most likely, you'll never have to worry about this stuff (see Recipes 18-2 and 18-3).

Additional Information

You can stuff more information into a system definition, which is not necessary for ASDF to do its job but should be in place once you plan to publish your code. This includes your (the author's) name, license information, a version number, and maybe a short textual description of what your code does. QUICKPROJECT (see Recipe 18-3) will provide you with a template `.asd` file, where those fields are already present.

What About the Names?

We called our example file `foo.asd` and the system itself was named using the keyword `:FOO`, so except for the case (ASDF actively downcases symbol names; see Recipe 1-8), they have the same name. This is the usual way of doing it, and unless you have very specific needs, you should use this pattern.

(There's nobody preventing you from putting more than one system definition in an `.asd` file, but ASDF will only know about these definitions once it has loaded the `.asd` file. So this is generally a bad idea, except maybe for systems which are only supposed to be loaded *after* the "main" system has been loaded.)

Advanced Usage of ASDF

ASDF has a pretty elaborate object model that makes it almost infinitely extensible. It is capable of doing much more than loading and compiling Lisp code. It could just as well compile source code from other languages or manage resources like image files and these things have actually been done. You can also specify where your object files (the files created by `COMPILE-FILE`) will be stored (they don't have to clutter your source directory) and lots of other things.

Unfortunately, this book is too short to cover all of this, but the ASDF manual is quite good and you can also learn a lot from looking at how larger open source libraries are organized.

18-2. Employing Open Source Libraries

Problem

You want to use a specific open source library.

Solution

Use QUICKLISP. Once you have QUICKLISP installed (see below), the process of adding a new library is just a matter of issuing a single form like

```
(ql:quickload "drakma")
```

to make a library like DRAKMA (see Recipe 18-7) available in your Lisp image. If necessary, QUICKLISP will download and compile the library for you. It will also take care of dependencies; that is, it will download and compile other libraries that your library depends on.

All the libraries mentioned in this book (and many, many more) are available via QUICKLISP.

How It Works

ASDF (see Recipe 18-1) will take care of compiling and loading libraries in one go. It'll also automatically load other libraries first, if needed. However, in order for this to work, all of these libraries have to be downloaded first and then put into a place where ASDF can find them. This involves manual *dependency tracking* (library *A* might depend on *B*, which in turn depends on *C*) and maybe version conflicts as well.

CTAN and CPAN are early examples of tools that automated such a cumbersome process. TEX had CTAN since 1992, and shortly thereafter, CPAN for PERL was modeled after it. Both are central repositories for open source libraries that extend the respective base languages and make downloading and installing of such libraries easy and painless; which includes automated dependency tracking and resolution of version conflicts, if possible.[9]

It took quite some time and several attempts that were only partially successful until something similar was available for COMMON LISP. But thanks to the efforts of Zach Beane, we now have QUICKLISP. While I'm writing this recipe (August 2015),

[9]There are similar repositories for other languages, but these two are the oldest, and in their heyday, they were very successful. In fact, many people argue that CPAN was maybe the most important factor for PERL's immense popularity in the 1990s and the first years of this century.

there are more than 1,200 libraries available via QUICKLISP, and I'm sure there will be significantly more before the book is finished. Loading such a library into your Lisp image (and downloading and compiling it, if necessary; and downloading and compiling dependencies, if necessary; and putting all the stuff into the right place) is done with one simple statement, as shown above. You just have to install QUICKLISP once—and that's also very easy.

Installing Quicklisp

Before you can use QUICKLISP for the first time, you will have to download the file `quicklisp.lisp` which at the time of this writing is at `http://beta.quicklisp.org/quicklisp.lisp`.[10] Then `LOAD` the file and afterward evaluate the following forms:[11]

```
(quicklisp-quickstart:install)
(ql:add-to-init-file)
```

This will write some code to your *init file* (see Recipe 22-5) so that the next time you start your Lisp image, QUICKLISP is already available. That's all. Wasn't that easy? (And you can throw away the file `quicklisp.lisp` now if you want.)

You can use `QL:UNINSTALL` to get rid of a library that you loaded and don't need anymore; and you can use `QL:SYSTEM-APROPOS` to see what's available.

Zach Beane maintains the QUICKLISP repository and updates it on a regular basis. To update your local mirror, use the command `QL:UPDATE-ALL-DISTS`. You can also update QUICKLISP itself, if necessary, with `QL:UPDATE-CLIENT`. QUICKLISP can do even more than that (like going "back in time" in case an updated library has broken your code), but you'll have to read its documentation for that.

One final remark: libraries are added to QUICKLISP if someone sends a request to add them and they are only ever rejected if they don't build on a reference system or fail to fulfill formal criteria (like having an acceptable open source license). Other than that, the fact that a library is available via QUICKLISP shouldn't be interpreted as some seal of quality. You can't even be sure if a certain library compiles on your particular system and actually works as advertised. (It would be almost humanly impossible, even for someone who got paid for it, to constantly test and evaluate all COMMON LISP libraries on all COMMON LISP compilers on various different operating systems...)

[10]Don't worry about the "beta" there. QUICKLISP has been around since 2010 and it works just fine. For the reasons why it's still "beta," see `http://lispblog.xach.com/post/122948651818/quicklisp-beyond-beta`.

[11]Actually, the better advice is to follow the instructions you'll see on the screen. QUICKLISP will guide you through the installation process and this will presumably still work, should this book be outdated at some point in the future.

Another small fly in the ointment is that apart from the aforementioned `QL:SYSTEM-APROPOS` (which only scans the *names* of the libraries), QUICKLISP can't help you with finding software that does what you need. For this, have a look at QUICKDOCS by Eitaro Fukamachi (and maybe also CLIKI).[12]

Using Quicklisp for Your Own Code

QUICKLISP isn't "just" a tool to make working with public open source libraries easier. You can also use it with your own code, which might only exist locally on your hard drive or in a private repository. The easiest way is to put such code into the `~/quicklisp/local-projects/` directory. QUICKLISP will then seamlessly integrate these projects as if they were part of the public QUICKLISP infrastructure.

This also applies to all libraries that ASDF can find (see Recipe 18-1). If you try to load a library FOO, which is available via QUICKLISP but is already on your hard disk so that it can be loaded with `(ASDF:REQUIRE-SYSTEM :FOO)`, then QUICKLISP uses this local copy and does not try to download FOO from the Internet. (This mechanism can obviously also be used to "pin down" a specific version of a library that you're relying on.)

18-3. Creating a Project's Skeleton Automatically

Problem

You want to start a new COMMON LISP project but you want to skip the grunt work of creating boilerplate code.

Solution

Use QUICKPROJECT. If QUICKLISP (see Recipe 18-2) is installed, you only need these two forms

```
(ql:quickload "quickproject")
(quickproject:make-project "/home/edi/lisp/fnork/"
                           :depends-on '(drakma lparallel))
```

to create the directory `fnork` at the place specified and fill it with four files, including a system definition that "knows" that the project depends on the DRAKMA and LPARALLEL libraries and that is automatically made available to QUICKLISP.

[12]To be found at `http://quickdocs.org/` and `http://cliki.net/`, respectively.

How It Works

Recipe 18-1 describes how a Lisp code project is typically organized into several files. If you follow these guidelines, then every project will always start with more or less the same steps, and this is what QUICKPROJECT (written by Zach Beane who also created QUICKLISP) automates for you.

What was described above is practically all you need to know, and from there on, every project will likely differ and it wouldn't make sense to automate more. However, if you're starting new projects pretty often, then you might want to look at other options that QUICKPROJECT has to offer, like automatically adding author names and license information or adding files from a template directory.

Note that while QUICKPROJECT will make the new project available to QUICKLISP immediately after its creation, it won't be available after you restart your Lisp image unless you took care of this; for example, by adding your project to a specific directory. (See Recipes 18-1 and 18-2 for details.)

18-4. Avoiding Wheel-Reinvention

Problem

There's this one piece of functionality of which you're wondering why it isn't in the COMMON LISP standard. Do you really have to write it yourself?

Solution

Have a look at the ALEXANDRIA library.[13] Chances are that it has what you're looking for.

How It Works

On the one hand, probably every programming language contains things some of its users find superfluous; whereas on the other hand, it will lack certain features that people would like to have. You can't be all things to all people...

Still, COMMON LISP might have more "gaping holes" than other languages; partly for historical reasons (as it was created as a "compromise" of several competing Lisp dialects) and partly because its standard hasn't changed for decades.

[13]Which is, of course, available via QUICKLISP (see Recipe 18-2).

The ALEXANDRIA library tries to fill some of these gaps in a strictly portable (and "conservative") way. And it is pretty successful at that, as it has topped the QUICKLISP download charts for years now.

We're already referencing ALEXANDRIA from other parts of this book, but here are some samples of what you might find in there:

- Conversion of alists and plists into hash tables (see Chapter 6):

```
CL-USER > (alexandria:plist-hash-table '(batman gotham-city
                                          superman metropolis
                                          spider-man
                                            new-york-city)
                                        :test 'eq)
#<EQ Hash Table{3} 2008FAD3>
```

- Helpful combinations of control structures and variable bindings:

```
CL-USER > (alexandria:when-let (symbol (find-symbol "LET"))
            (symbol-package symbol))
#<The COMMON-LISP package, 3/4 internal, 978/1024 external>
```

- Partial application[14] and function composition:

```
CL-USER > (let ((mod3 (alexandria:rcurry 'mod 3)))
            (funcall mod3 5))
2
```

- Functionality for lists and conses (see Chapter 2) you might have missed:

```
CL-USER > (defparameter *a* (list 1 2 3 4 5))
*A*
CL-USER > (alexandria:appendf *a* (list 6 7 9))
(1 2 3 4 5 6 7 9)
CL-USER > *a*
(1 2 3 4 5 6 7 9)
CL-USER > (setf (alexandria:lastcar *a*) 8)
8
CL-USER > *a*
(1 2 3 4 5 6 7 8)
```

- Utilities for sequences:

```
CL-USER > (alexandria:shuffle (list 1 2 3 4 5 6))
(2 1 6 5 4 3)
```

[14]See https://en.wikipedia.org/wiki/Partial_application.

```
CL-USER > (alexandria:map-combinations
           (lambda (subseq)
             (format t "~{~A~^-~}~%" subseq))
           '(1 2 3 4 5)
           :length 3)
1-2-3
1-2-4
1-2-5
1-3-4
1-3-5
1-4-5
2-3-4
2-3-5
2-4-5
3-4-5
(1 2 3 4 5)
```

- Mathematical functions like linear interpolation:

```
CL-USER > (alexandria:lerp 1/10 40 60)
42
```

- And a lot more...

18-5. Using Libraries to Write Portable Code

Problem

You want to write code that runs on as many different COMMON LISP implementations as possible.

Solution

There are lots of libraries that act as "portability layers" and that can help you with this task. We'll discuss some of them below.

How It Works

If you're writing open source software and you're interested in wide dissemination, then it's certainly a good idea to publish code that can run on more than one Lisp.

But this can even be helpful if you're only coding for yourself, as you thus won't depend on one implementation.[15]

As long as you're using standard COMMON LISP, you're writing portable code by definition. But as soon as you're in the dreaded "implementation-specific" territory, things become complicated and you will have to start using *feature expressions* (see Recipe 10-10) to make your code agnostic of the differences between the various compilers. Luckily, you're not the first one facing this task; for many areas, there already exist libraries that enable you to write code almost as if all Lisps were equal.

Here are some of them—all of which are installable with QUICKLISP (see Recipe 18-2) and many of which are also discussed in other chapters:

- APPLY-ARGV is one of several libraries to access the command-line arguments that your program was provided with (see Recipe 22-2).
- BORDEAUX THREADS is meant to make writing multithreaded apps portable (see Chapter 11).
- The CFFI library (see Chapter 19) aims to be a rather comprehensive unification of the foreign function interfaces of many Lisps.
- CL-CUSTOM-HASH-TABLE provides a portability layer for custom hash tables (see Recipe 6-5).
- The CL-FAD library tries to achieve similar behavior across different Lisps regarding pathname handling on Windows, Unix, and Mac OS (see Recipe 15-10).
- CLOSER TO MOP is a comprehensive portability layer for the Metaobject Protocol (see Recipe 13-11).
- With EXTERNAL-PROGRAM you can execute other programs from your Lisp in an implementation-independent way (see more in Recipe 22-6).
- FLEXI-STREAMS provides a uniform interface to external formats (Recipe 3-3).
- INTROSPECT-ENVIRONMENT tries to unify environment access (Recipe 10-9), although so far it only covers a few open source Lisps.
- TRIVIAL-BACKTRACE can be used to programmatically generate a backtrace in an implementation-independent way (see page 480).
- TRIVIAL-DUMP-CORE unifies the process of saving an image for SBCL, CLISP, and CLOZURECL (see Recipe 22-4).
- TRIVIAL-FEATURES tries to ensure consistent `*FEATURES*` (see Recipe 10-10) across multiple implementations.

[15] Also, due to different diagnostic capabilities and compilation strategies (see Recipe 17-15), different compilers might be able to point out different flaws and weaknesses of your code. It might thus be a good habit to run your code on different Lisps from time to time.

- TRIVIAL-GARBAGE deals with several topics related to garbage collection (see Recipes 6-7 and 22-10).
- TRIVIAL-GRAY-STREAMS (see Recipe 14-14) unifies Gray streams.
- USOCKET provides a portable TCP/IP and UDP/IP socket interface.

You have to keep in mind, though, that some of these libraries provide a unified *interface*, but the underlying *behavior* might still differ from one Lisp to the other; CLOSER TO MOP and TRIVIAL-GRAY-STREAMS come to mind. Others (e.g., CFFI or BORDEAUX THREADS) necessarily have to use a lowest common denominator approach, because implementations are so different that many interesting features can't be unified at all.

18-6. Utilizing Regular Expressions

Problem

You want to scan strings with regular expressions.

Solution

Check whether your implementation has out-of-the-box regular expressions; or use a library like CL-PPCRE.[16] In CL-PPCRE, the most general operator is `PPCRE:SCAN`, which would be used like so to find the first occurrence of double vowels in a string:

```
(ppcre:scan "([aeiou])\\1" "This example is too simple and cheesy.")
```

The first argument is a regular expression (often fondly called *regex*) in PERL syntax, and the function will return up to four values. In this case, these values are

```
17
19
#(17)
#(18)
```

where `17` and `19` denote the position[17] of `"oo"` in the string, and `17` and `18` denote the position of the first of these two characters corresponding to the part in the regular expression with parentheses around it.

If you are just interested in the string `"oo"` and not in its position within the original string, CL-PPCRE has several convenience functions for you. Likewise, there are

[16]Which is, of course, available via QUICKLISP (see Recipe 18-2).

[17]Positions are meant to be understood as in `SUBSEQ` (see Recipe 7-5).

macros to loop through a string and find or act on *all* occurrences of a pattern and there are functions to modify strings based on regexes (see below).

How It Works

Regular expressions are originally a concept from theoretical computer science,[18] but were adopted pretty early as a useful tool by the Unix community. In particular, regular expressions were used extensively in PERL. It is probably fair to say that PERL made regexes popular (and established an informal "industry standard" for their syntax), but also gave them a bad reputation, as many PERL hackers used them as a kind of silver bullet, even in situations where they were not appropriate.

If used considerately, regular expressions can be very helpful, though. COMMON LISP programmers always had access to regular expressions; either because they came bundled with their compiler[19] or because they used libraries. But CL-PPCRE (originally released in 2002) was the first widespread regex library that worked consistently on all implementations and tried to be as compatible with PERL as possible.[20] (But it also has features like *filters* and *property resolvers*, which have no counterpart in PERL.) It has since become the *de facto* standard for regexes in COMMON LISP.

I'm assuming that you're already familiar with regular expressions to a certain extent. Unfortunately, this recipe can't provide an introduction to regular expressions; but if you've never used them before, you probably won't need CL-PPCRE anyway.[21] If you *have* used them before, whether in PERL or in one of the many languages that employ almost the same syntax, you should feel right at home, so let's take a closer look.

Regex Syntax

Whenever a regular expression is required in CL-PPCRE, you can simply use a string in the syntax you'll hopefully be familiar with.[22] There's one point that might be a bit confusing at first; it can already be seen in our first example: backslashes will usually have to be doubled. This is because backslashes are metacharacters in

[18]The regular expressions used in most programming languages today are much more powerful than the ones that were originally used to describe so-called *regular languages*, though.

[19]This is, for example, the case with CLISP, ALLEGROCL, and LISPWORKS.

[20]It is probably worth noting that in spite of the similarity in name, CL-PPCRE is not in any way related to the popular C library PCRE. In particular, it doesn't employ this library but is rather written in pure COMMON LISP.

[21]If, however, you know the basics but need a refresher, you might want to have a look at THE REGEX COACH (to be found at `http://weitz.de/regex-coach/`), which is based on CL-PPCRE. In terms of downloads, it is certainly one of the most popular COMMON LISP applications ever written.

[22]Except for arcane differences described in the CL-PPCRE documentation the syntax coincides with the one found at `http://perldoc.perl.org/perlre.html`.

regex syntax, but they are also metacharacters in COMMON LISP's syntax for literal strings. So the first backslash is there to tell Lisp that the second backslash is just that—a backslash.[23]

Other than that, a Lisp string can simply stand in as a regular expression. This entails all that comes with regexes; particularly, they are almost unreadable and begin to look like line noise once they become moderately complex. The good news is that CL-PPCRE allows you to describe regular expression in an alternative syntax: as S-expressions that represent the regexes as trees. Try something like

```
(pprint (ppcre:parse-string "([a-z])|42+"))
```

and you'll see what I mean. Specifically, the tree will immediately show that the + in the regex above only applies to the digit 2 (as opposed to the number 42) and so on.[24] And as we're talking about S-expressions, you can use the whole COMMON LISP machinery (see Chapter 2) to manipulate and analyze them, which is far easier and less error-prone than dissecting strings. (Plus, you can build up S-expression regexes from "known parts" using so-called *synonyms*.) So, whenever a string is acceptable as a regular expression, an S-expression is too.

Scanners

When a regex is provided as an argument to a CL-PPCRE function as a string or as an S-expression, it will first be converted into an internal representation called a *scanner*. You can view these scanners as opaque objects and don't need to be concerned with what they actually are,[25] but you might want to keep in mind that depending on the complexity of the regex, this conversion might take some time. The idea is that this time should be spent only once and that the scanner will be an optimized representation of the regex, better suited for the task of scanning a string.[26]

That's why there's a function PPCRE:CREATE-SCANNER to create such scanners. It's used internally by PPCRE:SCAN and all other functions that scan strings, but it is exposed as part of the API so that you can create scanners and store them. Each function that accepts regexes (as strings or S-expressions) will also accept such scanners instead. (And will be much more efficient with scanners, as no conversion will happen.)

---

[23]If you're a dyed-in-the-wool PERL hacker and plan to use CL-PPCRE regexes a lot, you might want to have a look at the CL-INTERPOL library, which will relieve you of the need to always type two backslashes.

[24]The full syntax is described in the CL-PPCRE documentation.

[25]Ok, so you're nosey. They are closures, or rather "chains" of closures.

[26]Although the closures themselves employ some Lisp-y techniques, the idea of processing a regular expression before it is used is far from being original or revolutionary. It's what pretty much every regex engine does. Some call this "compilation" of the regular expression, some use other names.

CL-PPCRE also employs compiler macros (see Recipe 17-9) for the same reason. If you have a form like

```
(ppcre:scan "a|b+" string)
```

in some function FOO and compile FOO, then the string "a|b+" will be converted into a scanner and the scanner will become a part of FOO, so that when FOO is called, no further regex conversion needs to happen (and you don't have to worry about using PPCRE:CREATE-SCANNER).

As is the nature of compiler macros, this will only work if the compiler can determine that the regex is *constant*; so sometimes you *will* have to manually create scanners to avoid needless repeated regex conversions.

To drive the point home, consider these two simple functions:

```
(defun foo-1 (regex)
  (dotimes (i 100000)
    (ppcre:scan regex "Frunobulax")))

(defun foo-2 ()
  (dotimes (i 100000)
    (ppcre:scan "a|b+" "Frunobulax")))
```

Compare them using (TIME (FOO-1 "a|b+")) and (TIME (FOO-2)) after compiling them. (See page 513 for the TIME function.) Although both function calls will do exactly the same thing semantically, the differences in terms of memory allocation and time spent should be quite noticeable.

Convenience Features

As we already saw above, the function PPCRE:SCAN will return (packaged as two positional values) the part of the string where the regex matched plus (as two vectors) the same information for all capture groups, if there are any. To quote the movie *Pulp Fiction,* sometimes this is a little bit more information than you needed. That's why CL-PPCRE provides a function that will return the match itself as a string:

```
(ppcre:scan-to-strings "([aeiou])\\1"
                       "This example is too simple and cheesy.")
```

This will return the following two values:[27]

[27]Of course, PPCRE:SCAN provides *more* information. Here you can't see just from looking at the results, where in the string the "oo" came from or whether the "o" was the first or the second character of the match.

```
"oo"
#("o")
```

Another variant of the vanilla scan is one where you want all matches:

```
(ppcre:all-matches-as-strings
 "([aeiou])\\1"
 "This example is too simple and cheesy.")
```

This will give you the list `("oo" "ee")` and there's also `PPCRE:ALL-MATCHES` which is to `PPCRE:ALL-MATCHES-AS-STRINGS` what `PPCRE:SCAN` is to `PPCRE:SCAN-TO-STRINGS`.

And speaking of *all* matches, sometimes you don't want to cons up a list of all matches, but you want to iterate through them and do something with them. There are several `DO-` macros in CL-PPCRE that will help you with that. Much like `DOLIST` iterates through a list and binds a variable to each list element in turn, these macros iterate through a string and bind one or more variables each time the regex matches:[28]

```
(defun digital-root-1 (target-string)
  (let ((sum 0))
    (ppcre:do-matches-as-strings (match :digit-class target-string)
      (incf sum (parse-integer match)))
    (if (< sum 10)
      sum
      (digital-root-1 (princ-to-string sum)))))

(defun digital-root-2 (target-string)
  (let ((sum 0))
    (ppcre:do-matches (start end :digit-class target-string)
      (incf sum (parse-integer target-string :start start :end end)))
    (if (< sum 10)
      sum
      (digital-root-2 (princ-to-string sum)))))
```

Above are two (quite naïve) functions that do the same thing[29] but use different CL-PPCRE macros. The first one is a bit easier to read and understand, while the second one is to be preferred if you need to be concerned about efficiency.

[28]This also demonstrates an S-expression regex (see above).

[29]They compute the digital root (see also page 79) of their argument (which should be the string representation of an integer written in decimal notation) and will tacitly skip all non-digit characters.

Modifying and Dissecting Strings

Two other tasks typically executed with regexes are replacing matched substrings of a string with something else and splitting a string into parts based on where some regex matches. This can be done with CL-PPCRE as well.

I'll just show a simple example session to whet your appetite and refer you to the documentation otherwise:

```
CL-USER 1 > (ppcre:split "\\W+" "The  quick brown
fox
jumps over the lazy dog.")
("The" "quick" "brown" "fox" "jumps" "over" "the" "lazy" "dog")
CL-USER 2 > (ppcre:regex-replace-all "[aeiou]" "foul" "e")
"feel"
T
```

In the first example, we split the sentence at each point where one or more "non-word characters" (according to PERL regex syntax) occur. This also worked across line boundaries. In the second example, we replaced all vowels by the string "e". There's much more to do with these facilities, of course.

CL-PPCRE can't split arbitrary sequences (like lists or vectors) instead of strings, and surprisingly, this is something COMMON LISP also can't do out of the box. But there's a popular small library called SPLIT-SEQUENCE that does exactly that.

More Information

Let me close this recipe by pointing you at the section called *Hints, comments, performance considerations* at the end of the CL-PPCRE documentation. It contains some useful information that you might want to give some consideration. (Well, I should say so because I wrote it. But, really, give it a try!)

18-7. Obtaining Data via HTTP

Problem

You want to programmatically grab data—for example, a picture or the HTML source of a web site—via HTTP.

Solution

Use the DRAKMA library (which you can install using QUICKLISP; see Recipe 18-2).

For example, to retrieve the HTML source code of a web page as a string, you just need its URL:

```
(drakma:http-request "http://weitz.de/erdos.html")
```

How It Works

It is probably not much of an exaggeration to say that every resource you can access over the HTTP protocol[30] can be retrieved using DRAKMA. You are not limited to textual data, as in the example above; you can also read binary data and have it returned as a stream (see Chapter 14):

```
(with-open-file (out "/tmp/lisp_logo.jpg"
                     :element-type '(unsigned-byte 8)
                     :direction :output)
  (cl-fad:copy-stream
   (flexi-streams:flexi-stream-stream
    (drakma:http-request "http://weitz.de/regex-coach/lisp_logo.jpg"
                         :want-stream t))
   out))
```

In this case, we asked the web server for a picture and from the reply (from the *headers*, to be exact) DRAKMA can automatically infer that the data sent is to be interpreted as binary. We use the `:WANT-STREAM` keyword argument to tell the library that we don't want a vector of octets (see Recipe 5-9) as a return value but rather a stream. And we then use CL-FAD (see Recipe 15-10) to copy the picture data to a local file.[31]

Pretty much everything in DRAKMA is done with just one function: `DRAKMA:HTTP-REQUEST`. But this one function is extremely flexible because it has more than three dozen (!) keyword parameters which, for example, can be used to specify parameters or cookies to send with the request, to send authorization data, to ask for partial transfers, to set timeouts, and so forth. The function will also return not just one value (which typically is the payload) but seven, containing detailed status information about the server's reply.

We could provide several more examples demonstrating the usage of these keyword parameters or we could discuss how DRAKMA can deal with redirects, different char-

[30]See `https://en.wikipedia.org/wiki/Hypertext_Transfer_Protocol`.

[31]The reason for using the FLEXI-STREAMS library (see Recipe 3-3) in this case is explained in the DRAKMA documentation.

acter encodings, chunked transfers, or secure connections. However, that would be a waste of space because its documentation already comes with almost a dozen tutorial-style examples. DRAKMA is designed to "do the right thing" by default and should thus be fairly easy to use in most scenarios, while at the same time being flexible enough for the remaining use cases.

Parsing HTML

A resource available via HTTP doesn't have to be a web page coded in HTML, but many are, and you might want to parse such a page programmatically. There are several available Lisp libraries that can do that for you,[32] and we'll just provide a quick example using CL-HTML-PARSE:[33]

```
CL-USER> (cl-html-parse:parse-html
           (drakma:http-request "http://lisp.org"))
;; output edited to fit page width
((:HTML
  (:HEAD (:TITLE "John McCarthy, 1927-2011")
         ((:STYLE :TYPE "text/css") "
    BODY {text-align: center}
  "))
  (:BODY
   (:H1 "John McCarthy")
   ((:IMG :SRC "jmccolor.jpg"
          :ALT "a picture of John McCarthy, from his website"))
   (:H3 "1927-2011")
   :BR :BR "
"  ((:A :HREF "http://www-formal.stanford.edu/jmc/")
    "John McCarthy's Home Page")
   :BR "
"  ((:A :HREF "http://news.stanford.edu/news/2011/october/...")
    "Obituary"))))
```

The main thing to note here is that the return value is an S-expression, which is now amenable to all the Lisp tools available for querying and manipulating lists and conses (see Chapter 2).

[32]See `http://www.cliki.net/html%20parser`.

[33]A port of the parser that comes with ALLEGROCL.

18-8. Creating Dynamic Web Sites with Lisp

Problem

You want to serve web content from your Lisp application; that is, you want to do the inverse of what we did in Recipe 18-7.

Solution

Use the library HUNCHENTOOT (available via QUICKLISP; see Recipe 18-2).

To start a very basic, no-frills web server, you just need to evaluate one form:[34]

```
(hunchentoot:start (make-instance 'hunchentoot:easy-acceptor
                                  :port 4242))
```

You can now enter the URL `http://127.0.0.1:4242/` in a web browser on the same machine and you should see a web page with a Lisp logo and a link to the HUNCHENTOOT documentation. This content is already served by your Lisp image.

What you are seeing is so-called *static content* residing in the `www/` subdirectory of the HUNCHENTOOT source tree. You could add more HTML files and pictures there, but as long as you're not doing more than that, it is not immediately obvious why you would want a Lisp web server when you could have performed the same task with the ubiquitous APACHE or with more lightweight solutions like NGINX or LIGHTTPD instead.

The whole thing becomes much more interesting once you start serving *dynamic* content—content that depends on the input sent by the client and/or the state of your application. For a simple example, enter this form:[35]

```
(hunchentoot:define-easy-handler (test-handler :uri "/test")
    ((name :init-form "Pumpkin"))
  (format nil "<!doctype html>
<title>Common Lisp Recipes</title>
<body>Yo, ~A!  The Lisp time is ~A.</body>"
          name (get-universal-time)))
```

You will now have defined a Lisp function called `TEST-HANDLER`, which you can call as `(TEST-HANDLER)` and also with a keyword argument as `(TEST-HANDLER :NAME "Bruce")`. In both cases, the return value should be a string containing HTML; and

[34]We are using a keyword argument to instruct HUNCHENTOOT to listen on port 4242. The default port is 80, which is the standard HTTP port, but with most modern operating systems, you won't be able to use it unless you are running your Lisp with admin rights.

[35]See Recipe 22-9 for `GET-UNIVERSAL-TIME`.

a different string each time you call the function, based on the keyword argument and the current time.

More importantly, though, you can now also call the function and see its return value from your browser by entering URLs like these:

```
http://127.0.0.1:4242/test
http://127.0.0.1:4242/test?name=Clark
```

How It Works

COMMON LISP has a proud tradition of being used as a language to implement web servers. Already in 1994, the venerable CL-HTTP[36] served the White House Publications web site. It is still available today, together with several alternatives with different strengths and priorities.[37] We're using HUNCHENTOOT in this recipe because it is the most popular (and has been for quite some time).

The job of a web server is to handle incoming *requests* from *clients*—for example from DRAKMA (Recipe 18-7), but typically from web browsers. It has to be able to cope with several requests from different clients coming in at the same time. It has to maintain network connections to these clients. It has to decide what to send to the clients based on the *request method* and on the *resource* requested. And it is expected to do other things on the side, like logging.

Within HUNCHENTOOT, this job is done by *acceptors*, *taskmasters*, and *handlers*. Here's a *very* rough picture of how HUNCHENTOOT works:

- The *acceptor* listens for requests on a specific address and port; that is, you first have to create and start an acceptor before anything happens.[38] That was the first thing we did above.
- Each acceptor works together with its *taskmaster*, which in a way is responsible for assigning the work once requests come in. (The work itself will still be done by the acceptor, but the taskmaster might decide to distribute it over several threads.)
- Then the acceptor will, for each request, analyse it, decide which *handler* to call, and provide the handler with the necessary information. The job of the handler is to generate the reply's content, which the acceptor in turn sends to the client.

The interaction between acceptors, taskmasters, and handlers is defined and documented in terms of CLOS classes and a protocol of generic function calls. The

[36]By John C. Mallery, see `https://en.wikipedia.org/wiki/CL-HTTP`.

[37]See `http://www.cliki.net/web` for an overview. If you want a super-fast Lisp web server, have a look at WOO by Eitaro Fukamachi, see `https://github.com/fukamachi/woo`.

[38]You can have several active acceptors at the same time, but only one per address/port combination.

purpose of this slightly complex setup is that you can customize HUNCHENTOOT's behavior (by subclassing and specializing) to your heart's content.

But luckily you don't have to. There's a class of acceptors called `HUNCHENTOOT:EASY-ACCEPTOR`, which is intended to make the generation of dynamic web sites as easy as possible. With such an "easy acceptor" running, you can add new handlers and associate them with resources using the function `HUNCHENTOOT:DEFINE-EASY-HANDLER` as we did above. This works a bit like `DEFUN` in that it defines a function (which *is* the handler) but with a few differences:

- The function not only has a Lisp name (`TEST-HANDLER` in our case) but is also associated with a resource on the web server, which in the example was `/test`. This means that when a request for this resource comes in, the acceptor knows that the handler `TEST-HANDLER` is to be called.[39]
- When the handler is called, the GET and/or POST parameters sent by the client (if any) will have been translated in such a way that they appear to be normal function arguments; as was the case for the `NAME` parameter in our example.
- The function is responsible for generating the reply's content. This is typically done by returning a string (such as HTML) or a sequence of octets for binary data. (But there are other means available, like writing directly to a network stream.)

`HUNCHENTOOT:DEFINE-EASY-HANDLER` is not the only way to create handlers for easy acceptors. You can also simply define them using `DEFUN` and then select them using a *dispatcher*. For a very simple example, just evaluate these two forms:

```
(defun my-other-handler ()
  "<!doctype html>
<title>Common Lisp Recipes</title>
<body>I'm a constant string.</body>")

(push (hunchentoot:create-prefix-dispatcher "/foo" 'my-other-handler)
      hunchentoot:*dispatch-table*)
```

The first form defines your new handler, `MY-OTHER-HANDLER`, which always unconditionally returns the same HTML string. And the second form (a) creates a dispatcher that will call this handler whenever the resource starts with `/foo` and (b) activates this dispatcher by adding it to the list of all dispatchers consulted by the easy acceptor.

You can test this new handler from your browser using this URL:

```
http://127.0.0.1:4242/hunchentoot/foo
```

[39]You can be more flexible, though, and provide a test function instead of a string so that one handler can be made responsible for a whole class of resources.

Or with any other one as long as it starts with `/foo`:

```
http://127.0.0.1:4242/hunchentoot/foobarbaz
```

As we just saw, a normal handler (as opposed to the "easy handler" we defined earlier) doesn't receive any function parameters. So, how does it get at the information that the client might have sent?

For example, like so:

```
(defun my-other-handler ()
  (format nil "<!doctype html>
<title>Common Lisp Recipes</title>
<body>I'm not a constant string.<br>
And these were the GET parameters:~{ <span>~S</span>~}.</body>"
          (hunchentoot:get-parameters*)))
```

Redefine `MY-OTHER-HANDLER` as above and then try a URL like this one:

```
http://127.0.0.1:4242/foo?x=1&y=2&zzz=42
```

This shows that `HUNCHENTOOT:DEFINE-EASY-HANDLER` is just a convenience macro, which, among other things, prepares the parameters for you and relieves you of the work of hanging the handler off of a dispatcher. But it also shows a very handy feature of web development in Lisp: any changes you make to your program are instantly visible from the client side. Except for the web browser, you can have a development cycle that is almost as interactive as the one you're used to from the REPL.

HUNCHENTOOT is too voluminous to treat in one recipe of this book, but you might want to try out the examples it comes with in order to get more acquainted with it and see more of its features. With the web server from above (on port 4242) still running, evaluate this in your REPL:

```
(ql:quickload "hunchentoot-test")
```

You should now be able to visit the following URL with your web browser:

```
http://127.0.0.1:4242/hunchentoot/test
```

This will show various little test pages and also the Lisp source code of these pages.

For another usage example of HUNCHENTOOT, see Recipe 20-1.

Generating HTML

When writing a web client you are often interested in *parsing* HTML (see page 583); in your web server, you typically want to *generate* it. You could do that with calls to FORMAT as above, but that'll be cumbersome and ugly in the long run. To make this a nicer task, there are essentially two different strategies in widespread use in the Lisp world.

- One way is to use a *templating engine* (as is also done in many other languages). You generate the HTML as a string or a file and put special *tags* in there, which the engine will then replace with content at run time. That's not so different from using FORMAT, but it usually has a nicer syntax and additional amenities. To give you a flavor of what this could look like, let's briefly use the CLIP engine by Nicolas Hafner[40] to generate essentially the same handler we had on page 587:

```
(defun my-other-handler ()
  (let ((template "<!doctype html>
<title>Common Lisp Recipes</title>
<body>I'm not a constant string.<br>
  And these were the GET parameters:
  <splice iterate=\"params\">
    <span lquery=\"(text (prin1-to-string *))\"></span>
  </splice>
</body>"))
    (clip:process-to-string
     template :params (hunchentoot:get-parameters*))))
```

- The other approach is rarely found in other languages. It is to manipulate the syntax so that you can use Lisp's own S-expressions to describe the output, interspersed with code, and have it transformed to HTML automatically. Let's again rewrite our handler, this time using Eitaro Fukamachi's CL-MARKUP:[41]

```
(defun my-other-handler ()
  (cl-markup:html5
   (:title "Common Lisp Recipes")
   (:body "I'm not a constant string." (:br)
          "And these were the GET parameters: "
          (loop for param in (hunchentoot:get-parameters*)
                collect (cl-markup:markup
                         (:span (prin1-to-string param))))
```

[40] For alternatives see http://www.cliki.net/templating%20library.

[41] For alternatives see http://cliki.net/html%20generator. In the examples mentioned above, HUNCHENTOOT uses CL-WHO.

```
            ".")))
```

Web Frameworks

With a Lisp web server like HUNCHENTOOT and maybe a library for generating HTML, in theory, there's nothing stopping you from writing cool and impressive dynamic web applications. However, doing something like this is not as easy as it sounds. Not because it's complicated in the sense of being hard to understand, but because there are typically so many mundane things to take care of. That's why—as in other programming languages—many so-called *web frameworks* have evolved; they usually sit atop a web server and aim to abstract away most of the grunt work of creating a "typical" web application.

There are several such frameworks available for COMMON LISP[42] but to do justice to at least one of them, we'd have to talk too much about stuff that hasn't anything to do with Lisp. So I'll just leave it at that and let you try out what's out there and make a decision.

(See also the remarks about JAVASCRIPT on page 591; see Recipe 19-11 about JSON.)

[42]See for example `http://www.cliki.net/web%20framework` for an overview.

19. Interfacing with Other Languages

Once upon a time, Lisp ruled the world...

Well, OK, not really. But there used to be a time when you could buy horribly expensive but impressive computers called *Lisp Machines* where the whole operating system was written in Lisp and Lisp was the dominant (or sometimes the only) programming language. Those times are long gone, though, and COMMON LISP has since had to learn to cooperate in a world that is dominated by other programming languages. In this chapter, we'll mostly concentrate on the major players like C or JAVA but there's a lot more stuff out there, some of which should at least be mentioned.[1]

- Some COMMON LISP implementations (like CLOZURECL or LISPWORKS) come with built-in support for calling out to Apple's OBJECTIVE-C programming language.
- Some COMMON LISP implementations (like ALLEGROCL or LISPWORKS) come with built-in support for Microsoft's OLE technology.
- ALLEGROCL and LISPWORKS can communicate via CORBA. (There's actually an official CORBA mapping for COMMON LISP, which can be found at `http://www.omg.org/spec/LISP/1.0/`.)
- For integration with JAVASCRIPT, have a look at PARENSCRIPT (installable with QUICKLISP; see Recipe 18-2) and CL-JAVASCRIPT.[2] And see Recipe 19-11.
- The RDNZL library[3] provides an interface between COMMON LISP and the .NET framework from Microsoft.
- The web page at `http://cliki.net/FFI` lists open source libraries that purport to interface COMMON LISP with languages like APPLE SCRIPT, TCL/TK, PERL, PYTHON, COBOL (!), and others.
- If you google "f2cl" you'll find a compiler that translates FORTRAN 77 code to COMMON LISP.
- Have a look at page 557 for some implementations where you can mix assembly code with Lisp.

---

[1] And you might also want to look at Recipe 22-7.

[2] See `http://marijnhaverbeke.nl/cl-javascript/`.

[3] See `http://weitz.de/rdnzl`.

The first seven recipes of this chapter deal with C and comprise a large part of this chapter. If you've never worked with a Lisp foreign function interface before, it is probably a good idea to read them all in the order that they are presented here. In another chapter, Recipe 11-6 shows an application of what is discussed here.

For most of the C examples, we'll use SBCL on Linux, but at least the Lisp parts should work essentially unchanged with other Lisps or on other operating systems as well.

19-1. Calling C Functions from Lisp

Problem

You want to call a function from Lisp that is provided by an external C library.

Solution

Use your Lisp's *foreign function interface.*

The following example was performed on a 64-bit Linux system with SBCL. We're using the CFFI library (more below), which can be installed via QUICKLISP (see Recipe 18-2).

Create a file called `test.c` containing the following C code:

```
double power (double base, int exponent) {
  int i;
  double result = 1.0;

  for (i = 1; i <= exponent; i++)
    result *= base;
  return result;
}
```

Compile this into a shared library:[4]

```
gcc -fpic -shared test.c -o test.so
```

Now, in Lisp, we make the system aware of the existence of our new library and load it into our address space:

[4]See `https://en.wikipedia.org/wiki/Library_%28computing%29#Shared_libraries`.

```
;; where the file test.so we just created is located
* (cffi:load-foreign-library "/tmp/test.so")
#<CFFI:FOREIGN-LIBRARY TEST.SO-643 "test.so">
```

We can now call the function power from Lisp like so:

```
* (cffi:foreign-funcall "power"
                        :double 1.4142135623730951d0
                        :int 2
                        :double)
2.0000000000000004d0
```

Here we provide as arguments

a) the name of the C function,

b) for each argument of the C function, a keyword specifying the C type (more about that below) followed by the argument's value as a Lisp object, and

c) the return type of the C function (also as a keyword).

As this will get tedious rather quickly, we can define a "wrapper" Lisp function around the C function:[5]

```
* (cffi:defcfun "power" :double
    (base :double)
    (exponent :int))
POWER
```

The symbol returned by this macro is the name of a function we can now call like any other Lisp function (except that the argument types have to match the ones we used when defining the wrapper):

```
* (power 2.5457298950218306d0 4)
42.00000000000001d0
```

How It Works

Pretty much every COMMON LISP these days has a so-called *"foreign function interface"* (FFI)—sometimes also called *"foreign language interface"* (FLI)—which can be used to call C functions from Lisp. (One notable exception is ABCL, which due to it

[5]Note that the order is reversed here; we start with the function's return type. Also, we don't have to use the same names for the arguments as we used in the C code. The names we provide are just used for argument list display in the IDE or by tools like debuggers.

being a part of the JAVA ecosystem, has an FFI that calls into JAVA. This is explained in Recipe 19-10.) As C is the *lingua franca* of computers nowadays, this should allow you to access a vast quantity of code that wasn't originally written with COMMON LISP users in mind.

Because FFIs aren't covered by the standard, very different implementations have evolved over the years. But apart from different names there's a common core of functionality that all FFIs share and that is made accessible in a uniform way by the CFFI library, created by James Bielman and Luís Oliveira.[6] (Google search results for CFFI might be interspersed with links to a PYTHON library of the same name. These two are not related; except that they are both about calling into C from another language.)

CFFI is a compatibility layer that wraps around your Lisp's FFI. It won't add an FFI to your Lisp if it doesn't already have one. Which implies that there's actually no need for you to use CFFI unless you're intending to write portable open source code (or author Lisp books); but it won't hurt either. Some Lisps will offer specific FFI niceties that aren't covered by CFFI, but for most typical use cases, CFFI will have all you'll need.

So, to enable us to call a C function from Lisp, the FFI has to do the following things:

(i) It has to *load* the foreign library that the function belongs to (and for that, it has to *find* it first).

(ii) It has to locate the C function that we want to call in the library and it has to call it like another C function would call it.

(iii) It has to convert from Lisp to C types when calling the function and from C to Lisp types when it returns.

Let's look at each of these tasks in turn, at least as far as we as users of the FFI are concerned.

How the FFI Finds and Loads Shared Libraries

First of all, the C code we want to interact with needs to be contained in a *shared, dynamically linked library* (see footnote 4). We won't be able to call C functions from executable binaries, from static libraries, or from object files created as an intermediate step by compilers. The libraries we need can typically be recognized by their suffixes: `.dll` on Windows, `.dylib` on OS X, and `.so` on Unix-like systems.

[6] There's a similar library called UFFI (by Kevin Rosenberg) which actually predates CFFI and which is still used by some popular Lisp libraries like CLSQL (see Recipe 21-2). But because of active development and bigger mindshare you should opt for CFFI unless you need to work with legacy code that uses UFFI. (And even then you might consider using CFFI's UFFI compatibility layer.)

In our example above, `CFFI:LOAD-FOREIGN-LIBRARY` had no problem finding the library because we specified its exact location in the file system. This isn't always a good idea, though, especially if you want to write code that can run unmodified on different machines where the library could be in different places. Luckily, you don't have to. If you don't specify an absolute directory, libraries, by default, will be searched using the same mechanism the underlying OS uses. Roughly, and making no claims of completeness, this works like so:

- On Linux, the directories `/lib` and `/usr/lib` as well as those listed in the file `/etc/ld.so.conf` are searched. You can temporarily prepend directories to this list using the environment variable `LD_LIBRARY_PATH`.
- On OS X, the directories `~/lib`, `/usr/local/lib`, and `/usr/lib` are searched. Furthermore, the environment variables `LD_LIBRARY_PATH`, `DYLD_LIBRARY_PATH`, and `DYLD_FALLBACK_LIBRARY_PATH` are used.
- On Windows, the search process can't be described in two or three sentences, but it involves, among other things, the directory the application (i.e., the Lisp system) was started from, the current directory, the *system directory*, the *windows directory*, and the `PATH` environment variable; whereas the search *order* can depend on various settings.

This means that on my Linux system, where the library `libjpeg.so` is installed in a standard location, I can load it using

```
(cffi:load-foreign-library "libjpeg.so")
```

or even more portably by

```
(cffi:load-foreign-library '(:default "libjpeg"))
```

where `:DEFAULT` means: "Use the standard suffix of the operating system." (This might also work unchanged on OS X or Windows if I'm lucky.) Or I could have used

```
(cffi:load-foreign-library '(:or "libjpeg.so.3" "libjpeg.so"))
```

instead, providing two alternative names to try in order.

CFFI provides a macro to define various search strategies and alternative names for a shared library. It is used like so:

```
(cffi:define-foreign-library gd-lib
  (:darwin (:or "libgd.3.dylib" "libgd.dylib"))
  (:windows (:or "gd.dll" "libgd.dll"))
  (t (:default "libgd")))
```

In this example we provide two alternative names for OS X (née :DARWIN), two for Windows, and a fallback option that just uses the "native" suffix.

The library isn't loaded yet; you'd have to do that with

```
(cffi:load-foreign-library 'gd-lib)
```

(Note that we now use the symbol from the definition above and not a string or a pathname.)

There are even more ways to control how libraries are found, but you'll have to read the documentation for that.

It is pretty obvious that you can't expect to load, say, a Windows DLL into SBCL on Linux. What's less obvious, but a common source of problems, is that there can be incompatibilities even on the same operating system. There's a 32-bit version of LISPWORKS on the same Linux system I used above, but if I try to load `test.so` there, I get an error message containing the following information:

```
wrong ELF class: ELFCLASS64
```

Likewise, if I recreate `test.so` as a 32-bit library like so

```
gcc -m32 -fpic -shared test.c -o test.so
```

the 64-bit SBCL can't load it anymore. If you have such a conflict, your only viable option is to acquire the correct version of the library (or to recompile it if you have access to the source code).

Finally, on Linux I can just do this without loading a library:

```
* (cffi:foreign-funcall "hypot"
                        :double 3d0
                        :double 4d0
                        :double)

5.0d0
```

This works because `hypot` is part of the standard C library,[7] which was already loaded by SBCL when it started up. System libraries like this one usually don't have to be loaded explicitly.

How the FFI Calls C Functions

Once the library is loaded, the next step is to find and call a function. The function we want to call is a piece of machine language that "expects" to be called in a certain

[7]See `https://www.gnu.org/software/libc/manual/`.

way and there are many things to watch out for, for example:

- Are parameters passed via the stack (see page 510) or via registers or is it a mix of both?
- What is the order of parameters on the stack and how are they aligned?
- Which registers are *caller-saved* and which are *callee-saved*?
- Where do function return values end up?
- Who cleans up the stack after the function has finished?

This is all part of the *calling convention*[8] and the answers to the questions above depend on the processor architecture, the operating system, and the compiler that created the shared library. Luckily, most of this is taken care of by the FFI automatically so we don't have to worry about it. (But see page 599.) Still, we should have at least a vague understanding of all the things that *could* go wrong; which also explains why we can't just take any old file consisting of machine code and utilize it.

The question we're more concerned with right now is how the function is *found* so that it can be called. This is mostly a non-issue for C[9] as all functions in a shared library are available and can be looked up by name[10] unless they're explicitly made "invisible" using the `static` keyword. But there's one thing that can potentially harm us:

Create a file `test2.c` with these contents:

```
double power(int exponent) {
  int i;
  double result = 1.0;
  for (i = 1; i <= exponent; i++)
    result *= 2.0;
  return result;
}
```

Then compile it, like above:

```
gcc -fpic -shared test2.c -o test2.so
```

On the Lisp side, you can now do the following:

```
(cffi:load-foreign-library "/tmp/test.so")
(cffi:load-foreign-library "/tmp/test2.so")
```

[8] See `https://en.wikipedia.org/wiki/Calling_convention`.

[9] But it *is* for C++; see Recipe 19-9.

[10] Try `nm -D test.so` to see that the `.so` file kept the name (which is called a *symbol* in this context) of the function `power`.

But if you now call power, which of the two C functions called "power" will be called?

This is why you can always associate a foreign function with the library it originates from so that there's no ambiguity. The safer way to execute our example from the beginning would thus have been like so:

```
(cffi:define-foreign-library test-lib
  (t "/tmp/test.so"))
(cffi:load-foreign-library 'test-lib)
(cffi:defcfun ("power" :library test-lib) :double
  (base :double)
  (exponent :int))
```

Here we define the library before loading it and give it a name (the symbol TEST-LIB) and then use this name when defining the wrapper function POWER.

But if we now do the same for test2.so, how do we distinguish the Lisp wrappers? They'll both be called POWER, right?

No. While CFFI provides convenience features that will automatically translate the C name power to the Lisp symbol POWER and even something like fast_power to FAST-POWER, you can always override this by providing your own Lisp name.[11]

So, how about this?

```
(cffi:define-foreign-library other-test-lib
  (t "/tmp/test2.so"))
(cffi:load-foreign-library 'other-test-lib)
(cffi:defcfun ("power" one-arg-power :library other-test-lib) :double
  (exponent :int))
```

This is the right way to do it but it *still* won't work because at least on Linux C has a so-called *flat namespace*, which means that there is always only one function called power, no matter what you do. CFFI tells you about this by adding the symbol CFFI-FEATURES:FLAT-NAMESPACE to *FEATURES* (see Recipe 10-10). On OS X and Windows, you don't have a flat namespace and the above will work.

As a final remark, you can also call a function you only have the address of. See the documentation of CFFI:FOREIGN-FUNCALL-POINTER for that.

How the FFI Converts Between C and Lisp Types

When we call the C function power, our arguments are a Lisp floating-point number and a Lisp integer. The C function wants two such arguments, but both will have a

[11] You can also use your own default translation instead of CFFI's. Look up the documentation for its functions CFFI:TRANSLATE-NAME-TO-FOREIGN and CFFI:TRANSLATE-NAME-FROM-FOREIGN.

representation in memory it won't understand.[12]

So, the job of the FFI is to translate from Lisp arguments to arguments that a C function expects; and then to translate the return value of the C function back to a suitable Lisp representation. Neither C nor Lisp have hard-and-fast rules for how exactly their types have to be represented in memory,[13] but still there are a couple of default mappings provided by `CFFI`:

- The C integer types will always be mapped to Lisp integers. When integers are converted from C to Lisp, there's no problem with overflow. When there's a conversion from Lisp to C, the FFI should make sure no bad things happen.[14]

  C integers can be specified with keywords resembling their C types like `:INT`, `:UNSIGNED-CHAR`, or `:LONG`, with shortcuts like `:USHORT`, or by explicitly denoting a specific number of octets as in `:INT8` or `:UINT32`.

- `float` and `double` on the C side will almost always be mapped to `SINGLE-FLOAT` and `DOUBLE-FLOAT` on the Lisp side which should more or less "just work." (See Recipe 4-6 for more details.)

- The C type `void` is `:VOID` on the Lisp side.

Compound C types (arrays, structs, unions, strings) and pointers will be discussed in other parts of this chapter; see Recipes 19-2, 19-3, 19-4, and 19-5 (which also show more examples of how the types listed above can be used).

The "`stdcall` Problem"

When I talked about calling conventions on page 597, I wasn't complete honest when I said that you don't have to worry about them. It is true that you don't have to worry on 64-bit architectures, or on non-Intel architectures, or on OS X, Linux, or other Unix-like operating systems. But on 32-bit Windows versions there are two different calling conventions in use that are so different[15] that calling a C function with the wrong convention will almost certainly lead to disaster.

The two conventions are called `cdecl` (which is what is used on almost all other systems that employ the `X86` architecture) and `stdcall`. The rule of thumb is that you need to use `stdcall` if you're calling Windows library functions and that otherwise `cdecl` is typically used. But if in doubt, you should definitely check.

[12]The Lisp floating-point number will be *boxed* (see page 525) and the Lisp integer will be a fixnum (see Recipe 4-2). The numbers on the C side on the other hand will be in the native format of the processor.

[13]For example, a `long int` in C sometimes is four octets long and sometimes eight. On the Lisp side it is even more complicated (see Recipes 4-1 and 4-2).

[14]If I try to call our function from above as `(POWER 2D0 (EXPT 2 31))`, SBCL will refuse to do it and tell me that the second argument is not of Lisp type `(SIGNED-BYTE 32)`.

[15]This includes for example different conventions about whom—caller or callee—has to clean up the stack after a function call.

Like most C compilers, CFFI supports both conventions (at least on Windows) and you can set the calling convention with a keyword argument when calling a C function or when defining a wrapper with CFFI:DEFCFUN.

19-2. Working with C Pointers

Problem

You need to call C functions that want pointers as arguments or which return pointers.

Solution

We'll look at two different ways to create pointers to objects on the Lisp side, which can then be fed to C functions. What we're doing here will be discussed in more detail below.

We're assuming that you know the basics of CFFI (see Recipe 19-1) and so we won't repeat those here. So, we'll just show a C function and will below continue in Lisp at the point where you've compiled the C code into a shared library, which you've loaded from within Lisp:

```
void swap (int *a, int *b) {
  int t = *b;
  *b = *a;
  *a = t;
}
```

The purpose of this function obviously is to swap two integers which is done (and can only be done) through pointers.

As above, we create a Lisp wrapper for this function:

```
(cffi:defcfun swap :void
  (a :pointer)
  (b :pointer))
```

We'll now create two objects suitable for the SWAP function:

```
CL-USER> (defparameter *a* (cffi:foreign-alloc :int))
*A*
CL-USER> *a*
;; output is implementation-dependent
```

```
#.(SB-SYS:INT-SAP #X7FFFE4001160)
CL-USER> (cffi:mem-ref *a* :int)
0
CL-USER> (setf (cffi:mem-ref *a* :int) 42)
42
CL-USER> (cffi:mem-ref *a* :int)
42
CL-USER> (defparameter *b*
           (cffi:foreign-alloc :int :initial-element 23))
*B*
CL-USER> (cffi:mem-ref *b* :int)
23
```

And now we use them (and clean up afterward):

```
CL-USER> (swap *a* *b*)
; No value
CL-USER> (list (cffi:mem-ref *a* :int)
               (cffi:mem-ref *b* :int))
(23 42)
CL-USER> (cffi:foreign-free *a*)
NIL
CL-USER> (cffi:foreign-free *b*)
NIL
```

As promised, here's a different way of doing it:

```
CL-USER> (cffi:with-foreign-objects ((a :int) (b :int))
           (setf (cffi:mem-ref a :int) 42
                 (cffi:mem-ref b :int) 23)
           (print (list (cffi:mem-ref a :int) (cffi:mem-ref b :int)))
           (swap a b)
           (list (cffi:mem-ref a :int) (cffi:mem-ref b :int)))
(42 23)
(23 42)
```

How It Works

Whereas *pointers* (the memory addresses of other objects) are the bread and butter of C, they are an alien concept for a language like COMMON LISP (or JAVA for that matter). So, if you're exchanging data between Lisp and C and C wants pointers to your Lisp data, then the FFI not only has to convert types (see Recipe 19-1), it also has to figure out a way to generate a pointer to that data.

And there's a second problem. Although your Lisp implementation will certainly *know* where Lisp objects are, it can't just give their address to C because the garbage collector might move objects around, so that the address may no longer be valid somewhat later.

The solution is that space for the "foreign" objects is allocated where C would do it as well and in the same way that C would do it.

One way we demonstrated above is to use `CFFI:FOREIGN-ALLOC`, which essentially works like C's `malloc`.[16] (And as in C, we have to make sure we relinquish the space once we're done with it. The Lisp equivalent to C's `free` is `CFFI:FOREIGN-FREE`.) The function `CFFI:FOREIGN-ALLOC` returns a CFFI pointer object and the example shows how it can be used. We can get and set its value using the accessor `CFFI:MEM-REF` and we can use it as an argument where a C function expects a pointer.

The second way to allocate such objects is with the `CFFI:WITH-FOREIGN-OBJECTS` macro we've also seen in action already. This macro has the advantage that we don't have to take care of freeing the objects we allocated as this will automatically happen once it has finished. The other advantage is that objects created this way will usually[17] be allocated on the stack; see Recipe 17-7 for a discussion of stack allocation.

There are other things you can do with pointers like accessing their actual machine address (an integer) with `CFFI:POINTER-ADDRESS` or creating a pointer like C's `NULL` with `CFFI:NULL-POINTER`.

If a C function returns a pointer, it'll too be a CFFI pointer and we can use it just like a pointer we generated ourselves. (Except that we should *not* free it unless this is part of the function's contract.)

Typed Pointers

In C source code, pointers usually have a type, but once the compiler is done with the source, the shared library we're using consists of machine code for which *everything* is just a bunch of bits. Likewise, a CFFI pointer can, in theory, point to everything.[18] That's why we have to tell `CFFI:MEM-REF` the type of the pointer each time we're using it.

We could have defined `SWAP` like so

```
(cffi:defcfun swap :void
  (a (:pointer :int))
```

[16]This is not to say that this actually *uses* the C function `malloc`, though. Different Lisps will have different ways to allocate foreign data. You might want to have a look at the ALLEGROCL FFI documentation for an overview of its variety of allocation strategies.

[17]Stack allocation will only happen if the FFI underlying CFFI can do it (most can), and there might be other restrictions like the size of the object.

[18]Like a pointer to `void` in C.

```
  (b (:pointer :int)))
```

but that wouldn't have made a difference. We could still do something like this (note the use of :DOUBLE)

```
(cffi:with-foreign-objects ((a :int) (b :double))
  (setf (cffi:mem-ref a :int) 42
        (cffi:mem-ref b :double) 23d0)
  (print (list (cffi:mem-ref a :int)
               (cffi:mem-ref b :double)))
  (swap a b)
  (list (cffi:mem-ref a :double) (cffi:mem-ref b :int)))
```

without getting an error message; but very likely without getting a useful result either...

To get a clearer picture of what is happening here, let's try this:

```
CL-USER> (defparameter *test*
           (cffi:foreign-alloc :short
                               :initial-contents (list 42 23)))
*TEST*
CL-USER> (cffi:foreign-type-size :short)
2
CL-USER> (cffi:foreign-type-size :float)
4
CL-USER> (list (cffi:mem-ref *test* :short)
               (cffi:mem-ref *test* :short 2)   ;; *TEST* + 2 (octets)
               (cffi:mem-ref *test* :float))
(42 23 2.1122753e-39)
```

We're using the :INITIAL-CONTENTS initarg to CFFI:FOREIGN-ALLOC in anticipation of the next recipe. It just means that we want to have *two* integers of type short next to each other with the values 42 and 23 respectively. We're then asking CFFI for information about the size (in octets) of short and float.[19] And as one short occupies two octets, and we're on a little-endian machine, the four octets starting at the address *TEST* will look like so (with the integer values we entered marked in gray):

0	0	1	0	1	0	1	0	0	0	0	0	0	0	0	0	0	0	0	1	0	1	1	1	0	0	0	0	0	0	0	0

It just so happens that this bit pattern is the IEEE 754 representation (see Recipe 4-6) of the Lisp float 2.1122753e-39 we saw in the output and this strange metamor-

[19]On this particular machine, mind you. Although these two types will rarely, if ever, have different sizes on other machines.

phosis is only possible because CFFI allows us to use CFFI:MEM-REF with any type whatsoever.

The reason for this behavior of CFFI is that it acts as a kind of lowest common denominator between various Lisps' FFIs. There certainly are implementations that have *typed* pointers and use them. As an example, let's try this in LispWorks without going through CFFI.

We load the library and define the function:

```
(fli:register-module 'foo :real-name "/tmp/foo.so")

(fli:define-foreign-function swap
    ((a (:pointer :int))
     (b (:pointer :int)))
  :module 'foo
  :result-type :void)
```

If we now evaluate this form

```
(fli:with-dynamic-foreign-objects ((a :int :initial-element 42)
                                   (b :int :initial-element 23))
  (swap a b)
  (list (fli:dereference a) (fli:dereference b)))
```

the result is (23 42) as expected.

However, this form (again, note :DOUBLE)

```
(fli:with-dynamic-foreign-objects ((a :int :initial-element 42)
                                   (b :double :initial-element 23d0))
  (swap a b)
  (list (fli:dereference a) (fli:dereference b)))
```

will lead to an error message.[20]

19-3. Accessing and Generating C Arrays

Problem

You want to work with C arrays (or create arrays in Lisp that can be used from C).

[20]You can also have untyped pointers or "coerce" typed pointers to other types, though.

Solution

C arrays have a lot in common with C pointers, so in a way, this is a "sequel" to Recipe 19-2.

We'll use the following C code, and as above we're assuming that it was compiled into a shared library and loaded with CFFI (see Recipe 19-1).

```
double sum (double *arr, int size) {
  int i;
  double result = 0.0;
  for (i = 0; i < size; i++) {
    result += arr[i];
  }
  return result;
}

double set_arr (double *arr, int index, double new_value) {
  arr[index] = new_value;
  return new_value;
}
```

We're first working with the function sum[21] to demonstrate how we create a C array in Lisp and hand it over to a C function.

```
CL-USER> (cffi:defcfun sum :double
           (arr :pointer)
           (size :int))
SUM
CL-USER> (defparameter *arr*
           (cffi:foreign-alloc :double
                               :initial-contents
                                 (loop for x from 1 to 10
                                       collect (float x 1d0))))
*ARR*
CL-USER> (cffi:mem-aref *arr* :double 3)
4.0d0
CL-USER> (sum *arr* 10)
55.0d0
```

And with the help of the set_arr function, we can see how a C function actually modifies our array:

[21]Note how we use the Lisp symbol SUM to name the function. Compare with Recipe 19-1 where we used strings to look up C functions. This is again CFFI's name translation mechanism in action.

```
CL-USER> (cffi:defcfun "set_arr" :double
           (arr :pointer)
           (index :int)
           (new-value :double))
SET-ARR
CL-USER> (cffi:mem-aref *arr* :double 7)
8.0d0
CL-USER> (set-arr *arr* 7 42d0)
42.0d0
CL-USER> (cffi:mem-aref *arr* :double 7)
42.0d0
;; don't forget this!
CL-USER> (cffi:foreign-free *arr*)
NIL
```

How It Works

In C, arrays work very much like pointers. Specifically, if `arr` is an array, then `arr[i]` is equivalent to `*(arr + i)`, where the latter involves adding the integer `i` to the *pointer* `arr` and the result depends on the type of `arr`.[22]

CFFI mimics this behavior. You allocate arrays like you'd allocate individual objects and the result is a pointer. (You can specify initial contents as above, but you can also just use the `:COUNT` keyword argument.) You then use `CFFI:MEM-AREF` which works like C's square brackets.[23]

Giving C Access to Lisp Arrays

Although the usual approach is to create C arrays on the "foreign heap," if you want to interact with C, some Lisps can actually expose their "own" arrays to C. This is not supported by CFFI, but we'll demonstrate how this can be done in LISPWORKS.

You create your arrays like you'd usually do it (see Chapter 5), but they need to be specialized (see Recipe 5-9), and moreover, you will need to specify that you want *static allocation*, which means that the garbage collector won't move them around (and thus possibly confuse C):

---

[22] If `arr` is an array of `float` elements which each occupy four octets, then the actual *address* computed by the compiler will be what `arr_add + 4 * i` would be if `arr_add` were the address of `arr` as an integer.

[23] Note that you can also use `CFFI:MEM-REF` with an index as at the end of Recipe 19-2, but in this case the index is always measured in octets.

```
(defparameter *arr*
  (make-array 10 :element-type 'double-float
              :initial-contents (loop for x from 1d0 to 10d0 by 1d0
                                      collect x)
              :allocation :static))
```

These arrays will still be managed on the Lisp side, so you don't have to worry about calling `free` once you're done with them.[24]

We would now wrap our sum from above like so (note the `:LISP-ARRAY` type):

```
(fli:define-foreign-function sum
    ((arr :lisp-array)
     (size :int))
  :result-type :double
  :module 'foo)
```

And this is how it works:

```
CL-USER 1 > *arr*
#(1.0D0 2.0D0 3.0D0 4.0D0 5.0D0 6.0D0 7.0D0 8.0D0 9.0D0 10.0D0)
CL-USER 2 > (aref *arr* 5)
6.0D0
CL-USER 3 > (sum *arr* (length *arr*))
55.0D0
```

19-4. Handling C Structs and Unions

Problem

The C library you want to interact with uses structs and/or unions.

Solution

This is also supported by CFFI. As in the previous recipes of this chapter, we'll use a simple example to demonstrate the functionality you'll need.

This is the C code that we compile into a shared library and load with CFFI (see Recipe 19-1):[25]

[24]But the Lisp garbage collector can't possibly be aware of C holding references to your arrays. In this case, you need to prevent it from collecting the array by holding a reference on the Lisp side too.

[25]I refrained from using the library function `sqrt` in order to keep things as simple as possible.

```
struct complex {
  double real;
  double imag;
};

double magnitude_squared (struct complex *c) {
  return c->real * c->real + c->imag * c->imag;
}
```

Using this function from Lisp is now as easy as this:

```
CL-USER> (cffi:defcstruct c-complex
           (real :double)
           (imag :double))
(:STRUCT C-COMPLEX)
CL-USER> (cffi:defcfun "magnitude_squared" :double
           (c :pointer))
MAGNITUDE-SQUARED
CL-USER> (cffi:with-foreign-object (c '(:struct c-complex))
           (setf (cffi:foreign-slot-value c '(:struct c-complex)
                                          'real)
                 3d0
                 (cffi:foreign-slot-value c '(:struct c-complex)
                                          'imag)
                 4d0)
           (sqrt (magnitude-squared c)))
5.0d0
```

For unions, we'll combine them with structs to show how compound C types can be nested. This will be our C code:

```
union result_union {
  double rval;
  unsigned long ival;
};

struct result_struct {
  char exact;
  union result_union val;
};

void factorial (int n, struct result_struct *r) {
  int i;
  // assumes long has 64 bits
```

```
  if (n < 21) {
    unsigned long result = 1;
    for (i = 1; i <= n; i++)
      result *= i;
    r->exact = 1;
    r->val.ival = result;
  } else {
    double result = 1.0;
    for (i = 1; i <= n; i++)
      result *= i;
    r->exact = 0;
    r->val.rval = result;
  }
}
```

This is the Lisp code to define the union and struct types as well as the wrapper for the C function (together with a helper function on the Lisp side to retrieve the correct numerical value from the result):

```
(cffi:defcunion result-union
  (rval :double)
  (ival :unsigned-long))

(cffi:defcstruct result-struct
  (exact (:boolean :char))
  (val (:union result-union)))

(cffi:defcfun factorial :void
  (n :int)
  (r :pointer))

(defun fact (n)
  (cffi:with-foreign-object (r '(:struct result-struct))
    (factorial n r)
    (let ((result-union
            (cffi:foreign-slot-value r '(:struct result-struct)
                                     'val)))
      (if (cffi:foreign-slot-value r '(:struct result-struct) 'exact)
        (cffi:foreign-slot-value result-union
                                 '(:union result-union) 'ival)
        (cffi:foreign-slot-value result-union
                                 '(:union result-union) 'rval)))))
```

We can now use it like so:

```
CL-USER> (fact 20)
2432902008176640000
CL-USER> (fact 23)
2.585201673888498d22
```

How It Works

If you've understood how to work with pointers and arrays (see previous recipes), then structs and unions shouldn't be a problem. As we can see from the examples, we first use CFFI:DEFCSTRUCT and CFFI:DEFCUNION to define the types and then CFFI:FOREIGN-SLOT-VALUE (for both) to access individual parts. The second example shows that structs and unions can be nested and you can also mix them with arrays. Any hierarchy of compound types you can come up with in C can also be modeled in CFFI.

In case you found the above a bit verbose, there's CFFI:DEFCTYPE, which is a bit like C's typedef in that you can define *names* (Lisp symbols) for your types, which you can then use as abbreviations. If you now also *use* (as in USE-PACKAGE) the CFFI package, the code from above looks a bit less intimidating:

```
;; using RESULT-UNION from example above
(defctype r-union (:union result-union))

(defcstruct result-struct
  (exact (:boolean :char))
  (val r-union))

(defctype r-struct (:struct result-struct))

(defun fact (n)
  (with-foreign-object (r 'r-struct)
    (factorial n r)
    (let ((result-union (foreign-slot-value r 'r-struct 'val)))
      (if (foreign-slot-value r 'r-struct 'exact)
          (foreign-slot-value result-union 'r-union 'ival)
          (foreign-slot-value result-union 'r-union 'rval)))))
```

A few more things worth noting:

- When defining structs (as when defining wrappers for C functions), names don't matter to the compiler (so, instead of, say, RVAL we could have used RV), but order obviously does because it determines how the individual parts of the struct or union are laid out in memory.

(But names matter to whoever reads your code, so—unless you have a good reason not to—you should generally use matching names.)

- You usually shouldn't have to worry about alignment and padding in structs, but if the authors of the C code you're using have used things like `#pragma pack` to alter the way the compiler would typically lay out things, then CFFI has options to override the size that individual parts of a struct will occupy.
- If you dereference a pointer to a struct using `CFFI:MEM-REF`, you'll get a *plist* (see Recipe 6-9):

```
CL-USER> (cffi:foreign-alloc '(:struct c-complex))
#.(SB-SYS:INT-SAP #X7FFFE40011A0)
CL-USER> (cffi:mem-ref * '(:struct c-complex))
(IMAG 0.0d0 REAL 0.0d0)
```

- Note the usage of the type `(:BOOLEAN :CHAR)` which signals that a) the size of this slot is only one octet and b) we want the C integers automatically translated to Lisp booleans (so that 0 is `NIL` and everything else is `T`).

Passing Structs by Value

One thing that's not so easy is passing structs to and from C *by value*. We have so far passed pointers around, but we could have written our function from above like so:

```
double magnitude_squared (struct complex c) {
  return c.real * c.real + c.imag * c.imag;
}
```

That's something that most[26] COMMON LISP FFIs can't do out of the box, unfortunately. If you need this feature, you should try the CFFI-LIBFFI subsystem of CFFI, which makes passing structs by value possible with the help of the `libffi` C library.[27]

19-5. Converting Between Lisp and C Strings

Problem

The C code you're working with uses strings and you want automatic conversion between the C representation of a string and its Lisp counterpart.

[26]But have a look at ALLEGROCL's FFI!

[27]See `https://en.wikipedia.org/wiki/Libffi`.

Solution

As usual, we'll work with a simple example. We're going to show how you can pass Lisp strings to C functions without having to worry too much about the differences between the two languages.

This is our C code:

```
void convert (unsigned char in[], unsigned int out[]) {
  int i = 0;
  while (in[i]) {
    out[i] = in[i];
    i++;
  }
  out[i] = 0;
}
```

It just makes a copy of its input, and we'll use it to demonstrate what arrives at the C side.

For that, we'll use this Lisp code:

```
(cffi:defcfun convert :void
  (in :string)
  (out :pointer))

(defun show (str)
  (cffi:with-foreign-object (arr :uint (* (length str) 2))
    (convert str arr)
    (loop for i from 0
          for c = (cffi:mem-aref arr :uint i)
          until (zerop c)
          collect c)))
```

If we now use it, we'll see this (note the *umlaut* character in the input):

```
CL-USER> (show "Läther")
(76 195 164 116 104 101 114)
```

For most of the characters, we see their ASCII code (see Recipe 3-1), but for the second character, we see two integers—that's the UTF-8 encoding[28] of this letter.

We could have defined the Lisp wrapper like so:

[28]See https://en.wikipedia.org/wiki/UTF-8.

```
(cffi:defcfun convert :void
  (in (:string :encoding :latin-1))
  (out :pointer))
```

And in that case, we'd have this outcome (where the second letter is mapped to one octet only):

```
CL-USER> (show "Läther")
(76 228 116 104 101 114)
```

How It Works

C strings and Lisp strings are very different beasts. Whereas strings in Lisp (see Chapter 3) are arrays of characters (with both `CHARACTER` and `STRING` being defined types of the language), strings in C are essentially just sequences of octets. At first, This might seem to be a detail of no particular importance, but in fact, this is a huge difference. While in a Lisp string it is always clear what, for example, the tenth character is, in a C string, it is neither obvious what the tenth character is nor *where* it is; it depends on the interpretation, viz. the encoding.

CFFI will take care of encoding strings when sending them to C and decoding them when they come from C, you just have to tell it which encoding to use. In our example, we first used the default encoding UTF-8 and then we asked for ISO-8859-1[29] explicitly.

CFFI uses the BABEL library[30] for this task and you can thus get a list of available encodings like so:

```
(babel-encodings:list-character-encodings)
```

CFFI also does two other things when sending a Lisp string to a C function which maybe weren't totally obvious:

- C strings need a null byte as an end marker that Lisp strings don't need. This end marker is added automatically. (And this also works the other way around, if C strings are converted to Lisp strings.)
- The array of `char` objects the Lisp string is converted to needs to be allocated (and later freed) in a "C-friendly" way (as described in Recipe 19-2). This is also done automatically.

[29]See `https://en.wikipedia.org/wiki/ISO/IEC_8859-1`.

[30]See `https://common-lisp.net/project/babel/`.

If performance is of importance, be aware that this kind of automatic conversion entails *copying* from Lisp to C strings and vice versa, so you probably want to avoid it in tight loops or for huge strings. (Or check if your Lisp offers a non-copying technique like the one described on page 606.)

19-6. Calling Lisp Functions from C

Problem

You are working with C code with *callbacks*; that is, with functions that accept functions as arguments. And you want to implement these functions in COMMON LISP.

Solution

This is actually quite easy. As a minimal example, consider this C code:

```
void test (int n, void (*func)(int)) {
  (*func)(n * n);
}
```

`test` accepts an integer as its first argument, squares it, and then feeds the result to a function which is its second argument. This must be a function that accepts an integer and returns nothing.

To implement a function in Lisp we could use as the `func` argument, we'd write something like this:

```
(cffi:defcallback print-hex :void
    ((n :int))
  (format t "--> ~X" n))
```

You can now use the callback like so:

```
CL-USER> (cffi:foreign-funcall test
                               :int 32
                               :pointer (cffi:callback print-hex)
                               :void)
--> 400
; No value
```

How It Works

In C, *callbacks*[31] aren't used as often as in functional programming languages, but they have their uses in user interface libraries, event handling, or as arguments to various algorithms (for example, the `qsort` function of the GNU C library).

The example above should be rather self-explanatory. Use the `CFFI:DEFCALLBACK` macro to define a function almost as if with `DEFUN` except that each argument will have to have a CFFI type and you'll need to declare a return type as well.

The name of this function can then be used with the macro `CFFI:CALLBACK` (or the function `CFFI:GET-CALLBACK`) to produce a pointer. (Which is what C wants. While in Lisp functions are first-class objects, in C you obviously want a pointer to the function.)

19-7. Generating FFI Code Automatically

Problem

You need to interface with a big C library and you don't want to manually write lots of wrapper code like in the last recipes.

Solution

There are some tools available that claim to be able to do this job for you. (But don't expect too much...)

We'll use SWIG[32] as an example. Let's assume that we have a C header file `foo.h`, which contains function prototypes and type declarations from some of the previous recipes:

```
double power (double base, int exponent);
void swap (int *a, int *b);
double sum (double *arr, int size);
double set_arr (double *arr, int index, double new_value);

union result_union {
  double rval;
  unsigned long ival;
};
```

[31]See `https://en.wikipedia.org/wiki/Callback_%28computer_programming%29`.
[32]Available from `http://www.swig.org/`.

```
struct result_struct {
  char exact;
  union result_union val;
};

void factorial (int n, struct result_struct *r);
void convert (unsigned char in[], unsigned int out[]);
void test (int n, void (*func)(int));
```

If you now invoke SWIG like so

```
swig -cffi -module bar foo.h
```

it will generate a file `bar.lisp` for you, which will contain all the `CFFI:DEFCFUN`'s and so on you've seen on the previous pages…

How It Works

If you're thinking about generating the FFI code necessary to interface with a C library automatically with some kind of tool, you will need the library's source code or at least the header files. The library in itself doesn't contain enough information to glean things like function signatures and struct declarations from it.[33]

While in theory, it would be possible to parse the C code from Lisp,[34] all authors who worked on tools like this eventually decided to rely on existing C compilers.

SWIG is such a tool and has been around for almost twenty years. It is impressive and complicated (it comes with 800 pages of documentation!) and includes support for COMMON LISP. SWIG can generate CFFI code (see above) and also code for the native FFIs of ALLEGROCL and CLISP.

There are at least two alternatives to SWIG that are specifically targeted at COMMON LISP:

- VERRAZANO[35] is available via QUICKLISP (see Recipe 18-2) and based on GCC-XML,[36] but there seems to be no active development and its status is a bit unclear.

[33]Of course, the library's documentation might contain this information. But you probably won't find a tool which RTFM for you…

[34]The Lisp Machines had C compilers written in Lisp (see `http://www.mirrorservice.org/sites/www.bitsavers.org/bits/TI/Explorer/zeta-c/`), and there's also an interesting project at `https://github.com/vsedach/Vacietis`.

[35]See `https://common-lisp.net/project/fetter/`.

[36]See `http://gccxml.github.io/HTML/Index.html`.

- LISPWORKS comes with a built-in *Foreign Parser* that relies on the C preprocessor of the platform it runs on and generates code for its native FFI.

It is beyond the scope of this book to explain these three tools in detail. They can all be pretty helpful if you're willing to grapple with them, but be warned that large C libraries are typically so complex and riddled with macros, conditional compilation, and special features that you'll rarely get good results without considerable manual intervention.

19-8. Embedding C in Common Lisp

Problem

You want even tighter integration with C than what was described in previous recipes. You want to be able to intermingle C with Lisp.

Solution

As you might expect, this is generally not an option. But with an implementation like ECL, you can actually do it quite easily. Here's the example from Recipe 19-1 directly embedded into a Lisp function:

```
(defun power (base exponent)
  (ffi:c-inline (base exponent) (:double :int) :double "{
    int i;
    double result = 1.0;

    for (i = 1; i <= #1; i++)
      result *= #0;
    @(return) = result;
}"))
```

After compiling this function, we can now do the same we already did in the first recipe of this chapter:

```
CL-USER> (power 1.4142135623730951d0 2)
2.0000000000000004d0
```

But we can also do something we couldn't do before:

```
CL-USER> (power 2 10)
1024.0d0
```

(When using CFFI, the first argument had to be a Lisp `DOUBLE-FLOAT`. Here we are calling a Lisp function that will accept an integer and convert it to a C `double` automatically when the C code is called.)

How It Works

The idea that you could simply "inject" some lines of C code into a COMMON LISP program might seem as unrealistic as intermixing JAVA and FORTH code.[37] But if you're using a Lisp implementation that uses C as an intermediate language (see page 560), this suddenly doesn't sound so strange anymore.

We've used ECL (for *Embeddable Common Lisp*) above, which makes this very easy via its `FFI:C-INLINE` special operator. It works like this:

- You provide it with a list of forms and a corresponding list of C types (i.e., keywords ECL's FFI can understand).

  That's what `(BASE EXPONENT)` and `(:DOUBLE :INT)` were for. Note that any *form* is OK here, so you could have, say, `(* 2 EXPONENT)` instead of `EXPONENT`.

- The values of these forms are converted according to the provided C types and can then be inserted into the C code with the escape forms `#0`, `#1` to `#9`, followed by `#a` and so on.

  (Which means that the string holding the C code is actually a *template*.)

- You use the `@(return)` form, as above, to set the return value. You can also use `@(return 1)` or `@(return 2)` to set a second or third return value, and so on.

  The C return type is also declared (that's the `:DOUBLE` at the end of the line) and ECL will then automatically convert the value back to a corresponding Lisp type.

Note that there's also a special form called `FFI:C-LINES` that is intended for things like global variable declarations or `#include` directives.

ECL can even do similar things with C++ (see Recipe 19-9).

19-9. Calling C++ from Lisp

Problem

You want to call a function from Lisp that is provided by an external C++ library.

[37] Although even *that* has probably been done already…

Solution

Although one might think this would be very similar to what we did in Recipe 19-1, unfortunately, it is a lot more complicated. We'll use a very simple piece of C++ code as the basis for this recipe and we'll discuss various ways to make it available from COMMON LISP.

The initial code consists of a header file `Compl.h`[38] with the class definition

```
class Compl {
private:
  double realpart;
  double imagpart;
public:
  Compl (double r, double i);
  double magnitude_squared ();
};
```

and a source file `Compl.cpp` with the implementation:

```
#include "Compl.h"

Compl::Compl (double r, double i = 1.0) {
  realpart = r;
  imagpart = i;
}

double Compl::magnitude_squared () {
  return realpart * realpart + imagpart * imagpart;
}
```

Let's suppose we want to create a `Compl` object and call its `magnitude_squared` member function from the Lisp side to achieve something similar to what we did in Recipe 19-4.

If we compile the code into a shared library like so

```
g++ -fpic -shared Compl.cpp -o Compl.so
```

we won't see the *symbol* (see footnote 10 in this chapter) `magnitude_squared` in the file. Instead, we see strange stuff like "`_ZN5Compl17magnitude_squaredEv`." Certainly not what we expected or wanted to call from Lisp.

Here's something that will work (if we add it to the end of our `Compl.cpp` file):

[38] We're not using the name `Complex` in order to avoid name conflicts with `CL:COMPLEX` later.

```
extern "C" {
  double mag_helper (double r, double i) {
    Compl c = Compl(r, i);
    return c.magnitude_squared();
  }
}
```

We have created a helper function and declared it to have C *linkage*, meaning that it must be compiled in such a way that it looks like a C function from the outside. We can now call mag_helper from Lisp using an FFI. The helper function has, on the other hand, access to the C++ classes and member functions and thus acts as a "bridge" between us and the code we want to use.

But this is not the only way to do it (and sometimes it's not possible). Read on.

How It Works

What we saw above, the "_ZN7Compl17magnitude_squaredEv," was *name mangling*[39] in action. In C++, different functions can have the same name, so the compiler needs to find a scheme to map them to unique symbols and pack information about their signature and other things into the symbols as well. Unfortunately, this is not standardized, so different compilers implement name mangling in different ways and thus even C++ linkers typically can't cope with libraries generated by other compilers.[40] So, there's not much hope that a COMMON LISP library will be able to call arbitrary C++ code.

The example above has shown one way to attack the problem: add "bridging" code to arbitrate between C++ and Lisp. This will work, but there's one big catch: you need to have access to the source code and be reasonably proficient in C and C++ to do this.

But even if you don't have the source code, you can write a "bridging library" which does what our mag_helper from above does, but is itself a shared library. You would then load both libraries into your Lisp's address space and use one to access the other. You'll still need to write the C++ code, of course.

Automating the Process

Or you can use a tool like SWIG (see Recipe 19-7) to automate this process for you, ideally dispensing you of the need to write bridging code. Let's see how we would

[39]See https://en.wikipedia.org/wiki/Name_mangling.

[40]Name mangling is not the only reason this is hard. There's also the question of how the this implicit parameter is passed, and so on.

integrate the code from above with SWIG:

We'd start with this:

```
swig -c++ -cffi -module compl Compl.h
```

This will generate three files for us:

- A file `Compl_wrap.cxx` with C++ bridging code far more sophisticated then what we did above.
- A Lisp file `compl.lisp` with low-level CFFI code to access this bridging code.
- A second Lisp file, `compl-clos.lisp`, with code to work with the C++ objects as if they were CLOS objects!

Now we add the line

```
#include "Compl.h"
```

to the beginning of the `.cxx` file and compile it to a shared library:

```
g++ -fpic -shared Compl.so Compl_wrap.cxx -o Compl_wrap.so
```

In Lisp, after loading CFFI we then evaluate these four forms:

```
(cffi:load-foreign-library "Compl.so")
(cffi:load-foreign-library "Compl_wrap.so")
(load (compile-file "compl.lisp"))
(load (compile-file "compl-clos.lisp"))
```

Now this will work:[41]

```
CL-USER> (defparameter *c* (make-instance 'compl :r 3d0 :i 4d0))
*C*
CL-USER> (magnitude-squared *c*)
25.0d0
```

(SWIG will also generate wrappers for C++ code for ALLEGROCL's native FFI.)

The caveats about large libraries mentioned in Recipe 19-7 still apply, of course, but this is certainly very helpful!

[41]Full disclosure: there were small bugs in the Lisp code generated by SWIG. Still, it has obviously been used successfully for some larger projects, so it's definitely worth a try. (And maybe you think it's more fun to debug Lisp code than to debug C++ code...)

ECL and Clasp

Another approach for interaction with C++ would be to not view C++ as a "foreign" language but to rather use the same ecosystem (like ABCL is a part of the JAVA world; see Recipe 19-10). That's what ECL does, and we described this kind of tight integration already in Recipe 19-8 (which you should have read before proceeding). You can do this with C++ just as well if ECL has been built with support for C++.[42]

For our example above, you can first load the `Compl.so` shared library with

```
(ffi:load-foreign-library "/tmp/Compl.so")
```

and then compile and load this file:

```
(ffi:clines "#include \"/tmp/Compl.h\"")

(defun mag (real imag)
  (ffi:c-inline (real imag) (:double :double) :double "{
    Compl c = Compl(#0, #1);
    @(return) = c.magnitude_squared();
}"))
```

In ECL you can now do this:

```
CL-USER> (sqrt (mag 3 4))
5.0d0
```

An alternative could be to use CLASP,[43] which is a fairly new COMMON LISP implementation. A large part of it is implemented in C++ and it was built from the ground up with the idea of cooperation with C++ in mind. CLASP is still a moving target and whatever I could write here would probably be obsolete once the book is in print, but if you're a C++ hacker interested in COMMON LISP, then maybe you should keep an eye on CLASP.

19-10. Using Java from Lisp

Problem

You want to interact with JAVA from your Lisp program.

[42]If you're building from source, you'll need the `--with-cxx` configuration option.
[43]Available at `https://github.com/drmeister/clasp`.

Solution

There are several ways to do that. Our main example will use the ABCL (for "ARMED BEAR COMMON LISP") implementation. We'll discuss alternatives further down below.

Our aim will be to ape this JAVA code snippet in Lisp:

```
import java.util.TimeZone;
import java.util.Date;
import java.text.SimpleDateFormat

// ...

  TimeZone tz = TimeZone.getTimeZone("Europe/Berlin");
  DateFormat df = new SimpleDateFormat("yyyy-MM-dd'T'HH:mm'Z'");
  df.setTimeZone(tz);
  String result = df.format(new Date());
```

We'll start by invoking the static method `getTimeZone` of the JAVA class `TimeZone`:[44]

```
CL-USER> (jclass "java.util.TimeZone")
#<java class java.util.TimeZone>
CL-USER> (jmethod * "getTimeZone" "java.lang.String")
;; output edited to fit page width
#<method public static synchronized java.util.TimeZone
         java.util.TimeZone.getTimeZone(java.lang.String)>
CL-USER> (jstatic * ** "Europe/Berlin")
#<sun.util.calendar.ZoneInfo
  sun.util.calendar.ZoneInfo[id="E.... {89B8340}>
```

We first use `JCLASS`[45] to look up the class by name and get a reference to it. We then use this class reference with `JMETHOD` to get a reference to the `getTimeZone` method. To fully identify the method, `JMETHOD` also needs its signature; that is, we have to tell it that the method we're interested in accepts one argument of type `String`.[46] We finally call the method with `JSTATIC` utilizing the method reference as well as the class reference. Note that we use a Lisp string as the argument which ABCL automatically converts to a JAVA string.[47]

In case you found this too verbose, there's a much shorter way to do it:

[44]For the meaning of `*` and `**`, see Recipe 16-11.

[45]Note that symbols like `JCLASS` are from ABCL's `JAVA` package, which is *used* by the `CL-USER` package.

[46]In JAVA 7 there's only one method of this name which accepts one argument, so we could have used the alternative syntax `(JMETHOD * "getTimeZone" 1)` instead. With JAVA 8, that won't work anymore because the call would be ambiguous.

[47]There are also "raw" versions of most of these functions that don't convert from and to Lisp types.

```
CL-USER> (jstatic "getTimeZone" "java.util.TimeZone" "Europe/Berlin")
#<sun.util.calendar.ZoneInfo
  sun.util.calendar.ZoneInfo[id="E.... {2DBFD4D4}>
```

Here we use *dynamic dispatch* (via JAVA's reflection API) which means that both the class as well as the method are looked up by name (and signature) when JSTATIC is called. While this is certainly more convenient, it comes with a performance penalty and there are also some other caveats. (See the ABCL manual for details.)

Now let's see when exactly I wrote this recipe:

```
;; continued from above
CL-USER> (jnew "java.text.SimpleDateFormat" "yyyy-MM-dd'T'HH:mm'Z'")
#<java.text.SimpleDateFormat
  java.text.SimpleDateFormat@6b2e8.... {15503B70}>
CL-USER> (jcall "setTimeZone" * **)
NIL
CL-USER> (jcall "format" ** (jnew "java.util.Date"))
"2015-06-23T09:59Z"
```

Here we see that JNEW is used to call a constructor, which creates a new instance of a class. And that JCALL is for instance methods what JSTATIC is for static methods. Note again how the return value of the format method is automatically converted to a Lisp string.

See Recipe 20-3 for a nicer syntax for JAVA interaction and for examples of JAVA calling back into ABCL. That recipe will also show you how to access JAVA arrays.

How It Works

ABCL is currently unique among COMMON LISP implementations in that it is hosted on the JVM.[48] Which means that it consists of a bunch of JAVA classes and that it is distributed as a plain old jar file like any other JAVA program. That's why ABCL is perfectly suited to communicate with JAVA—which is always "there" anyway.

While the solution above demonstrated the basics of how to call JAVA from Lisp, you can also do it the other way around: host ABCL as a so-called "inferior Lisp" from a JAVA program. But this is something we won't go into here. You'll have to study the documentation.

[48]See https://en.wikipedia.org/wiki/Java_virtual_machine.

Alternatives

There are some other Lisps that, although not hosted on the JVM, have built-in support for interaction with JAVA. The oldest most likely is ALLEGROCL with its "JLINKER." To use it, you start like this:

```
(require 'jlinker)
(use-package :net.jlinker)
(jlinker-init :jni)
```

The JLINKER-INIT call is to actually establish a connection to some JAVA process. JLINKER-INIT offers a whole variety of options for that. In this case, we decided to communicate via the JNI[49] so that Lisp and JAVA share one address space and one OS process. (But we could as well start JAVA in a separate process and communicate via sockets. The rest of the example would work just the same.)

To do what we did above we can use exactly the same syntax:[50]

```
(let* ((time-zone-class (jclass "java.util.TimeZone"))
       (time-zone
        (jstatic (jmethod time-zone-class "getTimeZone"
                                          "java.lang.String")
                 time-zone-class "Europe/Berlin"))
       (date-format-class (jclass "java.text.SimpleDateFormat"))
       (date-format
        (jnew date-format-class "yyyy-MM-dd'T'HH:mm'Z'")))
  (jcall "setTimeZone" date-format time-zone)
  (jcall (jmethod date-format-class "format" "java.util.Date")
         date-format (jnew "java.util.Date")))
```

But as you will have noticed, we had to be a bit more explicit in this case. This is because JLINKER resolves ambiguities differently. Whereas for ABCL it seems to be clear that

```
(jstatic "getTimeZone" "java.util.TimeZone" "Europe/Berlin")
```

must refer to a method with a `String` argument, JLINKER thinks that the Lisp string `"Europe/Berlin"` could also be a JAVA `ZoneId` object.

JLINKER also offers a `LispCall` class on the JAVA side so that you can call back into Lisp from JAVA classes.

Another Lisp with built-in support for JAVA is LISPWORKS. The initialization sequence in this case looks like so:

[49]See `https://en.wikipedia.org/wiki/Java_Native_Interface`.

[50]ABCL apparently "borrowed" the JLINKER syntax.

```
(require "java-interface")
(use-package :lw-ji)
(init-java-interface
 :jvm-library-path
   ;; where jvm.dll is (if not on PATH)
   "C:/Program Files/Java/jre1.8.0_31/bin/server/jvm.dll"
 ;; optional (for calling Lisp from Java)
 :java-class-path
   (namestring (lispworks-file "etc/lispcalls.jar")))
```

If we now once again follow our original plan, it'll look like so:

```
CL-USER 1 > (call-java-method "java.util.TimeZone.getTimeZone"
                              "Europe/Berlin")
#<Jobject java.util.TimeZone  = #x000000000A5F6EC8>
CL-USER 2 > (create-java-object "java.text.SimpleDateFormat"
                                "yyyy-MM-dd'T'HH:mm'Z'")
#<Jobject java.text.SimpleDateFormat  = #x000000000A5F6F10>
CL-USER 3 > (call-java-method
              "java.text.SimpleDateFormat.setTimeZone" * **)
NIL
CL-USER 4 > (call-java-method "java.text.SimpleDateFormat.format" **
                              (create-java-object "java.util.Date"))
"2015-06-23T21:28Z"
```

It should be obvious that `CALL-JAVA-METHOD` is the equivalent of `JSTATIC` *and* `JCALL`; whereas `CREATE-JAVA-OBJECT` has to be used instead of `JNEW`. Also, class and method names always have to be spelled out in full including the package. But once they've been used they are cached and can be abbreviated, so after executing the code above, this will work:

```
(call-java-method "getTimeZone" "Europe/Amsterdam")
```

There's also a more Lisp-y and in the long run less verbose way to achieve the same effect:[51] If you evaluate the form

```
(import-java-class-definitions "java.util.TimeZone")
```

it will automatically generate Lisp functions for all methods, constructors, and fields of this class. You can inspect them with

```
(with-output-to-string (out)
```

[51] And it can be done in JLINKER in a similar way.

```
  (write-java-class-definitions-to-stream "java.util.TimeZone" out))
```

and also write these definitions to a file.[52] You can now refer to getTimeZone like so:

```
;; note that we use a string because it's lowercase
CL-USER 5 > (use-package "java.util")
T
CL-USER 6 > (timezone.gettimezone "Europe/Paris")
#<Jobject java.util.TimeZone  = #x000000000A47DD88>
```

Finally, here is (without a detailed explanation) an example to demonstrate that it's relatively easy to call back from JAVA into Lisp. We define a "proxy" on the Lisp side that is an implementation of a JAVA interface with Lisp functions for the methods.

```
CL-USER 7 > (defparameter *counter* 0)
*COUNTER*
;; this will become the "run" method below
CL-USER 8 > (defun add-something ()
              (incf *counter* 42))
ADD-SOMETHING
CL-USER 9 > (compile *)
ADD-SOMETHING
NIL
NIL
CL-USER 10 > (define-lisp-proxy proxy-example
               ;; the interface to implement
               ("java.lang.Runnable"
                ;; we could have more than one method here
                ("run" add-something)))
PROXY-EXAMPLE
CL-USER 11 > (create-java-object "java.lang.Thread"
                                 ;; "instantiate" the proxy
                                 (make-lisp-proxy 'proxy-example))
#<Jobject java.lang.Thread  = #x000000000A576E38>
CL-USER 12 > *counter*
0
CL-USER 13 > (call-java-method "java.lang.Thread.start" **)
NIL
CL-USER 14 > *counter*
42
```

All three JAVA interfaces, ABCL's as well as those of ALLEGROCL and LISPWORKS, have a lot more to offer than can be covered in one recipe. You'll have to study their

[52]Or you could define just those Lisp functions you need and give them arbitrary names.

documentation for that.

There's also CL+J,[53] which purports to offer similar capabilities for some open source COMMON LISP implementations. However, it is currently not available via QUICKLISP (see Recipe 18-2), has no documentation, and rates itself as having only "beta" quality. Probably not something you want to use for production software, but maybe worth hacking on...

Let's close with a "historical" tidbit. Rich Hickey, now of CLOJURE fame, wrote two different libraries[54] in the beginning of this century that were both intended to facilitate access from COMMON LISP to JAVA (and in one case also Microsoft's .NET). The code hasn't been maintained for a while, but there's probably quite a lot of interesting stuff in there in case you're thinking about implementing JAVA interaction yourself. (One of these libraries is still part of the CLOZURECL distribution.)

19-11. Reading and Writing JSON

Problem

You need to communicate with programs that encode data using JSON.

Solution

There are several possible solutions. We'll demonstrate one approach using the YASON library (installable with QUICKLISP; see Recipe 18-2) written by Hans Hübner. (See below for alternatives.)

Let's first see how JSON is parsed and what we'll get on the Lisp side:

```
CL-USER 1 > (yason:parse "1")
1
CL-USER 2 > (yason:parse "2.0")
2.0
CL-USER 3 > (yason:parse "\"I am a string\"")
"I am a string"
CL-USER 4 > (yason:parse "null")
NIL
CL-USER 5 > (yason:parse "true")
T
CL-USER 6 > (yason:parse "false")
NIL
```

[53] See https://common-lisp.net/project/cl-plus-j/.

[54] See http://jfli.sourceforge.net/ and http://foil.sourceforge.net/.

```
CL-USER 7 > (yason:parse "[1, 2.0, \"foo\", null, false]")
(1 2.0 "foo" NIL NIL)
```

That's already almost all except for *objects* which are the most versatile data structure on the JAVASCRIPT side:[55]

```
CL-USER 8 > (yason:parse "{\"one\":1, \"two\": 2.0, \"three\":true}")
#<EQUAL Hash Table{3} 2009437B>
CL-USER 9 > (loop for key being the hash-keys of *
                  using (hash-value value)
                  collect (list key value))
(("three" T) ("two" 2.0) ("one" 1))
```

Note that we got a hash table (see Chapter 6) on the Lisp side with strings as keys. (But you can implement your own ways to represent the keys if you want.)

YASON has several "switches" to modify the parsing behavior shown above. We'll show some of them in action parsing the same strings again. This should be self-explanatory:[56]

```
CL-USER 10 > (let ((yason:*parse-json-booleans-as-symbols* t))
               (yason:parse "true"))
YASON:TRUE
CL-USER 11 > (let ((yason:*parse-json-arrays-as-vectors* t))
               (yason:parse "[1, 2.0, \"foo\", null, false]"))
#(1 2.0 "foo" NIL NIL)
CL-USER 12 > (let ((yason:*parse-object-as* :alist))
               (yason:parse "{one:1, two:2.0, \"three\":true}"))
(("one" . 1) ("two" . 2.0) ("three" . T))
CL-USER 13 > (let ((yason:*parse-object-as* :plist))
               (yason:parse "{one:1, two:2.0, \"three\":true}"))
("one" 1 "two" 2.0 "three" T)
```

(Although the last value returned is technically a *plist* according to the standard's glossary, it won't play nicely with the standard plist functions described in Recipe 6-9 because the keys can't be compared with EQ.)

Now for the other way around. Let's encode some data. By default, the output will be sent to *STANDARD-OUTPUT*:

```
CL-USER 14 > (yason:encode 3)
3                                                    ;; <- YASON output
3                                                    ;; <- return value
```

[55]For the meaning of *, see Recipe 16-11.

[56]Something like {one:1} (where the key is not a string) is not valid JSON, but we use it here for brevity and to show that YASON nevertheless accepts it.

```
CL-USER 15 > (yason:encode 3.141)
3.1410000324249268                                    ;; see below
3.141
CL-USER 16 > (yason:encode t)
true
T
CL-USER 17 > (yason:encode nil)
null
NIL
CL-USER 18 > (yason:encode '(1 2 #(3 4)))
[1,2,[3,4]]
(1 2 #(3 4))
CL-USER 19 > (let ((hash (make-hash-table)))
               (setf (gethash "42" hash) "forty-two"
                     (gethash "one" hash) '(42))
               (yason:encode hash))
{"42":"forty-two","one":[42]}
#<EQL Hash Table{2} 2221F787>
CL-USER 20 > (yason:encode-alist '((:42 . 42) (:foo "foo")))
{"42":42,"FOO":["foo"]}
((:|42| . 42) (:FOO "foo"))
CL-USER 21 > (yason:encode-plist '(:42 42 :foo "foo"))
{"42":42,"FOO":"foo"}
(:|42| 42 :FOO "foo")
```

YASON offers precise user control over how data is encoded to JSON, but you'll have to read its documentation for that.

Two remarks:

- We used strings as input for our examples, but YASON works just as well with streams (see Chapter 14) and this is probably what you'll use when communicating with other programs.
- YASON uses the Lisp reader (see Chapter 8) and printer (see Chapter 9) to parse and encode numbers. This entails that for example YASON parses the string "-0" to the Lisp number 0,[57] whereas Google Chrome parses it to the JAVASCRIPT number -0. This is not an error, mind you, as JSON is considered to be "agnostic about numbers."

  Also note what we got when we encoded the number 3.14. If you were surprised, have a look at Chapter 4.

[57]But it parses "-0.0" to -0.0.

How It Works

JSON is for JAVASCRIPT what S-expressions are for COMMON LISP: the most "native" way to serialize program data you could imagine. And like S-expressions (and as opposed to, say, XML; see Recipe 19-12), JSON is easy to read for humans and it is also rather easy to parse and generate for computer programs, even if they're not written in JAVASCRIPT. This and the ubiquity of JAVASCRIPT has made JSON a pretty popular data format in the years since its inception. It is also often used as a lightweight alternative to XML even if JAVASCRIPT isn't involved.

As of July 2015, there are at least six (!) different JSON libraries available for COMMON LISP. Naturally, they will all *basically* do the same thing although they'll differ here and there.

If you're just using JSON sparingly, you can probably pick anyone of them and be done with it. If you have very specific needs, Sabra Crolleton has made an extremely thorough comparison which can be found at `https://sites.google.com/site/sabraonthehill/home/json-libraries`. (Of course, you might first want to check if this comparison is still up-to-date when you read this.)

19-12. Reading and Writing XML

Problem

You need to deal with XML data.

Solution

Use (for example) the *Closure XML* library, written by Gilbert Baumann and David Lichteblau, which is available via QUICKLISP (Recipe 18-2) under the name CXML.

We'll start demonstrating its usage with a very simple XML file `note.xml`:

```
<?xml version="1.0" encoding="UTF-8"?>
<note>
  <to>Fur Trapper</to>
  <content>
    <heading color="red">Warning</heading>
    <body>Don't Eat The Yellow Snow!</body>
  </content>
  <from>Nanook</from>
</note>
```

Let's try one of several approaches to parse this file:

```
CL-USER 1 > (cxml:parse #p"note.xml" (cxml-xmls:make-xmls-builder))
("note" NIL "
  " ("to" NIL "Fur Trapper") "
  " ("content" NIL "
    " ("heading" (("color" "red")) "Warning") "
    " ("body" NIL "Don't Eat The Yellow Snow!") "
  ") "
  " ("from" NIL "Nanook") "
")
```

This gives us a simple S-expression tree representation of the XML document.[58] This format is actually modeled after another, much simpler, Lisp XML parser called XMLS.

The first thing to note is that parsing is usually done using `CXML:PARSE` (but see below) and that this function wants at least two arguments. The first argument describes the input and can be a pathname like above but also a stream or a Lisp string. The second argument describes a *handler*. Parsing using `CXML:PARSE` is what is called "SAX parsing" in the XML world[59] and it can be implemented in CXML by providing your own objects for which you specialize the methods you're interested in; for example, like so:

```
(defclass my-handler (sax:default-handler)
  ((indentation :initform 0
                :accessor indentation)))

(defmethod sax:start-element ((handler my-handler)
                              namespace-uri local-name
                              qname attributes)
  (declare (ignore namespace-uri qname attributes))
  (incf (indentation handler) 2)
  (format t "~VT~A~%" (indentation handler) local-name))

(defmethod sax:end-element ((handler my-handler)
                            namespace-uri local-name qname)
  (declare (ignore namespace-uri qname))
  (decf (indentation handler) 2))
```

We created our own class, which inherits from `SAX:DEFAULT-HANDLER`. This means that we'll get default methods for all SAX events we decide not to handle ourselves. We then just write methods for what should happen at the beginning and at the end

[58]In case you're wondering what the `NIL`s are for, they are the attributes of the individual elements.
[59]`https://en.wikipedia.org/wiki/Simple_API_for_XML`.

of an element: incrementing and decrementing an indentation value and printing the element's name.

This will now work like so:

```
CL-USER 2 > (cxml:parse #p"note.xml" (make-instance 'my-handler))
  note
    to
    content
      heading
      body
    from
NIL
```

So, CXML-XMLS:MAKE-XMLS-BUILDER from above also just returns an object; and based on its class, certain handlers will be called, which will eventually build up the S-expression that we got. There are more pre-built handlers in CXML. The function CXML-DOM:MAKE-DOM-BUILDER will, for instance, return a handler that can be used to generate a DOM[60] of the XML document implemented as nested CLOS objects.

CXML offers yet another way to parse XML which is called *Klacks*. Whereas SAX parsing is "push-based," *Klacks* is "pull-based" in that your program drives the parsing process (instead of your methods being called by the parser).

And, of course, CXML also offers various different ways to serialize data to XML.

We'll refrain from showing more examples here, as we would need too much space to do justice to all of CXML's features. It comes with extensive documentation, including several "quick-start examples," though, so you shouldn't have problems using it.

How It Works

It is probably fair to say that many Lispers perceive XML as bloated and overly complex, and they can't quite understand what XML has to offer that can't be done with their beloved S-expressions. But even if you fully agree with this, you might be in a situation where you'll need to parse XML data coming from another application or generate XML data for someone else to consume.

The good news is that there are plenty of XML libraries for COMMON LISP available. (See http://cliki.net/xml.) The bad news is precisely that there are so many libraries and that it is hard to see the forest for the trees. It seems that these libraries mostly differ in their approach; whether they are "hands-on" or rather want to faithfully implement the XML standards, whether their main aim is to provide a

[60]See http://www.w3.org/TR/DOM-Level-2-Core/core.html.

"no-questions-asked" bridge between XML and Lisp data structures or if they rather want to make the parsing process as customizable as possible, and so on.

We decided to use CXML here because it offers a couple of simple convenience features (some of which we demonstrated) but is also very versatile and extensible. But in the end, you'll have to select the best XML library for your purposes yourself.

19-13. Using Prolog from Common Lisp

Problem

You want to run PROLOG code without leaving Lisp. (Or you have a problem that cries for a declarative solution in a logic programming language, but you want to solve it as part of a larger COMMON LISP program.)

Solution

Use the PAIPROLOG library (installable with QUICKLISP; see Recipe 18-2).

Here's a simple session. We first add some facts to the database:

```
CL-USER 1 > (use-package :paiprolog)
T
CL-USER 2 > (<- (father anakin luke))
FATHER
CL-USER 3 > (<- (father anakin leia))
FATHER
CL-USER 4 > (<- (father luke ben))
FATHER
```

Now we query the database:

```
CL-USER 5 > (?- (father ?x leia))
?X = ANAKIN;
No.
CL-USER 6 > (?- (father anakin ?x))
?X = LUKE;
?X = LEIA;
No.
```

Note that whenever a semicolon is displayed above, we actually typed the semicolon which means that we want the *next* answer. (We could have typed a dot instead to stop.) The "`No.`" at the end means that there are no more answers.

Now we add a rule:

```
CL-USER 7 > (<- (child ?x ?y) (father ?y ?x))
CHILD
```

As the direction of the arrow suggests, such rules are meant to be read from right to left. *If* ?y is the father of ?x, *then* ?x is a child of ?y.

We can now ask more questions:

```
CL-USER 8 > (?- (child ?z anakin))
?Z = LUKE;
?Z = LEIA;
No.
CL-USER 9 > (?- (child ?a ?b))
?A = LUKE
?B = ANAKIN;
?A = LEIA
?B = ANAKIN;
?A = BEN
?B = LUKE;
No.
```

Finally, one more rule and another automatic inference done by the PROLOG system:

```
CL-USER 10 > (<- (grand-child ?x ?z) (child ?x ?y) (child ?y ?z))
GRAND-CHILD
CL-USER 11 > (?- (grand-child ?a anakin))
?A = BEN;
No.
```

How It Works

It is moderately easy to implement PROLOG in COMMON LISP. If you're not too concerned with efficiency and convenience features, you can write an interpreter in about 50 lines of code. A well-known example is the PROLOG interpreter and compiler that Peter Norvig wrote for his book *Paradigms of Artificial Intelligence* (*PAIP*). This PROLOG is available, in slightly modified form, as PAIPROLOG, and it should run in every COMMON LISP implementation. (And *PAIP* would probably be the best documentation you can get for it.)

If you're serious about using PROLOG from Lisp, you might want to check out the commercial offerings which presumably have much better performance and more features:

- ALLEGROCL offers ALLEGRO PROLOG which is based on the *PAIP* implementation but is apparently heavily optimized and has lots of additional features.
- LISPWORKS offers KNOWLEDGEWORKS which is a "toolkit for building knowledge based systems" and which includes COMMON PROLOG, an implementation *not* based on *PAIP*, but rather on the *Warren Abstract Machine*.[61]

[61]See `https://en.wikipedia.org/wiki/Warren_Abstract_Machine`.

20. Graphical User Interfaces

Many a Lisp "newbie" has been seen complaining that while COMMON LISP is a cool language, it is and always was pretty weak as far as graphical user interfaces (GUIs) are concerned. If you know a bit about the history of Lisp, this sounds quite ridiculous because the GUI of the famous *Lisp Machines* was written in Lisp and arguably way ahead of its time.[1]

What is true is that if nowadays you want to create graphical user interfaces that work equally well on a variety of operating systems, and if you want to do this without a lot of effort and also at no cost, then some other languages will offer far better environments for this task.[2]

Still, it is certainly neither impossible nor does it require Herculean efforts to wrap a GUI around your COMMON LISP application. We'll show four completely different approaches in this chapter. Due to the complexity of GUIs in general, the recipes will all be longer than usual, but will still only scratch the surface. (You could certainly write a whole book about this topic.) At the end of the chapter, there's also one recipe about Lisp on mobile devices.

What all these recipes (except the last one) have in common is that they are intended to work on Windows and OS X and Linux (and maybe other operating systems as well). One approach that we won't go into, but is worthwhile exploring, is that of directly using your operating system's built-in GUI libraries. This will require quite a bit of knowledge about these libraries and the usage of your Lisp's foreign function interface (see Chapter 19), but some implementations offer pretty good ecosystems for such tasks. (CLOZURECL's support for OBJECTIVE-C and Apple's COCOA[3] API is a good example.)

A general issue of GUI programs is that they will have some kind of *event loop* which endlessly waits for user input, like key strokes or mouse movements, and acts upon them. Whether this disrupts the interactive nature of working in COMMON LISP is

[1] And while we're talking about things way ahead of their time, in case you've never heard of CLIM, you might want to have a look at it because it is really worth studying (see `https://en.wikipedia.org/wiki/Common_Lisp_Interface_Manager`, and follow the links from there). On the other hand, while CLIM is interesting and some of it is even impressive, it is not an option for real-world applications that are supposed to run on today's computers.

[2] This is often due to the fact that these environments are backed by large companies giving away stuff for free because they make their money elsewhere. Unfortunately, the days when Lisp companies were large enough to do that are long gone.

[3] See `https://en.wikipedia.org/wiki/Cocoa_%28API%29`.

largely a matter of how the GUI is implemented. It is usually a good idea if the code responsible for the GUI runs in a thread (see Chapter 11) separate from the REPL thread.

20-1. Using a Web Browser as the GUI for Your Lisp Program

Problem

You want to generate a graphical front end for your application that can be used by anybody with a modern web browser.

Solution

Use a library like JQUERY UI and hook it up to your Lisp via AJAX.

What follows is an absolutely minimal example, without any bells and whistles,[4] just to get the general idea across.

Create a file called `index.html` with the following contents:

```
<!DOCTYPE html>
<html>
  <head>
    <meta charset="utf-8">
    <link rel="stylesheet"
          href="http://code.jquery.com/ui/1.11.4/themes/overcast/jquery-ui.css">
    <script src="http://code.jquery.com/jquery-2.1.4.min.js"></script>
    <script src="http://code.jquery.com/ui/1.11.4/jquery-ui.min.js"></script>
    <script>
     $(function() {
       $("#foo").autocomplete({
          source: "/get-symbols"
       });
     });
    </script>
  </head>
  <body>
    <div class="ui-widget">
      <input id="foo">
    </div>
  </body>
</html>
```

[4] Specifically with no considerations about security or reasonable default behavior in the case of "stupid" user input.

Put this file into a newly created empty directory, which for the purpose of this example we'll call /path/to/gui/.

In your Lisp, load YASON and HUNCHENTOOT via QUICKLISP (see Recipes 18-2, 18-8, and 19-11) and perform the following two steps:

```
(hunchentoot:start
  (make-instance 'hunchentoot:easy-acceptor
                 :document-root "/path/to/gui/"
                 :port 4242))

(hunchentoot:define-easy-handler (get-symbols :uri "/get-symbols")
    (term)
  (setf (hunchentoot:content-type*) "application/json")
  (with-output-to-string (*standard-output*)
    (yason:encode
     (sort
      (mapcar 'string-downcase (apropos-list term :cl))
      'string<))))
```

You should now be able to open http://localhost:4242/ in your web browser. And if you start typing in the input field, you should see an autocomplete list based on the output of APROPOS-LIST (see Recipe 16-8) similar to this:[5]

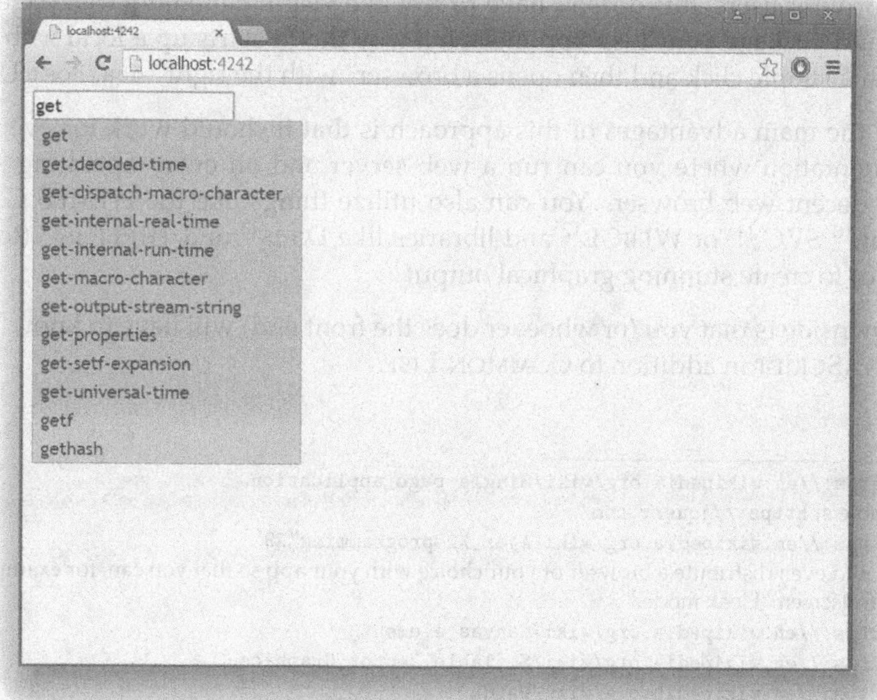

[5]Screenshot from Google Chrome on Windows 7.

How It Works

Using a web browser as a front end for COMMON LISP applications has been possible since 1994 (see page 585). However, in the age of HTML5 and with today's modern browsers, the situation is far more convenient and Google and others have created whole office suites running as single-page applications[6] (SPA) in a browser window.

We can leverage this approach as well, using COMMON LISP as the back end for an SPA. The general structure will look like this:

(i) Create the front end using HTML, CSS, and JAVASCRIPT, utilizing libraries of your choice. In our example, we used JQUERY[7] and its user interface library, JQUERY UI.

(ii) On the Lisp side, add a web server to your application.

(iii) Use AJAX[8] for the communication between the front and back ends.

You might even want to view this as a "model-view-controller" (MVC) pattern, where you can decide how much of the model and controller work will be done on the JAVASCRIPT side.

There are lots of frameworks to choose from. What you'll want is something that provides enough "hooks" to call back to your Lisp server whenever there's relevant user interaction—like when a button is pressed or a menu item is selected.

And, for your users, this doesn't have to feel like visiting a remote web page at all. You could package your Lisp app in such a way that it starts up a local web server through a simple click and then opens a browser[9] with the right `localhost` URL.

One of the main advantages of this approach is that it should work for every Lisp implementation where you can run a web server and on every operating system with a decent web browser. You can also utilize things like the HTML5 CANVAS element,[10] SVG,[11], or WEBGL[12] and libraries like D3.JS[13] and THREE.JS[14] (to name just two) to create stunning graphical output.

The downside is that you (or whoever does the front end) will have to know HTML and JAVASCRIPT in addition to COMMON LISP.

---

6 See `https://en.wikipedia.org/wiki/Single-page_application`.

7 Available at `https://jquery.com/`.

8 See `https://en.wikipedia.org/wiki/Ajax_%28programming%29`.

9 You could even distribute a browser of your choice with your app so that you can, for example, start it in fullscreen "kiosk mode."

10 See `https://en.wikipedia.org/wiki/Canvas_element`.

11 See `https://en.wikipedia.org/wiki/Scalable_Vector_Graphics`.

12 See `https://en.wikipedia.org/wiki/WebGL`.

13 See `http://d3js.org/`.

14 See `http://threejs.org/`.

As another drawback, one could add that there's currently no COMMON LISP library to support this way of generating user interfaces out of the box. But the main task of such a library would be to facilitate communication between the JAVASCRIPT side and the Lisp web server. And as you've seen above, this can be done with a minimal amount of code. I don't really see how a library could help here, except perhaps by tying you to a specific JAVASCRIPT solution.

What the Example Does

Here's a walkthrough of our example above, in case you want more details:

- The `<body>` part of our HTML page essentially only contains an `<input>` element with the ID `foo`.

  It is wrapped in a `<div>` of class `ui-widget`, which is not necessary for the functionality described here, but allows the contained elements to be styled by JQUERY UI "themes."

- In the `<head>` part of the page, we're loading the JQUERY and JQUERY UI libraries as well as the already-mentioned "theme." This is done through the `code.jquery.com` CDN[15] to make it easier to reproduce the example.

  If you want to create an application that doesn't connect to the Internet, you can, of course, download these libs and add them to the files served by your Lisp web server.

- What follows is a short JAVASCRIPT function that uses a JQUERY mechanism to make sure it is not executed before the whole page has finished loading. It associates a *widget* responsible for displaying the autocomplete texts with the HTML `<input>` field and then tells it to use the URL

  ```
  http://localhost:4242/get-symbols
  ```

  whenever the text in the `<input>` field changes. (We only needed to specify the `/get-symbols` part. The `localhost:4242` part is due to what we entered into the browser.)

- On each change, the widget will send a request like

  ```
  http://localhost:4242/get-symbols?term=get
  ```

  where "`get`" would be the current contents of the `<input>` field. It expects as a reply a list[16] of strings to populate the drop-down menu, and it wants the list to be encoded as a JSON array.

[15] See `https://en.wikipedia.org/wiki/Content_delivery_network`.

[16] It doesn't have to be a flat list like here. See the JQUERY UI documentation for other options.

- On the Lisp side, we start a web server and tell it to listen on port 4242. We also tell it that its *document root* should be the directory where we put our HTML file. As we used the name `index.html` for this file, it will be served once we enter

  ```
  http://localhost:4242/
  ```

  into a browser.

- The last step is to define a HUNCHENTOOT *handler*, which in this case is a function which is invoked whenever a request like

  ```
  http://localhost:4242/get-symbols?term=get
  ```

  is made. The function is set up to receive the parameter called `term` as a string, calls `APROPOS-LIST` with this string, sorts and downcases[17] the output, and then feeds the result to the YASON library, which takes care of formatting the list as a JSON array. This is what the handler returns and what will be sent to the client (the autocomplete widget) that made the request.

20-2. Building Applications with the "Lisp Toolkit"

Problem

You want a cross-platform solution for a graphical user interface that doesn't have to be particularly fancy and posh. (Or maybe you want to quickly create a prototype for something that will be fancy and posh in the future.)

Solution

Use LTK.

Like in the previous recipe, we'll build a simple demo. In addition to LTK itself (which you can install through QUICKLISP; see Recipe 18-2), you will need to have TK. If TK isn't already installed (check if a program called `wish` can be started from the command line) or available through a package management system like APT, then you are most likely on Windows. In that case, an easy way to get it is the ACTIVETCL distribution.[18]

[17]Note that symbols are automatically converted to strings here; see Recipe 1-9.

[18]See `http://www.activestate.com/activetcl`. TK was originally written for and is still tightly knit to the TCL programming language, thus the name. But that doesn't need to bother us if we just want to use LTK.

It should now be possible to call[19] the program `wish` from your Lisp image. If that's not the case, you'll need to set your `PATH` environment variable[20] or tell LTK where `wish` can be found, like so:

```
(setf ltk:*wish-pathname* "c:/Tcl/bin/wish.exe")
```

Check if it worked by evaluating `(LTK:LTKTEST)`.

Now compile and load the following code:

```
(defparameter *size* 400)

(defun gui ()
  (ltk:with-ltk ()
    (let* ((vals (list 2 3 4))
           (canvas (ltk:make-canvas nil :width *size* :height *size*))
           (spinbox
            (make-instance 'ltk:spinbox
                           :width 3
                           :command
                             (lambda (val)
                               (sierpinski canvas
                                           (parse-integer val)))
                           :master nil
                           :values vals
                           :text (first vals))))
      (ltk:wm-title ltk:*tk* "Sierpinski")
      (ltk:configure canvas :background :white)
      (ltk:pack canvas)
      (ltk:pack spinbox)
      (sierpinski canvas (first vals)))))

(defun sierpinski (canvas level)
  (ltk:clear canvas)
  (labels ((square (x y size)
             (let ((rectangle
                    (ltk:create-rectangle canvas x y
                                          (+ x size) (+ y size))))
               (ltk:itemconfigure canvas rectangle :fill :red)
               (ltk:itemconfigure canvas rectangle :outline :red)))
           (recurse (x y size level)
             (let ((step (* 1/3 size)))
               (square (+ x step) (+ y step) step)
```

[19]See Recipe 22-6.

[20]See Recipe 22-1.

```
            (when (plusp level)
              (dolist (next-x (list x (+ x step) (+ x step step)))
                (dolist
                    (next-y (list y (+ y step) (+ y step step)))
                  (recurse next-x next-y step (1- level)))))))
    (recurse 0 0 *size* level)))
```

After evaluating (GUI), you should now see a more or less square window showing a Sierpinski carpet,[21] the depth of which you can control with a *spin box* at the bottom:[22]

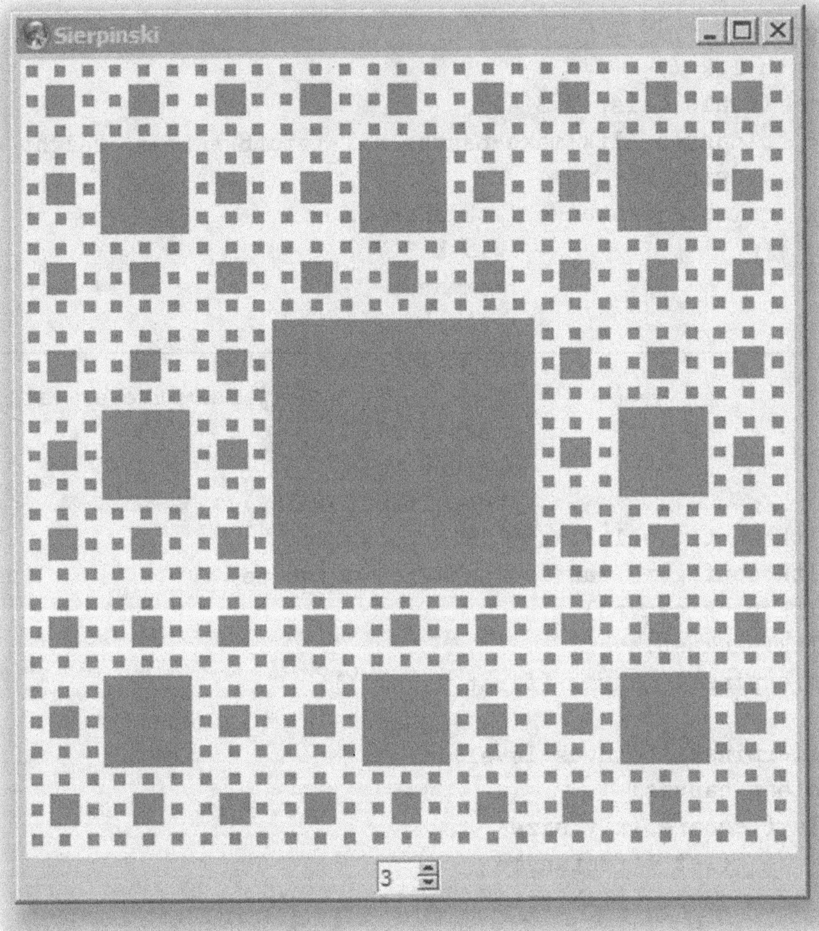

[21]See https://en.wikipedia.org/wiki/Sierpinski_carpet.

[22]Screenshot from TCL/TK 8.5 on Windows 7.

How It Works

LTK calls itself "the easy way to do Lisp GUI programming" and that's probably right. There are various other COMMON LISP GUI libraries,[23] which—like LTK—provide some kind of binding[24] to an existing solution in another language, and most of them will likely be faster or offer more features. But in terms of simplicity and ease of use, LTK is hard to beat.

LTK (originally written by Peter Herth) works by "outsourcing" all the GUI work to the TK[25] widget toolkit, which means that TK has to be installed before you can use it. LTK will then establish a connection to the `wish` shell and use it to communicate with TK. So, like in Recipe 20-1, we have a separate program running independently of our Lisp image, which is responsible for the GUI grunt work. (And in both cases, this involves communication of text commands through a network stream. This is OK for many apps, but it might cause performance problems[26] in certain scenarios.)

Note that there are two other bridges from COMMON LISP to TCL/TK: one called CLTCL and one called CL-TK. All three approaches should essentially enable you to perform the same tasks, but LTK seems to have the most "Lisp-y" API (while CL-TK is likely faster because it can communicate "directly" through Lisp's foreign function interface).

One final remark: I used LTK with SBCL on Windows without any problems. But it seems there are long-standing problems with LISPWORKS on this operating system. However, if you're using LISPWORKS, you probably won't need something like LTK anyway (see Recipe 20-4).

What the Example Does

LTK comes with reasonably good documentation,[27] but let's nevertheless have a closer look at our example code. (For brevity, we'll leave out the `LTK:` package prefix in the following discussion.)

- `WITH-LTK` is a convenience macro that establishes a connection to the `wish` shell so that LTK can communicate with TK. It also starts TK's event loop, which means that the macro doesn't return before we explicitly exit the GUI (for example, by clicking on the close box of the TK window).

[23]See `http://www.cliki.net/gui` for a list (which is probably incomplete).

[24]We use the term *binding* in a broader sense here. Most libraries really establish a binding in the sense that they call "foreign code" (see Chapter 19), while some, like LTK, use a (network) stream to communicate with an external process.

[25]See `https://en.wikipedia.org/wiki/Tk_%28software%29`.

[26]And TCL/TK itself is not particularly fast either...

[27]And you might want to have a look at `https://en.wikibooks.org/wiki/Common_Lisp/External_libraries/Ltk` as well. A general understanding of TK will also be helpful. For that, a good starting point is `http://www.tkdocs.com/tutorial/index.html`.

You can also dispense with WITH-LTK and handle the event loop yourself.

- A GUI in TK is comprised of so-called *widgets*, which in LTK are mapped to CLOS objects. You generally create widgets with MAKE-INSTANCE but many of them also have their own convenience functions, like MAKE-CANVAS.
- We create a *canvas* of a specific size to draw on and a *spin box*[28] to switch between recursion levels.
- While the meaning of most arguments in the last step should be obvious, two deserve some explanation. One is that widgets can have a *master* widget that they are in (for example, a *frame*). We use NIL here because ours are top-level widgets.

  The second is the :COMMAND initarg for the spin box, which is a *callback*—a function that is called whenever the user changes the value in the spin box.
- To change a widget's attributes, you use CONFIGURE after its creation. This is how we set the canvas's background color to white.
- The WITH-LTK macro automatically bound the global special variable *TK* to TK's *top level*. We use it with the *window manager* function WM-TITLE to change the title of the main window.
- Once widgets are created, they need to be placed on the window. That's what the call to PACK in our example does. There are various options to PACK that we didn't use and there are also other ways to arrange widgets, like PLACE or GRID.
- The function SIERPINSKI finally does the drawing. The parts that are interesting for us are the functions CREATE-RECTANGLE to draw a rectangle (and there are also things like lines, arcs, polygons, ...) and ITEMCONFIGURE, which shows that as with widgets, the items drawn on a canvas must be configured after their creation to change their appearance.

20-3. Creating Common Lisp GUIs Through Java

Problem

You want to use a JAVA GUI as the front end for your COMMON LISP back-end code.

[28]See https://en.wikipedia.org/wiki/Spinner_%28computing%29.

Solution

We'll use ABCL for the examples (and you might want to read Recipe 19-10 first, which also hints at how you could achieve similar results with other COMMON LISP implementations).

The first example is essentially the "Hello World" example from Oracle's SWING tutorial, which we'll try to reproduce from Lisp. In ABCL's REPL, evaluate the following three forms:

```
(require 'abcl-contrib)
(require 'jss)
(use-package :jss)
```

This is so that we can use a nicer syntax[29] than that of ABCL's "JAVA FFI," demonstrated in Recipe 19-10.

Now define and compile the following function:

```
(defun say-hello ()
  (let ((frame (new 'JFrame "Hello ABCL"))
        (label (new 'JLabel
                    "The crux of the biscuit is the apostrophe.")))
    (#"add" (#"getContentPane" frame) label)
    (#"pack" frame)
    (#"setVisible" frame t)))
```

If you've ever done something with SWING, this should all look familiar to you—except for the Lisp-y syntax (which we'll talk about shortly). In JAVA, the next step is to create an *anonymous class* implementing the interface `java.lang.Runnable` (the `run` method of which would call `SAY-HELLO`) and to feed this class to SWING's `invokeLater`. In ABCL, you do it like this:[30]

```
(#"invokeLater" 'SwingUtilities
                (jinterface-implementation "java.lang.Runnable"
                                           "run" #'say-hello))
```

You should now see the following window:

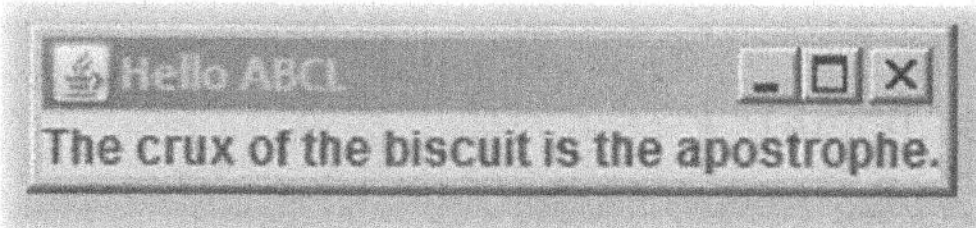

[29]Which, by the way, relies on modifying the Lisp reader. See more in Chapter 8.

[30]I was using ABCL 1.3.2 and according to their documentation the `JINTERFACE-IMPLEMENTATION` part is "partly not finished," so you might want to check if there's a newer version and if the API has changed.

Keep reading for a slightly more interesting example where JAVA calls back into Lisp.

How It Works

One of the big advantages[31] of JAVA is that it comes with standard libraries for graphical user interfaces. If you know how to utilize them and can access JAVA from your Lisp, why not just use them?

A natural choice for such an approach is ABCL, which we use here. But every COMMON LISP with good JAVA integration should do (see Recipe 19-10 for alternatives).

What the Example Does

The code above is more or less a verbatim translation of what you'd do in JAVA: create a `JFrame` and a `JLabel`, add the label to the frame's content pane, and so on. What's new is that we use a specific reader syntax (see Recipe 8-10) for method invocation; `#"pack"`, for example, means that we want ABCL to query (at run time) for a method called `pack` for the corresponding object instance fitting the supplied list of arguments. The `#"invokeLater"` call shows how this is supposed to be done with static method calls. Also, the order of arguments is reversed to be more like in Lisp: the method comes first, then the object.

Other than that, you should understand what's happening if you know JAVA. The function `JINTERFACE-IMPLEMENTATION` will be discussed below.

A Better Example

A more typical approach for larger projects would be to code a significant amount of the GUI directly in JAVA—maybe with the help of a WYSIWYG GUI designer[32]—and implement only callbacks to Lisp. This is what our next example is supposed to demonstrate. We start with this JAVA code:

```
package de.weitz;
import javax.swing.*;
import java.awt.*;

class Plane extends JPanel {
  int size;
  boolean points[][];
```

[31] JAVA also has some big disadvantages as not only Lisp hackers will happily attest. But I'll refrain from pursuing this topic here...

[32] Historical tidbit: did you know that the forebear of Apple's *Interface Builder* was written in Lisp?

```
  Plane(PointSetter ps, int size) {
    this.size = size;
    this.points = new boolean[size][size];
    ps.fill(points);
    this.setPreferredSize(new Dimension(size, size));
  }
  public void paintComponent(Graphics g) {
    super.paintComponent(g);
    for (int x = 0; x < size; x++) {
      for (int y = 0; y < size; y++) {
        ((Graphics2D) g).setPaint(points[x][y] ?
                                  Color.black : Color.white);
        ((Graphics2D) g).drawLine(x, y, x, y);
      }
    }
  }
}

public class Mandelbrot extends JFrame {
  public Mandelbrot(PointSetter ps, int size) {
    final Plane plane = new Plane(ps, size);
    add(plane);
    setTitle("Mandelbrot");
    pack();
  }
  public void display() {
    javax.swing.SwingUtilities.invokeLater(new Runnable() {
        public void run() {
          setVisible(true);
        }
      });
  }
}
```

This code brings up a GUI window (a `JFrame`) and fills it with a `JPanel`, where black or white pixels are drawn according to the contents of a boolean array called `points`. `points` is supposed to be initialized by the `fill` method of a `PointSetter` object.

Save this code to a file called `Mandelbrot.java` and put it into a directory called `weitz` inside a directory called `de`. For this example, let's suppose that `de` resides in the `/tmp` directory.

For `PointSetter`, you'll need to save this code

```
package de.weitz;
```

```
public interface PointSetter {
  public void fill(boolean points[][]);
}
```

to a file `PointSetter.java` and add it to the directory where `Mandelbrot.java` already is.

This defines a JAVA *interface*, but we'll need to provide an actual implementation of the `fill` method before it can be used. That's what will happen on the Lisp side.

Now compile the JAVA code. From the command line, you'd do it like so:

```
cd /tmp/
javac de/weitz/PointSetter.java
javac de/weitz/Mandelbrot.java
```

Back in ABCL, we now use the same invocation sequence as above, except that in the first line, we additionally tell the Lisp image where the JAVA classes we just created can be found:

```
(add-to-classpath "/tmp/")
(require 'abcl-contrib)
(require 'jss)
(use-package :jss)
```

The Lisp code to fill the boolean array[33] is this (which you should compile and load):

```
(defparameter *size* 400)

(defun set-points (java-array)
  (loop for x from -2d0 to 1d0 by (/ 3d0 *size*)
        for i from 0 do
        (loop for y from 1.5d0 downto -1.5d0 by (/ 3d0 *size*)
              for j from 0
              for c = (complex x y)
              when (loop repeat 100
                         for z = c then (+ (* z z) c)
                         always (< (abs z) 2d0)) do
                (jarray-set java-array +true+ i j))))
```

The interesting part here is that the argument to this function is a JAVA array, so we have to use `JARRAY-SET` instead of `AREF` (see Chapter 5) to access it. Also note that we use the ABCL constant `+TRUE+` (instead of just `T`) for the JAVA constant `true`.

[33]This is a very simple and unoptimized way of computing the *Mandelbrot set* (see `https://en.wikipedia.org/wiki/Mandelbrot_set`).

The final step now is the implementation of the JAVA interface `PointSetter`. This is done by `JINTERFACE-IMPLEMENTATION`, which is given the (package-qualified) name of an interface and a plist with strings as keys and Lisp functions (to implement the methods named by the strings) as values. This is roughly what an *anonymous class* in JAVA does:

```
(let ((mandelbrot
       (new "de.weitz.Mandelbrot"
            (jinterface-implementation "de.weitz.PointSetter"
                                       "fill" #'set-points)
            *size*)))
  (#"display" mandelbrot))
```

You should now see this:

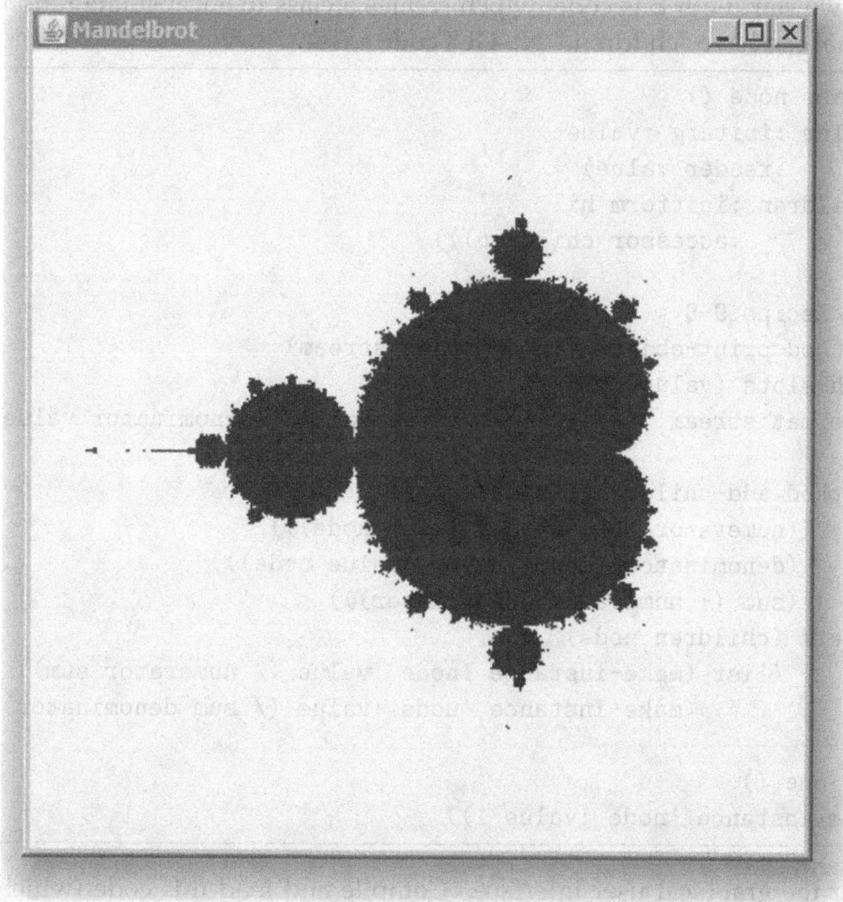

20-4. Using CAPI to Build Graphical User Interfaces

Problem

You want to create cross-platform GUIs with LISPWORKS's CAPI.

Solution

For the following example, you will obviously need LISPWORKS. The so-called "Personal Edition," which you can download from their web site for free, will suffice, though.

So that we have something that is a bit less boring than a button yelling *"Hello World,"* we start with this code, which creates a class to encapsulate rational numbers[34] that can have "children." No GUI code so far.

```
(defclass node ()
  ((value :initarg :value
          :reader value)
   (children :initform nil
             :accessor children)))

;; see Recipe 9-8
(defmethod print-object ((node node) stream)
  (with-slots (value) node
    (format stream "~A/~A" (numerator value) (denominator value))))

(defmethod add-children ((node node))
  (let* ((numerator (numerator (value node)))
         (denominator (denominator (value node)))
         (sum (+ numerator denominator)))
    (setf (children node)
          (list (make-instance 'node :value (/ numerator sum))
                (make-instance 'node :value (/ sum denominator))))))

(defun one ()
  (make-instance 'node :value 1))
```

Now for the graphical user interface. Compile and load this code (which will be explained below):

[34]Our aim is to implement a graphical representation of the *Calkin-Wilf tree* (see `https://en.wikipedia.org/wiki/Calkin%E2%80%93Wilf_tree`; see also Recipe 4-5).

```
(capi:define-interface calkin-wilf-tree ()
  ()
  (:panes
   (tree
    capi:tree-view
    :reader tree
    :roots (list (one))
    :children-function #'children
    :action-callback (lambda (node interface)
                       (unless (children node)
                         (add-children node)
                         (capi:tree-view-update-item (tree interface)
                                                     node nil)))
    :action-callback-expand-p t)
   (reset-button
    capi:push-button
    :text "Reset"
    :callback-type :interface
    :callback (lambda (interface)
                (setf (capi:tree-view-roots
                       (tree interface))
                      (list (one))))))
  (:layouts
   (default-layout
    capi:column-layout
    '(tree reset-button)
    :adjust :center))
  (:default-initargs
   :best-width 400
   :best-height 400
   :title "Calkin-Wilf Tree"))
```

If you now evaluate this form

```
(capi:display (make-instance 'calkin-wilf-tree))
```

you should see a window with the fraction `1/1` shown in the upper-left corner. If you double-click the number, it'll "spawn" the two "children" `1/2` and `2/1`, which you can again double-click, and so on. You can also click the symbols next to the numbers to collapse and/or expand parts of the tree. Or click the button labeled "Reset" to start from scratch.

After some time and some clicking around, the window might look like so:

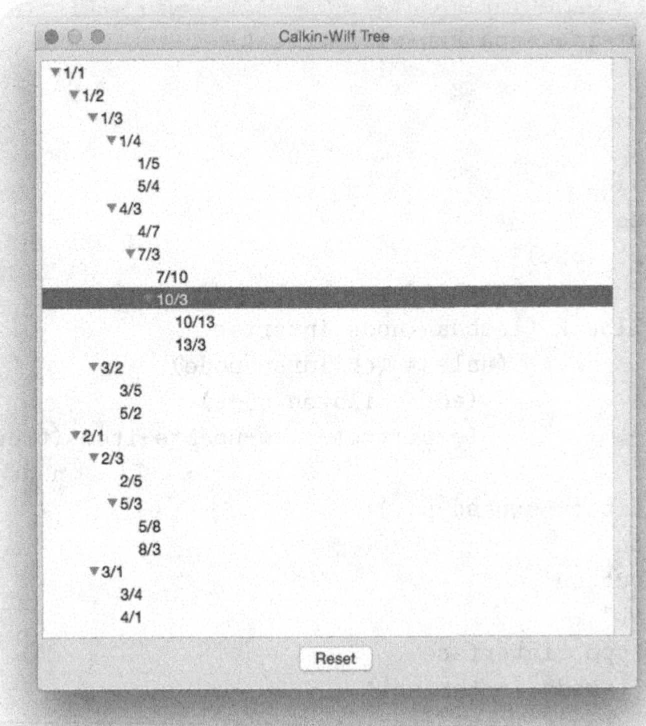

This should work on all desktop operating systems supported by LISPWORKS.

How It Works

At the moment, LISPWORKS is the only[35] COMMON LISP implementation that comes with a GUI library that's completely implemented in Lisp, fully integrated with the rest of the product, and cross-platform in the sense that essentially the same code will work on Windows, Mac OS, Linux, and even some Unix variants.

The library is called CAPI ("Common Application Programming Interface") and it uses the "native" libraries of the host operating system to draw GUI elements and provide interaction with the user (similar to JAVA's AWT). It has been used for many different applications[36] and is also the basis of LISPWORKS's own advanced IDE.

CAPI is huge—the PDF version of its *User Guide and Reference Manual* has more than 1,300 (!) pages—, so we can only give a very rough overview and emphasize some important points here:

---

[35]ALLEGROCL's *Common Graphics* comes close, but according to their documentation currently (as of June 2015) uses GTK instead of COCOA on Macs and can't be used with SMP versions of the compiler unless you're on Windows.

[36]Some of them are listed at `http://www.lispworks.com/success-stories/index.html`.

- CAPI uses an object-oriented approach throughout, where all UI elements are instances of CLOS classes that can be used directly, subclassed, and manipulated through methods.[37]
- The top-level GUI element, which corresponds to an OS window and contains the other elements, is called an *interface* in CAPI.
- Inside an interface, the individual elements (called *panes*) are arranged with the help of *layouts*.
- You can construct a complete interface programmatically at run time if you so wish, but the usual approach is to define most of it statically using a macro called `CAPI:DEFINE-INTERFACE`, which is an extended variant of `DEFCLASS`.
- Almost all GUI elements provide various *callbacks* so that you can define arbitrary Lisp functions to be called whenever the user does something (presses a button, fills a text field, drags and drops an item, and so on).
- Displayed CAPI interfaces automatically set up and operate the "message pump" of the underlying OS library,[38] so you usually don't have to care about this. You should be aware, though, that this will likely happen in a thread different from your REPL or application thread. This implies that if you want to modify the user interface from an arbitrary thread, you'll need to do it in the right way. (Unless you are in a callback that already runs in the UI thread.) CAPI provides functions like `CAPI:APPLY-IN-PANE-PROCESS` to do this for you.
- LISPWORKS comes with an *Interface Builder* that is supposed to help you to design GUIs using a WYSIWYG approach. It isn't half as powerful and convenient as some of the drag-and-drop GUI builders available for other languages, but it might nevertheless be a good starting point if you're new to CAPI.

While CAPI's own user guide is quite good, it isn't written in a tutorial style where you are escorted through various examples of increasing complexity. But the LISPWORKS distribution comes with a lot of examples worth looking at and you might also want to look at the CAPI *Cookbook* by David Johnson-Davies.[39]

What the Example Does

Here's a closer look at the example's GUI code (which essentially consists only of one Lisp form). (For brevity, we'll leave out the `CAPI:` package prefix in the following discussion.)

[37]The hierarchy of CAPI classes can be seen at `http://weitz.de/capi-overview/`.
[38]See `https://en.wikipedia.org/wiki/Event_loop`.
[39]To be found at `http://capi.plasticki.com/`.

- The DEFINE-INTERFACE form starts like the DEFCLASS macro: we define a class called CALKIN-WILF-TREE. We could have specified superclasses and slots but didn't do that in this case. (But our class will automatically inherit from CAPI's INTERFACE class.)
- The part starting with :PANES contains definitions for individual *panes* (UI elements) that will become part of the interface (and also slots of the class). In this case, we have two panes: a *tree view* and a *push button*.
- Each individual pane definition starts with the slot name and the pane's class and is followed by several keyword/value pairs used to customize the pane.
- TREE-VIEW is one of the many built-in CAPI classes. It is responsible for most of the functionality we saw in the running example. We just provide one or more roots for the tree and a function to compute the children of an individual tree node, which in this case happens to be the CHILDREN accessor we had already defined.
- We also specify a function (called the *action callback* of the tree view) to be called whenever the user double-clicks a node. It adds two children to the node if there aren't any already and then asks the tree view to update the corresponding part of the tree. (The :ACTION-CALLBACK-EXPAND-P option tells the tree view to expand the node in case of a double-click in addition to calling our callback.)
- The button is customized by providing a text to show and a callback to call when it is pressed. (The callback resets the tree's root to its original state.)
- In the case of the button, we can also see that we can specify per pane how callbacks are called; that is, which arguments they receive. In this case, we want the callback to receive the interface itself as its only argument.
- In the :LAYOUTS section, we define how panes are geometrically arranged in the interface by specifying *layouts* to hold the panes. (Layouts can also be nested.) The syntax is as with panes: a name for a slot followed by the layout class.

  We just want the two panes to be arranged in a column and centered.
- Finally, with :DEFAULT-INITARGS, we declare a preferred size and a title for our window. We could also have provided this information at instance creation time, though.
- To actually create an OS window corresponding to our interface class, we instantiate a CALKIN-WILF-TREE object using MAKE-INSTANCE and then call the function DISPLAY.

20-5. Using Lisp on Mobile Devices

Problem

You want to use COMMON LISP on mobile devices like iPhones, iPads, or Android smartphones or tablets.

Solution

We'll walk through a very simple iOS example using MOCL. (Ways of doing this with Android or other Lisps are discussed below.) You'll need to have Apple's XCODE ready to use and you should have already installed MOCL following the instructions it comes with.

This example is intended to provide just enough information to emphasize how you connect Lisp with a mobile app and how coding for mobile devices differs from your normal Lisp workflow. The more typical way to create such apps will be discussed below.

OK, here we go:

(i) In XCODE, create a new "single view iOS application." For the purpose of this example, we'll call it `Test` and save it on the desktop.

The default settings should be fine for this project. Make sure the language selected is OBJECTIVE-C.

(ii) In the file `ViewController.m`, at the end of the body of `viewDidLoad`, add this code:

```
UILabel *label = [[UILabel alloc] initWithFrame:self.view.frame];
NSString *foo = @"Hello World";

[label setFont:[UIFont fontWithName: @"Helvetica" size: 48.0f]];
[label setText:@"Hello World"];
[label setTextAlignment:NSTextAlignmentCenter];
[label sizeToFit];
[[self view] addSubview:label];
[label setCenter:[self view].center];
```

(iii) Build and run your code to make sure that you're seeing "Hello World" in the emulator.

(iv) Create a file `code.lisp` on the desktop with these contents:

```
(declaim (call-in listify))
(defun listify (arg n)
  (format nil "(~{~A~^ ~})"
          (loop repeat n collect arg)))
```

The CALL-IN declaration (see Chapter 17 for more about declarations) is specific to MOCL and tells the compiler that our LISTIFY function should be made accessible to OBJECTIVE-C. You'll see in a minute that MOCL will typically take care of conversion between Lisp and OBJECTIVE-C types automatically, but you can also declare argument and return types if needed.

(v) We now compile our Lisp code from the command line:

```
mocl -m64 --ios ~/Desktop/Test ~/Desktop/code.lisp
```

It should be obvious that the switches tell MOCL to (also) compile for 64-bit devices (32-bit support is included by default) and to target the iOS platform.

(vi) MOCL will now have created a folder called mocl in your project directory.

From XCODE, use the menu command *Add Files to "Test"* to add this whole folder to your project. Make sure that *Create Groups* is checked.

(vii) In the *Build Phases* tab, under *Link Binary With Libraries*, add the libz.dylib library.

(viii) In the file AppDelegate.m, add the line

```
#include "mocl.h"
```

at the top and add

```
cl_init();
```

to the end of the body of didFinishLaunchingWithOptions. This is necessary so that MOCL can perform some initializations when the app starts up on your mobile device.

The #include line has to be added to each file that calls MOCL functions. This also applies to the next step.

(ix) In the OBJECTIVE-C code we added above, optionally remove the line where foo was declared and change the setText line to

```
[label setText:listify(@"42", 3)]
```

You should now be able to test your app with the emulator and see this:

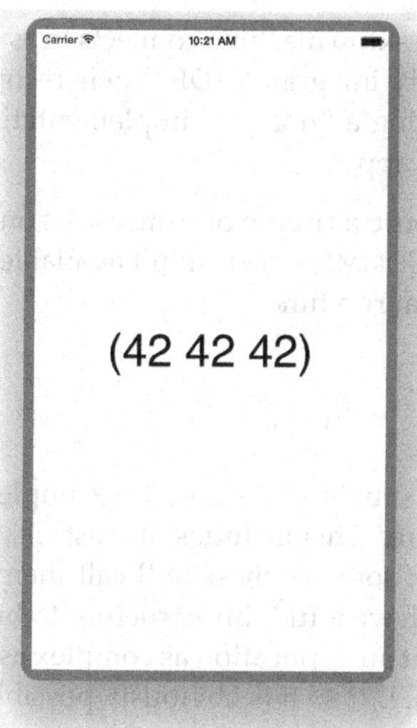

How It Works

Having the ability to run a large and complicated language like COMMON LISP on a comparatively small and slow device like a cell phone is still something pretty new. Of the existing approaches that I'm aware of (as of June 2015), MOCL[40] seems to be the most mature so far; so I'm using it for this example.

MOCL is one of those Lisps that compile to C as an intermediate language (see page 560) and from its acknowledgements, one can see that its heritage goes as far back as the CLICC compiler from the University of Kiel.[41]

MOCL can also create Android apps with pretty much the same workflow. (The only relevant difference is that on the Lisp side, MOCL has a nice special syntax for OBJECTIVE-C calls, whereas it currently doesn't have an equivalent for the JAVA calls on Android.)

Above we added a label programmatically to have a minimal example up and running quickly. The more typical approach would be to create your GUI using the corresponding tools for the platform (XCODE or ANDROID STUDIO) and to then add code that calls back into Lisp in the right places.[42]

Due to the nature of the target platforms, the development and coding experience will necessarily be a bit different from what you're used to in COMMON LISP. MOCL, for example, offers a "run time REPL" (which is provided by the target device as a

[40]See `https://wukix.com/mocl`.

[41]See `http://www.informatik.uni-kiel.de/~wg/clicc.html`.

[42]There are some good introductory screencasts at `https://wukix.com/mocl-screencasts`.

server your development desktop machine connects to as a client), but this obviously won't be the same as a fully integrated IDE. Their recommendation is to develop and test your Lisp code using a "normal" implementation, like SBCL, before you integrate it with the mobile app.

Also, iOS and Android impose a couple of restrictions on binaries, which entail that some dynamic features of COMMON LISP aren't available; for example, definition of functions, classes, or types at run time.

Alternatives

There are a various open source COMMON LISP implementations that can compile to the ARM architecture. This includes at least CLOZURECL, ECL, GCL, and SBCL. But as of June 2015, some of these still call themselves "work-in-progress" and none of them seem to have a full infrastructure to build mobile apps comparable to MOCL's. (But note that an application as complex as MAXIMA has already been ported to Android using ECL,[43] so it is obviously possible to "get things done.")

LISPWORKS released a new version of their product a few weeks before I wrote this chapter. They now offer runtime versions for Android and for iOS, which seem to provide a development environment similar to that of MOCL.[44] The basic idea is that you develop and test your code in LISPWORKS as usual, and then deliver (see Recipe 22-4) binaries for the corresponding platform(s). CAPI (see Recipe 20-4) won't be available, though; that is, you'll create the GUI as with MOCL.

---

[43]See `https://sites.google.com/site/maximaonandroid/`.

[44]See `http://www.lispworks.com/documentation/lw70/LW/html/lw-123.htm` and `http://www.lispworks.com/documentation/lw70/LW/html/lw-119.htm` for more information.

21. Persistence

Most larger applications will sooner or later need some kind of *persistence*—the ability to save data to non-volatile storage (for example, your hard disk), so that it can outlive the program that created it. Whole libraries could be filled with the literature that has already been written about various aspects of persistence, and yet this chapter is comparatively short.

That's because, on the one hand, there are many good and battle-tried databases out there that aren't written in Lisp but can be *used* from Lisp, while, on the other hand, on the Lisp side, there currently isn't such a thing as "the standard solution for object persistence."

For the former category, there is a huge class of COMMON LISP libraries[1] that provide access to existing database systems. Many do it in a straightforward way by simply providing a more or less verbatim translation of access invocations. It wouldn't make much sense to write about them here because you'll essentially just have to learn how to use the underlying database.

Others pile layers of abstraction atop the underlying database to make the result as "Lisp-y" as possible. As an example, we'll introduce the CLSQL library in the second recipe, which not only provides access to many professional SQL databases but also adds a convenient object-relational mapping for saving CLOS objects in an RDBMS.

While CLSQL and comparable approaches rely on external applications and/or foreign libraries (see Chapter 19), the rest of the chapter deals with "pure" Lisp solutions for persistence—from simple serialization to a high-performance object database meeting the classic ACID[2] requirements.

But for a production-quality persistence solution fitting your application's demands, you should view this chapter as only a quick introduction to *some* of the options, and thoroughly investigate what else is out there as well.

[1]See for example `http://cliki.net/database`.

[2]See `https://en.wikipedia.org/wiki/ACID`.

21-1. Serializing Your Data

Problem

You want to be able to simply write Lisp objects to a file and read them back in.

Solution

Use the CL-STORE library. It can be customized in various ways (see its documentation), but basically you just need two functions: `CL-STORE:STORE` and `CL-STORE:RESTORE`. Here's a simple example:

```
CL-USER> (defclass quux () ((a :initarg :a :reader a)))
#<STANDARD-CLASS QUUX>
CL-USER> (defpackage frob)
#<PACKAGE "FROB">
CL-USER> (defparameter *thing*
           (let* ((list (list :foo))
                  (hash (make-hash-table)))
             (setf (gethash 42 hash) list)
             (vector #\x "x" (make-instance 'quux :a 42)
                     (intern "X" :frob) list hash)))
*THING*
CL-USER> (cl-store:store *thing* "/tmp/store")
#(#\x "x" #<QUUX {100704A013}> FROB::X (:FOO)
  #<HASH-TABLE :TEST EQL :COUNT 1 {100704A043}>)
```

At this point, we have created a vector consisting of several Lisp objects and we have written it to a file `/tmp/store`. We can now do something like this:

```
;; continued from above
CL-USER> (defparameter *other-thing*
           (cl-store:restore "/tmp/store"))
*OTHER-THING*
CL-USER> *other-thing*
#(#\x "x" #<QUUX {10033719D3}> FROB::X (:FOO)
  #<HASH-TABLE :TEST EQL :COUNT 1 {1003371F93}>)
CL-USER> (eq (aref *other-thing* 4)
             (gethash 42 (aref *other-thing* 5)))
T
CL-USER> (a (aref *other-thing* 2))
42
```

CL-STORE can also be used with *streams* (see Chapter 14) instead of files, so it is not only useful for persistence but also for, say, sending data over a network.

How It Works

According to its documentation, the library CL-STORE[3] by Sean Ross is "intended to serve the same purpose as JAVA's `ObjectOutputStream` and `ObjectInputStream`."

From a Lisp point of view, it does what we described in Recipe 14-13, but in a more general way; it can serialize most objects that usually don't have a readable representation, like packages or hash tables. It will also serialize your own CLOS objects without the need for you to write `PRINT-OBJECT` methods (see Recipe 9-8). And it'll automatically resolve circularities (see page 427), which we could observe in our example with the `EQ` test above.

CL-STORE concentrates on one task; which is a good thing. It does nothing more and nothing less than writing *one* object[4] to a file or a stream and reading it back in.

To be able to restore instances of a CLOS class, the class must be known to the Lisp system. Which means that, if you start a fresh image and immediately evaluate the form

```
(cl-store:restore "/tmp/store")
```

then you'll get an error message. The same holds for symbols and their packages; that is, even without the `QUUX` instance in `*THING*` you'd get an error because of the `FROB::X` symbol.

To "fix" this, you can save the class and the package as well;[5] that is, you'd define `*THING*` like so before storing it:

```
(defparameter *thing*
  (let* ((list (list :foo))
         (hash (make-hash-table)))
    (setf (gethash 42 hash) list)
    (vector (find-package :frob) (find-class 'quux)          ;; <- added
            #\x "x" (make-instance 'quux :a 42)
            (intern "X" :frob) list hash)))
```

Here are some other things to watch out for:

[3]Which can be installed with QUICKLISP (see Recipe 18-2).

[4]This is like with JSON (see Recipe 19-11), where you also only read or write one object. And remember that this is also necessary to detect all circularities.

[5]You can also only call `CL-STORE:RESTORE` *after* you've loaded the *code* to define the class and/or the package.

- Saying that *the* object is read back in is only a manner of speaking. The object returned by `CL-STORE:RESTORE` will *not* be `EQ` to the one stored by `CL-STORE:STORE`; in general, it will not even be `EQUALP` (see Recipe 10-1) to it.[6]
- CL-STORE doesn't use the Lisp printer and reader as in Recipe 14-13, and thus the files that it creates aren't human-readable.
- Functions can't be serialized,[7] and as a consequence, initforms of class definitions can't be serialized either.
- Serializing something with one Lisp implementation and deserializing it with another one is not guaranteed to always work. Strings could, for example, be a problem for portability (see Recipe 3-1).

For other approaches to serialization in COMMON LISP, see `http://www.cliki.net/serialization`.

21-2. Accessing Relational Databases

Problem

You want to store your Lisp objects in an SQL database (or read data from there).

Solution

The CLSQL library provides a flexible approach to talk to various SQL databases. We'll go through a simple, albeit somewhat longish, example where we'll create a database and then use different means to query it.

We are going to use the SQLITE database[8] for this example, as it is the easiest to set up. The example should work more or less the same with MYSQL, POSTGRESQL, ORACLE, or ODBC, except that the initial step of creating and getting access to a database might be more difficult because of access rights and other complications.

While acquiring CLSQL itself is easy due to QUICKLISP (see Recipe 18-2), this does not include the database software. If you want to, say, talk to a POSTGRESQL database, a POSTGRESQL server has to be up and running. You should also know how to access it and you should have at least a basic knowledge of SQL.

For our example to work, the SQLITE shared library (typically called `libsqlite3.so` or `sqlite3.dll`) has to be installed in a place where the *foreign function interface* (see Chapter 19) can find it.

---

[6]Try `(EQUALP *THING* *OTHER-THING*)` in our example.

[7]But you can of course serialize their names.

[8]See `https://www.sqlite.org/`.

Once that is done, we can start, like so:[9]

```
CL-USER> (clsql:connect '("/tmp/worldcup.db") :database-type :sqlite3)
;; lots of compiler output here if this is done for the first time
#<CLSQL-SQLITE3:SQLITE3-DATABASE /tmp/worldcup.db OPEN {10058EA593}>
```

This will create a file /tmp/worldcup.db that will be our database and establish a *connection* to it, which will automatically be used (see CLSQL:*DEFAULT-DATABASE*) when we evaluate other forms during this example.

For the next step, load this code:

```
(clsql:def-view-class final ()
  ((city :accessor city
         :initarg :city
         :type string)
   (year :accessor year
         :initarg :year
         :db-kind :key
         :type integer)
   (winner :accessor winner
           :initarg :winner
           :type keyword)))
```

The CLSQL:DEF-VIEW-CLASS macro is similar to DEFCLASS but adds SQL-specific options. We're essentially defining a CLOS class FINAL, but we are also specifying a type for each slot (which is not mandatory in CLOS) and for one slot, we're declaring that it shall be used as a (primary) *key*, because we are now going to create a database table from this class:

```
CL-USER> (clsql:create-view-from-class 'final)
; No value
```

To check that this was actually done, you can now connect to the database from the console[10] (using something like sqlite3 /tmp/worldcup.db) and issue the following command (note the dot):

```
.schema
```

Let's now create a CLOS instance and add it to our new database:

```
CL-USER> (make-instance 'final :city "Rome" :year 1934 :winner :ita)
#<FINAL {100681A8D3}>
```

[9]To connect to other databases, you usually need to provide authentication information like a username and a password. Search for *connection specification* in the CLSQL manual.

[10]See https://www.sqlite.org/cli.html.

```
CL-USER> (clsql:update-records-from-instance *)
(1934)
```

If you're still connected from the console, try something like this to confirm that a row was added to the country table:

```
select * from final;
```

Although this was quite easy so far, we can make it even easier and automatically insert newly created instances into the database by setting `CLSQL:*DB-AUTO-SYNC*` to a true value:

```
CL-USER> (let ((clsql:*db-auto-sync* t))
           (loop for (city year winner) in '(("Paris" 1938 :ita)
                                              ("Bern" 1954 :deu)
                                              ("Solna" 1958 :bra)
                                              ("Santiago" 1962 :bra)
                                              ("Mexico City" 1970 :bra)
                                              ("Munich" 1974 :deu)
                                              ("Madrid" 1982 :ita)
                                              ("Rome" 1990 :deu)
                                              ("Pasadena" 1994 :bra)
                                              ("Yokohama" 2002 :bra)
                                              ("Berlin" 2006 :ita)
                                              ("Rio" 2014 :deu))
                 for final = (make-instance 'final :city city
                                                   :year year
                                                   :winner winner)
                 finally (return final)))
#<FINAL {10073FBF83}>
;; oh wait, we made a mistake in the last object; let's fix it:
CL-USER> (let ((clsql:*db-auto-sync* t))
           (setf (city *) "Rio de Janeiro"))
"Rio de Janeiro"
```

We could now check our database from the console again, but we can do it from Lisp as well:

```
CL-USER> (clsql:select 'final :flatp t)
(#<FINAL {1007E14093}> #<FINAL {1004939F13}> #<FINAL {100493A1C3}>
 #<FINAL {100493A473}> #<FINAL {100493A723}> #<FINAL {100493A9D3}>
 #<FINAL {100493AC83}> #<FINAL {100493AF33}> #<FINAL {100493B1E3}>
 #<FINAL {100493B493}> #<FINAL {100493B743}> #<FINAL {100493B9F3}>
 #<FINAL {100493BCA3}>)
CL-USER> (describe (first (last *)))
```

```
#<FINAL {100493BCA3}>
  [standard-object]
Slots with :INSTANCE allocation:
  CITY            = "Rio de Janeiro"
  YEAR            = 2014
  WINNER          = :DEU
  VIEW-DATABASE   = #<CLSQL-SQLITE3:SQLITE3-DATABASE /tmp/worldcup...
; No value
```

(Note that the city is really shown as "Rio de Janeiro", so the "last minute change" we made was propagated to the database as an update.)

We have so far shown a direct mapping between CLOS classes and SQL tables. But you don't have to work like this. Next, we'll show various ways to query our new database,[11] some of which won't involve CLOS at all:

```
;; this is for the [...] syntax used below
CL-USER> (clsql:enable-sql-reader-syntax)
; No value

CL-USER> (clsql:select 'final :where [= [city] "Rome"] :flatp t)
(#<FINAL {1004F17BD3}> #<FINAL {1004F17E93}>)
CL-USER> (mapcar 'winner *)
(:ITA :DEU)

;; now we lose the CLOS objects and read the data "directly"
CL-USER> (clsql:select [winner] [count [*]]
                       :from [final] :group-by [winner])
((":BRA" 5) (":DEU" 4) (":ITA" 4))
("WINNER" "COUNT(*)")

;; you can also transmit SQL statements as strings if you prefer
CL-USER> (clsql:query "select distinct winner from final")
((":ITA") (":DEU") (":BRA"))
("WINNER")

;; various looping constructs are available
CL-USER> (clsql:do-query ((winner) [select [distinct [winner]]
                                            :from [final]])
           (princ winner))
:ITA:DEU:BRA
":BRA"
```

[11]We won't discuss these in detail. Most of them are more or less self-explanatory if you know SQL. The rest you'll have to look up in the CLSQL manual.

```
;; and even a modified LOOP (which will work in /some/ Lisps)
CL-USER> (loop for winner being the records
                    of [select [winner] :from [final]]
                count (string= ":ITA" winner))
4
```

How It Works

CLSQL, by Kevin Rosenberg, is a library that provides a unified interface to many different SQL databases. It began as a "clone" of COMMON SQL (which comes bundled with LISPWORKS and has been around since the early 1990s). The APIs of both libraries are very similar. (Up to the point that Nick Levine's very helpful COMMON SQL tutorial at `http://www.lispworks.com/documentation/sql-tutorial/` is applicable to CLSQL, with just a few minor modifications.)

We only scratched the surface so far. For example, we didn't see transactions, joins, explicit updates and inserts, sequences, and so on. But CLSQL comes with almost 250 pages of documentation, and lots of examples are available in the source tree and online, so you aren't left alone if you want to explore this library further.

There are several other libraries that can connect COMMON LISP to relational databases. For example, if you are sure that you'll only ever use POSTGRESQL, then POSTMODERN by Marijn Haverbeke seems to be a very good choice. It comes with a nice domain-specific language called "S-SQL," which provides a Lisp-y syntax for SQL queries[12] and doesn't rely on foreign libraries (as is also the case for CLSQL with the `:POSTGRESQL-SOCKET` database type).

21-3. Keeping Your Database in RAM

Problem

You want to work with all of your data in RAM and you only want to use persistence for exceptional situations (like recovery, in case your program has to be shut down).

Solution

A good solution for such a scenario is the BKNR.DATASTORE library. We'll walk through a very simple scenario.

[12] You'll find a lot of good examples for it at `https://sites.google.com/site/sabraonthehill/postmodern-examples`.

We start (after loading the library with QUICKLISP; see Recipe 18-2) by evaluating the following form to create a new CLOS class:[13]

```
(defclass final (bknr.datastore:store-object)
  ((city :accessor city
         :initarg :city)
   (year :accessor year
         :initarg :year)
   (winner :accessor winner
           :initarg :winner))
  (:metaclass bknr.datastore:persistent-class))
```

Except for the *metaclass* (see page 393), this looks like a vanilla CLOS class. But we'll see in a moment that objects of this class will be special because changes to them will be automatically propagated to a *transaction log*.

We'll now create a *datastore*, which from the view of the file system, will just be a directory that'll get filled with some files soon:[14]

```
CL-USER> (let ((object-subsystem
                (make-instance
                  'bknr.datastore:store-object-subsystem)))
           (make-instance 'bknr.datastore:mp-store
                          :directory "/tmp/store/"
                          :subsystems (list object-subsystem)))
initializing store random state
restoring #<MP-STORE DIR: "/tmp/store/">
#<BKNR.DATASTORE:MP-STORE DIR: "/tmp/store/">
CL-USER> bknr.datastore:*store*
#<BKNR.DATASTORE:MP-STORE DIR: "/tmp/store/">
```

The second form shows that our new datastore is now stored in a global special variable to act as *the* datastore for all subsequent transactions.

As in Recipe 21-2, we'll now just create a few objects (and we'll create them with MAKE-INSTANCE as usual).

```
CL-USER> (loop for (city year winner) in '(("Rome" 1934 :ita)
                                            ("Paris" 1938 :ita)
                                            ("Bern" 1954 :deu)
                                            ("Stockholm" 1958 :bra))
           for final = (make-instance 'final :city city
```

[13]You might want to compare to the definition on page 665.

[14]It wouldn't really be necessary to use BKNR.DATASTORE:MP-STORE here; BKNR.DATASTORE:STORE would suffice. BKNR.DATASTORE:MP-STORE is meant to serialize concurrent access to the store from multiple threads (see Chapter 11).

```
                                          :year year
                                          :winner winner)
                 finally (return final))
#<FINAL ID: 3>
;; Oops, let's fix that...
CL-USER> (bknr.datastore:with-transaction ()
           (setf (city *) "Solna"))
"Solna"
```

If you now look into the /tmp/store/ directory, you'll find a file there that contains (in some binary format which is not human readable) information about the four objects we just created.

Let's simulate a power outage by closing down our Lisp image (for example, using the *,q* shortcut from the SLIME REPL). Now start the Lisp anew and repeat everything we did above, *except for* creating the objects (the LOOP form). Once you create the datastore, you'll see a message like this one:

```
loading transaction log /tmp/store/current/transaction-log
```

This means that the objects that we created in the previous session are now in the current image. Let's try it:

```
CL-USER> (bknr.datastore:store-objects-with-class 'final)
(#<FINAL ID: 0> #<FINAL ID: 1> #<FINAL ID: 2> #<FINAL ID: 3>)
CL-USER> (describe (first (last *)))
#<FINAL ID: 3>
  [standard-object]

Slots with :INSTANCE allocation:
  DESTROYED-P   = NIL
  ID            = 3
  LAST-CHANGE   = 3651303637
  CITY          = "Solna"
  YEAR          = 1958
  WINNER        = :BRA
; No value
```

It may not be immediately obvious how this differs from evaluating a CLSQL:SELECT form (see page 666). The difference is that in the CLSQL case, the objects were loaded from the database as a result of evaluating the form, whereas here the four FINAL objects were already in the Lisp *image* (see Recipe 16-1) and only had to be found[15] and returned.

[15]By their class in this example. But there are, of course, better ways to do that. See what page 672 has to say about *indices*.

At this point we've just seen the most basic usage of this library. For a discussion of the concepts involved, see below.

How It Works

The main idea behind libraries like BKNR.DATASTORE is called *object prevalence*. It is assumed (and a basic requirement) that your database fits into and permanently resides in RAM. Given the amount of memory today's computers have, this is possible for a vast majority of databases; most are easily less than a gigabyte (GB). And even if you wanted to set aside 256 octets of address information for each citizen of the EU's most populated country (Germany), you'd only need around 20 GB; a few weeks before I wrote this, Lenovo announced *laptops* with 64 GB of RAM.

Once your entire data is in RAM, working with it actually gets a lot easier because you can now just use normal Lisp functions to access your objects. The only downside is that you have to prepare for, say, a power failure or a regular shutdown of your program; how do you work with your data in RAM and at the same time create a safe backup on disk that is always in sync with it?

The strategy is to look at the overall *state* of the system (of all objects that belong to the *store*) and view each change (like adding or modifying an object) as a *transaction* that alters this state. So, in our example we had an initial (empty) state and five transactions—four implicit ones when we added four objects and one explicit one when we changed one object.

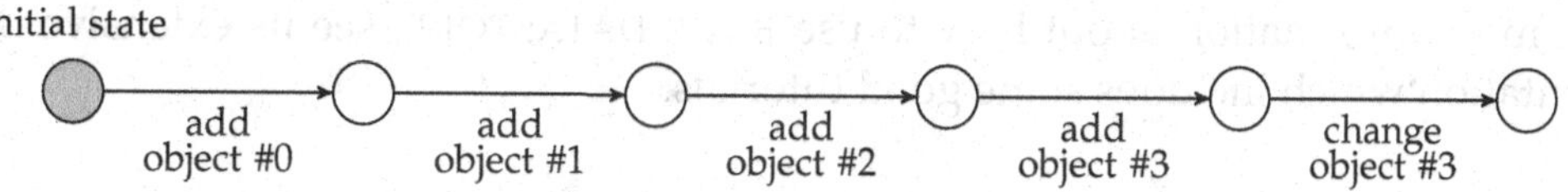

The transactions were written to a *transaction log* in the file system, and when we restarted the image, the system was first put in its initial state and then the log was "played back." This is essentially what an RDBMS does as well, except that in the case of prevalence, all objects are in RAM all the time and the transaction log is more like a "safety net." (Of course, you can also define your own transactions, which can comprise several operations in an all-or-nothing manner. Or you can insert *snapshots* of the whole system into the transaction log in order to speed up the playback process.[16])

The first usable object prevalence solution was a JAVA library called PREVAYLER, which was released in 2001. Shortly thereafter, Sven Van Caekenberghe published a COMMON LISP variant of it called CL-PREVALENCE. BKNR.DATASTORE by Manuel Odendahl and Hans Hübner builds on its concepts, but is more robust and offers more features.

[16]The subsystem we used in our example provides snapshotting out of the box.

One feature that we didn't investigate so far—because it is nice but essentially orthogonal to persistence—is the ability to add *indices* to your data for quick look-up. To give you an idea of how they work, quit your Lisp again and then proceed like above, except that this time you should use the following extended class definition:

```
(defclass final (bknr.datastore:store-object)
  ((city :accessor city
         :initarg :city)
   (year :accessor year
         :initarg :year
         :index-type bknr.indices:unique-index                    ;; added
         :index-reader final-by-year                              ;; added
         :index-values all-finals)                                ;; added
   (winner :accessor winner
           :initarg :winner))
  (:metaclass bknr.datastore:persistent-class))
```

After opening the store again,[17] you can now do things like this:

```
CL-USER> (final-by-year 1934)
#<FINAL ID: 0>
T
CL-USER> (length (all-finals))
4
```

For more information about how to use BKNR.DATASTORE, see its extensive documentation which includes some good tutorials.

21-4. Using a Lisp Object Database

Problem

You want to use an object database that is "Lisp all the way down."

Solution

Use ALLEGROCACHE. We'll use the same data we already used in Recipe 21-3. To follow this example, you'll need ALLEGROCL, but the free trial version will suffice.

First, to load the necessary code, evaluate this form:

[17] Or, as an alternative, don't quit your Lisp; just enter the new class definition, and then evaluate `(BKNR.DATASTORE:RESTORE)`. That will also work.

```
(require :acache)
```

At that point you'll get an error because you'll need to load a specific version of the code. Follow the instructions and pick any version, preferably the newest one.

We'll now define our class. Evaluate this form:

```
(defclass final ()
  ((city :accessor city
         :initarg :city)
   (year :accessor year
         :initarg :year
         :index :any-unique)
   (winner :accessor winner
           :initarg :winner))
  (:metaclass db.ac:persistent-class))
```

Note the :INDEX option for the YEAR slot and the *metaclass*. This is pretty similar to what we did on page 672.

In the next step, we'll create a database (which like in Recipe 21-3 will be a directory on disk):

```
CL-USER> (db.ac:open-file-database "/tmp/db/"
                                   :if-does-not-exist :create
                                   :if-exists :supersede)
#<AllegroCache db "/tmp/db" @ #x20bd6caa>
CL-USER> db.ac:*allegrocache*
#<AllegroCache db "/tmp/db" @ #x20bd6caa>
```

As we can see, the database is stored in a global special variable. It will be used as the default for the following operations.

We now create a couple of objects and modify one, exactly like in previous recipes.

```
CL-USER> (loop for (city year winner) in '(("Rome" 1934 :ita)
                                           ("Paris" 1938 :ita)
                                           ("Bern" 1954 :deu)
                                           ("Stockholm" 1958 :bra))
               for final = (make-instance 'final :city city
                                                 :year year
                                                 :winner winner)
               finally (return final))
#<FINAL oid: 15, ver 5, trans: NIL,  modified @ #x2115ab9a>
;; Oops, the same error again...
```

```
CL-USER> (setf (city *) "Solna")
"Solna"
```

At this point, these objects have already been written to disk. But they aren't really persisted yet because we've been in an implicit *transaction* which we need to commit:

```
CL-USER> (db.ac:commit)
T
```

Now we can proceed. As with BKNR.DATASTORE, we can quit the Lisp image, start a new one, load the ALLEGROCACHE code, and then open the database (this time without the `:IF-EXISTS` option):

```
(db.ac:open-file-database "/tmp/db/")
```

Now we can retrieve an object from the database using the index that we defined:

```
CL-USER> (db.ac:retrieve-from-index 'final 'year 1958)
#<FINAL oid: 15, ver 5, trans: 8,  not modified @ #x20ba1502>
CL-USER> (describe *)
#<FINAL oid: 15, ver 5, trans: 8,  not modified @ #x20ba1502> is an
    instance of #<DB.ALLEGROCACHE:PERSISTENT-CLASS FINAL>:
 The following slots have :INSTANCE allocation:
  DB.ALLEGROCACHE::OID          15
  DB.ALLEGROCACHE::SLOTS        NIL
  DB.ALLEGROCACHE::NEW-SLOTS    NIL
  DB.ALLEGROCACHE::DCLASS
     #<DB.ALLEGROCACHE::FILE-DASH-CLASS @ #x20b0540a>
  DB.ALLEGROCACHE::VERSION      5
  DB.ALLEGROCACHE::PREV-VERSION NIL
  DB.ALLEGROCACHE::TRANS        8
  DB.ALLEGROCACHE::MODIFIED     NIL
 The following slots have nonstandard allocation as shown:
  CITY :PERSISTENT                     "Solna"
  YEAR :PERSISTENT                     1958
  WINNER :PERSISTENT                   :BRA
; No value
```

(Note that we didn't have to load the `DEFCLASS` form. ALLEGROCACHE retrieved the class definition from the database when loading the `FINAL` objects.)

How It Works

What we did above was, as far as the API is concerned, almost the same we did in Recipe 21-3. The main difference is that in this case, the objects don't reside in RAM but are in a database on disk (as in CLSQL).

If you want such a database that can seamlessly store CLOS objects and is implemented in "pure" Lisp without the need to talk to external programs or load foreign libraries, then with the COMMON LISP implementations currently in use, ALLEGROCACHE is the only choice; at least if you want something that is also ACID-compliant and has good performance.

ALLEGROCACHE is built on a fast *B-tree*[18] implementation (like, for example BERKELEY DB[19]), which you also can access directly. In addition to things you'd expect from a database (like transactions and cursors), you'll also find more "Lisp-y" stuff in there like, say, *maps* and *sets*. For more information, see its tutorial and its reference manual.

Sadly, in terms of features and performance, there's nothing comparable to ALLEGROCACHE in the open source Lisp world so far. The closest might be the RUCKSACK library by Arthur Lemmens.

[18]See `https://en.wikipedia.org/wiki/B-tree`.

[19]See `https://en.wikipedia.org/wiki/Berkeley_DB`.

22. The World Outside

This chapter is mostly about stuff that happens "around" your Lisp program. Unless you're on a Lisp Machine (see page 591), there'll be an operating system underneath your Lisp system, and from its point of view, your application is just one of many. Likewise, there will be other programs on the same machine. We'll discuss how you can start and interact with such other programs. We'll also discuss how you can turn your Lisp code into something that's behaving as if it were "just another program."

We'll then look at functionality related to time (which, too, is a part of the "external environment" according to the HyperSpec), and finally, there'll be a recipe about garbage collection. The latter definitely isn't happening *outside*, but it's an area you should rarely have to deal with and thus somehow orthogonal to whatever else you're coding.

22-1. Accessing Environment Variables

Problem

You want to read (and maybe also modify) the value of an environment variable.

Solution

We'll show how to do that on a couple of different Lisps. For the ones not mentioned here, have a look at their documentation.

On SBCL:

```
* (sb-posix:getenv "HOME")
"/home/edi"
* (sb-posix:setenv "WAKA" "Jawaka" 1)
0
* (sb-posix:getenv "WAKA")
"Jawaka"
```

As the name of the package already suggests, SBCL faithfully implements the POSIX[1] specification. In particular, the third argument to SB-POSIX:GETENV (whether to overwrite existing environment variables) *must* be an integer.

On CLOZURECL:

```
? (ccl:getenv "HOME")
"/home/edi"
? (ccl:setenv "WAKA" "Jawaka")
0
? (ccl:getenv "WAKA")
"Jawaka"
```

This is similar to SBCL, except that CCL:SETENV works a bit more like a Lisp function; the third argument is optional and is interpreted as a generalized boolean. (So, use NIL instead of 0 here.)

The ECL version is like that of CLOZURECL, only the package is called EXT there.

On CLISP, it is even more Lisp-like because environment variables are set using SETF:[2]

```
[1]> (ext:getenv "HOME")
"/home/edi"
[2]> (setf (ext:getenv "WAKA") "Jawaka")
"Jawaka"
[3]> (ext:getenv "WAKA")
"Jawaka"
```

It's the same on ALLEGROCL,[3] where the function is called SYS:GETENV, and on LISPWORKS, where its name is LW:ENVIRONMENT-VARIABLE.

How It Works

Environment variables[4] are something that originally came from Unix but has also been available on Windows for a long time. Sometimes you need to read the value of an environment variable, sometimes (for example, when starting an external process; see Recipe 22-6) you even want to change it.

Although this is not part of the COMMON LISP standard, pretty much every implementation provides functions to do that, albeit with different names. If such a

[1]See https://en.wikipedia.org/wiki/POSIX.

[2]See Recipe 10-8.

[3]ALLEGROCL also offers a second, POSIX-like approach in its *Operating System Interface* package.

[4]See https://en.wikipedia.org/wiki/Environment_variable.

function is really missing in your Lisp, you should be able to program it yourself quite easily using its foreign function interface (see Chapter 19).

If an environment variable doesn't exist, all the reader functions above will return `NIL`. Which makes sense because otherwise you'd get a string, which—even if it's empty—is *true* if viewed as a generalized boolean.

To *remove* an environment variable, SBCL, CLOZURECL, and ALLEGROCL offer access to the POSIX function `unsetenv`. On ECL, you can instead use `EXT:SETENV` with the "new value" `NIL`. Likewise, on CLISP and LISPWORKS you use the `SETF` functions with `NIL` to get rid of an environment variable.

The Windows Registry and Application-Specific Settings

Information which on a Unix-like system is typically stored in environment variables or configuration files is often stored in the so-called *Registry*[5] on Windows. Most Lisps don't have specific support for it, but at least ALLEGROCL and LISPWORKS have. For example, to find out the number of cores (see also Recipe 11-6) of your CPU with LISPWORKS, you could do this:

```
(length (win32:collect-registry-subkeys
         "Hardware\\Description\\System\\CentralProcessor"
         :root :local-machine))
```

In addition to that, LISPWORKS offers a neat facility to store persistent per-user settings. This is done with the same functions across all supported operating systems; but on Windows, it uses the Registry, whereas on other operating systems, it uses configuration files. See *User Preferences* in their manual for more information.

22-2. Accessing the Command-Line Arguments

Problem

You want, typically in a stand-alone program, to read the command-line arguments your program was provided with.

Solution

In most implementations, these arguments are available as a list of strings in a global variable. Here are some examples:

[5]A system-wide hierarchical database. See `https://en.wikipedia.org/wiki/Windows_Registry`.

Implementation	Variable
ABCL	EXT:*COMMAND-LINE-ARGUMENT-LIST*
CLOZURECL	CCL:*COMMAND-LINE-ARGUMENT-LIST*
CLISP	EXT:*ARGS*
CMUCL	EXT:*COMMAND-LINE-STRINGS*
LISPWORKS	SYS:*LINE-ARGUMENTS-LIST*
SBCL	SB-EXT:*POSIX-ARGV*

On ECL, you instead call the function EXT:COMMAND-ARGS, and on ALLEGROCL, you call SYS:COMMAND-LINE-ARGUMENTS.[6]

How It Works

C programs always start with the main function, the arguments of which (traditionally called argc and argv) are the program's *command-line arguments*—information provided to it when it was started; for example, by typing them on the console after the program's name. Due to the way one usually works with COMMON LISP, command-line arguments are rarely relevant. They might be, though, when you are writing a stand-alone program; see Recipe 22-4.

On most implementations, the first string in this list will be the name of the executable itself (as it would be for a C program), but that's not always the case. Some Lisps will preprocess the list and only give you a "censored" version.[7]

There are several libraries[8] available that aim to unify command-line access across different implementations and to provide help with *parsing* the arguments. Take your pick.

22-3. Querying Your Lisp for Information About Its Environment

Problem

You want to programmatically figure out things like the operating system, the CPU, or the name of the machine that your Lisp runs on.

---

[6] And they have more commands concerned with the command line. See ALLEGROCL's documentation.

[7] Compare for example CLISP's EXT:*ARGS* with the result of evaluating (EXT:ARGV).

[8] See http://www.cliki.net/command-line%20options%20parser.

Solution

The standard offers a couple of functions that you can use, which I've all wrapped here so that you can test which replies you'll get on your machine:

```
(defun test ()
  (list (short-site-name)
        (long-site-name)
        (lisp-implementation-type)
        (lisp-implementation-version)
        (machine-instance)
        (machine-type)
        (machine-version)
        (software-type)
        (software-version)))
```

We'll compare the output of various Lisps below.

You might also want to look at Recipe 10-10.

How It Works

All the nine functions from above are supposed to return a string containing some information (or `NIL` in case that information is not available) about the running Lisp and the software and hardware it is running on.[9]

Here are the results of running the test from above in four different Lisps on the same Linux PC:

Function	CLOZURECL	SBCL	ECL	CLISP
SHORT-SITE-NAME	"unspecified"	NIL		"nanook"
LONG-SITE-NAME	"unspecified"	NIL		■
LISP-IMPLEMENTATION-TYPE	"Clozure Common Lisp"	"SBCL"	"ECL"	"CLISP"
LISP-IMPLEMENTATION-VERSION	"Version 1.10-r16196 (LinuxX8664)"	"1.2.13"	"13.5.1"	■
MACHINE-INSTANCE	"nanook"			"nanook [127.0.1.1]"
MACHINE-TYPE	"x86_64"	"x86-64"	"x86_64"	
MACHINE-VERSION	"Intel(R) Core(TM) i5-4590T CPU @ 2.00GHz"		NIL	"x86_64"
SOFTWARE-TYPE	"Linux"			■
SOFTWARE-VERSION	"3.16.0-45-generic"			"GNU C 4.8.2"

(The entries marked with ■ in the last column were too long to fit. For the long site name, `CLISP` provides a string, including the machine name `nanook`, but also a lot of information about the Linux system underneath. For the Lisp implementation version, you get a string with the version number plus information about when and where the binary was built. Finally, the software type is a huge string containing details about how exactly `CLISP` was built using GCC.)

[9]If there *is* any other software underneath. A Lisp Machine could presumably return `NIL` for the last two functions.

As you can see, the results are implementation-dependent, and even with just four Lisps, there's no function where all agree about what exactly should be returned. If you're writing a program that will run on various machines but always on the same Lisp, it makes sense to, say, use a function like `MACHINE-INSTANCE` to check whether you are on a specific PC, or to use `MACHINE-TYPE` to figure out the CPU. But for a portable program, unfortunately, these functions are almost useless.

22-4. Delivering Stand-Alone Executables

Problem

You want to deliver your Lisp program to users who aren't necessarily Lisp programmers or even computer-savvy.

Solution

How you package your Lisp program with "batteries included" depends on your implementation. We'll show how to do it for some of the more popular open source Lisps.[10] (For the commercial ones, see below.)

We're going to create (of course) a "Hello World" example. For all examples below, first please compile and load the following function:[11]

```
(defun hello ()
  (format t "Hello World!~%The time is ~A.~%" (get-universal-time)))
```

- To create an executable from SBCL, you'll need to evaluate this form:

  ```
  (sb-ext:save-lisp-and-die #p"foo.exe" :toplevel #'hello
                                        :executable t)
  ```

  But read the following notes before trying it yourself:

  – The first argument is the pathname of the executable file that you're going to create.[12]

  – The `:TOPLEVEL` keyword argument is a function that will run when the executable is started.

[10] ABCL is not included because with it you currently (as of August 2015) can't do it. A feature to create a stand-alone `.jar` file is planned for version 1.4. See `http://abcl.org/trac/ticket/383`.

[11] See Recipe 22-9 for `GET-UNIVERSAL-TIME`.

[12] This also works with SBCL on Windows. But if you want to be able to start your new program from the Windows console, the filename should end with `".exe"` as in the example.

  - The name `SB-EXT:SAVE-LISP-AND-DIE` is not a joke. The Lisp system will immediately exit after successfully executing this function![13]
  - Run SBCL from the console. This will *not* work from within `SLIME` because only one thread may be running when the image is saved.

  You should now have a file `foo.exe` which you can start like any other program and which will print the expected message.

- On CLOZURECL, the process is pretty much the same, except that you don't have to worry about your Lisp image "dying:"

```
(ccl:save-application #p"foo.exe" :toplevel-function #'hello
                                  :prepend-kernel t)
```

- With CLISP, you'd do something like this:

```
(ext:saveinitmem #p"foo.exe" :init-function (lambda ()
                                              (hello)
                                              (ext:quit))
                             :executable t
                             :quiet t :norc t)
```

  The call to `EXT:QUIT` is necessary so that our program stops after printing its message. If we just use `#'HELLO` as the init function, we end up in the CLISP REPL when running our executable. Likewise, the last two keyword arguments are there to make the executable behave less like an interactive development environment and more like a "normal" binary executable. (They instruct the generated executable to not print a banner at startup and to not read the init file; see Recipe 22-5.)

- Finally, on ECL you have to put the `HELLO` function from above into a Lisp source file, which for the purpose of this example will be `/tmp/hello.lisp`. You then do this:

```
(compile-file "/tmp/hello.lisp" :system-p t)
(c:build-program #p"foo.exe" :lisp-files '(#p"/tmp/hello.o")
                             :epilogue-code '(hello))
```

  The `:SYSTEM-P` keyword argument we passed to `COMPILE-FILE` directs the compiler to create a static object file (`.o`) instead of the usual FASL file. This file is needed in the next step. The `:EPILOGUE-CODE` keyword argument is a *form* to execute, while on the other Lisps you specify a *function* to call.

[13] If you don't want that and you are on a Unix-like system, use `SB-POSIX:FORK` to fork a child process that calls this "deadly" function. But make sure that the parent process is single-threaded.

All of the functions shown here offer several other customization options that you'll have to look up in the documentation of the respective Lisp. Also, there's a library called TRIVIAL-DUMP-CORE that aims to provide a unified interface to this functionality for the first three Lisps, but naturally doesn't offer all the implementation-specific customization possibilities.

For other deployments options, some of them Unix-centric, have a look at the libraries BUILDAPP, CL-LAUNCH, LISP-EXECUTABLE, and CLON. (See also Recipe 22-2.)

How It Works

Even a program that's compiled to machine code isn't necessarily just a blob of binary data that can run on any computer. Depending on the programming language or on what it does, the program might rely on the presence of a *runtime library* or a *runtime system*.[14] For a COMMON LISP or JAVA program this will, for example, include the garbage collector (see Recipe 22-10), which is something you didn't code yourself, but nevertheless expect to be present when your program runs.

So, if you want to give your program to someone else so that they can run it on their machine, in theory, you could give them the source code and ask them to install your development environment and build the application themselves. But if you don't want to put this technical burden upon them, or if you don't want to give your source code away, or if the compiler you used isn't available to them, you will need to provide enough infrastructure so that the code generated by your Lisp compiler will do what it's supposed to do.

To pick up the JAVA example again, there are roughly two choices:

(i) You're hoping that JAVA's *runtime environment* (JRE) is already installed on the user's machine and just send them a `.jar` file. Should they not have the JRE, you direct them to a web site from where they can more or less easily install it.

(ii) You package the JRE together with your `.jar` files so that you can be sure it is installed. (This might even be necessary if you want to assure that a specific version of the JRE is present.)

The first option is rarely viable for COMMON LISP because Lisp runtimes are typically not installed on many computers and installing a Lisp compiler isn't usually a routine task.[15]

[14]Programs targeted at "end users" often also come with various resource files that have to be put in specific places and might also need to make certain settings related to the operating system. This is what so-called *installers* are for, but that's beyond the scope of a book about Lisp.

[15]There are exceptions. On a Linux system, several Lisps might be available via your distribution's package manager.

Thus, we have concentrated on the second option: how to deliver a COMMON LISP program, including all the necessary infrastructure in a way that's as painless as possible for the recipient. They will get just one file, which they can execute without further installations.

What happens under the hood is that the whole Lisp *image* (see Recipe 16-1), which includes the "runtime library," is saved. This means that you'll typically first compile and load all your application code (which in our case was just the `HELLO` function) and then call the function to create the executable as described above.[16]

Delivering Programs with the Commercial Lisps

ALLEGROCL and LISPWORKS used to have two advantages in the area of application delivery, which are both largely irrelevant nowadays:

- They could do it a long time ago, whereas most open source Lisps acquired this ability comparatively late.
- They offer sophisticated techniques (called "tree shaking") to reduce the size of the created files.[17] (For example, an uncompressed executable created with SBCL can easily be more than ten times as big as a LISPWORKS executable with the same functionality, and delivered with aggressive tree shaking options.)

Nevertheless, they probably still have the best support for creating stand-alone programs. (Search their documentations for "delivery" if you want to know more.) But note that these features are usually not available in the free trial versions that both companies offer.

22-5. Customizing Your Lisp

Problem

There are a couple of things that you're always doing after starting up your Lisp implementation and you want to automate them.

[16]We saw that the process on ECL differs somewhat due to its implementation strategy (see page 560). There's no image to be saved, but instead your application has to exist in the form of *object files* that will be linked with ECL to create the executable.

[17]This is a complicated process (requiring the programmer's assistance) because due to the dynamic nature of COMMON LISP, it is essentially impossible for the compiler to prove that a certain feature can be safely removed from the image.

Solution

Use your Lisp's *init file*. That's a file that (if it exists) should contain COMMON LISP code, which will be executed before you'll end up in the REPL.

How It Works

Although not mandated by the standard, each of the current COMMON LISP implementations looks for a file with a specific name[18] at startup, and if it finds this file, it executes the Lisp code in there.

This file is a good place for code that you want to be sure is executed each time before you enter the REPL. QUICKLISP (see Recipe 18-2) can, for example, put code there so that it is immediately available. And behind that code, you could put a form like

```
(ql:quickload "foo")
```

if you're always using the FOO library. Or you could use the init file to set `*READ-DEFAULT-FLOAT-FORMAT*` (see Recipe 4-6) to a value different from the default.

Here's a list, stolen from the QUICKLISP source code, of init file names for almost a dozen different implementations:

Implementation	Init File
ALLEGROCL	`.clinit.cl`
ABCL	`.abclrc`
CLOZURECL	`ccl-init.lisp`
CLASP	`.claspr c`
CLISP	`.clisprc.lisp`
CMUCL	`.cmucl-init.lisp`
ECL	`.eclrc`
MANKAI COMMON LISP	`.mkclrc`
LISPWORKS	`.lispworks`
SBCL	`.sbclrc`
SCIENEER COMMON LISP	`.scl-init.lisp`

Your Lisp will usually look for the init file in your *home directory* if you're on a Unix-like system. On Windows, this is a bit more complicated, as it doesn't have a real

[18]Some implementations will even go through a list of possible init file names and look for them in a specified order. Or they will look for a system-wide init file as well as a user-specific init file. But for most use cases, it's obviously sufficient to use just one of these files consistently.

equivalent for this. Different Lisps use different user-specific directories on Windows. If you can't find the location in your documentation, probably your best bet is to let QUICKLISP figure it out (see page 570).

Some notes:

- Many Lisps accept command-line arguments (see Recipe 22-2) to temporarily specify a different (or no) init file. Some will also allow you to change the init file name and location permanently.
- The init file is a text file and usually loaded with `LOAD`, which for all current implementations, except for CLOZURECL, implies that the code is interpreted.[19] But some Lisps will look for a FASL file (see page 429) with the same name first and load that instead if it's present.
- If the init file is loaded with `LOAD`, then certain things aren't doable. For example, `LOAD` binds `*PACKAGE*` (see Recipe 1-1) and `*READTABLE*` (see Recipe 8-7) and thus changes to them won't have any effect for their values once you're in the REPL.
- For this reason, some Lisps (for example, SBCL) don't use `LOAD` but rather process the init file using `READ` and `EVAL`.
- Some Lisps provide additional means to customize the startup process. See SBCL's `SB-EXT:*INIT-HOOKS*` or LISPWORKS's *action lists*.
- Some Lisps will also accept command-line arguments like `--load` or `--eval` so that you can load files or evaluate forms on startup independently of the init file's contents.
- The free trial version of LISPWORKS will ignore init files.

Saving an Image

If the code in your init file does a lot of things, this may have a noticeable effect on your Lisp's startup time. If that bothers you, then a solution to this problem is to *save an image*[20] with all of your customizations loaded and to use that instead of the default image. This process is very similar to that of creating an executable (see Recipe 22-4) and even uses the same function on many Lisps.

For example, to save an image with SBCL:

```
(sb-ext:save-lisp-and-die #p"/tmp/my-image")
```

[19] You can `LOAD` compiled code from the init file, though.

[20] See Recipe 16-1 for more about "images."

This is explained on page 682. The only difference is that we neither provide the :EXECUTABLE keyword argument nor a *toplevel* function (so that instead the default function, which is the REPL, will be run). To use this image, start SBCL like so:

```
sbcl --core /tmp/my-image
```

The process is similar on other Lisps.

22-6. Running External Programs

Problem

From Lisp, you want to execute an external program and presumably communicate with it somehow.

Solution

Every current COMMON LISP implementation can do this, but they don't all support the same features. We're going to use Greg Pfeil's compatibility library EXTERNAL-PROGRAM[21] to demonstrate what you can do. The examples should work at least with SBCL and CLOZURECL on Unix-like operating systems. For other platforms see below.

Let's start with this:

```
CL-USER> (external-program:run "date" nil)
:EXITED
0
```

We ran the program date, and as a result, we were notified that the external process exited with exit code 0. However, we didn't see the program's output.

To see it, we have to provide the program with a (Lisp) stream. For date, this stream will become its stdout.

```
CL-USER> (external-program:run "date" nil :output *standard-output*)
Tue Sep 15 19:46:46 CEST 2015
:EXITED
0
```

[21]Which you can install with QUICKLISP; see Recipe 18-2.

(Instead of a stream, we could have used other arguments; for example, a pathname to send the output to a file. See EXTERNAL-PROGRAM's documentation for all options.)

The second argument for EXTERNAL-PROGRAM:RUN, which we haven't used so far, is a list of command-line arguments (see Recipe 22-2) for the external program:

```
CL-USER> (external-program:run "date" '("-u")
                                :output *standard-output*)
Tue Sep 15 17:46:57 UTC 2015
:EXITED
0
```

If we want to capture and analyze the program's output, we can use a string stream (see Recipe 14-7):

```
CL-USER> (with-output-to-string (out)
           (external-program:run "date" '("-R") :output out))
"Sat, 08 Aug 2015 10:03:49 +0200
"
```

And we can also use streams for the other direction; that is, we can control the program's stdin:

```
CL-USER> (with-input-from-string (in (format nil "One~%Two~%Three~%"))
           (external-program:run "wc" '("-l")
                                 :output *standard-output*
                                 :input in))
3
:EXITED
0
```

What the examples had in common so far is that we always waited until the external process was finished. See below for a more "interactive" way to run another program.

How It Works

So that we don't run into problems with buffered output that might spoil our examples, we'll create our own little "filter" program.[22] Compile the following C code

[22]Let me emphasize that this is really just a toy example to demonstrate the usage of the EXTERNAL-PROGRAM library. If you're trying something similar with other programs without taking the necessary precautions, you will very likely run into general deadlock problems that have nothing to do with Lisp.

with a command like `gcc -o foo foo.c`:

```
#include <stdio.h>

int main (void) {
  int c;
  while ((c = getchar()) != EOF) {
    putchar(c);
    if (c == '\n')
      fflush(stdout);
    else
      putchar(c);
  }
  return 0;
}
```

Our program `foo` reads characters from `stdin` and writes them back to `stdout` *twice*, except for the newline character that it views as a request to flush `stdout`.

To test this from the Lisp side, we do the following:

```
CL-USER> (external-program:start "/tmp/foo" nil
                                 :input :stream :output :stream)
#<EXTERNAL-PROCESS (/tmp/foo)[20047] (RUNNING) #x302001279C4D>
CL-USER> (defparameter *p* *)
*P*
CL-USER> (defparameter *in*
           (external-program:process-input-stream *p*))
*IN*
CL-USER> (defparameter *out*
           (external-program:process-output-stream *p*))
*OUT*
```

Instead of `EXTERNAL-PROGRAM:RUN`, we're now using `EXTERNAL-PROGRAM:START`; it starts the process but doesn't wait for it to complete. Instead, it returns an object representing the process, which we store in `*P*`.[23] We also used the keyword `:STREAM` this time instead of providing existing Lisp streams. This means that streams were created for us, which we can, as seen above, extract from the process object.

We'll now use these streams to communicate with `foo`. Note that the *input* stream of the process is an *output* stream, as seen from the Lisp side, and vice versa for the other stream:

```
;; continued from above
```

[23]For the meaning of `*`, see Recipe 16-11.

```
CL-USER> (format *in* "addressee~%")
NIL
CL-USER> (finish-output *in*)
NIL
CL-USER> (read-line *out*)
"aaddddrreesssseeee"
NIL
CL-USER> (format *in* "committee~%")
NIL
CL-USER> (format *in* "mississippi~%")
NIL
CL-USER> (finish-output *in*)
NIL
CL-USER> (list (read-line *out*) (read-line *out*))
("ccoommmmiittttteeee" "mmiissssiissssiippppii)
```

We're sending some text to `foo` and then read its reply. We're using `FINISH-OUPUT` (see Recipe 14-2) to make sure our output really arrived before we start reading.

We could go on like that, but the general idea should be clear now. Finally:

```
;; continued from above
CL-USER> (external-program:process-status *p*)
:RUNNING
NIL
CL-USER> (close *in*)
T
CL-USER> (external-program:process-status *p*)
:EXITED
0
```

This showed that we can query the process object stored in `*P*` for its status. At first, the process was still running, but then we closed the stream, and as a result, the process exited with exit code 0.

EXTERNAL-PROGRAM offers other possibilities that we haven't shown here. For example, you can modify the environment (see Recipe 22-1) of the process you're starting, you can send (Unix) signals, or you can provide a callback function that is called whenever the status changes.

EXTERNAL-PROGRAM won't offer all options for all Lisps, though. Its documentation contains a "support matrix" table with an overview of restrictions for several COMMON LISP implementations. But because something doesn't work with EXTERNAL-PROGRAM on your Lisp doesn't necessarily mean that it's impossible. (See the LISPWORKS case in the next paragraph.) If in doubt, you should consult your implementation's documentation.

Let's close with an implementation-specific example. Some of the code from above won't work with LISPWORKS, although in principle, it is supported by EXTERNAL-PROGRAM. But if you sift through LISPWORKS's documentation, you'll find the function SYS:OPEN-PIPE, with which you can replicate our foo "interaction:"

```
(with-open-stream (stream (sys:open-pipe "/tmp/foo" :direction :io))
  (format stream "mississippi~%")
  (finish-output stream)
  (read-line stream))
```

This also works on Windows if you compile foo with VISUAL STUDIO.

22-7. Embedding Lisp

Problem

You want to use COMMON LISP from a program written in C/C++ or JAVA.

Solution

ECL is a COMMON LISP implementation that has the word "embeddable" already in its name, so it seems an obvious candidate for this recipe. Once we've shown how to embed ECL into a C program, we'll then show different approaches further down below.

We'll first create a file hello.lisp with these contents:[24]

```
(defun hello ()
  (format t "Hello World!~%The time is ~A.~%" (get-universal-time)))
```

And from ECL, we compile it to a shared library hello.so:

```
(compile-file "/tmp/hello.lisp" :system-p t)
(c:build-shared-library #p"/tmp/hello.so"
                        :lisp-files '(#p"/tmp/hello.o")
                        :init-name "init_mylib")
```

This is very similar to what we did on page 683, except that we now have the keyword argument :INIT-NAME. This is a name for a function the C program will have to call to initialize our library.

[24]This was done on a Linux system, but should also work on other operating systems, maybe with different compiler and linker settings. Everything happens in the /tmp directory.

Now for our C program, which we'll put into a file test.c:[25]

```
#include <ecl/ecl.h>

int main (int argc, char **argv) {
  extern void init_mylib(cl_object);
  cl_boot(argc, argv);
  ecl_init_module(NULL, init_mylib);
  cl_eval(c_string_to_object("(hello)"));
  cl_shutdown();
  return 0;
}
```

cl_boot and cl_shutdown are standard functions to initialize and shut down ECL from within another program. We then use ecl_init_module to initialize our shared library using the name we defined above. And finally, we use cl_eval to call our Lisp function HELLO. (All of the functions used here are explained in the ECL documentation.)

We can now create our program:

```
gcc test.c hello.so -o test -lecl
```

And if we use it like so, we should see the "Hello World" message:

```
LD_LIBRARY_PATH=. ./test
```

How It Works

We've actually demonstrated two things at once:

- The full ECL system can be embedded in a C program and standard COMMON LISP functions can be called from there. In fact, all standard functions are implemented as C functions. For example, the function DENOMINATOR (see Recipe 4-5) is declared in the header files, like so:

  ```
  extern ECL_API cl_object cl_denominator(cl_object rational);
  ```

- Your own Lisp code can be compiled to a shared (or static) library and added to your embedded Lisp.

[25]This assumes that ecl.h is installed in some standard location, like /usr/include/ecl/ecl.h. If you installed ECL using a package management system like APT, this should be the case.

Doing this is the *raison d'être* for ECL and it is thus particularly good at that. But some other Lisps can do it as well:[26]

Creating Shared Libraries with LispWorks

With some Lisps (notably ALLEGROCL and LISPWORKS), you can also create shared libraries from Lisp code in a different way; namely, so that you provide Lisp functions that can be called from the C side as if they were vanilla C functions. We'll show a simple example of how this can be done in LISPWORKS.[27]

First, the actual Lisp code that we'll put into the file `code.lisp`:[28]

```
(fli:define-foreign-callable ("toLispTime" :result-type :long)
    ((year :int)
     (month :int)
     (date :int))
  (encode-universal-time 0 0 0 date month year))
```

We are essentially defining a normal Lisp function (which comprises the last line) but we're defining it in such a way that it can be called from "foreign" code using the name `toLispTime`. We also prescribe the types of the arguments and the return type in terms of C types. This is very similar to what we did in Recipe 19-1, except that it's "the other way around."

Now we create another file `deliver.lisp` with this code:

```
(load (compile-file "code.lisp"))
(lw:deliver nil "my_lib" 0 :dll-exports '("toLispTime"))
```

The function `LW:DELIVER` is what we would also use on LISPWORKS to create an executable (see Recipe 22-4), but here we use it to create a shared library, which the compiler will deduce from our usage of the keyword argument `:DLL-EXPORTS`. This argument provides a list of the *symbols* (not Lisp symbols; see footnote on page 597) to export. The number `0` just means that we don't want any *tree shaking* (see page 685) for this example.

If you now execute

```
/path/to/lispworks -build deliver.lisp
```

[26]In a way, what MOCL (see Recipe 20-5) is doing is also embedding—the Lisp code is embedded in a JAVA or OBJECTIVE-C app running on a mobile phone.

[27]Note that you'll need a version of the compiler that contains the function `LW:DELIVER`. This is not the case in the free trial version.

[28]This is on Linux but (with the obvious modifications) will work on all platforms supported by LISPWORKS. As in all examples, everything happens in the `/tmp` directory.

in a shell, you'll get a new file my_lib.so. (The suffix was automatically added to match the platform's conventions.) You can query this library with

```
nm -D my_lib.so | grep Time
```

to see that it indeed exports our function.

To test our library we use this file test.c

```
#include <stdio.h>

int main () {
  extern long toLispTime(int, int, int);
  printf("Date 1940-12-21 is Lisp time %ld.\n",
         toLispTime(1940, 12, 21));
  return 0;
}
```

and compile it like so:[29]

```
gcc -o test test.c my_lib.so -lpthread -ldl
```

We now have a C program test we can run:

```
LD_LIBRARY_PATH=. ./test
```

Embedding ABCL in a Java Program

Just as you can embed the whole of ECL into a C program, you can embed ABCL in JAVA (see also Recipe 19-10).

For an example, we'll again start with a file hello.lisp, but this time HELLO, will be a little different so that we can pass a parameter to it and have a meaningful return value.

```
(defun hello (name)
  (format nil "Hello ~A!~%The time is ~A.~%"
          name (get-universal-time)))
```

We now create a file Test.java containing this code:

[29]Note that a 64-bit version of LISPWORKS will create 64-bit shared libraries and a 32-bit version will create 32-bit shared libraries. You might have to use the corresponding flags for your C compiler to match the word sizes (see page 596).

```
import org.armedbear.lisp.*;

public class Test {
  public static void main(String arg[]) {
    Interpreter interpreter = Interpreter.createInstance();
    interpreter.eval("(load \"hello.lisp\")");
    Function hello = (Function) Packages.findPackage("CL-USER")
                                        .findAccessibleSymbol("HELLO")
                                        .getSymbolFunction();
    LispObject result = hello.execute(new SimpleString("ABCL"));
    System.out.print(result.princToString());
  }
}
```

This should be pretty obvious. We first have to initialize ABCL (which can take a bit of time when you're testing your program), then we `LOAD` our code by calling `EVAL`.[30] To get a handle to our function `HELLO`, we kind of simulate what the REPL does (see Recipe 1-1): we look for a symbol with the name `"HELLO"` in the `CL-USER` package and then query its *function cell* using `SYMBOL-FUNCTION`. The object we get has a JAVA method `execute` that corresponds to calling the function in Lisp. All objects from the Lisp side are represented as instances of `LispObject`, and there's a hierarchy below that, including classes like `Function` or `SimpleString`. Finally, `princToString` is a method to convert such a Lisp object to a JAVA string akin to how `PRINC` (see Recipe 9-1) would do it.

To compile and test this code, you can now proceed like this, assuming the two files from above and `abcl.jar` are in the same directory:

```
javac -cp abcl.jar Test.java
java -cp abcl.jar;. Test
```

The ABCL documentation for the interaction between JAVA and Lisp is currently still a bit scarce, but with the help of the source code, it shouldn't be too hard to figure out what to do.

22-8. Measuring Time

Problem

You want to measure the time between two events.

[30]And in this case, we're simply discarding the return value.

Solution

If you just want to measure the time a certain part of your code needs to run, the better solution will usually be the TIME macro (see page 513).

To understand the two other available options, consider this function:

```
(defun time-test ()
  (let ((run-time (get-internal-run-time))
        (real-time (get-internal-real-time)))
    (sleep 2.5)
    (format t "Run time: ~,6F seconds~%Real time: ~,6F seconds~%"
            (/ (- (get-internal-run-time) run-time)
               internal-time-units-per-second)
            (/ (- (get-internal-real-time) real-time)
               internal-time-units-per-second))))
```

If I run it on CLOZURECL, for example, I see something like this:[31]

```
? (time-test)
Run time: 0.001004 seconds
Real time: 2.500154 seconds
NIL
```

You should see *approximately* the same values, unless your Lisp is very busy with other threads.[32]

How It Works

The standard requires every COMMON LISP implementation to provide two timing functions. One is measuring *real time*, which is also sometimes called *wall time*, while the other is measuring *run time*, which is often called *CPU time*. Whereas it is clear what *real time* should be, the standard understandably dodges a precise definition of *run time* and paraphrases it as the "amount of time [...] during which computational effort was expended on behalf of the executing program." In particular, it doesn't specify how run time should be measured in the presence of multiple threads; see Chapter 11. (It seems that most Lisps will report the sum of the CPU times for *all* threads in this case; but you should consult your documentation or conduct some experiments to be sure.)

---

[31]Just for fun, you could also try (TIME (TIME-TEST)).

[32]The only exception I'm aware of is ABCL, which currently (version 1.3.2) reports a (wrong) run time value that is identical to the (correct) real time value.

In our example, the real time was about 2.5 seconds because that's how long it took for `TIME-TEST` to return. The run time, on the other hand, was almost zero because the program was sleeping most of the time.

For both functions, `GET-INTERNAL-REAL-TIME` and `GET-INTERNAL-RUN-TIME`, the *absolute* value returned is meaningless. The intended usage, like in our example above, is to take two timings and work with the *difference* between the two values.

The authors of the standard had enough foresight not to base these timing functions on a fixed physical unit like a millisecond. Instead, they decided that the values returned should be in (implementation-dependent) *internal time units*. In order to translate these to seconds, there's the constant with the long-but-telling name `INTERNAL-TIME-UNITS-PER-SECOND`. If we divide by this constant like above, the result is in seconds.

For most Lisps, the internal time unit currently is one millisecond.[33] If you want more fine-grained timings, you will have to implement this yourself using features of your operating system and the foreign function interface (see Chapter 19).[34] Be aware, though, that with multi-core systems and CPUs that can throttle their clock frequency, timings with an accuracy of microseconds or higher are a tricky business.

22-9. Working with Dates and Times

Problem

You need to work with *calendar time*; that is, with points in time expressed in years, months, days, etc.

Solution

COMMON LISP has standard functionality for so-called *decoded time* and *universal time*. Although in theory this would be enough for almost all date and time calculations, there's a library called LOCAL-TIME that adds lots of convenience features.

Let's start with some examples for what the standard has to offer:[35]

---

[33] With the exception of CLOZURECL and CLISP, which both claim to be able to measure in microseconds or better.

[34] Or sniff around using `APROPOS` (see Recipe 16-8) to find out that, for example, SBCL already has the function `SB-UNIX:UNIX-GETTIMEOFDAY`, which returns microseconds. SBCL can also count the processor's clock cycles, as one can see from its `TIME` output. This functionality isn't exported, though.

[35] See Recipe 16-11 for the meaning of `*` and `**`.

```
CL-USER> (get-decoded-time)
31
2
17
24
8
2015
0
T
-1
CL-USER> (get-universal-time)
3649417353
CL-USER> (decode-universal-time *)
33
2
17
24
8
2015
0
T
-1
CL-USER> (multiple-value-bind
             (second minute hour date month year day
                     daylight-p zone)
           (decode-universal-time **)
         (declare (ignore day daylight-p zone))
         (encode-universal-time second minute hour date month year))
3649417353                                        ;; <- same as above
```

This will be explained in detail below.

How It Works

COMMON LISP's *universal time* is simply the number of seconds since the beginning of the year 1900.[36] This is very similar to *Epoch time* on Unix, except that the latter starts 70 years later, and because of bignums, (see Recipe 4-1) you don't have to worry about "dangerous dates" in the future.[37]

As we saw above, there are functions to convert between universal time and *decoded*

[36]To be more precise, the universal time 1 corresponds to 00:00:01 on January 1, 1900 UTC.
[37]See `https://en.wikipedia.org/wiki/Year_2038_problem`.

time—an ordered series of nine values with the following meaning:

- The first six values represent the second, minute, hour, date, month, and year. So, the values 33, 2, 17, 24, 8, and 2015 from above correspond to the time 17:02:33 on August 24, 2015.
- The seventh value is an integer representing the day of the week, with the week starting on Monday (0) and ending with Sunday (6). So, the 0 from our example means Monday.
- The eighth value is a boolean that is true if daylight saving time is in effect. (This is the case in the example.)
- And the last value is the time zone expressed as an offset in hours from Greenwich Mean Time (GMT).

Some things to note:

(i) Like on Unix, leap seconds[38] are ignored.

(ii) The time zone offset doesn't have to be an integer; it just has to be rational (see Recipe 4-5) and a multiple of 1/3600 (i.e., one second). So you can also express time on the Chatham Islands correctly...

(iii) A universal time must always be non-negative, which implies that times before 1900 cannot be represented.

(iv) For convenience, if a year is given as a two-digit number, it is interpreted as the "obvious" year, which is closest to the current date:[39]

```
CL-USER> (encode-universal-time 0 0 0 4 12 1993)
2963948400
CL-USER> (encode-universal-time 0 0 0 4 12 93)
2963948400                                    ;; same as above
CL-USER> (encode-universal-time 0 0 0 21 12 1940)
1292882400
CL-USER> (encode-universal-time 0 0 0 21 12 40)
4448646000                                    ;; different (2040)
```

(v) For ENCODE-UNIVERSAL-TIME, you can either omit the (optional) time zone argument, in which case the local time zone, *including* daylight saving time (if applicable), is assumed; or you provide it, in which case you have to add daylight saving time, if necessary:

```
CL-USER> (nth-value 8 (get-decoded-time))
-1
CL-USER> (nth-value 7 (get-decoded-time))
```

[38]See https://en.wikipedia.org/wiki/Leap_second.

[39]I did this in 2015. Just in case you're reading the book several decades later...

```
T
CL-USER> (encode-universal-time 0 10 17 24 8 2015)
3649417800
CL-USER> (encode-universal-time 0 10 17 24 8 2015 -2)
3649417800
```

Above we are "one hour to the east" of Greenwich with daylight saving time in effect. We thus have to provide the argument -2 (and not -1) in the last form.

The local-time Library

As I already said above, in theory, you could do pretty much everything with dates and times with these four functions. For example, to add exactly 28 days to a given date, you can convert it to universal time, add (* 28 24 60 60), and then convert back to decoded time. But this will get unwieldy pretty quickly, and luckily, you don't have to: the LOCAL-TIME library[40] by Daniel Lowe adds a lot of convenience features related to date and time calculations.

Dates and times are represented in LOCAL-TIME as *timestamps*, which have a printed representation in ISO 8601[41] format:

```
CL-USER> (local-time:now)
@2015-08-24T18:20:07.223379+02:00
CL-USER> (local-time:encode-timestamp 123456789 0 10 12 23 12 1965)
@1965-12-23T12:10:00.123456+01:00
```

(The first argument in the second form above represents fractions of a second in nanoseconds. Whether this will be taken into account and to which degree depends on the implementation you're using.)

There are functions to convert back and forth between these timestamps and Lisp universal times (and Unix times). And you can parse textual representations of dates and times into timestamps, like so:

```
CL-USER> (local-time:parse-timestring "1965-12-23")
@1965-12-23T01:00:00.000000+01:00
CL-USER> (local-time:parse-timestring "1965-12-23T12:20:12")
@1965-12-23T13:20:12.000000+01:00
CL-USER> (local-time:parse-timestring "1965-12-23T12:20:12-05")
@1965-12-23T18:20:12.000000+01:00
```

[40]Installable with QUICKLISP; see Recipe 18-2. (Note that some parts of this library rely on POSIX features and might not work as expected on Windows.)

[41]See https://en.wikipedia.org/wiki/ISO_8601.

LOCAL-TIME also has objects representing *time zones*, which you can use in computations and which you can retrieve by name from the IANA time zone database:[42]

```
CL-USER> (local-time:reread-timezone-repository)
; No value
CL-USER> (local-time:timestamp-subtimezone
          (local-time:encode-timestamp 0 0 40 18 24 8 2015)
          (local-time:find-timezone-by-location-name "Europe/Moscow"))
14400
T
"MSD"
```

The code above reads in the database and then loads the time zone for Moscow and relates it to a specific timestamp. The three return values mean that

a) the offset from GMT for this point in time is four hours (14400 seconds),

b) daylight saving time is in effect in Moscow (which explains why the first value isn't three hours), and

c) the standard abbreviation for the time zone is "MSD."

Another area where LOCAL-TIME can be helpful is formatting of dates and times, like so:

```
CL-USER> (defparameter *timestamp*
          (local-time:encode-timestamp 0 13 5 19 24 8 2015))
*TIMESTAMP*
CL-USER> (local-time:format-timestring nil *timestamp*)
"2015-08-24T19:05:13.000000+02:00"
CL-USER> (local-time:format-timestring
          nil *timestamp*
          :format local-time:+rfc-1123-format+)
"Mon, 24 Aug 2015 19:05:13 +0200"
CL-USER> (local-time:format-timestring
          nil *timestamp* :format
          '(:long-weekday ", " :day " " :long-month))
"Monday, 24 August"
```

There's more that this library can do, but you'll have to look at its manual for that. As a final teaser, here's its reader syntax (see Chapter 8) with some date/time arithmetic:

```
CL-USER> (local-time:enable-read-macros)
; No value
CL-USER> @2015-08-24T19:05:13
```

[42]See https://en.wikipedia.org/wiki/Tz_database.

```
@2015-08-24T21:05:13.000000+02:00
CL-USER> (local-time:timestamp< @2015-08-24T19:05:13
                                @2015-07-14T20:00:33)
NIL
CL-USER> (local-time:timestamp+ @2015-08-24T19:05:13 10 :day)
@2015-09-03T21:05:13.000000+02:00
```

22-10. Working with the Garbage Collector

Problem

You want to query or explicitly invoke the garbage collector.

Or you want to be notified when some Lisp object is garbage collected.

Solution

We'll use the TRIVIAL-GARBAGE library,[43] written by Luís Oliveira, which is a typical compatibility library (see Recipe 18-5) in that it doesn't add new features to your Lisp but just exposes some existing features in an implementation-independent way.

Here's an example session with CLOZURECL, which will be explained below:

```
CL-USER> (room)
Approximately 17,432,576 bytes of memory can be allocated
before the next full GC is triggered.
                  Total Size             Free                 Used
Lisp Heap:    38141952 (37248K)   17432576 (17024K)   20709376 (20224K)
Stacks:       46601840 (45510K)   46567736 (45476K)      34104 (33K)
Static:       20227808 (19754K)          0 (0K)       20227808 (19754K)
376763.620 MB reserved for heap expansion.
NIL
CL-USER> (trivial-garbage:gc)
NIL
CL-USER> (room)
Approximately 32,899,072 bytes of memory can be allocated
before the next full GC is triggered.
                  Total Size             Free                 Used
Lisp Heap:    46399488 (45312K)   32899072 (32128K)   13500416 (13184K)
Stacks:       46601840 (45510K)   46567736 (45476K)      34104 (33K)
Static:       20227808 (19754K)          0 (0K)       20227808 (19754K)
```

[43] Which can be installed via QUICKLISP; see Recipe 18-2.

```
376755.750 MB reserved for heap expansion.
NIL
```

How It Works

Garbage collection (which was invented by John McCarthy in 1959 for, you guessed it, the first ever Lisp implementation) is something you usually shouldn't notice—that's the whole point of having it. It's unobtrusive, it makes your life as a programmer much easier, and there are certain types of errors that are quite common in languages without automatic memory management, which simply can't happen if you have a garbage collector.[44] But there's nothing in the standard that forces an implementation to actually *have* a garbage collector (although all present Lisps have one), and consequentially, there aren't any standard functions that explicitly deal with garbage collection.

The only exceptions (kind of) are `TIME` (see page 513) and `ROOM`. As we saw above, `ROOM` will print an overview of the current state of your Lisp's internal memory management. Its output is thus as implementation-dependent as that of `TIME`, and most of the details will only make sense once you've studied your Lisp's documentation. (It'll also accept an optional argument for output that provides even more details.)

But at least we can see that after the call to `TRIVIAL-GARBAGE:GC`, the amount of "free" heap space[45] has noticeably increased, whereas the amount of "used" heap space has decreased. As you'll know, it's the job of the garbage collector to do exactly this (increasing the available space by "cleaning up," i.e., by reclaiming space used by objects that are not needed anymore) and it'll usually do this automatically whenever appropriate (see also page 532). The function `TRIVIAL-GARBAGE:GC` is there so that you can invoke this process manually.

What will happen exactly if you call this function (or what will be different if you use its `:FULL` keyword argument) will depend on the garbage collection strategy,[46] which can differ between implementations and between architectures. As a rule of thumb, you'll rarely need to invoke the garbage collector explicitly, except maybe for testing purposes (as in the example below). And if you need to, your only sensible choice is to acquaint yourself with the specifics of your Lisp's memory management first.

---

[44]On the other hand, garbage collection can sometimes also impose performance penalties on your program; see Chapter 17. But that's a bridge you shouldn't cross before you come to it.

[45]See page 532.

[46]See `https://en.wikipedia.org/wiki/Garbage_collection_%28computer_science%29` for a first overview and `https://en.wikipedia.org/wiki/Tracing_garbage_collection` for strategies typically seen in the Lisp world.

Finalizers

Depending on your application, one area where you might want to interact with automatic memory management is what is usually called *finalizing*. Most Lisps can notify you once an object is garbage collected. But why would you want to do that?

As a typical application, let's assume you have a class of `FOO` objects that, when initialized, will acquire some resource that is not under the control of your Lisp (because otherwise the garbage collector could take care of it). Such a resource could be, say, a "foreign" object (see Chapter 19) that needs to be freed manually.[47] Once such a `FOO` object is collected, you can be sure that it won't be needed anymore in any part of your program, and you can thus release the resource.

We'll show an example where we simulate the "resources" by a simple stack (see Recipe 2-9) of numbers:

```
CL-USER> (defparameter *resources* (loop for i below 10
                                         collect i))
*RESOURCES*
CL-USER> *resources*
(0 1 2 3 4 5 6 7 8 9)
CL-USER> (defclass foo ()
           ((resource :initform (pop *resources*))))
#<STANDARD-CLASS FOO>
CL-USER> (defparameter *objects* (loop repeat 5
                                       collect (make-instance 'foo)))
*OBJECTS*
CL-USER> *resources*
(5 6 7 8 9)
```

We now have in `*OBJECTS*` a list of five `FOO` objects, each of which is holding in its `RESOURCE` slot a number that was removed from the stack `*RESOURCES*`.

Now we add the finalizers:

```
;; continued from above
CL-USER> (dolist (object *objects*)
           (trivial-garbage:finalize
            object
            (let ((resource (slot-value object 'resource)))
              (lambda ()
                (push resource *resources*)))))
NIL
```

[47] The source of libraries like BURGLED-BATTERIES or RDNZL contains "real-world" usage examples.

For each object in *OBJECTS*, we register a function of no arguments, which will be called once the object is garbage collected. This function will put the "resource" back onto the stack.

Let's test the finalizers. This is again with CLOZURECL, and you might see slightly different output on another Lisp:

```
;; continued from above
CL-USER> (setq *objects* (cdr *objects*))
(#<FOO #x302000C1F8FD> #<FOO #x302000C1F8AD>
 #<FOO #x302000C1F85D> #<FOO #x302000C1F80D>)
CL-USER> *resources*
(5 6 7 8 9)                                   ;; <- see comments below
CL-USER> (trivial-garbage:gc :full t)
NIL
CL-USER> *resources*
(0 5 6 7 8 9)
CL-USER> (setq *objects* nil)
NIL
CL-USER> (trivial-garbage:gc :full t)
NIL
CL-USER> *resources*
(4 3 2 1 0 5 6 7 8 9)                         ;; <- order might differ
```

We started by removing the first element of *OBJECTS*. As there now was no way to refer to this object anymore, the garbage collector was free to get rid of it. So, in theory, it could have already been collected by the next step (thus the comment above), but typically this will happen (much) later. We therefore initiate garbage collection manually, and afterward we see that a "resource" was added back to *RESOURCES*, which was the finalizer's job. We then do the same for the other four objects.

Garbage collection and finalizers are tricky stuff, so there are various things to look out for:

- It would have been tempting to create the finalizers like so:[48]

  ```
  (dolist (object *objects*)
    (let ((obj object))
      (trivial-garbage:finalize obj
                                (lambda ()
                                  (push (slot-value obj 'resource)
                                        *resources*)))))
  ```

  But that won't work, as the second argument to TRIVIAL-GARBAGE:FINALIZE

[48]See Recipe 7-9 for why we have to rebind OBJECT to OBJ.

would be a function closing over the object, and thus preventing it from ever being garbage collected...

- Not only "accidental closures" prevent an object from being collected. A typical mistake made when testing would have been to replace the form

```
(setq *objects* (cdr *objects*))
```

with this one:

```
(pop *objects*)
```

This seems to have exactly the same effect, but it will also bind the object removed from `*OBJECTS*` to the REPL variable `*` (see Recipe 16-11), so that it can't be collected (yet).

- You obviously shouldn't make any assumptions about *when* objects will be collected. You also shouldn't expect a certain *order* in which finalizers will be called. (And on multithreaded Lisps, you should be prepared for finalizers to be invoked in arbitrary threads.)

- And in some cases, you can't even be sure whether objects will be collected *at all*—even if no reference to them exists anymore. (Your Lisp might decide to move objects which have lived "long enough" into a "high generation"—a collection of objects that won't be touched even by a "full" garbage collection.) Again, you'll have to consult your documentation for details.

- The bottom line is that using finalizers is tricky. You definitely don't want to use them for resources that *must* be freed "on time" or in a deterministic way.

- Finally, as TRIVIAL-GARBAGE is one of those lowest-common-denominator libraries, there are certain things you can't do with it, although you might be able to do them in specific implementations. For example, in some Lisps, the finalizers can be functions which accept the soon-to-be-collected object as an argument, and they can inspect the object and even prevent it from being collected. This can't be done in a portable way.

(See also Recipe 6-7.)

Index

Printed in the United States
By Bookmasters